WITHDRAWN

THE HISTORY OF HUMAN POPULATIONS

Volume I
Forms of Growth and Decline

THE HISTORY OF HUMAN POPULATIONS

Volume I
Forms of Growth and Decline

P. M. G. Harris

PRAEGER

Westport, Connecticut
London

Library of Congress Cataloging-in-Publication Data

Harris, P. M. G.
    The history of human populations : v. 1. forms of growth and decline / P. M. G. Harris.
        p.   cm.
    Includes bibliographical references (p.   ) and index.
    ISBN 0–275–97131–7 (alk. paper)
    1. Population—History.   I. Title.
    HB851.H286   2001
    304.6'09—dc21   00–061110

British Library Cataloguing in Publication Data is available.

Library of Congress Catalog Card Number: 00–061110
ISBN: 0–275–97131–7

First published in 2001

Praeger Publishers, 88 Post Road West, Westport, CT 06881
An imprint of Greenwood Publishing Group, Inc.
www.praeger.com

Printed in the United States of America

The paper used in this book complies with the
Permanent Paper Standard issued by the National
Information Standards Organization (Z39.48–1984).

10 9 8 7 6 5 4 3 2 1

For Marianne

"My dear Miss Duchesne, ..."

Contents

Illustrations

TABLES

Preface

The extended undertaking of which this book reports the first stage began with an effort long ago just to pattern population increase in colonial New England. Finding a way to model these demographic changes more effectively unexpectedly opened up very general, perhaps universal, insights into how historical populations have grown or declined. Populations from Republican Rome and Han China to the present, on every continent and across a full range of societies, economies, and cultures, from the global total of *homo sapiens* down to the smallest villages and hamlets, all have enlarged or shrunk in just a few repeated and related types of trend.

The inquiry unfolded like this: While the constant proportional multiplication noted by Benjamin Franklin (later adopted by Thomas Robert Malthus) does still best characterize the demographic expansion of mainland British North America and then the society formed out of those Thirteen Colonies from the 1670s to the 1850s (no mean feat), it turns out that for several decades before that time far faster initial growth steadily slowed to the rate implied by Franklin's assessment.

This constantly decelerating pattern of population increase was soon identified also in the early settlements of the Chesapeake, both collectively and locally, and in the opening phases of other New World colonization, both British ones and those controlled by competing European powers. Meanwhile, examining the population history of the fifty varied colonies/states that have formed the United States made it clear that by far the most frequent type of demographic expansion—in the 17th, 18th, 19th, and 20th centuries alike—has been just this one general or basic growth curve, G. Its formula, though, holds imbedded in it the same 3 percent rate of proportional change as found in the simple exponential representation of Franklin's trending (called the F formula here).

In a similarly connected fashion, the way the U.S. population as a whole expanded from the 1850s to World War II could best be captured, it was discovered, by another mathematical "relative" of the G curve. This is a "halfway," H, modification whose rate of deceleration falls in between the rapid slowing of G and the unbending proportional constancy of F. Such patterning is both simpler and more accurate than the once-impressive "logistic" formulation of Pierre-François Verhulst and the Johns Hopkins colleagues Raymond A. Pearl, Lowell J. Reed, and Alfred J. Lotka, who revived his kind of modeling in the 1920s. Among these preliminary probings of North American regional growths, furthermore, G was the overwhelmingly most common or general form, F appeared very much in the exceptional, expandable frontier conditions claimed for it by Franklin and Malthus, while H seemed to characterize populations involved in sustained economic change.

The generality of these findings held up and extended as the population histories of other "New World" settlements were examined—in Canada, the Caribbean, Australia and New Zealand, and Southern Africa. For societies, provinces or districts within them, and also racial or ethnic subpopulations, the three patterns prove to account for growth in comparable historical contexts with about the same frequencies of occurrence. As the survey turned to Latin America, however, two additional phenomena required accounting. First, Iberian invasions of the 1500s are known to have decimated native American populations, a proposition made quantifiable by the meticulous and inventive work of Sherburne F. Cook and Woodrow Wilson Borah and others that appeared from the 1970s onward. Second, in modern times Latin America has been noted for the "population explosion" that modern commentators have made fashionable for discussing developing countries. "Demographic disaster," however, proves historically—on Pacific islands from the later 1700s to World War II as much as in Spanish America between 1492 and about 1650—to have taken a decelerating D form that represents simply the G curve turned upside down. "Explosion," meanwhile—proportionally *accelerating* increase—is repeatedly captured by G both inverted vertically and reversed horizontally with respect to time (called the E curve). A sixth, fortunately very rare, C type of trend in population size accelerates downward toward total collapse or extinction, apparently where populations fail to maintain a niche upon which they once depended.

The question then became whether the same forms account for population trends in the Old World societies where most people have lived. The surge of interest in historical demography that had occurred in many countries across the 1950s, 1960s, and 1970s provided a substantial literature that could be sampled to see just how globally general the six trend forms discovered in the New World actually were. Meanwhile, the ebb of historical fashion did not prevent more sophisticated, if fewer, relevant studies about demographic history from continuing to emerge across the 1980s and 1990s. Most of the material is still heavily European because of the nature of the records; but some splendid deeply historical work has been carried out on Japan and China, and studies of quite recent perspective flourish for all sorts of places.

Taken together, such rich bequests from previous investigations make a global analysis possible. This indicates that though the frequencies of the trend types have varied from one part of the world to another, and from one kind of population to another, the six G-related patterns suffice to account for sustained trends of demographic increase and decline everywhere—in all kinds of historical settings, across all recorded eras, at every level of population from the smallest local aggregates to the total for humankind.

The first step towards understanding how any one of these six types of trend appears is to observe the nature of the historical contexts in which the form has repeatedly occurred. Such characterization is established throughout the chapters of the present volume. Attention is given to how alternative modeling—not from the G-based "family" of six curves—might mathematically fit the data discussed. Equally important in feeling confident about the proposed conclusions, though, is how well a hypothesized demographic patterning suits what is known about the historical events and processes going on around it, confirming and clarifying—fitting in with—what is familiar in the literature or providing new insight from the population movement observed. Will modeling with the six proposed curves help those who best know the evidence and its context in doing their own work? Clearly, their application and evaluation of my approach will lead to some refinements. But will those particular changes then weaken or strengthen the general interpretation proposed here?

It is movements in births, deaths, and migration that add up to yield demographic growth or decline. The volume that follows this one analyzes historical trends of fertility, mortality, and transfer from one population to another, engaging familiar interpretations like those of demographic transition or stable populations and offering fresh insight. These three familiar inputs into the renewal of populations, it turns out, themselves through time follow patterns already evident in the G-based paths for population size. Such movements have much to do with how growth and decline keep taking just a few repeated forms. A final volume of the extended study then applies what has been learned about the processes of populations across time to reassess the large and lively literature that exists on the interaction between demographic and economic change. Some familiar ideas still carry weight; but some changes in interpretation are also required.

In a far-reaching survey like this, the first order of indebtedness is to those who, across half a century of fruitful inquiry, have built up the literature of historical demography. Hopefully, in spite of mistakes that will have occurred in such a sweeping treatment of other peoples' expertise, they will feel more stimulated than aggravated by the way their work has been incorporated into the broader picture through my treatment.

Over the long endeavor of this project (at times it seemed that at best another Willie Maryngton was in the making), much assistance was crucial. Work supported by the Center for the Study of the History of Liberty at Harvard University gave rise to the first ideas and helped in launching their investigation. Research assistance and study leaves from Howard and Temple Universities and segments of the work done on grants from the National Science Foundation and the National Endowment for the Humanities went into developing this line of inquiry. In the latter activities, Lois Green Carr, Russell R. Menard, and Lorena S. Walsh perennially helped steer my applications to the colonial Chesapeake away from the brink of the unreal.

Several successive assistant directors of Temple's Social Science Data Laboratory, especially Ira J. Goldstein, patiently piloted a novice through the incessant surf of learning curves that the hurricane-force winds of technological change have driven at investigators across the later 20th century. So did Billy G. Smith. Dane Morgan at an early stage raised hope that there was a cure for the middle-aged mathematical ignorance that made so much demographic literature so intimidating. At a time when universities are "managed" on an industrial model by administrators and boards of trustees who do not understand what "industry" they are in, the precious intellectual community of the academy was kept alive by several colleagues from Temple's faculty, most notably David R. Hill, John A. Paulos, and William L. Holmes, who let me participate in their classes to try to make up deficiencies. At many tough teaching times since then I have come to realize just how much was asked of them and how generous they were. Eugene P. Ericksen, in critiquing a preliminary version of my argument, demonstrated how colleagues with quite different political stances can nonetheless help in each other's work. Ann R. Miller, though she could not publish an overview of my investigation in the journal she then edited, gave invaluable encouragement at a critical time. Through the 1990s members of the History Department at Indiana University, Indianapolis, have given not just facilities but friendship, while participants in the Economic History Workshop and the Population Institute for Research and Teaching at Indiana University, Bloomington, especially George C. Alter and Elyce J. Rotella, have provided that lively environment of intellectual exchange (including constructive criticism) for which we join the profession and put up with its credit hours generated, workload revisions, responsibility-centered budgeting, and endless change for change's sake.

Cynthia M. Harris (regrettably no relative) grasped the significance of this work and arranged for its publication in an exceptionally supportive and professional fashion. One could not ask for a better editor. Rebecca Ardwin kept the production process going in a clear and dependable way. Thanks are also due to Linda B. Robinson for a skilled and helpful editing of the text and illustrations of what must have been a rather challenging script.

Most of all I owe to my wife, Marianne S. Wokeck. She has patiently shared me with this project since we first met and endured without complaint consequences of my being so involved in it. Her love, her loyalty, her daily support year-in and year-out, her steadying good sense, and her understanding as a colleague of the research process and the profession have made the work possible and enjoyable. To her this volume is dedicated.

Indianapolis, May 6–June 6, 2000

Introduction

As the 200th anniversary of Thomas Robert Malthus's *Essay on the Principle of Population* goes by, it seems appropriate to examine once again the much-debated issues of how human populations grow and decline. A global review of the historical evidence indicates that a fundamentally new and different approach is needed for looking at the manner in which the peoples of the world have flourished or atrophied. Previous interpretations have misunderstood the nature of the trends that expansion, contraction, and related change in demographic process and composition have taken in historical populations and therefore have failed to grasp properly the causes and consequences of these recurring patterns.

Actual historical populations, it turns out, have most often increased or decreased in ways that Malthus, several fruitful precursors, and many successors across the past two centuries have not yet comprehended. In addition to frequently restating the ideas of Malthus himself and earlier insightful thinkers of the 18th century like Benjamin Franklin and Adam Smith, later writers have advanced various new theories of their own. These range from having population numbers gradually determined by limits to available resources long before crises arrive, or channeled through demographic stabilization into manageable proportionally constant growth, to gripping scenarios of devastating decline or overwhelming, uncontrollable population explosion. It proves to be the case that these diverse views, accumulated across the ages, are more simply and closely related to each other than anyone has recognized. All partial truths, their proper value is realized only when their connections to each other through the processes of human replacement are perceived and understood.

This book begins the far-reaching reinterpretation being offered by establishing the shapes that demographic growth and decline have actually followed and identifying the kinds of historical contexts in which these six fundamentally related patterns have typically appeared. Succeeding volumes then in turn demonstrate how most demographic change—in human reproduction, age structure, migration, and mortality—also follows just the same few simple and closely connected trends over time, as do alterations in the economies that support or curb demographic growth. Populations expand or shrink in just a few repeated forms, in short, because the processes that make them grow or decline themselves move in such fashion. Ultimately, the shapes of these basic, recurring paths prove to be determined by the nature of *homo sapiens* as a biological organism: how we wear out and die off and replace ourselves. Such findings, if they stand up to evaluation and application by others, have far-reaching implications for both knowledge and method in many studies of humankind.

RECONSIDERING SOME BASIC ISSUES OF THE SOCIAL SCIENCES

To launch such a comprehensive inquiry, an extensive historical survey reexamines here what the information available says about the nature of population growth and decline. The evidence comes from all continents, from all types of documented societies and communities, from the time of the Roman Republic and Han Dynasty China to the present. Out of this review emerges a new way of patterning change in the size of populations over time that is more accurate, more economical, and more powerful than analyses previously offered. The fundamental phenomenon, that which is most commonly encountered, is constantly proportionally decelerating growth at a single recurring rate. This form of trend appears most of the time, as expanding populations typically exploit, but soon begin to exhaust, limited changes in their environments. The new model for this repeated general occurrence—called the G curve, for short—is more empirically correct and more interpretatively insightful than the "logistic" curve, which has heretofore been applied to situations of restrained expansion.

Three exceptional forms of demographic increase, each associated with distinctive conditions of growth in the societies and economies involved, also occur, under special historical circumstances—for instance, the continual doubling every 20 to 25 years that was adopted by Malthus from Benjamin Franklin's colonial observations. These other shapes, however, are all much less common than the underlying G pattern. Each, furthermore, can be shown to be just a mathematical mutation of that one basic growth formula, a simple transformation of it on a plane. So can two paths of decelerating and accelerating decline, which stressed populations sometimes experience. In other words, all six formulas that are necessary to account for historical trends in population size, and that suffice for that purpose, provocatively prove to be rooted in the same simple mathematics. That raises important questions concerning how these close linkages among patterns come about.

In searching out reasons for such relatedness, the following volume of this global study explores historical movements in reproduction, death, and migration and shows how these much-examined processes, which together determine population size, have themselves also adhered to the same few patterns of change across time. Trends in fertility, mortality, and relocation out of one population into another, that is, prove to take just the same small set of mathematically connected paths that are observed here in the ways population numbers expand or atrophy. That next fundamental and general step of discovery helps reconceptualize fruitfully what is known about basic demographic processes ever since substantial evidence about them begins, in the 1500s—or perhaps even in the 1200s in the case of a few localities within Europe. Some familiar arguments about what caused what, and why—for instance, in the "demographic transition" to modern population dynamics—have to be revised in light of this new perspective on the actual historical patterning of demographic change.

Further probing shows, finally, that the underlying mathematical shape of constantly proportionally decelerating growth, the G curve, upon which the other trends in population size and demographic process are based, keeps recurring because of the way that the nature of human mortality across most of the life cycle shapes change in age structure and thereby affects how all demographic processes pass through populations. In this manner, all interactions between population and environment, all demographic and economic and social changes, potentially have imbedded in them the same type of repeated patterning over time. This is a finding that every social scientist in every part of the world will have to take into account, and many decision-makers in government and business will be wise to understand.

The new interpretation, if proven correct under the usual and appropriate bombardment of scholarly and scientific application and criticism, lifts explanation above the prevailing, too loosely stated debate about the tension between population and resources to yield a more sophisticated, more general, and more effective understanding of how growth and change actually work. In this fresh formulation, the nature of demographic dynamics themselves, what has been called the "hard mathematical core" of demography (Coleman and Schofield 1986, "Introduction," 5), shapes how both populations and their environments evolve. In such reinterpretation, population theory is elevated from a passive, mostly reactive junior partner among the social sciences to a primal explanation of how and why, and with what consequences, changes in all aspects of the collective life of humankind exhibit repeated forms.

How populations grow, for what reasons they grow, and what consequences their growth generates were already central concerns as the classical early modern population debate began to take shape two and a half centuries ago, in the

1750s. They remain so today, permeating and shaping all the social sciences. Indeed, views first posited in the 18th and early 19th centuries still structure much of the theory to be found in contemporary population studies and related discussions in disciplines like economics and sociology.

At least since Benjamin Franklin's "Observations on the Increase of Mankind" and Adam Smith's *Wealth of Nations*, the response of populations to the fruitfulness of their environments has provided a central core of issues about how populations grow and what difference that makes (Franklin 1751, 227–34; Smith 1776, 74–85). The most famous, and the most bleak, formulation was of course offered by Thomas Robert Malthus in his 1798 *Essay on the Principle of Population*, which recently experienced its bicentennial anniversary. Compared with other participants in the evolving international debate, Malthus judged that significantly fewer and less pleasant options were all that was available for bringing the explosive and virtually unlimited power of human multiplication into balance with the quite restricted potential that existed for expanding the resources that are required to make life possible, let alone enjoyable.

He significantly softened this dismal prognosis in the revised and much expanded *Essay* of 1803.[1] Still, the emphasis that Malthus put upon the way natural increase will always outrun the capacity to expand sustenance stimulated an attempt to model his argument in quantitative terms that would account for the way growth is continually affected by environmental limits, not just through extraordinary crises. In 1838 the Belgian mathematical biologist Pierre-François Verhulst developed and published a "logistic" formula to represent such circumstances. In this modeling, competition becomes more intense among individuals as populations rise towards some ceiling determined by resources. As a consequence, while growth can become faster and faster up to half the maximum population the environment will support, past this point it becomes slower and slower as it approaches the eventual upper limit (Verhulst 1838, 113–17). The resulting pattern through time of Verhulst's "law" has a symmetric "S" or sigmoid shape in arithmetic scale, whose point of inflection between accelerating and decelerating increase is located at half the ultimate maximum that is possible.[2]

This formulation, as applied by Verhulst and by others thereafter, served to model quite effectively U.S. population growth from the late 1700s through the early 1900s, and Belgian demographic increase from the early 1800s to this very day (Verhulst 1845, 1847; Keyfitz 1968; M. Braun 1976). The logistic function was enthusiastically readopted by Raymond A. Pearl and Lowell T. Reed in the 1920s and by their Johns Hopkins colleague Alfred J. Lotka, who applied the formula to all sorts of biological and economic growth as well as to human population increase, and even to the course of certain chemical reactions (Pearl and Reed 1920; Lotka 1925, 83, 289–92, 122–27, 328–29, 369). While the baby boom that followed World War II seemed to vitiate the pattern for the most publicized application of the logistic to human multiplication—to the expansion of the population of the United States—and demographers began to regard

Verhulst's formula as just a "museum piece" no longer of practical value in predicting future paths of growth in population (Keyfitz 1985, 22), the density-dependent approach toward an ultimate "carrying capacity" inherent in the logistic "law" is sufficiently satisfactory still to make Verhulst's equation the most favored formula for biologists today when they confront growth either across populations or within individual organisms.[3]

Students of human life, meanwhile, have not just given up on the notion of environmental limits to demographic increase. After all, that is the central point of Malthus, one of the few generally recognized sources of demographic theory, whom most undergraduates still encounter during their earliest exposure to the social sciences. The oversimplified historical analysis of Verhulst and his early 20th century followers, however, has been replaced by a more complex—if often rather vague—reconceptualization in which a sequence of different maximum or optimum population sizes succeed each other as supporting environments shift or evolve and as the opportunities they produce are soaked up by demographic growth (Coleman 1986; Livi-Bacci 1992).

Other scholars have argued, however, that such a passive, one-sided type of interpretation is inadequate, even if its workings have been made rather more flexible. Several decades ago, after all, the archaeologist V. Gordon Childe reminded us that "Man makes himself": the outstanding feature of *homo sapiens* as an organism (perhaps for the worse as well as for the better, we now sometimes argue) is to be able to alter the environment of the species more decisively than can other fauna and flora. Such potential is not without its champions in the modern debate on population. Most important, the Danish economist Ester Boserup has argued how population pressure itself promotes the technological change that; in the longer run, makes possible something of the bootstrap self-help in expanding resources that Malthus so bluntly belittled (Boserup 1965; also Simon 1977). It is not necessary, furthermore, to discard the whole underlying Franklin-Malthus concept that natural increase tends to outrun growth in what is needed to support a population in order to challenge presently prevailing views concerning just *how* a maximum size is approached and to show that what regulates the path along which growth repeatedly slows is not population density alone, as those who model too superficially with the logistic formula have implied.

The purpose of this book is to demonstrate a more accurate, simpler, and more insightful way in which human population growth can be generalized and understood. From our far-ranging historical inquiry the most common and basic form of population increase for mankind turns out to be one of constant proportional deceleration, called the G curve, the fundamental growth curve. This path approaches an upper limit, like Verhulst's logistic, but it does so in a different way—and for reasons quite distinct from what has previously been argued in the literature, from classical theory to modern interpretation.

In the new mode of thinking offered here—as, long ago, in the minds of

Franklin, Smith, Malthus, and Verhulst—demographic increase without the restriction of some limiting effect constitutes a rare exception. This unusual pattern has occurred historically in much the same extraordinary "frontier" conditions that Franklin identified as characteristic of the British colonies of the 18th century, a finding that Malthus incorporated into his analysis as necessary for permitting, in exceptional cases, the uninhibited "geometric" natural increase of which he thought the species capable. In other words, we shall encounter this rare constant exponential form of growth in the New World, where it was first reported by Franklin two and a half centuries ago, or in situations in which societies have enjoyed through other means some comparable open end for expansion.[4]

Two other exceptional forms of demographic growth also appear here and there: the accelerating "population explosion" that was first found and feared in Third World societies about 1960 and the kind of slowly decelerating increase that the United States followed approximately from 1850 to 1950, which Verhulst so effectively projected with his logistic curve (von Foerster et al. 1960; Verhulst 1845; Pearl and Reed 1920). And populations sometimes do become smaller. One form of contraction is the kind of initially devastating but eventually bottoming-out decline that was experienced by New World natives after the European invasion that Columbus initiated. Publicized by Rodolpho Barón Castro in 1942, this phenomenon of "demographic disaster" has been much discussed in the historical literature since the 1960s and was brought to the foreground again recently by the quinquicentennial 1492 debate on contact among Europe, Africa, and the New World (Barón Castro 1978; S. F. Cook and Borah 1971, 1974, 1979). A distinctly different type of population loss, though, involves *accelerating* erosion, which picks up speed as it goes and leads ever more rapidly towards extinction. Because total disappearance is a fate that, thus far, has been observed only among species other than *homo sapiens*, it is too often assumed that we cannot experience it. It would be foolish to think, though, that we are any more immune to slipping down such a road toward extinction than were the dinosaurs. A few human populations have in fact declined this way historically for a while.

Each of these five other, less frequent patterns of change in population size (1) is rare compared with the most general "G" form of continually compressing growth and (2) is closely based mathematically on that most usual formula for demographic increase. In short, history shows that there is one small family of six trends for sustained change in population size, all of which are rooted in—which at most constitute simple transformations of—a single function for limited growth.[5] This basic formula is somewhat like Verhulst's logistic curve in the phenotypical respect of having an "S" shape in arithmetic scale, but it is quite unlike that familiar "law" in both origin and consequences, in how it works and what it implies.

If population change over and over again follows just a few such related forms, what generates such patterns? Are the determining factors lodged within demographic dynamics themselves—in the ways people reproduce, move from place to place, and die off—or do they come from the economic or social contexts in which people live? If, on the other hand, the numbers of producers and consumers repeatedly change (for whatever reason) along only a few paths, can these patterns escape reappearing in economic and social developments as well? The historical generalizations about population growth and decline that are established here open up a wide range of likely connections among processes that the social sciences will have to rethink carefully.

HOW THE ARGUMENT BUILDS

This volume of the broader study establishes general conclusions about the shape of growth and decline in the world history of populations. Chapter 1 begins the undertaking by developing better ways for depicting, connecting, and understanding three forms of expansion from successive phases of the demographic experience of the United States. This society has repeatedly served as a seminal case study for debate in the literature. These distinctive but closely related paths of expansion are (1) the constant doubling or simple exponential increase at a 3 percent rate from the 1670s through the 1850s that Franklin identified in 1751 (called the F trend here); (2) a rapidly decelerating growth pattern that was followed by the colonies before about 1675—the mathematically fundamental G trend, which has not yet been effectively identified and understood; and (3) the more slowly slowing expansion from the 1850s through the 1930s (according to an H modification of the curvature of deceleration, roughly halfway between G and F) that was approximated quite effectively, though not as simply and insightfully as it might have been, by Verhulst and by early 20th century analysts who followed his logistic example. All three types of trend are shown to be based upon the simple mathematics of the .03 rate of exponential change that is inherent in the G formula. This makes the successive phases of American demographic development across the last four centuries not so disconnected as they at first may seem.

Chapter 2 then applies these three models to the several dozen histories, between 1607 and the 1990s, of the populations of colonies/states within the territory that became the United States. Do the kinds of circumstances in which the three different forms of increase appeared for the national population in its distinctive phases—extensive or "frontier" expansion (F); lasting, accumulative economic change (H); and swiftly dissipated opportunity to increase (G), which lacks the extra "room" of these two special conditions—apply to identifiable stages of relatively *local* demographic growth as well? It being established that they have since records begin within the bounds of the present United States, Chapter 3 moves outward to examine how well these same three patterns of population increase fit and account for the expansion of other northern European colonizations around the world: in Canada, in the Caribbean, in Australia and New Zealand, and in South Africa. Did societies founded by not one but several different colonizing powers experience population increase in the same few ways, both as a whole and in their principal subpopulations? The component parts studied include distinct ethnic and racial groups and both enslaved and free peoples, not just territorial units.

While northern European "New World" colonizations may compose one consistent category in demographic history, what about the earlier Iberian invasions of the Americas? The tales of those conquests ring with death and disaster. It turns out in the regional historical survey of Chapter 4, however, that—no matter how severely it started out—such population loss in the 16th and early 17th centuries regularly began to decelerate. With time, proportionally less and less of the remaining population disappeared. The shape of this recurring D trend of *decline*, furthermore, was nothing other than the most common, rapidly slowing growth curve, G, turned upside down (1/G). Thus expansion and atrophy seem most often to have followed the same formulation historically. And when Latin American populations subsequently recovered and grew on into their modern dimensions, they mostly followed the same three growth patterns found in Chapters 1, 2, and 3 for other ex-colonies.

The difference, though, is an exciting one. Many South and Middle American populations have "exploded," experiencing proportionally *accelerating* growth. This phenomenon (called the E curve), however, instead of taking the hyperbolic trajectory claimed for it by startled observers in the 1960s, proves to be just the GI form of growth reversed in time as well as turned upside down (G inverse or G^i). Therefore, both of the new shapes of change in population size that are encountered when moving into Latin America from other New World ex-colonial societies, D decline and E explosion, are also tightly tied to the same underlying mathematics of the G curve. Furthermore, as Barón Castro pointed out in the 1940s, when explorers, traders, missionaries, and romantics came ashore on Hawaii and the islands of the South Pacific in the late 1700s and early 1800s, they brought with them to populations there the same patterns of decimation and then recovery as the conquistadors had carried to the Americas centuries before.

What, then, of the "Old World"? Since the debates of Franklin, Hume, Wallace, and others in the 1750s—half a century before Malthus—it has been argued that population growth followed different rules in Europe and Asia. That perception turns out to be both true and untrue. Change has followed the same few forms, not distinct ones. It is the *frequency* of their occurrence that has distinguished the Old World from the New.

As Franklin argued in 1751, constant F-type doubling every 20 to 25 years, of the sort experienced by his American colonies, was not a European phenomenon historically. Before the 1500s, in fact, known European populations expanded only in the basic rapidly decelerating G form or contracted in its simply upside-down D version, as with the Black Death of the 1300s or the decimation of Roman manpower during the protracted Second Punic War. Chapter 5 generalizes these patterns of growth and decay for nations; Chapter 6 extends the evidence to some insightfully illustrative sets of regions within European countries, including territories that as yet had no modern national cohesion: like parts of "Germany" in the age of the Thirty Years War, or Provence and Tuscany in late medieval times. Then, beginning in the last decades of the 16th century, England, Sweden, and most notably the Dutch maritime province of Holland— followed by other parts of northern and western Europe—began to support more accumulative, only slowly decelerating growth at national and/or regional levels. This tendency to have demographic increase in such an H pattern—the kind of trend later followed in the United States in the period 1850–1940 (and probably anew since World War II)—generally spread southward and eastward across much of the continent to reach Russia in the 18th century and Italy and Serbia in the 19th century.

This was not the only change in the pattern of demographic increase, however, as Europe passed from the medieval to the modern. Across most of the 18th century the population of England began to "explode," to experience proportionally *accelerating* increase in E form—as, say, Mexico across the middle of the 20th century. Several other national and regional populations of Europe followed suit for some of the time before World War II. The chronology and geography of these movements suggest that "population explosion" may historically have had a closer connection with modern economic development than has usually been assumed. It also could underlie aggressive politico-economic expansionism, as neighbors of early 20th century Germany discovered.

Asia and Africa pose evidential problems for population history. Japan and, in certain ways, China offer very useful information. Some of it reaches back two millennia. Elsewhere the evidence is likely to be thin, mostly recent, and often unreliable. Chapter 7 surveys the records available for these two less-well-documented continents. Accelerating or "exploding" demographic expansion in Asia and Africa is widely known in our own time. Less recognized is the presence of slowly decelerating increase, supported by economic growth, that has been occurring not only in the "Little Tigers" during recent decades but in India and Pakistan and which has been the repeated pattern for China since the 1740s—a century before the United States took up such an H trend. Selected regional patternings from within a few Asian nations further enrich our understanding of what kind of growth has been connected to what kinds of historical circumstances. Finally, lessons of the overwhelmingly 20th century evidence from Africa are teased out as best possible.

Chapter 8 and 9 examine the histories of more local populations. The first shows how the sizes of leading cities around the world have expanded almost universally just in the basic G form. Very rare E, F, or H exceptions are easily understood against their particular historical contexts. Urban decline, meanwhile—whether in Geneva between 1540 and 1590 or in center cities of the United States and Canada between 1940 and 1990—has likewise almost totally followed the D pattern of G upside down. Meanwhile, the curves of the little G family also help account better for the way in which the general process of urbanization as a national or international phenomenon has evolved. In these new terms, for instance, the far-reaching, thought-provoking analysis of city development in Europe between 1500 and 1890 that Jan de Vries offered not long ago (1984) can fruitfully be reinterpreted and revised.

Whereas prominent cities with substantial historical records are not unlimited in number, lesser local populations must be sampled—still more drastically than patterns for regions within countries. Chapter 9, nevertheless, demonstrates the way in which the number of inhabitants in small geographical areas like counties and even more narrowly in towns, villages, manors, hamlets, pueblos, and far-flung Pacific atolls have characteristically changed size only in the simplest G and D (1/G) forms. This is true for all parts of the world that can be studied and for all eras for which we have records, reaching back from the present to the 13th century in Europe and to the 1600s in Tokugawa Japan, a part of China, and both Spanish and English America.

The conclusion of this volume summarizes when and where the six related but distinctive shapes of G-based change in population size have been discovered. First, in order to provide an overall framework for interpretation, internationally aggregate growth patterns are identified from the late 1800s or early 1900s through to standard projections for 2025: for total world population, the numbers of persons living in less and more economically developed regions of the globe, and the peopling of the various continents. These movements are shown to be rather different from and to augur rather different consequences than do currently conventional presentations (for example, Livi-Bacci 1992, 147, 202). Then, the overwhelming predominance of the simplest forms—G gain and 1/G (D) loss—in both historically early and geographically local populations is summarized, and the implications of their prevalence across the most basic demographic units is explored. In contrast, proportionally *accelerating* growth or decline, the E and C curves, each in its own way headed out of control, has been relatively rare in the historical record. The ways these threatening paths have not been allowed to continue, particularly the manner in which accelerating increase has swung over into decelerating demographic expansion, reframe the issues that relate population explosion and economic development, from northwestern Europe in the 1700s to many "Third World" societies today. Finally, the modern form of only slowly decelerating growth (H) is shown to be connected over and over again with economic change that allows for the extra people, while simple, nondecelerating constant doubling in size (the F trend) has appeared historically either where a way of life has spread with little restraint along physical frontiers or where, in some recent contexts, another kind of extensive economic growth has substituted for its more familiar Franklin-Malthus "New World" geographic counterpart.

To establish that just six related curves seem to have provided the paths along which all historically recorded populations have grown or declined is a considerable achievement. In turn, though, this discovery raises some very challenging questions. How have such universally shaped trends been generated? What relates their distinctive forms so closely to each other? What has led one population to enlarge or atrophy in one way, another in a different fashion? Active minds will be leaping ahead to search for the answers. Thus it is important for readers to know what comes next that cannot all be fitted between the same book covers.

First of all, it is necessary to dig inside the dynamics of how populations are molded, to look at the ways in which fertility, mortality, and migration have contributed historically to changes in the size of populations. What forms do variations in rates of birth, death, and relocation from one place to another themselves take over time, and how are these related to demographic growth or decline? For what reasons, either internal to the dynamics of demographic change or through interaction with the evolving economic, social, and natural environments in which people live, do such movements occur?

A second volume of this study first of all demonstrates how rates of birth, death, and migration also have followed four of the six G-based patterns discovered here to govern alterations in the size of populations. This next part of our investigation then advances to probe inside the key processes of migration, reproduction, and mortality that shape population growth and decline in order to comprehend how the various G-based shapes for trends in births, deaths, and relocation are themselves generated by dynamics internal to demographic regimes. While stimuli that initiate demographic changes can come from external origins such as health conditions, the economy, or shifts in culture, the *paths* followed by such movements through time appear to be dictated instead by certain basic characteristics of the way developments of many sorts pass through populations. This is why populations over and over again grow or decline according to only a few long-term patterns—patterns also exhibited by many processes of economic or social change in which the number of people engaged plays a role.

Indeed, several types of *economic* change that are conventionally believed to shape, or to result from, patterns of population growth also prove repeatedly to take G-related trends. A third volume of our inquiry demonstrates that point. This finding turns both the analysis of demographic increase and decline and the study of their relationships to the way peoples are supported into a mathematics of how various G-shaped movements interact and combine. Some of the principles of population behavior that are involved in this interpretation have already begun to be formulated in familiar theories of demographic transition, on the one hand, and stable populations, on the other. And there has now accumulated, of course, a lengthy and lively literature on the interplay between population and economy. Drawing upon a wide range of findings and interpretations from demographic and economic history and theory, however, the new analysis offered will show the way to simpler, more accurate, and more insightful conclusions about the nature of the developments at work and their connections to each other. A successful journey down that road of promise, though, begins here with a better understanding of the manner in which, and the contexts in which, populations have expanded and declined historically.

NOTES

1. In her introductory comments on the nature and extent of changes between the first and second editions (Malthus 1872, xxvii–xxxvi), Himmelfarb stresses how far the differences "have been largely ignored, both by Malthus' contemporaries and by later commentators" (xxxiii). Indeed, now the subtitle became *A View of Its Past and Present Effects on Human Happiness; with an Inquiry into Our Prospects Respecting the Future Removal or Mitigation of the Evils Which It Occasions*, coming back almost full cycle to the attitudes of Condorcet and of Godwin (who claimed foul at having his main criticism adopted without credit, xxvii).

2. Modern explanations and applications of the logistic are available in Keyfitz 1968, 76, 213–18, and M. Braun 1976, 59–60.

3. As evident from a keyword CD search of *Biological Abstracts* from 1988 through 1992.

4. In the sparsely occupied northern regions of the Western Hemisphere, Native Americans were too thinly spread and too decimated by disease to interfere much with the "openness" of the horizon for European settlement there. Most remnants, in spite of occasionally effective resistance, were soon removed from the land.

5. Lotka showed the way a comparable transformation of the logistic might model population decline towards a new equilibrium, but applied a different approach to *accelerating* growth in his critique of the picture that W. R. Thompson drew of invasion by parasites (1925, 85). Benjamin Gompertz used a double exponential curve of G's generic type to pattern mortality across the life cycle. The important difference is that G, unlike his formulation, has a *fixed* exponential coefficient of .03 rather than an open parameter that can vary. "G" here stands for basic growth curve, not Gompertz, though as early as the 1820s this fruitful thinker was pioneering in directions upon which the present study builds (Gompertz 1820, 1825, 1862).

Chapter 1

New Viewpoints on an Old Topic: What Form Does Population Growth Take —and Why?

Issues concerning how populations increase or stop expanding and what consequences such growth processes produce have been embedded at the core of the social sciences since the inception of these disciplines in early modern times. While over the past two centuries some stimulating interpretations have been put forward and widely used, a generally effective way to model how populations grow or decline has in practice proved elusive. Actual population histories have failed, over and over again, to do what theories have expected of them.

Most familiar among the more classical of these interpretations, of course, is Malthus's formulation of 1798, in which he argued that only "arithmetically" expandable resources for human life cannot help being overrun cataclysmically by "geometrically" exploding population increase unless "restraints" of one kind or another are imposed (Malthus 1798). The basic principle of constantly multiplying population was in fact one among several ingredients of Malthus's argument that were already widely known in the 18th century. In 1751, in his "OBSERVATIONS concerning the Increase of Mankind, Peopling of Countries, &c.," the colonial observer Benjamin Franklin had noted that unrestricted New World population was doubling every 20 to 25 years and gave reasons for this phenomenon that largely remain valid today (Franklin 1751, 227–34).[1] Then, in 1760, the fertile Swiss mathematician Leonhard Euler worked out the principle of steady proportional natural increase in exponential terms, treating the long-range effect of constant mortality and a level birthrate in a way that presaged modern stable population theory (Euler 1760). And, indeed, to view the growth of population in British North America through much of its history as an example of such simple exponential increase—like a bank deposit left sitting at constant, daily compounded interest—is still highly justified even after two centuries of controversy about the mechanisms of such growth and of improvements in the data. From the 1670s to the 1850s, for close to two centuries, a steady expansion at 3 percent does characterize very adequately the demographic increase of the thirteen mainland British North American colonies and the United States that they became.

The next question in the accumulative effort to understand better the dynamics of growth concerned what pattern demographic multiplication—with only limited resources of land, technology, trade, and the like—might be expected to follow if the kinds of restraints seen by Malthus and others came to bear continuously, not in a macrocosmic disaster or some erratic succession of crises. In 1838, while the Malthusian debate still glowed warm, indeed, in the very year in which Charles Darwin read the *Essay on the Principle of Population* and found in it an important component for his theory of natural selection (Vorzimmer 1969, 537; Darwin 1898, 2: 68), the Belgian mathematical biologist Pierre-François Verhulst presented a formula for population growth in which a maximum was set by limited resources. He constructed this new conceptualization to reflect more and more intense competition among individuals as a population with such restricted assets becomes larger (Verhulst 1838, 113–17). This "logistic" curve, as he called it, was subsequently used by Verhulst in 1845 to model the size of the American population from 1790 through 1840 in a way that would predict future numbers quite accurately up to World War II. In 1847 he made similar projections for certain European countries.

Considerably later, in 1920, Raymond Pearl and Lowell J. Reed called renewed attention to that sigmoid formula of Verhulst and showed how well it had anticipated American population growth all the way through World War I. They were, furthermore, only two of many scientists since the early 20th century who have employed the logistic also to depict growth in plants and animals. Another was their Johns Hopkins colleague Alfred J. Lotka, a founder of modern demography, who in his *Elements of Physical Biology* of 1925 utilized formulas of Verhulst's type to analyze epidemics, prey-predator relationships, dominant-recessive gene balances, the progress of certain chemical reactions, and even the spread of American railroads (83, 289–92, 122–27, 328–29, 369). Subsequently, now for several decades, the logistic has been a widely employed formula for depicting growth and change in populations, including cultural and economic phenomena such as the dissemination of new weedkillers or novel hybrids of corn among farmers or the spread of innovation in industries (Braun 1976, 59–60; Mansfield 1961). In 1932 Charles Winsor undertook an exploration of the usefulness of other S-shaped curves relative to the logistic, most notably the cumulative normal after Friedrich Gauss and the arc-tangent, and concluded that the logistic was most effective.

Despite all its usefulness in several types of literature over the past century and a half, however, there are serious reasons for questioning the value of Verhulst's logistic as an adequate general formulation for limited or slowing population increase. As I returned to take a more careful look at the basic historical evidence on American population growth—the data that made the reputation of both the Franklin-Malthus and the Verhulst-Pearl-Reed models—it became clear that for all of the major epochs of demographic growth in this country the logistic is not as helpful as it should be.

To begin, while an application of Verhulst's curve does characterize change in the size of the American population well from about 1700 to the 1940s (no trivial achievement), national demographic experience since World War II has in fact produced *many* more people in the United States than even the ultimate maximum for such a modeling (approximately 197 million) would allow. This is a fact impressed upon students by demographers like Nathan Keyfitz (1985, 22) in urging the abandonment of general curves in the analysis of populations. Second, the Verhulst formulation calls for *much* larger populations before 1680 than the colonies really had. Third, from the 1670s through the 1850s, a pattern of simple exponential growth in the fashion indicated by Franklin, Euler, and Malthus is in fact somewhat more accurate, as well as simpler, than the logistic as employed by Verhulst and then later by Pearl and Reed.

Presented in this volume are new ways of modeling growth that account more adequately both for the much-invoked example of U.S. population history and for many other instances of expansion and change across the worldwide experience of humankind to which simple exponential or log-linear increase and the logistic have previously been applied. This reconceptualization of the shapes taken by demographic growth and change was inspired years ago by an insight as to how to depict more effectively the pattern of British North American population increase before 1680. The new formulation is related to the solutions provided by both Euler and Verhulst and employs the identical fixed exponential coefficient that best fits American demographic experience in the long era for which simple proportional multiplication of the Franklin-Euler-Malthus sort is indeed the appropriate model. But it represents a distinctly different way of looking at growth and, likewise, at demographic decline or collapse. Furthermore, it raises quite different implications about the causes and consequences of population increase or atrophy and about the mechanisms of other growths or changes in human experience—such as economic ones—that follow patterns of comparable form.

This chapter begins the argument by discussing how the new model was derived; how it improves upon, but still relates insightfully to, previous widely employed ways of looking at growth; and where it might usefully replace these older, more familiar approaches. The initial discussion here focuses upon getting beyond the time-honored, partially valid but ultimately inadequate propositions of log-linear and logistic growth. But a groundwork is laid for later demonstration of the ways in which recent conceptualizations of "demographic disaster," "population explosion," "demographic transition," and "stable population theory" can also profitably be redrawn and reinterpreted. In other words, this chapter represents just the first step of what will be a comprehensive overhaul of how we depict and explain the nature of demographic growth and decline and the character of processes that produce or reflect such trends in the size of populations.

DISCOVERING STEADY PROPORTIONAL OR EXPONENTIAL GROWTH: THE ENLIGHTENMENT'S DEMOGRAPHY FROM FRANKLIN TO MALTHUS

While it is impossible from this distance to determine whether he worked it out himself or was instead disseminating the findings of one or more of his many associates, correspondents, and gossips on both sides of the Atlantic, it is clear that as of 1751 Benjamin Franklin quite accurately perceived what by then had already been for generations the actual pattern of increase in the population of the American colonies. He wrote in that year in his soon widely read "OBSERVATIONS concerning the Increase of Mankind, Peopling of Countries, &c." that the British settlers of North America were doubling every 20 to 25 years (Franklin 1751, 228, 233). In actual fact, from the 1670s through the 1850s this population grew at an instantaneous exponential rate of 3 percent ($e^{.03}$), meaning that it doubled over and over again every 23.1 years. Part A of Figure 1.1 shows this "F" phenomenon in semilogarithmic scale, on which a straight line represents steady proportional or exponential growth.

Franklin's conclusion from his observations was that any population—human, animal, or plant—expands continually in such a fashion until it fills out the limits of its supply of food and other resources. "There is in short, no bound to the prolific Nature of Plants or Animals, but what is made by their crowding and interfering with each others Means of Subsistence" (233). He then addressed himself to those conditions that restricted the growth of human populations: urbanization, which—he said 250 years ago—increases single living to produce low fertility and holds down the net balance of births to deaths; limited land for supporting families; lack of freedom of action, both in slavery and in the economic environment of legally unfettered men; loss of trade; the importation of luxuries at the expense of necessities; and bad government, which makes property insecure and taxes excessive (230–31). In this reasoning, it should be remembered, he was sending a political message to England, arguing that the growth of population, settlement, and—contrary to the tenets of the Navigation Acts—even manufacturing in the colonies was a "good" thing for the Motherland, which the government now in charge in London should not undo after Robert Walpole's decades of "salutary neglect" in colonial policy. Discounting Franklin's special pleading, it is important to note that he did nonetheless perceive a variety of real interactions of population growth with both limited and unlimited resources.

Leonhard Euler, "the most prolific mathematician in history" (Bell 1965, 139), took up the topic of a proportionally increasing population in his "Recherches générales sur la mortalité et la multiplication" of 1760. In this paper he dem-

Figure 1.1
Old and New Ways of Modeling Population Growth

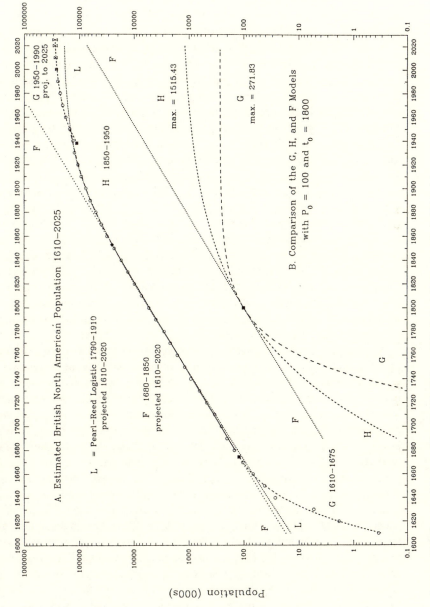

A. Estimated British North American Population 1610–2025

L = Pearl–Reed Logistic 1790–1910
projected 1610–2020

F 1680–1850
projected 1610–2020

H 1850–1950

G 1950–1990
proj. to 2025

G 1610–1675

B. Comparison of the G, H, and F Models
with $P_0 = 100$ and $t_0 = 1800$

H max. = 1515.43

G max. = 271.83

Population (000s)

Sources: U.S. Bureau of Census, *Historical Statistics* and *Statistical Abstracts*; note 6; Table 1.1.

onstrated that, given fixed mortality and an excess of births over deaths that is constantly proportional to the size of the population, both the total population and the number of births will increase exponentially. Also, there will emerge a stable age distribution within the population. This is the first known historical step toward the stable population theory that became so important for modern demography in the 20th century (Euler 1760).

What Euler contributed in 1760 to the evolving understanding of demographic growth that is being reexamined here was twofold: First, he combined mortality via the concept of the life table with fertility, while Franklin had stressed postponement and denial of marriage, not the death rate, as the regulatory mechanism that holds back population increase in response to limits encountered in mankind's supporting environment.[2] Second, he modeled population growth not by "geometric" multiplication as did Franklin in his doubling time—and Malthus in 1798, and Darwin still in 1859 (Franklin 1751, 228, 233; Malthus 1798, 20, 23; Darwin 1859, 3: 79–82)—but exponentially as in constant, instantaneous interest on a bank account. Indeed, Euler had recently been the discoverer of the exponential function (to the base $e = 2.718\ldots$), the inverse of Napier's logarithm, for which he published an infinite series in 1748. In 1760, this much-traveled Swiss mathematician was situated in Berlin (Bell 1965, 148). It is quite possible, however, that Franklin's "Observations," which were circulating widely in Europe by then, were known to him. It is also conceivable that Euler's earlier work on the exponential function was known in Philadelphia by 1751; but Franklin's argument, as it is written, seems to be rooted instead simply in his familiarity as a political leader of active mind with past and current demographic estimates for the colonies.

Adam Smith, on the other hand, most probably did have knowledge of Franklin's relevant argument (among other mid-century contributions) when in 1776 he wrote the sections of *The Wealth of Nations* that discuss interaction of population growth and the economy. In these paragraphs he accepts the principle that, given a steady level of wealth, labor will multiply beyond the opportunity for employment and subsistence. The curb on this process, in his view as opposed to that of Franklin, was not delay of marriage or low fertility among working people. To the contrary, Smith recognized that by his time the poor produced more children than the rich. Instead, he argued, "poverty, though it does not prevent the generation, it is extremely unfavorable to the rearing of children." This childhood mortality was the mechanism, Smith maintained, by which the supply of labor adjusted to the demand for workers in broad biological terms, making available or denying the resources necessary for their offspring to stay alive. "It is in this manner that the demand for men, like that for any other commodity, necessarily regulates the production of men; quickens when it goes on too slowly, and stops when it advances too fast" (1776, 74–85). Neither Franklin nor Smith made the interaction of population and resources in a society very dramatic. Both were pragmatic, hope-filled sons of the Enlightenment. Each argued that, given sensible policy, things would continue to work out, as they had been doing all along. The "correct" policy in each of their views consisted mostly of leaving well enough alone. For Franklin the Pennsylvanian, the goal was to restrain over-management of colonies by the Motherland; for Smith, living in the golden age of the Scottish Enlightenment and enveloped by the optimistic energy of the industrial revolution, the objective was similarly to hold back within Britain any political temptation to interfere in trade or in economic change. Neither of these two, furthermore, ever tried to model graphically or quantitatively just *how* population would adjust to resources via the mechanisms that they identified.

Thomas Robert Malthus was different. He, too, maintained vigorously that intervention in the name of public policy was inappropriate. He did so at first, however, in a strikingly gloomy way that flatly denied mankind's capacity to master the environment or control procreation and stressed the role of misery and vice in keeping population within limits that resources could support. It would seem that this *philosophical* view, as much as the originality or enduring accuracy of his observations about how populations adjust to limited resources, is what thrust Malthus visibly onto center stage in world controversy. In 1798, when *An Essay on the Principle of Population* appeared in its original, harshest form, debate over the social price being paid for the new industrial economy emerging in Britain raged intensely. This controversy was fueled, on the one hand, by Smith's tempting contention that the "invisible hand" of the market would put everything right and, on the other, by very evident disruption and distress being generated within the population by economic growth and change. Public recognition of these problems of industrialization among other things gave the older landed, commercial, and professional leadership of the country a handy moralistic whip with which to drive challenging upstart manufacturers back into their place. Malthus's analysis in effect retorted that such misery and misfortune was *endemic* to the very essence of society. William Godwin in England and the Marquis de Condorcet in France had just published perfectionist arguments that because essentially Man could control his destiny, problems of population and resources would work themselves out through the development of natural science and engineering (Godwin 1797, 168–84; Caritat 1795, 173–202). Malthus rejected these views unequivocally. The explosive potential of humankind for reproduction could never be overcome by policy or by technology. Given *any* quantity of resources, population increase would soon eat them up, because—said Malthus, in a categorical statement that even today's undergraduates seem to retain—resources can only be expanded "arithmetically" while population increases "geometrically." To hammer his point home he contrasted what he saw as the mathematical potential of these two forms of growth in a way that deeply persuaded many readers (1798, 14, 23–26). This graphic contrast of the two forms of expansion—a slower one for resources, a rapidly multiplying one for population, he claimed—not only made Malthus appear scientifically sophisticated in his argumentation but also rendered him darkly fatalistic in moral tone and cataclysmic in historical implication. The more continual, controllable mechanisms of "moral restraint" were given more emphasis within the array of feasible solutions only in the second edition of the *Essay*, in 1803. As the case was first stated, particularly in the way that the dreaded but inescapable crossing-point of the two trajectories of growth was introduced, the reader was left with the impression of surging population increase recurrently colliding with a ceiling of only slowly growing resources in a fashion that could only be "corrected" by misfortune and disaster.[3]

The increased role allowed to "moral restraint" in later versions of the *Essay* allowed a smoothing out of the head-on collisions of surging population with the just gradual increment that was possible in resources. Of course, vice and disease—highest on Malthus's original list of adjusting mechanisms—could also be considered to be relatively continuous in their impact on a population. Still, neither Malthus nor anyone else in the early decades of the debate worked out an appropriate model as to *how* a more constant, gradual interaction of resources and population might operate in response to the types of restraints that had been identified by Malthus and his predecessors when they perceived limited opportunity and inevitably intensifying competition for it among members of a growing population.

CONTINUOUS PRESSURES OF MULTIPLYING POPULATION: POST-MALTHUSIAN THEORY FROM VERHULST TO LOTKA

Such a modeling was finally offered in 1838 by the Belgian mathematical biologist Pierre-François Verhulst. He proposed a "logistic" curve of population increase for those circumstances under which a ceiling on growth is present because resources to sustain life are limited. Continually increasing competition for finite assets will, he argued, progressively slow growth toward a halt as population expands under such conditions. The model he put forward for these circumstances takes an "S" shape in arithmetic scale, as illustrated by "L" (for logistic) in the lefthand panel (or A panel) of Figure 1.2, while the exponential form focused upon by Franklin and Euler a century earlier ("F"—for Franklin—in the righthand or B panel of the figure) climbs upward more and more rapidly with time.

The Euler model of growth (the exponential form for geometric increase with a constant doubling time, which was used by Franklin and Malthus) can be expressed mathematically as:

$$P_t = P_0 e^{r(t-t_0)}.$$

In this equation, P_t is the population size at some point in time, t, for which projection is desired, either forward or backward, from a known population of P_0 at time t_0; r is the exponential rate of increase (for instance, .03 in the American population from the 1670s through the 1850s in Figure 1.1); and e is the base of the natural logarithm, approximately 2.72. In a century, for example, $P_t = P_0 e^{.03(100-0)}$ gives a predicted population size of 20.09 times P_0. Such

Figure 1.2
Four Growth Curves in Arithmetic Scale

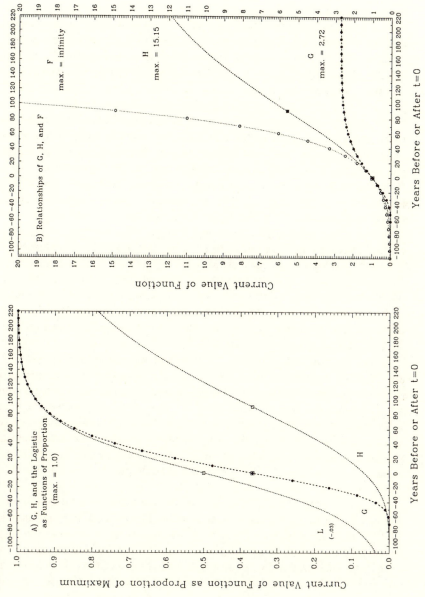

Source: Table 1.1.

growth, as has been noted, produces a straight line in semilogarithmic scale, as part A of Figure 1.1 presents for the American population across its middle years from the 1670s through the 1850s. In the equation, expansion goes upward in this direction forever, as part A of Figure 1.1 shows the actual American population after the 1850s clearly did *not*.

To correct for the limits that finite resources begin to put upon population increase as it proceeds, Verhulst introduced into his model a ceiling, here called P_{max}, which is equivalent to twice P at time $\emptyset$, beyond which available resources will not let population grow. To employ notation comparable with that of other formulas used here, for him:

$$P_t = P_{max} / [1 + e^{-r(t-t_0)}].$$

Figure 1.2, which depicts four different growth models discussed in this chapter in *arithmetic* scale, illustrates in panel A how demographic growth according to Verhulst's "L" formula begins, after half the maximum population has been reached at time 0, to slow down to parallel, not exceed, the asymptotic limit of P_{max}, which is set at 1.0 in this graph.[4] The later and larger t becomes, the smaller $e^{-r(t-t_0)}$ gets, and $1 + e^{-r(t-t_0)}$ approaches 1, with P_t consequently approaching P_{max} in a continually slower and slower fashion. In this manner, Verhulst modeled a gradually stronger and stronger effect of limited opportunity for further growth upon the rate of increase in population. This would be suitable for those "restraints" conceived by Malthus (or anybody else) that come to bear continuously rather than cataclysmically as population expands in a context of only finite resources. Verhulst's reasoning in essence introduced a mathematical factor to represent more and more competition among individuals within a population as it grows larger and closer to the limit of its means of support (Lotka 1925, 64–66; M. Braun 1976, 45–48).

Fitting an r of .03134 with t_0 in 1914, and forecasting a P_{max} (or $2P_0$) of 197,230,000, Verhulst in effect predicted quite accurately the pattern that the U.S. population would follow for the next century (M. Braun 1976, 51; Verhulst 1845). Projections from this calculation are labeled "L" (for logistic) in Figure 1.1. Up into the 1940s that model, as used by Verhulst in 1845 and then revived by Pearl and Reed in 1920, in fact very accurately projects American population size decade after decade, while the steady exponential pattern of the Franklin-Euler-Malthus or F type calls for growth that simply was not sustained after about 1850.

Following World War II, however, this logistic model is not nearly so effective as it ought to be. It calls for a maximum population of 197 million, while by 1990 the United States already held 249 million residents and even lower-bound projections (*Statistical Abstracts [Stat. Abs.]* 1991, 15, Series 19) indicated about 262 million by 2025, just a generation ahead, as shown in part A of Figure 1.1. These minimal estimates for the future as of 1991 are indicated by the upward-pointing triangles in the figure. Furthermore, the logistic as applied by its promoters really does not account for the nature of American population increase from the 1670s to the 1850s as accurately as the simpler straight exponential formula, F. Particularly before 1710, as part A of Figure 1.1 shows, the .03134 exponential is too steep; a rate of .0300 provides a more accurate slope for the data. Finally, to apply the formula of Verhulst backward before 1680 is to project population sizes for the British North American mainland through the first seventy years of colonial history that are almost as preposterous as those produced by the steady exponential model—many, *many* times too large. Clearly, the actual population of the colonies at first grew from very small numbers much more rapidly than $e^{.03}$, slowed persistently over time to converge on exponential growth at that rate during the 1670s, and then remained in or "stuck" at this slope of trajectory for close to two hundred years: the phenomenon noticed by Franklin about halfway through that second, long F phase of American demographic history.

Still, Verhulst's formula has proven to be a very useful one for a variety of purposes in both social and natural science. The growth of not just human but biological populations of several kinds, the increase in weight or height of individual animals and plants, the dominance of favored types in a gene pool, the expansion of an industry like the railroads, the spread of a cultural practice such as using fertilizers, and even the behavior of a chemical energy storage system like a battery have all been approximated with prima facie success by models of Verhulst's type. Prey-predator relationships, the competition of species, and the dynamics of epidemics have also been analyzed usefully with formulas based upon the same logistic equation. For convenience of reference, these illustrations come mostly just from Lotka's book of 1925. Many others have appeared since; and to the present time the logistic is still employed as one of the main models for depicting and explaining biological growth and also some underlying dynamics within demographic processes.[5] Thus, if a more accurate way of modeling continuously resource-restrained human growth can be identified, it offers promise for a wide range of uses, both for analyzing increase of change in populations of humankind and for reassessing and reworking the many varied other applications to which Verhulst's formula has been put in the social and natural sciences. In short, a new, improved conceptualization could be at least as fundamental and as general a way of looking at growth and change as the logistic, which, though at times it has been overworked and oversold, has served many purposes well.

CONSTANTLY PROPORTIONALLY DECELERATING GROWTH: A MORE ACCURATE, SIMPLER, AND MORE INSIGHTFUL GENERALIZATION OF THE HISTORICAL BEHAVIOR OF HUMAN POPULATIONS

The inadequacies of the logistic for U.S. growth in the period after World War II led contemporary demographers to turn away from attempts to model population increase mathematically (contrast Keyfitz 1968, 213–19, to Keyfitz 1985 [1977], 23). Such skepticism has also characterized their reaction to more recently proposed patterning, such as a hyperbola to capture "population explosion," which became a major demographic and environmental concern in the 1960s and 1970s (Keyfitz 1968, 219–20; von Foerster et al. 1960). Ironically, it was during these same years that witnessed professional opinion stiffen against general modeling, that my own search to correct for the enormous error of both the Franklin-Euler-Malthus and the Verhulst-Pearl-Reed models in patterning increase during the first seven decades of American population history before 1680 provided a basic insight about how to develop a better method for depicting and interpreting demographic growth in a general fashion. That new way of modeling population change, the basis of this book, builds upon valid if incomplete insights of the old Franklin-Malthus and Verhulst formulations, shows how they proved inadequate, and provides new solutions that, while closely related in some ways to the old proposals, account for actual histories of population change more accurately, more parsimoniously, and more fruitfully than those predecessors.

My reformulation began in the following way: The steady exponential model for working backward in time to project smaller populations from larger ones is $P_t = P_0 e^{-r(t-t_0)}$. Part A of Figure 1.1 shows how drastically actual early population size in the British North American colonies departed from that retrograde projection, F, even if that was truly the trend from about 1675 onwards for almost two centuries. In some way the model had to be made instead to fall more and more below this exponential line the further back in time the population was to be estimated. One way of doing this was to take the $e^{-.03(t-t_0)}$ of the steady proportional Franklin-Malthus growth equation, F, and make it into an exponent: $e^{[e^{-.03(t-t_0)}]}$. In that fashion, $P_t = P_0 e^{[1-e^{-.03(t-t_0)}]}$, which is the same as saying that $P_t = P_{max}/e^{[e^{-.03(t-t_0)}]}$, since at t_0 $P_t = P_{max}/e$. This point of inflection in the new model—which is called "G" for general growth curve because of its historical ubiquity and the mathematical basis that it provides for all other demographic trends—is analogous to what is found in Verhulst's logistic at t_0, except that there, in the L formula, $P_0 = P_{max}/2$ (.5 of the maximum) rather than $P_{max}/2.72$ ($1/e$ or .3679 of the maximum). Table 1.1 compares the formulas. Further, while in arithmetic scale both curves are S-shaped, that of Verhulst is symmetrical before and after the point of inflection at t_0, but the new G model is not. It is bigger to the top and right than to the bottom and left. This contrast stands out in panel A of Figure 1.2. Part A of Figure 1.1, meanwhile, shows how this new formulation, G, with a t_0 in 1675 and a P_0 at that time of approximately 121,700 European settlers, servants, and slaves, much better fits the actual pattern of available estimates for the number of people in Britain's mainland North American colonies from 1610 through 1670 (*Historical Statistics [Hist. Stat.]* 2: 1168, series Z 1–19).[6] That the actual population fell below the long-term trend around 1630 reflects the impact of Opechancanough's attack of 1622, in which one quarter of the Virginia settlers died and others were sent scurrying home to England. Subsequently, the exceptional surge of Puritan migration to New England in the 1630s drove the total British North American population *above* the curve as of 1640. Well-established history, in short, read-

Table 1.1
Four Formulas for Population Growth

"F"	"G"
Franklin-Euler-Malthus[a]	General Model for Limited Growth
(1751, 1760, 1798)	(proposed here)
$P_t = P_0 e^{.03(t-t_0)}$	$P_t = P_0 (e^{1 - e^{-.03(t-t_0)}})$

"L"	"H"
Verhulst's Logistic[b]	Half-Way Decelerating form of G
(1838, 1920)	(proposed here)
$P_t = 2P_0 / 1 + e^{-r(t-t_0)}$	$P_t = P_0 [e^{e(1 - e^{-.03(t-t_0)}/e)}]$

[a]Euler (1760) used the exponent parameter form: $P_t = P_0 e^{r(t-t_0)}$; Franklin (1751) argued a doubling time of 20 to 25 years that implied the constant .03 exponent; and Malthus took up Franklin's New World analysis as the unrestrained pattern.
[b]Verhulst (1838), and Pearl and Reed (1920) after him in reviving this formula, left r open from population to population but in practice found a value of $-.03134$ for U.S. growth in the 19th century.

ily explains the obvious deviations from the model curve at these points in time.

In the 1960s I happened to construct this type of double exponential formula for decelerating population growth from early American data and began to apply it widely, as in succeeding chapters here, dubbing it "G" for general growth curve. Too many years passed before I realized that way back in the 1820s Benjamin Gompertz, the English mathematician and actuary, had first introduced modeling of this generic double-exponential type, in reverse with respect to time, to approximate decreasing survivorship with age in human populations (Gompertz 1820, 1825, 1862).[7] While biologists have occasionally employed such a formulation for growth, however, the Gompertz representation has appeared much, much less frequently in their literature than has Verhulst's logistic. It is even more rarely used in any way by students of *human* populations. Gompertz's view of the relationship of mortality to age itself began to be substantially revised by subsequent writers (beginning with Makeham 1867).

The *difference* between my G and the Gompertz formula, however, is an important one and must be clearly understood. Neither Gompertz nor his successors in biological or social science have specified that a *single* exponential value comparable to the .03 of the G function constitutes the basis for change in a population. They leave the door open for an *unlimited "family"* of coefficients. In contrast, I maintain that only one constant exponent, .03, is needed for growth and decline (and some other kinds of trends) in our species. Thus, a formulation for decline after Gompertz, as put into the notation used here, becomes $P_t = P_0 e^{[1-e^{-r(t_0-t)}]}$ while in my growth equation, $P_t = P_0 e^{[1-e^{-.03(t-t_0)}]}$. In the former expression, the exponential coefficient, r, constitutes a third parameter, a value that is allowed to vary, along with P_0 and t_0; in the G formula proposed here, in contrast, .03 is *fixed* as a constant (in lieu of r), and there are only two parameters in the equation.[8] In G, in other words, we are working with a much simpler—but also a much more limiting and demanding—representation than Gompertz or his modern followers (most in biology rather than the social sciences) have applied.

In depicting the early American evidence, it is clear, however, that the slowing of population increase along the curving G path across the early 17th century then "stuck," or stopped decelerating, when the rate reached simple $e^{.03}$ (the exponent for the F formula) at t_0 in the 1670s, and remained constant at this straightforward or log-linear proportional F pace through almost two centuries of continental expansion. Then, when the geographic spread of the United States could no longer sustain steady proportional increase of that sort, beginning in the 1850s (not at 1890, when Frederick Jackson Turner timed the closing of the "frontier"), the decline below the exponential line for the U.S. census data in part A of Figure 1.1 was considerably gentler than a resumption of the new model of decelerating growth as found for 1610–1670 would have produced. (That hypothetical G for 1860 to 1950 is presented as a lightly drawn curve in Figure 1.3, which magnifies the modern end of part A of Figure 1.1 for easier inspection.)

The new formula, G, derived from the early colonial demographic experience can, nevertheless, also serve as the foundation for a very accurate and insightful way of looking at U.S. population increase in the century-long era that began in the 1850s. It serves as the basis for a modified *half*-speed decelerating model, "H," that fits the data as well as the familiar logistic does over this third major phase in American demographic history, from the 1850s to the Great Depression, but does so more economically (with fewer open variables or parameters). The necessary transformation in G is made by slowing down the curvature of the logarithm—the sharpness of the bend in proportional scale—by the constant e. This graphic difference between G and H shows up best in the B section of Figure 1.1. A calculation of $P_t = P_0 [e^{e(1-e^{-.03(t-t_0)/e})}]$, which diminishes the deceleration of G by $1/e$, produces from a base population of $P_0 = 26,060,000$ in 1854 the estimates for 1860 through 1930 that are designated "H" in Figure 1.1. (This path is projected forward through 1954 for comparative purposes that are taken up shortly.) In Figure 1.2, the curvature of H is compared abstractly in

Figure 1.3
Modeling U.S. Population 1850–2050 (enlarged and revised)

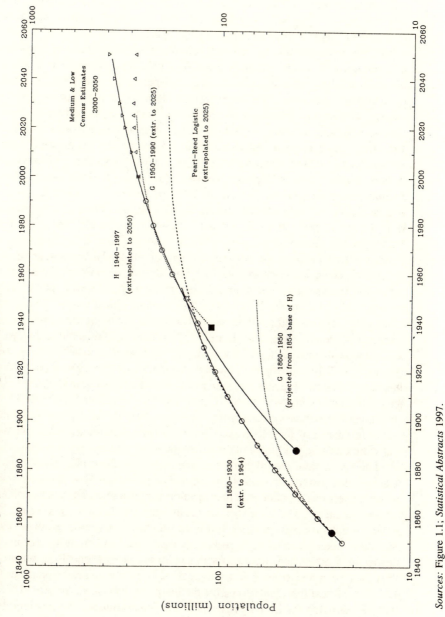

Sources: Figure 1.1; *Statistical Abstracts* 1997.

arithmetic scale with that of its base formula G set to the same zero year. While G goes to a ceiling of 2.72 (or e) times the value for the base year, the maximum for H is eventually 15.15 or e^e times the level at year 0. In another important difference, the point of inflection for H is not 1.0 at t_0, as for G, but 5.575 at +90.61 years. (See panel B in Figure 1.2.) This is where the function equals 1/e or .3679 of its maximum (panel A of the figure).

The projections of this second new formula, H, surpass those of Verhulst in accounting for U.S. population increase from 1850 through 1930, when the low birthrates of the Depression decade began to pull down the 1940 total below the expected trajectory. Then, from around 1950, a new phase of demographic increase surged above this old H path, as the enlargement of the right end of part A of Figure 1.1 shown in Figure 1.3 most clearly indicates. According to Bureau of the Census estimates *in 1991* of future U.S. population size, it seemed—as I worked on this chapter several years ago—that a G curve with its base at 1938 (the fit of the formula to data for 1950–1990) would best account for the path of expansion forward to 2025 or so. The census data, low and middle future estimates by the Bureau as of 1991, and the G curve projected from the 1950–1990 returns are plotted in Figure 1.1 (*Stat. Abs.* 1991, 15, Table 16, Series 14 and 19).

As of 1997, however, the Bureau had new, significantly different projections for what seemed to be happening to births, deaths, and net migration. These called for more sustained demographic increase than previously expected, rising to some 393 million by 2050 rather than topping out under 300 million as predicted six years before. If these revised calculations remain approximately correct, U.S. population growth from the 1940s into the 2040s, rather than taking a G trend, will have followed for a century a fresh H path with t_0 near 1888 (Figure 1.3). This still replaces the old trajectory of 1850–1930 with a steeper increase but retains the same H pattern of slow deceleration in the new expansion. The famous postwar "baby boom," though still marching across the age structure of America year by year, has—in short—been incorporated into a sustained pattern of long-term growth rather than generating a briefer G surge that would more quickly lose its momentum.

If I had been more careful in my calculations of several years ago, I would have noted that a G pattern for 1950–1990 and an H for 1940–1990 were both possible, approximately equal candidates for projection as of that time. The census evidence for 2000, though, would have soon settled the choice in favor of the H shape. Projection by any method is perilous, however. Bureau of the Census estimates based on current assumptions about fertility, mortality, and migration (as favored by Keyfitz in rejecting the logistic, for example) are at least equally problematic. They have been revised over and over again significantly in recent years because they have proved repeatedly to be off the mark (for instance, *Stat. Abs.* 1977, 7; 1985, 9; 1991, 15). As Gregory Spencer of the Census Bureau said candidly about the population projections of his office some time ago, forecasting by this technique inevitably involves error.[9] Although crucial transition points will always occur (as in the 1670s, 1850s, and 1940s in part A of Figure 1.1), if a general tendency for population growth to follow just a few G-related paths can be proven (as will be argued in subsequent chapters), prediction for substantial periods of time can be made easier and more reliable. Meanwhile, just how alterations in fertility, mortality, and migration fit in with such ongoing G-based net growth patterns, on the one hand, or signal and set off new, retargeted trends of demographic increase, on the other, can be more readily understood.

In short, while the logistic and its simplistic reasoning based just upon competition for one unchanging limit to resources may indeed offer an unreliable explanation of how populations grow, the possibility of *some* general patterning to population increase perhaps should not be tossed out too casually with the particular shortcomings of Verhulst's projections and reasoning. This caution is especially pertinent when all the new modeling, as later phases of this study will show, can be rooted in the way familiar demographic dynamics, like those of the life table, work to digest shifts in levels of migration, fertility, and mortality in standard, repeated G-based patterns. In other words, it is not necessary to choose just between projecting from the unchanging resource-limit hypothesis of the logistic, on the one hand, and the inputs from components of fertility, mortality, and migration that are favored by modern demographers, on the other—as Keyfitz (1985, 23), for one, has posed the false dichotomy. The two kinds of dynamics, demographic and economic, can (and must) instead be wedded into one "demonomic" interpretation. Indeed, the basic current problem in predicting population size from expected rates of migration, fertility, and mortality is precisely not recognizing that these contributing factors themselves alter in G-related forms as populations adjust through their age structures (the topic of the second, following volume of this study).

Though three models have been put forward here to replace much past interpretation, it is important to remember that H involves just a very simple modification of the way G bends. And the old familiar Franklin-Malthus simple exponential, doubling every 23.1 years, the F formula, is nothing but the special case of the slope of G at its zero year, projected forward and backward at this fixed .03 exponential rate. Table 1.1 reviews the close mathematical connections that exist among the formulas of the three models, F, G, and H, that appear extensively throughout this volume. It also contrasts them with the logistic (L).

Subsequent chapters probe why the H curve was appropriate for the circumstances of the United States during 1854–1930 (probably again since 1940) and how F could be the shape for the long era of 1675–1854. Such explanation starts with a survey of the kinds of populations in which these other patterns—exceptions to G, but in fact mathematically based upon that function—have occurred historically and of the conditions in which the various repeated G-connected forms of demographic change apparently have emerged. Like the logic of unrestricted New World opportunity that was invoked two centuries ago by Franklin and Malthus, there turn out to be easily understandable and readily acceptable reasons why some populations at some times have multiplied in the two more robust and persistent but infrequent F and H forms rather than the usual and basic, more swiftly decelerating G trend.

It must be realized here from the beginning, however, that without any modification at all the fundamental new model, G or $P_t = P_0 e^{(1 - e^{-.03(t - t_0)})}$, is in fact the *norm* for human population increase, absent certain exceptional conditions. It proves to be a very generally appropriate method for depicting population expansion across a wide variety of historical contexts. Not only national but *local* growth has behaved this way in many diverse historical settings, as some examples in Figure 1.4 illustrate. For instance, the population of Washington County, Rhode Island, filled out according to such a trajectory from 1708 to 1782—and perhaps broadly continued to do so on through the early 1800s (Rossiter 1909, 163). Alerting us to the potential applicability of the G function for demographic increase in cultures quite different from the original example of the United States, so did the growth of the French Indian Ocean colony of Mauritius take G form from 1735 through 1787 and again 1787 through 1817 (Deerr 1950, 2: 280). The pattern, furthermore, is not relevent just for rural areas, since Boston expanded roughly the same way from 1700 through 1790 (Rossiter 1909, 11), while the population of Missouri, which included the two large cities of St. Louis and Kansas City, multiplied closely according to G from 1810 all the way through to 1950 (*Hist. Stat.* 1: 30, series A-195). In the chapters that follow, most national, regional, and local populations around the world will be shown to have increased similarly.

Meanwhile, *components within* populations can be shown to have expanded historically in the same manner, as Figure 1.4 also illustrates. Urbanization has evolved this way: The total population of all U.S. cities with over 500,000 persons, for instance, expanded in such a pattern from 1890 through 1970 (*Hist. Stat.* 1: 11, series A-44 and A-45). To exemplify the applicability of the same curve for ethnic or racial groups, African-Americans in Tennessee can be seen to have multiplied via G—first as slaves and then as free persons—from 1770 through 1940 (*Hist. Stat.* 2: 1168, series Z-19; 1: 34–35, series A-200). Economically distinctive categories of people, too, have expanded historically along G paths. "Taxables" in colonial Essex County, Virginia, for example—white men and slave adults of both sexes thought capable of producing tobacco—increased along this kind of track from 1693 through 1774.[10] In other words, populations as a whole (both local and more aggregate ones), racial or ethnic groups within them, urban and rural subpopulations, and economic segments such as adult workers or dependents may all prove generally to have expanded historically according to the new basic pattern, G. While small populations like the Essex County taxables or the few thousand people who inhabited colonial Boston demonstrate that there can be some substantial temporary variation around the underlying G trend, that fundamental pattern nonetheless captures the long-term shape of demographic increase over and over again. This generalization can be shown to characterize growth not just in one North American

Figure 1.4
The Applicability of G Growth to Different Kinds of Populations and Subpopulations

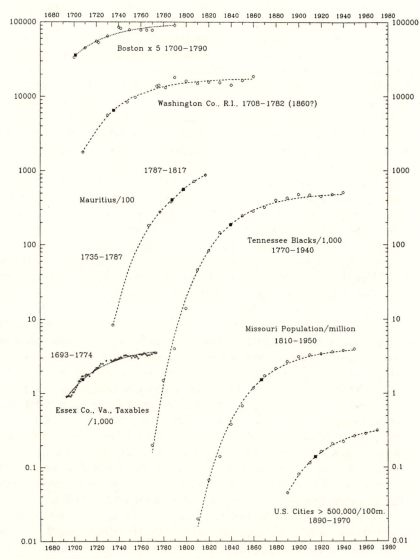

Sources: Rossiter 1909; Deerr 1950; *Historical Statistics;* note 10.

society, from whose population experience the G model was originally discovered, but perhaps also in the demographic histories of many diverse cultures across many distinct epochs of world history. These findings and their implications for our understanding of many aspects of human life are the topics of the chapters that follow.

As the discussion proceeds, furthermore, it will in turn be demonstrated how newer conceptualizations of growth or decline that have appeared in modern demography, such as "the demographic transition," "population explosion," "demographic disaster," and "stable population theory," can also best be understood in terms of transformations of the one basic G function. Thus, the new G pattern, whose centrality and generality have begun to unfold here, does not only of itself provide a widely useful tool for depicting population increase across time and space and across varying cultures and economies more accurately and more simply than its predecessors. It also forms the underlying basis for *all* modelings or depictions of growth and decline that continue to be fruitful. The way this handful of trends are very simply connected to each other through the mathematics of G provokes some fundamental rethinking about the nature of demographic processes, which succeeding stages of this study explore and develop.

In turning like this to apply G-related modeling to demographic history very broadly, certain decisions about method and interpretation should be made clear. The initial insight, developed in Figure 1.1 and Table 1.1, was that successive phases of the much-invoked series for population size across time in the United States *could* all be promisingly modeled with very simply related mathematical formulas that each shared the .03 exponential coefficient. These patternings entailed (1) the old familiar constant exponential of Franklin and Malthus for the later colonial and early national periods; (2) subsequent gradually slowing growth into the early 1900s to improve upon the logistic modeling of Verhulst; (3) a phase of early very fast but rapidly decelerating expansion in the 17th century settlements, which no one has patterned yet, and (4) a second phase of slowly slowing modern growth since 1940. That schema offers simplicity in conceptualization and also clues as to how the perceived mathematical interconnectedness yet differentiation of the formulas come about. But how good are the fits of the data to the curves proposed? Not all points fall right on the calculated trend lines. Would other formulas suit the evidence better?

Today it is easy to run segments of data series through computer programs that try thousands of formulas to see what results. First of all, though, for what are we looking? The more parameters (coefficients that are allowed to vary) that one uses in an equation, the easier it is to obtain a closer fit (reduce the mean squared error around the proposed model). Since the era of Occam's razor, however, parsimony is also prized in intellectual inquiry.

One way of giving credit to simpler models is via the F test, which weighs the number of degrees of freedom that participate in achieving a certain reduced level of error. We shall rank the results of attempted models in this form. Meanwhile it should be noted that any glitch in a data series, especially one with only few points of observation available, is likely to make some form of curve especially suitable to this particular set of evidence. Instead, we are seeking a justifiable and useful *generalization*, a pattern of change through time that works well over and over again. The unsystematic appearance of formulas with higher F values here and there is inevitable if there is any idiosyncracy in the data; and historical data are indeed idiosyncratic. We just do not want to encounter some alternative model that starts out-performing the chosen one over and over again, whether that alternative is a form proposed in some other interpretation of demographic change, a pattern we have simply missed, or the straight arithmetic line, which suggests that anything more complex is inappropriate.

The upper part of Table 1.2 presents three characteristics of the basic F, G, and H models as these have been applied in Figure 1.1 to four successive phases of population growth between 1610 and 2030 in what is now the United States. Particulars are also presented for some potentially competitive patternings that offer special insight. From left to right these findings are: the exponential coefficient of the curve examined (which determines its slope or bend; the F, G, and H formulas all set this at .03); the rank of the formula's F value among over 3,000 models commonly employed in scientific inquiry that have been attempted (some of which are so inappropriate for the present circumstances that they blow up in computation); and the size of that F statistic.

For the U.S. data of 1680–1850 the simple log-linear equation $\ln y = a + bx$ with an exponential coefficient b of .0295 ranks 2nd among more than 3,000 equations fitted. The same formula with exponent *fixed* at .0300 (i.e., the proposed F function) comes 8th. The fit of Verhulst's logistic equation is only number 143 on the rank list of results (and has an exponential coefficient of .0309, compared with the .0314 found by Verhulst and Pearl and Reed).[11] The F value of the logistic is less than half of that for the Franklin-Malthus formula. Thus, simple exponential growth at an instantaneous .03 rate represents U.S. population increase from the 1670s through the 1850s quite well, clearly better than logistic projections. No simple competitor, furthermore, is suggested from the top of the list of F statistic findings for all the other curves attempted.

Estimates for colonial population growth from 1610 through 1670 rely upon only seven dates and entail quite crude calculations about a very tenuous demographic foothold in the New World. The error is high for all approximations (the F statistics are all much smaller than for the trend of the next 180 years). Still, the G curve with exponent fixed at .03 comes in 10th among over 3,000 models tried. Whereas to leave the exponential coefficient open increases r^2 slightly, the degree of improvement does not justify employing the additional parameter. Open G (G_o, equivalent to the equation of Gompertz reversed in time) in fact generates an F statistic less than half the size of my simpler G. The exponent for G_o is .0251, furthermore, which suggests that the fixed .0300 of G is not far off the mark. The logistic formula, in contrast, is a poor competitor here, coming in at only 1,235th place with an F just one fifth the size

Table 1.2
The Fit of the Proposed Models and Some Competitors

Data:	Model	Exponent	F Rank	Value of F
U.S. 1680-1850	Open F	.0295	2	138,035
n = 18	F	.0300	8	75,908
	Logistic	.0309	143	33,184
U.S. 1610-1670	G	.0300	10	835
n = 7	Open G	.0251	159	358
	Logistic	.0561	1,235	180
U.S. 1850-1930	H	.0300	1	14,658
n = 9	Open H	.0273	147	7,951
	Logistic	.0286	312	6,148
	Line	(1.28)	2,686	486
U.S. 1940-2030	Line	(2.40)	9	25,987
n = 11	H	.0300	156	14,636
	Open H	.0272	769	8,380
	Logistic	.0023	1,545	7,010
Missouri,	G	.0300	1	5,657
1810-1950	G Open	.0344	2	5,202
n = 15	Logistic	.0507	81	1,720
Tenn. Blacks,	G	.0300	1	2,637
1770-1940	G Open	.0297	67	1,237
N = 18	Logistic	.0441	124	795
Big Cities,	G	.0300	3	1,646
1890-1970	G Open	.0292	77	714
n = 9	Logistic	.0256	1,094	429
Essex Taxables,	G	.0300	6	2,776
1693-1774	G Open	.0428	9	2,403
n = 71	Logistic	.0566	340	1,621
Washington Co.,	G	.0300	1	134
1708-1860	G Open	.0376	20	68
n = 15	Logistic	.0610	267	46
Boston,	G	.0300	3	76
1700-1790	G Open	.0459	231	43
n = 12	Logistic	.1450	430	37

Sources: Figures 1.1 and 1.3.

of that for G and an exponent of .0561, almost double that promoted by Verhulst and by Pearl and Reed. Nothing very definitive is decided, however, by so few observations from such uncertain early historical information.

The bottom part of Table 1.2, nevertheless, demonstrates how well G fits the additional, illustrative data of Figure 1.4. Only applications to series with quite a few dates are considered (omitting the two four-point trendings for Mauritius 1735–1787 and 1787–1817). These findings show two things: (1) G averages a rank of 2.5 in over 3,000 modelings for the six historical cases (coming in first half of the time) compared with average ranks of 67 for G_o and 389 for the logistic fit; and in every instance simple, straightforward G "beats" both those additional-parameter formulas in terms of the F statistic. (2) The exponential coefficient for G_o though averaging rather high (.0366) compared with the fixed model's .0300, displays much less variation than the coefficients required by the six logistic challengers (.0292 to .0459 as opposed to .0256 to .1450), while the best and most certain data—for Missouri population, Tennessee blacks, and U.S. cities over 500,000—have the three exponential parameters closest to the theorized .0300 (.0344, .0297, and .0292 respectively, for an average of .0311). In sum, though more data are needed to clinch the argument, it appears as though looking out for G patterns in evidence of demographic growth will be neither a futile nor a misleading endeavor.

What, then, about the proposed H trends of 1850–1930 and 1940–2030 (best seen in Figure 1.3)? For the former, the case is clear. H with exponential coefficient fixed at .03 is the very best of over 3,000 fittings tried (the third layer of Table 1.2). Left to float in a calculation of H_o, the exponential coefficient becomes .0273. Both H-type models appreciably improve upon the logistic, for all its past touted success over this historical span.

For the subsequent period from 1940 through middle-level Bureau of the Census projections to 2030, once more fixed H "beats" H_o, which in turn improves upon the logistic. The exponential coefficient for H_o here is .0272, again close to the expected .0300 of H. Now, however, the 1940–2030 trend incorporates a much later and flatter segment of the curving H pattern than that for 1850–1930 as Figure 1.3 displays the modelings.[12] As H (or G, for that matter) stops bending so much as it did in its early stages, other formulas can compete more readily in fitting the evidence. Here H, though better than both H_o and the logistic, ranks only 156th among the 3,000 curves tried. In particular, the simple arithmetic line, $y = a + bx$, rises in power. In this particular application it places 9th, with almost double the F value of H, whereas the line was a horrible fit for 1850–1930 (only 2,686th in rank among the available array of curves). As other cases with relatively flat patterns of change are encountered, in H or in some other, no longer so vigorously curving G-based shape, the question becomes this: What is of more analytical value, knowing that the forms are still being repeated, if only in their waning stages, or ignoring them because with increasing flatness they are losing their statistical clout? Much of the choice would seem to depend upon the insight that the curves, however shallow and statistically less competitive they become under these conditions, still provide into the population growths they depict and the nature of the processes by which these occur.

One more procedural question needs consideration. Where do old trends stop and new ones begin? If the division of time were viewed differently, would a different form of curve fit better?

While computer programs exist for lengthening and shortening trends and retesting their shapes, these will not be applied here, though readers interested in certain cases may want to bring such measures to bear in their own evaluations. Dealing with several thousand historical trends in population size and demographic behavior as this study does, to use such techniques is first of all impracticable. Further, they do not seem necessary. Instead, templates are employed to start with a visual estimate as to what segment of data is following what form. This procedure identifies quite well the relatively simple, repeated successions of G-based patternings that have occurred in growth and other movements in population history, the following chapters will show. It also spots situations where alternative trending seems possible and more than one fitting needs to be considered. An illustration of this is contained in Figure 1.3. Taken alone, data for 1950–1990 could be represented well by a G curve. That would leave the census number for 1940 hanging below the H trend for 1850–1930 and suggest that the Pearl-Reed logistic might be a better model for 1850–1940 than an H. Statistical comparison of the two formulas for that altered span of time (not shown in Table 1.2), however, demonstrates that the H is still preferable, though the logistic moves closer if 1940 is included in the calculation. In the meantime, evidence for 1997 (let alone currently preferred projections for subsequent years) show that 1940 should instead be incorporated into the trend for 1950–2030 since this postwar H pattern runs pretty much right back through the post-Depression level of that year.

Readers may find more sophisticated testing of alternative turning points and what they do to the shapes of the trends involved to be appropriate in certain cases of concern to them. On the whole, however, much simpler technique would seem to capture most of the less-clear transitions and set forth how these at times might be depicted and interpreted in more than one fashion. The possibility of alternative trending here and there and thoughts about what it would take to come to a decision will not be neglected, as subsequent chapters examine the ways in which G, F, H, and three other G-based patterns account for historical paths of demographic growth and change and open up insight into how these movements occurred and affected the life of the populations involved.

NOTES

1. The essay was first published by S. Kneeland, Boston, 1755. Initially it was sent to Peter Colinson and Robert Jackson in England. (Colinson replied September 27, 1752.) The piece was circulated for several years before it was published. Besides Kneeland's

printing, as an appendix to an essay by William Clarke, "Observations on the late and present Conduct of the French, with Regard to their Encroachments upon the British Colonies in North America," all or parts of Franklin's argument appeared in *Gentlemen's Magazine*, November 1755, *Scots Magazine*, April 1756, and the *London Chronicles*, May 20, 1760 (Labaree 1961, 4: 358, note 8).

2. In the international debate that was evolving, David Hume in 1752 stressed the role of restraints proceeding from "difficulties in men's situation," for which he gave plague and—by implication—bad government as examples (Hume 1854, 3: 413–15). Robert Wallace, in contrast, followed Franklin's emphasis on the "number and fruitfulness of marriages" in his 1753 argument (15–20, 161–63). Several classic discussions dealing with the population growth are usefully excerpted in Appleman 1976.

3. This is a model still liked for the history of European population by Carlo Cippola (1979, 111).

4. The "L" illustration in Figure 1.1 is based upon the Pearl-Reed (1920) application of Verhulst's logistic formula to U.S. population from 1790 through 1910. Figure 1.2, in order to facilitate schematic comparison with G, sets the exponential coefficient of the logistic at $-.03$ rather than $-.03134$, which was the best fit for many years of actual U.S. population increase, in the views of Verhulst and Pearl and Reed.

5. For recent demographic applications see Keyfitz 1968, 76, 213–18. By 1977 (in the first edition of Keyfitz 1985, 23), however, Keyfitz argued that, for predicting population size, the value of the logistic was useful only in ecological models, not demographic ones. "As a means of forecasting, the logistic has become something of a museum piece."

6. Figures for Maryland and Virginia (Series Z 13 and Z 14) and therefore intercolonial totals, however, are amended by Russell R. Menard's (1980) suggested corrections. These are most accessible to readers in McCusker and Menard 1991, 136.

7. Ralph Gray brought to my attention the nature of the G curve as a near relation of the Gompertz formula and the fact that Gompertz's equation was once in a while used in economic analysis.

8. Another way of expressing G, without so many superscripts, is logarithmic in form: $\ln[1 - \ln (P_t/P_0)] = -.03t$, in which ln is Napier's natural logarithm.

9. *New York Times*, February 5, 1989, 30.

10. St. Mary's City files. Data gathered by Russell R. Menard and Alan L. Kulikoff. The level of the series is adjusted for division of the county in the early 1730s.

11. In its lists of results from fitting, the *TableCurve* program uses the abbreviated term "logistic" for the logistic peak function, not for the transitional S-shaped logistic curve of Verhulst, which it labels "sigmoid." The two models should not be confused. In this case the coefficients and the F value are almost identical. Sometimes they differ markedly, however. To our patterns of data, the nonlinearly calculated logistic is quite generally a better fit than its linearly computed counterpart (curve 8011 vs. 601 in the *TableCurve* array).

12. With data not beginning until 52 years after the t_0 for the formula, 1888, rather than right at that point for the earlier H.

Chapter 2

Patterning the Parts as Well as the Whole across Four Centuries of American Demographic Increase

If the constantly proportionally decelerating G function, its more slowly slowing modification H, and the simple .03 exponential equation F adequately pattern the expansion of the American people from the first successful European colonization in 1607 into the foreseeable future, how *generally*, then, do they account for increases in populations? Are these three forms of trends products simply of U.S. continental experience, part of a demographic exceptionalism in New World life that was first argued long ago by Franklin and Malthus? Or do they represent patterns of growth that are more common, perhaps universal? In what kinds of historical contexts, furthermore, do the three different, if mathematically connected, trends respectively appear? From knowing where each occurs, what clues arise concerning dynamics of human life that might produce the G, F, and H forms of population increase?

A first step toward answering these questions is available within the American population, in the growth histories of the thirteen colonies that composed early British North America and the fifty states that eventually evolved from them. How well do the proposed G, H, and F patterns represent successive stages of increase in these several dozen regional populations? When, in which colonies or states, and under what circumstances have the three distinct, if related, forms of demographic expansion appeared? And what, in turn, does knowing where these different patternings occur do to enlighten understanding of how life in the diverse parts of this large society of the Western Hemisphere evolved? How insightful, in other words, is modeling demographic growth with the new formulas for interpreting the ways in which various localities shared or did not share various aspects of their historical development? How useful a tool is the new depiction of population increase likely to be for topics of historical inquiry other than demography, at the same time that it fruitfully reorders and reshapes questions about how population processes themselves operated?

INSIGHTS FROM POPULATION GROWTH IN THE ORIGINAL AREAS OF MAINLAND BRITISH NORTH AMERICA SINCE THE 1600s

To discover that four centuries of overall U.S. demographic growth can effectively be summarized by just three mathematically related functions, as demonstrated in Chapter 1, tempts one to speculate as to how far increases in *many* types of populations can be generalized in like manner. These same preliminary findings, though, also raise some fundamental procedural questions that must be addressed before more far-ranging applications of the formulas can be undertaken and any broader claims advanced.

On the one hand, it is essential to establish the generality of the growth patterns proposed. In what kinds of populations or subpopulations do the different, if related, F, G, and H trends appear? What is known about the characteristics of particular demographic units that followed one path of expansion or another—of the environments in which the people concerned lived out their lives—that will help decipher the processes by which one course of growth rather than some alternative was taken? Do similar forms of change in size reflect comparable underlying dynamics of demographic development and response to economic and social change?

Simultaneously, however, it is also necessary to evaluate somewhat further how well the proposed curves actually work as tools for description or explanation. The landscape of intellectual inquiry is cluttered, horizon to horizon, with abandoned claims for general patterning that soon proved unpersuasive. Do each of the preferred growth trajectories in fact depict the empirical evidence better than other possibilities? Is the suggested G, or its modification H, over and over again a better fit for conditions of slowing growth than the logistic sigmoid or the cumulative normal curve or some other already familiar model for transition? Do the three proposed trend types even improve upon a straight line or a simple log-linear slope at some rate other than .03 for capturing the shape of substantial periods of change? Even accepting as better the underlying principle of constant proportional deceleration that is imbedded in the new curves, finally, would some value for the exponential constant other than the proposed .03 be more accurate? These are not always easy assessments to make, but the best must be done to probe such questions effectively.

A logical place to begin an evaluation of the generality of the new interpretation would seem to be among those early settlements in the New World which composed the aggregate 17th-century population for which the G function was initially discovered to be a promising descriptive formulation for change over time. The analysis thus starts with particulars for the original mainland British

North American colonies that became the United States, examining their growth both in the early years and in later, better recorded eras of their history. How accurately, how insightfully, and how universally, do the G, F, and H functions proposed in fact represent demographic increase in the types of historical developments that these settlements and their populations have experienced?

Table 2.1 in four parts, A through D, depicts the way that the demographic growth of sixteen pre-Revolutionary regions of what became the United States of America would seem best to be patterned by G-related curves.[1] The evidence begins with the establishment of Jamestown and follows growth, colony by colony and then state by state, up through figures from the 1990 census and projections preferred by the Bureau of the Census for the first quarter of the 21st century (*Hist. Stat.* 2: 1168, Series Z 2–19; 1: 24–37, Series B 195.[2] *Stat. Abs.* 1997, 35). For purposes of analysis, all data from all areas were graphed. Some illustrations of different kinds of sequences of G-based trends appear, in semi-logarithmic or ratio scale, in Figure 2.1 for Virginia, Connecticut, Pennsylvania, and South Carolina. Virginia, the largest of all the colonies, has experienced both H and F exceptional forms of demographic increase, in recent years as well as during her early history. In contrast, Connecticut is one of several early colonies/states whose population across four centuries has apparently grown only via a series of G trends. Pennsylvania illustrates robust, enduring multiplication that was shared by various mid-Atlantic regions in the 18th and 19th centuries, while South Carolina shows a shift from sustained pre-Revolutionary demographic dynamism to subsequent expansion only via the rapidly decelerating G form.

Transparent templates for the G function and its related formulas were tried out upon the graphs for all sixteen pre-Revolutionary colonies/states in order to estimate the kinds of trends present in various segments of each series and the necessary initial parameters for nonlinear curve-fitting designed to minimize proportional error.[3] The fitted curves were then examined visually, considering, for instance, whether the flatter bend of an H would represent the evidence more tightly than a more sharply decelerating G, or whether a more accurate modeling could be obtained by starting or ending a chronological phase at a different point in time. Sometimes a better alternative became clear. Once in a while an observation or estimate stood out that, unlike evidence around it, defied inclusion in a G-based trend. In a few cases, which will also be discussed, modeling might reasonably go more than one way. On the whole, though, it appears that the 103 fitted trends cited in Table 2.1 represent quite well the growth movements of 16 parts of colonial America from their earliest years of settlement through near-term projections for the early 21st century.

Table A.1 in Appendix A demonstrates that this conclusion is not merely a mirage. It compares the proposed G-based trendings that are graphed as examples in Figure 2.1 (from four among the sixteen colonial areas of what became the United States) on the F-statistic basis introduced for Table 1.2 of Chapter

Table 2.1
Demographic Growth Trends in Early U.S. Colonies/States by Region

A. The 17th Century South

Virginia	Maryland	North Carolina	South Carolina
1607-1670 G 1668	1634-1710 G 1696		
1670-1710 H 1671			
1710-1770 F -		1670-1730 F -	1670-1690 G 1733
	1720-1760 G 1733	1730-1750 G 1752	1700-1720 G 1730
			1720-1770 H 1768
1780-1870 G 1774	1770-1840 G 1768	1760-1840 G 1785	1780-1870 G 1790
	1840-1870 G 1834	1840-1870 G 1823	
1870-1930 G 1863	1870-1910 G 1858	1870-1910 G 1869	1870-1940 G 1872
	1920-1940 G 1897	1920-1970 G 1914	1950-1970 G 1923
1940-2025 H 1908	1940-2025 G 1950	1970-2025 H 1909	1970-2025 G 1959

B. New England

Massachusetts	Rhode Island	Connecticut	New Hampshire
1640-1660 G 1655			1640-1680 G 1638
1660-1690 G 1675	1640-1680 G 1679	1640-1700 G 1680	
1710-1780 G 1723	1680-1710 F -	1700-1740 G 1719	1680-1730 G 1703
	1720-1810 G 1744	1750-1840 G 1752	1730-1760 G 1754
1790-1850 accel.	1790-1850 accel.		1760-1880 G 1788
1840-1870 G 1844	1840-1870 G 1844	1850-1880 G 1845	
1880-1950 G 1883	1880-1940 G 1885	1890-1940 G 1893	1880-1940 G 1849
1950-2025 G 1919	1940-2025 G 1914	1950-1970 G 1947	1950,1960 ?G 1927
		1970-2025 rG 1920	1970-2025 G 1963

C. Middle Atlantic

New York	Pennsylvania	New Jersey	Delaware
1640-1670 G 1659			
1670-1710 G 1691			1650-1690 G 1683
1710-1750 G 1729	1690-1720 G 1707	1670-1730 G 1718	1690-1720 G 1715
	1730-1760 G 1754		1720-1760 G 1753
1750-1780 G 1767	1760-1820 F -	1730-1840 H 1745	1770-1840 G 1766
1790-1830 G 1820			
1830-1900 H 1818	1830-1880 H 1831	1840-1890 H 1855	1840-1940 H 1803
1900-1950 G 1897	1890-2025 G 1886	1890-1950 G 1903	
1950-1970 G 1924		1950-1970 G 1944	1950-1970 G 1956
1980-2005 rG 1892		1970-2025 rG 1935	1980-2025 G 1958
2010-2025 G 1954			

D. Other Once-Colonial Areas

Maine	Vermont	West Virginia	Georgia
			1740-1760 G 1781
			1760-1790 G 1803
1780-1930 G 1814	1790-1810 G 1814	1790-1840 H 1806	1790-1820 G 1818
	1810-1940 rG 1787	1840-1870 G 1844	1820-1870 G 1836
		1870-1890 G 1876	1870-1950 G 1874
1940-1970 G 1897	1940-1960 G 1883	1900-1950 G 1899	1930-1980 accel.?
1970-2025 G 1941	1970-2025 G 1949	1950-1970 1/G?	1980-2025 G 1973
		1980-2025 1/G?	

Sources: U.S. Bureau of Census, *Historical Statistics* 2: 1168, 1: 24–37; and *Statistical Abstracts* 1977, 1985, 1991, 1993, 1997. Note 6 in Chapter 1.

Figure 2.1
Patterns of Population Growth in Some U.S. States Colonized before the Revolution

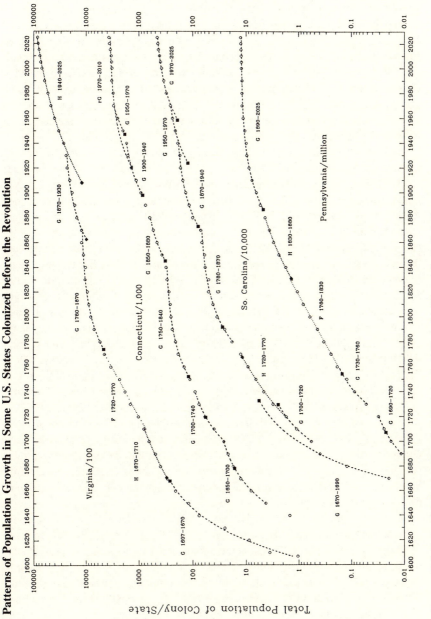

Sources: U.S. Bureau of Census, *Historical Statistics* 2: 1168, 1: 24–37; and *Statistical Abstracts* 1977, 1985, 1991, 1993, 1997. Note 6 in Chapter 1.

1. This procedure, once again, weighs both the goodness of fit of the model to the data and the number of adjustable parameters employed in the formula to achieve this degree of accuracy. For each historical segment of demographic growth in each colony/state that incorporates five or more observations or estimates of population size across a span of at least forty years, the fixed G or H model with .03 exponent is compared with its alternative having open or floating exponent and also with the familiar linear and logistic modes of trending. With regard to log-linear patterning, the eye records satisfactorily what curve-fitting shows: This constant exponential formula, contrary to what stable population theory implies and to how social scientists so often look at data, is of little use except in the one .03 slope of unusual F-slope circumstances. That is, almost everything on a semi-logarithmic graph such as Figure 2.1 *bends*.

Table A.1 first of all presents the F values from respective curve-fittings for the four models considered.[4] This not only indicates which of the four formulas works best but shows how some differences between models are proportionally much larger than others. Results in part A of the table for states that were once British colonies show that, for 9 of 11 hypothesized G segments of demographic increase in Figure 2.1 that involve a reasonable amount of data, the basic G curve with exponent fixed at .03 is the best fit among the four competitors displayed here. Of the two exceptions, for Virginia 1870–1930 the arithmetic line should be the choice; for Connecticut 1900–1940, the logistic curve after Verhulst. In its nine strong performances the G formula, furthermore, averages 16th among more than 3,000 curves that were tried, though it falls well back into the pack in the two Virginia and Connecticut instances of poorer fit. Meanwhile, the exponential coefficients used by the open or extra-parameter version of the G formula—G_o—in the 11 cases addressed in Table A.1 average .0262. While this is lower than the expected .03, it offsets the rather *high* results found in 7 similar fittings for putative G trends in Table 1.2 of Chapter 1. Together, that is, all 18 potential Gs explored so far have an average exponent of .0296, very close to the hypothesized .03. This finding, along with the fact that the F value of G_o only for Virginia 1870–1930 outscores the results from basic, *fixed* G among the 11 cases of Table A.1, indicates that the standardized two-parameter formula with .03 constant is going to suffice as a tool for representing movements of the G sort. No third parameter to let the exponential coefficient be something other than .03 is required.

There are only four cases of H-type or slower deceleration in demographic increase for once-colonial states in Figure 2.1 and part B of Table A.1. In three of these, however, the H formula with fixed .03 exponent is the best model. (Once again, the log-linear alternative is an obvious loser.) The weak example from contemporary Virginia, for which the logistic edges into the lead, heavily depends upon Bureau of the Census projections for the next quarter of a century. The average exponent for the four applications of the open version of H, meanwhile, comes to .0282. That makes a mean of .0279 when combined with the two nationwide instances from Table 1.2 of Chapter 1, for a total of six apparent

H trends encountered so far. Meanwhile, log-linear fits for Virginia 1710–1770 and Pennsylvania 1760–1830, where F trajectories have been hypothesized, yield exponents of .0297 and .0291 respectively, to accompany the .0295 that was found in the last chapter for the United States as a whole in 1680–1850.

Finally, the attempted fitting of over 3,000 formulas to each of the G and H trends of Table A.1 indicates that other familiar models for change through time are quite unlikely to represent the kinds of movements observed in demographic increase. Nonlinear equations of transition besides the sigmoid of Verhulst—such as the cumulative function of Gauss and the logistic dose response; peak equations like those of Gauss and Lorentz, the log normal and the logistic peak functions, and formulas for extreme value and complementary error peaks; wave equations like those of sin and sine^2—all prove to do poorly for these data that can reasonably be modeled by G or H. One or another of those different formulas gives a good fit once in a while, but no sign of consistent competition emerges. The same is true for hundreds of intercept, polynomial, and rational equations. In short, what seems to be a G, or an H, or an F trend most likely is one.

There can be no guarantee here that some other way of segmenting the time series and/or the use of one or more different functions might not provide better fitting in terms of accuracy, simplicity, or generality. As the evidence of this and following chapters accumulates, however, the burden of proof would soon seem to shift to those who would claim that they can pattern so much historical information with so few and so closely related formulas and so little error as is possible with the proffered G-based functions. There do remain occasional anomalous data points, such as 1890 for Connecticut in Figure 2.1. There also will persist periods in certain series that might reasonably be modeled with more than one combination of G-related curves. The significance of outlying evidence and alternative possibilities for trending will be noted and discussed throughout this study. But it seems appropriate here to move ahead to another way of evaluating the kind of modeling proposed.

That is, what do the kinds of trendings offered in Figure 2.1 and Table 2.1 accomplish for historical understanding? On the one hand, do they make sense when held up against what is already known about how regional populations expanded and changes in the conditions under which people lived that may have affected such demographic growth? On the other, do they provide fruitful fresh insight into what is *not* yet properly comprehended—for instance, about how particular areas of the United States flourished or languished at certain times, not just demographically but in economic and social development?

The first thing to note, best seen from Table 2.2, is that the large majority of trends identified for population growth in the sixteen early areas of British American settlement and their successor states are of G form. No less than 52 of 69, or 75 percent, of trends lasting at least forty years and based upon at least five data points have this basic decelerating shape; so do 84 of 103 fitted trends in

Table 2.2
The Frequency of G and Various G-Based Trends in the Population Sizes of U.S. Colonies/States

Once-Colonial States (*n* = 16)   Later States (*n* = 34)

Trend Type:	Longer Series	Shorter Series	Total	Longer Series	Shorter Series	Total
F	3	1	4	0	1	1
H	10	0	10	6	2	8
accel.	3	0	3	0	0	0
1/G	1	1	2	0	3	3
rG	4	0	4	5	9	14
G	48	32	80	55	48	103
Total	69	34	103	66	63	129

All Colonies/States (*n* = 50)

	Longer	Shorter	Total
F	3	2	5
H	16	2	18
accel.	3	0	3
1/G	1	4	5
rG	9	9	18
G	103	80	183
Total	135	97	232

Sources: Tables 2.1, 2.3.

all, or 81 percent. This predominance of G curves pertains in the 17th and 18th centuries; it also persists in the 19th and 20th. Colonies/states like Maryland, Connecticut, New Hampshire, Maine, and Vermont—5 of 16 areas covered in Table 2.1—have known demographic growth in no other form than G. South Carolina, Massachusetts, and Georgia have experienced only one phase of their population increase along some other G-related path.

Among the exceptions to these predominating G movements, just four trends of the Franklin-Malthus constant exponential form emerge: for North Carolina 1670–1730, Rhode Island (briefly) 1680–1710, Virginia 1710–1770, and Pennsylvania 1760–1820 (Table 2.1). The latter two were, in their respective periods, large colonies with established economic systems and room for substantial further interior settlement. Geographically extending "frontier" expansion is easily understood also for North Carolina 1670–1730. The population of this extensive area began on a small scale through overflows from neighboring Virginia and South Carolina. It expanded in F fashion across eastern coastal regions until that $e^{.03}$ slope was replaced by even steeper G-shape surging as heavy migration (including many Germans and Irish swinging south from Philadelphia and other northern ports of entry) moved into North Carolina's interior piedmont region across the decades leading up to the Revolution. New England historians, meanwhile, will even understand how, following the destruction of the once-powerful Narragansetts in Metacom's War (1675–1676), Rhode Island became an inviting interior frontier at the very time when conflict with Canada for more than two decades shut off, or destroyed and thrust back, settlement in Maine, New Hampshire, the Connecticut Valley, and even places not far from Boston. Graphing and curve-fitting not shown here, finally, suggests that something like F trends *might* have appeared in New Hampshire 1680–1760 and New York 1690–1780, though the successions of G curves reported in Table 2.1 seem to fit the data more tightly than these alternative plottings, given the evidence available at present.

No F-type demographic increase appears after 1820 in these sixteen parts of the future United States. That does not mean, of course, that later-settled post-Revolutionary states might not be found in their turn to display the form in certain expansive situations. It is essential to understand, however, that in all four instances where log-linearity definitely applies in Table 2.1—among over 100 phases of local growth in all—the same single F pattern of the simple exponential with coefficient fixed at .03 suffices to represent the trend taken. No *other* log-linear slope emerges. In other words, the supposition of much demography (since Euler in 1760) that populations tend to stabilize around log-linear trends of growth (or decline), in an unlimited array of paths from very shallow to steep, is undermined by this historical evidence. Only the G-based .03 trajectory of F occurs. This growth pattern appears to represent an exploitation of certain exceptional environmental circumstances, situations that resemble on a more local scale the context of the continentally expanding American population as a whole from the 1670s through the 1850s, the "frontier" society from which first Franklin, and after him Malthus, drew their fundamental insight.

Did the 10 instances in which slowly decelerating H-type demographic increase appeared in the 16 once-colonial areas covered in Table 2.1 similarly occur in conditions like those of 1850–1930 for the United States as a whole, where this form of expansion was discovered in Chapter 1? For America in aggregate that was a period of substantial and sustained economic development and urbanization.

To speak of urbanization in Virginia 1670–1710 makes little sense. This was, however, an era of significant economic growth, as the tobacco culture of the Chesapeake took mature shape in the Tidewater region, including the introduction of slavery as a mainstay of the labor force, the rise of large planters at the expense of lesser farmers, and some substantial diversification or fleshing out of economic activity. The ensuing F trend of demographic increase for 1710–1770, one might say, then reflects the extension of this regional system into the large interior of Virginia (when towns for marketing and providing services for the expansion finally developed in a significant way). What tobacco was to Virginia, rice was to South Carolina. Introduced in the 1690s to a colony started only in the 1670s, rice culture took off after the Peace of Utrecht (1713), spreading across suitable coastal wetlands from Georgia to southern North Carolina, making Charleston a fast-rising colonial urban hub. In the 18th century indigo joined rice as an internationally successful South Carolina product. From these development processes would seem to come the H trend for demographic increase in the colony from about 1720 to the Revolution.

Historians, like modern travelers, tend to overlook New Jersey between the more obvious centers of Philadelphia and New York. Yet the grain and livestock farming that built both those much-studied ports thrived in between them, and parts of the region became bases for important colonial and early national craftsmanship and industry. While Pennsylvania, comparably endowed with resources and transportation in its southeastern zones, also possessed a large interior whose settlement tended to dominate the overall pattern of demographic increase at this stage (producing the F trend of 1760–1820 shown in Table 2.1), New Jersey did not. Thus population growth there in H fashion from 1730 through 1840 probably reflects the way economic development, not expanding settlement, left its imprint upon demographic increase. Much the same seems to have been the case in the mountainous region of northwestern Virginia, the counties that split off to become West Virginia during the Civil War. This area with little inviting farmland but many active iron works and other industrial enterprises saw its population, too, swell in H fashion from 1790 (or sooner) to 1840 (Adams 1986).

Another four cases of H-type, only slowly decelerating demographic expansion, appeared in the Middle Atlantic region of the United States in the *19th* century in the four neighboring states of New York 1840–1890, New Jersey 1830–1900, Pennsylvania 1830–1880, and Delaware 1840–1940. As first canals and then railroads bound the ocean and its ports to the Great Lakes and the Mississippi heartland, economic growth and urbanization both thrived in this region. To have these particular states of the eastern seaboard see their populations increase so distinctly in the H pattern that was characteristic in 1850–1930 for the country as a whole seems appropriate for a zone that was so pivotal for the industrial and transportation revolutions of 19th century America. To have the residents of Virginia and North Carolina seemingly multiply, much later, in parallel H paths in 1940–2025 and 1970–2025 then raises questions about the location and the nature of American economic development in the 20th century and about the growth that followed the Great Depression. Apparently similar interactions of economic change and demographic increase are at work today in the post-industrial era as well, not in all "Sun Belt" states but in some of them—and perhaps in other portions of the country, too.

What, though, about the early 19th century industrialization of New England? There, a quite different form of demographic increase seems to have accompanied economic development. Between 1790 and 1850, in these two pioneering industrial states with their famous water-powered factories on the Merrimack, Charles, Fall, and Blackstone Rivers, the populations of Massachusetts and Rhode Island seem to have expanded in some *accelerating* manner, starting gradually but growing proportionally faster and faster instead of slower and slower. Was this previously unencountered exceptional pattern also based upon the G formula? Under what kinds of conditions did it occur? These questions are best answered where further pertinent historical evidence presents itself. But the possibility that such a trend was also followed by the population of modern Georgia between 1930 and 1980 hints that early 19th century factory industrialization may not have been the only historical setting for accelerating demographic increase.

Still another new form of change in population size appears for West Virginia, first from 1950 to 1970 and then—after some brief growth—from 1980 into the new century. Here the number of residents *declined*. That atrophy, however, looks as though it might take the form of G upside down, starting fast but apparently decelerating at something like the familiar .03 pace. Once again, proper analysis of this extra pattern awaits the examination of historical settings in which the phenomenon may be more common. Still, these 5 exceptional cases among the 103 covered in Table 2.1 serve as a warning that other paths of change in population size may occur, but allow that these in turn could also prove to be related to the basic G function.

For the most part, however, just successions of G curves sufficiently pattern demographic increase in the sixteen early parts of the United States currently under consideration. And almost all of the time in these sequences a steeper G segment (one with a later base year or t_0) replaces the old one. Something inspires and allows fresh growth, which is then played out in the usual type of deceleration. In Table 2.1, nevertheless, appear three instances in which a *slower* or *flatter* phase of G follows the previous one. These *retrogressive* transitions (with the new curve designated "rG" in Table 2.1) all appear in very recent years in a cluster of neighboring states: New York 1980–2005 (after which growth is currently projected to resume by the Bureau of the Census); and New York's Siamese sisters to the east and southwest, Connecticut (Figure 2.1) and New Jersey, from 1970 into the second or third decade of the new century. In these places, somehow a "ceiling" of development seems to have been hit, abruptly forcing more modest trajectories of further demographic expansion upon the region.[5] Is this a phenomenon that is common to other historical circumstances in which growth overshoots its mark? What causes such sudden or sharp-angled change of direction in pattern rather than the usual succession of G's, and what consequences does it have?

Finally, in the same fashion seen for the contiguous 19th century H's of the Middle Atlantic states, the demographic accelerations of industrializing Massachusetts and Rhode Island, or the present-day rot spreading across the hinterland of the Big Apple, the cross-state or cross-colony sharing of G patterns, too, can confirm or improve our knowledge of how regional developments evolved and affected population change. The expansion of the antebellum Old South, for instance, shows up in G trends that were shared by the populations of Maryland, Virginia, and the Carolinas from just before the Revolution into the middle of the next century (Figure 2.1 and Table 2.1). Equally parallel was subsequent demographic increase in these four states from 1870 into the early 1900s. Insightful, though, is the way industrialization and better transportation gave fresh growth to Maryland 1840–1870 and new tobacco cultivation brought extra population increase to North Carolina about the same time, while Virginia and South Carolina kept plodding along in the old G tracks until "the war" (Gates 1962, 110–15).

Insightfully, also, Massachusetts, Rhode Island, and Connecticut shared G trends of demographic expansion for approximately 1840–1870 and then again 1880–1940, without taking New Hampshire or Maine along. New Hampshire began to pick up more general New England patterns in the 1880s and forged ahead after 1970 with the steepest contemporary regional G trajectory of all. Though less vigorous than that, Maine's demographic expansion since 1970 has matched the G that Connecticut attempted 1950–1970 before giving way to slower growth and has exceeded modern paths of increase for Rhode Island and Massachusetts. Similarly, the populations of New York, New Jersey, and Pennsylvania swelled along mostly parallel G curves from about 1890 to 1950. After World War II, however, this ever-slowing trajectory remained the pattern for Pennsylvania, while the other two states experienced fresh growth. Likewise, from the late 1600s into the early 1700s population increases in New York, New Jersey, Pennsylvania, and Delaware took comparable G paths. For reasons undoubtedly connected with the subsequent economic surge of "the best poor man's country," and the flood of German and Irish immigration that this attracted, however, only Pennsylvania and Delaware experienced new G-type demographic growth approximately from 1720 to 1760.

In the end, though, one of the most important findings of the analysis summarized by Table 2.1 is how closely demographic growths occurring in quite *different* social and economic contexts can resemble each other. For instance, if one aggregates the population increase of the Chesapeake (Maryland and Virginia), on the one hand, and of New England, on the other, across the 17th century, virtually identical G curves result (Harris 1983; 1992, 56–57). In the former region, settlement is generally considered to have been driven by investment in producing a staple, tobacco; and the labor force expanded mostly with bound servants imported from Britain. In the latter, a heavy early migration of free people in families, which soon produced substantial natural increase, was the mode of demographic growth, while religious freedom constituted a large part of the motivation for that brief initial migration. Yet settlement took hold and expanded along strikingly similar G-shape lines in these two distinct and widely separated early colonial regions. Furthermore, the G form of seminal development in other and later colonies, which embraced diverse religious and national groups and exploited quite varied New World economic opportunities, indicates that the origins of this parallel G *shape* in early New England and the Chesapeake could hardly be determined by conditions in 17th century England such as real wage trends, the availability of capital, and the like, which are too often invoked to explain those patterns of colonization.

STARTING TO GENERALIZE FROM THESE PRELIMINARY FINDINGS: DEMOGRAPHIC EXPERIENCE IN THAT MAJORITY OF U.S. STATES THAT WERE "SETTLED" AFTER THE REVOLUTION

For a limited number of oldest regions within the United States, whose population has so often served as material for building demographic theory, the simple G curve by itself has been shown to represent the shape of most trends of recorded or estimated historical growth. In addition, however, the exceptional F and H patterns first encountered for the United States as a whole for approximately 1675–1850 and 1850–1930 have been found suited for certain periods of demographic change in a few parts of the country under conditions that seem to resemble the circumstances of extensive settlement and economic development in which they were first observed in national demographic history. The survey so far has also shown that two other forms of change in population size, a decelerating type of decline and some kind of accelerating growth, may be needed in order to account for all of the historical movements encountered.

What does the experience of the other thirty-four states of the United States then add concerning the generality of these findings? Table 2.3 lists what graphing and curve-fitting of the kind employed for Table 2.1 show about the shape of trends in these twice-as-numerous areas that were more recently "settled" by Europeans, brushing aside or destroying the indigenous inhabitants. Figure 2.2 presents a few more visual examples of the trending that results as all areas are graphed and analyzed. Louisiana illustrates further the occasional local appearance of the H type of expansion in the 19th century, here in the New South rather than the Mid-Atlantic region. Oregon is one of a few western states (part F of Table 2.3) that display this form of growth of late. The populations of Illinois and Utah, meanwhile representing quite different parts of trans-Appalachian America, have enlarged markedly over time, but only via a sequence of G trends. Iowa, finally, serves as an example of several states of the Plains whose early robust population increase suddenly encountered ceilings of much slower growth (part G of Table 2.3).

Once again, among these thirty-four later-established regional populations shown in Table 2.3, expansion in just the G form predominates. It is even more common here than among the earlier, once-colonial states presented in Table 2.1 (117 of 129 trends or 90 percent, as Table 2.2 indicates, compared with 84 of 103 or 81 percent). No accelerating growth appears, and just one case of constant $e^{.03}$ or F-type increase. That the latter occurred in Florida in the early 20th century should come as no surprise.[6] Three instances of sustained demographic decline emerge, all on the Great Plains: Nebraska 1930–1950, Oklahoma 1930–1950, and—longest of all—North Dakota 1930–1970. Such decay occurred in the Depression, following the Dust Bowl, before the postwar collapse of coal emptied out the hollows of West Virginia (Table 2.1).

Table 2.3
Demographic Growth Trends in Later U.S. States by Region

A. Early Trans-Appalachia

Kentucky	Tennessee	Ohio	Indiana
1770-1820 G 1823	1770-1830 G 1838		
1820-1840 rG 1809	1830-1860 rG 1824		
1840-1870 G 1835		1810-1890 G 1845	1820-1910 G 1857
1870-1920 G 1861	1870-1920 G 1862		
1920-1960 G 1883	1930-1960 G 1911	1900-1940 G 1893	1920-1940 G 1885
1970-2025 G 1935	1970-1990 G 1946	1950-1970 G 1936	1940-2025 G 1929
	1990-2025 G 1965	1970-2025 rG 1902	

B. New South

Louisiana	Mississippi	Alabama	Florida
1810-1830 G 1837			
1830-1860 G 1853	1800-1860 G 1857	1820-1860 G 1855	1830-1850 G 1853
1870-1940 H 1848	1870-1970 G 1871	1870-1920 G 1873	1850-1890 G 1868
		1920-1970 G 1895	1880-1900 G 1893
			1890-1920 F ·
1950-2025 G 1937	1970,1980 ?G 1947	1970,1980 ?G 1945	1920-1940 G 1933
	1990-2025 G 1950	1990-2025 G 1950	1950-1970 G 1973
			1970-2025 G 1980

C. Mississippi-Great Lakes

Illinois	Michigan	Wisconsin	Missouri
		1860-1880 G 1865	1810-1950 G 1867
1810-1890 G 1872	1840-1910 G 1876	1880-1940 G 1881	
1890-1940 G 1888	1910-1950 G 1915		
1950-2015 G 1922	1950-1970 G 1937	1950-2025 G 1933	1950-1990 G 1917
	1970-2025 rG 1910		1990-2025 G 1951

D. Near Southwest

Arkansas	Texas	Colorado	New Mexico
1810-1860 G 1876			1850-1880 G 1850
	1850,1860 ?G 1896		
1880-1940 G 1881	1870-1920 G 1896	1860-1910 G 1906	1890-1940 G 1904
1950,1960 decline	1920-1940 G 1909	1910-1940 rG 1891	
1970-1990 G 1957	1950-1970 G 1943	1950-1990 H 1946	1940-1970 G 1944
1990-2025 G 1960	1970-2025 H 1939	1990-2025 G 1977	1970-1990 G 1966
			1990-2025 G 1984

Table 2.3 (*Continued*)

E. Southwest-Pacific

Utah	Nevada	California	Arizona
1850-1940 G 1896	1860-1940 G 1896	1870-1900 G 1887	1870-1940 G 1918
1950-1970 G 1948	1950-2000 H 2018	1910-1940 G 1930	
1970-2025 G 1978	2000-2025 rG 1966	1940-1980 G 1959	1950-1970 G 1971
		1980-2005 G 1968	1970-2025 G 1986
		2005-2025 G 1997	

F. Northwest-Pacific

Oregon	Washington	Wyoming
1870-1940 G 1904	1870-1910 G 1927	1870-1970 G 1914
	1910-1940 rG 1898	
1940-2025 H 1922	1940-2025 H 1931	1990-2025 H 1927

Alaska	Hawaii	Idaho
1880-1940 G 1878		
	1910-1950 G 1921	1870-1970 G 1918
1940-1980 G 1970	1950-1970 G 1948	
1980-2025 G 1981	1970-2000 G 1963	1970-2025 G 1974
	2000-2025 ?H 1947	

G. Great Plains

Minnesota	Iowa	Nebraska	Kansas
1860-1900 G 1900	1840-1860 G 1900	1860-1900 G 1920	1860-1880 G 1913
1900-1950 rG 1886	1870-1900 rG 1871	1900-1930 rG 1872	1880-1930 rG 1870
	1910-2025 G 1871	1930-1950 1/G?	1930,1940 decline
1950-1990 G 1930		1950-1990 G 1907	1940-1990 G 1911
1990-2025 G 1955		1990-2025 G 1951	1990-2025 ?H 1868

So. Dakota	No. Dakota	Montana	Oklahoma
1870-1890 G 1937	1870-1890 G 1947	1870-1920 G 1919	1890-1910 G 1937
1910-1930 rG 1877	1910-1930 rG 1877	1920-1940 flat	1910-1930 rG 1903
1940-1990 rG 1864	1930-1970 1/G	1950-1990 G 1924	1930-1950 1/G
1990-2025 G 1953	1990-2025 G 1937	1990-2025 G 1968	1960-2000 G 1942
			2005-2025 G 1969

Sources: U.S. Bureau of Census, *Historical Statistics* 2: 1168, 1: 24–37; and *Historical Abstracts* 1977, 1985, 1991, 1993, 1997.

Figure 2.2
Patterns of Growth in Some Post-Revolutionary U.S. States

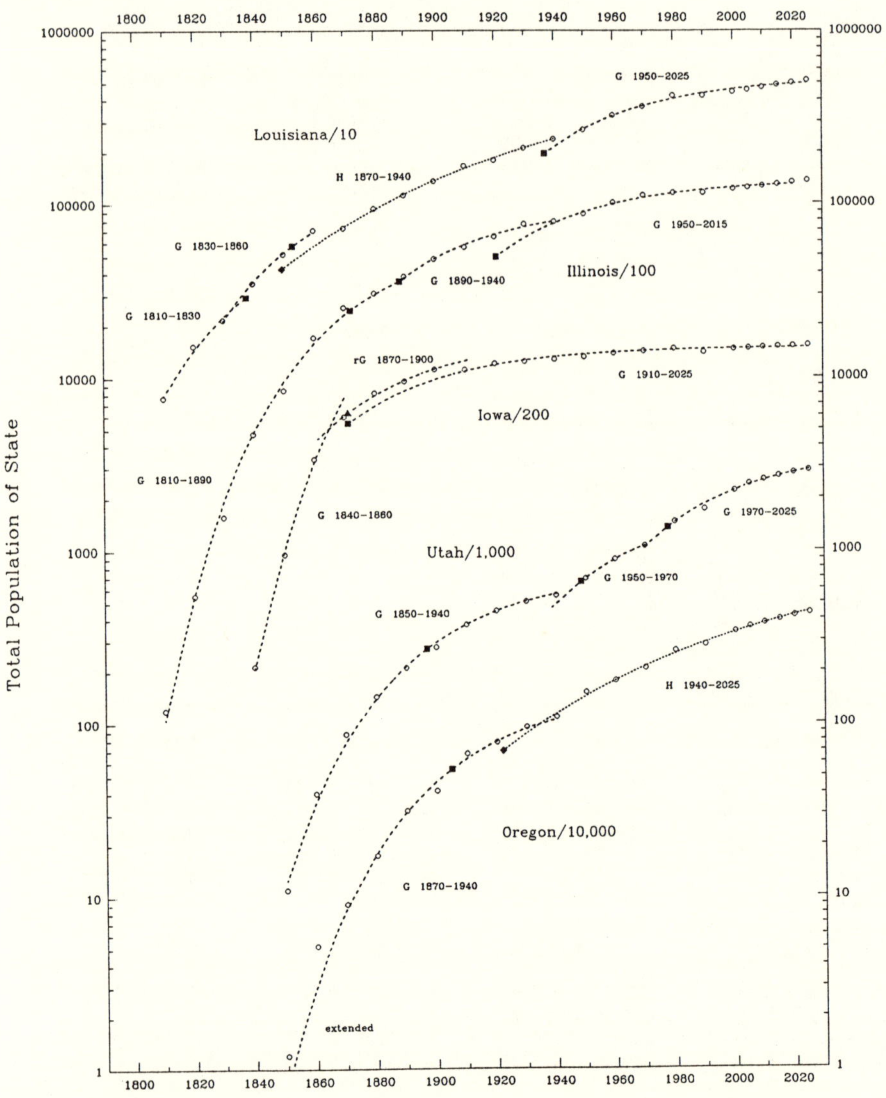

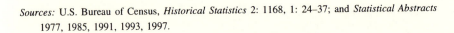

Sources: U.S. Bureau of Census, *Historical Statistics* 2: 1168, 1: 24–37; and *Statistical Abstracts* 1977, 1985, 1991, 1993, 1997.

Eight trends of H shape provide the most significant exception to the pervasiveness of more swiftly decelerating G increase. The form in Louisiana 1870–1940, almost exactly parallel with the national H for 1850–1930, would seem to reflect how that state prospered from its position as outlet for the immense Mississippi-Missouri-Ohio network of riverine trade. The populations of Washington and Oregon have expanded this way since World War II, joined for a while by Colorado 1950–1990 and most recently by Texas 1970–2025 and perhaps by Wyoming in the 1990s. These regional increases appear likely to involve the kind of marriage of population growth and economic change found with the H pattern elsewhere. While similarly postwar in timing (1950–2000), the H trend for Nevada was much steeper, involving takeoff from a smaller local base; but this notorious expansion of glitter-land seems currently to be switching over into a more rapidly decelerating G form, if recent Bureau of the Census projections are correct. Also dependent upon such projections are possible H trajectories for the populations of Hawaii and Kansas across the early years of the 21st century. That for Hawaii resembles in timing and slope the paths for the H trends cited for states of the western continental United States: Washington, Oregon, and Wyoming. The one for Kansas, if it continues to unfold along projected lines, will be much flatter, more like the current H paths for Virginia and North Carolina. Have comparable histories of recent economic development and demographic vigor somehow been shared by these last three states in so separate parts of the country, or is the parallel just coincidental?

Retrogressive successions of G curves by flatter rather than steeper segments of the same shape of trend (rG's, with earlier rather than later base years or t_0's for the G formula) first appeared at the colony or state level in Vermont at about 1810 (in Table 2.1). After the Revolution, recently settled Vermont briefly started to become a new breadbasket for America, supplying the markets of New England, Montreal, and New York with grain. This boom did not last long, however, as fresh agricultural settlements in western New York, Ohio, and Ontario went into production and better transport brought their output eastward. Dozens of Vermont towns disappeared off the map, and many residents left to seek more promising fortunes further west. This out-migration included Joseph Smith, who was murdered in Illinois after promoting his provocative word in New York, Ohio, and Missouri; John Humphrey Noyes, who transferred complex marriage from Putney, Vermont, to Oneida, New York, before moving on to Canada; and the Donners, who, having tried Illinois, went on to eat and be eaten in the California pass that bears their name.

Table 2.3 shows how comparable sudden failures of regional systems to sustain the demographic growth they initially inspired have appeared elsewhere in American history, too. These abrupt changes in direction by once-bumptious local growths have often resulted from agricultural and extractive over-commitment. Lately, they have also been the product of industrial vulnerability. The graphed consequences of these historical collisions of excessively ambitious population increase with limits to what regional economies could achieve look the same, for whatever reasons they have occurred.

In the first westward thrust across the southern Appalachians in the early 19th century, Kentucky and Tennessee were "over-speculated," too. Confronting aggressive engrossers while holding unclear land titles, new settlers soon found it more attractive to keep on going into the New South, Missouri, or the lower portions of Ohio, Indiana, and Illinois (Gates 1962, 11–15). The Lincoln family represents one example. The suddenly flattening change of direction in population growth appeared here in the 1820s, about a decade and a half after Vermont's sudden loss of steam.

Subsequently Iowa in the mid-1860s, Kansas, Nebraska, and the two Dakotas around 1890, and Minnesota about 1900 similarly saw vigorous spurts of agricultural growth, expanding settlement and production, collide with ceilings of economic reality. Here, overoptimistic grain production abruptly encountered gluts in world markets in which Canada, Russia, Australia, and Argentina had become successful competitors. Meanwhile, railroads squeezed farmers in order to make the most of the profits that remained. Such tensions fed first the Granger movement of the 1870s and then Populism in the 1890s.[7]

In like fashion, rapid population growths in Colorado, Montana, and Washington subsequently hit ceilings around 1910. Here the excessively ambitious frontier wagered on mining, ranching, and lumbering. Oversanguine hopes for a last land grab in Oklahoma produced a demographic surge that similarly and simultaneously capped out suddenly, while the two Dakotas now experienced second downward tilts in their trajectories of development. In this particular early 20th century wave of frontier frustrations, the international competition in mining, livestock, and logging featured Australia, New Zealand, Argentina, and western Canada. Ensuing struggles among workers, small producers, big operators, railroads, and financiers set a stage for the heroics/villainies of giants like Big Bill Haywood and his "Wobblies," Eugene Debs, William Jennings Bryan, James J. Hill and Edward H. Harriman, and J. Pierpont Morgan.

As noted, the Dust Bowl and the Great Depression caused significant population *loss* in Nebraska, North Dakota, and Oklahoma for two or more decades after 1930, developments that John Steinbeck and W.P.A. photographers have most famously and indelibly depicted. Then even as the United States emerged as the dominant national economy after World War II, the hollows and mines of West Virginia emptied out, chiefly for work in the factories of the Midwest, as oil (increasingly imported oil) replaced coal in the factories, offices, and homes of America. Quite recently, too, beginning about 1970, historically familiar sharp-angled lids on further population increase have reappeared in America. This time, retrogressive G successions in Michigan and Ohio (Table 2.3) join those in New Jersey, Connecticut, and New York (Table 2.1) to identify a broad zone of eastern "Rust Belt" America across which old industrial forms of economic development have encountered capping limits. The global competition now came from Japan, Korea, Taiwan, and Europe.

In sum, in almost every twenty-plus-year "Kuznets cycle" or "long swing" of economic development since 1800, some economic and demographic frontier within the United States has been stranded by the downturn while attempting more rapid expansion than could be maintained.[8] Virtually every time, some state populations suffered demographic as well as economic scars from having their unrealistic expectations lopped off, expectations that growth would continue forever and never be set back. The main mechanism for local adjustment, when it came, seems to have been migration. Some people stopped coming to where the attraction had been; others left. The history of colonial frontiers such as the valleys of the Appalachians, the upper Connecticut River settlements, or the exposed coastal communities of New Hampshire and Maine before about 1720, furthermore, suggests that such breaks in population growth caused by suddenly hitting ceilings or actually suffering decline in overextended times also occurred *before* the 19th century case of Vermont. The earlier reversals were just more local and have to be traced in terms of the populations of counties and towns, not colonies or states. The "over-ambitious frontier," whether in simple agricultural expansion or in more complex modern economic growth (as for the Michigan to Greater New York belt after 1970), probably has been a recurring feature throughout American population history since close to its beginning (see Barbados about 1640 in Chapter 3).

Ironically, these costly, upsetting collisions of mounting population with ceilings on resources have been regular, recurrent features of the history of North America, the socioeconomic context that Malthus used to represent the exceptional circumstances in which demographic multiplication could *escape* the restraints that brought about such crises! Meanwhile the normal, overwhelmingly usual way in which population was restrained in colonies or states of this country since 1607 has been not sudden or cataclysmic but *continuous*, as Verhulst argued a century and a half ago in his criticism of Malthus.

In new states formed after nationhood as much in those that began as British colonies, furthermore, to observe which places followed these predominantly G-shape paths along with what others both confirms the results of the new mode of trend analysis against the background of what is already familiar and provides some fresh insight as to which regional populations were going through what kinds of experiences when. For instance, like the once-colonial plantation areas of the Chesapeake and the Carolinas, already noted in Table 2.1, the new post-Revolutionary states that had substantial slave populations—Kentucky, Tennessee, Louisiana, Mississippi, Alabama, and Arkansas—all, Table 2.3 shows, enjoyed demographic growth after the Civil War in G form with t_0's near 1870. Missouri, meanwhile—as Figure 1.4 demonstrates—kept up a G trajectory with similar timing that had been followed there already since initial settlement. These findings indicate that in this later 19th century era certain basic adjustments were being shared across all the erstwhile slave-holding states, whether from demographic response among newly freed persons or as some reflection in population growth of the economic reconstitution of plantation America.

More recently, Alabama, Mississippi, and Arkansas shared postwar G growths having base years roughly in the 1940s with Texas, New Mexico, Utah, Oklahoma, Louisiana, Indiana, and Wisconsin (Table 2.3). In the first three of these states, the parallel trends were shifted downward by some demographic stagnation in the 1980s (if not, perhaps, by problems with the 1990 census). In Louisiana, Indiana, and Wisconsin, in contrast, the same postwar G trajectories are continuing unaltered into the new century, while in Utah, New Mexico, and Oklahoma fresh, stronger trends of G shape have appeared. Texas, finally, has seen much more persistently robust H-type expansion of population since 1970. In short, some states that have been lumped together in the "Sun Belt" paradigm have in fact not behaved the same way demographically even though they started off expanding together after World War II. That popular grouping also disregards the similarities of some "Sun Belt" areas with quite differently situated states like Utah, Wisconsin, and Indiana. More work is needed on the reasons for such regional parallels and divergences.

In these and in other ways that readers can readily explore for themselves, both shared and differing population patterns that emerge from Table 2.3, as previously from Table 2.1, mostly suit known local or regional histories. In some other instances they seem to call for some rethinking about what demographic and other changes have in fact taken place, posing further questions that will have to be addressed in trying to explain just how things transpired. Both familiar and innovative results from this kind of inquiry attest to the value of examining population growth with the new analytical instrument of the G curve and its less frequent "relatives" like F and H. The approach *should* make sense in terms of what is already known, yet also open up insights into what has been missed so far.

Once again, however—as for the initial group of erstwhile colonies in Table 2.1—not all data for the post-Revolutionary states of Table 2.3 fit neatly into the proposed summarization by means of G, F, and H trends. Most noticeably, a possible underlying G trend for Alaska 1880–1940 has to cut through the marked up and down swings of the Yukon gold rush at the turn of the century. Similarly, Colorado population size for 1870 is well below what seems otherwise to have been an underlying G pattern 1860–1910 (and is not included in the curve fitting). In Nevada, in contrast, 1870 and 1880 are exceptionally *high* points for a population that otherwise generally seems to have multiplied along a G pattern from first exploitation before 1860 until a tinsel-and-neon, gangster-developed one-armed phoenix arose from the now otherwise silver-bare soil of the state in the 1940s. It would seem that the momentum of mining mania, blunted in Colorado by the Indian wars of the 1860s, shifted to Nevada for a time. The fabulous Comstock lode was discovered there in 1859, and many ore-seekers of the ever-moving mining frontier poured into the area seeking their fortunes.

To discuss the way that the proposed modeling via G and its related F and H curves does not account for the data well at certain points of time in certain places is to raise again the question of goodness of fit. How does the accuracy of the trends offered in Table 2.3 for thirty-four post-Revolutionary U.S. states, for which better, census-based data more generally exist, compare with what was discovered for the sixteen once-colonial territories of Table 2.1? Results for the more substantial trends among the five states graphed for illustration in Figure 2.2 are given in parts C and D of appendix Table A.1.

Where G curves were proposed for trends of at least forty years and five data points (part C), fixed G is always better than the open G_o version with the extra parameter, and the logistic curve, and the simple arithmetic line. In fact, except for Illinois 1950–2025 (dependent heavily upon Bureau of the Census projections for the next quarter of a century), the average rank in F statistic value for the basic G formula is about 12 in over 3,000 curves tried for each case. The average coefficient for open G (G_o) in lieu of the fixed .03 in these 8 new instances comes to .0259. But taking all 26 examples of G trends valuated so far, including 11 from part A of Table 2.2 for the illustrations of Figure 2.1 and 7 more that were previously explored in chapter 1, the average is .0284, not far off the hypothesized .03. That is why G_o rarely improves upon the simpler fixed G.

Where H trends are suspected, the two extra cases of Oregon 1940–2025 and Louisiana 1870–1940 in part D of Table A.1, with relatively high coefficients, raise the average for all eight graphed H segments so far to .0294. Thus H_o is also of no additional help compared with H. No sufficiently long instances of F growth appear in Table 2.3, leaving the average for the 3 previously encountered specimens at .0294. In both the Oregon and the Louisiana examples, H beats the line and the logistic as well as H_o. It comes, respectively, 3rd and 1st among all 3,000-plus formulas tried.

In short, trends that appear to take G or H or F shape in Figures 2.1 and 2.2 and other unprinted graphings from which Tables 2.1 and 2.3 are drawn really are, overall, best generally patterned by those respective formulas, though individual exceptions can occur. What looks like a G or an H or an F path is one. From here on, then, it does not seem necessary to spend a great amount of effort in agonizing appraisal when patterns like those illustrated in Figures 1.1, 1.4, 2.1, and 2.2 emerge in other graphs. This mode of trending, though not a universally perfect fit, is a very useful and representative one, though departures from the models should continually be noted and explored as best possible.[9]

Skeptical readers may still wish to remodel in other ways all the data for all population units covered across all four centuries of U.S. demographic history that have been examined here to see whether, by employing different time segments and different formulas, they can attain less total error or do as well as the G or G-related H and F fits that I have offered with fewer total parameters (by lumping periods, for example). There may after all exist out there somewhere a better way of systematizing the aggregate evidence. This, however, is the issue, not whether one or several proposed G trends in the graphs might be replaced by open-ended, tailor-made fitting to reduce the error case by case. That clearly can be done, but what purpose would it serve? On the other hand,

accumulating evidence on the uniformity, simplicity, and effectiveness of the
G-based curves proposed here makes it seem unlikely that a better summarization of trends exists. It just remains impossible to anticipate all other conceivable competitive modelings in advance. Motivated readers are thus urged to
try to improve upon what is offered here, since only that kind of bombardment
by challenging methods and interpretations provides the ultimate test for the
kind of discovery that is claimed.

In all, though, detailed analysis of the histories of fifty colonies and states of
the United States, across four centuries from 1607 to the present, shows in Table
2.2 that 201 among 232 trends in population size simply took the basic G form.
Only in a handful of cases did log-linear expansion appear, always close to the
.03 rate first approximated by Franklin in 1751. This is the F slope, which is
nothing but the rate of change in G at the zero year for the formula. Another
rather more frequent exceptional pattern—with more gradual proportional deceleration or more slowly bending growth than G—similarly took only the one
H shape, in which the curvature of G is softened by $1/e$. This form of trend was
first discovered for the total U.S. population 1850–1930 (Chapter 1) to improve
upon the logistic curve employed by Verhulst and his followers. The exceptions
to G in these U.S. data, in other words, are few and far between; and both F
and H types are closely connected with the G formula. Two other patterns, of
demographic decline and of accelerating as opposed to decelerating growth, have
been encountered infrequently; each of these, too, could turn out be another
"relative" within the family of G, the scant evidence so far suggests.

Trends identified as looking like G or H or F when graphed in the figures,
furthermore, prove through some quantitative probing generally to be fitted best
by such formulas, not one of many other models that are widely employed to
depict change through time. It seems worthwhile, therefore, to apply the same
simple visual method for identifying trends to other bodies of data as the analysis
of this study moves ahead. The challenge for critics of that approach is to
demonstrate a way of fitting so much change through time so well so simply,
through so few formulas that are so closely related to each other.

The value of the patterns proposed must also be assessed by what they indicate to be substantively similar or different among the local histories within
which the plotted populations lived. Preliminary exploration, as offered here,
would seem to indicate that the G, F, and H trends of Tables 2.1 and 2.3 do
indeed identify real distinct and shared local experiences and suggest some insightful things about how and why American colony or state populations grew
as they did when they did.

Weighed all together, these American findings suggest that it is now worthwhile to take this kind of analysis of growth forward to populations other than
those from within the one country in which all the models were discovered, the
United States. To that more far-reaching task of demonstrating generality our
study now turns, step by step, beginning with populations that seem most likely

to have shared historical dynamics with the people who began as colonists of mainland British North America.

NOTES

1. Settlement in Maine, Vermont, and West Virginia was originally contained in one or another of the thirteen colonies, but for much of the time can be separated out.

2. Corrections for Series Z 13 and 14 (Maryland and Virginia) to 1730 are from Menard 1980, appendix. His estimations for South Carolina (1989, Table 3 n.p.) are, except for 1740, so close to those of Sutherland in *Historical Statistics* as to require no adjustments.

3. The logarithms of the models were fitted to the logs of the data so that small absolute error in small early populations would receive the same weight as proportionally comparable departures from the predicted trend in more modern and therefore much larger populations. For G, for example, the fit was $f = \ln[P_0 e^{(1-e^{-.03(t-t_0)})}]$; then exp(f) was taken to get the G model values for successive dates.

4. To simplify comparative calculations, *TableCurve* fits were made in terms of arithmetic, not proportional, error. Within any span of trend examined, this gives extra weight to later, larger populations at the expense of early, smaller ones, unlike the way curves were fitted for graphing (both Figures 2.1 and 2.2 and comparable unpublished plottings for all other data) and for Table 2.1. This shortcut in assessment can disadvantage models proposed in terms of proportional error, as are all G-related trends discussed here. In other words, the new models enter the competition with something of a handicap.

5. The economic stagnation of the three-state area was noted, for example, by the *New York Times*, January 6, 1995.

6. The demographic growth of California came close to log-linear between 1900 and 1940, but a G for 1910–1940—one of a series of three such relatively short decelerating curves between 1870 and 1980—seems more likely.

7. The sequencing of the two political reactions from the more eastern prairies to the Great Plains, about a quarter-century apart, was vividly set forth by Richard Hofstadter (1955, 99–100).

8. For one cataloguing of these up-and-down movements and references to the relevant literature since the 1920s, see Harris 1969, 255–92.

The populations of Louisiana, Mississippi, Alabama, Arkansas, and probably Texas were notably set back by their experiences in the Civil War. That this loss was not shared by older southern states or by Kentucky and Tennessee, through which armies fought and supplied themselves constantly for half a decade, suggests that interruption of development by the war, not military action as such, was the source of interrupted expansion.

9. For the colony/state segments summarized in Tables 2.1 and 2.3, comparative F statistics have been run for over 100 G trends of prescribed length and amount of evidence, not just the 19 listed in Table A.1 from the illustrations of Figures 2.1 and 2.2. The larger group yields results similar to those of Table A.1.

Chapter 3

Common Patterns of Growth for All New Settlements? Evidence from Other Northern European Colonizations

If these findings about demographic growth in parts of the United States across the centuries identify phenomena that are in any way general in human life, comparable changes in population size ought to appear at least in some other, similar historical circumstances. To begin, have a certain class or category of "new," overseas European colonial populations as a whole grown historically according to the same few fundamental patterns?

It is possible to identify several societies that though not exactly identical in their experiences, also began with colonization by northern European powers in the 17th and 18th centuries. In the Western Hemisphere, Canada and the settlements of the Caribbean on the whole had many things in common with the Thirteen Colonies that became the United States: British, Dutch, French, and Scandinavian investment and exploitation; substantial immigration from the Old World; and expansion that was little impeded by small and relatively weak indigenous populations. Even further afield, settlements in Australia, New Zealand, and South Africa also shared at least certain crucial characteristics found in North American history. For this worldwide category of once-colonial populations that were begun under and long held under northern European control, was demographic growth in G form, with occasional exceptions of F and H shape, also the norm?

THE EXPANSION OF CANADA AND HER PROVINCES— AND THE FATE OF HER NATIVE PEOPLES

While tensions and treasured differences persist, most citizens of the United States and Canada in more sober and sportsmanlike moments must admit that they are, in all, closer to each other than to anybody else. Over almost four centuries now, much of what the two nations have experienced has been similar. Therefore, if societal and regional patterns of demographic growth exist that resemble those found in the United States, Canada should be the first place in which to start looking for them.

Figure 3.1 plots the historic growth of population in New France–Canada as a whole and illustrative regional examples from French "Canada"–Lower Canada–Quebec, Acadia–Nova Scotia, Upper Canada–Ontario, Manitoba, and the Northwest Territories as first French and then British invaders moved in and multiplied. Table 3.1 lists models for historical estimates and more modern census data for all portions of the country. As for the United States, trends for each area for all known time have been graphed and fitted, though not all can be displayed here. Three subzones within New France have been tracked to 1698, and modern information for Native Canadians and Inuit (Eskimo) is analyzed.[1]

In brief, the history of demographic growth in Canada down to the provincial or territorial level can be outlined accurately and informatively in 60 phases of expansion via the fundamental growth curve G (7 of them retroactively timed), just 2 segments of more slowly decelerating H increase, only 1 spurt of simple exponential F multiplication, and 2 cases where local population or native population can be shown to have grown in an upwardly curving, *accelerating* fashion. In 6 instances some sort of demographic decline appears.

The one place where the F pattern emerged was for Canada as a whole 1680–1730. No equivalent to 18th century Virginia or 20th century Florida appears with F growth among the many regions within Canada. As in the United States, however, no log-linear trajectory at any other rate but .03 presents itself anywhere, further undermining the predictions of stable population theory. Canada's total population took on the Franklin-Malthus trend at about the same time as her larger sister to the south; but this F trajectory was followed for just half a century, not the almost two centuries (roughly 1670–1850) found in the Thirteen Colonies and the country they became (see Figure 1.1). Since 1790, moreover, following just a half-century of slowly decelerating H-type expansion, even total population for Canada has multiplied only in a succession of four G spurts, a pattern that the United States as a whole has not displayed since the 1670s. It apparently requires more than just continental space to generate demographic growth in the F form.[2]

The population of French "Canada" (which later became Lower Canada, and still later the province of Quebec) also expanded in H form approximately 1715–1775, without any prior F, just taking off in such a trajectory from its opening G of 1625–1706. The fact that in the United States the H pattern of population increase has been so consistently associated with periods of economic growth suggests that new thinking might be required concerning the nature of the economy of New France. This has perhaps been too casually dichotomized into a weak agricultural settlement and a subverting, unregulated fur trade. There may have been more diversification and integrated development than that involved in this case of 18th century French colonial demographic growth.

Figure 3.1
Four Centuries of Population Growth in Canada

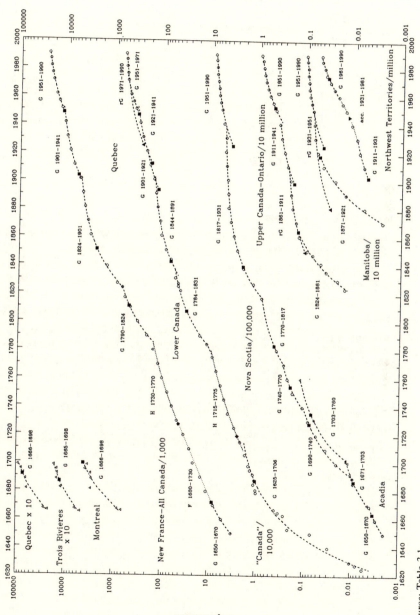

Population

Source: Table 3.1.

Table 3.1
Successive Phases of Population Growth in Canada, Her Provinces, and Her Native Peoples

New France/All Canada	Lower Canada/Quebec	Acadia/Nova Scotia	Newfoundland
1650-1670 G 1672		1650-1670 G 1664	1640-1720 G 1678
1680-1730 F ·	1625-1706 G 1687	1671-1703 G 1687	
1730-1770 H 1727	1715-1775 H 1719	1703-1760 G 1735 A	
		1690-1740 G 1728 NS	1720-1750 G 1721
		1740-1770 G 1755	
1790-1824 G 1811	1784-1831 G 1807	1770-1817 G 1783	
1824-1901 G 1851	1844-1891 G 1842	1817-1931 G 1839	1845-1869 G 1838
1901-1941 G 1903	1901-1921 G 1893		1869-1935 G 1859
	1921-1941 G 1912		
1951-1990 G 1947	1951-1971 G 1946	1951-1990 G 1925	1945-1971 G 1942
	1971-1990 rG 1925		1971-1990 rG 1916

Quebec	Trois Rivières	Montréal
1666-1698 G 1691	1665-1698 G 1686	1666-1698 G 1699

New Brunswick	Upper Canada/Ontario	Assiniboia	Prince Edward I.
1824-1881 G 1843	1824-1861 G 1864	1831-1856 G 1849	1841-1881 G 1847
1891-1911 rG 1837	1861-1911 rG 1850		1891-1921 acc. loss
			1901-1931 1/G decline
1911-1931 G 1874	1911-1941 G 1898		1931-1956 G 1881
1941-1990 G 1924	1951-1990 G 1952		1956-1990 G 1927

Manitoba	Alberta	Saskatchewan	British Columbia
1871-1921 G 1918	1901-1911 G 1962	1901-1911 G 1963	1881-1941 ?G 1922
1931-1951 rG 1881	1921-1951 rG 1911	1911-1931 rG 1922	1881-1911 ? accel.
1951-1990 G 1925	1951-1976 G 1958	1931-1951 acc. loss	1911-1941 G 1919
	1976-1990 G 1970	1951-1990 G 1901	1951-1990 G 1963

Yukon	Northwest Territories	Native Canadians	Inuit
1901-1921 1/G decline	1911-1931 G 1903	1911-1929 1/G decl.	
	1931-1961 accel.	1929-1961 accel.	1921-1961 G 1944
1941-1990 G 1960	1961-1990 G 1974	1961-1986 G 1961	1961-1986 G 1976

Source: Note 1.

Earlier, in the 17th century, the initial G-shape surge in the originally faltering settlements that had strung themselves up the St. Lawrence was timed rather later (with its t_0 in 1687) than those in Newfoundland (1678), and especially Acadia (1664), as Table 3.1 indicates.[3] This interregional mix made the opening G pattern for all of Canada have its t_0 at 1672, almost exactly coterminous with the one for the British mainland colonies to the south, while opening growths for particular regions within Canada were arrayed around this timing not unlike individual British colonies in Table 2.1.[4]

The parallel nature of these findings is very important for understanding the demographic history of the Western Hemisphere. Conditions in England, such as real wages or demand for a staple like tobacco, which have been invoked promiscuously to explain patterns of immigration and population growth for British North America in the 17th century, scarcely account for how the French occupied Canada. Some other way of explaining the pattern of the European invasion of North America is required.

The populations of Nova Scotia and Newfoundland, Table 3.1 shows, generally expanded via just sequences of the more common G trend up into the early 1800s (though data for Newfoundland is puzzling or absent for several decades following 1750). By then there was a tendency for Lower Canada–Quebec, Nova Scotia, and Newfoundland to grow via parallel G's through the remainder of the 19th century. In this they were joined by New Brunswick, Prince Edward Island, Upper Canada–Ontario, and the territory to the west of that (for the time being called Assiniboia).

This type of expansion could not be sustained in New Brunswick and Ontario. The first slightly, the second more markedly, had to adjust for ceilings. For New Brunswick in the East, the course correction into a slower or retrogressively timed G trend (rG) came just after similar sudden slowings in Kentucky and Tennessee; inland in Ontario, the change to a flatter growth trajectory was forced in the 1860s, not unlike what happened in Iowa (Table 2.3 and Figure 2.2). In Canada's western grain lands—in Manitoba (Figure 3.1), Alberta, and Saskatchewan—new vigorous population increase into the early 1900s even more strikingly crashed into upper limits set by slower rG trends around 1920 or 1930. This is, once more, what happened as part of a general Great Plains phenomenon south of the border, only just a little earlier: in Nebraska, Oklahoma, Minnesota, and the two Dakotas (Table 2.3).

In very modern times, too, Newfoundland and Quebec have shared the kind of capping of growth that has been found in New York, New Jersey, Connecticut (Table 2.1), and reaching westward back along the Great Lakes through Ohio and Michigan (Table 2.3). At about 1970, new G growths in these provinces that had commenced in the 1940s hit ceilings and were capped by a retroactive G curves with t_0's back at more like 1920. In consequence, Canada's pathway to the Great Lakes via the St. Lawrence can be seen to have experienced recent demographic limitation very much like the principal historic U.S. Hudson-Mohawk-Erie access to the Midwest. Fading flow from the continental heartland to and from Atlantic markets, which have been constricted by the pressure of vigorous European and Pacific competition, seems to have had much the same kind of regional demographic impact lately in Canada as in the United States as comparison of the local population trends indicates. In general, then, starting in the early 1800s parts of Canada, like certain regions of the United States, repeatedly have been caught out on a limb in successive over-expansions of continental settlement in response to temptations of international markets.

Outright sustained population *decline*, meanwhile, appeared in the early 1900s on Prince Edward Island. Looking at 1901–1931, this seems to have taken 1/G form. If 1891–1921 is instead considered as the period of decline, what emerges may be atrophy that started slowly but picked up speed with time. (This, it will be seen, can be modeled as G(r)—G reversed with respect to time.) Population loss in the latter, previously unencountered, *accelerating* form also may have occurred in Saskatchewan through the 1930s and 1940s while, in the United States, Nebraska, North Dakota, and Oklahoma lost people in the more usual decelerating 1/G fashion. Far more drastic proportionally was the way the population of the Yukon Territory collapsed via 1/G as the Klondike Gold Rush petered out between 1901 and 1921. Canada's Indians also saw their numbers atrophy across the first three decades of the 1900s. Then, however, into the 1960s Native Canadians experienced upwardly *accelerating* population growth, a pattern shared by the Northwest Territories as a whole, in whose population they predominate. (Such ever-faster growth will be shown to take the form 1/ G(r) or G reversed both vertically and with respect to time.) Both of these subpopulations, though, have settled back into proportionally decelerating G expansion since about 1961.[5] For the Inuit (the Eskimo), demographic increase after 1921 took the ubiquitous proportionally decelerating G form instead. The reasons for this difference between recent growths for two types of native peoples in Canada—one accelerating, the other decelerating—would seem to deserve systematic exploration.

In short, population in French Canada as a whole started out to grow very much as the British American population did below the border, first in an opening G surge and then in following F and H phases. Compared with Canada's bigger neighbor to the south, however, this succession of growth stages was greatly compressed in time. The F lasted 40 years, not 180; the H persisted 50 years, not 90. By as early as 1790, demographic expansion for Canada—now under British control—had become a series of just G growths. As a society, Canada has been less expansive than her big sister to the south, a difference that was already evident by the time of the fateful outbreak of war in 1754.

In contrast, *regional* demographic growth trends *within* Canada have been very similar to patterns within the United States. Indeed, they often visibly reflect dynamics shared by the two neighbors. This parallelism is most obvious in the original French and English colonial growths and in how continental expansion was repeatedly capped by retroactively timed G trends across the 19th and early 20th centuries, most notably in the great continental plains that the two contiguous nations share and in the fate of their once-dominant arteries of trade from heartlands to the Atlantic. Once again, however, in Canada as in the United States, G was the prevailing form of expansion to be found locally, over and over and over again. Exceptions of provincial or territorial growth that took the F and H shapes were even rarer in Canada than below the border. And a few other instances of demographic increase or decline, though they raise possibilities of models beyond the three stressed so far, are rare and seemingly also related to the curvature of the basic G function.

On the whole, patterns of national and regional demographic growth in Canada confirm what has been argued about the Thirteen Colonies and their offspring United States. The proportions and the timings in the recipe for expansion have varied, not the ingredients. Given these discoveries, it now becomes appropriate to extend the claim for generality in how populations grow more venturesomely to countries whose histories diverge noticeably further from U.S. conditions than the experience of Canada.

EUROPEAN AND AFRICAN OCCUPATION OF THE WEST INDIES: GROWTH PATTERNS DURING THE SHIFT TO SLAVERY

The 17th and 18th century European colonies of the Caribbean are best known for sugar, slavery, and conditions that killed Europeans with disease and Africans with work. No less than five quite distinctive political and economic regimes—those of England, France, the Netherlands, Denmark, and Spain[6]—controlled Caribbean colonies whose purpose was to exploit the tropical natural riches of the region for national and personal profit. The majority of these West Indian enterprises were located on small islands, in contrast to the vast North American continental expansion of Canada and the United States. Most embraced the monoculture of sugar with a single-mindedness of commitment seldom found for a staple of the mainland. These settlements primarily constituted both small and specialized operations. Their colonizing populations started out largely composed of young European servant men only to change drastically—in some places almost totally—to African slaves. Under these so contrasting conditions for living, administered in the interests of such diverse national powers, did West Indian populations grow in the same way that has been observed in the more moderate and balanced circumstances of the North American settlements that became the United States and Canada?

This in fact was the case. Table 3.2 lays out how G-based trends account for the growth of total, white, and black populations in twenty-one colonies of the West Indies up through 1780 or so.[7] Figures 3.2a and 3.2b present examples of insightful patterns and pattern sequences from Antigua, Barbados, Jamaica, and St. Domingue (later called Haiti). All data from all places in the table, however, have been graphed and modeled.

Table 3.2
Trends in the Total, White, and Black Populations of the Early West Indies

A. Total Populations

Barbados (B)	Nevis (B)	Montserrat (B)	Antigua (B)	British Virgins (B)
1628-1650 G 1690	1640-1660 G 1665	1650-1690 G 1678	1650-1670 G 1684	1670-1690 G 1677
1650-1670 rG 1644	1660-1740 flat	1700-1730 rG 1623	1670-1710 G 1703	1690-1720 G 1716
1680-1710 flat	1740-1780 G 1722	1730-1770 G 1731	1710-1780 G 1710	1720-1770 G 1736
1710-1770 G 1693				

St. Christopher (BF-B)	Bermuda (B)		Bahamas (B)	Jamaica (S-B)
1650-1660 flat	1650-1680 G 1671		1650-1670 G 1686	1650-1700 G 1693
1660-1680 1/G loss	1680-1710 1/G loss			1710-1770 H 1698
1680-1700 G 1671	1700-1770 G 1688		1710-1730 G 1703	
1730-1780 G 1698			1740-1770 G 1750	

		Martinique (F)	Cayenne/Guiana (F)	St. Dominique (S-F)
		1650-1710 G 1680	1670-1690 G 1674	
		1710-1750 G 1723	1690-1710 acc. loss	
		1760-1780 G 1723	1720-1780 G 1739	

St. Croix (F-Dan)	Guadeloupe (F)	St. Thomas (Dan)	St. John (Dan)	Dominica (F-B)
1650-1680 1/G loss	1650-1670 G 1672	1680-1720 G 1721	1720-1740 G 1764	1720-1760 G 1758
1680-1700 G 1652	1670-1720 acc. gain	1740-1770 rG 1701	1740-1770 rG 1701	
1700-1720 1/G loss	1710-1760 G 1731			
1730-1760 G 1739	1760-1780 G 1764			

Grenada & Grens. (F-B)	Surinam/Guiana (Du)			
1650-1710 ?G 1652	1690-1740 G 1711			
1710-1750 G 1757	1740-1770 G 1739			
1760-1780 G 1786				

Cuba (S)	Puerto Rico (S)			
1620-1700 G 1638	1765-1812 G 1788			
1700-1792 H 1693	1812-1836 G 1821			
1817-1877 G 1822				

Table 3.2 (*Continued*)

B. White Populations

Barbados (B)	Nevis (B)	Montserrat (B)	Antigua (B)	British Virgins (B)
1650-1680 1/G loss	1640-1660 G 1654	1650-1670 G 1679	1650-1740 G 1668	1670-1780 G 1675
1680-1710 acc. loss	1660-1680 1/G loss	1680-1780 1/G loss		
1720-1780 1/G loss	1690-1750 1/G loss		1750-1780 acc. loss	
	1760-1780 G 1764			

St. Christopher (BF-B)	Bermuda (B)		Bahamas (B)	Jamaica (S-B)
1650-1720 1/G loss	1650-1680 G 1671		1650-1700 G 1686	1650-1670 G 1693
	1680-1700 1/G loss		1700-1720 1/G loss	1680-1740 1/G loss
1730-1780 1/G loss	1700-1770 G 1682		1720-1740 G 1696	1750-1780 acc. gain
			1740-1770 G 1744	

St. Croix (F-Dan)	Guadeloupe (F)	Martinique (F)	Cayenne/Guiana (F)	St. Dominque (S-F)
1650-1690 1/G loss	1650-1670 G 1676	1650-1720 G 1673	1670-1690 ?G 1658	1650-1680 acc. gain
1700-1730 acc. loss	1670-1730 acc. gain	1720-1740 G 1719	1690-1710 acc. loss	1680-1750 rG 1688
1740-1760 acc. gain	1740-1780 acc. gain	1740-1780 1/G loss	1710-1740 G 1708	1750-1770 G 1744

Grenada & Grens. (F-B)	Surinam/Guiana (Du)	St. Thomas (Dan)	St. John (Dan)	Dominica (F-B)
1650-1680 ?G 1647	1670-1690 G 1704	1680-1720 G 1692	1720-1780 ?G 1700	1710-1730 G 1739
1680-1710 1/G loss	1710-1730 rG 1659	1730-1770 1/G loss		1730-1760 G 1764
1710-1770 G 1740	1740-1780 G 1747			

Cuba (S)	Puerto Rico (S)
?	1765-1812 G 1787
1817-1841 G 1819	1820-1836 G 1834

Table 3.2 (Continued)

C. Black and Colored Populations

Barbados (B)
1650-1670 G 1681
1670-1710 rG 1636
1720-1770 G 1701

Nevis (B)
1680-1700 G 1675
1710-1780 G 1705

Montserrat (B)
1650-1690 acc. gain
1690-1720 rG 1638
1720-1780 G 1721

Antigua (B)
1660-1780 G 1714

British Virgins (B)
1700-1720 G 1729
1720-1770 G 1745

St. Christopher (BF-B)
1650-1710 G 1670
1730-1780 G 1712

Bermuda (B)
1650-1690 G 1676
1700-1770 G 1695

Bahamas (B)
1730-1770 G 1758

Jamaica (S-B)
1670-1690 G 1710
1710-1770 H 1701

St. Croix (F-Dan)
1650-1700 G 1632

1740-1770 G 1790

Guadeloupe (F)
1650-1670 acc. gain
1670-1730 acc. gain
1730-1770 acc. gain

Martinique (F)
1650-1710 G 1691
1710-1750 G 1727
1760-1780 G 1732

Cayenne/Guiana (F)
1660-1680 G 1717
1680-1710 rG 1649
1720-1760 G 1735

St. Dominique (S-F)
1650-1670 G 1696
1670-1730 G 1730
1730-1760 H 1725

Grenada & Grens. (F-B)
1710-1730 G 1765
1730-1750 rG 1749
1760-1780 G 1789

Surinam/Guiana (Du)
1690-1740 G 1713

1740-1760 G 1744
1760-1780 acc. loss?

St. Thomas (Dan)
1680-1720 G 1729
1740-1780 rG 1710

St. John (Dan)
1720-1740 G 1769
1740-1780 rG 1723

Dominica (F-B)
1720-1760 1759

Cuba (S): Slaves
1768-1841 F .

Cuba: Free Colored
1768-1841 G 1792

Puerto Rico (S): Slaves
1776-1820 F .
1820-1836 G 1836

Puerto Rico: Free Colored
1776-1836 G 1787

Puerto Rico: Free Black
1776-1836 G 1788

B = English/British, BF = British and French, F = French, Du = Dutch, Dan = Danish, S = Spanish.
Sources: McCusker 1970, 2: 548-747; Gemery 1980, 211; Deerr 1949, 1: 279-81.

Of 131 trends of growth shown in Table 3.2, as many as 114 or 87 percent took G form.[8] This compares with 89 percent for the United States and 92 percent for Canada. (See summary Table 3.4 at the end of this chapter.) Of these G growths, furthermore, about the same proportion were retrogressive, cases in which a flatter segment of the curve followed a steeper one rather than the other, usual way around. The total population of Barbados hit a ceiling like this about 1650 (Figure 3.2a), as the surge to replace tobacco and servants with sugar and slaves confronted the limits of this one small island; many dissatisfied and adventurous Barbadians overflowed to the Leewards, Jamaica, the Carolinas, and even New Jersey—taking their bound labor with them (Dunn 1972, 75, 110–16, 152–54). Similarly, as Denmark tried to use her maritime prowess to buy into tropical plantation production in the 18th century, early trajectories of expansion on St. Thomas and St. John could not be sustained past about 1740, when failing St. Croix was purchased from France. In between, total population growth on Montserrat also had to shift to a more modest course in the 1690s.

About the turn of the century, too, *white* settlement in Surinam, which had taken off in 1670–1690 after the area was swapped back to the Netherlands following the Second Anglo-Dutch War, had to assume a flatter G trajectory. Simultaneously, an *accelerating* surge of small French planters, servants, and buccaneers into the western half of Hispaniola, at the expense of Spain, gave way to demographic growth in which there was much slower increase of whites, who—turning to sugar cultivation—could afford to introduce more and more slaves. That the accumulation of slaves, too, could overshoot the mark and have to change path is illustrated by Barbados about 1670, Cayenne 1680, Montserrat 1690, and Grenada and the Grenadines just shortly before St. Thomas and St. John. Misestimation of frontier potential was as common to the Caribbean as it was to Canada and the United States.

Where West Indian demographic expansion could persist for a substantial period of time without the inexorable deceleration of G was, not surprisingly, on the large islands. More slowly bending H trends appeared in the black populations of Jamaica and St. Domingue in the 18th century and therefore in their total populations, which were composed overwhelmingly of slaves (Figure 3.2b).[9] The other occurrence was on Cuba over a similar period. Here the increase of the *slave* population actually took the constantly expanding F form during 1768–1841, but was slowed down by the substantial proportions of white and free colored persons on the island, who both multiplied only in sharply decelerating G shape even as the opportunity to further expand sugar production in the West Indies shifted from Jamaica and St. Domingue to the still larger Spanish holdings.

Cane had been introduced on Cuba in the early 1500s, but the jealous growers of southern Spain used their influence at court to choke back their New World colonial competition. Meanwhile, the riches to be had from adventuring in Mexico drained off manpower, capital, and energy. Modern Cuban sugar production did not really take off until the later 1700s. By then, unlike most other places

Figure 3.2a

Total, White, and Black Populations in the Colonial West Indies: Antigua and Barbados

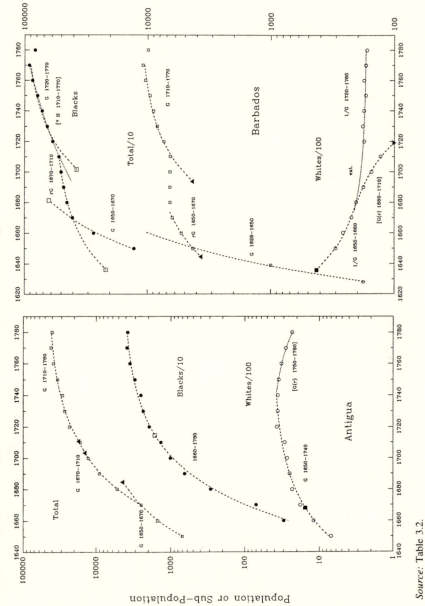

Source: Table 3.2.

Figure 3.2b

Total, White, and Black Populations in the Colonial West Indies: Jamaica and St. Domingue

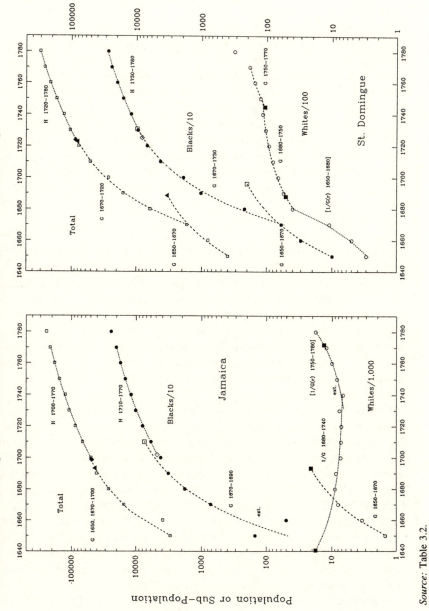

Source: Table 3.2.

in the Caribbean, the island also possessed a substantial population of free people of color, which first rose from about ⅔ the size of the slave population to more like ⅝ in 1792, then dropped back to ⅓ by 1841 as slave importing to Cuba surged across the first half of the 19th century and total slave numbers grew in the F trajectory. Free whites, though, remained over 40 percent of Cuba's population as of 1841, unlike the situation on most sugar islands. Cuba continued to be a big, diverse colony in spite of its massive, later-developing proclivity towards sugar and slaves.

Much the same was true of Puerto Rico. On this island, however, as late as 1836 slaves composed only about ⅑ of the total population, being outnumbered by whites 4½ to 1 and by free persons of color 2½ to 1. In Puerto Rico, free blacks were also recorded separately. Their number came to some 60 percent of the size of the slave population. Still, amid these blends of free and bound, black, white, and racially mixed peoples that were so very different from what mostly pertained across the colonies of the Caribbean in the later 1700s, both the total population and the subpopulations of Puerto Rico and Cuba probably multiplied according to the same few G-based patterns of growth discovered to be so general elsewhere.

It was particularly in the frequency of H-type growth that the distribution of trends in the West Indies differed from those of the United States. That pattern seems to be accompanied historically by economic growth and diversification, which are conditions not typical of smaller Caribbean islands. In contrast to most West Indian colonies, even across the 18th century up to the great slave rebellion, many whites and blacks continued to farm coffee and food crops on a small scale in the interior of St. Domingue, while plantations focusing on provisions, tropical foodstuffs, and cattle likewise thrived in Jamaica alongside sugar. Much the same must have been the case on vast Cuba, which became sugar-oriented still later in West Indian history. Where the economy was large and diverse, the H form did appear.

Noticeable in Table 3.2 are ten instances in which population grew along an *accelerating* path, curving upward in semi-logarithmic scale via a curve of $1/G(r)$, as illustrated for whites in Jamaica and St. Domingue in Figure 3.2b. Only on Guadeloupe between 1670 and 1720 did this so far rare form of expansion appear in the total population of a colony. Two phases of growth in this shape for the white population (1670–1730 and 1740–1780) and three for the black (1650–1670, 1670–1730, and probably 1730–1770), furthermore, bring to six out of ten the number of demographic expansions of that type that occurred just on this one island. Others emerged among the slaves on Montserrat 1650–1690 and among whites on St. Domingue 1650–1680, as French colonists of low standing and limited capital discovered the opportunities to be had from under-protected Spanish territory, and on St. Croix 1740–1760, as Danish resources were pumped in to revive settlement after purchase from the French. The tenth case took place among Jamaican whites from 1750 to 1780 or later. Their accelerating accumulation may have something to do with what was happening to the ordinary folk of Britain in this period. Just what went on in Guadeloupe to generate so much repeated demographic growth of the unusual upwardly curving form needs to be evaluated as well as records allow. Later chapters will say more about the conditions under which this distinctive type of expansion has taken place elsewhere historically.

The outstanding difference between the Caribbean and the mainland to the north was that European settler populations on many islands suffered substantial periods of significant *decline*. Over and over again there came a point at which the number of whites dropped off quite sharply. On island after island the number of Europeans shrank as production turned to growing sugar with slaves. Many died, few replaced themselves with children, and smaller and smaller numbers of fresh immigrants could be induced to come. European decline began about 1650 on Barbados, St. Christopher (for both English and French), and St. Croix; at 1660 on Nevis; near 1680 on Montserrat (replacing those troublesome Irish servants there), Bermuda, Jamaica, and Grenada and the Grenadines; at more like 1700 in the Bahamas. Only on St. Christopher, Bermuda, and St. Croix (twice), however, was such loss sufficient to bring down *total* population in the same fashion. Later declines in a decelerating shape, once more something like 1/G, appeared in Barbados 1720–1780, Nevis 1690–1750, St. Christopher 1730–1780, Martinique 1740–1780, and St. Thomas 1730–1770. By this later wave of losses in European population, slavery was well established. Yet since no black population can be seen to have dropped off this way in the West Indies before 1780, the white losses seem to represent some further shift for these places in the ratio of Europeans to Africans that accompanied the social and economic change of the 18th century.

The precise shape and timing of these decelerating trends of Caribbean loss are explored at the beginning of the next chapter, where more striking and more general cases of this form of demographic disaster are encountered elsewhere in the Americas. It is important to note here, however, that on Antigua, the British Virgins, Guadeloupe, Martinique, and St. Domingue and in Cayenne and Surinam no such marked late 17th century or early 18th century drop-off in the number of whites appeared. Regarding the two English colonies, sugar cultivation on Antigua was held back by a lack of water and the Virgins were always marginal to the industry (Dunn 1972, 34). French Guadeloupe, Martinique, Cayenne, and especially St. Domingue and also Dutch Surinam, in contrast, were in the thick of cane production. Apparently, however, they either attracted fewer white servants in their earlier years and from the start depended more on slavery (though the French part of St. Christopher and St. Croix shared the servant phenomenon with most British Caribbean colonies) or managed better to keep their white settlers alive and in the colony. These differences between English and French or Dutch peopling of the West Indies deserve some systematic study in terms of their economic, social, and racial implications. Were the English, for example, less willing to take female partners of color, or were the French and Dutch more able to get European women to their colonies, perhaps by establishing better opportunities for small planters?

Another kind of decay, beginning slowly but picking up speed with time, appeared four times among whites: 1690–1710 in Cayenne, strong enough to drag down total population the same way; without such broader accompaniment on Barbados 1680–1710, St. Croix 1700–1730, and—later—on Antigua 1750–1780. The G(r) shape and likely causation of this rarer, accelerating type of demographic atrophy, too, will be addressed specifically as more instances appear.

Along with these less frequent other patterns, finally, the array of predominating G-shaped increases across the Caribbean seems to make good sense when related to what is known of the development of the region. It also connects demographic growth in the West Indies to that of the mainland in insightful ways. For example, early G surges of white population increase on Nevis, Montserrat, Antigua, the British Virgins, Bermuda, Guadeloupe, Martinique, Grenada and the Grenadines, and Cuba, in French Guiana, and possibly on Barbados, St. Christopher, and St. Croix up through 1650 resemble initial G-shape growths previously encountered in the Chesapeake, New England, and New Amsterdam (Table 2.1), on the one hand, and Acadia and Newfoundland (Table 3.1), on the other. Then, just as later new waves of settlement followed later G paths up the St. Lawrence from Quebec through Montréal and into the middle Atlantic region and the Carolinas, accompanied by some second phases of G-shaped growth in older mainland colonies of New England and the Chesapeake, so later European footholds in the Bahamas, Jamaica, Surinam, St. Thomas, and St. John swelled demographically, along with second growths for whites in Bermuda and Martinique and the retrogressive G path into which European occupation of St. Domingue settled after 1680.

Similarly, Barbados, Bermuda, Nevis, Montserrat, and St. Christopher (after the English took control of the whole island) experienced later, secondary expansions of their *slave* populations that paralleled steeper first growths for blacks on Antigua, the British Virgins, Jamaica, and St. Domingue and in Cayenne and Surinam.[10] Meanwhile, overenthusiasm in introducing slaves onto Barbados and Montserrat during the third quarter of the 17th century was corrected back to the kind of more subdued G path that French St. Croix had been following all along (all three with base years in the 1630s).

As British, French, and Dutch colonists were lured to the New World and began to multiply there in parallel G-shaped surges, an intercontinental process that involved more than one country of origin and settlements that stretched from the Newfoundland fisheries to the canefields of Cayenne, so did the Atlantic slave trade produce parallel growths of Africans from place to place across the Caribbean. Cross-national dynamics were at work both in motivating European colonization and in creating demand for slaves. The repeating trends of

Table 3.2 show this. They also demonstrate, nevertheless, that—wherever and with whomever populations grew—the basic form in all these diverse contexts of colonization by northern European powers was G. The related curves H and F were infrequent phenomena in the colonial Caribbean, as in the history of the United States and Canada. The population record of the West Indies up to the time of the American and French revolutions, however, shows more signs of decline—in both decelerating 1/G and accelerating G(r) forms, it seems—than were observed on the North American mainland, and a few additional cases of accelerating 1/G(r) demographic expansion.

Before moving on to explore systematically such less familiar and less frequent shapes of change in population size, however, it will pay to consider the following: Have conditions somewhat like those of the Western Hemisphere's northern European settlements in the United States, Canada, and the Caribbean appeared elsewhere in world experience? And do the G-based generalizations that account for how populations have so far been seen to change size apply equally there?

SIMILAR COLONIZATION QUITE AROUND THE GLOBE: DEMOGRAPHIC INCREASE IN AUSTRALIA, NEW ZEALAND, AND SOUTHERN AFRICA

Australia, New Zealand, and South Africa were also developed as northern European colonies between the late 1600s and the early 1800s. To what extent do their histories of growth resemble what has been observed in North America?

Figure 3.3 presents the shape and timing of population increase in Australia and her component states and territories (Cameron 1982, 90; Knibbs 1915, 116). Part A of Table 3.3 lists these trends to facilitate comparison.

The Australian population as a whole over no period of recorded time has followed anything but G patterns of expansion. Even more than Canada, this third continent-spanning frontier society departed from the pattern of the United States in its overall history of growth. It never developed a rolling, persisting frontier with F-type expansion, as the British and French North American mainland colonies did by about 1680, three-quarters of a century into the history of their settlement. Nor did Australia or any of her regions ever put together the kind of mix of gradual but long-term economic and demographic development that seems to have been associated with the more slowly decelerating H-type modification of G that has been found in the United States approximately 1850–1940 and in Canada, more briefly, 1730–1770.

Australia's early growth, of course, was overwhelmingly driven by the transportation of convicts from Britain. This dumping of offenders and unfortunates started in the 1780s, when the erstwhile American colonies, in particular Maryland, would no longer relieve Britain of her undesirables. Robert Hughes's fine book (1987) on transportation in Australia's early years seems to indicate that

Figure 3.3
Total Population in Australia and Her States and Territories

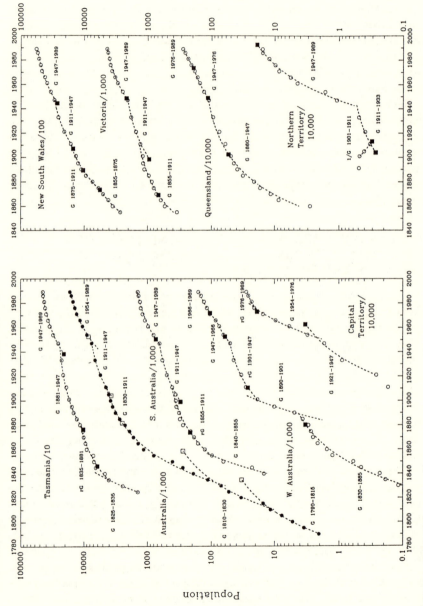

Source: Table 3.3.

there unfolded successive phases of British penal policy and practice that are likely to have generated the first three G curves of expansion for the century: for 1790–1815, 1810–1830, and 1830–1911.

A first, germinal but struggling phase for Australia—including Van Diemen's Land (later called Tasmania)—took place up to the end of the Napoleonic Wars. This was followed by a fresh flood of transportation during the difficult postwar period in Britain. The beginning in the 1830s of a longer third spurt of G shape for Australia's population growth seems related to several developments. In Britain, the crash of 1837 was disastrous, greatly swelling the ranks of the unemployed and the desperate, those who were likely to become entangled with the law and shipped overseas. Simultaneously a "bounty system" for free immigrants was instituted in 1837 to foster a better quality of population in Australia amid severe criticism of how the penal operations were working (Hughes 1987, 496–97). Meanwhile, this was just about when free residents of New South Wales began to outnumber convicts, as shown by the first census in 1828 (354). In other words, Australia's own demographic processes, especially natural increase, now began to do most to generate the third, much longer G-shaped trend of national population growth from this point in time to World War I.

The original version of Figure 3.3 was calculated before Hughes's book became available. The patterns presented there not only draw unanticipated support from his argument but seem, reciprocally, to help periodize his beautifully constructed and worded presentation. This is the kind of fruitful interaction between curve-fitting per se and other forms of historical insight that should occur over and over again for all sorts of different places and times if the demographic analysis of this volume is correct.

Turning to the proposed growth patterns for Australia's eight states and territories, the question, once again, is whether these make good sense in terms of what is known of the history of this nation's settlement and development. Even to someone who is not well versed in Australian particulars, there appear to exist at least certain internal consistencies and readily explicable variations among the experiences of the individual sections of the country as Figure 3.3 and Table 3.3 present them via G trends.

To work backwards in time from the most common to the most diverse local development, all regions not surprisingly witnessed a new surge of population growth after World War II. In Tasmania, New South Wales, Victoria, and South Australia and also as long as about 1970 in Queensland and Western Australia, these recent curves from 1947 were virtually parallel: All had zero years between 1938 and 1952 (Table 3.3). The sparsely settled Northern Territory, however, and also the Capital Territory (to about 1976) began much stronger booms after World War II along trajectories that would not reach the base year for G (its t_0) until the 1990s. Why Queensland and Western Australia have had second postwar spurts of growth in very recent years will have to be left up to local historians; but even to outsiders more familiar with images of yachting and

Table 3.3
Demographic Growth Trends "Down Under"

A. Australia

ALL AUSTRALIA
1790-1815	G 1834
1810-1830	G 1858
1830-1911	G 1881
1911-1947	G 1904
1954-1989	G 1952

New South Wales
1855-1875	G 1873
1875-1911	G 1889
1911-1947	G 1907
1947-1989	G 1944

Victoria
1855-1911	G 1869
-	
1911-1947	G 1898
1947-1989	G 1948

Queensland
1860-1947	G 1902
-	
1947-1976	G 1949
1976-1989	G 1974

Northern Territory
1901-1911	1/G loss
1911-1933	G 1904
1947-1989	G 1992

Tasmania
1825-1835	G 1871
1835-1881	rG 1846
1881-1947	G 1876
1947-1989	G 1938

South Australia
1840-1855	G 1897
1855-1911	rG 1873
1911-1947	G 1899
1947-1989	G 1950

Western Australia
1830-1885	G 1880
1890-1901	G 1944
1901-1947	rG 1910
1947-1966	G 1952
1966-1989	G 1971

Capital Territories
1921-1947	G 1962
1954-1976	G 2000
1976-1989	rG 1973

B. New Zealand

ALL NEW ZEALAND
1858-1881	G 1895
1881-1901	rG 1878
1901-1945	G 1901
1945-1991	G 1944

European Origin
1841-1867	G 1905
1864-1901	rG 1892
1901-1945	G 1901
1911-1991	G 1940

North Island (N)
1858-1901	G 1899
-	
1901-1945	G 1914
1951-1991	G 1950

Auckland (N)
1864-1901	G 1890
-	
1901-1945	G 1921
1951-1991	G 1951

Wellington (N)
1867-1945	G 1905
-	
1945-1991	G 1939

Hawke's Bay (N)
1858-1880	G 1911
1886-1945	rG 1900
1945-1976	G 1945
1981-1991	1/G loss

Taranaki (N)
1871-1936	G 1911
-	
1945-1976	G 1923
1976-1991	flat

South Island
1858-1867	G 1924
1867-1945	rG 1880
1945-1991	G 1930

Otago (S)
1861-1881	G 1895
1881-1945	rG 1845
1945-1976	G 1940
1976-1991	? loss

Marlborough (S)
1867-1891	G 1893
1896-1945	rG 1883
1945-1981	G 1940

Southland (S)
1867-1886	G 1911
1886-1936	rG 1884
1945-1976	G 1937
1981-1991	1/G loss

Canterbury (S)
1867-1881	acc. gain
1881-1901	rG 1860
1901-1945	G 1893
1945-1976	G 1943

Table 3.3 (Continued)

Maori
1858-1896 1/G loss
1896-1921 G 1870
1926-1945 G 1926
1951-1991 G 1965

MAURITIUS:

Whites
1735-1817 G 1781

TOTAL POPULATION
1904-1921 G 1894
1921-1951 G 1926
1960-1990 G 1970[un]

Nelson (S)
1874-1945 G 1877
1945-1981 G 1934

Chinese
1935-1956 G 1956
1961-1986 G 1980

Slaves
1735-1787 G 1789
1787-1817 G 1799

Blacks
1904-1921 G 1894
1921-1951 G 1921
1960,1970 ?G 1967
1970-1985 G 1968

Westland (S)
1867-1916 1/G loss
1916-1951 G 1887
1956-1981 1/G loss

Indian
1945-1986 G 1982

C. Southern Africa

TOTAL POPULATION
1735-1787 G 1788
1787-1817 G 1799

Coloured
1904-1921 G 1881
1921-1946 G 1921
1946-1985 H 1963

Fijian
1951-1986 G 1985

SOUTH AFRICA:

Cape Whites
1701-1723 G 1705
1723-1748 G 1732
1758-1773 G 1761
1774-1795 G 1779
1795,1806 ?G 1818
1820-1891 F -

Asian
1904-1936 G 1900
1940-1970 G 1959

Pac. Isl. Polynesian
1951-1981 G 2007

Other Whites[a]
1842,1891 ?G 1886

All Whites
1891-1936 G 1905
1946-1985 H 1921

N = North Island; S = South Island; [a] = Orange Free State, Transvaal, Natal; [un] = U.N. estimates

Sources: Australia: Cameron 1982, 90; Knibbs 1915, 116; U.N. *Demo. Ybk.* 1985, 1990, 1993; Bloomfield 1984, 42–45, 54–55; N.Z. *Ybk.* 1992, 62–67; Ross 1975, 227–28; S.A. *Ybk.* 1985, 22–23; *Statistieke* 1990, 16.

beach life than other particulars for the Land of Oz, these two regions would appear to be frontiers of recent Australian development.

Earlier, furthermore, a G trajectory leading up to the 1940s from a zero year between 1898 and 1910 was common almost everywhere across the country. The exceptions were the then brand-new Capital Territory, whose population surged much more vigorously 1921–1947, and the long-developed island of Tasmania, where the previous G spurt from about 1881 was, unlike what happened in most states, simply not superceded by new growth in the early 1900s.

In the 19th century, though, there was appreciably more variation in how the regional populations of Australia increased. Some territories had been settled later than others, or their early growth had been shaped by distinctive local conditions. In the simplest patterns, the people of Victoria and Queensland multiplied along single G curves all the way from where local records begin to World War I or later. In Victoria, a G for 1855–1910 with base year at 1869 was succeeded by the widely shared interregional curve from the eve of World War I to the aftermath of World War II. In Queensland, the path started in 1860 *was* that almost universal interwar G.[11] The population of Tasmania also grew in a prolonged G curve that began in the later 1800s. In this case, though, the continuing trajectory was a G like the one that Victoria's population, across the straits, followed for 1855–1911. Population increase in New South Wales took much the same track from 1855 through 1875; but then a somewhat faster new G (with later t_0 at 1889) intruded between there and 1911. Reasons for these movements in those particular states should be evident to local historians. *Loss* of people in the early 1900s in the Northern Territories, meanwhile, quite clearly seems to reflect what was happening to the Aboriginals living there in the early 1900s (Jones 1970, 4). Those native Australians composed the bulk of the population in this thinly settled region.

Finally, at one time or another during their early demographic history, four Australian states experienced the kind of suddenly capped expansion with a retrogressive succession of G curves that this study so far has most prominently encountered in North America's Great Plains. Tasmania apparently had such a sharp-cornered frustration of rapid growth very early, somewhere around 1840. A "roaring boom in sheep-farming and wool exports" took off in Tasmania in the 1820s, further inflaming an already blazing guerilla war with the natives, whose game lands were being overrun by sheep. By 1834 the last Tasmanians occupied "a benign concentration camp" on an island in Bass Strait, where they continued to die off rapidly of now more natural causes, especially if that term includes alcohol. Before long, though, the white man's boom came to an end, anyhow, as land left to seize gave out (Hughes 1987, 414–24). Further, "without assignment, there could have been no colony in Van Diemen's Land. Its economy would have died because . . . there was no labor but convict labor" (380). The implication of this would seem to be that that when such use of convict workers by the civilian population was ended in the early 1840s, Tasmania was especially vulnerable. Meanwhile, the worldwide depression of these years was also hard on the island. In the first half of 1845, no less than 5 percent of Van Diemen's Land's people actually left the island for greener pastures on the Australian mainland (521, 527). In short, evidence abounds for why the trajectory of early, ambitious population increase in Tasmania across the 1820s and 1830s could not be sustained.

In South Australia, the original growth spurt broke about twenty years later, around 1855. By this time, transportation of convicts to the eastern parts of the country was being terminated and shifted to Western Australia (578–79). That free inhabitants of South Australia were glad to see the prisoners go is perhaps one indicator that early development there had hit a ceiling and that the labor of convicts no longer made it worth putting up with their moral influence on the agriculture-oriented life of the region. Another clue as to what was happening may be that the gold-mining boom in neighboring Victoria peaked in the mid-1850s (Eichengreen and McLean 1994, 296). There was little mineral wealth in South Australia itself, but the farmers there grew wheat to feed regions that did have mining booms and sheep booms. Indeed, until the late 1800s South Australia was the leading Australian zone for producing wheat.

In Western Australia, convicts powered the opening G curve of population increase 1830–1885. As the eastern areas of the country tried to protect their now rapidly civilizing purity against any further flow of prisoners near mid-century, Western Australia—as Hughes puts it—"was greedy; it wanted to get as many 'government men' as it could, and extract as much profit from their labor as possible" (578). The new demographic boom of the 1890s, which followed, was powered by exciting mining opportunities. Its momentum ran out in the early 1900s, however, as gold production from Western Australia dropped off (Eichengreen and McLean, 296).

Interestingly, population growth in Australia's Capital Territory also encountered a lid of this retroactive rG type—very recently, in the 1970s. There are no reports of jungle retaking the streets of Canberra, as from that other modern planned capital de novo, Brasilia. But central government in Australia looks as though it enlarged in a way after World War II that could not sustain the G trend of its 1954–1976 expansion in population into more recent years.

In New Zealand (Figure 3.4 and part B of Table 3.3), the whole society started out with a G-shaped demographic surge that could not be kept up for long. By about 1880 the fast opening spurt of demographic increase there (from the 1840s, the data for European settlers indicate) was replaced by a slower, flatter one for 1881–1901. This subsequent trend had its t_0 at 1878, much as in Australia for 1830–1911 (Figure 3.3). From here on, population increase in New Zealand continued to parallel that for Australia, with G's for 1901–1945 and 1945–1991 that very closely matched trends for 1911–1947 and 1954–1989 in the big continental island to the northwest (Bloomfield 1984, 54–55, 42, 44–45; New Zealand, *Official 1992 Yearbook*, 62–67).[12]

The early ricochet off a ceiling in the 1860s into retroactive, slower G increase for the later 1800s occurred in the *European* portion of the New Zealand pop-

Figure 3.4
The Populations of New Zealand, Her Ethnic Groups, and Selected Regions

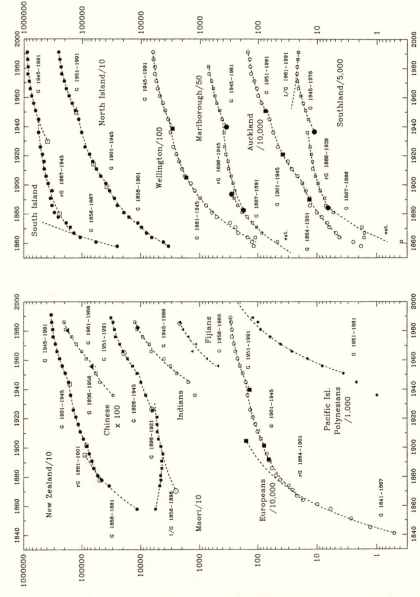
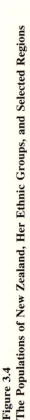

Source: Table 3.3.

ulation. It took place principally on South Island, where a gold boom tapered off after 1865 and the initial craze to exploit the international wool market of the 19th century soon used up the best or most convenient range for sheep. Whaling and sealing were other profitable activities that attracted initial settlers to New Zealand but did not thrive for long. Gold likewise provided an early driving force for growth in the Auckland District on North Island, where population similarly increased more rapidly into the mid-1860s than the trend thereafter could sustain. Opening booms of other South Island districts, however—notably Southland, Otago, Marlborough, and Canterbury—broke only rather later, in the 1880s, a further indication that excessive hopes from farming, not just mining, contributed to the unsustainable trajectory of early expansion.[13]

Population on South Island and in its individual districts then grew more slowly into the early 20th century than the peoples of North Island and its divisions, as Figure 3.4 illustrates. Part B of Table 3.3 demonstrates how in the north, the G trends all had base points clustered around 1900. To the south, there was considerable local spread in pattern—from actual decline in Westland to increase in Marlborough and Southland that briefly paralleled trends on North Island but gave way to slower, retrogressively timed G curves by about 1890. As a result, in this era of scaling back growth, the population of South Island as a whole followed a G curve that had its t_0 more like 1880 than 1900, making for appreciably flatter growth than is evident on North Island.

On North Island, in contrast, new and steeper G-shape increase appeared for 1901–1945. This surpassed what was experienced both on South Island and in most parts of Australia. The surge came primarily from Auckland, however, since 19th century curves persisted in Wellington and Taranaki, while in Hawke's Bay the G for 1886–1945 was actually retrogressive to (flatter than) what had preceded it. Within the old Auckland District (now administratively divided), furthermore, it was South Auckland and especially urban Central Auckland that drove demographic expansion. In the latter, for 1926–1961 population even increased along a proportionally accelerating, upwardly bending trajectory. As in Australia, furthermore, following World War II local G spurts were geographically general, and also generally parallel in timing—with a few exceptions—from one provincial district to another across New Zealand.

Boundary changes in recent years make it hard to tell what has been happening in Westland, Nelson, and Marlborough since 1981 and perhaps skew the trend in Table 3.3 for Canterbury in the past decade as well. But populations in Southland and Otago (the rest of South Island) and in Hawke's Bay and East Coast on North Island seem to have joined Westland in decline. Only Northland, the upper tip of New Zealand, has seen fresh demographic expansion since the end of the war, in effect joining its neighbors South and Central Auckland in a steeper than typical G trajectory.

Chinese, Indians, Fijians, and Pacific Island Polynesians, in faster and faster growth paths respectively (part B of Table 3.3), have contributed substantially to this Auckland-centered urbanization. Since the 1920s, multiplication among the Maori has also noticeably exceeded the current rate for those from European stock, though these native people of New Zealand shrank significantly in number across the second half of the 19th century, according to a now familiar decelerating pattern that seems to resemble G upside down. They then began to recover during 1896–1921, but expanded appreciably slower than the European majority.

There is, in sum, readily understandable patterning for these findings concerning the growth of geographic and ethnic subpopulations in New Zealand. Though a definitive relating of demographic trends to other local experience through time must in the end be executed by knowledgeable scholars closer to the evidence, once again the G and G-based trends that appear in the population numbers seem to make sense against their historical contexts and to help understand what was going on from place to place and time to time.

From southern Africa, also, are available two relatively long-running histories of colonial demographic increase with which to extend our generalizing still further. The first comes from a relatively obscure sugar colony located half a world away from the Caribbean; the second constitutes a well-known invasion of the tip of this substantially populated continent by Europeans.

Mauritius, in the Indian Ocean several hundred miles east of Madagascar, was occupied by the Dutch off and on from 1638 through 1712 to support their challenge to the Asian commerce of Portugal. This handy jumping-off place for eastern operations was next settled by the French in 1721. They turned it into a sugar island as well as a base for servicing their empire in India (from here Madras was captured from the British in 1746) and a lair for privateers and pirates attacking trade with India. The British subsequently took possession of the island during the Napoleonic Wars, in 1810.

For the French period of colonization, a fairly good sense of the way population multiplied is available (Deerr 1950, 2, 280; Figure 1.4, this book). The number of whites seemingly increased fairly much along one extended G curve from 1735 to 1817, though an overshoot at 1767 appears. When French sugar growers were dislodged as certain Caribbean islands became British prizes in the peace of 1763, did they relocate to Mauritius? The slave population expanded in roughly parallel fashion as far as 1787, but the French Revolution and the revolt of Haiti apparently fostered fresh investment in the sugar culture of the island; a new, steeper G surge of slave numbers—and therefore total population—emerged for 1787–1817. This carried the ratio of blacks to whites from about 3½:1 in 1735 to more like 11:1 by 1817.

The tip of South Africa was also settled by the Dutch, in 1652, as a key base for their intrusion into the Portuguese East. This Cape Colony was invaded periodically; but it became lastingly British only in 1841, gaining independence in 1910, a few years after the Boer War. Population trends can be approximated for European settlers for 1701–1891; and the numbers for several different kinds of South Africans can be followed since 1904, though there appears to have been some substantial undercounting in census figures (South Africa, *Yearbook* 1985, 22–23; *Statistieke* 1990, 16; U.N., *Demo. Ybk.* 1992, 146).

The European population of the Cape from about the 1820s to 1891 seems to have multiplied in the simple exponential path of F, following what previously may have been G growth from 1795 up into the early 1800s. Before that, the number of South Africans of European stock (not including indentured servants) increased in four successive short G curves 1701–1723, 1723–1748, 1758–1773, and 1773–1795, as part C of Table 3.3 summarizes (Ross 1975, 221). Intercontinental struggles in the War of Spanish Succession, the War of Austrian Succession, and the American and French Revolutions would seem to have periodized this sequence of trends through encouraging or interrupting trade and colonization by the Dutch and their English and French competitors.[14] Though immigration continued, the small population of the Netherlands could not pour large numbers of fresh settlers into South Africa. Instead, the upward drift underlying these G curves across the 18th century was primarily the consequence of natural increase among the colonists (Ross 1975, 221, 227–28).

Indeed, by the 1800s—following that series of short early G surges—the intruding white population in South Africa expanded much like contemporary northern European colonizations in America and Canada (Figures 1.1 and 3.1), according to a non-decelerating F trend. Then, as of the early 1840s, Europeans began to burst northward out of the bounds of the original Cape Colony. About 14,000 Boers who refused to accept life under the new British rule pushed inland in the Great Trek to occupy what became the Orange Free State, Transvaal, and Natal. An estimate for European settlers in all three regions is not available again until about 1890. The hypothesis proposed here, however, suggests that this expansion probably took the kind of G form offered in Table 3.3, which is based upon the only data available: for 1842 and 1891. Subsequently, from 1891 to 1936, the white population of all South Africa increased along another G trajectory. This fresh growth started out steeper than the Cape Colony's old F trend, as discovery of diamonds in the Orange Free State in 1867 and gold in Transvaal in 1886 drew floods of non-Dutch fortune-seekers into the interior (triggering old-settler resistance to British development policy and soon instigating the Boer War). Since World War II, interestingly, the *white* population of the Republic of South Africa (but that part alone) has apparently increased in an H trend. As observed elsewhere, this pattern seems to be associated with sustained and mixed economic development, a condition that probably has applied to the white segment of this prosperous but racially and economically divided nation in recent decades—though not to most South Africans. It will be interesting to see how, and how much, the new political conditions of the country change this divergence of patterns.

The black majority increased roughly parallel to the white subpopulation from the first census of 1904 until the 1920s. Growth for both groups was not markedly different from there to 1951, even though white demographic expansion started on an H trend while black increase took a new G trajectory. Modern distinctions have magnified since the 1950s, with black numbers surging in a fresh, third G path above the continuing (and decelerating) H for whites.[15] The implication seems to be that new demographic growth reached blacks through postwar changes in health and perhaps nutrition, but they did not share equally in the additional stimulus from economic change that helped produce H-form growth among whites.

So-called "coloureds" of officially designated mixed race expanded much like blacks in all three modern phases of South African demographic increase, Table 3.3 indicates. The main difference is their slower growth to 1921. Asians (mostly of Indian origin, like the young lawyer M. Gandhi) multiplied rather more steeply up to the Great Depression than other groups besides whites. They probably have increased in two recent G curves since 1946, but it will take later data to settle definitively on the best modeling. Like blacks, since World War II both coloureds and Asians have increased more robustly than whites; but these two subpopulations have taken more swiftly decelerating G tracks in doing so. They seem most likely so far still not to have shared in the more sustained H trend evident for whites and may not have partaken in the economic dynamics that have allowed South African whites to multiply in this less rapidly slowing fashion (though for both "coloureds" and Asians since 1946 an alternative H pattern is possible).

Thus, four colonized areas situated far around the world from North America experienced expansion of population in the same G-based forms as the more frequently singled-out "New World" societies of the United States, Canada, and the West Indies. Furthermore, these settlements in Australia, New Zealand, Mauritius, and South Africa—which, like most of the North American colonies, were British, French, and Dutch in origin—witnessed demographic increase at respective stages of their development and under comparable conditions of growth that resembles how population multiplied in similar circumstances in mainland North America and the Caribbean.

The accumulative summary of Table 3.4 shows how among 522 trends of increase that have been identified in societies once colonized by northern European powers, as many as 470 (90 percent) seemingly took the G form. The reader, with or without the aid of further data, may wish to remodel some of these growth segments.[16] Still, the preponderance of G forms is so great that likely revisions will not disturb the general conclusion that G is the norm for demographic increase in these diverse societies and their principal subpopulations.

Chapter 2 established that regional populations (for individual colonies or states of the United States) as well as entire societal peoples have generally increased in G form. The current chapter has extended that finding for geographical components of countries to areas within Canada, Australia, and New Zealand.[17] More novelly, this chapter has also shown how racial and ethnic subgroups within populations, not just territorial ones, have also followed G

Table 3.4
Frequencies of Trend Types in "New World" Societies of Northern European Origin

Trend Type:	U.S.A.	ALL OTHERS	Canada	WEST INDIES: Whites	Blacks & Others	Total Pop.	ALL W.I.
F	5	4	1	0	2	0	2
H	18	9	2	0	2	3	5
Accel. Gain	3	13	2	5	4	1	10
rG	18	31	7	2	6	4	12
G	183	238	53	25	34	43	102
All Growths	227	295	65	32	48	51	131
% G or rG	88.5%	91.2%	92.3%	84.3%	83.0%	92.2%	87.0%
1/G Loss	5	27	3	14	0	4	18
Accel. Loss	0	9	3	4	1	1	6
All Trends	232	331	71	50	49	56	155

Trend Type:	Australia	New Zealand	Southern Afr.	ALL THREE	GRAND TOTAL
F	0	0	1	1	9
H	0	0	2	2	27
Accel. Gain	0	1	0	1	16
rG	4	8	0	12	49
G	29	39	15	83	421
All Growths	33	48	18	99	522
% G or rG	100.0%	97.9%	83.3%	96.0%	90.0%
1/G Loss	1	5	0	6	32
Accel. Loss	0	0	0	0	9
All Trends	34	53	18	105	563

Sources: Figure 1.1; Table 2.2; Tables 3.1, 3.2, 3.3.

paths in their expansion. The Indian and Inuit peoples within Canada; whites, free blacks, and slaves in twenty-one Caribbean colonies of England, France, the Netherlands, Spain, and Denmark and on the Indian Ocean island of Mauritius; the native Maori and immigrant Europeans, Indians, Chinese, Fijians, and Pacific Island Polynesians in New Zealand; and blacks, whites, "coloureds," and Asians in South Africa all have enlarged overwhelmingly in G fashion.

This finding implies a significant role for G-shaped trends in how the compositions of populations change, not just how they expand. What dynamics taking such increasingly familiar G-based paths might determine how the balance between immigrant and native shifts in new societies, or how various waves of newcomers replace each other? Do such processes similarly sculpt the models by which fundamental characteristics of populations such as gender ratios and age structures alter with time? These are issues that penetrate down to the very roots of demographic analysis. They form the topics toward which the global historical generalizations of this volume lead.[18]

The present chapter has also further enlightened the phenomenon that might be called "ambitions cast too high": instances where original trajectories for demographic increase could simply not be followed for long and had to be replaced by flatter, more modest, retrogressively timed G's. This kind of sharp-cornered, backward-adjusting transition from one G trend to the next was first encountered (see Chapter 2) among the states of the U.S. Plains and West, as initial 19th century hopes to grow grain, mine, ranch, and harvest timber drew early investment and settlement to an expansion whose pace could not be sustained. Now it has been seen that certain areas of Canada, Australia, and New Zealand and even Caribbean islands like Barbados, Montserrat, and St. John also experienced overreaching initial demographic increase in similar situations in the 17th and 18th centuries, not just the 19th and 20th centuries. An over-ambitious attraction of people could be hazarded on sugar and other tropical produce as easily as upon gold, grazing, grain, or timber—or smokestack industry in our own time.

What seems to have happened in all these cases, however, from Barbados around 1650 to regions of the United States and Canada today is that a local focus on making a living in a particular profitable way—be it wheat-farming, growing sugar cane, lumbering, mining, cattle-ranching, sheep-raising, or "rust belt" manufacturing—encouraged settlement and demographic development that could not be maintained as the region's economy came up against certain realities. Resources for such specialized exploitation of opportunity were always limited—by suitable space for farming or grazing, by the extent of reserves of ore or timber, and so forth. The early returns were so promising, however, that they encouraged what proved to be an unrealistic pace of increase in population trying to take advantage of them. At some point, then, the likelihood of over-shooting demographic increase revealed itself quite suddenly: in exhaustion of veins of ore or shifts in world commodity markets (often driven by new international competition) that quite abruptly changed the terms under which some or all local people could make a living.

Regional experts will have to spell out the particulars in each case. On the surface, however, the situations encountered seem to share certain basic features. For most of available history, they represent overeager staple-oriented settlement of some sort or other. If this interpretation is correct, there will appear almost no cases of the phenomenon among Old World populations. In the colonization of Asia or Africa, for instance—and perhaps Central and South America as well—the invading group was probably too small relative to the native one to make total demographic increase so sensitive to such narrow, specialized market forces. That hypothesis can be assessed in the chapters that follow.

If this interpretation holds up, abrupt disruption and pain from having excessive demographic expansion overrun limited increase in resources turns out to be a rather different phenomenon from what Malthus emphasized. He wrote of human reproduction outrunning possible increments in basics such as food and shelter. Open-ended New World settlement might avoid such encounters, he said; Old World life could not. In general, though, Quetelet and Verhulst were more correct in assuming that this kind of stress between population and sustenance would usually be worked out more gradually as limits began to be approached, not left until some crisis point of collision.[19] Meanwhile, a very real need for frantic adjustment in paths of demographic growth turns out to have been be a fairly common phenomenon in frontier populations since the 1600s (just where Malthus said it need not happen). There, early growths were driven by migration rather than human reproduction; and a specialization for international markets provided stimulus for settlement. These are crisis dynamics quite different from those of Malthus. They may be the product, furthermore, only of relatively recent times and may occur just on the margins of modern international economic systems.

While the G form of change in population size overwhelmingly predominates—mostly with steeper (later dated) segments of the curve succeeding earlier ones—across other formerly colonial societies besides the Unites States, the exceptions once again seem to be mathematical "relatives," simple transformations of the G function. The slowly decelerating and non-decelerating patterns H and F have been less common in Canada, the Caribbean, and "Down Under" than in the United States (Table 3.4). They appear to have occurred in similar historical contexts, but those circumstances of unhindered frontier expansion and sustained economic development have been less abundant.

There have also emerged 16 cases (4 percent of growths outside the United States) in which demographic increase has apparently proportionally *accelerated*, most notably in the white and black subpopulations of the sugar-dominated colonial Caribbean. Meanwhile, several "New World" populations or subpopulations have been seen to *decline*: most in continually slowing trajectories; a few in ever-quickening downward paths. (About half of the former occurred just among the European peoples of the early West Indies, Table 3.4 indicates.) In each of these three exceptional circumstances to the so-far more familiar G, H, and F patterns, though, graphing suggests some form of curving that might be related to G. It is now time to explore this possibility systematically. More frequent examples of these as yet unspecified patterns appear in those parts of the New World that were colonized by the Iberian powers, Spain and Portugal.

NOTES

1. For Canada and her regions up to 1780: McCusker 1970, 1: 586; Henripin 1972, 5; Charbonneau 1975, 30, 40; and Gemery 1980, 211 (Newfoundland 1640). For later periods: Urquhart 1965; Leacy 1983; Ministry of Supply and Services 1981, 80–81; Dominion Bureau of Statistics 1953, 1: 1–1 and 14 (Series A-2); Department of Agriculture 1876; and Statistics Canada 1991, 82–83, 90. All may be found in the Bibliography under Government Documents, Canada.

2. The hollow trangle for the national population estimate in 1780, lying above both the preceding H curve and the succeeding G pattern and not included in either, probably reflects the impact of Tory migration that followed disturbances to the south.

3. The hollow upward triangles for Acadia from 1671 through 1770 plot the growth of just the *French* component remaining in that population. After about 1690, British settlement of what they called Nova Scotia became more and more substantial, though control of the region had been contested since the early 1600s.

4. Within French "Canada", the local settlements of Trois Rivières (t_0 in 1686) and Quebec (1691) not surprisingly somewhat preceded upriver Montréal (1699) in the dating of their G growths. The latter served as the jumping-off place for the continental fur trade frontier.

5. Table 3.1 indicates, as an alternative patterning, that expansion in this upwardly curving shape may also have occurred in British Columbia's early years, between about 1881 and 1911, a view that the opening growth of the city of Vancouver supports (Chapter 8).

6. Portuguese Brazil and Spain's mainland possessions are covered in Chapter 4.

7. Only fragmentary and sporadic data or estimates are available for Louisiana, Florida, Santo Domingo (the Spanish half of Hispaniola), St. Lucia, St. Vincent, and Tobago through 1780. I have encountered no substantial information for populations in St. Martin, Trinidad, or British Honduras (now Belize) before the very end of the 18th century.

8. Some rough approximations noted as "?G" are not included in this calculation.

9. Figure 3.2a indicates how a rather flatter H trend segment might be possible among the slaves of Barbados 1710–1770, though this form probably did not appear in the total population of the 18th century.

10. Sugar cultivation was held back on Antigua by lack of water (Dunn 1972, 34). Population growth on St. Domingue and Surinam was restrained until questions of jurisdiction were settled (favoring French over Spanish, Dutch over English claimants respectively). Jamaica, St. Domingue, and the mainland Guiana colonies of Surinam and Cayenne could keep on taking more slaves longer because they comprised large areas. Unlike the case in the 1600s, growth of sugar production in the 18th century tended to be French rather than British. This happened for two reasons: On the one hand, France held suitable places with more room for increased planting (unlike, say, Barbados and

the Leewards). On the other, English producers and their merchants were increasingly monopolistic within Britain and British North America and inclined to take profits from manipulated prices there rather than push for a greater share of world markets by extending output (Sheridan 1974, 66–74).

11. One might split this long trend for Queensland into two successive G's, one to 1911 and another thereafter; but the base years and population sizes at t_0 are so close as to make the division hardly necessary.

12. The creation of new districts and regions after 1976 makes modern continuity with historic governmental units difficult in several areas.

13. In Canterbury, for the period 1867–1881, demographic increase actually followed an *accelerating*, upwardly curving path.

14. The population estimate for 1713 is especially low, and that at 1753 lies temporarily high. The first phenomenon can hardly be the effect of the smallpox epidemic of 1714, as Ross argues (1975, 221), though a later outburst of the disease in 1755 may well have cut back new growth that had started in the late 1740s.

15. The U.N. estimates for total population since 1970 suggest significant undercounting of blacks in official South African statistics, probably due in large part to territorial and reporting rearrangements that were imbedded in the late, unlamented apartheid policy. It will be interesting to see what the new government produces in the way of revised historical evidence.

16. Proposed trends in any figure that are labeled with a question mark are not included in the counts of Table 3.4. The challenge, it should be remembered, is not to best any one proposed G with an alternative form but to account for as much information as simply and effectively *everywhere* as the simple fixed-exponent G curve does.

17. Within South Africa, also, total and racial populations for the region of Natal/KwaZulu can, for instance, be shown to have expanded in G sequences from the early 1900s through 1980 (Grobbelaar 1985, 2).

18. A succeeding volume is devoted to these issues.

19. Though demographic catastrophes have of course occasionally occurred historically, as in the infamous Black Death of the later Middle Ages (Chapters 5, 6, and 9).

Chapter 4

Other Striking but General G-Based Trends: "Demographic Disaster" and "Population Explosion" in Latin America, the Caribbean, and Oceania

Thus far several instances have been encountered in which populations shrank rather than enlarged. Such atrophy has been observed in some states of the United States in recent years, among native Canadians and the total populations of one or two provinces of that northern country, for the original peoples of both Australia and New Zealand, and in the populations of a few rural provincial districts within New Zealand during the past decade or two. Most notable to this point, though, has been the first rapid then progressively slowing contraction of European populations as slavery and sugar production spread across several Caribbean colonies of various European powers in the 17th century (part B of Table 3.2). This pronounced and repeated atrophy of white populations in the West Indies, along with other more sporadic cases of decay elsewhere, raises a general and fundamental question that must now be considered systematically: If the G function is the form taken by population *growth* in most historical circumstances, does the same curve upside down, 1/G, also typically characterize demographic *decline*? There is considerable evidence that it does.

Demographic disaster, in which populations rapidly deteriorate, shrinking eventually to a mere fraction of their former size, has long captured the imagination of historians and social scientists. Whether the most likely cause for such striking decay was war, famine, disease, economic competition, cultural disintegration, or some combination of these blights, cases where demographic numbers have "crashed"—where the populations of societies, regions, cities, or even small communities have withered or almost disappeared—have widely been regarded as provocative and informative events in human experience. It is now shown how classic cases of such demographic decay in history have in fact taken the path across time of the upside-down general growth function G, that is, constant proportionally decelerating *loss* of population via 1/G. Henceforth this will be called the "D" curve of reaction to *disaster*.

Beyond the disappearance of most of the European element in several 17th and 18th century Caribbean populations that has already been noted in Chapter 3 (along with a handful of more modern contractions in North America), there lurk the infamous demographic losses experienced by the native inhabitants of Mexico and South America subsequent to Spanish conquest in the 1500s and a less well known but equally devastating decay of Pacific island peoples as they suffered contact with foreign explorers, traders, whalers, missionaries, romantics, and empire builders from the late 18th century into the early 20th. These cases suggest how demographic decline according to the D formula may be just as widespread historically—if fortunately not so frequent—as the constant proportionally decelerating G trend for population growth.

As the demographic history of Latin America is examined to incorporate its famous early population collapses into generalizations concerning how populations change size, it is appropriate also to assess whether subsequent colonial *recoveries* from demographic disaster south of the Rio Grande, and likewise modern population growth there, have followed G-based forms. For such expansion, previous observations from northern European colonizations in other parts of the world predict a predominance of G trends, embellished only by contextually comprehensible exceptions of more sustained demographic increase via H or possibly the constant exponential F.

Another pattern for change in population size may be needed here, however. It is for demographic developments like those of many Latin American countries since World War II that the concept of "population explosion" was advanced forty years ago (von Foerster et al. 1960). The idea of possibly *accelerating* demographic increase has received considerable attention in recent decades, though weaknesses in the excessive notion that populations might explode indefinitely in something like the hyperbolic path originally proposed have been remarked for some time (Keyfitz 1985, 22–23; 1968, 219–20). Already in this present study several instances of likely accelerating growth that have appeared (for example, those in Table 3.2) have been seen to give way to the standard proportionally decelerating G trajectory of expansion. Of course, F or H trends might in other circumstances become possible successors as well. It is necessary to examine carefully just where and when such "explosions" have occurred in the more numerous cases known to have appeared in Latin America, to see if their steepening trajectories are also in some way related to G, and to learn how such threatening supra-Malthusian expansions have come to an end. Such an investigation of proportionally accelerating growth tests the usefulness of G-based analysis for one of the most sensational and mobilizing topics of 20th century demography: the threat to world resources from the rapid multiplication of humankind.

Table 4.1

Loss of White Population in the 17th and 18th Century West Indies via the D Trend (1/G)

Place	Colonizer	Years of Decline	0 Year for D
Barbados	England	1650-1680	1636
"	England	[1680-1710]	[accel.]
Barbados[2]	England	1720-1780	1624
Jamaica	England	1680-1740	1641
St. Croix	France	1650-1690	1646
Cayenne	France	[1690-1710]	[accel.]
Nevis	England	1660-1680	1670
Montserrat	England	1680-1780	1675
Bahamas	England	1700-1720	1676
St. Christopher	Total E & F	1650-1720	1677
"	England	1660-1700	1679
"	France	1650-1700	1686
Bermuda	England	1680-1700	1685
Martinique	France	1740-1780	1691
Nevis[2]	England	1690-1750	1695
Grenada	France	1680-1710	1699
St. Christopher[2]	England	1730-1780	1720
St. Thomas	Denmark	1730-1770	1729

[2]Represents a second local phase of D-type population loss.

[ ] Denote a phase of accelerating decline.

Sources: See Table 3.2.

THE COLLAPSE OF EUROPEAN POPULATIONS IN THE 17TH AND 18TH CENTURY WEST INDIES

Chapter 3 has already revealed cases in which the European populations of certain Caribbean colonies declined substantially for considerable periods of time. Table 4.1 recapitulates that information. It indicates the years through which atrophy of this part of the population probably followed the 1/G or "D" form of constant proportional deceleration, beginning to fall off rapidly and then progressively slowing down relative to the number of whites who still remained.

The first point to be noted from the table (and from Figures 3.2a and 3.2b) is that such declines in population of European origin—in British, French, and Danish settlements alike—did approximate the shape of 1/G or D for response to *disaster*. (Marked in brackets are two instances of *accelerating* demographic loss, which will be discussed shortly.) Table 4.1 orders these historic declines of white population mostly according to the zero year in the D formula, as this is fitted to the available population estimates in each case, and states the range of years across which white population loss according to that trajectory occurred. Some European populations suffered more than one D decline.

Without taking quantitative steps to evaluate curve-fitting for the proposed model, the eye determines quite well that D (simply 1/G) is indeed at least a likely formula for summarizing population loss in these cases, whose patterns usually depend on rather rough approximations of 17th and 18th century population numbers anyhow. All likely D trends, not just those illustrated in Figures 3.2a, and 3.2b, were graphed and fitted in the process of preparing Table 4.1 (and Table 3.2, from which it is drawn).

The second point to note from Table 4.1 is the timing of white demographic decay via D across the colonies of the different European powers in terms of "Years of Decline." By about the 1650s, the English populations of Barbados, St. Christopher, and Nevis and the French settlers on St. Christopher and St. Croix were already shrinking along a D curve. Of the English possessions, Barbados was first to turn to cultivating sugar and to employing African slaves for that purpose. St. Croix, first occupied by the Dutch and the English in 1643, produced a flourishing sugar industry under its new owners, the French, soon after 1650. St. Christopher, invaded in 1624, was the seedbed island for both English and French colonization in the Caribbean and offered considerable agricultural land that was suitable for sugar. Other settlements in the Leewards were initially far less successful, though Nevis, even if "mainly one great mountain," began to lose whites about the same time (Dunn 1972, 18–23).

In the 1680s, the Europeans of these four islands were joined in decay by the British settlers of Montserrat, Bermuda, and Jamaica and the French colonists of Grenada. Contemporaneously, a *second* drop in population according to the D form occurred on Nevis.[1] In the British Bahamas, Danish St. Thomas, and French Martinique, however, decline of Europeans along the D trend appeared only in the 18th century, accompanied by further D-type loss of white population on St. Christopher and, more shallowly, on Barbados.

In sum, smaller islands that made early commitments towards a monoculture of sugar grown by slaves were the first to squeeze out much of their white populations. That is not a fact just noticed here (Dunn 1972, Chapters 3 and 4). Where local conditions delayed or prohibited so much concentration on sugar, European populations began to shrink only rather later—or never did, as in the large and agriculturally diverse colonies of St. Domingue, Cuba, Puerto Rico, and Surinam (Dutch Guiana) and marginal or mountainous fringes of the West Indian sugar industry like Dominica and the British Virgins. As plantation slavery, chiefly to grow sugar, took hold in preference to a prior form of development in which small independent farmers had grown less labor-intensive crops (principally tobacco and foodstuffs) with servant workers from Europe, a shift from white to black population occurred in most settlements of the Caribbean. This swing to slavery, in essence a competition between labor systems, pushed out many resident white settlers to less developed places—or to marginal ways of making a living such as buccaneering and piracy. It also held back new colonists from coming to the West Indies (either as free persons or as servants). Wherever Europeans atrophied, confronted with poor terms of competition in the face of slave-powered specialization in sugar and decimated by disease, that decline usually followed the D form.

There are important implications here for how the proportional compositions of populations change (by type of employment as well as by race or ethnicity) and for many other ways in which economies alter through time. The central role of G-shaped processes in those kinds of historical transitions is pursued in a later volume, as the argument of this study continues to unfold.

THE DEVASTATION OF NATIVE AMERICANS BY SPANISH CONQUEST FROM THE EARLY 1500s TO THE LATE 1600s

The best-known demographic declines in modern history are the crashes of Native American populations that occurred in Mexico and South America subsequent to the Spanish Conquest of the early 1500s. In some places, as much as 99 percent of the indigenous people disappeared. Did these notorious destructions of population, too, follow the D (1/G) curve?

One of the most important contributions made to demographic history in recent decades has been the monumental survey and sophisticated analysis of Meso-American population since 1492 that Sherburne F. Cook and Woodrow Borah conducted. Figure 4.1 plots several examples of demographic loss in central Mexico that they provide (1: viii, 82, 105). What it shows, first of all, is that the native or aboriginal population of all central Mexico fell off in D fashion from 1532 or a little sooner through 1585, with a zero year for the formula at 1566, and then again from 1585 through 1605, with a t_0 for D in 1593. More moderate earlier population loss is also evident between 1518, the year before Cortez's first attack on the heart of the Aztec empire, and 1532, by which time Spanish dominion had been extended across much of the countryside for about a decade. It is impossible to tell from this distance, however, precisely when within that fourteen-year period the curve of loss observed after 1532 began. Meanwhile, the entire population of central Mexico shrank in almost exactly parallel fashion over the half century from the 1530s to the 1580s, since it was so far composed predominantly of native peoples. Between the 1580s and the early 1600s, however, a now-greater proportion of Europeans and persons of mixed origin apparently kept the total population of the region from falling as steeply as just its indigenous component.

From the start, some types of Indian settlements were hit harder than others. Figure 4.1 demonstrates distinctions that Cook and Borah (1971) stress between the demographic experiences for residents of coastal and plateau areas (1: 82). Aggregate plateau population quite clearly dropped off in something like two successive D curves in 1532–1580 and 1580–1608. The pattern for coastal regions, as Cook and Borah sum them up, is much choppier. The level for 1595 breaks back above the preceding D of 1548–1580 (much like the retrogressive *growth* or rG sequences found first on the U.S. and Canadian plains); and the value for 1532 is not as high as the 1548–1580 curve would project, suggesting either that still another, flatter D may have been present in the early 1500s or that decline did not start in earnest until the 1540s.

Is this fragmented series for coastal residents then evidence that the D formula

Figure 4.1
Loss of Population in Early Colonial Central Mexico

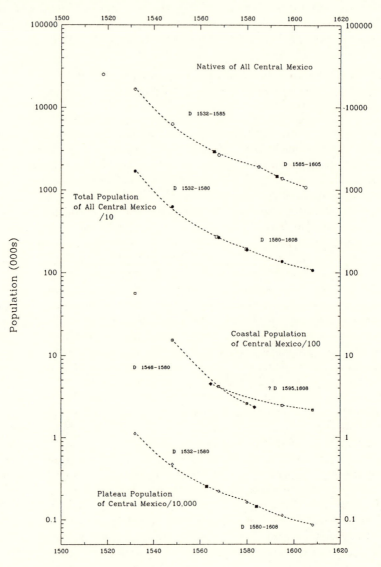

Source: Cook and Borah 1: viii, 82, 105.

is in fact unsuitable for summarizing population loss in such contexts? To the contrary, it appears. Separate background graphings made for composing Table 4.2 for the three "coastal" locales of Banderas, Purificación, and Zacualpan, which Cook and Borah selected for emphasis in their interpretation, show with ample evidence across time how the D-type declines to the 1580s cut deeper (had later t_0's) than in "plateau" central Nueva Galicia and Mixteca Alta or topographically mixed Avalos, where single uninterrupted D-type declines ran from about 1550 to 1650. Beginning in the late 1500s, then, second D-shape losses took each of the local "coastal" population sizes lower still.[2] In Purificación and Zacualpan, however, these second D trends began at higher levels than where the preceding D curves ended, as has been noted for aggregate "coastal" population in Figure 4.1. Thus local evidence presented by Cook and Borah supports the argument for an offset or elevated transition between D curves that has been proposed for the combined category of total "coastal" settlement of which these three places were part.

Figure 4.2 depicts demographic atrophy via the D pattern across the 1500s and 1600s that the data and estimations of Cook and Borah reveal for some fairly large zones of central Mexico. Their evidence for the smaller areas of Motines, Colima, and Avalos and for Yucatán has also been graphed and fitted for inclusion in Table 4.2, though it is not offered visually.[3] Figure 4.3 presents trends of decline (and subsequent recovery) revealed by various researchers concerning Hispaniola, the Cuchumatán Highlands of Guatemala, Costa Rica, and the Quimbaya, Pamplona, and Sabana de Bogatá regions of what is now Columbia.[4] Data from N. D. Cook on the decline of tributarios in Peru and the north, central, and south portions of her coastal and sierra zones between 1570 and 1620 have also been graphed and analyzed for Table 4.2.[5] Some of these losses followed a single D trend over the period studied; others unfolded in two stages, sometimes with a little recovery before the new D curve began.

North of Mexico, too, scholars have surmised that major population loss took place among Amerindians following contact with Europeans or even just indirect exposure to their diseases as carried by other native peoples. Estimates of numbers there, however, are even more ephemeral than for the jungles and remote highlands of Central and South America. No attempt is made to graph them here; but readers should understand that the process of decline was probably about the same. It is just that the Spanish colonial power, which regarded native people as potential converts, laborers, and taxpayers, kept better records of their number than Northern European invaders, who saw Amerindians principally as a nuisance to be removed from desirable land and provided their own labor in the form of children, white servants, or African slaves. Much the same seems to be the case for the sugar-conscious 16th century Portuguese settlements in Brazil: The increase of Africans can be approximately followed, but not the disappearance of natives.

Three important findings emerge from the downward trends in Figures 4.1, 4.2, and 4.3 and graphings like them that were made in order to create the

Table 4.2
First and Later Declines in Colonial Spanish American Populations by Base Year for the D Formula

A. First Recorded Declines

Population	Years of D	0 Year	Conditions
Costa Rica	1522-1622	1504	Mixed
Colima	1548-1600	1542	C
Cuchumatán H.	1520-1580	1543	P
Peru C. Sierra	1570-1600	1552	P
Peru N. Sierra	1570-1590	1561	P
Mixteca Alta	1532,1569?	1562?	P
C. Mex. Plateau	1532-1580	1563	P
Peru C. Coast	1570-1590	1565	C
Avalos	1548-1654	1569	Mixed
Peru S. Sierra	1570-1620	1573	P
Quimbaya	1539-1568	1573	P
Zacualpan	1525-1568	1573	C
Pamplona	1532-1602	1575	P
S.W. Jalisco	1548-1680	1575	C
Hispaniola	1496-1548	1576	Mixed
Peru N. Coast	1570-1590	1577	C
Peru S. Coast	1570-1590	1578	C
Nueva Galicia	1560-1620	1578	Mixed
C. Mex. Coast	1548-1580	1583	C
Motines	1560-1590	1584	C
Yucatán	1543,1549?	1587?	C
Banderas	1548-1590	1593	C
Purificación	1548-1590	1596	C

B. Subsequent Declines

Population	Years of D	0 Year	Conditions
*			
Colima	1600-1640	1578	C
Cuchumatán H.	1580,1671?	1584?	P
Peru C. Sierra	1600-1620	1572	P
Peru N. Sierra	1600-1620	1585	P
Mixteca Alta	1569-1660	1579	P
C. Mex. Plateau	1580-1608	1584	P
Peru C. Coast	1600-1620	1589	C
*			
*			
Quimbaya	1585-1628	1626	P
Zacualpan	1578-1608	1603	C
Pamplona	1623-1778	1633	P
*			
Hispaniola	1548-1573	1585	Mixed
Peru N. Coast	1600-1620	1600	C
Peru S. Coast	1600-1620	1595	C
Nueva Galicia	1620-1650	1591	Mixed
C. Mex. Coast	1595,1608?	1563?	C
Motines	1590-1630	1593	C
*			
Banderas	1590-1661	1620	C
Purificación	1608-1661	1615	C
Sabana de Bogotá	1673-1687	1607	P
Colima[3]	1640-1700	1612	C
Motines[3]	1630-1700	1625	C
Sabana de Bogotá[3]?	1681-1708	1689	P

C = Coastal; P = Plateau or Highland; *Only one D decline; [3] = 3rd local D decline.

Sources: Fernández et al. 1977; Cook and Borah 1971, 1974; Lovell 1981; Villamarin and Villamarin 1981; note 5.

Figure 4.2
Some Other Mexican Population Trends, 1548–1980

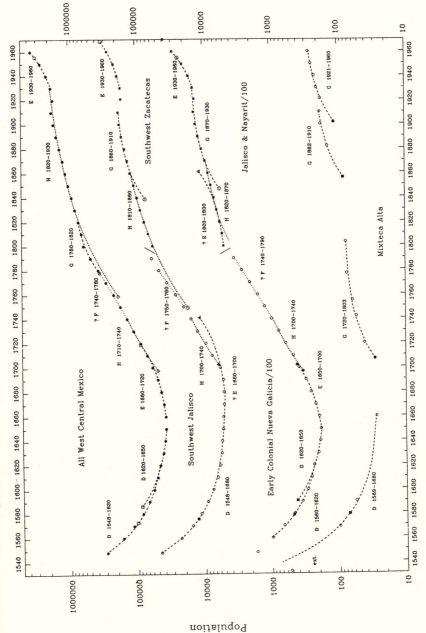

Sources: Tables 4.2 and 4.3.

105

Figure 4.3
Population Loss and Recovery Elsewhere in Early Spanish America

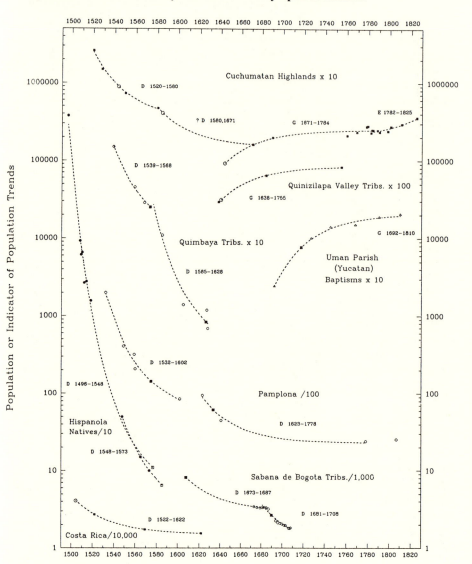

Source: Note 4.

summary of Table 4.2. First of all, the much-studied, much-publicized population loss of early Spanish America over and over again took the D form, as expected from occasional evidence for decline seen in Chapters 2 and 3 and the patterns for losses of Europeans in the Caribbean. From Hispaniola to central Mexico and Yucatán, through Guatemala and Costa Rica into northeastern, central, and southwestern Colombia, and thence into northern, central, and southern Peru, both highland and coastal populations contracted in D (1/G) form as Amerindians encountered Europeans and deadly aspects of "Colombian exchange" carried by their invasion. The evidence that this is so, which comes from several different scholars, leaves some open ends here and there for debate about interpretation and further investigation. As a whole, however, it seems convincing.

In their "Essay on Method," in fact, Cook and Borah themselves barely missed grasping the nature of the repeated proportionally slowing change in population size that D and G represent for decline and growth respectively. They were aware that their "coefficient of population movement" decreased with time during these early colonial demographic disasters, that is, the rate of relative loss slowed down (1: 89–93). What they failed to observe was that various contractions through successive eras of change, which they correctly periodized, in fact took the *same* shape of deceleration and that this form was 1/G, or D. Perhaps their conviction that "living populations, either at present or in the past, do not necessarily follow in detail highly schematized mathematical relationships. They are influenced by all sorts of pressures such that the time course may become very complex and may effectively defy the rigid application of ultra-simple numerical rules" (1: 89) was itself so rigid as to blind them to what they nearly discovered: that, for reasons that are established in this present study, demographic change that does indeed commence for varied and mixed causes nonetheless tends to follow just a few standard patterns as it develops across time.

A second general point to note from the figures and the table is that decline in some populations took place according to a single prolonged D curve, while in other situations two or even three drops in this shape occurred. What generated one pattern of decay rather than the other? Of nine documented populations that probably experienced just a single sustained decline of D shape before starting to climb back in some fashion, only two involved relatively small areas: southwest Jalisco and Avalos. The Mixteca Alta, central Nueva Galicia, all west central Mexico, the Yucatán Peninsula, Costa Rica as a whole, Peru in its entirety, and that colony's most populous region, the South Sierra all represent relatively large areas inhabited by numerous and complex peoples. Of the two smaller exceptions, Avalos was noted for being "remarkably well administered and prosperous" "by the standards of the sixteenth century" (Cook and Borah 1: 110). There seems to be a clue here that should help decipher the processes by which populations of different scope and complexity reacted to the kinds of disease, hardship, and disorganization that were brought about by invasion. In local circumstances, for instance, does unfamiliar illness strike populations that lack immunity in two waves, perhaps reflecting the involvement of successive generations? On a larger aggregate scale, though, do local differences in the timing of trends iron out this two-step transition into a single curve of decline, smoothing it over with how the social and economic consequences of demographic disaster come to bear more broadly?

Third, to compare the timing of the widespread D curves of demographic decline and the related matter of what proportion of the people disappeared seems to help in understanding somewhat better how decay took place. Cook and Borah, for instance, considered the difference between hot and wet coastal conditions and more cool and dry plateau environments to be determinative in how populations shrank (1: 79). In Table 4.2 there is indeed some tendency among the first recorded declines for plateau or highland regions to have earlier years for the D curve, and therefore rather flatter population losses (part A).[6] Consequently, demographic atrophy over the first four or five recorded decades was proportionally more severe in lowland than in upland regions—for instance, 95 percent in "coastal" west central Mexico as opposed to 85 percent in the "plateau" areas of Cook and Borah. Exceptions of relatively light early attrition in coastal Motines and Colima, furthermore, set the stage for not one but two subsequent D-type demographic declines in these locales, as Table 4.2 indicates. Heavy loss was just delayed. Nevertheless, in the coast-encircled peninsula of Yucatán population had begin to *grow* steadily already by the 1580s.

The climate, in short, may not have been so important as the degree of intrusion upon local life that the Spaniards made at various stages of contact. For instance, in the inland Colombian regions of Quimbaya and Pamplona (and perhaps also the Sabana de Bogotá) *second* D declines in population (part B of the table), beginning in the late 1500s or early 1600s, were comparatively strong. These in many ways, furthermore, paralleled contemporary new demographic losses in the coastal central Mexican areas of Colima, Motines, Banderas, Purificación, and Zacualpan, as presented by Cook and Borah. What experiences might such widely separated populations have shared at this time? Where were the economic, missionary, or political interests of the invaders attracted during various phases of colonization? How disruptive were such new European activities for native people, and what options did they have for resisting or evading them?

Apparently more successful cultural and military resistance in Mayan areas has already been mentioned. Marginality to the unfolding invasion could be another factor. Costa Rica, for example, was conquered late, only after 1550.[7] By the time the Spanish attained control, apparently half or more of Costa Rica's demographic loss had already been suffered, presumably by the spread of disease from areas that had experienced earlier European contact.[8] That may have something to do with how the population of the region was in the end cut less deeply and disastrously: Unfamiliar disease and the social and economic disorganization of conquest did not strike simultaneously. Local peoples may have been somewhat hardened to the new biological hazards before full contact and occupation took place.[9]

Students of the particular regions involved will have to provide the detailed and definitive answers. The new G-based comparative approach towards analyzing change in population size, however, seems to indicate rather better what the "coastal"/"plateau" distinction advanced by Cook and Borah may really mean for demographic history in colonial Spanish America, and what kinds of further research will more adequately clarify the dynamics by which native populations drastically fell away after contact was made with European invaders.

RECOVERY AND MODERN GROWTH AMONG LATIN AMERICAN AND CARIBBEAN PEOPLES: PARALLELS TO NORTHERN EXPERIENCE, BUT SOME THREATENING POPULATION EXPLOSION

Even colonial populations that almost totally disappeared in the 1500s and early 1600s eventually began to recover. Remaining natives developed resistance to once-devastating diseases and adjusted to new ways of life that had been forced upon them. European immigrants and African slaves arrived, and a mixed population evolved. In this process of reexpansion, the peoples of Iberian American enlarged along the same few related paths of growth seen to have been followed by the settlements of northern European powers (Chapters 2 and 3).

Figures 4.4a and 4.4b add further examples to illustrations of this kind of patterning in Latin America that already appear in Figures 4.2 and 4.3. Figure 4.5 presents a few growth histories from the Caribbean forward from where Figure 3.2 in Chapter 3 left off in the late 1700s. Tables 4.3, 4.4, and 4.5 summarize all the G-related trends of population size that have been established in graphing: not only the cases presented in the figures but every available substantial recorded population history of Middle America, South America, and the modern Caribbean.

Table 4.3 follows population *recovery* in various parts of Mexico and Guatemala, whose early demographic declines have just been examined. The first thing to note from it is how in several areas proportionally *accelerating* growth appeared in the later 1600s as D-type decline finally ground to a halt. (In Nueva Galicia, west central Mexico, Avalos, and perhaps southwest Jalisco during Era I in the table; later in Colima, after 1720.) Accelerating demographic increase has appeared here and there in other New World populations surveyed in Chapters 2 and 3. Now it emerges with substantial frequency. Such "population explosion" has been much publicized as it occurred recently among modern Third World peoples. (Era VI of Table 4.3 contains examples for several areas of Mexico.) This kind of proportionally accelerating growth turns out, however, to be a fairly frequent phenomenon also three centuries earlier during the recovery

Table 4.3

Later Colonial Demographic Recovery and Modern Population Growth in Certain Areas within Mexico and Guatemala

Era:	I			II			III		
Location:	Years	Trend	Base Date	Years	Trend	Base Date	Years	Trend	Base Date
Nueva Galicia	1650-1700	E	1702	1700-1740	H	1697	1740-1790	F?	-
W. C. Mexico	1660-1720	E	1729	1710-1740	H	1697	1740-1780	F?	-
S.W. Jalisco	1680-1700	E?	1741	1700-1740	H	1702	1750-1790	F?	-
Avalos	1650-1720	E	1731	1720-1750	H	1684	1750-1790	H	1755
MEXICO									
Colima	1640-1700	D	1612	1720-1760	E	1761	1803-1831	G	1746
Motines	1630-1700	D	1625	1710-1740	G	1703	1760-1800	G	1759
Mixteca Alta				1720-1803	G	1707	1740-1800	G	1737
Umán Parish Baptisms (Yuc.)				1692-1810	G	1717	(cont.)		
Yucatán	1583-1639	G	1563	some form of loss			(cont.)		
Cuchumatán Highlands	1678-1784	G	1644				1789-1842	G	1778
Quinizilapa Valley	1638-1755	G	1640						

Era:	IV			V			VI		
Location	Years	Trend	Base Date	Years	Trend	Base Date	Years	Trend	Base Date
MEXICO	1831-1873	H	1740	1873-1910	H	1819	1921-1960	E	1951
W. Central Mexico	1820-1930	H	1759	(cont.)			1930-1960	E	1956
Jalisco & Nayarit	1800-1830	E?	1861	1870-1930	G	1847	1930-1960	E	1955
"	1820-1870	H	1744	1860-1910	G	1839			
S.W. Zacatecas	1810-1860	H	1749	1850-1880	G	1849	1930-1960	E	1968
Motines	1810-1850	H	1790	1870-1910	E	1895	1940-1960	E	1957
"				1920-1950	G	1920			
Aguascalientes	1810-1900	G	1820	1850-1900	rG	1755	1940-1960	E	1963
Colima	1810-1850	G	1821	1882-1910	G	1856	1903-1960	G	1944
Mixteca Alta		?		1854-1921	G	1836	1921-1960	E	1902
All Yucatán Peninsula	1789-1842	G	1778	1881-1921	G	1858	1921-1980	E	1964
Yucatán State				1846-1910	G	1746	1921-1980	E	1971
Campeche							1921-1980	E	1955
Quintana Roo							1940-1980	E	1939

Sources: Cook and Borah 1971, 1974; Robinson 1981b; Lovell 1981; Lutz 1981.

of Middle American populations after the demographic disasters of Spanish conquest.

Meanwhile, Figure 4.2 and similar graphing for Table 4.3 that are not shown here provide enough data to perform curve-fitting that demonstrates how such population explosion, whether in colonial or in recent times, has repeatedly followed the shape of the inverse of the G function (G^1), switched both top to bottom and left to right. Called the E curve for *explosion*, this formula represents nothing but another simple transposition of G on the plane in semi-logarithmic scale. In Chapter 3 it was labeled, tentatively, $1/G(r)$. One of the hottest topics of 20th century historical demography thus turns out to involve just another manifestation of the G function at work. Simultaneously, explosion in this form proves to be a phenomenon of historical scope far beyond the recent decades with which it has commonly been identified. Important questions arise as to whether the same mechanisms of social and economic change generated E-type explosion in 17th century as have been at work to this effect in modern times.

Generally, these exploding populations of colonial west central Mexico swung over into robust but decelerating expansion of the H form in the 1700s (Era II in the table). Is the same change of trajectory taking place in well-known exploding populations of the present day, in countries like India or Bolivia or Egypt?

Subsequently, across the second half of the 18th century (Era III), demographic increase in Nueva Galicia, southwest Jalisco, and west central Mexico as a whole for a time came close to following the F trend. That the pace (from .025 to .028) for these simple exponential multiplications was somewhat less than the .03 found elsewhere historically could result just from how Cook and Borah smoothed their data; or it might in reality distinguish about the only three cases in this worldwide survey in which constant exponential growth at some rate other than .03 is encountered. Some fresh work with the Mexican data would be helpful.

Not all populations in Mexico and Guatemala grew this way up to the early 1800s. Already by the 1580s Yucatán seems to have been repopulating in G fashion. By the middle of the 1600s expansion of this more usual historical shape was also taking place in two parts of present-day Guatemala. The Quinizilapa Valley lay in the south, between Guatemala City and the Pacific (Lutz 1981, 186). The Cuchumatán Highlands stood in the west, along what is now the Mexican border. Though Yucatán as a whole lost people in some form across the first half of the 18th century, in the peninsula's parish of Umán baptisms increased across the 1700s in a G trend that closely resembled the contemporaneous G paths of demographic growth in Motines and the Mixteca Alta. The latter lasted on past 1800 like the Umán trend (Robinson 1981, 156). Meanwhile, fresh G growths in Colima, Motines, and Yucatán were not unlike the pattern for Mexico as a whole in 1803–1831.

What made the recovery of population in some parts of Mexico and Guatemala up into the early 19th century take the more standard sequence of G trends rather than a succession of E, H, and F paths as in some areas of west central Mexico? Did the nature of economic exploitation or development differ? How far had the indigenous population been run down before recovery commenced? Parts of west central Mexico were especially noted for their silver. That may have aggravated population loss at first, but then subsequently provided a basis for the kind of economic development that is generally seen to accompany H-type population increase historically. What happened to social life there? How did cultural differences shape the course of demographic disaster and recovery? For instance, the early G rebounds of the 1500s and 1600s appeared in *Mayan* zones of Yucatán and Guatemala. There is an interesting agenda for further research here.

In a fourth phase of Mexican demographic increase, after independence was won from Spain in the period of 1811–1821, the people of the country as a whole and the populations of most regions for which we have records expanded to about 1870 in H fashion. More rapidly decelerating G exceptions character-ized Aguascalientes, Colima, and Yucatán. From the kinds of economic settings observed for demographic trends of H shape in other historical contexts, the implication is that Mexico as a whole and certain regions within the country were experiencing some substantial development in this era. Though not as robust as for New York, New Jersey, Pennsylvania, and Delaware in comparable decades (part C of Table 2.1), these H trends are a reminder to North Americans that Mexico was not just a moribund society in the years during which we seized much of her territory. It would be useful to know more about the supporting environments in which these regional demographic growths of the H form could be sustained in 19th century Mexico and by what movements in fertility and mortality and migration they were achieved.

Through the later decades of the 1800s and up to the successive upheavals of the 1910s and early 1920s, however—Era V in the table—regional popula-tions in Mexico generally grew in G form. The H for Mexico as a whole, as north of the border, resulted from the staggered timing of those local G trends. In Jalisco and Nayarit, Southwest Zacatecas, Motines, the Mixteca Alta, the Yucatán Peninsula as a whole, and Yucatán State within it, these G's were quite parallel, with base years clustered around 1845.[10] In contrast, population increase in the Campeche part of Yucatán was very flat in 1846–1910, a pattern to which Colima reverted following more rapid G expansion in the preceding period. In at least this one small part of Mexico occurred the kind of retrogressive suc-cession of a steeper G by a flatter rG that has been encountered in "oversettled" frontiers of the United States, Canada, Australia, and New Zealand. It would be interesting to know more about how this happened in that particular part of west central Mexico—and only there, within the known set of data.

Beginning about the 1920s, finally, populations across Mexico tended to "ex-plode" in E trends (Era VI in Table 4.3).[11] In all three states of Yucatán this accelerating surge was still gathering momentum as late as 1980. By about 1950, however, it looks as though decelerating increase took over in Colima. Though the form here is G rather than H, the transition is reminiscent of what happened in several locations in the early 1700s (Era II in the table) and in Colima itself rather later. The interested reader can explore whether similar "topping out" into G or H trends has occurred elsewhere in Mexico since 1960 or so with the aid of recent census data on individual states.

Information on what has been happening lately to E-shape "explosions" in several other Latin American countries since World War II is one of the principal insights of Table 4.4. This summarizes graphing and analysis of what is known, or can be reasonably estimated, about movements in the sizes of societal populations in Middle and South America since records begin. Figure 4.4a presents trend fittings for Mexico, Brazil, Argentina, Costa Rica, and El Salvador, which have the longest series of historical evidence in Latin America. Figure 4.4b shows the patterns in countries with shorter historical records. The extensive international zone covered in the table and the figures, stretching from Baja California to Patagonia, displays very much the same mix of trends—all based upon the G formula—that the evidence of Table 4.3 has produced for post-disaster recovery and modern expansion in local Mexican and Guatemalan populations.

The table groups countries by the kinds of sequences of growths they have had in the 20th century. Seven populations (group I) have experienced explosion of the standard E form and then followed it with F trends—like several parts of west central Mexico in the 1600s and 1700s (Table 4.3 and Figure 4.2). In six other countries (group II), explosion gave way by the 1950s or 1960s to rapidly decelerating G increase. Little Uruguay (III) has had nothing but a series of G expansions since the early 1800s. Finally, the populations of Brazil, Argentina, and Paraguay (IV)—particularly the first two—have grown robustly via H and F paths, but without ever accelerating in explosive fashion.[12]

Clearly, by the time "population explosion" became recognized as a threat to ecology and economy in the 1960s, everywhere in Latin America demographic multiplication of this accelerating type was in fact *coming to an end* (Table 4.4). True, though, what followed in Mexico, Guatemala, Honduras, Panama, Venezuela, Ecuador, and Peru amounted to very challenging growth of the Franklin-Malthus sort, maintaining a heavy pressure (doubling about every 23 years) upon the resources of society.

Two centuries ago Franklin, and Malthus after him, thought that spacially open "frontier" conditions of new societies allowed populations to multiply in the F form. This interpretation might apply to Argentina in the second half of the 19th century and thinly settled Paraguay in 1950–1990, or to drastically depopulated zones of west central Mexico in the 1700s (Era III in Table 4.3). It hardly fits recent Mexico, Guatemala, Honduras, Panama, Venezuela, Ecuador, and Peru. Instead, it is necessary to enlarge the concept of "frontier" or geographically unrestricted populations to include those for which the support of constant exponential demographic expansion in the F form comes not from

Table 4.4

Sequences of Modern Population Growth in Middle and South America

I. Explosion Followed by Constant F Expansion

Ecuador		
1850-1900	G	1837
1900-1930	G	1889
1930-1960	E	1955
1950-1990	F	·

Peru		
1790-1836	G	1750
1836-1876	G	1833
1900-1930	G	1888
1920-1961	E	1962
1972-1990	F	·

Guatemala		
1848-1920	G	1843
·		
1920-1950	E	1943
1950-1990	F	·

Colombia		
1770-1825	G	1747
1825-1870	G	1830
1905-1930	G	1908
1930-1960	E	1952
1960-1990	G	1966

Mexico		
1803-1831	G	1746
1831-1873	H	1740
1873-1910	H	1819
1921-1960	E	1952
1940-1990	F	·

[III. All G]

Uruguay		
1825,1850	?G	1826
1852-1908	G	1883
1908-1950	G	1909
1950-1970	G	1932
1975-1990	G	1933

II. Explosion without F Succession

Costa Rica		
1700-1751	G	1685
1778-1824	G	1773
1836-1864	G	1826
1864-1892	E	1886
1883-1930	G	1893
1920-1963	G	1946
1963-1990	G	1973

El Salvador		
1769-1796	G	1734
1796-1821	G	1790
1878-1900	G	1865
1900-1940	G	1901
1940-1971	E	1962
1960-1990	G	1968

Chile		
1800,1813	?G	1764
1813-1843	G	1813
1843-1907	H	1813
1907-1930	?H	1845
1940-1960	E	1967
1970-1990	G	1960

Nicaragua		
1900,1906	?G	1890
1920-1940	G	1916
1930-1960	E	1955
1950-1971	G	1957
1971-1990	G	1989

Bolivia		
1826-1920	G	1812
1930-1968	E	1964
1958-1973	G	1962
1976-1990	G	1985

IV. No Explosion, but Strong Growth

Brazil		
1585-1660	G	1593
1690-1823	H	1710
1823-1872	H	1806
1900-1940	H	1885
1950-1970	F	·
1970-1990	G	1972

Argentina		
1778-1809	H	1709
1809-1839	H	1764
1857-1895	F	·
1895-1970	H	1905
1970-1990	G	1959

Paraguay		
1886,1900	?G	1880
1920-1950	G	1925
1950-1990	F	·

Honduras		
1801-1900	G	1810
·		
1900-1930	G	1908
1930-1960	E	1957
1950-1974	F	·
1974-1990	G	1987

Panama		
1900-1930	G	1891
1930-1960	E	1954
1950-1976	F	·
1976-1990	G	1975

Venezuela		
1802,1825	?G	1791
1838-1855	G	1849
1855-1900	G	1848
1926-1961	E	1949
1961-1976	F	·
1976-1990	G	1988

Source: Note 12.

Figure 4.4a

Trends of Growth in Modern South and Middle American Populations: Mexico, Brazil, Argentina, Costa Rica, and El Salvador

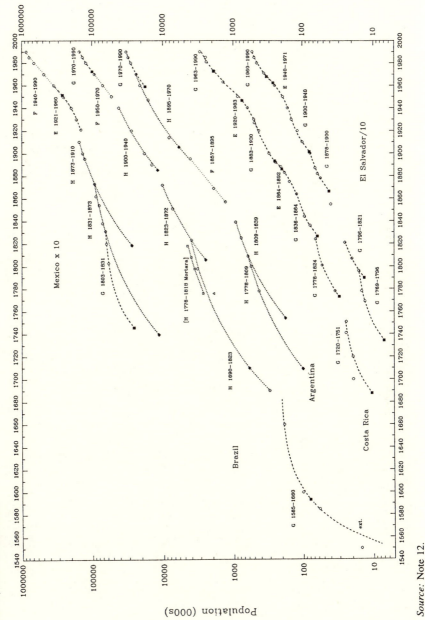

Source: Note 12.

Figure 4.4b
Trends of Growth in Modern South and Middle American Populations: Bolivia, Peru, Colombia, Venezuela, Chile, and Uruguay

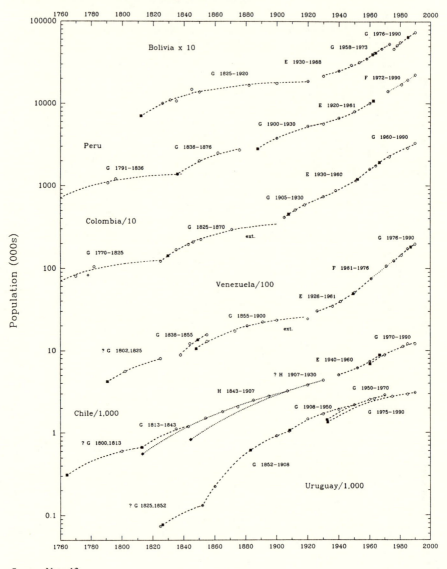

Source: Note 12.

occupying new territory but from some other way of regularly adding resources—perhaps through extensive economic growth that services "core" international economies as frontier societies once did, but with assets like cheap
labor in lieu of fresh land and its agricultural products, fish, timber, and furs,
or metals. This possibility needs to be pursued carefully as our global survey
moves to other parts of the world, especially modern Asia and Africa.

By the 1970s, however, the pace of expansion dropped off significantly below
the F slope via G-type deceleration in Venezuela, Panama, and Honduras. In
Costa Rica, El Salvador, Nicaragua, Colombia, Bolivia, and Chile, furthermore,
E-type explosions across the middle of the century had given over directly into
G tends by about the same time. A question of interest for local scholars concerns how six exploding Latin American populations "fell out of orbit," so to
speak, directly into G-type decelerating increase while the seven others of group
I instead settled into a steady aggressive F path of doubling every twenty to
twenty-five years. Those who know the histories of local population policies,
demographic behavior, change in values, and economic development ought to
be able to construct consistent and convincing explanations for the locations of
the two distinct sequences of pattern observed here. In turn, the types of successions of trend that we note may help these scholars identify the population
processes at work, set up the issues to be resolved, and organize the further
comparative inquiry that will provide the needed answers.

Over the last quarter century, in short, across all of Latin America population
explosion has disappeared, and also most of the F expansion that followed it in
some societies. Such transition from accelerating to decelerating growth, with
or without an intermediate stage of constant proportional increase, it must be
remembered, has not been achieved by some miraculous "hidden hand." Much
hard work, religious and political debate, and fundamental change in living
patterns has been required to slow the engine of demographic growth in these
ways. Those who sit and wait, assuming that things will take care of themselves
because population explosion has come to an end elsewhere, will be overrun by
fellow citizens, with all the consequences that such crowding typically entails.

Looking at Table 4.4 back in time, before the start of modern population
explosion in Latin America after World War I, one sees that most growth took
the G shape and that many of these G growths were largely parallel from country
to country. To begin with, preceding independence from Spain, generally similar
G trends with base years located from 1734 through 1750 occurred in Mexico,
Colombia, Peru, and El Salvador, and somewhat later and steeper ones for Costa
Rica, perhaps Chile and Venezuela, and as a second spurt for El Salvador in
1796–1821.

Then, from independence into the later 19th century or early 20th, a new
wave of G-shape growth appeared. These Bolivarian booms were flattest in
Honduras, Bolivia, and Chile, average in Costa Rica, Uruguay, Colombia, Peru,
and Ecuador, and strongest in Guatemala and Venezuela. Finally, from about
1900 into the interwar years, the high-water mark of Yankee imperialism, a

third common set of G expansions emerged: weakest in Peru, Ecuador, Paraguay, Nicaragua, and Costa Rica; strongest in El Salvador, Honduras, Colombia, and Uruguay, accompanied by second spurts in Nicaragua and Paraguay. What was the stimulus to such fresh demographic increase that Venezuela, Bolivia, and Guatemala failed to share at this time: better health (perhaps precisely because of foreign intervention); opportunities for participating in world markets (as in banana exports); altered values and expectations that eroded traditional views and practices? Table 4.4 tries to present the sequences of the various countries so that even more detailed parallels and contrasts among these predominant G curves catch the eye of readers interested in explaining the similarities or dissimilarities of demographic expansion in this part of the world.

Mexico, Brazil, Argentina, and sometimes Chile, however, stand out in the table as having experienced quite different series of growth patterns across their known demographic histories. All four populations have enlarged vigorously, Brazil and Argentina with as many as three H trends each.

Brazil from as early as 1690 and Argentina from where her record begins in 1778 shared a parallel H path of only slowly slowing multiplication up into the early 1800s. This trajectory with base year near 1710 very much resembled the H trends found in parts of west central Mexico across the first half of the 1700s (era II of Table 4.3). It also was much like the H trends for populations in Cuba 1700–1792, St. Domingue 1720–1780, Jamaica 1710–1770 (part A of Table 3.2), New France 1715–1775 (Table 3.1), and perhaps Virginia 1670–1710 and South Carolina 1720–1770 (Table 2.1). In short, Brazil and Argentina in the 18th century seem to have shared an H-type demographic increase experienced by some colonies of France and England as well as Spain and Portugal. A promising working hypothesis for explaining this parallelism should involve the way these various settlements from the St. Lawrence to the Río de la Plata— whether they primarily produced furs, precious metals, sugar, tobacco, rice, or cattle—generally participated in the 18th century growth of Atlantic trade in a way that others did not. While the development of the African slave trade was important for Brazil, Cuba, St. Domingue, Jamaica, Virginia, and South Carolina, it was less significant by far for west central Mexico and irrelevant in Canada. The essential economic dynamic was thus also broader than this particular thriving if notorious aspect of intercontinental business in the 1700s.

In the early 1800s, Brazil and Chile, and rather more flatly Argentina, experienced another round of H-type demographic increase joined by Mexico and at least several individual parts of that country (Era IV in Table 4.3). These H trajectories now closely resembled paths of that shape for the populations of Delaware, New York, Pennsylvania, and New Jersey (Table 2.1). Once more, widely spread New World populations swelled in similar ways, now in the mid-Atlantic region of the United States and central Mexico in the north and Argentina, Chile, and Brazil in the south, but nowhere in between or to the north and west. Once again, the nature of local ties to international markets (and the immigration involved with these economic developments) would seem to have determined the parallelism in paths.

By about 1920 or 1930 Chile and Mexico became countries experiencing the slow early stages of population explosion—along with almost all the rest of Latin America. After a brief spate of F-type frontier expansion in 1857–1895, however, Argentina joined Brazil in still another round of H-form increase across the first half of the 20th century. Presumably this was related again to connections that these two more developed countries of Latin America had to international economic growth, which were not shared by other nations of South and Middle America. In spite of a brief era of F expansion in Brazil 1950–1970, over the last quarter of a century her population and that of Argentina have experienced the same kind of rapidly decelerating G pattern found in Chile, Colombia, Panama, El Salvador, or Costa Rica. For one thing, the women of Brazil—the world's largest Catholic country—have en masse been taking up birth control practices that diverge from the policies of their church.

Finally, there has as yet been not even one sustained D decline in Middle or South America since the 17th century. What are evident, though, are sudden, short drops or breaks in population growth in Mexico in the 1910s, Chile in the 1960s, and Bolivia and Uruguay in the late 1970s. These are known to be epochs of civil war or of efforts to eliminate parts of the local population.[13] This lack of modern D trends is unlike what has been observed among the states of the United States, the provinces of Canada, the districts of New Zealand, and Yucatán and Colima within Mexico. The peoples of mainland Middle and South America have, in the modern era, so far constituted consistently *growing* populations.

The modern Caribbean remains the one last substantial area of the Western Hemisphere whose trends of demographic increase have not been analyzed. In most places there is unfortunately a gap for the late 1700s and early 1800s in reliable records with which to model growth trends. McCusker's careful review of the early colonial evidence stops in 1780 (1970, 1: 593–655, 2: 656–712). Deerr's information for the sugar colonies is not the latest and best (1949, 278–81 and passim). Emancipation of slaves by the English in 1834 and the French in 1848 apparently affected the completeness of counts of the many persons who now became no longer such valuable property.[14] Modern series like those of Roberts (1966, 63), Sánchez-Albornoz (1974, 169), and Mitchell (1993, 31–43) as a rule start only in the 1840s or 1850s.

Nevertheless, for the past century and a half—in some places for longer—it is possible to trace population increase in twenty-five societies of the Caribbean region, carrying forward to the present, with more-or-less modern materials, colonial inquiries begun as part of Chapter 3. A sampling of the likely G-based trends that emerge for the West Indies are graphed in Figure 4.5. These illustrations cover large populations like those of Haiti, Cuba, the Dominican Republic, and Puerto Rico and also movements on small islands or island groups such as the Netherlands Antilles, Bermuda, and the U.S. Virgin Islands (acquired from Denmark at the time of World War I). Table 4.5 summarizes observed

Figure 4.5
Some Modern Demographic Increase in the Caribbean

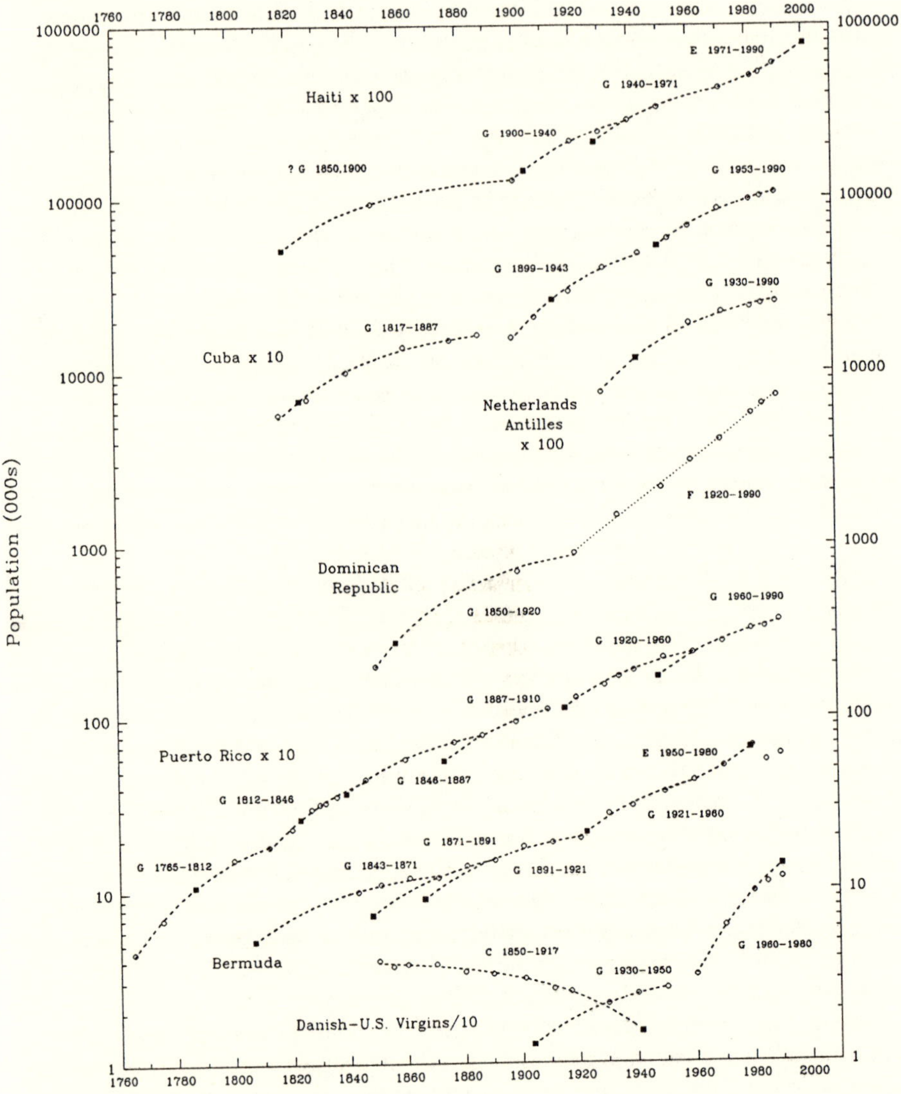

Source: See Table 4.5.

trends in population size for all twenty-five societies. The particulars of each have been graphed and fitted to G-related patterns, though they are not all presented in figures.

The first thing to note from the table is that among trends of growth in the modern West Indies there have been fewer exceptions to the basic G pattern than among the populations of mainland Latin America.[15] No H trend appears, and only one F (in the Dominican Republic in 1920–1990). There are only three accelerations of the E type—in contemporary Haiti (aggravating this poor country's many problems), for some reason in Bermuda 1950–1980, and in Guadeloupe across the first third of the 20th century.[16] One case of retrogressively timed succession between G's in Guyana, the rG of 1911–1931, reminds us again that this kind of reaction to overambitious development could occur south of the Rio Grande as well as in the United States and Canada.

Meanwhile, whereas sustained demographic decline has been virtually unknown in modern mainland Latin America, several instances appear in the Caribbean. The first type, originally rapid but steadily decelerating D, emerged in Barbados, Grenada, and Montserrat across the last half-century or so of slavery in the British West Indies (terminated in 1834). A second demographic drop of this form occurred on Barbados in 1901–1921, paralleled by similar loss on Antigua and, a little earlier, the British Virgins. Perhaps a seventh trend of this sort applies to Montserrat for 1946–1970.

A second and different form of population loss, starting slowly but accelerating with time, is evident on Antigua in 1774–1807, St. Kitts and Nevis in 1891–1921, and most persistently in the Danish Virgins from 1850 to 1917, when they were sold to the United States. This shape of shrinking has been noted here and there before, in Chapter 3.

The possibility that this rare trend for change in population size, too, might be a mathematical relative of G has been raised. It was tentatively labeled Gr. Now there seem to be enough data—most clearly from the Danish Virgins Islands—to declare that this pattern of ever more rapid decline, called the C curve for the total *collapse* toward which the trajectory heads, is indeed nothing but G reversed with respect to time. Its historical settings so far suggest that this form of atrophy occurs where a way of life begins to prove unsuitable. For instance, French planters started to give up on St. Croix in 1700–1730, before their government disposed of the island to the Danes. In turn, after the population of St. Croix and the other Danish Virgins had taken the C path across the second half of the 19th century, as oversupply squeezed world markets in tropical produce, especially sugar, Copenhagen in turn was willing to sell the group off to Washington. Local historians of various territories involved should be able to determine whether the mechanisms causing C decline were similar from place to place or could instead reflect the product of more than one set of dynamics.

Among the predominating G-type growth trends in Table 4.5, finally, appear certain intersocietal parallels that merit further attention. An attempt is made in the table to group these G's by base year for the curves and time span through

Table 4.5
G-Based Growth Patterns in the Modern Caribbean

Cuba			Haiti			Puerto Rico		
						1765-1812	G 1786	A
1817-1887	G 1825	C	1850,1900	?G 1819	C	1812-1846	G 1823	C
						1846-1887	G 1839	D
						1877-1910	G 1873	E
1899-1943	G 1913	F	1900-1940	G 1904	F	1920-1960	G 1916	F
			1940-1971	G 1928	G			
1953-1990	G 1950	H	1971-1990	E 2001	*	1960-1990	G 1948	H

Jamaica			Trinidad & Tobago			Dominican Republic		
1787-1844	G 1769	A						
1861-1891	G 1846	D	1844-1861	G 1833	D			
1891-1921	G 1868	E	1871-1931	G 1883	E	1850-1890	G 1867	E
1946-1976	G 1929	F				1920-1990	F -	*
1976-1990	G 1948	G	1946-1990	G 1948	G			

Suriname			Guyana			Cayenne		
			1841-1861	G 1838	D			
			1861-1891	G 1864	E	1901-1926	G 1870	E
1920-1950	G 1916	F	1911-1931	rG 1836	rD			
1950-1990	G 1955	G	1946-1985	G 1949	G	1946-1961	G 1952	G
						1961-1974	G 1974	H
						1982-1990	G 1994	I

Belize			St. Vincent			St. Lucia		
			1764-1834	G 1759	A			
			1834-1921	G 1828	C	1844-1861	G 1827	C
1881-1911	G 1868	E				1861-1921	G 1854	E
1911-1946	G 1894	F	1931-1970	G 1927	F	1946-1980	G 1937	F/G
1960-1985	G 1962	G	1980-1990	G 1966	G			
						1980-1990	G 1984	H/I

which they occurred (by labeling each category with a capital letter). It is possible that some of these clusterings happened by chance. Others, though, seem to link populations that might well have genuinely shared experiences. The big societies of Cuba, Haiti, and Puerto Rico, for example, all followed comparable G's (group "C") in the middle of the 19th century and again across the first decades of the 20th (category "F") and show some other similarities, though Puerto Rico displays extra G trends and Haiti went into population explosion in the 1970s. Likewise, there are several shared movements along the mainland fringe of the Caribbean in Cayenne, Guyana, Suriname, and Belize, while Jamaica and Trinidad and Tobago, on the one hand, and several small islands, on the other, seem to have gained (and lost) people in comparable ways. The similarities and contrasts among these trends raise some useful thoughts concerning the distribution of demographic, economic, medical, and social change across the West Indian region during various stages of its modern history.

Table 4.5 (*Continued*)

Barbados			
1770-1834	D	1736	a
1845-1901	G	1825	C
1901-1921	D	1877	b
1946-1990	G	1913	F

Grenada			
1780-1834	D	1766	a
1834-1851	G	1843	D
1881-1911	G	1874	E
1946-1976	G	1931	F/G

Antigua			
1774-1807	C	1841	*
1807-1851	G	1754	A
1901-1921	D	1866	b
1946-1990	G	1941	G

St. Kitts-Nevis			
1861-1891	G	1843	D
1891-1921	C	1952	*
1946-1976	G	1930	F/G

Danish/U.S. Virgins			
1850-1917	C	1941	*
1930-1950	G	1904	F
1960-1980	G	1990	I

British Virgins			
1871-1891	D	1865	b
1921-1960	G	1898	F
1960-1990	G	1958	G

Dominica			
1780-1805	G	1781	A
1844-1901	G	1803	B
1901-1946	G	1887	E/F
1946-1990	G	1936	F/G

Martinique			
1835-1894	G	1819	C
1905-1936	G	1884	E/F
1961-1990	G	1911	F

Guadeloupe			
1789-1861	G	1747	A
1852-1906	G	1831	C/D
1901-1936	E	1946	*
1961-1990	G	1920	F

Bahamas			
1851-1881	G	1841	D
1881-1911	G	1853	D/E
1921-1943	G	1901	F
1953-1990	G	1970	H

Bermuda			
1843-1871	G	1807	B
1871-1891	G	1848	D
1891-1921	G	1866	E
1921-1960	G	1923	F
1950-1980	E	1979	*

Montserrat			
1774-1807	D	1703	a
1851-1990	G	1834	D
1946-1970	?D	1912	c

Netherlands Antilles			
1930-1990	G	1942	G

A,B, . . . Successive contemporary clusters of G trends
a,b, . . . Successive contemporary clusters of D trends
*   Trend forms other than G or D
/   Borderline of two clusters.

Sources: McCusker 1970, 1: 593–655, 2: 656–712; Deerr 1949, 1: 278–81 and passim; Roberts 1966, 63; Sánchez-Albornoz 1974, 169; Mitchell 1993, 31–43.

Overall, the arrays of Latin American and Caribbean population trends appearing in Tables 4.4. and 4.5 underscore the importance of certain approaches when one attempts to comprehend better the nature of population growth or decline. First of all, though the mix of trends varies in this part of the world— with more frequent accelerating growth of the E type, for instance, and some rare accelerating population loss in the C form—the limited family of six G-based curves once more suffices to account well for the demographic increases and declines observed historically. No other formulas are necessary.

Second, it is essential to distinguish, unlike some commentators, "explosion" that specifically involves proportionally ever more rapid growth from fast expansion of the F type or during early stages of H or G trends before they decelerate. "Rapid" is not necessarily "exploding." The implications for how movements derive and what consequences they are likely to have are quite different in those divergent circumstances.

Third, E-type acceleration, D-form decline, slowly decelerating H expansion, and the constant proportional F multiplication introduced by Franklin long ago have not historically been as peculiar to certain eras or places as it is easy to think. F is modern as well as colonial. H is Latin American as well as North American. Explosion could occur in the 17th century, not just the 20th.

Fourth, knowing the repeated shapes of trend taken by population size helps in seeing what is coming. Most notably, many E-form explosions were evident in national data by the 1920s and 1930s and were in fact over by the time the alarm bells were rung for them in the 1960s. Analysts no longer need be that far behind the curve.

Finally, sifting through the ways that certain kinds of trends do or do not resemble each other from country to country produces valuable clues as to how the histories of Latin American and Caribbean peoples might help in understanding the ways in which the different types of G-based trends come and go. Identifying these similar or disparate trajectories of growth in Middle and South American and West Indian populations in turn can provide insight into how various movements in local demographic, social, economic, and even political history came about and left their impact upon the peoples who hosted them.

DID TRENDS FOR REGIONS WITHIN THESE COUNTRIES FOLLOW COMPARABLE PATTERNS?

Within the United States, Canada, Australia, and New Zealand, it has been seen that state, provincial, or territorial growth patterns—not just national ones—have also taken G-based forms. Sometimes these more local trends have mimicked the societal aggregate; sometimes they have pursued their own paths. Does such *regional* applicability of the G family of curves to population increase and decline also pertain inside the demographically active and insightful nations of Latin America?

Reliable, relatively extensive and unbroken state or district series that are not plagued by boundary changes do not exist in large quantity for the populations of South and Middle America. Three comparatively long records, however, which have relatively regular evidence that reports on largely consistent geographical areas, cover the major subdivisions of Brazil from 1808 to 1985, Venezuela 1873–1981, and Chile 1835–1970. For demonstration, G-based curves have been fitted to movements for the states and districts of Brazil, as illustrated in Figure 4.6. Local trends in Venezuela and Chile have simply been estimated by using templates of the various G forms in order to attain some rough comparisons.[17]

Within Brazil, Table 4.6 shows, historical patterns in population growth for the most part distinguish the states of the North from those of the South. In Amazonas, Pará, and Maranhão—down the Amazon and eastward along the northern coast of Brazil—G growths arrayed around a modern E explosion have been the pattern. Here has unfolded a sequence of trends already familiar from several South and Middle American nations (Table 4.4). Such a patterning has also pertained in the states of Rio Grande do Norte, Sergipe, and Bahia, which jut still further out toward Africa along the northeastern coast of the country. In other parts of Brazil, only Rio de Janeiro and Paraná, situated further down the Atlantic litoral, join this group of 6 northern states in having just G and E growth this way among the 26 areas of the country for which records exist. In Amapá and Roraima along the northern fringes of the Amazon Basin, meanwhile, only G growths have occurred (without any E), which is shown in part I of Table 4.6. This pattern has also applied to Rondônia, the Distrito Federal (Brasilia), Minas Gerais, and Guanabara (now incorporated as the northern part of the state of Rio de Janeiro): roughly a belt of in-between zones draped west to east across the tapering hips of bulging Brazil.

In contrast, for most states of the southern section of the country (Rio Grande do Sul, Santa Catarina, Mato Grosso, Acre to the far west, São Paulo, Goiás, and Espírito Santo) and for some in the Northeast (Alagoas, Pernambuco, Paraíba, Ceará, and Piauí) at one time or other the more robust F or H forms of expansion have occurred. São Paulo, Espírito Santo, and Piauí have additionally witnessed some of the E-type explosion that has been evident in the more "Third World"–looking growth sequences of northern Brazil.

Broadly, this division of Brazilian demographic history by South and North distinguishes the more developed and richer regions of the country from the more primitive and poorer ones (Merrick and Graham 1979, 9). It is in such more robust and complex economic conditions that the H form of demographic increase has been encountered elsewhere, as in North America. The regional Brazilian data build that generalization still further. Similarly, the F trend appears within Brazil only for the booming plantation frontier of São Paulo in 1854–1890, the present-day deep interior penetration of Acre, and mid-20th century Santa Catarina, where some of the best modern agriculture of Brazil evolved and spread.

Such broad regionalization between northern and southern parts of the country mostly reaffirms conventional categorization. Table 4.6, however, makes it possible to proceed beyond this crude dichotomy to identify finer patterns among the particulars for individual states. For this purpose successive G, E, and H trends are classified in the table by their timing (their t_0's), using numbers, capital letters, and lower-case letters respectively. Those who study regional agriculture, industrialization, urbanization, migration, health, and natural in-

Figure 4.6
Growth Patterns in Some States of Brazil since 1808

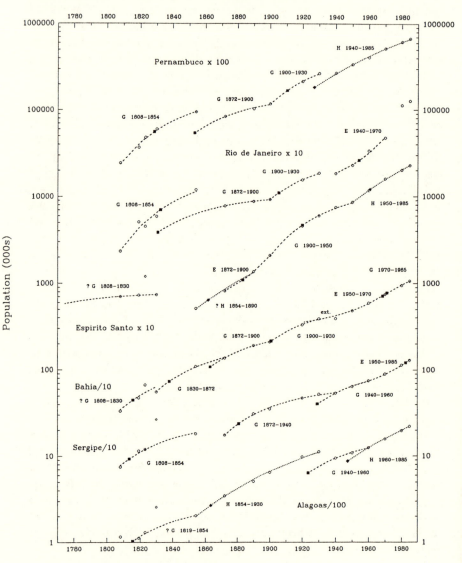

Sources: Ludwig 1985, 47; Brazil, Fundaçao 1988, 55.

crease within Brazil should be able to identify the particular local dynamics that have made demographic development parallel in some areas at some times, divergent in other places and eras. Even the inexpert eye perceives many thought-provoking patternings in the table.

Looking at G-related trendings for the regions of Brazil as part of a broader international context likewise provides valuable insights. For instance, while most population explosions in Latin America and the Caribbean have been clustered in one period of time and have followed roughly parallel E curves—whether nationally in modern times or regionally in the 18th century demographic recoveries of central Mexico—for the states of Brazil, in contrast, the table demonstrates that the distribution of growth in the E form by era and by the timing of the upward-surging curves themselves was much less focused. Less than half of the total cases of local explosion paralleled national E trends for neighboring populations like those of Bolivia, Peru, Ecuador, Colombia, and Venezuela shown in Table 4.4, even though it was mostly the comparably equatorial states of Brazil whose populations did surge in this way. While one might think that the chronological scattering of whatever E's did exist for state populations within Brazil kept this national population from taking E form, that hypothesis collapses when template approximations for likely E trends in the states of Venezuela and the provinces of Chile are examined. In Venezuela, it is true, the regional E's very do much cluster parallel to the national one. In Chile, though, there has been even more temporal dispersion of local E trends than in Brazil. The total population of Chile nevertheless expanded in E fashion 1940–1960 even if in the company of only two provinces. Meanwhile, about half the state populations of Brazil have experienced E growth, almost the same proportion as within Venezuela and Chile. It has not been lack of local E growths as such that prevented proportional acceleration for the total Brazilian population, but how local patterns of all types summed up into the national one. In this process, the nature of local migration clearly made a big difference.

In short, national E growth does not *have* to be powered by repeated parallel local trends, though it *can* receive much of its dynamic from that source. Probably principally through interregional migration, population explosion in the E trajectory, like the other exceptional forms of growth H and F, can appear in whole countries as a composite of local trends of increase that do *not* take the E shape. This is reminiscent of the way G growths in the colonies/states of the future United States were found, in Chapter 2, to be the building blocks of long F and H trends for the population as a whole in 1670–1850 and in 1850–1940.[18] What forces, then, have been at work to shape population size on the aggregate and the local levels? Both demographic behavior and economic change would seem to bear on each. How are the parts then integrated into a whole?

Finally, even among the most common type of growths, the G trends, insightful groupings appear across the local populations of Brazil—and also Chile and Venezuela. The reader may wish to refine the clusterings that are suggested by the numbered categories of Table 4.6 and revise some of the proposed trends

Table 4.6
Parallels and Divergences of Growth in the States of Brazil

I. States with G Growths Only

Minas Gerais

1808-1854	G 1827	(5)
1872-1900	G 1872	(7)
1900-1930	G 1904	(9)
1950-1985	G 1949	(12)

Amapá

1950-1985	G 1983	(14)

Guanabara

1872-1920	G 1893	(8)
1920-1940	G 1918	(10)
1950-1970	G 1958	(12)

Rondônia

1950-1970	G 1981	(14)

Roraima

1950-1970	G 1970	(13)
1970-1985	G 2001	(15)

Distrito Federal

1960-1985	G 2011	(15)

II. States with E Explosion as Well as G Growth

Paraná

1819,1854	?G 1778	(2)
1872-1900	G 1889	(8)
1900-1930	G 1917	(10)
1920-1950	E 1929	[C]
1950-1970	G 1982	(14)

Rio de Janeiro

1808-1854	G 1833	(5)
1872-1900	G 1831	(6)
1900-1930	G 1905	(9)
1940-1970	E 1954	[D]

Bahia

1808-1830	G 1816	(4)
1830-1872	G 1838	(5)
1872-1900	G 1863	(7)
1900-1930	G 1901	(9)
1950-1970	E 1971	[E]
1970-1985	G 1969	(13)

Sergipe

1808-1854	G 1813	(4)
1872-1940	G 1881	(8)
1940-1960	G 1930	(11)
1950-1985	E 1983	[F]

Rio Grande do Norte

1808-1900	G 1830	(5)
1900-1940	G 1914	(10)
1930-1970	E 1965	[E]
1960-1985	G 1965	(13)

Pará

1808-1823	G 1802	(3)
1854-1890	G 1842	(6)
1900-1930	G 1920	(10)
1940-1980	E 1959	[E]
1970-1985	G 1991	(14)

Amazonas

1819,1854	?G 1802	(3)
1872,1890	?G 1899	(8)
1900-1940	G 1899	(9)
1940-1970	E 1960	[E]
1970-1985	G 1986	(14)

Maranhao

1808-1872	G 1818	(4)
1872-1920	E 1915	[B]
1900-1940	G 1908	(10)
1940-1960	E 1945	[D]
1960-1985	E 1979	[F]

Table 4.6 (Continued)

III. States with H Expansion as Well as G Growth

Pernambuco

1808-1854	G 1829	(5)
1872-1890	G 1853	(7)
1900-1930	G 1910	(10)
1940-1985	H 1927	{d}

Goiás

1808-1854	G 1829	(5)
1872-1900	G 1865	(7)
1900-1940	H 1918	{d}
1950-1985	G 1972	(13)

Rio Grande do Sul

1808-1854	G 1845	(5)
1872-1890	G 1890	(8)
1900-1930	G 1912	(10)
1940-1985	H 1930	{d}

Mato Grosso[a]

1808-1854	G 1828	(5)
1872-1900	H 1864	{b}
1900-1950	H 1924	{d}
1960-1985	G 1988	(14)

Paraíba

1854-1890	G 1859	(7)
1900-1940	G 1914	(10)
1940-1985	H 1909	{c}

Alagoas

1819-1854	G 1815	(4)
1854-1930	H 1863	{b}
1940-1960	G 1924	(11)
1960-1985	H 1947	{e}

Ceará

1808-1854	G 1814	(4)
1872-1900	G 1829	(6)
1900-1930	G 1900	(9)
1930-1960	H 1930	{d}
1960-1985	H 1948	{e}

IV. States with More Unusual Growth Patterns

Santa Catarina

1808-1830	G 1789	(2)
1830-1872	H 1843	{a}
1872-1900	G 1880	(8)
1900-1930	G 1917	(10)
1920-1970	F ·	*
1970-1985	G 1968	(13)

Sao Paulo

1819-1854	G 1823	(5)
1854-1890	F ·	*
1890-1940	G 1911	(10)
1930-1960	E 1951	[D]
1960-1985	H 1982	{g}

Espírito Santo

1808-1830	G 1734	(1)
1854-1890	H 1862	{b}
1872-1900	E 1883	[A]
1900-1950	G 1920	(10)
1950-1985	H 1961	{f}

Piauí

1872-1920	E 1908	[B]
1920-1970	E 1962	[E]
1960-1985	H 1967	{f}

Acre

1950-1985	F ·	*

(1), etc. Denotes successive clusters of G trends
[A], etc. Denotes successive clusters of E trends
{a}, etc. Denotes successive clusters of H trends
*   Denotes F trends (which have no zero year)
[a]   Includes the new state of Mato Grosso do Sul 1980 and 1985

Sources: Ludwig 1985, 47; Brazil, Fundaçao 1988, 55.

involved. Still, many comparable parallels of G paths should emerge across all three countries.

In conclusion, within the three quite different countries of Latin America represented by Brazil, Venezuela, and Chile, patterns of population increase from area to area present valuable clues as to how local growth took various G-based forms. Shared patterns imply the possibility of shared demographic and economic dynamics generating the common paths of change in population size. Where populations grew differently, the course of economic expansion and/or demographic behavior almost certainly diverged, too. Fruitful ways of organizing local history are offered. Furthermore—as among the component geographical units of the United States, Canada, Australia, and New Zealand, which have been discussed in previous chapters—local trends within these Latin New World lands did not slavishly imitate national outlines. This repeated finding suggests that interregional migration and perhaps natural increase, too, must also follow some G-connected form if disparate state or provincial trends are going to fit together to constitute distinct national patterns of G-based demographic increase.

EXPOSING PACIFIC ISLAND PEOPLES TO OUTSIDERS: SIMILAR DISASTERS AND RESURGENCES IN THE 1800s AND 1900s

To cite the conquest of Mexico, Central America, and most of South America by Spain in the 16th century evokes images of armored, unscrupulous adventurers, the enslaving of native populations, fatal labor in the mines, and coerced settlement on great ranches and plantations. Diego Rivera painted the murals for this history. It is important to realize, though, that when European and American explorers, whalers, traders, missionaries, empire builders, and romantics intruded into the far-flung island "paradises" of the South Pacific in the 18th, 19th, and 20th centuries, this modern invasion of "civilization" wiped out local populations in much the same way. Captain Cook, the mutineers of the *Bounty*, Ahab's crew, and the evangelical, pre-pineapple Doles brought disease and social destruction with them almost as disastrously as had Columbus, Cortez, and Pizarro. Moreover, population loss from death (and from the impact of cultural and social disorganization upon reproduction) decimated Pacific islanders according to exactly the same pattern of decline—the D curve—as had been experienced by Amerindians three centuries before and thousands of miles away.

The overall cost of these encounters to the peoples of Oceania has for some time been known to be comparable to those of earlier catastrophes in Latin America. The Salvadorian demographer Rodolfo Barón Castro pointed out that fact in 1942.[19] What can be added now, however, is that these Pacific disasters followed similar D-shaped paths. That point is demonstrated for some of the larger islands and island groups in Figure 4.7, which also indicates how these

Figure 4.7
Demographic Devastation and Recovery on Larger Islands and Island Groups in the Pacific

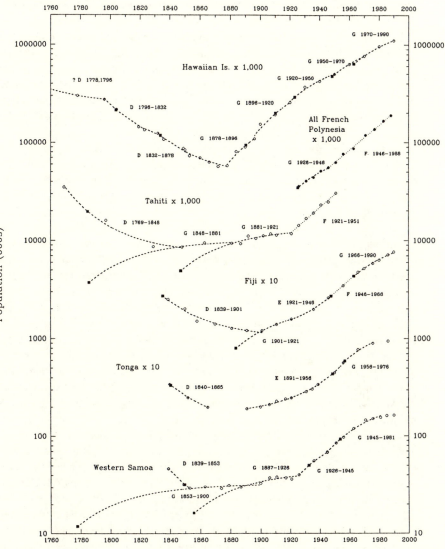

Source: See Table 4.7.

populations have similarly rebounded thereafter in other familiar G-connected forms. The invaluable work of Norma McArthur (1967), three decades ago, in sifting through the available census reports, estimates, and more or less informed guesses about the number of people who were living on certain islands at various points of time makes such analysis feasible.

Because some records do not begin until the middle or even the end of the 19th century, it is not possible to tell precisely how much loss was sustained everywhere, or whether this was experienced in just one or in more than one D trend. For Tahiti and the Hawaiian Islands, however, it is evident that the decline was severe, about 75 to 85 percent.[20] Most disastrous of all was the annihilation of the native people of Tasmania between 1803 and 1855, along something like the two D trajectories summarized in Table 4.7.[21]

Losses in Fiji for 1839–1901, Tonga for 1840–1865, Western Samoa for 1839–1853, and what became U.S. Samoa for 1839–1849, which entailed declines of 48, 44, 37, and 53 percent respectively, at first glance may appear in Figure 4.7 to be less devastating. This is largely the case, though, simply because no records exist giving the sizes of earlier populations, which the typical hazards of contact had done much to erode well before local demographic data begin. Explorers, whalers, traders, and others had reached these islands well before the 1840s. It was just record keeping, not disease, death, and disorganization, that had to await the missionaries. These arrived at Fiji, for instance, only in 1835.[22]

By the middle of the 1800s, however, in Tahiti, the Hawaiian Islands, the two Samoas, and the Northern Cook group population sizes began to rebound. Table 4.7 shows this, along with the way that such growth everywhere took G form. No explosion is found, as by Cook and Borah in several areas of west central Mexico in the early 1700s (Table 4.3). Instead, ubiquitous G recovery after D decline makes demographic revival in the South Seas a century ago look more like the reexpansion in more remote places of Middle America such as the Mixteca Alta and Yucatán in Mexico or the highlands of Guatemala. As in the Mayan G-shaped recovery in Yucatán across the second half of the 1500s, furthermore, G growth in Oceania appeared appreciably sooner than the century-and-a-half lag that was typical from the onset of decline to visible recovery in most local populations of early Mexico and Central America. The implication is that something about the nature of Spanish colonization in central Mexico, perhaps its harsh and systematic exploitation of native labor, *kept* the size of the population down longer after the big initial damage was done, sometimes eventually allowing expansion in the almost imperceptible elevation of the early E curve, sometimes simply involving a prolongation or renewal of D-shaped decline before G recovery could at last begin. Investigation of what those dynamics were (and why places like Yucatán, also subservient to Spain, did not have them) would seem a fruitful inquiry for the future. Meanwhile, Fiji and the Lower Cook Islands provide exceptions in which Pacific populations, too, could have longer delays than typical in this part of the world before demo-

Table 4.7

Patterns of Decline and Growth on Pacific Islands since the Later 1700s

A. Comparing Trends across the Pacific

Tahiti

1769-1848	D	1785
1848-1881	G	1786
1881-1921	G	1847
1921-1971	F	.

All French Polynesia

1926-1946	G	1925
1946-1988	F	.

Natives of Tasmania

1803,1835	?D	1857
1835-1855	D	1888

Hawaiian Is.

1778-1796	D	1726
1796-1832	D	1804
1832-1878	G	1834
1878-1896	G	1890
1896-1920	G	1910
1920-1950	G	1923
1950-1970	G	1948
1970-1990	G	1963

Western Samoa

1839-1853	D	1850
1853-1900	G	1778
1887-1926	G	1856
1926-1945	G	1933
1945-1981	G	1954

Guam

1901-1920	G	1891
1920-1940	G	1925
1960-1990	G	1960

All Cook Is.

1902-1916	G	1832
1926-1951	G	1917

Northern Cook Is.

1850,1871	?D	1848
1871,1899	?G	1838
1902-1916	D	1862
1916-1951	E	1973

U.S. Samoa

1839,1849	?D	1872
1853-1900	G	1806
1900-1912	G	1895
1912-1950	E	1938
1960-1990	G	1963

Tonga

1840-1865	D	1841
?		
1891-1956	E	1949
1956-1976	G	1957

Fiji

1839-1901	G	1835
1900-1921	G	1884
1921-1946	E	1948
1946-1966	F	.
1966-1990	G	1963

Leewards

1902-1911	G	1917
1911-1956	E	1948

Lower Cook Is.

1845-1902	D	1825
1902-1936	E	1947
1926-1951	G	1919

B. Continuities and Variations within the Hawaiian Islands

	First Decline			Second Decline			Some Recovery		
Kauai	1779,1805	?D	1759	1805-1872	D	1833	1872,1896	?G	1899
Oahu	1779,1805	?D	1760	1831-1878	D	1811	1878-1896	G	1893
Maui	1779,1805	?D	1760	1831-1878	D	1839	1878-1890	G	1884
Molokai	1779,1805	?D	1766	1805-1896	D	1838			
Hawaii	1779-1823	D	1770	1823-1878	D	1845	1878-1896	G	1892
Niihau	1779,1805	?D	1797	1805-1860	D	1832	1860-1878	D	1897
Lanai	1779,1805	?D	1802	1823-1872	D	1853	1872-1896	D	1900

Sources: McArthur 1967; J. Cook 1821; Schmitt 1968; see notes 21, 22, 24.

graphic increase reappeared (only around 1900, rather than half a century before that). What made for these particular delays?

Once growth began, Hawaii, Western Samoa, Guam, and the Cook Islands as a whole experienced no other form of demographic increase save repeated decelerating G surges. In contrast, in U.S. Samoa, Tonga, Fiji, the Leewards, and also the Lower and Northern Cook groups taken separately, distinct paths of E-type explosion emerged after a while, in the first half of the 20th century. All of these accelerating trends, except for the rather steeper Northern Cook example, were remarkably parallel. A single pattern of population explosion was generally shared by the six Pacific populations that experienced that form of increase. Further, this timing makes those Pacific islands accompany in their explosions by far the most numerous clustering of E-shape demographic accelerations in the history of Latin American nations and regions. Their E trends, in other words, paralleled those of Guatemala, Costa Rica, Guadeloupe, Venezuela, Mexico, Colombia, Panama, Nicaragua, Ecuador, and Honduras among whole societies, and most known recent regional E growths within Mexico and Venezuela. Mere coincidence seems unlikely to have accounted for these similarities. Instead, certain widely felt international changes of the modern era—probably in health—most likely produced this parallelism from southern zones of the Americas right across the Pacific. That hypothesis seems worth researching carefully.

Some F-type expansion also forms part of the recent tale of the South Pacific: in Tahiti for 1921–1971, all French Polynesia (of which Tahiti composes a major part) for 1946–1988, and Fiji more briefly, for 1946–1966. McArthur's data end about 1970, while the U.N.'s recent information (*Demo. Ybk.* 1975–1993) deals only with aggregations of some of the islands discussed here. Hence population sizes for the last two or three decades for several island groups are difficult to integrate into Table 4.7 without digging into particulars of French or New Zealand colonial records. Still, where recent years *are* covered, G growth with a base year around 1960 also seems rather universal, the one exception being French Polynesia, where the F continues. In other words, after more than half the recorded island groups experienced E explosion, they settled into the same decelerating G pattern that was shared by Pacific populations that had never taken an exploding path. Here another generality, found scattered across thousands of miles of open sea, in places controlled by a diversity of indigenous and colonial governments, and involving widely varying mixes of peoples, demands to be explained. How did changing conditions of health, fashions of family formation, economic change, and patterns of migration produce such similar explosion in so many far-flung places half a century ago, and even more common G growth more recently?

Finally, population trends on individual islands within the Hawaiian group (at the bottom of Table 4.7) show how the numbers of local peoples changed via G-based forms also within the overall aggregate (Schmitt 1968, 42, 70). Just as has been observed within several populations of North, Central, and South

America and Australia and New Zealand, not all local change had to be parallel. The most similar developments across all seven islands were D declines from the early 1800s to about 1875. Subsequently, the trends became noticeably more divergent from island to island. On Kauai, Oahu, Maui, and Hawaii very comparable G growths then appeared, in a timing much like that found for the early 1900s on Guam, U.S. Samoa, and Fiji (Table 4.7). On Molokai, the D that had begun in 1805 continued and was not reversed by G expansion even by the 1890s. On the smallest of the seven major islands, Niihau and Lanai, however, *third* D-shape atrophies took place in the later 1800s. In consequence, these two places lost about 96 and 99 percent (or more) of the population they had held when Captain Cook came to the islands. That puts their damage in a class with the worst demographic disasters of Hispaniola and Mexico under the Spanish Conquest. Comparatively, next smallest Molokai saw 90 to 94 percent of its people disappear, Kauai 88 to 91 percent, the "big island" (Hawaii) 87 to 89 percent, Maui 81 to 84 percent, but Oahu just 68 percent. On Oahu native losses in the 19th century were, most of any island, offset by invaders of many types who sought to exploit this center of trade and economic development for the strategic mid-Pacific archipelago.

Finally, data for individual islands may help select the best estimates to employ for the Hawaiian group as a whole in the earliest years of contact. Here is another instance in which summarizing with the G family of curves clarifies issues concerning which evidence may be most trustworthy and helps lay out what further research is necessary to form final conclusions and how such investigation might proceed.[23]

In sum, population disaster in response to contact with biologically long-separated outsiders cut down the peoples of the Pacific as deeply as when first Iberian, then northern European invaders intruded upon the Americas in the "Columbian exchange" three centuries before. Such mid-ocean demographic catastrophe, furthermore, took the same D path that has been found to fit the disappearance of population in places like Hispaniola, Mexico, and Peru. As in the Americas, too, sometimes demographic loss in the Pacific followed a single dip of devastation; sometimes it occurred in two or more successive D-shape shrinkages. Then, when populations adjusted to the new circumstances (which they apparently did more rapidly in relatively modern Oceania than they did in some parts of early colonial Mexico), Pacific peoples universally recovered first via G growths. This sets them apart from certain colonial Latin American cases of recovery that have been documented, though it aligns them with others, particularly demographic rebounds among the Maya. In the 20th century, too, some island peoples, though not all, have experienced the E-type "Third World" population explosion that has been so common in Latin America, while not in the Caribbean or North America. Furthermore, they have done this parallel in timing and acceleration with the most numerous E growths found among the nations and subregions of Middle and South America. This far-flung similarity seems more likely to involve a genuine international phenomenon than to represent mere coincidence. Finally, almost universal parallel G growth in the Pacific across recent years indicates that very general inter-island dynamics are, once again, driving population change for Oceania in our own time.

OVERVIEW: JUST A FEW G-BASED TRENDS IN NEW WORLD POPULATIONS

Historically, the path of population decline has been determined by the G curve every bit as much as the course of population growth. Upside down, in its D form, the basic proportionally decelerating function captures the trajectory of demographic loss that has been followed under widely varied international conditions. Whatever its causes or contexts, population loss overwhelmingly takes this one G-based track. A few exceptional cases of *accelerating* decline have been noted here and there in the parts of the world studied so far. Yet these follow a path that is itself nothing but G reversed with respect to time, the C curve of faster and faster collapse, the sixth member of the family of G functions.

Population explosion, another hot topic in recent demography, turns out simply to adhere to a similar transposition of G, the proportionally accelerating E curve. This aggressive, threatening form of growth has occurred, however, way back in 18th century Spanish America as well as in the "developing" countries of recent times whose demographic expansion at an increasing proportional rate caused so much concern starting in the 1960s. The phenomenon is more historically general than previously supposed; and its shape is closely related, through the mathematics of G, to other forms of demographic increase, a fact that has not been recognized so far.

In all, populations in more and more parts of the world and in more and more eras of history are found to change size according to—and only according to—the G family of six related curves. These trends effectively and insightfully depict what has happened to widely diverse peoples who have lived in markedly different contexts of culture, scientific knowledge, health, politics, economy, and so forth.

Such far-flung manifestations of change in population size according to a few forms based upon G, however, have not been evident in the same *mix* for every set of "New World" circumstances. Table 4.8 summarizes, from all data sets surveyed so far, the varying frequencies from region to region of the six repeating G-based trend types discovered. These geographical distinctions in distribution offer some contextual clues concerning how best to go about explaining the ways in which the different trends come about.

First of all, as has been said many times, G itself—the simple, unadjusted, and untransformed pattern of proportional growth, which constantly decelerates at the .03 rate—is overwhelmingly the most frequent shape of demographic expansion. For all parts of the world examined so far, of 861 national or regional

Table 4.8
The Distribution of Trend Types Found in New World Populations*

Region of the World	G	H	F	E	Total Gains	D	C	Total Losses	All Trends
Detail									
U.S.A.	201	18	5	3	227	5	0	5	232
Canada	60	2	1	2	65	3	3	6	71
Pre-1800 Caribbean	114	5	2	10	131	18	6	24	155
Modern Caribbean	74	0	1	3	78	6	3	9	87
Australia & New Zealand	80	0	0	1	81	6	0	6	87
Southern Africa	15	2	1	0	18	0	0	0	18
Pacific Islands	28	0	3	6	37	19	0	19	56
Early Spanish Colonial Areas	23	9	3	15	50	43	0	43	93
Modern Latin American Nations	45	9	10	14	78	0	0	0	78
States of Brazil	64	15	3	14	96	0	0	0	96
Aggregates									
Latin America	132	33	16	43	224	43	0	43	267
Caribbean & Pacific Islands	228	5	6	19	246	43	9	52	298
U.S.A. & Canada	261	20	6	5	292	8	3	11	303
Australia, N.Z., S. Africa	95	2	1	1	99	6	0	6	105
TOTAL	704	60	29	68	861	100	12	112	973

*Without tentatively hypothesized trends marked "?" in preceding tables, except 3 ?F's of Table 4.3.

Source: All tables of Chapters 1–4.

trends of increase not less than 704, or 82 percent, took the G form. H, F, and E trends represent only 6, 3, and 7 percent of the growth patterns respectively. Outside Latin America, G accounts for as much as 90 percent of the observed expansions. Among losses of population, meanwhile, some 100 of 112 cases involve simply decay along the path of 1/G—the D curve of proportional decline, which also constantly decelerates at the standard rate of .03. There appear just 12 instances of demographic loss in the unusual trajectory of accelerating C.

The exceptions to the predominant G form of population increase for New World populations have not been evenly distributed geographically. Of 112 observed trends of demographic loss, for instance, five of every six (95) occurred in the Caribbean, Latin America, or among Pacific island populations. While the cases in the United States, Canada, Australia, and New Zealand are insightful, they are—so far—very rare. Most New World population loss in the places and periods surveyed occurred as native populations encountered invasion in the Americas or Oceania or as Europeans failed to fare well in tropical plantation systems.

Even more geographically focused have been accelerating E trends. As many as 43 of 68, or 63 percent, of the instances encountered have been located just in Latin America. Not only in our own times, moreover, but also in the 17th and 18th centuries as they began to recover from the effects of the Spanish Conquest, these societies from Mexico to Chile have been most familiar with "population explosion." Though there are a small number of exceptions evident in very early stages of settlement, two historical settings for E trends seems to be typical. On the one hand, such explosion occurs after disaster has at some point in time cut back a population significantly, as in Mexico in the 1600s or some Pacific populations in the 1900s; on the other, the limitations seem to be taken off populations that have not previously been cut back that way. This second set of circumstances appears to involve not only better health but more generous resources that will support such accelerating demographic growth without producing disaster. At worst, some form of decelerating demographic increase follows, not decline. Malthus, in other words, misjudged both how fast humankind could multiply free of restraint (in upward-curving rates often breaking well above his argued ultimate doubling time of 20 to 25 years) and how vigorously resources could be expanded or thinned at least enough to keep such exploding populations alive for substantial periods until they could begin to slow in growth. It is time to stop teaching his "arithmetic-geometric" model to students as an example of anything but early modern intellectual history.

In Latin America and Oceania, furthermore, as in northern European colonizations of North America, the West Indies, the Antipodes, and southern Africa, the F model of demographic increase has not cropped up only where substantial geographical frontiers existed, as Malthus argued after Franklin. Especially in recent times, it has also appeared (mostly in certain nations of South America and a few populations of relatively big Pacific islands) where economic extension other than sheer spacial openness has enlarged the opportunity to support more people. Malthus was wrong here, too. Meanwhile, slowly decelerating growth of the H form has unfolded over and over again where it seems that accumulative, persistent economic development has taken place, where incremental improvements in resources (or how they can be used) have kept the perimeters of new demographic opportunity expanding—in parts of Mexico and southern South America as in previously observed cases from North America and a few places in the Caribbean.

All this generality of change in some G-based form or another, either the basic G or its exceptional modifications H, F, E, D, and C, implies that something very fundamental to humankind underlies the G shape. The quest to find that controlling dynamic and to understand its workings structures a large project that only begins to unveil here.

The next stage of that inquiry, though, still remains a comparative geographic one. From Franklin forward to the present day, students of population have argued that in their change of size more mature or more developed peoples follow courses different from the paths taken by newer, simpler, or less economically advanced ones. Already, parallels among the demographic histories of the United States, Canada, Australia, and New Zealand, on the one hand, and the population experiences of Latin America, the Caribbean, and the Pacific, on the other, warn that some of these claims of contrast are incorrect. But determining just how much generality there is in population growth and decline around the world and across time and securing a satisfactory understanding of the conditions in which the six different fundamental G-based types of trends occur require knowledge of the patterns of the Old World: of Europe, Asia, and Africa.

NOTES

1. Barbados, in contrast, seems to have experienced *accelerating* atrophy among its settlers of European origin during the war years of 1688–1713 (see Figure 3.2a).

2. The exceptional high 1644 number for little Banderas is not used in fitting the later D there.

3. Most of these longer series reflect the interpolated trends constructed by Cook and Borah at decadal intervals to about 1800 (1: 310) and the timing of Mexican censuses thereafter.

Though there are only two early years with estimates, 1543 and 1549, it looks as though the population of Yucatán, the sturdy southern jaw of the Gulf of Mexico opposite the long northern overbite of Florida, may have atrophied along a D path to about 1560. If the early base of about 800,000 Indians there at the start of conquest in 1528 that Cook and Borah calculate is correct, the implication is that the steep demographic decline via D form (if that indeed was the path taken) began about 1538. If higher estimates by Morley (1.35 million), Jakeman (1.6 million), or Lange (2.29 million) are more accurate, then the possible D through the data of the 1540s commenced around 1534, 1533, or 1530 respectively. Cook and Borah cite the literature, including some estimates lower than theirs (2: 23). For their own calculation, see the discussion leading up to page 38.

The Spanish conquest of the Maya in Yucatán, under royal concession to Francisco de Montejo, was not an easy one; it encountered stubborn and effective resistance. The initial 1527 expedition was pulled out in 1529, that of 1531 withdrawn by 1535. Only in 1540 did the third invasion finally occur. This was not successfully completed until 1547 (2: 5). In other words, the hypothesized D decline is reasonably consistent with what is known of when heavy intrusion by the Spanish began, though smallpox had reached Yucatán earlier in the 1500s and significant demographic loss may have been under way before the Spanish tried to subdue the surviving Maya of the region militarily.

4. For particulars of the evidence and the sources for *Hispaniola*, see Cook and Borah (1: 376–401). By averaging estimates of 150 natives left in 1565 and 100 in 1573, they calculated 125 for 1570. I employ the two figures separately. As independent pieces of evidence, they combine with information for 1548 to form a second local decline of D shape. Similarly, rather than averaging reports of 200 in 1535 and 1542 and 500 in 1548, as they do, I suggest—until someone can prove otherwise—that the last may be a better contemporary guess than the other two numbers; once again it rests very close to the D trend beginning in 1496 that would be calculated without it. In this fashion, analysis via the G-based curve D of what is often very soft or sparse documentation in historical studies can pinpoint bits of data that seem to line up with each other and others that do not and may require some rethinking. Hispaniola illustrates how widely scholarly estimates for early colonial years vary. N. D. Cook (1993; 1998, 23) considers even the 4,000,000 lower initial estimate that Figure 4.3 takes from Cook and Borah far too high.

For the *Quimbaya*, near modern Cali in Colombia, see Cook and Borah (1: 417). How tributarios were defined at various times and in various places is discussed in 1: 17–46. The relative positioning of numbers for 1559 and 1568 suggest the validity of Cook and Borah's conclusion that "Friede may well be substantially correct in his figure of 15,000 tributarios" for 1539, when the first contact with Spaniards occurred (422). Therefore, I have used Friede's estimate for this early date in the graph. For the Province of *Pamplona*, up against the modern Venezuelan border in northeastern Colombia, see Cook and Borah, 1: 422–26.

Cuchumatán Highlands: Lovell 1981, 204. *Costa Rica*: Fernandez et al. 1977, 222. *Sabana de Bogotá*: Villamarin and Villamarin 1981, 78. Their own graphs for particular localities within the area appear on their pages 66 through 77.

5. The data, from a 1970 manuscript by N[oble]. D. Cook, were published by Sánchez-Albornoz (1974, 44). The interested reader is invited to plot Cook's estimates of *population*, which appear in the same table. These move in generally downward *accelerating* trends that are very different from the D tracks for tributarios. There is a problem everywhere of how to get from tributarios to estimates for all people; at this stage of his work, Cook seems to have made translations that shrank aggressively with time.

In his 1981 book, however, his native population estimates for all of Peru curve much like the number of tributarios he previously identified. Indeed, if his preferred estimate of 9.4 million for pre-Spanish natives (114) is placed in the later 1520s, it lines up with a D curve for his total Indian population 1570–1620 (94) that has its t_0 in the early 1570s. This compares with a base year in the early 1560s for the D trend I found (before his book came out) for all Peruvian tributarios he had formerly reported for 1570–1620—

not a bad match. In his final study, the regional figures before 1570 (94) are backward projections based on certain assumptions, from which his estimation of the initial total Indian population then departs.

6. Colima and the central coast of Peru are exceptions in the lefthand half of the table.

7. Hector Perez-Brignoli, "The Indian Population of Central America, XVI to XX Centuries," talk presented to the Population Institute for Research and Training, Indiana University, December 4, 1992.

8. The description that Cook and Borah give (2: 38) suggests that, similarly, European disease came to the Maya of Yucatán considerably before effective conquest. But that did not keep population loss among them from reaching three-quarters or more, unlike Costa Rica's much shallower decline. Of course, about 75 to 85 percent atrophy still represents noticeable improvement over the possible 99 percent loss on Hispaniola.

9. As among the Iroquois, situated in the heartland of northeastern colonial British North America in contrast to more exposed neighboring tribes of New England, the lower Delaware, and the lower St. Lawrence.

10. Yucatán had experienced a devastating "War of the Castes" in the 1840s since its early 19th century G expansion (Cook and Borah, 2: 127–28). From deaths in the fighting, from emigration, and from flight to unoccupied neighboring areas within Mexico, the population of Yucatán fell something like 45 percent between 1842 and 1854— approximately along a D trend, background graphing indicates.

11. For southwest Zacatecas, Jalisco and Nayarit, and Aguascalientes, the data come from Cook and Borah, 1: 373; for Yucatán and its states, 2: 125–126. For Mexican areas that constitute modern states, supplementary data for 1970 and 1980 are taken from B. R. Mitchell (1993, 31).

12. Modern data come from Mitchell 1993, 1–8, and U.N. *Dem. Ybk.* 1975, 1980, 1985, and 1990.

For earlier and supplementary figures, *Brazil*: Simonsen 1962, 271; Neiva 1966, 55; Merrick and Graham 1979, 26–31, 48. *Argentina*: Recchini de Lattes and Lattes 1975, 23, 30; Comadrán Ruiz 1969. *Costa Rica*: Fournier 1969, 24; Fernández et al. 1977, 222. *El Salvador*: Barón Castro 1978, 208, 211, 213, 239, 244, 252, 264, 272, 293, 493. *Mexico*: Alba 1982, 18. *Venezuela*: Carillo Batalla 1967, 19–20. *Peru*: Centro de Estudios 1972, 9–61. *Paraguay*: Rivarola et al. 1974, 10–17. Trends for the three Guianas and British Honduras (now Belize) are addressed shortly, along with modern demographic histories for the Caribbean.

13. Whether the shift down in level near 1855 in Venezuela represents losses from the series of revolutions involving the ascendancy of the Monagas family or just a change in how population was estimated, particularly after the emancipation of slaves at this time, will have to be decided by local scholars.

14. Deerr's data for 1834 seem especially questionable in many places. Only a few of those estimates are used here.

15. Belize, formerly British Honduras, Guyana (British Guiana), Cayenne (French Guiana), Surinam (Dutch Guiana), and Bermuda are included with islands or island groups of the Caribbean. Additional evidence for Surinam comes from Lamur (1973, 136).

16. The U.N. estimate for de jure population in Bermuda in 1980 is much lower than the census total reported by Mitchell and used here, 54,000 as opposed to 68,000.

Missing evidence around World War II may make some other Caribbean E surges possible in this period if better data become available. But in the many cases of Table 4.5 in which records *do* cover the World War II era, other E explosion is pretty much ruled out.

17. For Brazil's states, the most complete series are in Ludwig (1985, 47). Census projections for 1985 are also used to extend the analysis for these units more recently (Brazil, Fundaçao 1988, 55). The other local materials cited are available in Mitchell 1993, 37–39, 42. Data sets for Mexican states since 1895 (31), departments of Colombia since 1905 (39–40) and Peru since 1862 (41), and provinces of Argentina since 1869 (36) are other materials with which interested readers might work if they can bridge occasional significant gaps in time and adjust for some apparently substantial alterations in boundaries.

18. Similarly, H expansions for Brazil as a whole in 1823–1872 and 1900–1940 and for Chile 1843–1907 were compound results from mixtures of quite divergent local growth patterns.

19. He connected the scale of losses in the Sandwich (Hawaiian) Islands, among the Maoris of New Zealand, on Tahiti, and in Tasmania with the devastation wreaked long before in Central and South America (1978, 141–42).

20. McArthur (1967) discusses Tahiti (240, 247, 261, 315, 320). A guess of 30,000 for 1792 by Boatswain's Mate James Morrison, one of the mutineers of the *Bounty*, before he was captured and executed, is omitted here as being too high (245).

The decline for Hawaii is based upon the calculation of 400,000 at the start of this period that was made by Captain James King, who completed Cook's account of the last voyage after Cook was killed (J. Cook 1821, 7: 118–19). Subsequent commentators have generally favored lower figures. These decisions are heavily based, however, upon reports of missionaries that smaller numbers present later indicate less population earlier, a rather circular reasoning it would seem. Evidence of patterns for individual island populations within the Hawaiian group (graphed and fitted for Table 4.7) suggests that King's approximation may not be so inaccurate after all. For a history of the estimations as well as the data, see Schmitt (1968, 18–45), whose 300,000 judgment for 1778–1779 is used for Figure 4.7.

21. Hughes (1987, 414–24) presents the depressing details of both conquest and the fatal "protection" that followed. The story ends with the skeleton of a long-suffering woman, the last survivor, first displayed as a prize specimen and then hidden in a museum basement (to 1976). Hughes' account includes estimates of native numbers at 1803, 1835, 1843, and 1855.

22. Tasman had been there as early as 1643. Tonga had been discovered by the Dutch in 1616; Tasman had come by in 1643; Cook visited in 1773 and named the group the Friendly Islands; and English missionaries appeared in 1797 to combat cannibalism (islands both cannibal and "Friendly"?). The Dutch had been to the Samoan group by 1722. The early name for this archipelago, the Necessity Islands, reminds us that those harvesting the biological riches of the South Seas or traversing them for trade depended upon these widely scattered oases of dry land for water, food, shelter from bad weather, materials to make repairs, and sex. The deadly forms of contact with Europeans and Americans came fully to bear in most places well before serious demographic estimates began to be made.

Slaving was another demographic danger for island peoples. In 1862 and 1863 the Northern Cook Islands, for instance, were among the places exploited by slavers who had a contract to deliver 10,000 Polynesians to work the copper mines of Peru and the guano deposits on the Chincha Islands (McArthur 1967, 184).

23. Island-by-island estimates that Schmitt favors over those of King, which are used for Table 4.7, require that the population on Lanai doubled between 1779 and 1805, that those of Molokai and Niihau increased two and a half times or more, while the number on Kauai increased by a third, and the peoples of Oahu and Maui lost a third while Hawaii declined a sixth. Is there information on inter-island migration or local differentials in mortality and fertility to support this complicated patterning? Or do the frequently parallel hypothesized D curves of "First Decline" in Table 4.7, even though they are based on just two dates having information, better portray the evidence?

Chapter 5

The Growth and Decline of Old World Peoples: Insights from Europe, Where the Debate Began

So far, the new way of looking at population growth and decline proposed here has been tried out only upon colonial societies established by European powers in various other portions of the globe—in North, Middle, and South America, the Caribbean, Pacific Oceania, Australasia, and South Africa. The intent has been to explore as systematically as possible how far historical demographic patterns originally discovered in one such "New World" society, the 17th century British North American settlements and the United States they became, have been general to *all* populations of this type.

The richest and most extensive historical evidence about populations, however, exists for European societies. Furthermore, the demographic debate for most of its life since the middle 1700s has evolved primarily around European data and European issues. If the claim made here that populations historically have swollen or shrunk according to just six trends based upon the constantly proportionally decelerating G formula is to be of much value, the hypothesized patterning must also suit the European demographic experience. Meanwhile, because of long-standing demographic interest and often more sophisticated administration, European data generally reach back further across time and, in spite of some flaws, require less of the indirect estimation that is necessary in order to calculate population trends for New World societies before the 1800s. These European materials for many generations served as the principal ammunition for arguments about how populations grow or decline.

EVIDENCE FROM THE PRIME SOURCES OF MODERN DEMOGRAPHY: THE HISTORICAL EXPERIENCES OF EUROPEAN NATIONS

Table 5.1 summarizes what appear to have been the histories of growth and decline in thirty-one European societies since their records begin. Figure 5.1, a through c, depicts some of the longer trend sequences known.

There have occurred some important changes of political or reporting boundaries, which significantly affect any patterning of population size across time. I have tried to adjust for them as best possible. Experts on particular countries may be able to offer improved ways of doing this. There also emerge points of evidence here and there in the graphs (both those of the figure and other unpublished analyses done to construct Table 5.1) that, working with currently accessible data, simply do not fit the usual patterns. It will probably require further investigation to determine whether such historical information is only incomplete or incorrect or whether a trending different from what I offer is in fact required. The modelings suggested in the figures and in Table 5.1 seem, however, to find considerable justification in the data and ought at least to serve as a tentative basis for reconceptualizing how European populations have expanded or atrophied over time. These patternings in turn would seem to suggest some useful reinterpretations of just what demographic movements have appeared historically in certain types of situations and to provide some further insights as to how these trends came about.

The two chronologically divided panels of Figure 5.1a present paths of growth and decline in the populations of Italy, the Netherlands, England, Sweden, and Spain.[1] In each of these cases, the evidence begins in the 1500s and lasts for four centuries or more. The most frequent and regular information comes from the well-known series for Sweden that commences in the 1740s and from the quinquennial back-projections for England from 1541 through 1871 that were provided in 1981 by the monumental *Population History* of Wrigley and Schofield. Modern census data tend to come at intervals of about a decade, occasionally interrupted by wars or depressions. Elsewhere, evidence is more scattered; trends based upon it must be regarded as more tentative. Still, as in the Netherlands for 1500–1620 and 1620–1750 or in Sweden within the old boundaries for the years 1570–1720, a few spread-out observations nonetheless fit a particular G-based form very well and indicate a trend that makes sense against its historical context. Such findings would seem to generate a hypothetical patterning that is worth working with until fresh evidence proves different. In contrast, the Spanish H trend proposed for 1648–1768 somewhat misses a data point at 1717, which falls below the curve. The suggested trend based upon just three widely separated observations should therefore be regarded as only a very tentative possibility. It is, though, one that merits some serious consideration, it will be shown, because of how this national trend can be supported (in Chapter 6) with some local evidence and how such an assumption about the path of growth during the period fits the demographic history of Spain in with that of related countries that are examined. Such international comparisons are the objective of Table 5.1.

Figure 5.1a already indicates that sometimes European populations followed similar paths of change in size while sometimes they did not. In the left, early half of the figure, for instance, likely D declines in Italy, England, and Spain in the 1600s all have base years for their respective curves in the late 1500s, making these three historical losses of population quite parallel to each other. In marked contrast, the population of the Netherlands *grew* across the middle 1600s in a G curve, while that of Sweden increased, too, but apparently in the more slowly decelerating H form. Table 5.1 provides the dates across which each curve is argued to have been followed and gives the base year for each formula applied so that it can be judged just how parallel in time various trends were.

Moving from these first five national examples across the other eight cases graphed, most readers should find simply by eye that the proposed patternings generally suit the data quite well. Figure 5.1b fits trends to information on population size from Portugal, France, Norway, and Ireland, where evidence begins in the middle 1600s or earlier.[2] Figure 5.1c covers Finland, Denmark, Iceland, and Russia, countries with information or estimates available since the early 1700s.[3] Trends for Scotland, Belgium, Austria, Germany, and Hungary since the later 1700s,[4] Switzerland, Luxembourg, the Czech lands, Greece, and Bosnia and Hercegovina, starting only in the 1800s,[5] and discontinuous or brief evidence from Bulgaria, Romania, Poland, Montenegro, Serbia, and Albania[6] were analyzed graphically in order to construct Table 5.1, but are not presented visually here.

Figure 5.1 and Table 5.1 demonstrate, first of all, that most of the same forms of change in population size that were encountered in the New World also occurred in the Old, while no additional shape of curve is needed to account for European trends. Given the way numerous census figures or other calculations visibly adhere closely to the major underlying G-related trends proposed in Figure 5.1, it seems uneconomical to evaluate each curve fit proposed quantitatively against a virtually unlimited stock of potential competing patterns. The interested or unsatisfied reader can delve further into this matter as he or she chooses. The issue, though, is whether *all* the historical evidence in *all* places covered can be characterized so simply, effectively, and insightfully some other way, not whether some segments of the data here and there might be more closely modeled if an unlimited variety of alternative shapes were tried. It is clear that they can.

What shows up from Table 5.1 and the figures, second, is that the *mix* of trend types has differed significantly in Europe from the New World populations examined in Chapters 2, 3, and 4. First of all, in 136 growth trajectories identified for 31 nations as summarized in Table 5.1 (omitting those marked with "?"),[7] not a single case of the simple .03 exponential F appears! Franklin was

Table 5.1
Comparing Growth Trends in European Populations since 1500

England	Scotland	Denmark	Netherlands	Belgium
1541-1556 G 1507			1500-1620 G 1475	
1561-1656 H 1461				
1656-1686 D 1587			1620-1750 G 1574	
1686-1726 H 1492				
1726-1806 E 1822	1755-1821 E 1839	1735-1801 E 1857	1750-1839 E 1866	
1816-1861 H 1758	1811-1871 H 1741	1801-1845 H 1706	1815-1869 H 1728	1815-1866 H 1717
1861-1939 H 1794	1871-1911 H 1779	1850-1890 H 1775	1869-1889 H 1799	1876-1910 H 1790
		1890-1945 H 1833	1899-1947 H 1849	1920-1947 G 1874
1951-1990 G 1899	1891-1975 G 1896	1945-1990 G 1906	1947-1990 G 1931	1947-1990 G 1897
	1975-1990 D 1878			

Germany	Czech Lands	Switzerland	Hungary	F.R.G.
			1793-1817 G 1753	
	1818-1851 G 1790		1817-1880 G 1808	
1816-1864 H 1743	1851-1890 H 1739	1837-1888 H 1712		
1864-1910 E 1923	1880-1910 E 1945	1880-1910 E 1934		
			1880-1910 H 1811	
1910-1950 E 1977	1910-1930 E 2004	1910-1970 E 1985	1910-1941 E 1977	
1939-1990 G 1905	1947-1990 G 1913	1970-1990 G 1901	1949-1990 G 1897	1939-1990 G 1916

Sweden	Finland	France	Italy	Luxembourg
1570-1720 H 1447			1550-1625 G 1499	
		1675-1700 D 1566	1625-1675 D 1566	
1721-1748 G 1685		1700-1752 G 1650	1700-1771 G 1696	
1748-1783 G 1706	1723-1748 G 1702	1752-1792 G 1702	1771-1821 G 1717	
1783-1818 G 1737	1748-1793 G 1742	1792-1827 E 1876		
1823-1848 G 1795	1793-1808 G 1772	1826-1921 G 1774	1820-1861 G 1790	1839-1867 G 1796
	1808-1833 G 1801			
1848-1943 H 1757	1838-1873 G 1809		1861-1936 H 1755	1871-1895 G 1810
	1873-1908 G 1860			1895-1915 G 1868
	1908-1943 G 1878	1921-1936 G 1862		1922-1939 G 1889
1943-1990 G 1909	1943-1989 G 1911	1951-1990 G 1925	1951-1990 G 1910	1947-1970 G 1908
				1970-1989 G 1918

Table 5.1 (*Continued*)

Iceland	Ireland	Norway	Russia/U.S.S.R.	G.D.R.
	1600,1641 ?H 1518			
1703,1735 ?D 1651	1641,1672 ?D 1591			
	1672-1725 H 1595	1665-1735 H 1512		
1735-1775 G 1673			1719-1762 G 1693	
1769-1860 E 1890	1725-1791 E 1812	1748-1818 H 1632	1762-1815 H 1675	
1850-1890 G 1810	1777-1841 H 1729	1818-1893 H 1758	1815-1857 H 1707	
	1851-1961 D 1826	1893-1948 H 1797	1858-1897 H 1821	
1901-1940 H 1833			1897-1939 H 1830	
1950-1990 G 1946	1966-1990 G 1929	1948-1990 G 1917	1959-1989 G 1937	
				1946-1990 D 1886

Spain	Portugal	Romania	Albania	Bosnia & Herceg.
1540,1589 ?G 1496	1500-1636 G 1425			
1589,1648 ?D 1563				
1648-1768 ?H 1527	1636-1768 H 1547			
1768-1797 G 1718	1768-1835 G 1726			
1797-1887 H 1680				
	1841-1890 E 1920	1844-1912 E 1918		
	1890-1920 G 1853			1879-1910 G 1871
1857-1920 E 1952			1945-1960 E 1959	
1920-1960 H 1829	1920-1970 G 1897	1948-1990 G 1928	1955-1990 G 1964	
1960-1990 G 1932	1970-1990 G 1938			

Austria	Poland	Bulgaria	Serbia	Greece
1700,1774 ?G 1663				
1754-1828 G 1694				
1821-1857 G 1786	1823-1863 G 1793			
1850-1880 E 1910			1840-1863 G 1823	
1880-1910 E 1934	1863-1931 G 1863	1893-1920 G 1881	1863-1884 G 1852	1870-1907 G 1856
1923-1961 G 1847			1884-1910 H 1839	
1961-1990 G 1897	1946-1990 G 1931	1920-1956 G 1907		1920-1940 G 1914
		1956-1990 G 1912		1951-1971 G 1912
				1971-1990 G 1935

Montenegro

1857-1910 G 1854

Sources: Notes 1 through 6.

Figure 5.1a

Growth Trends in European Populations: Countries with Evidence since the 1500s

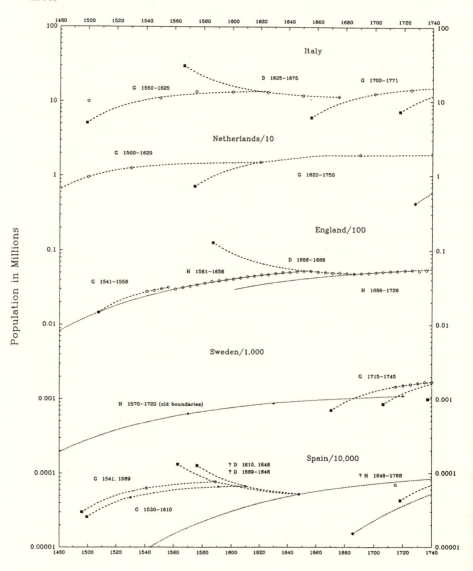

Figure 5.1a (*Continued*)

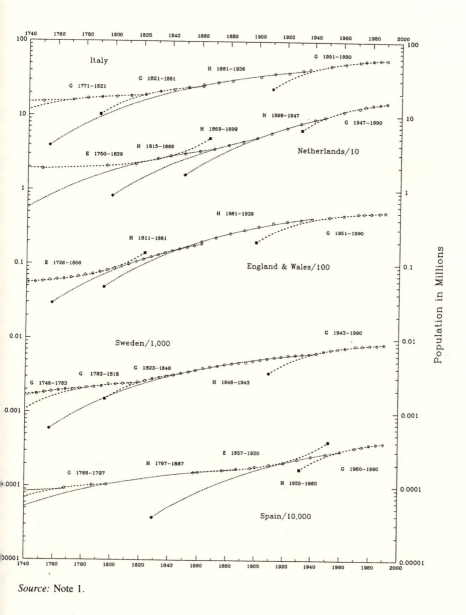

Source: Note 1.

Figure 5.1b
Growth Trends in European Populations: Countries with Evidence since the 1600s

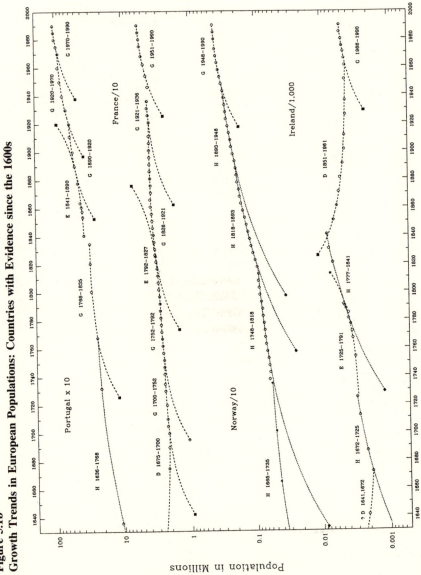

Source: Note 2.

Figure 5.1c
Growth Trends in European Populations: Countries with Evidence since the Early 1700s

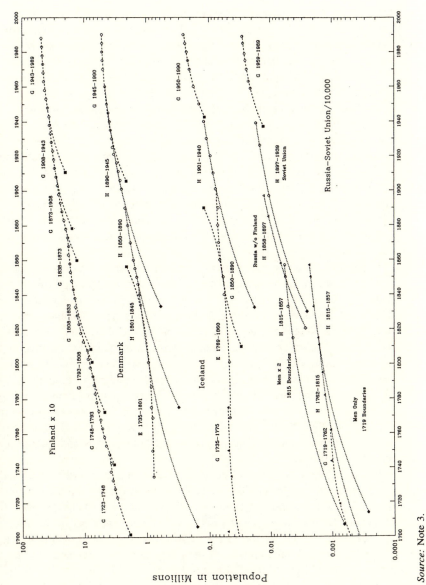

Source: Note 3.

153

right, and Malthus well advised to pick up his lead: somehow this has not been a phenomenon of Europe.

At the same time, though, *not one* case of log-linear growth (or decline) at *any other* rate than .03 appears in five centuries of European population history. Euler in 1760 and modern theorists of stable populations who have followed his path-breaking work, such as Alfred J. Lotka and R. R. Kuczynski, have been mathematically correct to assume that constant birth rates and death rates would lead to constant exponential population increase; but they have been historically wrong to think that such log-linear trends are a factor in actual human growth or decline, save in the exceptional case of the F-shaped expansion. Instead, aside from these unusual situations of F-type increase, change in population size—including developments on what might be expected to be the relatively stable demographic home ground of Europe—has been universally *curvilinear* in proportional scale. The appealingly elegant mathematics of stable population theory mislead the interpretation of historical reality. Verhulst's view of decelerating increase toward some current limit or carrying capacity posed the fundamental and usual nature of human population growth more realistically, though he failed to grasp the dominant G shape of such deceleration and the rather different implications that its mathematics hold for demographic process compared with his own logistic formulation.

In Europe, third, the more slowly bending H curve, which appeared just a handful of times in the accumulating New World evidence of Chapters 2, 3, and 4, fits 36 of 136 or as much as one quarter of the trends identified in national demographic histories. This more gradually slowing type of change—discovered in the United States for the period 1850–1940—has, however, been most common in certain *northern* European populations. Other countries, meanwhile, have not experienced a single case of such growth since their records begin, instead expanding only along one G curve after another (Finland in Figure 5.1c serves as an illustration). What is it that certain European populations have had in common to make them expand in this H form, which is appreciably more exceptional in New World societies? This is one of several basic questions that careful comparative analysis of national population trends and their accompaniments can probe.

Fourth, while all students of demographic history are aware that Ireland lost much population from the 1840s into the modern era, Figure 5.1b shows how this decline was just another instance of the same type of D (1/G) atrophy found in Chapter 4 to be so common for natives of the Americas in the 1500s and peoples of the South Pacific in the 1800s. The shifts in agricultural practices favored by English landlords when the Corn Laws were repealed and the devastating potato blight of the 1840s together powered population loss in Ireland. This struck in a catastrophic but decelerating way similar to the ravages of Mexico and South America by unfamiliar disease and forced reorganization of labor into mines and encomiendas by Spanish invaders. Less familiar to many readers, but known to national specialists, are significant though not so striking population declines in Italy, England, Spain, and France in the 1600s. What is offered as new insight here is that these earlier trends, too, probably took the D shape. So, also, did population losses following World War II in East Germany (the erstwhile German Democratic Republic [G.D.R.]) and probably also in Scotland. In all, there may be nine national cases of D decline in the population history of European nations as it can presently be documented since 1500.[8] Only the Irish disaster even came close in proportion to the infamous losses encountered in the New World; but everywhere, from the 16th century to the present, the G-based D curve has apparently constituted the repeating form taken by demographic atrophy in Europe.[9]

Finally, it may surprise some readers that "population explosion," a phenomenon discovered in, labeled for, and still mostly associated with "Third World" demographic behavior over the era following World War II, similarly has appeared in European countries—as many as 20 times among the 136 growth trends that can presently be identified.

In England 1726–1806, perhaps Ireland 1725–1791, Scotland 1755–1821, Denmark 1735–1801, and the Netherlands 1750–1839, the surges were largely coterminous. Following the Revolution, France briefly joined in this pattern for 1792–1827 before returning to her usually unbroken growth sequence of G after G. Ironically, writing in 1798 Malthus missed what was going on right under his nose. His own country and several others were in paths of demographic expansion that *accelerated*. These trends were potentially far more challengingly explosive than the *bête noire* he chose to make of Franklin's New World discovery, constant expansion at the .03 rate of F (doubling every 20 to 25 years). The Malthusian debate, furthermore, might have been both more temperate and more illuminating if analysts and prognosticators—then and also now—realized that by about 1790 in Ireland, 1800 in Denmark, 1810 in England, 1820 in Scotland, and 1825 in France the threateningly explosive E trends in fact were giving way to systematically *decelerating* patterns of growth: everywhere the H form, except for the even more rapidly slowing G in France. That is, after all, what the Costa Ricas, Colombias, and Tongas of the New World have been doing lately (Chapter 4 has just shown) in spite of the "wolf"-crying of doomsday theorists in recent decades.

In Iceland 1769–1860, Germany 1864–1910, the Czech lands (Bohemia, Moravia, and Silesia) 1880–1910, Portugal 1841–1890, and Romania 1844–1912 a later wave of E surges is also evident. This international upswing was followed by a second trend of accelerating growth in Germany 1910–1950 and initial E's in Switzerland 1910–1970, Hungary 1910–1941, and Spain 1857–1920 that all headed for zero years in their formulas after World War II. What produced this series of accelerating growth trends and induced them to march across half the countries of Europe in this way? Why did no such exploding surge occur in the other half? How were entry into and escape from the E pattern in these European countries some time ago similar to what other populations around the world have been experiencing much more recently? These are general and fundamental questions raised for further study by the unexpected discovery of so much "population explosion" within the Old World context of Europe. Examples of more specific issues include: the way having *two* successive E explosions of population between 1864 and 1950 may have contributed to how dangerous a neighbor Germany was in this historical period; how the E surge of England's population in 1726–1806 was related to industrialization there; or how that same 18th century acceleration may have made England an obsessively expansionist power, not a very tolerant and supportive "mother" for either American colonists or home-country workers.

For all these insightful observations about the occurrences of its F, H, D, and E relatives, however, the basic G curve remains, in Europe as elsewhere, the most frequent path taken by change in population size. In the evidence of Table 5.1, no less than 79 of 136 trends, almost 60 percent of all movements, still follow just this pattern in spite of the greater frequency of H in Europe than in New World settings and the surprising presence of several E surges there. For the full extent of their recorded demographic histories, 8 of the 31 European countries studied had population changes in no other form but G.[10] And among recent trends beginning since World War II, only 2 D's (in East Germany and Scotland) intrude among 29 G patterns. Even populations with very complex and very different demographic pasts are now uniformly experiencing G-type increase.

What Table 5.1 helps do is to group or categorize European populations by their historical patterns of growth. This facilitates identifying and analyzing what demographic processes and cultural or economic changes are likely to have caused or resulted from the growth trends observed, by pinpointing which populations changed when and how, together or separately. Such classification of European countries by their trends in population size divides naturally into two eras: an early period, from when information begins in the 1500s to somewhere around the 1720s, and the years since then.

PATTERNS OF GROWTH—AND DECLINE—IN EUROPEAN COUNTRIES TO THE EARLY 1700s

As Figure 5.1a and Table 5.1 indicate, the sizes of most European populations on which data currently exist moved generally together much of the recorded time before about 1620. Growth in the Netherlands, Italy, Spain, and (briefly) England took approximately parallel G form as follows, with Portugal apparently leading them somewhat in how far the local curve had slowed:

Portugal	1500–1636: G 1425
Netherlands	1500–1620: G 1475
Italy	1550–1625: G 1499

Spain   1530–1610: G 1500
England   1541–1556: G 1507

The fortunes of these five European countries were of course tightly conjoined in this early modern era. There were many opportunities for traders, priests, soldiers, savants, administrators, and diplomats to carry wealth, economic practice, family fashion and demographic behavior, dietary change, disease, and whatever medical knowledge existed at that time from one country to another as modern western European society evolved. Such transfers seem to have fostered roughly parallel demographic growth, no matter how the significance of particular contributing factors may turn out to have been weighted.

Among the few countries for which even crude information exists at this early time, it was Sweden that seems to have been out of step. There, the years 1570–1720 probably saw one long H increase in population (based mathematically on a t_0 at 1447). Interestingly, it was this Swedish pattern of growth that England joined when she broke, demographically as well as politically, from the Spanish-dominated pack of countries following the accession of Elizabeth I to the throne. England's H trend of 1561–1656, with its base year at 1461, is virtually identical with the likely 1570–1720 one for Sweden, as Figure 5.1a and Table 5.1 show. Why was that so?

A final, enduring shift to Protestantism after the death of Mary might be thought to be one element in England's taking on demographic behavior more like Sweden's than Spain's; but, then, the newly independent Netherlands were mostly Protestant, too. The break with Mediterranean dominance in business as well as church that Lawrence Stone (1947) and A. L. Rowse (1957) emphasized a half-century ago is another potential source of the English change. England under Elizabeth like Sweden under the Vasas began to evolve from a "periphery" of southern Europe towards part of a more modern northern European "core," to use the terminology of Immanuel Wallerstein (1980). England continued these developments to become a leader of the modern European "world-system," while Sweden exhausted her expanding economic and demographic resources in an ultimately futile effort to become a dominant continental military power.

Reduced international dependencies for England may have encouraged some improvement in health. The reconstruction of Wrigley and Schofield, though tentative this far back, does indicate a substantial drop in crude death rate for England during the early 1560s compared with the preceding two decades, a lower level that was maintained for some time.[11] While there is little evidence of how this occurred, one possibility, at least, is greater separation from the disease pool of more southern Europe that England gained as her ties to the continent were reduced in the middle 1500s.

Nonetheless, by the 1650s England's population reversed course to decline in a D form very much like those of several southern European countries, as follows:

Spain	1589, 1648: ?D 1563
Italy	1625–1675: D 1566
France	1675–1700: D 1566
England	1656–1686: D 1587
Ireland	1641, 1672: ?D 1591

Portugal, the Netherlands, and Sweden, though, apparently escaped such population loss. Iceland may have experienced similar atrophy between 1703 and 1735, but estimates begin only in the 18th century, and there is little evidence with which to construct a trend curve. While the Spanish calculation also must be built upon estimates for just two dates, conditions shared with the other countries to whose D patterns the Spanish one is so similar suggest that more than just coincidence is involved.

How can these international parallels and differences with respect to demographic decline be accounted for? Several local explanations have been offered or readily come to mind: a 17th century recurrence of plague (in Italy, Spain, and later in England), the depredations of other diseases that followed (France), the costs of the Thirty Years War and Louis XIV's ambitions (Spain and France), Irish uprising and Cromwell's re-invasion, migration to Ireland and the New World (England), the expulsion of the Moriscos (Spain), administrative ineptitude or irresponsibility (the Spanish monarchy, and perhaps also the Stuarts), and others.[12] Yet Portugal, the Netherlands, and Sweden avoided demographic decline during this mid-17th century era in spite of sharing war and its medical and economic consequences with nations that did. What united those three countries were pivotal positions in the Dutch north-south trade that revolutionized commerce in Europe at this time, especially bulk cargos like foodstuffs. It would seem that the interaction of demographic change with the evolving European "world-system" is the direction in which to look when trying to sort out the reasons for similarity and dissimilarity in national population histories in this period.[13]

Unfortunately, this far back there exists very little evidence with which to work in determining how health regimes, economic changes, wars, or political developments interacted with each other—or substituted for each other—to generate the international patterns of population growth and decline observed. Except for England, throughout this premodern period even crude birth and death rates come only from unsystematic local sources. Local populations are easily affected by quite idiosyncratic circumstances. What movements were general? Which were not? Data on economic change in this era before the 1700s, meanwhile, mostly entail fragmentary evidence on prices and wages or on those sectors of external trade that were regularly taxed, and even spottier clues about agricultural productivity, technology, or food supply. How, furthermore—from this distance and with the limited materials available—does one measure increasing or decreasing inequality and their consequences, the impact of systems of distribution, or the demographic effects of economic management or political administration? Such tasks are difficult and debatable enough even with 20th century data. The work, moreover, clearly has to be done by regional experts with full command of the nature of the sources and the local contexts from which the available information comes. Yet somehow the kinds of national or international possibilities raised here should be sorted out; and such inquiry must address satisfactorily how it was that some populations of the 1600s seem to have shared loss while others continued to grow.

Across the next era, from the middle or later 1600s into the middle 1700s, all documented European populations increased. They did so, however, in two distinct ways: some via the quickly slowing G curve, others according to the more gently decelerating, more sustained and robust H pattern, as follows (from Table 5.1):

Sweden	1570–1720: H 1447
England	1686–1726: H 1492
Norway	1665–1735: H 1512
Spain	1648–1768: ?H 1527
Portugal	1636–1768: H 1547
Ireland	1672–1725: ?H 1595

versus

Netherlands	1620–1750: G 1574
France	1700–1752: G 1650
Iceland	1735–1775: G 1673
Russia	1719–1762: G 1693
Italy	1700–1771: G 1696
Sweden	1721–1748: G 1706

That with independence the population of the Netherlands grew afresh, but soon stopped growing much, is not difficult to understand. Dutch fleets scored great victories from the East Indies to the Caribbean, but before long the global edge was being lost to England. Domestic Dutch opportunities for expanding a population remained limited, in spite of—perhaps largely because of—a high standard of living established in the "Golden Age." Meanwhile, King Louis kept battering at the border, draining away resources for defense (De Vries 1974; Schama 1987; De Vries and van der Woude, 1997; Israel 1995).[14]

As the nation rose to become a world power, the population of England interestingly returned to mimic the Elizabethan and early Stuart growth pattern of 1561–1656, in a new 1686–1726 H trend that was now rather fresher (with a t_0 45 years later) than the long-standing Swedish trajectory, which continued to 1720. Evidence for Norway unfortunately begins only spottily at 1665; but what is available indicates demographic expansion very parallel to that in England, across the North Sea. In Ireland, according to the older data of Connell (1975) an even steeper H trend of population increase took off and lasted to 1725. (Its later base year was at 1595, not in the early 1500s.) Such greater robustness in growth around 1700 suggests a vigor in Irish development that should not be obscured behind the wit of Jonathan Swift, though more recent calculations by Daultry, Dickson, and O. Gráda (1981, 624) suggest rather different modeling for Ireland's population in this era as note 2 has indicated.

That England, Ireland, Norway, and Sweden probably experienced relatively parallel demographic growth in the later 1600s and early 1700s, while known populations across the North Sea and the Baltic did not, must once again be explored in terms of several possible dynamics: changing health conditions, evolving economies, and still other factors that might contribute toward determining shared and divergent demographic histories. That the populations of Spain and Portugal, further down the Atlantic flank of Europe, probably took similar paths of expansion from the middle 1600s to the 1760s makes interpreting the international patterning even more of a challenge but also more of a prize. The rising involvement of Iberia with New World grains and flour by the end of this period suggests that growth in Atlantic trade (in which England and her regional partners Ireland and Norway shared directly or indirectly) provided the margin for sustaining demographic expansion in H form rather than via the more rapidly decelerating G path.

Malthus missed this type of substantial, sustained, but slowly slowing H growth in the populations of several European countries into the 18th century, including his own England. The demographic pressure building in these situations neither took the F shape he borrowed from Franklin as the biological potential of human multiplication, absent Old World limits on supporting life, nor found itself rapidly and continually curbed by the restraints that he stressed for normal, nonfrontier conditions. Among the growth trajectories found actually to exist historically, this latter "Old World" set of circumstances might be most closely represented by the near-equilibrium or almost stationary state that characterizes the later stages of the G curve.

Contemporaneous with these unnoticed cases of H-shape expansion in several countries, quite parallel G growths did occur across the first half of the 18th century in France, Iceland, Italy, and Russia. Also, after the costly Great Northern War, as Sweden pulled back from attempting to be an international powerhouse capable of dominating Germany, Poland, and Russia, population increase there switched from the one continuing H form it had apparently taken all the way since 1570 to follow a more rapidly decelerating G trajectory that resembled what appeared in those four other European societies. Fresh demographic expansion did come to Sweden with peace, but now it flattened out rapidly. In this new cleavage of Europe, running north to south rather than east to west, five Atlantic countries in an outer western ring from Norway to England and Ireland and thence to Portugal and Spain are distinguished in growth pattern from Russia, Sweden, and Italy, which had little access to the New World, from the Netherlands and France, which had both once been major players in the Atlantic but now were rapidly losing their influence there, and from relatively isolated Iceland. The further research that is needed to pin down precisely what caused what type of demographic development in each society seems likely to find differences in health, reproductive outlook, and sustenance that are in some way linked to advantages connected with access to Atlantic trade and New World resources.[15]

Up through about the 1720s, in short, three phases of demographic growth can be discerned in the populations of Europe for which data or reasonable estimates on size exist this early. Across these stages, H growth begins in Sweden and in England (after 1556). Then in the middle to later 1600s, Norway, Ireland, Spain, and Portugal come to share such patterns, though Sweden drops out around 1720 to follow only the G form of increase. More robust and sustained H growth, in other words, pivoted from an east-west axis across the North Sea and the Baltic extending from Sweden to England to a north-south axis down the Atlantic exterior of Europe from Norway to Spain. It seems not too rash to propose that this represented a shift from a North Sea–Baltic frontier of economic development within northern Europe to an international pattern of opportunity that was driven by New World resources instead. As this transition took place, perhaps paving the way for the 90-degree pivot during the middle phase of three demographic eras running from about 1500 to 1750, the populations of Spain, Italy, France, England, and Ireland all suffered about a half-century of D-shape demographic decline in the 1600s.

This patterning suggests some form or forms of quite well integrated change in the environments of European populations. It brings to mind again the analysis of shifts in international trade stressed by Ralph Davis (1973) and Immanuel Wallerstein (1974, 1980). Ironically, though, while the population of the Netherlands, whose riches soared with the development of Baltic trade and whose fleets, both naval and commercial, did so much to dominate the Atlantic in the first half of the 1600s, may have escaped the D-shape demographic decline of neighbors and competitors like France and England, this pivotal country—recently called "The First Modern Economy"—as a whole failed to share in the more robust and sustained H-shape population growth of several other powers both before 1620 and in the following century. Did a higher standard of living or the more intense focus on making the most of limited local resources that had much to do with generating such a high level of wealth and welfare in the Netherlands reduce fertility already this early in European history? Direct evidence on that point would be invaluable.[16]

Meanwhile, the populations of Portugal, displaced in much of her erstwhile world trade by the Dutch, and of Spain, no longer the hub of the Western universe, did nevertheless come by the middle 1600s to expand in durable H form. Does the experience of these two waning powers indicate that international trade, capital, and industrialization apparently did not have overriding demographic influence after all? Or have we simply misjudged the vigor of colonial exploitation and homeland development that remained in Iberia during this period, as the strong and recurrent H growth observed in the populations of central Mexico and Brazil in the later 17th and the 18th centuries (Chapter 4) might warn us not to do?

MODERN MOVEMENTS IN THE SIZE OF EUROPEAN POPULATIONS

Though shared D-shape decline briefly linked four or five countries in the 1600s demographically, it was the presence or absence of the robust and durable form of H growth that principally distinguished one group of European populations from another across the approximately two and a half centuries following 1500. In more modern times, since the early to middle 1700s, D decline in Europe has been rare, though it was indeed striking in the one instance of Ireland in the 19th century and looms in more moderate form on the horizon for several aging peoples today. While the tendency of some populations, but not others, to experience sustained H growth remains important in understanding demographic movements of the most recent 250 to 300 years, however, the simplest way to group modern European countries according to their patterns of population increase begins with a phenomenon not encountered on that continent before the 1720s.

This type of trend, interestingly, was accelerating E-shape expansion, the proportionally speeding-up form of increase dubbed "population explosion" as it was observed in less developed countries in the 1960s. That pattern, which has been witnessed extensively in Latin America, has also featured prominently in the demographic history of Europe, readers may be surprised to learn. If this fact had been known, perhaps earlier analysts would have viewed the "Third World" challenge of the 1960s with less alarm and better understanding of what was taking place. Such a proportionally *accelerating* growth pattern emerged historically in Europe, as Table 5.1 indicates, in four regionally focused waves of the following sort:

England	1726–1806: E 1822
Ireland?	1725–1791: E 1812
Scotland	1755–1821: E 1839
Denmark	1735–1801: E 1857
Netherlands	1750–1839: E 1866
Iceland	1769–1860: E 1890
France	1792–1827: E 1876

Austria I	1850–1880: E 1910
Germany I	1864–1910: E 1923
Romania	1844–1912: E 1918
Portugal	1841–1890: E 1920
Austria II	1880–1910: E 1934
Switzerland I	1880–1910: E 1934
Czech Lands I	1880–1910: E 1945
Spain	1857–1920: E 1952
Albania	1945–1960: E 1959
Hungary	1910–1941: E 1977
Germany II	1910–1950: E 1977
Switzerland II	1910–1970: E 1985
Czech Lands II	1910–1930: E 2004

As in prior eras of European population growth, the diffusion of the characteristic trend type began around the North Sea, this time without Norway, but including the Netherlands, Denmark (where regular information first becomes available at this time), and Iceland. The French population, too, started to participate in demographic "explosion" at the Revolution; but this E trajectory lasted just one generation and was gone by the 1820s. The spread of E growth across central Europe in later stages took the phenomenon to Germany (where after World War I a second E surge followed the first), Switzerland, and parts of what was the Austro-Hungarian Empire, but also southwestward into Spain and Portugal, now distinguishing these populations from those of the more northern Atlantic littoral via delay of their participation in "explosion." Southeastward, Romania and Albania each also became involved for a while in E-type growth.

Table 5.1 and Figure 5.1 make it clear that in documented European countries the observed E surges did *not* appear as recoveries after D declines, as has been seen to have happened sometimes in the colonial New World. Instead, explaining this pattern of growth in modern Europe should focus on economic changes that support accelerating demographic expansion and on developments in health and reproduction that might cause populations to multiply more and more rapidly, at least for a while, whether or not local economies expand with them. To begin to understand how these E growths contributed to European national demographic histories, from what origins they probably came, and how they posed challenges for local economies and governments, it helps to show the ways in which they fitted into the overall patterning of modern population growth in particular nations and spread from one place to another, but not everywhere.

To start, it can be noted that the E pattern of increase has never occurred since records begin for Norway, Sweden, Finland, Russia, Poland, the former

Yugoslavia, Bulgaria, or Greece. Nor, with the brief exception in the wake of the French Revolution already noted, has it appeared in Italy, France, Luxembourg, and possibly Belgium.[17] The first wave of E surges, taking place during the period approximately from 1725 to 1860, clustered geographically in England, perhaps Ireland, Scotland, Iceland, Denmark, and the Netherlands, all located at the North Sea corner of Europe. Later, from about 1850 to 1920, similar explosive population growth was experienced further south in Atlantic-facing Portugal and Spain, but also penetrated across central Europe through Germany, Switzerland, Austria, and the Czech lands as far as Romania. In even later periods, following World War I, the nearby populations of Hungary and probably Albania acquired accelerating trajectories of the E form, while Germany, Switzerland, and the Czech lands produced second surges of this E type (as Austria had done earlier). What was it, capable of generating such ever-quickening rates of population growth, that passed across Europe this way?

For England between 1726 and 1806 there are some clues as to what happened. The crude birthrate took an accelerating upward E path from the 1720s to about 1800 or later, while the crude death rate declined conversely in the ever-faster C form during 1736–1831 (Wrigley and Schofield 1981, 528–29). These are, of course, my terms of analysis applied to the data of the *Population History* and its revisers.[18] While the English population began to "explode" along an upward-curving E trajectory in response to those underlying demographic trends, moreover, real wages fell in almost mirror image, downward-accelerating C form from about 1740 through 1805 (Wrigley and Schofield 1981, 408). For the average worker—for most people, in other words—the English economy did not grow. As population increased, incomes fell in off-setting fashion. Two generations of ever-more-rapidly cheapening labor certainly facilitated industrialization in England, the establishment of factories and the geographical and social rearrangement of the labor force. They also, however, divided English society, at a cost in political and social pain that rising incomes after 1800, which Wrigley and Schofield enthusiastically celebrate, could scarcely assuage.[19] Much of English life and English discourse has remained ever since—for more than two centuries—estranged and embittered by these rifts of industrialization.

Exploding population, producing cheap wages that promote economic change and development? England leading up to 1800 begins to sound like South Korea or Mexico in recent decades. "Population explosion" after World War II, however, was long seen only as a *threat* to Third World development and well-being. It may remain so in some kinds of contexts: Having E-type demographic growth need scarcely be considered sufficient to lift the economies of Peru or Bangladesh by their bootstraps. But in certain conditions, the opening scissors of rising population and falling wages may *assist* "development," whether or not they erode the equity of a society and poison its polity.

Ever since the 1960s, when "population explosion" was leaping flashily into the lexicon of demographers, the Danish economist Ester Boserup (1965, 1983) has urged scholars to explore the economically positive side of population increase. It is imperative now to delineate more carefully just what the conditions of capital, technology, education, values, and perhaps personal freedom are that separate countries that can take advantage of accelerating population growth to develop their economies from those that just become poorer. For a start, England, Scotland, the Netherlands, and briefly France in the later 1700s and early 1800s—and quite possibly Denmark and Ireland (for a while) as well—seem like candidates for countries in which exploding trends of population increase were incorporated effectively into economic development. Later in time, Germany, the Czech lands, Switzerland, and possibly Hungary and Austria also seem like prima facie cases for changes not unlike those found previously in England. What Iceland, Spain, Portugal, Romania, and Albania may have experienced, as local populations multiplied for a while in E form, calls for more investigation.

Still, there seem to emerge here some provocative suggestions about how and where to proceed in analyzing the interplay between this particular proportionally accelerating E form of expansion in population and the economic growth that generally has been more characteristic of the chiefly northwestern and central European countries that had it than of other nations that did not. For instance, the estimates of B. H. Slicher van Bath show how agricultural yield ratios in England and the Netherlands, whose populations both had E surges in the 1700s, also curved sharply upward across the period (Pounds 1979, 180; Slicher van Bath 1963; 328–33). That form of agricultural productivity was similarly beginning to rise by 1800 in "Scandinavia and Central Europe," his work indicates. Within this other broad grouping of territory, it has become evident that early exploding demographic increase appeared in Denmark, later acceleration in Germany, the Czech lands, and Austria, but none in Norway, Sweden, or Finland. What happens when trends of agricultural productivity for these particular countries, or smaller groups of them, are appropriately disaggregated? Elsewhere in Europe, meanwhile, the E form of demographic increase was rare or late; and crop yields, according to Slicher van Bath, did not rise systematically across the 1700s and early 1800s. This discussion is just a crude introduction to connections with economic and social developments that are explored more fully elsewhere; but it should illustrate what kinds of historical reanalysis the demographic patterns reported here invoke and facilitate.

The E trend, however, is just one form of population increase that can be insightfully connected with regional variations in modern European economic growth and change. As happened off and on across the two and a half centuries before the middle 1700s, the presence of H patterns since then has likewise continued to separate a core of northern populations from the rest of the continent. England, Ireland, Scotland, Denmark, and the Netherlands all saw H trends follow their E surges of the late 1700s and early 1800s. Though Ireland dropped out of the pack with the crisis of the 1840s, Belgium (for which no national trend can be established before 1815) joined this group of populations in two parallel H growths from Waterloo to World War I (since when its pattern of demographic increase has shifted to resemble that of neighboring France).

Norway and Russia, though never experiencing E surges like the northern core countries, did have an uninterrupted sequence of H increases from about 1815 to World War II (Figures 5.1b and 5.1c). Finally, Iceland, in spite of a comparatively late E movement and a G trend in lieu of an H for the period 1850–1890, has largely mimicked this group of northern European nations in the patterning of its modern demographic growth. In short, a category of populations strung across the northern regions, from west to east, once again stands apart in history of population growth from the rest of Europe. Up to World War II, these countries over and over again supported long-lasting, usually recurrent, slowly decelerating trends of H increase as nations of the South did not. Since several of these countries of the northern core have not been noted for their poverty, they must have enjoyed some form of sustained economic growth as well.

As growth along similar lines penetrated further down into central Europe, Germany, the Czech lands of Bohemia, Moravia, and Silesia, Switzerland, and Hungary each enjoyed population increase in the H form in the middle or late 1800s, in this case *preceding* their rather later E surges, which have been previously been noted. This had been the sequence in England, too, from the H of 1686–1726 to the E of 1726–1806, though the E's in the Netherlands and Iceland were preceded by G trends instead (Table 5.1), while there is no early evidence with which to establish the succession for Scotland and Denmark. The Spanish population, like the English one a considerable time before, expanded in H trends both before and after its late E of 1857–1920. In Austria, Portugal, Romania, and Albania, however, recent E surges are known, but no modern H's appear. The combination of *both* E and H sometime since the mid-1700s, in other words, is to be found only in the inverted geographical "Y" of nations composed by Iceland, Ireland, England, and Spain down the Atlantic to compose one branch, and Scotland, Denmark, the Netherlands, Germany, Switzerland, the Czech lands, and Hungary reaching across the North Sea and penetrating into central Europe to form the other arm of the "Y." Elsewhere on the continent, this seminal sequence of E with one or more H's has not occurred.[20]

The populations of Sweden and Italy, both contiguous to this upside down geographical "Y" that penetrates western and central Europe, did grow in H form from about 1850 to 1940, sharing some of the patterning of the core belatedly and presumably also the economic development that made such demographic growth possible. As for France, with just its brief E after the Revolution, and Austria with two more modern E's but no H, however, the main and repeated form of expansion in these populations was G. Only the interruptions by H in Sweden and Italy, a late H in Serbia, and E's without H's in France and Austria interfere with a consistent pattern of just repeated G's in growth sequences that is documentable for France, Luxembourg, Italy, Finland, Sweden, Poland, Austria, Greece, Bulgaria, and with more fragmentary evidence for the Balkans, as set forth in Table 5.1.

The table also demonstrates how often these European G growths essentially paralleled each other throughout the modern era. Many, that is, had virtually identical base years or t_0's for the G curve that is fitted for a particular period or stage of demographic expansion. Interesting questions arise concerning how such similar widespread movements might have occurred across national boundaries.

What dynamics—demographic, economic, and/or cultural—for example, led Finland and Sweden, but simultaneously France, Italy, and Austria, to have G growths in their populations all with base years between 1684 and 1717? Or these same countries plus Luxembourg and Poland to experience later G expansions with t_0's each between 1772 and 1796? Many challenges are posed concerning how to identify and explain both the demographic and behavioral shifts that generated such trends and the economic changes that allowed such growths or resulted from them. A following volume analyzes in detail the considerable historical information that is known about movements in fertility, mortality, and migration in European societies. The economic movements that accompanied them are then fed back into the analysis in a third stage of this study. In the end, though, sorting out all the possible economic, medical, and cultural causes and consequences of the shared population growths noted in Table 5.1 and illustrated in Figure 5.1 will have to be the responsibility of many locally sophisticated scholars, experts who are sufficiently familiar with the many complicated pieces that must be fitted together regionally in order to obtain reliable answers. Nonetheless, the demographic parallels and divergences that appear here would seem to offer these investigators some stimulating and profitable undertakings, some corroborations of familiar interpretations, and also some fresh challenge and insight.

After World War II, however, the northern core populations and their partial imitators in central Europe and Iberia universally slipped into the G shape of growth, no longer expanding any differently from the twelve populations that had rarely witnessed anything but G increases since the 1700s. Some European peoples, as in the Soviet Union, Spain, and Poland, have enlarged along appreciably steeper postwar G curves than the rest. These departures seem to be related to the severity of local war losses and no longer substantially distinguish one geographical group of European peoples from others. A few countries have experienced more than one G growth of population since World War II, while Scotland and the former East Germany witnessed some demographic decline.

In the end, though, another major issue to emerge from this extensive survey of patterns of growth in European populations becomes how, after four and a half centuries of systematic differences between shifting clusters of countries, for the past five decades the shape of demographic increase in Europe has become so nearly universal. What integration of opportunities, values, and behavior has brought about such convergence? This is not an unfamiliar issue for contemporaries increasingly aware of the many ways—from fashion to film to finance—in which "the world has become smaller" and, in particular, of how many dynamics of European societies and economies are becoming more and more integrated across national boundaries, whatever mumbling and grumbling goes on around this process.

IS THE G FAMILY OF TRENDS ANCIENT HISTORY?
MANPOWER IN ROME FROM 508 B.C. TO 14 A.D.

Rome was a European state with central administration and regular record-keeping that existed long before the modern era. The interest of the Republic in keeping track of the number of its free, adult, male citizens—for military service and for taxation—has been exploited by P. A. Brunt (1971) to make some meaningful sense of how the size of the Roman population changed over time. His work allows us to explore whether the set of G-connected trends proposed in this present volume is a helpful tool in trying to understand what went on during a much different age from that which most demographic information perforce describes.

There has long been debate over just what kinds of people Roman censuses covered at various stages of history (Brunt 1971, 15–25). From 508 B.C. through 474, however, the numbers—whatever they represent—shrank from about 130,000 to something like 103,000, with the exception of 498, for which year 150,700 were calculated (13). The top panel of Figure 5.2 shows that the reported counts for 508, 503, 493, and 474 all line up to form a familiar D curve of decline. This was a difficult time, at which, says Brunt, Rome was "fighting almost for its existence."

Then, assuming that the rules of the census, or their application, did not change substantially, the population of Rome increased by about two-thirds from 465 to 393 and onwards to 340 along a familiarly shaped G curve, as the upper panel of Figure 5.2 next indicates. Such a path of demographic expansion seems compatible with the magnitiude of growth in the *Ager Romanus* that Blunt accepts from Beloch, and also with his own comment about Rome's occupation of Veii, one of the most powerful centers of the Etruscan League. In short, whatever the population *level* of the evidence up to 340 B.C. means, simply to omit 498 as an aberrant calculation and plot the rest, as Figure 5.2 does, produces trends of *direction* across time that seem to fit rather well Brunt's own description of how Roman history over this early century and a half from 508 to 340 B.C. should have affected population numbers, first in crisis, then in significant expansion (27). The analytical kit of G-based curves improves our understanding of sometimes elusive and uncertain classical evidence.

Another phase of demographic increase is indicated for Rome from 340 to 252 B.C. by the surviving census figures, whomever it was that they recorded. Territory held by Rome now increased even more; but acquired peoples were not automatically extended the benefits and duties of citizenship. Thus the impact of conquest upon the census of Romans was only indirect. Without widely disparate estimates for "the time of Alexander [the Great] (336–23)," of which Brunt, too, is suspicious,[21] these later figures fit well the G curve offered for the

Figure 5.2
Likely Patterns of Growth and Decline in the Manpower of Rome from 508 B.C. through 14 A.D.

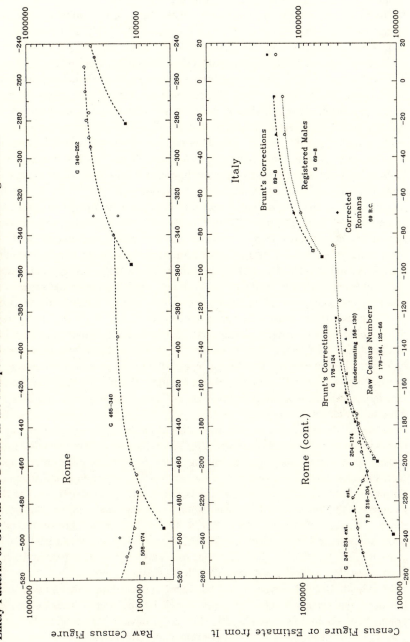

Source: Brunt 1971.

period in Figure 5.2. Subsequently, the census of 247/6 contained about 20 percent fewer of whatever group of men it was reporting than the preceding count of 252/1. This drop came during the First Punic War (264–241), at a frustrating stage of guerilla suppression. In all, the drop in numbers of the male population that shows up in the census seems quite likely to involve a real demographic loss, not just a shift in record-keeping.

Once again, though, the census numbers grew. The figures for 247, 241, and 234 generate a G curve that the bottom graph of Figure 5.2 shows, would just about run through the corrected 225 estimate of 300,000 adult male Romans offered by Brunt. This calculation is shown as a filled circle, past which the G path for the 247–234 data is extended (Brunt 1971, 54).[22] I have taken the liberty to extrapolate from this G curve a Roman number of 304,000 for 219–218. That was the point at which the costly Second Punic War (218–201) began. Combining this estimate with actual census figures for 209 and 204 produces the brief but steep D curve of decline next hypothesized in the figure. In this fourteen-year period of wartime crisis, the number of Roman men apparently shrank about 30 percent (from 304,000 to 214,000—perhaps dropping off rather less, if the later figures need some correction upward to be comparable to the higher quality of the 225 data). Such a proportion in so short a time represents heavy loss indeed. This, though, is the war in which Hannibal descended upon Italy across the Alps from the north, elephants and all, and campaigned successfully on Roman soil for a decade. The city was not attacked, but the countryside around it was either ravaged or turned against Rome. By 203, in contrast, the last phase of the struggle shifted to Carthage, whither Hannibal was recalled to defend his own capital against Scipio. What is known of the nature of the bitter war between these two superpowers of the western Mediterranean, in short, seems to support a D trend of demographic decline for Rome of the sort that the census figures for 209 and 204 and an extrapolation of the 247–234 trend to 218 together suggest.

In the peace that followed, the raw census numbers—whatever they represent—show a new G trend of growth 204–174, which seems not unnatural given the circumstances of the time. Beginning in the 170s, then, fresh demographic increase appeared. Corrections of census returns for selected years from 178 through 124 by Brunt fall along a G curve with base year at 197 B.C., as represented in the figure by filled square symbols for data and a hollow square for the t_0 (72). Raw census numbers for 179–164, 125, 115, and 86, on the other hand, suggest (as hollow circles) that this phase of Roman growth persisted 40 years longer (13, 70, 72). The base year for that G falls only a year and a half away from the t_0 for Brunt's adjusted 178–124 data.

Even with Brunt's corrections for soldiers overseas and other missed men, however, the census numbers sag (as shown by the hollow triangles on the graph) from about 158 through 130. The period of the Third Punic War (149–146) is less of a problem for the model than subsequent years. Brunt describes how victory over Carthage was followed by a growing concentration of wealth and land in the hands of a few. This fostered a degradation of the middling sort of Roman and seems to have involved some reduction in the rolls of citizens who would be reported by the census (61–83). The Gracchian allotments of land subsequently put many names back on the records and available to the censors— though it took a few years of litigation to effect the alterations. To have the politically driven and defined decline of *censi* in Figure 5.2 from 146 through 130 itself take what looks like a D path reflects the way social and economic changes, not just demographic developments—including tax collection and other forms of administrative activity—tend to follow G-connected patterns, a phenomenon that is revisited in subsequent sections of this study. It is interesting to observe a classical example this early.

Brunt concludes that numbers of the old type of Roman citizen, without new groups of allies and rebels who had been enfranchised under the *Lex Julia* of 90 B.C., stood at about 412,500 by the year 69 (83, 91, 97). The G curve fitted in Figure 5.2 to his corrected estimates for 178–124 (without the triangle-denoted, probably underreported years of this era) projects about 480,000 old-style Romans by 69. According to Brunt, the numbers "must have been higher in 90," as a G fitted to include the available raw registrations through 86 B.C. suggests. The 90 to 69 period witnessed civil war between Marius and Sulla and the great slave revolt led by Spartacus.[23]

The enfranchisement of Italian territory up to the Po River in 90 B.C. created about 700,000 additional citizens, producing a total of some 1,155,000 old and new free adult male Romans who should have been captured by the censors as of 69, according to Brunt (97). This number then grew to approximately 1,742,000 by 28 and 1,815,000 by the year 8 B.C.[24] Some were added as the region from the Po to the Alps (Cisalpine Gaul) received citizenship in 50. Brunt estimates only about 300,000 adult males in the area by 28, however. He considers the region then, unlike today, to have been thinly populated and hindered from demographic recovery by the kinds of damage sustained in its conquest. Other increments to the ranks of citizens came from the manumission of slaves into freedmen and the acceptance of provincials as citizens. In Brunt's view, though, "the old Italian stock" if anything declined rather than increased (103–12). The result of these somewhat offsetting changes, nevertheless, seems to have been that the free adult male population entitled to citizenship increased along a G curve from 69 through 8 B.C., whether one looks at Brunt's corrections for *incensi* or takes into consideration only the official registers. Between 8 B.C. and the Augustinian census of 14 A.D., though, it is Brunt's view that some of the steeper increase to 2,117,000 may have derived from having better records at the latter date for cross-checking who should be registered, not the actual presence of more eligible men (120). Thus the Italian population after 8 B.C., through the second half of the reign of Augustus in the new empire, may either have continued to grow fairly much along the G path followed from 69 to 8 or, with civil war ended and stability of several kinds enhanced, may have started off into a new phase of expansion. Only more and better evidence can determine which interpretation should be preferred.

What seems fairly likely, however, is that across more than 500 years from the founding of the Republic to its replacement by the Empire, the Roman free adult male population increased repeatedly along familiar G trends. In at least two periods of crisis, furthermore, demographic decay according to the also globally observed D curve appeared. The path of decline found to be followed by the conquered natives of 16th century Mexico or by the hard-pressed people of 19th century Ireland gives the formula for representing Roman losses during the first great crisis period of the young Republic in 508–474 or during the invasion of Hannibal in 218–203.

Finally, it is important to note that no form of growth other than the G curve appears in five centuries of Roman history. In spite of the extension of empire, with its expanding frontier, no F trend emerges. For all the economic reorganization involved in Rome's rise, furthermore—such as the intercontinentally networked grain trade or the kind of specialization illustrated by the fish sauce makers and distributors of Pompeii—at no time does a slowly decelerating H trajectory of demographic expansion occur. And there is no sign of any population explosion of the E type in Figure 5.2. We acquire, from an unusual classical perspective, some further historical evidence about the kinds of conditions under which these different forms of change within the G family of curves have or have not occurred.

BETWEEN THE ANCIENT AND THE MODERN: ENGLISH PATTERNS FROM DOMESDAY THROUGH THE BLACK DEATH, 1086–1377

Back before demographic history became internationally fashionable in the 1960s, Josiah Cox Russell produced one of the enduring classics of the field. In *British Medieval Population* (1948), he astutely and carefully teased out the available sources to produce a sense of how the population of England waxed and waned across much of the long era from the Norman conquest to the plague-wracked later 14th century. His calculations and estimations make it possible to obtain some sense of the underlying trends that capture these long-term movements.

In Russell's view, first of all, "the population grew rapidly in the early post-conquest period and then slowed up. Perhaps in the thirteenth century another period of rapid growth occurred which our evidence would seem to show had been retarded just before the plague" (259). His preferred computations of mean ratios of pre-plague extents to poll tax population produce the estimated populations for 1260, 1280, 1300, 1320, and 1340 that are depicted in Figure 5.3 (258, 247).[25] These do indeed indicate first rapid then slowing growth, as Russell claimed. What can be added here is that, if his estimates are correct, this de-

Figure 5.3
Possible Population Trends for England from 1086 through 1377

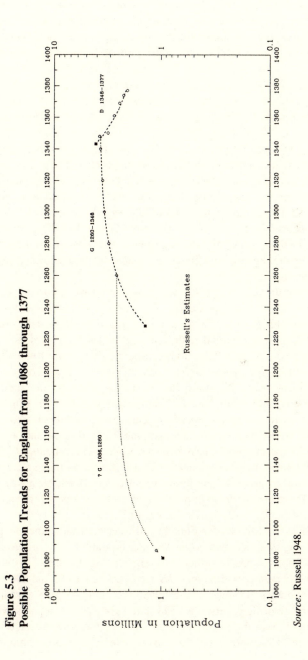

Source: Russell 1948.

celeration in increase clearly took the familiar G form with base year at 1228
across the long period from the defeat of Simon de Montfort by the young
Edward I to the victory of Edward III at Crécy. Russell himself perceived the
need for some sort of bending curve to represent his data: "We are justified in
feeling that an S curve would illustrate the development better than a compound
interest curve, but the plotting of the curve as yet would be largely hypothetical"
(260). No longer. The cross-culturally proven G curve provides the necessary
form.

For assessing Russell's other hypothesis of first rapid, then retarded growth,
for the period between 1066 and somewhere in the 1200s, there is very little
evidence. Figure 5.3, however, shows what a G trend based upon the data for
Domesday in 1086 and his first calculations for the 13th century, for 1250–
1269, would project. If the second G surge started somewhat sooner than this
first estimation (with midpoint at 1260), then the G back through 1086 would
be flatter and its base year rather earlier than the 1081 of the curve that is
tentatively fitted in the figure. Of course, there may well have been some ups
and downs during the century and a half period that has no information. Still,
as a hypothesis with which to work until additional evidence proves otherwise,
it might be appropriate for the time being to model Russell's educated guess
about decelerating growth across the 1066–1250 era with a G something like
that in the figure.

Depicting the demographic devastation caused when bubonic plague came to
England entails little speculation. Russell provided population estimates for
1348, 1350, 1361, 1369, 1374, and 1377 based upon mortality rates he calculated (263, 247). A D trend with base year at 1343 captures their decline quite
well, Figure 5.3 shows. Russell argued pointedly that the Black Death caused a
significantly higher proportion of casualties when it first arrived, in 1348, than
in subsequent years (263–64). That would help explain the suddenly low observation for 1349–1350. The 1377 number, also low relative to a trend that is
based mostly upon several preceding years, turns out probably to signal the start
of a new, second D curve of demographic decay that ran into the early 1400s.
This additional atrophy appeared in the wake of later bouts of plague and the
social and economic disorganization that followed so much sustained or recurrent mortality. That the long-term impact of the Black Death caused two successive D trends of demographic decay, not just one, is demonstrated more
clearly in Chapter 9 for certain locales of England.

This double blow of demographic disaster is a phenomenon that has been
found in the Americas when the Spanish brought strange diseases to the New
World. Chapter 4 has identified several such "double dips" of D shape among
the native populations of central Mexico between 1532 and the middle 1600s.
Russell estimates, however, that England lost about 45 percent of her population
in the first D decline between 1348 and 1374. That compares with more like
90 percent loss in the populations of Middle America between about 1530 and
1580, even before the second drop-off began. The demographic devastation of

Europe in the second half of the 14th century was serious enough, though, and followed the same kind of path that was later generated by the dark side of the Columbian exchange.

In sum, surveying almost half a millennium of European demographic history since about 1500, wherever and however far back in time the records permit, it is possible to discern insightful patterning of population growth from country to country across the continent that has not before been adequately identified and understood. Similar insights for historical reinterpretation can also be obtained across an earlier half-millennium for ancient Rome, from 508 B.C. to 14 A.D. The experience of England between about 1250 and 1377 likewise conforms to the hypothesis that premodern populations, as in Rome, just either expanded or shrank in proportionally constant G or D form.

Such gains in understanding can be had thanks to the new technique of looking at trends in terms of the G-based family of curves. These models not only fit the data well and conform to the historical contexts of the numbers. They also assist in reorganizing the demographic evidence more generally, in identifying similarities and dissimilarities from country to country that need to be explained, and in posing ways in which patterns of population history should be further analyzed for their underlying demographic dynamics and in turn connected with developments in the economic, biological, and cultural environments within which populations have increased or declined.

NOTES

1. As needed, U.N., *Demo. Ybk.* 1971, 1975, 1980, 1985, and 1990. Many series or sections of series come from Mitchell 1980, 29–37. A third edition of this valuable reference work adds some recent numbers but does not supplement or alter the historical data (Mitchell 1992, 3–11). Other sources used for national populations are as follows, by country.

Italy: Cippola 1965, 573; Felloni 1977, 4; del Panta 1979, 219; Instituto Centrale 1976, 13, and 1991, 55. For successive periods I have employed: 1500, Cippola, 1947 area; 1550–1625 and 1625–1675, Felloni, 1790 territory; 1600–1771, 1771–1821, and 1821–1861, del Panta, 1914 boundaries; 1861–1936 and 1951–1990, Instituto Centrale 1976 and U.N., *Demo. Ybk.*, for the 1971 area.

The Netherlands: For the period 1500–1750, van Houtte and van Buyten 1977, 81. Since 1795, Hofstee 1981, 125; U.N., *Demo. Ybk.*; Mitchell 1980 (for 1940).

England: For England 1541–1871, Wrigley and Schofield 1981, 528–529. For England and Wales 1861–1939 and 1951–1990, Office of Population Censuses and Surveys 1991a, 20.

Sweden: For 1520–1720 estimates within the boundaries pertaining before the end of the Great Northern War, Hofsten and Lundström 1976, 13. For population within the new borders 1715–1745, Lars Widén, "A retrojection back to 1700," Appendix 2 in Hofsten and Lundström, 172. For the era since 1748, Statistika Centralbyrån 1969, 86, 89, 91, 99, and U.N., *Demo. Ybk.* The 1721 figure for the new boundaries from Gille

1949, 19, and early data from Statistika Centralbyrån 1969, 86, for 1736–1745 fit into the estimations of Widén.

Spain: For 1541, 1589, and 1648–1768, Mauro and Parker 1977a, 37. Since 1768, official censuses without North African territories, but including the Balearic and Canary Islands, from Institutio National 1991, 69. Early estimates for continental Spain only, without the Balearics and the Canaries, for 1530–1610 come from Nadal 1984, 17 and 49.

2. Other sources are as follows, by country.

Portugal: Mauro and Parker (1977b, 64) contains estimates for 1500, 1580, and 1640. The G that fits this information is reported in Table 5.1 but not included in Figure 5.1b for the sake of keeping the scale of the graph more readable. Data for mainland Portugal 1636 through 1835 come from Morgado 1979, 333. His 1527 figure of 1.12 million is in line with the early estimates from Mauro and Parker. Beginning with 1841, numbers from Mitchell (1980) and then the U.N. include Madeira and the Azores.

France: For 1675–1735, estimates are synthesized from three series made available in Dupâquier 1979, 34, 35, 37. One is a back-projection from 1740 by Louis Henry, based upon estimated rates of growth per decade, starting in 1690; the second makes calculations retroactive to 1710 by means of the age pyramids found by INED for 1740, 1745, and 1750; the third works back to 1675 using rates of increase in rural baptisms and adjustments from rural population to the whole. Averages of the latter two methods are employed for 1710, 1720, and 1730. For 1742 through 1827 for the territory of 1861 calculations are taken from from Henry and Blayo 1975, 109. James C. Riley kindly made available a copy of this publication, which is unfortunately very difficult to find in the United States. For 1826–1951 Bourgeois-Pichat 1965, 498–99, covers present-day territory 1826–1866 and since 1921 but lacks Alsace-Lorraine 1871–1911. From 1951, the source is the U.N., *Demo. Ybk.*

Norway: Estimates for 1665, 1701, and 1735 are provided by Dyrvik 1972, 29–33. Since 1738, numbers for total population are taken from *Historisk Statistikk* 1978, 44–47, and the U.N.

Ireland: Estimates for 1600 and 1641 are in Cullen 1976, 389. Conceivably these indicate an H trend (with t_0 around 1520) for this period of substantial development under the early Stuarts. It was substantial, whether the Irish cared to have it or not. (That possible path, however, does not appear in the graph.) An upward correction for William Petty's contemporary population estimate for 1672—based upon the number of houses— which parallels in proportion Connell's similar modification of Petty for 1687, is adopted from McCusker 1970, 1: 550. This calculation yields about, 1,837,000 people rather than the 1,700,000 employed by Cullen for 1672. Together the 1641 and 1672 figures suggest that a D with base year back at 1591, as graphed, is a likely result of the demographic devastation that accompanied the Irish revolt and Cromwell's English revenge in the next decade. (McCusker's back-projections for 1660 and 1650 should not be used; they convey the impression of increase in a population that was almost certainly shrinking.) Connell 1975, 25, contains 1687–1791 estimates based on the hearth tax introduced in 1662, some of which are reported in Mitchell 1980, 36, note 37, and census figures for 1821–1841. Data thereafter come from Central Statistics Office 1991, 23. Beginning with 1926, these figures cover the Republic of Ireland only and are supplemented by numbers for Northern Ireland from Mitchell and the U.N.

My graphing shown in Figure 5.1b was, as noted, based upon Connell 1975. In 1981, Daultrey, Dickson, and Ó Gráda produced revised, lower calculations for the population of Ireland between 1706 and 1753 from different house counts and estimations of household size. While their data would keep the H trend for 1777–1841, in fact extending it back to 1749, a G for 1706–1732 would replace the 1672–1725 H indicated by Connell's calculations and no E pattern would emerge in between. Their own estimates of average household size, however, follow E curves in each of the four provinces of Ireland: 1706–1791 with t_0 around 1828 for Ulster, 1732–1791 (1840) for Leinster, 1732–1791 (1854) for Connaught, and 1749–1791 (1834) for Munster (not fitted mathematically, just estimated by template). According to the computations of Wrigley and Schofield (1981, 528–29) the crude birth rate for England rose in E fashion 1726–1816 toward a zero year at 1862, while the gross reproduction rate took and E path 1726–1816 with t_0 at 1851. This means that household size in Ireland (which was shaped mostly by the number of children) and fertility in England followed quite parallel paths.

The issue, in brief, seems to concern how the number of households was determined by Connell and by his critics from faulty official data. Someone with more expertise than I will have to decide. In the meantime, Table 5.1 and Figure 5.1b and various conclusions based upon them follow Connell, whose data make population behavior in Ireland look more like that of England. This decision would seem more compatible with the picture of 18th century economic vitality in Ireland and connection with Britain (and continental Europe) that Cullen develops (1986a and 1986b), though he himself apparently has adopted the population numbers of Daultrey et al. for this period (1994, 140).

3. Sources by country follow.

Finland: For 1723–1748 I have calculated the population trend implied by amounts and rates of births given in Juttikala 1965, 555. Since 1753 the data come from Finland, Tilatokeskus 1991, 80, 68.

Denmark: 1735–1775, Gille 1949, 19; 1769 onwards from Mitchell 1980 and U.N. See also Andersen 1979, 119.

Iceland: 1703–1775, Gille 1949, 19; 1976 and following from Mitchell 1980 and U.N.

Russia–Soviet Union: Kabuzan 1971, 52–57, presents numbers for males for Russia's 1719 boundaries for 1719–1857 and for the 1815 boundaries for 1815–1857. I have doubled these to approximate overall population size. Mitchell 1980, 36 (note 54) and 33, provides estimates of total population for the Russian Empire without Finland 1851–1897. In pages 36 (note 56) and 33 he gives population for the area of the Soviet Union 1897–1939. Figures for 1959–1989 come from Mitchell and the U.N.

4. Sources by country follow.

Scotland: 1755–1971, Mitchell 1980; 1975–1980, U.N., *Demo. Ybk.*; 1985–1990, Office of Population Censuses, *Population Trends*, 66: 55.

Belgium: For 1784–1829, Deprez 1979, 259. He tries to adjust for present-day territory. Thereafter, Mitchell 1980 and U.N. For the minor impact of new territory added in the 1920s, whose population did no more than offset Belgian losses during World War I, see Deprez 1979, notes e and f.

Austria: Klein 1973, 105. Extra figures on the Republic of Austria since 1971 are from Mitchell 1980 and the U.N.

Germany: Data for 1816–1864, from Mitchell 1980, refer to territory composing the German Empire in 1870, without areas ceded by Austria, Denmark, and France 1864–1871. For 1864–1910, the ceded areas are included. I have multiplied Mitchell's totals for 1923–1939 by 1.11 (the 1910 ratio his dual numbers imply) to obtain estimates for a territory of the same size as before Versailles; similarly, the sum of East and West Germany 1946–1990 (from Mitchell 1980 and the U.N.), is multiplied by 1.29, based upon the 1939 total for them relative to the size of the German population estimated then for Germany's pre–World War I boundaries (59.7 million vs. 77.2 million).

Hungary: Through 1910, the data are for Transleithania, the whole Hungarian portion of the Austro-Hungarian Empire, including Slavonia and Croatia (Mitchell 1980, 31 and 36 [note 34]). For 1910–1990, the Trianon boundary created at Versailles and adjustments made after World War II are followed. The figures come from Mitchell 1980 and the U.N. See also, Hungarian Central Statistical Office 1991, 25. Data given there for population within the boundaries of modern Hungary 1880–1910 follow an H curve virtually parallel to that for the larger territory of Transleithania for the same period.

5. Sources by country follow.

Switzerland: Mitchell 1980 and U.N., *Demo. Ybk.*

Luxembourg: Service Central 1990, B: 303.

The Czech lands: This means Bohemia, Moravia, and Czech Silesia through 1910 (Helczmanovzski 1979, 64, 66) and for 1921–1961 (Czechoslovakia, *Stat. Abs.* 1968, 19). The 1947–1990 data for the country following World War II come from Mitchell 1980 and the U.N.

Greece: Mitchell 1980 and the U.N. have the available figures. Enlargements of the population by accession of the Ionian Islands from Britain in 1864 and the Dodecanese from Italy in 1949 were minor, as were losses in Thessaly to Turkey around 1900. In contrast, acquiring Thrace, Epiros, and part of Macedonia from Turkey after World War I almost doubled the territory of Greece, while acquisition of Thessaly and Arta in 1881 enlarged existing territory about a quarter (National Statistical Services 1971, 18).

Bosnia and Hercegovinia: Mitchell 1980.

6. Figures for all these countries come just from Mitchell 1980, and the U.N. Boundary changes should be noted (Mitchell 1980, 35–37). Data for just Russian Poland appear in Mitchell 1980, 36, notes 46 and 47. Dual numbers for 1897 that Mitchell provides are used here to derive a multiplier with which to estimate what seems to be a parallel continuing trend for the territory of Versailles Poland to 1931.

7. Some early evidence for Portugal and for Ireland is not included on the graph, as mentioned in note 2. It is fitted, however, and the trends are included in Table 5.1 and discussed later.

8. Including D's marked "?".

9. The ninth case is only a possible one in Iceland. This is based upon just two estimates for 1703 and 1735 and is not graphed.

10. Finland, Luxembourg, Poland, Bulgaria, Greece, Montenegro, Bosnia and Hercegovina, and the former F.R.G.

11. But no rise in birth rate (1981, 528).

12. Cippola (1965, 573) stresses epidemics of 1630 and 1657. He argues that the 1657 event was the last for a long time. Looked at closely, the assessment of Pierre Goubert (1965, 467) implies that the likely D curve in France may have in fact started about the same time as the one in England, close to mid-century. Nadal (1984, 24–25, 38–43, 49, 56) cites both plague epidemics that Spain shared with her neighbors and an out-migration of Moriscos in three years (272,000 for 1609–1611) that equalled the total of Spanish people going to the New World between 1561 and 1625. J. H. Elliott (1977, 296–316) stresses the cost of poor government, military ambition, and inflation for the Spanish people at this time.

According to rates of population growth and natural increase generated by Wrigley and Schofield (1981, 528, Table A3.1), net emigration from England was in fact not as high relative to the domestic population, even in 1656–1660, as in certain other periods, and therefore did not constitute the engine of demographic loss 1656–1686. Meanwhile, the purchasing power of workers in England had bottomed out by the early 1600s. In spite of another dip in 1647–1650 (the late Civil War years), real wages in fact *rose* across the three decades of demographic decline (642–43), contrary to what American colonialists have too often concluded.

13. The territory that became "Germany" suffered worst of all demographically from fighting, disease, and starvation in the era of the Thirty Years War and its aftermath, but no nation with records existed at the time. For regional and local evidence of the severe losses there in this era, see Chapter 6, 8, and 9.

14. The preeminent Dutch maritime province of Holland, however, swelled in population during this era in an H trend very much like those of Sweden and England (Chapter 6).

15. The Netherlands remained strong in Asian trade throughout this period; but that commerce in unusual commodities did little to support or improve the lives of most Dutch people, compared with the foodstuffs coming from the Americas. Her other trades deteriorated (de Vries and van der Woude 1997, 409–29).

16. In support of such a hypothesis, the English data (Wrigley and Schofield 1981, 528–29) suggest that the crude birthrate in England fell in accelerating form between 1556 and 1661; and calculations by L. Livi, I. Zoller, and R. Bachi for the Jewish communities of several northern Italian cities indicate fertility decline in a similar pattern for 1681–1763 (Livi-Bacci 1977, 43). The succeeding volume to this one discusses historical patterns of fertility in detail.

17. "Possibly" because national records do not start soon enough in Belgium to be sure that growth there, which between Waterloo and World War I paralleled that in Netherlands, was not also similar during the preceding Dutch E phase.

18. Chapter 1 of the next volume has the details.

19. *Population History* 412. "Perhaps for the first time in the history of any country other than a land of recent settlement rapid population growth took place concurrently with rising living standards."

20. Unless Belgium had an E surge that ended before 1815 like her neighbors England and Denmark. The close match of her post-1815 H's to those of the Netherlands and Denmark suggest that just lack of data before 1815 may make the main difference for Belgium. Noticeably, the flow southward with time of this originally North Sea combination of demographic growth sequences yielded and divided around the resistant bastion of France.

21. The range for them is given with hollow diamonds on the graph.

22. At that date, thanks to earlier work by Beloch, Afzelius, and others, Brunt found it possible to establish an exceptional amount of detail about the numbers of adult males, all free persons, and territory occupied—not only for Romans but also for Latins, Samnites, Etruscans, and other associated peoples.

23. The G curve based on unquestioned raw census data between 179 and 86/5 calls for about 444,400 Romans in 69, compared with 375,000 old-style *censi* actually reported then. That represents about a 16 percent loss below the projection. The raw and the corrected data (which atrophied about 14 percent) present very much the same picture of demographic decay during this time of troubles.

24. I use the midpoint of the adjusted ranges given in Brunt 1971, 117.

25. His preference is explained on page 259.

Chapter 6

How Regional Changes of Population in Europe Underlay National Ones— from Andalusia to the Amur, from Trondheim to the Tisza

For several European countries extensive and reliable information is also available concerning how regional populations grew or declined within the national whole. Such evidence makes it possible, first of all, to compare Old World regional movements with those found elsewhere. If the distribution of *national* trends of growth has been different for Europe relative to parts of the New World, has that distinction also held for more *local* changes in population size? Are the varied relationships between regional and country-wide growth that have been found in the Americas and the Pacific also common to Europe?

As in the New World contexts that have been examined, furthermore, the kinds of growth experienced by particular types of areas within European countries provide extra insight into *how* population increased or atrophied. Additional clues emerge as to the probable relationships of one growth pattern or another to internal migration, urbanization, economic development, and perhaps also the distribution of people by ethnicity or religion.

Finally, regional information often covers spans of time for which no national total or only meager country-wide evidence exists. In other words, it extends and fills holes in the international patternings that have been introduced in the preceding chapter and strengthens tentative conclusions that have been offered about societal populations that had to be made on the basis of unsure or widely spaced estimates for certain periods of history.

Once one moves below the nationwide level, there are many regional populations that might be studied. Chosen here are examples for certain epochs from nine countries. Data for subpopulations within Norway 1735–1865, Ireland 1841–1991, and Spain 1585–1785 sample a north-south swathe of Atlantic Europe across four centuries. They illustrate situations in which regional populations mostly tended to move in step with national ones.

In Italy since 1750 and the Netherlands since 1795, in contrast, it is possible to distinguish clearly urbanizing, industrializing regions from persistently rural ones in insightful ways. The kind of population growth that goes with economic development is further established. Some of these findings reconfirm national clichés about particular regions; others reveal more subtle and more complicated distinctions in demographic development.

Available regional growth patterns within Austria 1617–1971, Germany 1639–1980, and the extensive reaches of the Hapsburg Empire outside Austria proper since 1786 serve two purposes. First they help clarify what transpired in central Europe, where the survey of national trends in Table 5.1 has indicated intermediary or transitional movements of population increase. These patterns of change fall between the characteristic North Sea sequence and the behavior of some southern and eastern populations that appear to have been immune to anything but G growth. Second, to see where and when additional H and E trends emerged helps in understanding further how these less usual patterns spread across some parts of Europe, not others; how territories of particular economic and cultural character have not yet had certain forms of growth, or have participated in them only at substantially later stages of European history.

Finally, there is the superficially strange, but ultimately not so different, land of the tsars. The sheer scale of territory and range of peoples, the great variety of life conditions, the substantial historical shifts in policy, outlook, and scope of control experienced by the Russian domain make regional records available there since 1719 invaluable to include. In spite of analytical difficulties stemming from war losses, boundary changes, and the like, a surprisingly clear sense of patterning for regional population growth within Russia and the Soviet Union can be obtained from the time of Peter the Great to 1970. This not only sets apart areas like Siberia and Muslim Central Asia in a readily anticipated manner; it also usefully distinguishes segments of European territory that participated in national development in certain ways at certain times.

In this extended survey, only a single subpopulation displays the F form of constant exponential population increase; and there is no log-linear growth at any rate other than .03. The F pattern, once again—at the regional level as well as the national one—is underscored as the New World phenomenon that Franklin proclaimed it in 1751. Further insight is obtained, though, about the conditions under which other exceptions to G increase occur, the H and E patterns, and how trends of all G-based forms in regional growth fit together within country-wide populations as these more comprehensive wholes themselves take G, H, or E trajectories of growth or experience D-type decline.

CONFIRMING AND CLARIFYING SOCIETAL PATTERNS
WITH LOCAL ONES ON THE ATLANTIC RIM OF EUROPE
BETWEEN 1585 AND 1990: TRENDS IN NORWEGIAN
BISHOPRICS AND IRISH PROVINCES AND FOR SPANISH
REGIONAL BAPTISMS

In Norway over the period 1735–1865, the records from which population trends can be established were collected by the four bishoprics. Graphing and curve-fitting, which are not displayed, indicate that the following patterns quite adequately account for regional and aggregate national growth in this era:

All Norway	1745–1815 H 1624	1815–1890 H 1758
Bergen	1745–1815 H 1617	1815–1865 H 1738
Trondheim	1745–1815 H 1624	1815–1865 H 1763
Kristiansand	1745–1815 H 1627	1815–1865 H 1758
Akershus	1745–1815 H 1630	1815–1865 H 1761

Generally, demographic growth in each region of Norway followed the national pattern very closely. Whatever dynamics of health, economy, or family fashion gave the population of Norway H-type increase in the later 1700s instead of the more slowly starting but accelerating E's found in Table 5.1 for Denmark, the Netherlands, and England across neighboring waters, and then lined up Norway with these countries in new H growth after 1815, those forces worked similarly in all parts of the country. So did whatever set Norwegian population increase apart from the patterns for neighboring Sweden (where four successive G-shape growths appeared instead between 1721 and 1848).[1]

The data of Drake, furthermore, indicate parallel trends of birth and death rates for the four regions across the two successive phases of H growth observed. Each local H trajectory of population expansion started because the diocesan birth rate shifted up; each slowed with time as the rate for births saw its lead over the rate for deaths progressively diminish (1969, 184–88, 192–95).

Drake stressed the importance of declining death rate for population growth in Norway during the period studied. The dissemination of the potato, however—noted by Malthus in his visit of 1799—is more likely to have driven this change up to 1800 or so than vaccination for smallpox, which came to bear for most people only in the 19th century. For this later period of demographic expansion, furthermore, the rise of the birth rate after independence from Denmark in 1815 was more significant than further reductions in the death rate.[2]

In Ireland, information on population growth for the four provinces of Leinster, Ulster, Munster, and Connacht is available for years since 1841.[3] The notorious decay of Irish population that began in the 1840s followed D patterns everywhere, Figure 6.1 indicates.[4] Up to the 1920s, Leinster and Ulster took the

Figure 6.1
Decline and Recovery in the Provinces of Ireland since 1841

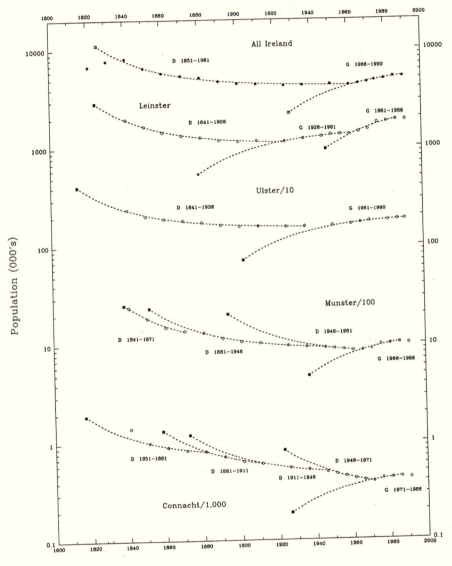

Source: Note 3.

country-wide course of a single long D decline, anchored on a t_0 in the early 1800s. In Munster in the south and Connacht in the west, however, more than one phase of atrophy appeared in regional population. In these two provinces, unlike the rest of Ireland, very late shrinkage took place even after World War II, most steeply in Connacht. The reasons for such distinctions in demographic decline—most notable in later decades—should be accessible to those who are familiar with details of the social and economic history of Ireland. Meanwhile, atrophy in all places seems to have taken the D form when and as it occurred.

Then, the recovery of Irish population in the 1900s also followed similar but distinctly timed trends from province to province across the country. The population of Leinster, incorporating Dublin and its eastern hinterland facing the Irish Sea and England, started to rebound first. This G began in the 1920s as most of Ireland gained independence from Britain and Dublin became the capital of a new republic. In the province of Ulster, G-shaped demographic recovery appeared only appreciably later, about 1960, approximately when a second, steeper post-independence surge showed up in Leinster. Recent growth in Munster and Connacht has come closer to paralleling that of Leinster in vigor than modern demographic increase in troubled Ulster; but recovery in these two provinces began only near 1970, and by 1991 there were signs of possible new demographic decay in these regions along with Leinster, though Ulster's population currently continues to move forward on a modest course of increase in spite of chronic strife there.

In short, modern Ireland turns out to have incorporated considerable regional homogeneity in her population trends, but more local diversity in growth and decline than occurred within Norway 1735–1865. How, and why, have local patterns of migration or of change in fertility and mortality area by area reflected or generated the regional G-based trends of growth that appear? It would seem that a useful framework for organizing and reinterpreting studies at the county or even more local level is made available by these findings.

Another country for which regional G-based patterns both clarify national trends and categorize local movements is Spain. Whereas there are available only scant and scattered estimates for the population size of some regions within the country between 1541 and 1797 (Mauro and Parker 1977a, 37), for eight major parts of Spain selected communities have continuous and extensive records of *baptisms* from 1580 through 1797 (Nadal 1984, 78–79).[5] These can serve as rough surrogates for trends of local population growth and decline through the two centuries across which Spain shifted from being the mightiest and richest European power to a considerably less dominating nation within the Western world. Table 6.1 presents the ways in which these baptismal totals changed over time relative to their local levels for a base period of the 1620s (1620–1629 = 1).

The average level for all eight regions for which evidence of baptisms is accessible first fell from the 1580s into the 1630s, possibly along a C type of

Table 6.1
Comparing Regional Trends for Baptisms in Spain, 1585–1785

<u>Average for Eight
   Regions</u>

```
1585-1635 ?C 1690*
1635-1685  G 1575*
..................
1685-1745  H 1529+
1745-1785  G 1698+
```

<u>Extremadura</u>	<u>Andalusia</u>	<u>Old Castile</u>	<u>Galicia</u>
1585-1655 C 1675*	1585-1615 D 1555	1605-1635 C 1646*	1615-1635 D 1588
1655-1675 G 1633*	1615-1675 G 1560*		
....	....		.....
1685-1745 H 1547+	1685-1745 H 1566+	1635-1745 H 1504+	1645-1745 H 1498+
1735-1785 G 1688+	1745-1785 G 1700+	1745-1785 G 1700+	1745-1785 G 1706+

<u>New Castile</u>	<u>León</u>	<u>Catalonia</u>	<u>Navarre & Vasco</u>
1585-1645 C 1685*	1585-1605 C 1643*	1595-1625 E 1675	1595-1635 G 1550
1645-1745 G 1595*	1605-1645 G 1556*	1625-1655 C 1698	1645-1715 G 1590*
....		....	.....
" " "	1655-1685 D 1619		" " "
	1685-1755 E 1768	1655-1745 H 1545+	
1745-1785 G 1706+	1735-1785 G 1700+	1745-1785 G 1722+	1715-1785 G 1677+

* Trends shared from region to region before about 1680.
+ Trends shared thereafter.

Source: Nadal 1984, 78–79.

downward accelerating curve.[6] These numbers subsequently grew from 1635
through 1685 fairly much along a G curve. This, however, was followed by a
rough H for 1685–1745. Figure 5.1a, in comparison, tentatively represented
three widely spaced *population* estimates for Spain as a whole from 1648 to
1768 by just one H trend. This, as noted, made evidence for 1717 fall somewhat
below the model. The succession of separate G, then H curves found here for
the average of baptisms in eight regions of the country would better fit that
meager available evidence for national population growth at 1648, 1717, and
1768, too. It would yield a stronger and clearer interpretation, confirming the
presence of H-type growth for Spain in the era but making it start a generation
later. Towards the end of the long era covered by the records for baptisms,
finally, the G for 1745–1785 shown in Table 6.1 is much like the G for total
Spanish population growth 1768–1797, as encountered in Figure 5.1a and Table
5.1. In all, the pattern for baptisms 1585–1785 confirms yet also improves upon
estimations that had to be made earlier from the thin evidence at hand for total
population in Spain over this long span of time.

   Turning to movements for individual regions, which are also summarized in
Table 6.1, the first thing that stands out is how trends in baptisms for all eight
parts of Spain *converged* in the later 18th century. From about 1735 or 1745

forward they all followed G trajectories that, on average, had their base years in the early 1700s.[7] In Catalonia, the hinterland of the major Mediterranean port of Barcelona, the growth was steepest (with t_0 at 1722); in the less prospering northwestern area of Navarre and Vasco, the G was flattest (base year at 1677), but it also began the earliest—about 1715. Probably one factor in this virtuallly nationwide G trajectory of demographic expansion between 1745 and 1785 was the intensified later 18th century trans-Atlantic shipment of foodstuffs, particularly grain. This outside origin of some significant sustenance probably fostered the uniformity of local growth trends across the various regions of Spain at this time; but it was not sufficient to generate a new phase of H expansion in the population, only a rapidly decelerating G.

Before the 1730s and 1740s there was more variation in growth from region to region within the country, if the number of baptisms serves as a reliable guide. Beginning in the middle to later 1600s, five of the eight recorded areas of Spain—first Old Castile and Galicia, then Catalonia, Extremadura, and Andalusia—saw baptisms increase in robust, only slowly decelerating H trends. In New Castile and in Navarre and Vasco growth continued to flatten out along G trajectories that had begun in the 1640s. No new trend replaced them. In León, the pattern was still more disparate: there was actually some D decline in the number of baptisms between 1655 and 1685; then, for about seven decades, the region probably experienced an accelerating E-type explosion in its number of baptisms. What opportunity for H-form demographic expansion passed these three regions by in the late 1600s and early 1700s? New Castile had been the political heart of Spain at the height of her rise to empire, dictating policy that did not always favor other areas. As the power of the monarchy weakened, did the center give back to the peripheries, demographically as well as politically and economically? In contrast, Navarre and Vasco represented distinctly marginal territory for the Spanish kingdom. Social and economic historians of Spain will have to sort out the details. Still, analysis of the likely demographic growth trends identified here raises some parallels and dissimilarities they could profitably consider.

Earlier, in contrast, in the late 1500s and early 1600s it was the movements of baptisms in New Castile, León, and the Extremadura that had determined the model for Spain. Table 6.1 contains lines across it to distinguish the patterns of this prior era from those of the period that followed; and widely shared trends of this time are marked "*". The successions of C decline, then G growth in baptisms that these heartlands of the Spanish interior experienced matched what happened to the average for all eight areas studied. Andalusia and Navarre and Vasco came into line with these regions in time for the G growth of the mid-1600s; but there had been considerable local variations before then.

It will take local experts to establish the reasons for these distinctive movements in particular parts of the country. Still, three things should be evident even from this preliminary survey of baptisms from region to region. First of all, the local patterns verify and clarify the form of growth and decline in national population across an era in which numbers for the whole country are scarce. Second, regional changes in population size became increasingly integrated with time, moving toward a single nationwide regime of demographic expansion by about 1740, while most local diversity appeared back in the later 1500s and early 1600s.[8] Finally, the geographical core of shared, pacesetting regional patterns for baptisms shifted from the interior heartland of New Castile, León, and the Extremadura, over the period 1585 to 1650 or so, to a rim of districts around the edge of Spain, in which the H growth of the later 1600s and early 1700s took hold, beginning with Galicia and Old Castile along the northern coast at about 1640. These shifts in parallelism and divergence for numbers of baptisms should be easy to associate with changes in the forces that brought population growth or decline to Spain over the long and determinative era between 1585 and 1785, such as how this country was governed, developed economically, chose to expend her resources among foreign and domestic undertakings, and increasingly relied on imports to sustain her population.[9]

CONTRASTING LOCAL AND NATIONAL CHANGE: REGIONS OF ITALY, PROVINCES OF THE NETHERLANDS AND BELGIUM, AND SELECTED DEPARTMENTS OF FRANCE FROM THE 1700s TO THE PRESENT

In other European countries, differing demographic growth patterns for particular regions add to already familiar local distinctions. Contrasts of northern and southern Italy, urban and rural provinces within the Netherlands and Belgium, and certain leading centers relative to the French countryside already structure regional depictions—from social science to editorializing to joke-making. The kernels of truth that germinate such persistent stereotyping, however, help toward understanding more about the way certain conditions of economy and society have accompanied particular forms of demographic expansion.

Local variations of population increase in Italy mostly reflect well-known differences in regional history and development within that country. A basic distinction between North and South—which surfaces in everything Italian from economic history and cuisine to folk prejudice and political tensions—stands out in Table 6.2. This is divided into A and B parts, which focus, in turn, upon trends of growth in the territories that existed before 1861 and changes of population size in the regions enumerated since then.[10] Figure 6.2 illustrates the historical patterns for those areas whose population size can be followed before 1813 and a few other territories. All trends summarized in Table 6.2, however, have been graphed and fitted in the usual way.

In the era up to 1770 or 1790 (later in Piedmont and neighboring Parma), a G trend with base year about 1695 characterized demographic expansion across northern Italy. This was the path of increase in what was to become the post-Napoleonic Kingdom of Sardinia and separately in its future parts of Piedmont,

Liguria, and the Island of Sardinia. A G trend of similar timing also appeared in Lombardy, Parma, and Venetia. While G-type growth also existed to the south in the Papal States and the Kingdom of the Two Sicilies during the same period, it was appreciably flatter, with t_0's for the curve at 1624 and somewhere around 1652 respectively. In Tuscany (situated between these two large northern and southern regions), Figure 6.2a contains a filled triangle at 1700 that indicates virtually no change in population size across the first half of the 18th century, or perhaps even a slight decline.[11] I am uncertain of accounting for all boundary changes in these early, politically very fluid years of modern Italian history. In general, however, it is clear that the populations of northern Italy expanded in very similar G trajectories, while peoples further to the south increased more slowly, if also along G paths.

From the 1770s or so until French occupation ended in the early 1800s, the populations of Piedmont and Liguria lingered in G trends begun long before. Demographic increase in Parma, though its pattern is unknown prior to 1770, took much the same flat trajectory (Figure 6.2b). More vigorous new G growth was characteristic elsewhere for the period from 1770 to 1820 or 1830. In Tuscany and Venetia, the trajectories were relatively flat, having their base years around 1715. G trends that appeared in the Papal States, the Kingdom of the Two Sicilies (and, separately, its two components of Sicily and Naples), and Modena were steeper (Figure 6.2b). Now it was generally the southern regions, less intruded upon by France, that witnessed somewhat stronger G growth in their populations. In Lombardy, increase to 1800 stayed along the old stagnating G curve of the 1700s; then, however, expansion became appreciably steeper for 1800–1838.

In the next era of modern Italian population increase, from about 1820 or 1830 up to the 1880s or later, the previously stagnant areas of Piedmont and Liguria commenced long trends of growth in the H form. This is the pattern generally found to be typical of economically developing regions. The implication is that Turin and Genoa, respectively, saw their hinterlands evolve more aggressively and diversely after the peace of 1815 than did Milan, Florence, Venice, Bologna, and other northern centers. These other northern Italian populations instead had a further wave of more rapidly slowing G-shape increase from about 1820 to 1861, like the Papal States, Naples, and Sicily, in an area stretching southward down the boot of Italy (Figure 6.2c). Later, however—about 1861—H growth did also appear in Tuscany. In short, regions of the Northwest experienced a type of growth not found in the central and eastern portions of northern Italy any more than in the conventionally different South. Precisely what was distinctive in the Northwest that generated such unusual H expansion in population? And why did it not occur elsewhere?

That the Italian population as a whole saw H growth in the later period of 1861–1936 is, on the other hand, mostly the product of the way local G increases from region to region summed up or fitted together into a national pattern. Among 19 areas with recorded populations since 1861, only Tuscany shows

Table 6.2
Patterns for Population Growth within Areas of Italy, 1700–1981

A. Pre-Unification Regions

ITALY	K. of Sardinia	Piedmont	Liguria	Tuscany
1700-1771 G 1696	1770,1800 ?G 1699	1700-1820 G 1698	1750-1790 G 1689	1750-1816 G 1720
1771-1821 G 1717			1816-1861 G 1792	
1820-1861 G 1790	1800-1861 H 1717	1820-1931 H 1697	1820-1881 H 1723	1861-1961 H 1749
1861-1936 H 1755				

Papal States	K. of Two Sicilies	Venetia	Lombardy	Modena
1700,1770 ?G 1624	1700,1750 ?G 1652	1750-1790 G 1694	1700-1800 G 1684	1770-1825 G 1734
1770-1825 G 1748	1770-1800 G 1737	1770-1833 G 1712	1800-1838 G 1778	
1825-1861 G 1794	1816-1861 G 1792	1833-1852 G 1801	1838-1861 G 1802	1833-1861 G 1816

Parma	Is. of Sardinia	Mainland Naples	Sicily
1770-1825 G 1690	1750,1770 ?G 1703	1770-1816 G 1726	1770-1825 G 1734
1825-1861 G 1776	1790-1858 G 1771	1816-1861 G 1790	1825-1848 G 1794
			1848-1871 G 1818

B. Regions after Unification

ITALY	Piedmont	Liguria	Tuscany
1700-1771 G 1696	1700-1820 G 1698	1750-1790 G 1689	1750-1816 G 1720
1771-1821 G 1717	" "		1816-1861 G 1792
1820-1861 G 1790	1820-1931 H 1697	1820-1881 H 1723	1861-1961 H 1749
1861-1936 H 1755	" "	1911-1951 G 1878	1961-1981 G 1908
1951-1990 G 1910	1951-1981 G 1923	1951-1971 G 1918	

Table 6.2 (Continued)

Venetia

1750-1790	G 1694
1770-1833	G 1712
1833-1852	G 1801
1861-1901	G 1831
1901-1951	G 1877
1961-1981	G 1917

Lombardy

1700-1800	G 1684
1800-1838	G 1778
1838-1861	G 1802
1861-1881	G 1816
1901-1936	G 1874
1951-1981	G 1930

Emilia

1861-1881	G 1809
1901-1961	G 1873
1961-1981	G 1902

Latium

1861-1881	G 1820
1901-1921	G 1875
1931-1981	G 1930

Umbria

1861-1881	G 1816
1901-1921	G 1853
1921-1981	G 1877

Trentino-Alto Adige

1861-1901	G 1774
1901-1936	G 1836
1951-1981	G 1912

Valle d'Aosta

1861-1901	[D 1741]
1911-1936	G 1818
1951-1981	G 1912

Abruzzi & Molise

1861-1881	G 1807
1881-1911	G 1832
1921-1936	G 1902
1936-1971	[D 1908]

Friuli-Ven. Giulia

1861-1881	G 1789
1881-1981	G 1855 . .

Marche

1861-1881	G 1799
1901-1981	G 1859 . "

Campania

1861-1881	G 1809
1881-1921	G 1834
1921-1971	[H 1845]

Sicily

1770-1825	G 1734
1825-1848	G 1794
1848-1871	G 1818
1881-1911	G 1854
1931-1981	G 1891

Sardinia

1750,1770	?G 1703
1790-1858	G 1771
1858-1881	G 1822
1881-1921	G 1848
1931-1981	G 1915

Calabria

1813-1881	G 1793
1881-1921	G 1832
1921-1961	G 1898

Apulia

1861,1871	?G 1820
1881-1921	G 1857
1931-1971	G 1910

Basilicata

1861-1881	G 1792
1881-1911	[D 1824]
1921-1961	G 1898

Source: Note 10.

191

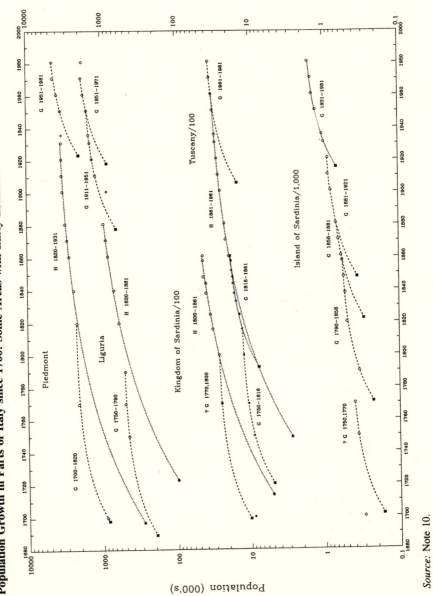

Figure 6.2a
Population Growth in Parts of Italy since 1700: Some Areas with Early Estimates

Population (000's)

Piedmont

Liguria

Kingdom of Sardinia/100

Tuscany/100

Island of Sardinia/1,000

G 1951–1981
H 1820–1931
G 1750–1790
G 1700–1820
G 1951–1971
G 1911–1951
H 1820–1881
H 1800–1881
? G 1770,1800
H 1861–1961
G 1816–1861
G 1750–1816
? G 1750,1770
G 1961–1981
G 1931–1981
G 1858–1881
G 1790–1858
G 1881–1921

Source: Note 10.

Figure 6.2b
Population Growth in Parts of Italy since 1700: Territories with Only Pre-Unification Estimates

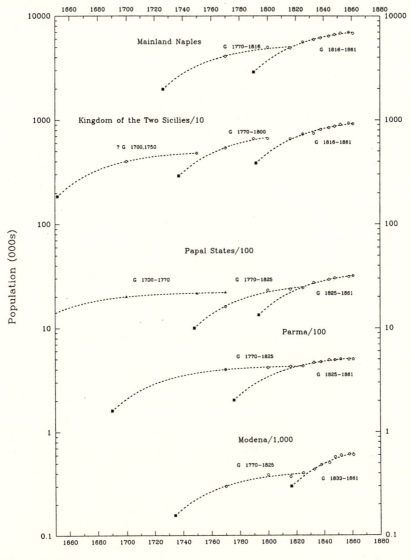

Source: Note 10.

Figure 6.2c
Population Growth in Parts of Italy since 1700: Areas of the South

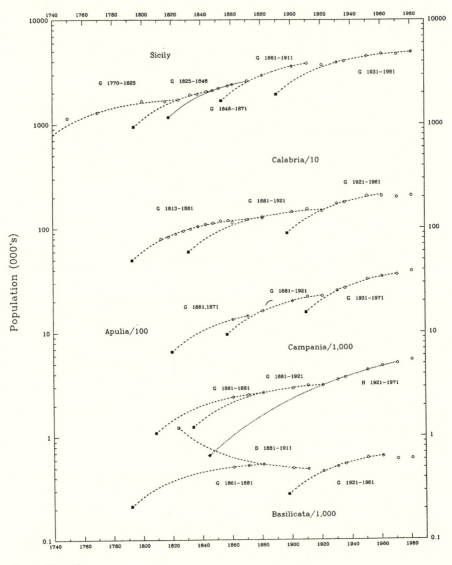

Source: Note 10.

signs of H expansion precisely parallel to the societal pattern over these years (as part B of Table 6.2 indicates). This phenomenon, in which a national H aggregates out of local G's, is already familiar from the United States between 1850 and 1940. Did *internal migration* among regions comparably produce an overall H out of component local G growths in Italy across the second half of the 19th century, even in a period during which Italy was one of the preeminent sources of international out-migration and the United States the leading receiver of immigrants? There seem to be some important research issues here. Further, why did Liguria fall out of its H trajectory in the 1880s or 1890s (unfortunately there are no data for 1891), though Piedmont could keep up this robust, only slowly decelerating pattern into the 1930s—across a span of more than a century? That Campania took on H growth in 1921–1971 undoubtedly must be understood relative to the way Naples expanded as center for the modern Mezzogiorno as the region's discontented flowed less toward America or Argentina and more into Italian cities.

Meanwhile, across the later 1800s most Italian regions experienced G growth, though in the lovely Valle d'Aosta from 1861 through 1901 population declined via the familiar D shape. Then into the early 1900s another wave of G expansions is evident across the regional populations of Italy. Once again, marginal areas saw the weakest surges; steepest G increases of population took place in Venetia, Lombardy, and Emilia in the heavily urban Po drainage of the North, joined by Liguria as this western coastal area around Genoa slipped out of its H trend. Over recent decades, finally, population increase across the regions of Italy has become significantly more homogeneous. No less than 16 of 19 areas have had new G growth approximately together, including Piedmont and Tuscany, which now both have shifted out of their former long-running H patterns. Slowest growth of late has been characteristic of the mountainous Apennine spine that reaches down the boot from Emilia through Umbria and Marche to Abbruzzi and Molise and on into the arch and toe of the country in Basilicata and Calabria. The steepest recent G's, in contrast, have occurred—equally unsurprisingly—around the large urban centers of Rome, Milan, and Turin (in Latium, Lombardy, and Piedmont, respectively). In the same metropolitan drift, the one part of Italy to acquire recent H growth for 1921–1971, as no longer exceptional regions of the Northwest abandoned it, has been Campania, the hinterland of Naples, though that trend may have come to an end by about 1980.

In general, this overview of known changes in population size within Italy since the early or middle 1700s first of all largely fits with familiar distinctions made between a rich, urbanized, developed but more socially and politically radical North and a poor, rural, conservative, and extralegally organized South. The historical patterning of demographic growth trends that is identified here, however, shows regionalization in Italy to be more complex than this cliché would suggest: Mountainous fringes, whether south or north, have in era after era enjoyed less robust population growth. Special circumstances—perhaps influences of revolutionized France, perhaps indigenous local developments of economic and social history—set apart some of the urbanized North from the hinterlands of other, more eastern cities of the Po watershed in sustained H growth for much of the 19th century. Since World War II, finally, old regional differences have been mostly blurred. The patterning of G-based regional population increase and decline that emerges in Table 6.2 and Figure 6.2a, Figure 6.2b, and Figure 6.2c, in other words, both confirms some things that are well known about Italian social and economic history and poses refinements and restatements of the issues that can help both to guide further interpretation of familiar evidence and to set up fresh research.

Unlike Italy, the Netherlands has witnessed over time a mixing of E-shape population explosion with multiple H growths—the sequencing that set apart the "core" countries of the Northwest from the remainder of Europe (Table 5.1). How did local Dutch populations behave as that seminal pattern of modern national demographic expansion unfolded? Part A of Table 6.3 arranges these local patterns to facilitate comparison and contrast. Figure 6.3a and Figure 6.3b plot discernible trends in population size for some of the provinces of the Netherlands.[12]

The first thing to note from part A of Table 6.3 is how the population of the maritime province of Holland swelled in H fashion from the early 1500s into the later 1600s. The data for Holland as a whole follow an H curve from 1514 through 1680 that has its base year at 1451 (Figure 6.3a). This resembles very closely the trends of identical shape for Sweden 1570–1720 (t_0 at 1447) and England 1561–1656 (t_0 at 1461) that Table 5.1 shows. Meanwhile, the earliest calculations for Norway, concerning 1665–1735, yield an H track with base year at 1512; and a comparable trend with t_0 at 1518 offers a possible fit for the 1600 and 1641 estimates for Ireland. The association of the origins of H-type demographic expansion with the economic rise of northwestern Europe approximately 1500–1650, hypothesized in Chapter 5, now becomes quite firm and clear. In particular—though data for Friesland and Zeeland are not available this early—participation in this H form of population growth by the maritime portion of the Netherlands, whose merchants came to dominate the east-west trade of the Baltic and North Sea, is isolated and identified.

Then came the crash. As the Netherlands faced toughening competition for her ocean trade, especially from England (which along with Colbert's France enacted trade laws to squeeze out the Dutch), the populations of her maritime zones declined. In this D-type contraction Friesland joined North and South Holland. Meanwhile, though, the two documented inland rural areas of Overijssel and Drenthe *expanded* demographically via G. There were apparently enough such areas with enough people in them to allow the population of the country as a whole to sustain its now almost flat G path begun in the early 1620s. But no more.

In the later 1700s, quite parallel E trends of demographic increase began in several provinces of the Netherlands. These gave the national population growth this shape during 1759–1839, comparable to England 1726–1806 and Scotland 1735–1821. As Britons moved to factories located in heretofore not much developed countryside in the Midlands, Lancashire, Yorkshire, and the Scottish Lowlands and had children there without customary farm-country restraints, so Dutch inland population gradually began to explode—often in areas known for their rural and town industry as well as commercial agriculture. The notion that E-type trends of demographic increase are connected with early, labor-intensive stages of industrialization, another hypothesis from the European national patterns of Chapter 5 (and some Latin American evidence of Chapter 4), is strengthened.

As for England in the early 19th century, populations in the provinces of Groningen, Friesland, and Overijssel bailed out of accelerating E tracks into decelerating but still robust H-type increase from the early 1800s to the 1870s. Meanwhile, though, explosion for the second half of the century spread to the provinces of North Holland, South Holland, and Limburg; and Gelderland, Utrecht, and North Brabant followed E's of the early 1800s with two or three more accelerations lasting well into the 20th century, a succession of E trends picked up also by Drenthe and Zeeland after the 1840s. Germany and Switzerland, situated along the upper reaches of the Rhine, display double E surges from the later 1800s until after World War II that resemble some of these trends of Dutch provinces at the other end of the river (Table 5.1). Later industrialization along this artery of western Europe is suggested.

Some of these subsequent explosions, as before, gave way to sustained H expansion before World War II (Utrecht, North Brabant, Gelderland). In contrast, successive E trends lasted until 1980 or later in Drenthe and Zeeland, a sequence apparently acquired by Friesland. Along with G patterns in other provinces, this mix of H and E trends has given the Netherlands as a whole the G shown there since 1947.

In Belgium across the border to the south, in contrast, not a single H growth has apparently occurred in any of the nine provinces since regular records begin in the early 1800s (part B of Table 6.3).[13] Meanwhile, there has been population explosion of the E type in only two provinces: West Flanders and Belgian Limbourg followed movements in neighboring parts of the Netherlands.

Otherwise, population increase in Belgian provinces since the age of Napoleon has been entirely a matter of successive G curves, in spite of two national H trends for the periods 1815–1866 and 1876–1910. One stage of G growth, across the first half of the 1800s, with a base year somewhere around the start of the century, was virtually universal across the regions of Belgium. Only some variation in provincial timing stretched the sum of these local G's out into a national H trajectory for 1815–1866. Once more it is seen that one way a society-wide H trend can occur is just through some staggered chronology of local G growths, as in Italy 1861–1936. Next, much the same thing happened from the 1860s to World War I. The exception was that now paths of E-type

Table 6.3
Varieties of Demographic Expansion in the Provinces of the Netherlands and Belgium and in Selected Departments of France*

A. The Netherlands

NETHERLANDS

1620-1750	G	1574
1759-1839	E	1866
1815-1869	H	1728
1869-1889	H	1797
1899-1947	H	1849
1947-1990	G	1931

Overijssel

1675,1723	?G	1659
1723-1795	G	1687
1764-1839	H	1863
1815-1879	H	1742
1889-1920	H	1827
1920-1947	G	1907
1947-1980	G	1935

Friesland

1660-1714	D	1616
1714-1796	E	1848
1815-1869	H	1737
1869-1899	G	1823
1879-1947	E	1979
1947-1980	E	2012

Groningen

1795-1830	E	1854
1830-1869	H	1740
1869-1899	G	1844
1899-1980	H	1810

South Holland

1514,1622	?H	1446
1622,1680	?H	1474
1680-1795	D	1612
1815-1849	G	1797
1839-1899	E	1901
1889-1980	H	1857

North Holland

1514-1650	H	1442
1680-1795	D	1651
1815-1849	H	1700
1839-1879	E	1896
1879-1920	H	1839
1920-1947	G	1901
1947-1980	G	1918

Limburg

1815-1859	G	1788
1859-1909	E	1929
1909-1947	G	1911
1947-1980	G	1936

Utrecht

1750-1830	E	1853
1839-1889	E	1909
1889-1920	E	1931
1930-1980	H	1897

North Brabant

1795-1839	E	1861
1839-1889	E	1923
1889-1930	E	1937
1930-1980	H	1902

Gelderland

1815-1839	E	1860
1839-1869	E	1902
1869-1909	E	1928
1920-1950	E	1964
1940-1980	H	1898

Drenthe

1672-1742	. G	1636
1742-1774	?E	1835
1764-1794	G	1701
1815-1849	G	1811
1839-1859	E	1876
1869-1909	E	1921
1920-1950	E	1971
1950-1980	E	1994

Zeeland

1815-1859	G	1796
1849-1879	E	1921
1879-1909	E	1943
1909-1980	E	2008

Table 6.3 (*Continued*)

B. Belgium*

BELGIUM
1815-1866 H 1717
1876-1910 H 1790
1920-1947 G 1874
1947-1990 G 1897

Luxembourg
1830-1900 G 1802
1910-1947 D 1855
1947-1981 G 1896

Hainaut
1801-1816 G 1768
1816-1856 G 1798
1866-1930 G 1845
1947-1981 G 1883

East Flanders
1811-1866 G 1778
1876-1910 G 1847
1930-1981 G 1870

West Flanders
1801-1866 G 1772
1846-1910 E 1942
1920-1981 G 1888

Namur
1816-1866 G 1803
1866-1910 G 1824
1920-1961 G 1821
1961-1981 G 1920

Brabant
1801-1866 G 1811
1866-1890 G 1846
1890-1947 G 1872
1961-1981 G 1917

Antwerp
1816-1866 G 1796
1876-1930 G 1871
1947-1981 G 1915

Liège
1806-1830 G 1764
1830-1866 G 1812
1876-1981 G 1852

Limburg
1830-1866 G 1791
1846-1910 E 1935
1920,1930 ?E 1938
1947-1981 G 1935

C. France (selected departments)*

FRANCE
1792-1827 E 1876
1826-1921 G 1774
1921-1936 G 1862
1951-1990 G 1925

Seine (Paris)
1811-1831 E 1847
1831-1931 H 1823
1841-1872 [G 1843]
1872-1946 [G 1868]
1946-1982 G 1908

Gironde (Bordeaux)
1801-1851 E 1894
1851-1954 G 1816
1962-1982 G 1930

Rhône (Lyon)
1801-1841 E 1854
1831-1872 G 1811
1872-1954 G 1844
1954-1982 G 1942

Bouches du Rhône (Marseilles)
1810-1841 G 1771
1831-1861 [E 1880]
1841-1881 G 1826
1891-1946 G 1866
1954-1982 G 1949

Nord (Lille)
1801-1851 H 1698
1831-1861 [E 1886]
1851-1911 H 1764
1946-1982 G 1918

Haute Marne
1801-1851 G 1749
1851-1891 D 1780
1891-1946 D 1858
1946-1968 G 1908

Saône et Loire
1831-1891 G 1778
1881-1911 D 1800
1911-1954 D 1867
1962-1982 G 1911

Vendée
1831-1911 G 1793
1911-1931 D 1874
1954-1982 E 2018

Loiret
1801-1851 E 1894
1841-1891 G 1800
1891-1921 C 1976
1921-1962 E 2010
1962-1982 G 1946

Hautes Alpes
1801-1851 G 1750
1831-1921 C 1950
1921-1954 D 1850
1954-1982 E 2015

Landes
1801-1881 G 1777
1881-1931 C 1977
1911-1954 D 1870
1962-1982 G 1924

Calvados
1801-1851 G 1735
1831-1901 C 1940
1891-1921 D 1836
1954-1982 G 1932

*Trends for Belgian provinces and French departments are only estimated, not fitted.

Sources: Notes 12 and 13; Mitchell 1992, 48–49 (France).

Figure 6.3a
Demographic Increase in Some Provinces of the Netherlands, 1514–1980: Growth and Atrophy in Evidence before 1800

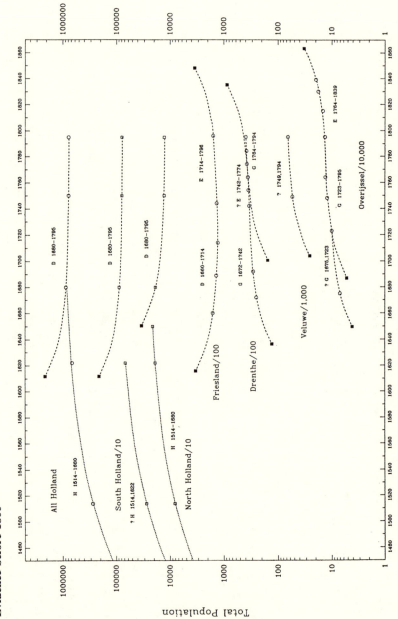

Source: Note 12.

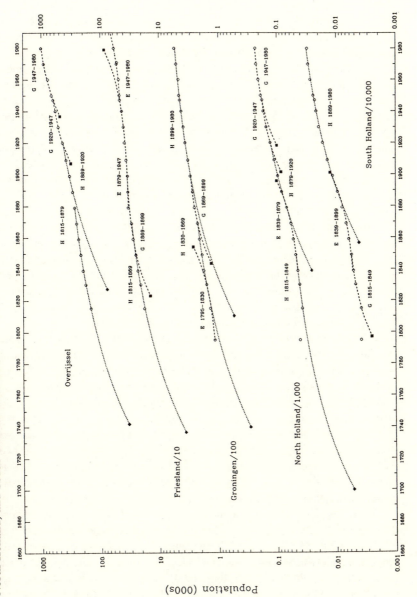

Figure 6.3b
Demographic Increase in Some Provinces of the Netherlands, 1514–1980: Overijssel, Friesland, Groningen, North Holland, and South Holland after 1800

Population (000s)

Source: Note 12.

201

population explosion began in Netherlands-bordering Limburg and West Flanders.

Like the H trends of 1815–1866 and 1876–1910, the two overall Belgian G-shape expansions since World War I have also involved the summing of chronologically varying local G's. This distribution from province to province serves as a reminder that societal G-type growths, too, can represent the piecing together of substantial inter-area migration and local differences in natural increase.

This overview of change in provincial populations across the Netherlands and Belgium underscores how some issues of demographic growth, its components, and its concomitants should be posed for the Low Countries. A careful comparison—province by province—of the migration, reproduction, aging, mortality, and economic change of these two neighboring Low Country populations, which generated such marked regional and national differences of demographic increase for societies so close to each other and so historically related, would seem to offer an especially fruitful step toward understanding better how G and H trends keep cropping up from country to country.

Though the data are available (for example, in Mitchell 1992, 48–50), it is not possible here to survey trends of demographic increase and decline for more than ninety departments across the succession of French republics that have evolved since the 1790s. What can be done, though, is to take at least a preliminary look at the patterns for a limited group of locales that might illustrate certain typical or distinctive categories of region within the country. Part C of Table 6.3 displays probable trends for twelve departments.

While the H trends of 1815–1866 and 1876–1910 for Belgium as a whole represent strictly composite results of local growth that nowhere themselves took H form, the E explosion in population that France experienced briefly as a nation in the early 1800s is simultaneously identifiable in the departments of all five major urban centers. In contrast, only one of the seven more rural areas examined—Loiret encircling Orleans—even possibly witnessed an E surge. Within France, in other words, proportionally accelerating demographic growth seems to have been an urban-centered phenomenon; and all the largest conurbations seem to have experienced it during the first half of the 19th century. Whatever domestic and demographic transformation took place to generate the upward-curving E trajectory, in France it occurred in and around major cities.[14]

The rare H phase of demographic expansion found in Seine, around Paris, for the years 1831–1931 might be replaced with roughly equal justification by two G's: one from 1841 through 1872, the other from 1872 through 1946—as the bracketed trends in the table indicate. Here the issue is how to treat the temporary effects of the events of 1848 and 1871 in France's beleaguered capital. French demographers will have to make the final choice. In Nord, however, the industrial region around Lille near the Belgian border, the two H's of 1801–1851 and 1851–1911 seem quite clear. Here is the one place in France where this sample survey finds trends of that shape for sure. Not surprisingly, they closely resemble the H's for all Belgium 1815–1866 and 1876–1910 and for all the Netherlands 1815–1869 and 1869–1889. In short, the northern industrial area around Lille seems—before becoming a victim of World War I—to have shared the demographic behavior of the nearby Low Countries more than that of the vast majority of France. Belgium somehow integrated local trends without H's to generate a sequence of national H growths up to World War I; France for some reason never produced this form of increase in aggregate.

Widespread local *loss* of population across the countryside interfered with any such synthesis of a modern national H trend for France. Part C of Table 6.3 displays some of the underlying particulars of this problem (cf. Spengler 1938). Among seven rural departments sampled, every single one saw population decline for a while between the middle 1800s and World War II. Meanwhile, not one of the five metropolitan areas examined witnessed any form of demographic atrophy. Internal migration within France was at work.

This loss of population across the French countryside, however, took two quite distinct forms. In Haute Marne, Sâone et Loire, and Vendée, the familiar D path was followed. Actually two successive D trends appeared in Haute Marne and Sâone et Loire, quite parallel downward adjustments from the later 1800s into the early 1900s, and from there to the end of World War II, respectively. Vendée, the table shows, joined in only for the second of these two slides.

In Loiret, Hautes Alpes, Landes, and Calvados, however, quite a different pairing of population declines occurred. The initial loss took the rare *accelerating* form of C (G reversed with respect to time). So far this unusual type of trend has been observed among European nations or regions only for *births* in some parts of Spain before 1650. In the New World such proportionally speeding-up C-shaped decline appeared only in a few outmoded or noncompetitive populations that began to lose their way of life, mostly small sugar islands of the Caribbean. What did these four departments of France share with other local peoples around the world that experienced C decline? How was their way of life perhaps becoming outmoded in the relevant periods? How was the generation of their demographic loss different from the dynamics of the D trends in Haute Marne, Sâone et Loire, and Vendée? Did the C form result from falling birth rates without offsetting improvement in health and net migration, as the applicability of the C form to some early modern Spanish birth trends might suggest? These would seem to be useful questions for framing further research in French local demography. Doubtless some of the necessary work has already been done and just needs to be reexamined in the new terms suggested here.

It is not that D decay failed ever to occur in departments that witnessed C decline. Excepting Loiret, where an unusual modern E explosion occurred in 1921–1961, the other three departments saw D patterns in the early 1900s, as their *second* stage of population loss, which closely paralleled those of Haute Marne, Sâone et Loire, and Vendée. What did Hautes Alpes, Landes, and—to a somewhat lesser extent—Calvados now share with those three other areas to generate largely comparable D's? How did their populations switch from accelerating C decline to initially faster but soon slowing D decay?

Since World War II, however, the famous international baby boom has apparently brought roughly parallel G growths to most parts of France, urban or rural. Local differences now are on the whole much less evident, as already noted in other countries. The two exceptions among twelve departments sampled here are Vendée and Hautes Alpes, where E explosions parallel to that of Loiret 1921–1962, but not begun until the 1950s, are still the current trend. These resemble E patterns that are lingering on in the Zeeland, Drenthe, and Friesland margins of the Netherlands (part A of Table 6.3), and lasted in Switzerland (Table 5.1) and the Tirol and Salzburg areas of Austria (Table 6.5) until the 1970s. What has generated this unusual surge in such widely separated places? For some, has it been a role as successful vacation lands? How many and what types of other parts of France have recently been sharing in such momentum-gaining demographic increase? These are questions that merit further exploration, it would seem.

Local evidence for the Netherlands, Belgium, a sampling of French departments, and Italy indicates, in short, substantial differences in the way regional trends underlay national patterns for this broad north-to-south swathe of western Europe since 1800 or earlier. The provincial populations of Belgium have been most homogeneous in their growth and most consistently G-dominated in their movements. Nevertheless, across the 19th century they produced in aggregate two examples of the H type of trend for the country as a whole, which no locality followed by itself. The regions of Italy, meanwhile, have divided conventionally between the urban North and the rest of the country, in a bifurcation for some reason not found in the nation of Brussels and Antwerp. Piedmont, Liguria, and Tuscany have for various periods of time seen their people multiply in H form, like Italy as a whole in 1861–1936. Elsewhere (including some other highly urbanized sectors of the North), nothing but G growth has appeared, along with occasional D decline in poor mountain areas, excepting an H in Campania with the expansion of Naples after World War II. In the Netherlands, in contrast, several local populations—first to the north around the Zuider Zee, then shifting to the Rhine-mouth areas of the south—have often closely reflected national sequences of E and H, the patterning that links this country's history of population increase with a group of demographically and economically core nations of northwestern Europe. France, unlike Belgium, mimicked the movements of this category of nations only in the brief E explosion that followed the Revolution. She had broken ranks to go her own way by the later 1820s. In the northern industrial area around Lille, however, the typical "North Sea" H's of the 19th century were locally replicated, extending the neighboring Low Country pattern of population growth at least a little way across the French border. Meanwhile, unlike what happened in Belgium, trends for the sampled departments of France show marked distinctions between urban areas, whose populations generally expanded in the typical national shapes of northwestern Europe (as in Italy, though the country-wide pattern there was itself different), and rural departments, in which substantial population loss of both D and C types and also very recent tendencies towards population explosion have set local movements apart from the national model.

Hopefully some readers have been inspired or provoked enough by the preliminary regional analyses offered here to advance further in explaining how these variations came about and were shared by some local populations within these countries, though not by others.

FILLING OUT THE PATTERNS FOR CENTRAL EUROPE: GROWTH WITHIN "GERMANY," AUSTRIA, AND THE HAPSBURG EAST FROM WHEN THE RECORDS BEGIN

The modern spread of typically northwestern European growth patterns into central and eastern parts of the continent—unlike, say, France and Italy or Sweden and Finland—is one of the principal findings shown in Chapter 5, which explored national trends for Europe. Yet recurrent boundary changes in this part of the continent make it difficult to follow these developments country by country over long, unbroken spans of time. Thus, to examine more local movements for some of the historically pivotal and better-documented areas within once and future nations of this part of Europe fulfills two important functions. On the one hand, it completes outlines that data at the national level cannot provide. Simultaneously, it further elucidates interrelationships between overall societal and constituent regional trends of demographic increase or decline, for a different zone of Europe. Selected for such internal analysis are Germany, Austria, and possessions of the Hapsburg Empire that lay beyond the core Austrian holdings.

There was no nation of "Germany" until the 1860s. Subsequently, as the result of successive wars, the country enlarged, shrank, violently expanded, then was divided and pared back even more drastically a second time. Examined here are changes of population size in certain territories that were recorded as part of the German Empire between 1871 and 1914. Being able to follow demographic change with some consistency in the largest central European area possible is the objective, not political correctness as to whose territory it was. For many regions once incorporated in the Second Reich, the general pace of growth can be followed from 1816 or sooner to the present, or until quite recent time. For a few areas, principally parts of Prussia, estimates reach back to the early 1700s.

Table 6.4 summarizes the fitted trends to facilitate comparison and contrast from place to place.[15] Figure 6.4a and Figure 6.4b illustrate some of the graphings. The evidence in the table falls into four eras: (A) whatever information exists before the Napoleonic Wars; (B) changes across the 1800s between the

Table 6.4
The Demographic Regionalization of "Germany" in Four Eras

A. Early Growths on Record

Phase:	I	II	III	IV
	Württemberg 1639-1679 G 1651	Neumark 1700,1740 ?G 1670	East Prussia 1720-1800 G 1717	Silesia 1765-1804 G 1756
		Silesia 1740-1765 G 1673	Pomerania 1740-1800 G 1722	West Prussia 1774-1816 G 1762
		Württemberg 1697-1759 G 1680	Neumark 1740-1780 G 1730	
			Württemberg 1759-1802 E 1830	

B. Life after Napoleon

Earlier G Trends

Hohenzollern	1816-1900	G 1765
Alsace-Lorraine	1816-1880	G 1771
Oldenburg	1816-1852	G 1772
Brunswick	1816-1858	G 1773
Württemberg	1816-1871	G 1777
Bavaria	1816-1864	G 1780
Hanover	1816-1871	G 1788
Hesse-Nassau	1819-1864	G 1789
Thuringian Sts.	1816-1861	G 1790
Schleswig-Holst.	1816-1845	G 1791
Mecklenburg	1819-1880	G 1792
Hesse	1816-1871	G 1792
Baden	1816-1849	G 1793
Pomerania	1816-1837	G 1806
East Prussia	1816-1855	G 1807
Brandenburg	1816-1871	G 1807
Posen	1816-1875	G 1809
West Prussia	1816-1828	G 1819

Later G Trends

Oldenburg	1852-1875	G 1809
Schleswig-Holst.	1845-1875	G 1811
Posen	1831-1875	G 1811
Pomerania	1837-1910	G 1819
East Prussia	1855-1890	G 1822
West Prussia	1855-1900	G 1825
Brunswick	1858-1871	G 1829
Hesse-Nassau	1861-1890	G 1841

H Expansion

Westphalia	1816-1864	H 1731
Prussian Saxony	1816-1871	H 1746
Silesia	1816-1880	H 1753
Rhineland	1816-1864	H 1756
Kdm. of Saxony	1816-1871	H 1772

Table 6.4 (*Continued*)

C. During the Second and Third Reichs			D. Two Cold-War Germanies	

No E Trend, Only Decelerating Growth

Hohenzollern	1816-1900 G 1765	1900-1939 G 1833		
Brunswick	1875-1933 G 1858	1925-1939 G 1860	Saxony (E)	1950-1971 D 1903
Kdm. of Saxony	1871-1910 H 1835	1939-1950 G 1878		

One E Trend, Over by World War I:

Westphalia	1864-1910 E 1903	1910-1939 G 1880	N. Rhine-West.	1950-1980 G 1923
Rhineland	1864-1900 E 1907	1900-1939 G 1874	Saarland	1946-1970 G 1924
Schleswig-H.	1855-1910 E 1924	1910-1939 G 1849	Schleswig-H.	1939-1980 G 1928
Hesse-Nassau	1864-1910 E 1925	1900-1939 G 1876	Rh.-Palatinate	1946-1970 G 1926
Hanover	1864-1900 E 1926	1900-1939 G 1870	Lower Saxony	1939-1980 G 1927
Oldenburg	1871-1900 E 1932	1900-1939 G 1879		
Hesse	1861-1910 E 1930	1925-1939 G 1880	Hesse	1939-1980 G 1926

Two E Trends, Including the Inter-War Period:

Brandenburg	1871-1910 E 1910	1910-1939 E 1974	Brandenburg (E)	1939-1971 G 1857
Thuringian Sts.	1861-1900 E 1923	1910-1939 E 1986	Thuringia (E)	1946-1971 D 1887
Baden	1849-1910 E 1930	1910-1939 E 1983	Baden-Württ.	1946-1970 G 1936
Bavaria	1864-1910 E 1933	1910-1939 E 1980	Bavaria	1939-1980 G 1923
Silesia	1880-1910 E 1936	1910-1939 E 1988	(to Poland)	
Posen	1864-1910 E 1940	(to Poland)		
Württemberg	1871-1910 E 1941	1910-1939 E 1980		
West Prussia	1890-1910 E 1942	1910-1933 E 1991	(to Poland)	
Alsace-Lorraine	1871-1910 E 1951	(to France)		
Mecklenburg	1880-1910 E 1968	1910-1939 E 1979	Mecklenburg (E)	1946-1971 D 1894

Only One Late E:

East Prussia	1855-1890 G 1822	1890-1933 E 1979	(to Poland)	
Pomerania	1816-1900 G 1814	1900-1933 E 1982	(to Poland)	
Prussian Saxony	1871-1910 H 1789	1910-1939 E 1984	Sax.-Anhalt (E)	1946-1971 D 1903

Source: Note 15.

Figure 6.4a
Three Centuries of Demographic Growth and Decline in Regions of Germany: Württemberg and Some Early-Documented Parts of Prussia

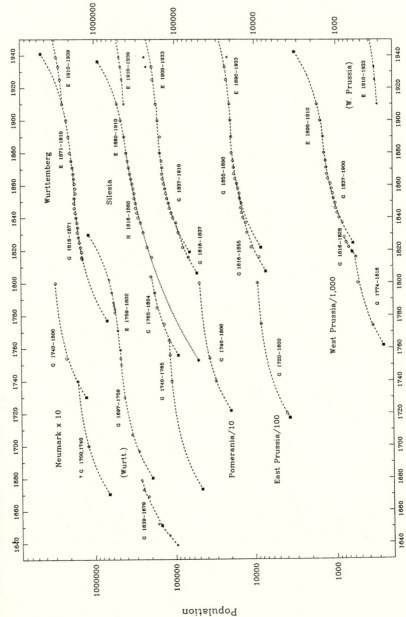

Source: Note 15.

208

Figure 6.4b
Three Centuries of Demographic Growth and Decline in Regions of Germany:
Westphalia, Rhineland, the Two Saxonies, Bavaria, and Thuringia

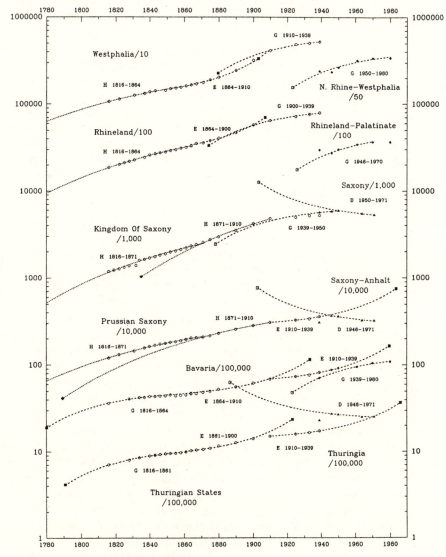

Source: Note 15.

Congress of Vienna and the consolidation of most of the rest of Germany through Prussian leadership; (C) the demographic growth of this enlarged Germany, somewhat pared by the Versailles Treaty, until the Third Reich took her to war again in 1939; and (D) the expansion—and contraction—of the divided peoples of West and East Germany in their reduced domain following World War II.[16]

Evidence from before 1800, most of it from territory that was being consolidated under Prussia, shows trends almost universally in G form, punctuated by the wars of the period. Certain parallels in the timing of these curves appear, part A of Table 6.4 and Figure 6.4a indicate. Sometimes these are just regional in nature; sometimes they link principalities from disparate parts of "Germany." Württemberg (the southwestern area around Stuttgart) displays an exceptional E trend for the second half of the 19th century. This, interestingly, resembles the comparably accelerating curve for England 1726–1806. Did Württemberg acquire this pattern of demographic expansion and put it to work economically, the same way England did?

Unlike England and other core North Sea countries, however, Württemberg did not then experience H-type expansion across the bulk of the 19th century. Part B of Table 6.4 shows, however, that other territories of Germany did: Westphalia and Rhineland in the West and Silesia and the two Saxonies in the East, from 1816 to about 1870. These H paths resemble those of England, Scotland, Denmark, the Netherlands, and Belgium following Waterloo (Table 5.1). For other documented parts of "Germany," G growth was the norm for this era, flatter (earlier in base year) in some regions than in others.

Did the German regional H trends of the 19th century accompany the same kind of economic development that was characteristic of several countries of northwestern Europe at the time? The answer is uncertain. On the one hand, Westphalia, Rhineland, and Silesia followed their H patterns with E growth up to World War I. In the latter they accompanied almost all other German territories and likewise the national population (part C of the table). This sequence is what England went through considerably earlier, first in 1686–1726, then in 1726–1806, not contemporaneously (Table 5.1 in Chapter 5). On the other hand, in the Kingdom of Saxony and Prussian Saxony H's for 1816–1871 were both followed by further H's for 1871–1910, parallel to or even steeper than comparable current trends in England. Some especially fertile opportunities for insight into relationships between demographic expansion and economic change would seem to exist in comparisons and contrasts of these five German regions.

Between the global wars of the 20th century (the second column of part C in Table 6.4), populations of territories in the West from Hesse northwards down the Rhine to the Danish border and in the Kingdom of Saxony expanded in G form. In contrast, slow-starting if accelerating increase was the norm elsewhere, generating by its majority among regions the national E for 1910–1950.[17] What economic, social, and perhaps political differences followed such lines of demarcation across this most dangerously expansionist country of Europe?

Finally, after World War II, G growth typical of many other European societies of late permeated the *Länder* of the Federal Republic. In the East, in contrast, demographic decline from the end of the war into the 1970s along the familiar D trajectory was almost as general: in Saxony, Thuringia, Mecklenburg, and Saxony-Anhalt, with base years for the formula all between 1887 and 1903. Only Brandenburg, the region of Berlin, experienced growth—in a G path, though this was much flatter than what was common in the West.

As a country, Austria never shared the H-type growth of the 19th century that Table 5.1 shows for Germany, Switzerland, and the Czech lands around her. Her population did display some signs of accelerating E expansion. Unlike the usual case in northwestern Europe, however, that tendency to explode was neither preceded nor followed by an H trend. This Austrian national sequence of G-E-E-G much resembled the regional patterns just observed for nearby eastern and southern Germany. Table 6.5 compares the movements for the provinces of Austria with each other and with the trends for Austria as a whole. Figure 6.5 illustrates some of these paths graphically (Klein 1973, 77, 105; Mitchell 1992, 46).

In the mining region of Styria, from 1617 (the eve of the Thirty Years War) to 1700 (when the Turks had been repulsed from Hungary), population increased along a G path with its base year back at 1571. This pattern suggests that the tentative G trend proposed for Austria as a whole in Table 5.1, though based only on estimations for 1600 and 1700, is not wildly incorrect. That seems even more likely when the second column of part A of Table 6.5 is examined. Across the early 1700s, population increases all over Austria—from Vorarlberg in the westward-running panhandle next to Switzerland to Burgenland eastwards along the Hungarian border—quite clearly unfolded closely together.

Much the same kind of parallelism then also held true during the later 1700s, as the clustering of G trends in Phase III of the table indicates. Here, however, Styria and the Tirol did not participate in the new growth; they just continued their G trends of Phase II instead. Around the turn of the century, though, Styria and Carinthia together in the south and also Salzburg in the northwest somehow saw their populations decay in the familiar D form. How that happened in these particular provinces but not others will have to be solved by local historians. Were the costs of the Napoleonic Wars especially heavy for these regions?

Between the defeat of Bonaparte and World War I, more internal variety appeared in the demographic history of Austria, part B of the table shows. Up through the middle of the 19th century (Phase V), populations in all eight provinces increased. In Lower Austria and neighboring Styria, however, very parallel H trends emerged, contrasting with the again largely similar G's of the other six regions (and Austria as a whole). Lower Austria (including Vienna) had, of any province, the highest proportion of its population employed outside forestry and agriculture in the 19th century (Helczmanovzski 1979, 35). How was Styria tied into this industrialization? Once again, the distribution of regional H patterns in population increase seems to associate locally with economic development.

After a short G-shaped burst in 1840–1857, which was shared only by Bur-

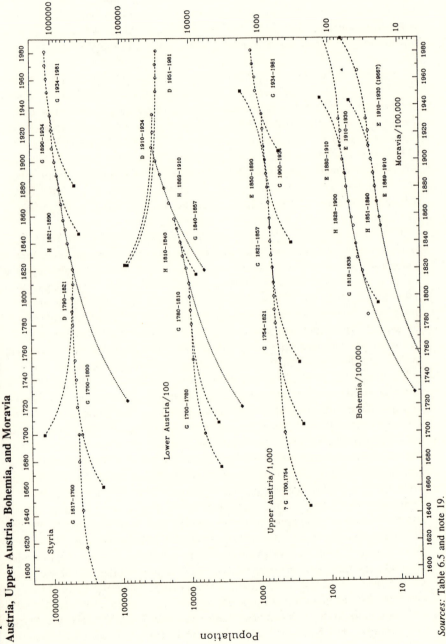

Figure 6.5
Population Trends in Five Parts of Austria-Hungary since 1617: Styria, Lower Austria, Upper Austria, Bohemia, and Moravia

Sources: Table 6.5 and note 19.

Table 6.5
Trends of Population Size in Areas of Austria

A. Through the Napoleonic Wars

Phase:	I	II	III	IV
AUSTRIA	1600,1700 ?G 1544	1700,1754 ?G 1665	1754-1821 G 1704	
Styria	1617-1700 G 1571	1700-1800 G 1661		1800-1821 D 1700
Upper Austria		1700,1754 ?G 1645	1754-1821 G 1706	
Salzburg		1700,1754 ?G 1635	1754,1780 ?G 1688	1780-1821 D 1720
Vorarlberg		1700,1754 ?G 1646	1780-1810 G 1736	
Tirol		1700-1821 G 1656		
Carinthia		1700,1754 ?G 1647	1754-1790 G 1683	1790-1821 D 1724
Lower Austria		1700-1780 G 1675	1780-1810 G 1708	
Burgenland		1700,1754 ?G 1681	1754-1810 G 1714	

B. From the Congress of Vienna to Versailles

Phase:	V	VI	VII
AUSTRIA	1821-1857 G 1784	1840-1880 E 1906	1880-1910 E 1936
Lower Austria	1810-1840 H 1719	1840-1857 G 1817	1869-1910 H 1820
Styria	1821-1890 H 1724		1890-1934 G 1847
Upper Austria	1821-1857 G 1752		1850-1890 E 1951
Salzburg	1821-1850 G 1751		1850-1890 E 1935
Tirol	1821-1850 G 1744		1857-1900 E 1955
Burgenland	1810-1857 G 1767	1857-1910 G 1814	
Carinthia	1821-1880 G 1780		1857-1910 E 1961
Vorarlberg	1821-1850 G 1791		1857-1910 E 1935

C. Since World War II

Phase:	VIII	IX	X
AUSTRIA	1923-1961 G 1847	1961-1990 G 1897	
Lower Austria	1910-1934 D 1824	1951-1981 D 1824	
Burgenland	1910-1981 D 1830		
Upper Austria	1890-1934 G 1839	1934-1981 G 1907	
Styria	1890-1934 G 1847	1951-1981 G 1883	
Carinthia		1934-1981 G 1901	
Vorarlberg	1923-1961 E 1973		1961-1981 G 1948
Salzburg	1923-1951 E 1964	1951-1971 E 1997	1961-1981 G 1940
Tirol	1910-1951 E 1974	1951-1971 E 1992	1961-1981 G 1940

Sources: Klein 1973, 77, 105; Mitchell 1992, 46.

genland (Phase VI), Lower Austria, which embraced the dominating imperial city, Vienna, took on H-shaped expansion again for 1869–1910. How did the intervening 1840–1857 G path between H's in the capitol region relate to the political and social events around 1848, which shook the Hapsburg empire significantly? Austria as a whole meanwhile experienced population explosion 1840–1880 and again 1880–1920. Such accelerating increase via the E curve appeared in five other provinces as of the 1850s. Upper Austria, Salzburg, the Tirol, Vorarlberg, and Carinthia were all slightly more rural than Styria. What demographic and related economic or cultural processes were at work to make their populations expand so differently, more like most regions of Germany (Table 6.4) than the heartland of their own country in Lower Austria and Styria? What did their experience share with the life of southern Germany that conditions in Lower Austria, Styria, and Burgenland did not?

Pursuing such cross-national relationships further, one can perceive from the time of World War I into the recovery years after World War II (in Phase VIII of the table) new, second-wave E trends in the westernmost provinces of Austria: Vorarlberg, Tirol, and Salzburg. These movements closely copied accelerations of the same type for the period 1910–1939 in Bavaria, Württemburg, and Baden across the border in southern Germany (part C of Table 6.4). The regions of northwestern Germany no longer experienced E trends in this era. What was it that some parts of Germany and Austria shared, which other portions of their own countries did not, that might generate such demographic similarities? In Salzburg and the Tirol still another wave of E surges appeared in 1951–1971, unlike anything in Germany but similar to the 1910–1970 E curve found in neighboring Switzerland (Table 5.1). Beginning in the 1960s, though, the populations of the Tirol, Vorarlberg, and Salzburg—again all moving together—finally bailed out of their sequence of explosions into G tracks of swiftly decerating growth. Once more these movements resembled what happened in nearby Bavaria and Baden-Württemberg, rather earlier, at the time of World War II, and more contemporaneously in Switzerland over the years 1970–1990.

Meanwhile, Lower Austria and Burgenland began at the time of World War I to *lose* population in D trends. These lasted at least into the 1980s. That the D for Lower Austria 1951–1981 is almost perfectly parallel to that for 1910–1934, but noticeably *lower*, presents stark statistical testimony as to what the Austrians did with Vienna's once-numerous Jews. Why these two particular provinces within all of Austria began to lose population at the time of World War I and along very parallel D paths, however, is a problem to be solved elsewhere.[18] The demographic decline of Lower Austria can be expected to reflect, at least in part, the dissolution of the complex empire of which Vienna had been capital.

In Upper Austria, Styria, and Carinthia, on the other hand, new G expansion—along largely similar tracks—has been the norm over recent decades. That has been the pattern also followed by Austria as a whole.

Local growth within Austria thus throws further insight upon European population history in several ways. To begin with, it shows how modern demographic movements and associated economic and social change began to erode the relatively homogeneous, nationwide succession of G increases that had prevailed up to about 1800, over an era of relative uniformity that probably lasted as much as two centuries—since before the Thirty Years War. First, demographic decay came to three regions across the early 1800s, the period of prolonged and costly conflict against France. Then—in the 19th century—Lower Austria and Styria, only a small minority of the eight provinces, managed the H expansion that has often been found associated with economic development in Europe and other parts of the world. As in the French experience with the industrial region around Lille and perhaps also the department of the Seine (Paris), this local H growth in Austria occurred within a country whose total population never advanced in that form.

In most parts of Austria, however, the years of the late 19th century and early 20th century witnessed the kinds of E accelerations of population size that have been discovered to be common in regions of nearby southern Germany. Cross-national comparisons, now including Austria, sharpen perception of the ways in which—according to patterns of population growth—southern and eastern portions of Europe departed from what has been observed in England, Scotland, Denmark, the Netherlands, and northwestern Germany. Demographic increase in much of central Europe—including most of Austria and Germany—behaved, in the early years of this present century, much in the fashion associated since World War II with "Third World" or "developing" countries; and in several places such patterns persisted as late as about 1970. These findings begin to build a rather different interpretative framework within which to decide how "demographic transition," a lately fashionable subject for students of population, spread across the peoples of the world via changes in fertility and mortality and making a living.

The Hapsburg Empire also controlled—and counted—the populations of regions that later became parts of Czechoslovakia, Hungary, Yugoslavia, Poland, and Romania. The series available for these diverse and so doggedly combative peoples are sometimes not very long; nevertheless, they helpfully extend the understanding that has been building here of how demographic growth unfolded across central and eastern Europe. Table 6.6 sets up comparison of the probable trends. Figure 6.5 plots examples from Bohemia and Moravia.[19]

The modern patterning for the area has been quite simple: Some regional populations have expanded in a fashion previously witnessed for parts of Germany. Others have followed sequences typical of nearby areas of Austria. The most numerous subpopulations of southeastern Europe, however, have either increased like neighboring—mostly Balkan—peoples in Bulgaria, Greece, Albania, and Poland or enlarged in the way that has been observed for Hungary. The table highlights these groupings and their national prototypes.

The Czech peoples of Bohemia and Moravia multiplied in H form through

Table 6.6
Comparing Trends across Southeastern Europe

A. German Pattern

GERMANY	CZECH LANDS	Bohemia	Moravia	Austrian Silesia
	1818-1851 G 1790	1818-1838 G 1795		
1816-1864 H 1743	1851-1890 H 1739	1828-1900 H 1729	1851-1890 H 1725	1857-1890 G 1834
1864-1910 E 1923	1880-1910 E 1945	1880-1910 E 1946	1869-1910 E 1944	1880-1910 E 1932
1910-1950 E 1977	1910-1930 E 2004	1910-1930 E 2005	1910-1930 E 1992	1910-1930 E 1978
1939-1990 G 1905	1947-1990 G 1913			

B. Austrian Pattern

AUSTRIA	Carniola/Slovenia	Görz, etc./Maritime	Dalmatia	ROMANIA
1754-1821 G 1694	1786,1818 ?D 1723			
1821-1857 G 1784	1818-1838 G 1786	1786-1857 G 1800		
1840-1880 E 1910				
1880-1910 E 1934	1828-1910 E 1963	1869-1910 E 1930	1869-1900 E 1927	1844-1912 E 1918
1923-1961 G 1847			1890-1910 G 1863	
1961-1990 G 1897	1948-1961 G 1909			1948-1990 G 1928
	1961-1981 G 1929			

C. Balkan Pattern

BULGARIA	Serbia	Croatia & Slavonia	Voivodina	GREECE
	1840-1863 G 1823			1843-1861 G 1815
	1884-1910 H 1839	1880-1910 G 1860		1870-1907 G 1856
1893-1920 G 1881	1921-1948 G 1908	1910-1931 G 1903	1921-1953 G 1855	1920-1940 G 1914
1920-1956 G 1907	1948-1981 G 1924	1948-1981 G 1910	1953-1981 G 1914	1951-1971 G 1912
1956-1990 G 1912				1971-1990 G 1935

POLAND	Slovakia	Bosnia & Herc.	Montenegro	Kosovo
1823-1863 G 1793		1879-1910 G 1873	1857-1910 G 1854	
1863-1931 G 1863	1890-1921 G 1844	1921,1931 ?G 1902	1910-1931 G 1902	1921-1948 G 1918
1946-1990 G 1931	1947-1980 G 1933	1948-1981 G 1939	1948-1981 G 1935	1948-1961 G 1943
				1961-1981 G 1964

Macedonia	ALBANIA
1921,1931 ?E 1947	1945-1960 E 1959
1948-1953 ?E -	1955-1990 G 1964
1953-1981 E 1994	

D. Hungarian Pattern

HUNGARY	Galicia & Bukovina	Siebenbürgen	Ruthenia	Donau-Tisza
1793-1817 G 1753				
1817-1880 G 1808	1828-1857 G 1788	1818-1869 G 1784		
1880-1910 H 1790	1857-1890 H 1780	1880-1910 H 1779		
	1890-1910 H 1808		1880-1910 H 1823	1880-1910 H 1836
1910-1941 E 1977				
1949-1990 G 1897				

Right Donau	Right Tisza	Tisza-Maros Plain	Left Donau	Left Tisza
1880-1910 H 1750	1880-1910 H 1753	1880-1910 H 1753	1880-1910 H 1765	1880-1910 H 1800

Source: Note 19.

most of the 19th century, like the population of Germany 1816–1864. More specifically, the H-type growth found in Westphalia, Rhineland, the two Saxonies, and Silesia (part B of Table 6.4) extended into neighboring Bohemia and Moravia as well as more distant Lower Austria and Styria within the Hapsburg holdings (phase V of Table 6.5). When Bohemia and Moravia thereafter went into the two successive modern E surges typical of Germany as a whole, several German territories, the western regions of Austria, and Switzerland in the late 1800s and early 1900s, Austrian Silesia followed suit.

The possible loss of population in Carniola (broadly, the area of today's Slovenia) between 1786 and 1818 along what might be a D curve with base year at 1723 (part B of Table 6.6) mirrors closely what Table 6.5 has indicated for Salzburg, Styria, and Carinthia in neighboring Austria. Highly parallel population *decline* in this period spread across a block of four contiguous Hapsburg-controlled regions from Salzburg, up next to Bavaria in the north, to Carniola, lying behind Fiume on the Adriatic. What did the peoples of this particular vertical strip of Austria-Hungary share to make them atrophy this way in the era of the wars against Napoleon?

Beginning in the early 1800s, Carniola, the neighboring area of Görz, Gradisca, and Triest (bordering Venice and the top of the Adriatic Sea), and Dalmatia southward down the coast likewise shared the kind of G trend that was typical of Austria's population to 1857, as part B of Table 6.6 summarizes. Across the later decades of the 19th century up to World War I, down the Adriatic is similarly found the kind of E surge typical of Austria in that period. Dalmatia later was made part of Croatia; but the growth of Slovenia (roughly what had been Carniola) after World War II still visibly followed quite closely the pattern of the population of Austria, with a second G trend that has resembled the most recent growth evident in the mountainous "panhandle" areas of Vorarlberg, Salzburg, and the Tirol. For some reason the national population of Romania shared the kind of E explosion evident in these Adriatic regions leading up to World War I, and also the Carniolan G curve of recent years.[20] This may be just coincidence; or it may not.

The "Balkan" pattern of part C of Table 6.6 is distinct from both the "German" and the "Austrian" ones. With four exceptions (an H in Serbia 1884–1910, and E's in Macedonia and Albania around World War II),[21] all growth across a large triangle of southeastern Europe from Croatia eastward to Bulgaria and south into Greece has taken the G form, and the G form only. The same has probably been true in the heartland of Poland, though some of the peripheral regions of the 1939 nation, both west and east, behaved differently.[22] There has existed much insightful parallelism, furthermore, among the G-shape demographic expansions of the diverse peoples who have inhabited this substantial area of southeastern Europe. To what extent have these similarities resulted from common ways in which practices affecting mortality and/or fertility have spread—even across bitterly clashing cultures? What role has been played by the economic development (or retardation of development) of these types of areas?

In Hungary and Carpathian regions northwards from Siebenbürgen (Transylvania) into Bukovina, Ruthenia, and Galicia, in contrast, steady and only slowly decelerating H expansion was ubiquitous in the late 1800s and early 1900s, as part D of Table 6.6 indicates. In the German Empire (Table 6.4), just the two Saxonies had H growth this late. In Austria, only the area around Vienna showed something like this pattern. The Right and Left Bank regions of the Danube in Hungary lie just downriver from Vienna, followed southeastward by the Right Bank of the Tisza and the Tisza-Maros Plain. Further eastward come the Left Tisza region and Siebenbürgen, and northward come Bukovina and Galicia.[23] Thus, over the years 1880–1910 H-type demographic growth reached outward to the south and east from Vienna, Austria-Hungary's capitol, across all of modern Hungary into the Carpathian regions and south into Serbia—through one contiguous heartland of what seems to have been turn-of-the-century development in this core of southeastern Europe. More accurately perhaps, Vienna and its Lower Austrian hinterland probably grew as this Danubian-Carpathian zone that they dominated prospered and expanded demographically in ways no longer found in the Czech lands by this time, rare in Germany and Austria, and missing in the encircling territories of what became Yugoslavia, Albania, Greece, Bulgaria, Romania, and Poland. Once again the H trend is associated with a coherent regionalism of likely economic development.

Overall there is beginning to develop a larger-scale picture of H-type population growth in Europe that, across time, spread southeastward from the countries around the North Sea up the Rhine and the Elbe, then down the Danube. Outposts of this distinctive zone of population growth appeared along the southern flank of its trans-European march: in the industrial centers of northern France, northern Italy, and Switzerland, and in Norway and then Sweden. The Austro-Hungarian material, for all its limitations, proves very helpful in systematizing further just what kinds of expansion have occurred in what kinds of places during the modern demographic development of Europe.

BRIDGING EUROPE AND ASIA: DEMOGRAPHIC INCREASE SINCE 1719 IN THE LAND OF THE TSARS

This sample survey of regional demographic growth patterns across Europe ultimately leads eastward into Russia. Historically that enormous country expanded to contain markedly diverse peoples who built lives out of forests, mountains, plains, and deserts that stretch thousands of miles from the Baltic to the Bering Straights, from the Arctic Ocean to the Caspian Sea. As a whole, the population of Imperial Russia and then the Soviet Union enlarged from 1762 through 1939 in a series of H trends without the E explosions or G growths found elsewhere in Europe. How did local demographic increase *within* the huge and varied territory of Russia contribute to this unusual national growth sequence? Did the distinctive local demographic patterns that have been observed spreading across Europe from the northwest to the southeast ever manage to penetrate the borders of this vast, strange land? Or, as a case of continental expansion in settlement and control, did population growth in Russia more closely resemble what happened in the United States and Canada than anything observed in Europe?

Under the tsars, as in ancient Rome, the principal purposes of counting heads (or "souls") were to raise taxes and troops. As elsewhere across history, individuals tried to slip through both these nets as best they could. From 1719 onward, however—beginning under Peter the Great during the Northern War against Sweden—a widely useful enumeration of males exists, province by province across the country. Russian scholars have collected and refined these series.[24] Table 6.7 summarizes the sequences of regional patterns that emerge from this survey, including *population* trends for selected economic regions of the Soviet Union up to 1970, retroactive to 1897 or 1851 as calculated by modern specialists on the U.S.S.R.[25] These primarily concern expansion into the East: the Urals, Siberia, the Caucasus, and Central Asia. In several regions of the West, two world wars and Stalin's program of agricultural collectivization caused drastic drops in population level, making reliable trending difficult. Still, movements before and after 1914 in some relatively less affected zones of European Russia can be considered as well. Many areas were acquired by Russia during the period studied, and their data begin well after 1719. Figures 6.6a, 6.6b, and 6.6c plot some of the trends in male population that have been fitted for the table. Figures 6.7a and 6.7b display movements for males and for total population in Russia's eastern frontiers.

Across almost seventy diverse territories of tsarist Russia and the U.S.S.R. one can readily observe diffusions of the regional patterning that has been found in the rest of Europe. Most simply, a band of six northwestern districts from present-day Lithuania, Latvia, and Estonia through southern Finland to the White Sea produced sequences of population growths, first G's and then an E in the late 1800s, that closely resembled movements in Prussian areas of northeastern Germany nearby (part A of Table 6.7 and Figure 6.6a).

Comparably, demographic growth sequences that included H-form increase extended from Hungary, Serbia, Galicia, and Ruthenia (Table 6.6) into western Russia. From Bessarabia, Kherson (the Odessa region), and Taurida (the Crimea and its hinterland) at the Black Sea to Pskov, Novgorod, and St. Petersburg just behind the Baltic frontier in the Northeast stretched a band of fourteen provinces that in the middle to late 19th century acquired this slowly slowing form of demographic expansion.[26] Mostly this followed earlier G trends.[27] Were these regional H growths once again associated with economic development, here in the age of Witte and Stolypin? Yet few E trends preceded or followed those provincial movements, unlike what happened in the nations and regions of northwestern Europe. What does that signify about the nature and origins of the

Table 6.7
Regional Patterns of Growth in Tsarist Russia and the Soviet Union from 1719

A. From the Baltic to the White Sea

1) Russian Regions

Courland
1815-1850	G	1784
1850-1897	G	1815
1885-1914	E	1951

Viborg
1762-1811	G	1740

Kovno
1863-1897	G	1848
1885-1914	E	1946

Livonia
1762-1811	G	1740
1811-1857	G	1786
1857-1897	G	1844
1885-1914	E	1928

Estonia
1762-1815	G	1731
1815-1857	G	1781
1833-1885	E	1911
1885-1914	E	1939

Olonets
1719-1815	G	1683
1815-1850	G	1774
1850-1885	G	1822
1857-1914	E	1934

Archangel
1719-1762	G	1618
1782-1811	G	1713
1815-1850	G	1783
1850-1885	G	1828
1863-1914	E	1927

2) Parallels in Northeastern Germany (from Table 6.4)

West Prussia
1774-1816	G	1756
1855-1900	G	1828
1890-1910	E	1942

Neumark
1740-1780	G	1730

All Brandenburg
1816-1871	G	1807
1871-1910	E	1910
1910-1939	E	1974

Pomerania
1740-1800	G	1722
1816-1900	G	1814
1900-1933	E	1982

East Prussia
1720-1800	G	1717
1855-1890	G	1822
1890-1933	E	1979

Posen
1855-1890	G	1820
1864-1910	E	1940

Mecklenburg
1816-1890	G	1803
1880-1910	E	1968

B. Russia's Main Western Frontier: From the Black Sea to the Gulf of Bothnia

Bessarabia
1833,1850	?G	1744
1857-1885	H	1824
1885-1914	H	1858

Podolia
1811-1857	G	1783
1857-1885	G	1841
1885-1914	H	1856

Kherson
1762-1811	E	1779
1815-1857	H	1740
1857-1885	G	1864
1885-1914	H	1867

Minsk
1811-1833	E	1862
1833-1857	C	1924
1857-1885	E	1889
1885-1914	H	1867

Mogilev
1781-1833	G	1743
1833-1857	C	1944
1857-1885	H	1805
1885-1914	H	1878

Taurida (Crimea, etc.)
1795-1857	G	1798
1863-1914	H	1867

Volyn
1815-1857	G	1766
1857-1885	H	1803
1885-1914	H	1872

Grodno
1811-1850	G	1787
1857-1914	H	1834

Vilno
1815-1850	G	1795
1885-1914	H	1847

Vitebsk
1762-1863	G	1720
1863-1914	H	1841

Novgorod
1762-1815	G	1738
1815-1857	G	1779
1857-1885	G	1835
1885-1914	H	1813

St. Petersburg
1762-1811	G	1738
1811-1857	G	1797
1863,1885	?H	1820
1885-1914	H	1872

Pskov
1744-1857	G	1728
1857-1885	H	1793
1885-1914	H	1831

Kiev
1811-1857	G	1781
1857-1885	G	1849
1885-1914	H	1859

Table 6.7 *(Continued)*

C. The Heartland of Muscovy

Moscow
1719-1762 G 1606
1782-1815 G 1738
1811-1857 G 1775
1857-1897 G 1853

Tver
1744-1815 G 1735
1811-1857 G 1772
1850-1897 G 1819
1863-1914 ?E 1932

Kaluga
1744-1815 G 1714
1815-1863 G 1764
1857-1897 G 1823

Smolyensk
1844-1857 G 1730
1857-1885 G 1824
1885-1914 E 1917

Ryazan
1719-1744 ?G 1678
1762-1815 G 1736
1815-1857 G 1786
1857-1897 G 1830

Tula
1719-1762 G 1695
1762-1815 G 1736
1815-1857 G 1765
1857-1897 G 1824

Nizhegorod
1744-1795 G 1720
1795-1850 G 1757
1850-1897 G 1829
1885-1914 E 1931

Vladimir
1762-1815 G 1719
1811-1857 G 1759
1857-1885 G 1821
1863-1914 E 1928

Kostrom
1719-1762 G 1663
1762-1850 G 1717
1850-1897 G 1829
1885-1914 E 1932

D. The Old Southern Frontier above the Steppes

Poltava
1744-1782 G 1696
1782-1857 H 1643
1857-1897 G 1846

Chernigov
1744-1857 H 1639
1863-1897 G 1850
1885-1914 ?E 1925

Kursk
1719-1762 G 1662
1762-1857 H 1680
1857-1897 G 1833

Tambov
1719-1762 H 1624
1762-1857 H 1708
1857-1897 G 1841
1885-1914 E 1934

Orel
1762-1850 H 1673
1857-1897 G 1837
1885-1914 E 1929

Penzen
1762-1850 H 1678
1850-1897 G 1826

Voronezh
1744-1795 G 1756
1795-1850 H 1730
1850-1897 G 1835

Simbirsk
1719-1762 G 1685
1762-1857 H 1694
1863-1897 G 1835

Saratov
1744-1782 G 1762
1782-1811 H 1758
1811-1857 G 1807
1863-1897 G 1844
1885-1914 E 1927

Samara
1863-1897 G 1854
1885-1914 E 1922

Orenburg
1744-1782 G 1748
1782-1811 H 1752
1811-1850 G 1811
1863-1914 H 1852

E. The Old Northeastern Forest Frontier

Yaroslav
1744-1850 H 1588
1850-1897 G 1807
1885-1914 E 1946

Vologod
1744-1811 H 1637
1815-1857 H 1715
1857-1897 G 1838
1885-1914 E 1928

Vyatsk
1719-1762 G 1724
1762-1815 H 1693
1815-1857 G 1765
1857-1897 G 1839
1885-1914 E 1933

Kazan
1762-1815 H 1667
1815-1850 G 1791
1850-1897 G 1838
1885-1914 E 1932

Perm
1719-1762 G 1720
1762-1815 H 1710
1833-1857 G 1810
1857-1897 G 1844
1885-1914 E 1925

Table 6.7 (Continued)

F. Pushing Southeastward across the Steppes

Yekaterinoslav	Kharkov	Don Military District	Astrakhan
1762-1795 G 1793	1744-1815 G 1749	1744-1782 G 1763	1815-1863 G 1784
1811-1857 G 1799	1815-1850 G 1776	1782-1815 G 1786	1863-1914 G 1878
1857-1897 G 1859	1857-1897 G 1849	1850,1863 ?G 1832	
	1885-1914 E 1925	1885-1914 G 1899	

G. Continental Expansion across Siberia

Tobolsk	Tomsk	Irkutsk	Siberia (Mitchell)	Tomsk + Irkutsk
1719-1762 G 1692	1744-1795 G 1748	1719-1815 G 1748		1744-1795 G 1746
1762-1795 G 1752	1815-1857 G 1807	1811-1857 G 1806	1851,1863 ?G 1808	1811-1857 G 1804
1815-1857 G 1800				

Ural Economic District	W. Siberia Econ. D.	E. Siberia Econ. D.	Far East Econ. D.	Siberia (Mitchell)	3 Siberian Econ. D.'s
1897,1926 ?G 1871	1851,1897 ?G 1864	1857,1897 ?G 1866		1885-1914 F .	1897-1939 F .
1926-1970 G 1916	1897-1970 G 1919	1926-1970 G 1928	1926-1970 G 1942		1926-1970 G 1926

H. Incorporating Explosive Populations in the Caucasus and Central Asia

North Caucasus E. D.	Transcaucasus E.D.	All "Caucasus"	Kazakh E.D./S.S.R.	Kazakh + Central Asia
1897-1939 H 1838		1851-1939 H 1861	1863,1885 ?G 1798	
	1897-1939 E 1948		1885-1914 H 1903	1897-1939 E 1952
	1939-1970 E 1982		1897,1926 ?E 1952	1939-1970 E 1966
1959,1970 ?G 1949	1970-1989 G 1951	1959,1970 ?G 1953	1939-1970 E 1966	
			1970-1989 G 1950	

Central Asia E.D.	Turkmen S.S.R.	Uzbek S.S.R.	Tadzhik S.S.R.	Kirghiz S.S.R.
1897-1939 E 1942	1926-1959 G 1912	1926-1959 G 1923	1926-1939 G 1927	1926-1959 G 1931
1926-1959 ?G 1924	1959-1989 H 1968	1959-1989 H 1974	1959-1989 H 1978	1959-1989 G 1966
1959-1989 H 1971				

Trends in other modern economic districts, where not disrupted severely by war, are related to the relevant tsarist provinces in the text and notes.

Source: Note 24.

Figure 6.6a
Numbers of Males in Some Provinces of Tsarist Russia:
The Far Northwest: The Baltic and Archangel

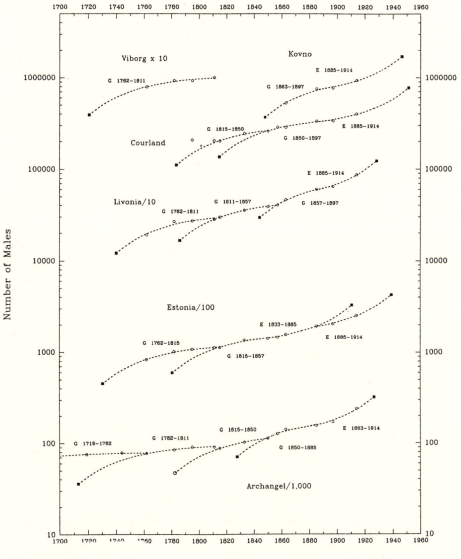

Source: Note 24.

Figure 6.6b
Numbers of Males in Some Provinces of Tsarist Russia: The Southwest

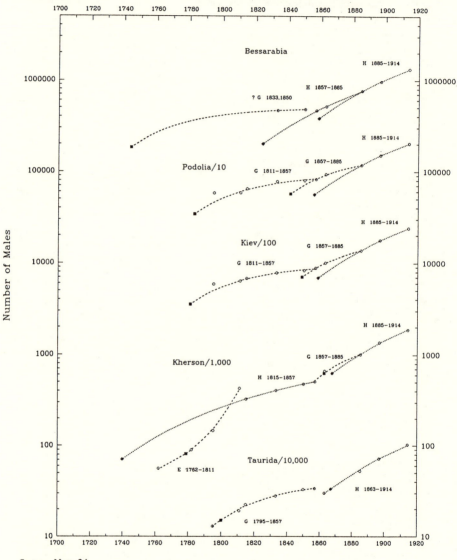

Source: Note 24.

Figure 6.6c
Number of Males in Some Provinces of Tsarist Russia: Some of the Old Southern Frontier above the Steppes

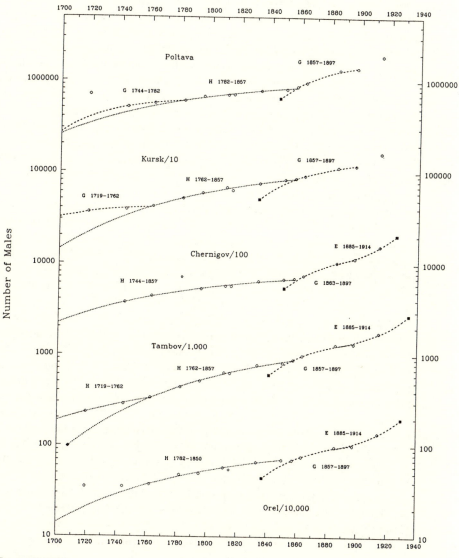

Source: Note 24.

development that occurred? How much of the H expansion, particularly in the southern half of this western belt, was due instead to the international grain trade, in which Russia participated vigorously in the late 1800s in competition with Canada, the United States, Argentina, and Australia?

The old southern frontier of Russia, on the other hand, experienced H-type demographic expansion a century earlier, by the middle or later 1700s.[28] Everywhere, more rapidly decelerating G patterns followed, though Orenburg, the jumping-off base for Central Asia at the southern end of the Urals, saw fresh H increase 1863–1914 while Tambov, Orel, Saratov, and Samara experienced accelerating growths around the turn of the century. A sequence of G-H-G-E resembling that of these four provinces likewise occurred in the old forest frontier north and east of Moscow: in Yaroslav, Vologod, Vyatsk, Kazan, and Perm (part E of the table). And part C of Table 6.7 shows how this E pattern of the late 1800s and early 1900s appeared, too, in some of the provinces of Russia's heartland around Moscow, where otherwise just series of G trends are evident from where local records begin to World War I.

Later in time, population numbers for the area embraced by the Central Economic Region of the modern Soviet Union—which included all or most of the former Tsarist provinces of Moscow, Kaluga, Ryazan, Tula, Smolyensk, Tver, Kostrom, Vladimir, and Yaroslav—for the years 1897, 1926, and 1939 indicate an H trend with a base year for the formula at about 1832 (Leasure and Lewis 1966, 5, 27). This track is almost identical to the H pattern for the nation as a whole over the same period (and for Serbia and the Donau-Tisza region of Hungary, or Voivodina, 1880–1910). Beginning in the 1890s, in short, the H-type demographic expansion found before that time in the more western regions of the country and neighboring areas of Austria-Hungary finally reached the Russian heartland. In several Russian provinces, moreover, this trend probably followed the kind of E phase that had preceded 19th century H growth during the industrialization of several countries and regions of more western Europe about a century before (Table 5.1).[29] Inspection of the 1897–1939 data elsewhere, moreover, shows that population in the neighboring economic region of Belorussia—composed of the old provinces of Grodno, Vilno, Minsk, Mogilev, and about half of Vitebsk—could easily also have increased in a quite parallel H path between 1926 and 1939, though the ravages of World War I and the subsequent Civil War that counterposed Reds, Whites, and Poles make it impossible to connect these points meaningfully with preceding 1897 or 1914 data (Leasure and Lewis 1966, 10, 27).

In the Southwest and South Economic Regions (respectively composed chiefly of what had been the provinces of Kiev, Podolia, and Volyn and constituting most of erstwhile Kherson and Taurida), meanwhile, parallel G trends with base years in the 1860s followed the H patterns of the three decades that led up to World War I (Leasure and Lewis, 12, 13, 27). The suggestion is that the national economic development that began in the last tsarist years and continued under the U.S.S.R. did not affect the populations of these southern areas in the same way as it did in the heartland around Moscow.[30] Further evidence from Soviet economic districts, finally, confirms that the turn-of-the-century H trend of the St. Petersburg, Pskov, and Novgorod area persisted into the 1920s. Comparably, the E paths of the Baltic zones (part A of Table 6.7) lasted to 1939 even if Estonia, Latvia, and Lithuania were now independent countries (Leasure and Lewis, 2, 3, 27). Because population numbers were driven down so much by forced collectivization between 1926 and 1939 in both the Volga and the Central Black Earth Economic Regions, it is impossible to say more about modern trends in this part of the nation since 1897.

Over the steppes across southern Russia, from the great bend of the Dnieper at Yekaterinoslav (Dnepropetrovsk), through Kharkov and the Don Military District into Astrakhan on the northern Caspian shore, stretched vast treeless grasslands that composed a loosely inhabited grazing frontier similar to the Great Plains of the United States or Canada. Demographic expansion in each of these territories (part F of Table 6.7) rose substantially over the long haul, more vigorously than in most of the tsarist provinces examined, but only along a series of successive G trends—as in the flatlands of North America.[31] The G's evident here for the half century up to 1897 are generally quite similar in timing to those of the older northern woodland and southern agricultural frontiers in part E and D of the table. It is just that other largely parallel G-shape trends for the early 19th century preceded them in Yekaterinoslav, Kharkov, the Don Military District, and Astrakhan rather than the H's of those sixteen provinces.

What these tsarist plains lacked, however, were the retrogressive successions of a steeper G by a flatter one that composed so distinctive a feature of demographic increase in the extensive grain-growing and grazing lands of the United States, Canada, Australia, and New Zealand. Was such overoptimistic settlement followed by a sharp-angled lowering of the trajectory of growth less likely to occur where one kind of people less totally replaced another? The Cossacks and Tartars remained substantial regional forces whereas the Plains Indians and the Australian Aboriginals did not. Or did the absence of overambitious, capped early growth *and* the persistence of earlier peoples both derive from a different way that investment and migration arrived on the steppes? Are we witnessing consequences of excessive growth stimulated by "the market" in contrast to less volatile governmentally promoted settlement?

Another loosely populated frontier for the land of the tsars lay over the Urals, in Siberia. Russian trappers, explorers, and traders pushed across this enormous, forbidding, lightly inhabited territory precisely as western Europeans started to colonize North America, establishing bases at Tobolsk in 1587, Tomsk 1604, Yeniseysk 1619, Jakutsk 1632, Irkutsk 1652, and at Ochotsk on the Pacific coast in 1649.

Originally, the population attracted to Siberia was meager. By 1719, however, the survey reported some 100,000 males in the *gubernia* of Tobolsk, 40,000 in Tomsk, and 27,000 still further east in the province of Irkutsk. Part G of Table 6.7 and Figure 6.7a show how these three regional populations swelled across

Figure 6.7a
The Eastern and Southeastern Regions of the Soviet Union: From the Urals to the Pacific: Colonizing Siberia

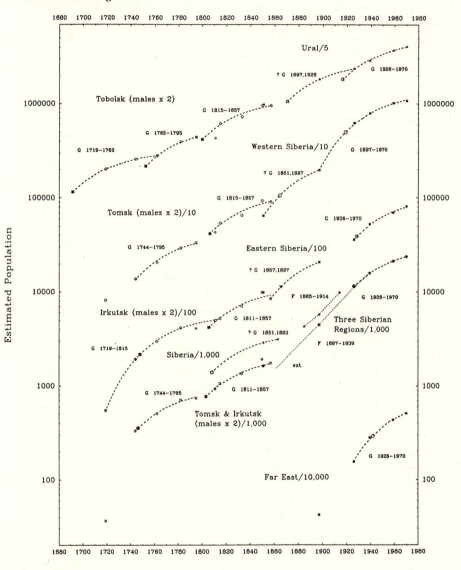

Source: Note 24.

the next century and a half.[32] This was always along G curves, as in most of the United States and Canada and all parts of Australia—three nations with lightly inhabited frontiers not unlike Siberia. Records for the modern economic regions of the U.S.S.R. that have incorporated parts of Siberia, furthermore, indicate that the G pattern of increase has continued to predominate in area after area also since the 1850s. In America, these local accumulations of demographic growth in G form could produce the F trend for aggregate populations, such as what Franklin first reported for the British American colonies in 1751. This kind of steady log-linear trend, however, has not been encountered in all of the demographic history of Europe that has been surveyed in these last two chapters. If such constant exponential growth, doubling about every twenty-three years, appeared anywhere in the Old World, should it not have emerged in Siberia?

It did. The data do not disappoint our interpretation. Tobolsk became part of the Ural economic region in the Soviet Union (along with Perm and Orenburg), and its local population numbers are hard to follow after Kabuzan's evidence runs out in 1857. But if we sum the three unambiguously Siberian economic regions of Western Siberia, Eastern Siberia, and the Far East, the numbers for 1897, 1926, and 1939 line up in what is almost exactly an F trend (in actuality, a slope of $e^{.0303}$). It is impossible to tell precisely how long before 1897 this F began, because to add up Tomsk and Irkutsk Provinces does not capture all 1851 population in Siberia beyond Tobolsk, as the data given for "Siberia" by Mitchell for 1851 and 1863 indicate.[33] Still, the F slope seems to have taken off from the preceding G about 1870, as backward projections of the 1897–1939 data for three Siberian economic regions from Leasure and Lewis and Mitchell's figures for Siberia 1885–1914 both suggest.[34] Such sustained exponential growth was in part fed by exiles from the chronic political disturbances and repressions of the late 1800s and early 1900s. By the 1920s, however, settlement in Siberia—forced and free—shifted over into the kind of decelerating G path indicated in the table.

In another sprawling economic region, the currently inflamed North Caucasus, the early years of this present century saw slowly decelerating H expansion of population instead, as part H of the table and the top plot in Figure 6.7b indicate. Another H growth, even steeper in slope, also probably occurred from 1885 through 1914 in the eastern steppe districts that were subsequently incorporated into the Kazakh S.S.R.: tsarist Uralsk, Turgai, Akmolinsk, and Semipalatinsk (Mitchell 1992, 58, 70). This tendency is shown ("Steppe Districts") near the bottom of Figure 6.7b. Data for 1863 and 1885, meanwhile, indicate a possible preceding G here, with base year at about 1798. Following the disturbances of World War II, it seems likely that G growth has again become the pattern for these territories, though rather later in Kazakhstan than in North Caucasus. Very much the same timing of recent G curve is found for the Transcaucasus economic region (Georgia, Armenia, and Azerbaydzan). In between, however, the populations of the Transcaucasus and the Kazakh S.S.R. exploded, probably in two successive E trends. It is possible that the North Caucasus (including

Figure 6.7b
The Eastern and Southeastern Regions of the Soviet Union: 19th Century
Conquests in the Caucasus and Central Asia

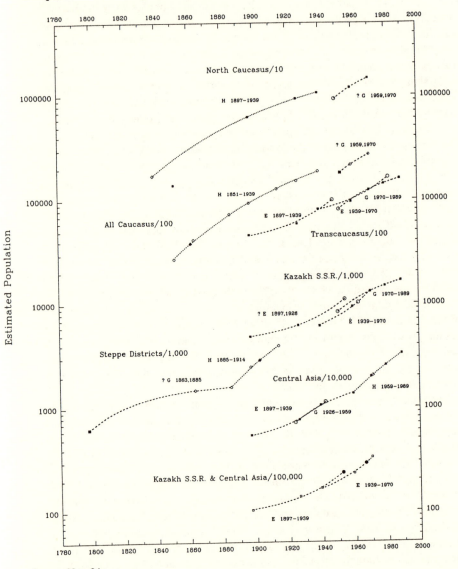

Source: Note 24.

Chechnya and Dagestan) shared the 1939–1970 movements, though not the preceding E across the first third of the century that was experienced by Transcaucasus, Central Asia, and probably Kazakhstan.

Most clearly, from 1897 through 1939 and again from the 1930s until about 1970, population increase in the Kazakh S.S.R. and the four republics of Central Asia collectively accelerated along successive E trajectories. Taking the regions separately, the E form in Kazakhstan is clear for the second period; in Central Asia, in contrast, the figure shows that what is more likely is a joint between a G for 1926–1959 and an H trend that followed. Each of the four S.S.R.'s separately can be shown to have experienced G growth for 1926–1959 and H expansion for 1959–1989. This transition, though, roughly allows an E for 1939–1970 not unlike that for Kazakhstan, thus making the combined pattern for the two large areas seem a good E fit. For just the economic district of Central Asia and its four component republics, however, the G then H sequence is patently more accurate, as the data from 1959 through 1989 demonstrate.[35]

Those demographic explosions from the Caucasus through Kazakhstan to Central Asia largely involved people who were non-Russian and Muslim. This differential demographic expansion has fed considerable concern about nationalism, conflict within the Red Army, threats to Russian minorities in Central Asia, dangers to sensitive military and industrial facilities, and so forth. Such tensions did not exactly disappear with the breakup of the U.S.S.R. The recent demographic increase in Central Asia, however, has become a decelerating one. It has slowed down, though, more quickly via G paths in North Caucasus, Transcaucasus, and Kazakhstan than the H trends to 1989 for the economic district of Central Asia and most of its republics indicate.

These many regional findings, which reach from Finland, Poland, and Romania to Alaska, further expand the ways in which local patterns carry our understanding of demographic growth beyond the indications of national trends. In the least, they permit substantial historical work on parts of Europe (and Asia) for which only recent or sporadic national data exist. Further, they make it possible to connect particular shapes of trend more tightly with the types of context in which they have appeared.

Most simply, constant exponential multiplication of the F sort has, as Franklin argued two and a half centuries ago, not been a European phenomenon. Since local records begin, only in the continental occupation of Siberia did such a trend appear anywhere between the Mediterranean and the Arctic, the North Atlantic and the Bering Straits.

The H type of persistent, only slowly slowing demographic expansion has more and more evidently been associated with economic development, probably in three somewhat similar but also rather different historical contexts. Before factory industrialization—as in England, the Dutch province of Holland, and Sweden by the later 1500s; Norway (and probably Portugal and Spain) a century later; or along Russia's old farm and forest frontiers beginning in the middle

1700s (parts D and E of Table 6.7)—agricultural improvement, rural industry, trade, and often urbanization allowed demographic increase without the drag of the G curve's rapid deceleration. More was produced, frequently by novel methods; and natural increase and migration rose to exploit the opportunity.

Similarly, modern industrialization allowed many European populations to grow for a while in H form before G deceleration set in after World War II. Some of these H's followed periods of population explosion that seem to be associated with early processes of "Industrial Revolution." Such H growths after E accelerations are found starting in the early 1800s in England, Ireland, Scotland, Denmark, the Netherlands and her northern provinces, the environs of Paris, possibly Belgium and Switzerland, and the tsarist Black Sea province of Kherson. They appear in northern France around Lille about 1850; in South Holland, North Holland, the *gubernia* of Minsk, and the Central Economic Region around Moscow as of the 1880s or 1890s; then in Spain and the south-central Dutch provinces of Utrecht, North Brabant, and Gelderland in the early 20th century; and perhaps in the Central Asian economic district of the U.S.S.R. as late as World War II.[36] While there may be some local coincidence here, the interplay of E-shape population explosion with the Industrial Revolution (facilitating the new manufacture and benefitting from it) in northwestern Europe, followed by sustained economic and demographic gains, rings true to a familiar tale. So do the subsequent diffusions from the northern to the southern Netherlands and within northern France, the way Russia began to industrialize late in the 1800s, and the very recent development of Central Asia.

In other countries and regions of Europe and northern Asia the modern phase or phases of E-form accelerating demographic expansion only *succeeded* H-type population growth: in Germany as a whole and her industrial centers of Rhineland, Westphalia, and Silesia; in the Czech lands of Bohemia and Moravia; and in Hungary. How did having population explosion *follow* a phase of H-type demographic increase with economic growth (as previously in England in the 1720s) affect the life of a society and its inhabitants? In the Kazakh economic district of the Soviet Union the E also came right after the H in the early 1900s. In certain provinces along Russia's old southern agricultural and northeastern woodland frontiers, some G growth intervened between the H and the ensuing E.[37] What difference, if any, did that make?

Some European countries and regions within them, on the other hand, have experienced slowly decelerating H expansion without any population explosion, before or after. Such was the case for Norway four times between 1665 and 1948 and for all her bishoprics between 1745 and 1865; for Italy and her Piedmont, Ligurian, and Tuscan regions starting in the 19th century, and the hinterland of Naples more recently; possibly for Lille and her environs in northernmost France 1801–1911; for the two Saxonies within Germany 1816–1910; for Lower Austria twice and Styria once; for Serbia briefly in 1884–1910; for most of Russia's western frontier and also the North Caucasus economic district, likewise in the later 19th century (part B of Table 6.7), and the Poltava,

Kursk, Penzen, Voronezh, Simbirsk, and Orenburg provinces rather earlier than that (part D).

On the other hand, several European territories had population explosion—mostly in the late 19th century—without ever achieving sustained growth in the H form. That was the case for France as a whole and the hinterlands of Bordeaux, Lyon, and perhaps Marseilles (just brief E's after the Revolution) and the largely rural departments of Loiret, Vendée, and Hautes Alpes much more recently; for the marginal Dutch provinces of Limburg, Zeeland, and Drenthe; for neighboring Belgian Limburg and West Flanders; for the large majority of the regions of Germany and Austria (and Austria as a whole); for Austrian Silesia, Carniola and the Adriatic coast, Albania, Macedonia, and Romania; for the Baltic and northeastern Arctic provinces of Russia, Kharkov, and the Transcaucasus. What consequences for the nature of economic development and the conditions of life arose when population increase accelerated without leading to sustained expansion of the H type?

In other areas of Europe, only series of G growths have occurred since records begin. At the national level, these local trends could aggregate into very vigorous expansion, like the F for Siberia or the two 19th century H's in Belgium. But the dominance of only G-shape increases suggests that Luxembourg and most provinces of Belgium; the Burgenland district of Austria; Finland and Poland; Greece, Bulgaria, Croatia and Slavonia, Slovakia, Bosnia and Hercegovina, Montenegro, and Kosovo; and likewise the Don Military District, Astrakhan, Tobolsk, Tomsk, and Irkutsk experienced a different kind of interplay between dynamics of economy and processes of population than what emerged in areas that at some point experienced H or E patterns or a combination of both. Everywhere, though, in Europe as in the New World, G has been the most common shape of trend. More needs to be learned about the changes of health, economy, migration, family practices, and attitudes that so repeatedly generate G growth from place to place, sometimes shared by various regions, sometimes strictly local.

Readers will be able to make some useful revisions of both the data and their patternings as presented here. And comparable local analysis can be extended substantially elsewhere within Europe.[38] Already from these selective European insights in their present form, however, there emerges a framework for better ways of understanding and organizing for further investigation how movements of fertility, mortality, the demographic transformations they have produced, migration, and various forms of economic and cultural change have interacted across human settlement to produce just a few G-based types of trend in population size so universally. These European historical findings cast a critical light upon past assumptions that either the New World or Europe followed demographic rules of its own. To the contrary, they shared common dynamics of population change (though with some significant differences of frequency) and, apparently, also common relationships of these demographic movements to economic development. What happens, though, when one looks at the remaining parts of the globe, at Asia and Africa?

NOTES

1. Alternative Norwegian trending with just G curves is most likely for the diocese of Akershus, bordered by southern and central Sweden, where there was the greatest tendency for the vital rates to fluctuate.

2. Drake's Chapter 3, 41–74, contains his rather different interpretation.

3. For the Republic of Ireland areas: *Stat. Abs.* 1991, 23. For Ulster 1841–1911, totals for counties Antrim, Armagh, Down, Fermanagh, Londonderry, and Tyrone and for Belfast are taken from Mitchell 1962, 21, 24–25. For years since 1926, Mitchell's total for Northern Ireland to 1971 (1980, 31) and from U.K. *Population Trends 1991* thereafter are added to figures for "Ulster (part of)" from the Irish *Stat. Abs.* 1991, 23.

4. The drop in Connacht, or northwestern Ireland, between 1841 and 1851 is the exception. Irish scholars may be able to explain this one regional departure from the general pattern or may instead show cause why a rough D for 1841–1871 should be preferred to the tighter fit that one gets for 1851–1881 (or why some other trending should be employed).

5. The missing areas are Valencia, Aragon, Murcia, Granada, and Asturias. Populations of the first three are known to have been most heavily disrupted by the expulsion of the Moriscos in the early 1600s (Nadal 1984, 49).

6. The average is taken here without trying to weight for the different size of the various regional populations, since the baptisms of only certain well-recorded parishes are employed to approximate trends for each area.

With no total population estimates available between 1610 and 1648, Figure 5.1a has hypothesized that demographic decline in Spain at this time instead took the kind of D path followed in England, Italy, and France. The different shape of loss for baptisms probably in part reflects the fact that five of thirteen regions are missing—including Valencia and Aragon, where 27 and 19 percent of the population were Moriscos (Moorish converts to Christianity) who were expelled during 1609–1611. Even in the present average for just eight regions, moreover, a D curve with base year near 1540 already approximates baptisms for 1585–1605 and 1635, omitting 1615 and 1625. Total Spanish baptisms for the 1610s and 1620s would almost certainly drop significantly relative to preceding years if the missing regions were included, because of the excised Morisco families.

In addition, using the number of baptisms as a surrogate for total population may involve distortion by what will be shown in a later phase of this study to be a very general tendency for birth rates to decline primarily in C form. Without knowledge of the offsetting death rate, to employ the number of baptisms as a surrogate for total population size will thus tend to skew a decline towards the C shape.

7. In Table 6.1, these and other similarities of trend from region to region and relative to the national average that appeared after the middle of the 17th century are highlighted by "+" for ease of comparison.

8. In effect, this interregional homogenization represents development in the opposite direction to that of modern Ireland, where—after sharing the disaster of the middle 1800s together—provincial populations went increasingly *different* ways over the century beginning about 1870.

9. A connection of these regional trends with changes in where and when urbanization took place in Spain is discussed in Chapter 8.

10. Some of these areas remained approximately the same before and after unification. Others did not.

For the era since 1861, Instituto Centrale 1976, 12. Prior to that time, Mitchell 1992, 54, supplemented with estimates from Felloni 1977, 2–3, and Cippola 1965, 571.

11. This may have truly been the case, or the effect may result just by moving from an estimate by Cippola for 1700 to one by Felloni for 1750.

12. The source for 1795–1930 and 1947 is Hofstee 1981, 124–25. This is supplemented for 1940 and 1950–1980 from Mitchell 1992, 55, which contains closely similar but not totally identical data for 1830–1930. Another useful series for the Netherlands is in Deprez 1979, 261. Provincial estimates from before 1795 come from van Houtte and van Buyten 1977, 81, and de Vries and van der Woude 1997, 52–55, 67–69.

13. These trends are estimated by use of a template only. But such inspection is supported by actual curve fitting for Belgian regions at a preliminary stage of this research. The main source is Mitchell 1992, 47. Other, slightly different numbers through 1947 are available in Deprez 1979, 260.

14. In the hinterlands of Marseilles and Lille the E trend is not necessary to account for the history of local growth since the early 1800s, just a possible fit. This is denoted by putting these trends in brackets in the table.

15. The data come from Mitchell 1992, 51–53 and 70; K. Stat. Amt 1914, 35: 3; and Köllmann, ed., 1980, 1. Valuable estimates for the Duchy of Württemburg and several parts of Prussia before 1800 are in Kellenbenz et al. 1977, 192.

16. East and West Prussia, Posen, Silesia, most of Pomerania, and some of Brandenburg became part of Poland. Of course, a new era of fascinating population movements across the various parts of Germany began in 1990.

17. Robert Lee has shown how in the preceding era of 1876–1895 death rates for the young (age 0 to 15) were consistently lower in Schleswig-Holstein, Hanover, Westphalia, Hesse-Nassau, and Rhineland than in East and West Prussia, Brandenburg, Pomerania, Posen, and Silesia (Lee, ed., 1979, 189). Unfortunately the one area he cites for the southwest is only little Hohenzollern. The evidence remains tentative, but a higher death rate seems to align the southwest with the east as part C of Table 6.4 here connects those regions via resulting growth sequences in the early 20th century. This insight suggests more about how the much-discussed "demographic transition," the way falling deathrates and birthrates interacted historically, moved across Europe, a topic taken up intensively in the volume that follows this one.

18. The high figure for 1934 in Burgenland is not included in the fitting of the curve.

19. The sources are: Helczmanovzski 1979, 64–67; Mitchell 1992, 3, 7, 9, 47, 69; also Czech Manuel Stat. 1932, 2; Stat. Abs. 1968, 19.

20. Transylvania, the Hungarian Siebenbürgen, was not a part of Romania until after World War I.

21. The 1948–1953 rise in Macedonia probably was a continuation of the 1921–1931 E, lowered in level by the war (and subsequent turmoil involving Greece). No dating of the base year is even approximated for such a short span of time.

22. Tables 6.4 ("Germany") and 6.7 (for Russia).

23. The area where the Danube and the Tisza come together is the modern Voivodina, which became part of Yugoslavia at Versailles. Thus the H trend with 1836 base there

for 1880–1910 not very surprisingly parallels the one with t_0 at 1839 for 1884–1910 in Serbia, just across the Danube to the south.

24. Kabuzan 1971, 59–181, presents the audits of 1719, 1744, 1762, 1782, 1795, 1811, 1815, 1833, 1850, and 1857 by province (*gubernia*). Earlier work by Rashin (1956, 44–45) gives figures for total population in 1863, 1885, 1897, and January 1914. Unfortunately, these are for European Russia only. I have divided Rashin's numbers by two to compare with Kabuzan's reports of males. This estimation is less and less accurate as one moves towards men-heavy frontiers; but the figures are all approximate anyway, and expert readers can redo the trends with their own preferred weightings by sex and by likely under-registration.

25. Leasure and Lewis 1966, 1–25, 27; Lewis et al. 1976, 412.

26. Part B of the table, with some illustration in Figure 6b. Numbers for Vilno up through 1857 also cover whatever part of Kovno, the western area of modern Lithuania, Russia held at the time.

27. Minsk and Mogilev display rare accelerating loss of the C form in the early 1800s, perhaps thanks to Napoleon's invasion. The opening explosion in Kherson, and the early H thereafter, may reflect the commitment that Catherine the Great made, via her favorite Potemkin, to this promising territorial acquisition along the Black Sea. Of course, possible changes in provincial boundaries are among the factors that those who know more than I about 19th century Russia will have to consider.

28. Part D of Table 6.7, with some examples in Figure 6.6c.

29. In Tver, Smolyensk, Nizhegorod, Vladimir, Kostrom, Yaroslav, Vologod, Vyatsk, Kazan, and Perm.

30. The population of the Moldavian Economic Region, consisting of about two-thirds of what had been Bessarabia, did nonetheless expand in H form for 1926–1959, approximately parallel to the Central Region and White Russia (Leasure and Lewis 1966, 11, 27).

31. One exception was possible E acceleration for 1885–1914 in Kharkov, the northwestern corner of this region, following the pattern of nearby Chernigov, Orel, and Tambov of the older agricultural frontier above the steppes.

32. Males are doubled to approximate all persons. This procedure represents something of an overstatement because of the prevalent sex ratios among pioneering Russians, but it leaves some room for uncounted native inhabitants, who were not quickly swept aside by the thin demographic intrusion onto their land.

33. The potential G curve for just these two data points in terms of total population, though, proves reassuringly parallel to the 1811–1857 G for just doubling males for the territory of the Tomsk and Irkutsk areas.

34. For Mitchell's data (1992, 58) the log-linear slope is .0286.

35. Data for 1897 and 1926 from Leasure and Lewis for the economic district of Kazakhstan only permit the possibility of an E trend of this type; they do not prove it. Still that hint is confirmed in two ways. First, subsequent Kazakh data for 1939–1970 indicate very much the same timing of E curve. In between, Stalin's forcing of the nomadic Kazakhs into agricultural collectives is known to have taken a heavy demographic toll. This disaster most probably produced the drop in level for the two successive parallel E curves between 1926 and 1939. Second, the population of the economic district of Central Asia (the recent Turkmen, Kirgiz, Uzbek, and Tadzhik S.S.R.'s) clearly exploded in much the same type of E trend for 1897–1939; and, when taken together, the Kazakh and Central Asian populations increased quite tightly along the kind of E curve

being argued. This suggests the possibility that some Kazakhs, under pressure to collectivize, "voted with their feet" and took off into supportive neighboring republics, though others who know more will have to assess the merit of that hypothesis.

36. Though a short G in between is possible.

37. In Tambov, Orel, Saratov, and perhaps Chernigov; in Yaroslav, Vologod, Vyatsk, Kazan, and Perm (parts D and E of Table 6.7).

38. Data exist for counties within England, Wales, Scotland, Ireland, and Norway from about 1800 and Sweden since 1750. All 90 departments and 8 other areas of France could be analyzed. Since the middle 1800s there is evidence for the cantons of Switzerland, districts of Portugal, and provinces and districts in modern Spain. Other internal particulars for various stretches of time also exist for Denmark, Finland, and Greece.

Chapter 7

Sketching Population History in Asia and Africa: Outlines of the Often Obscure

For all that has been revealed of them, European trends of demographic increase and decline fail to inform us about most of the population of the Old World. The large majority of such peoples have lived—and continue to live—in Asia and Africa. Unfortunately it is precisely where *homo sapiens* is most numerous that the historical evidence on numbers is least complete and reliable.

Over the years, nevertheless, accumulating scholarly efforts have cleverly and fruitfully estimated population trends for key countries such as China and Japan, where centralized administrations for long at least keep limited records that permit some reasonable approximation of population size across time. And even in the toughest challenges, like demographic quantification for sub-Saharan Africa, modern experts—notably at the United Nations—have made considerable progress in developing outlines of population change for at least the past half-century or so.

Turning to exploit these resources, this chapter begins with historical trends of growth and decline in the populations of Asian nations. It then again shifts the level of investigation downward to explore what some of the better sets of records reveal about regional demographic expansion and contraction within selected countries of Asia. Finally, we see what can be seen about what are generally less well documented movements of African populations from the relatively recent points in time for which evidence of them exists.

WHAT HAS HAPPENED WHERE MOST PEOPLE LIVE:
A NEW LOOK AT THE DEMOGRAPHIC RECORD OF ASIA

For thousands of years most of the world's population has lived in the large societies of Asia: China, India, and other territories, many of whose pre–World War II populations may never be very accurately known. In demographic debate, these nations have provided the classical examples used to demonstrate the "Malthusian" consequences of overpopulation: restraint by crises of starvation, war, disease, and economic disaster. In these allegedly extreme Asian examples of historical demographic development, what role has been played by the basic growth curve G, its exceptions F, H, and E, and decline according to D or possibly C? To be generally useful, the new models proposed must fit the history of these important populations, too.

They do. Figures 7.1a and 7.1b begin to demonstrate this result from John D. Durand's extensive and thoughtful review of what can be known about population growth across the ages in China (Durand 1960). Combining this survey with other modern estimates and with censuses for the years since 1851, it is possible to obtain a fairly reliable and insightful sense of the national trends for population growth and decline in that huge country across about three-quarters of the last two millennia.[1]

The form of the data varies; so does their quality. Still, there seems to exist enough information to demonstrate the relevance of G-based curves for modeling Chinese demographic history throughout. Indeed, such patterning appears to help make better sense than has previously been attained out of fragmented or contradictory evidence and to assist in resolving some of the problems that have beset scholarly interpretation so far.

The initial phenomenon—displayed in the first, topmost panel of Figure 7.1a—is a major loss of population between 2 A.D., in the last years of the Western Han dynasty, and the year 57, a quarter of a century after the Eastern Han dynasty arose. The new regime took hold only by stages, following a period of several major disasters for the Chinese people (Durand 1960, 218).

In the judgment of Durand, the official figure for about 21 million persons in the year 57 (the upward-pointing hollow triangle at that date on the graph) is too low. His reestimates for 57 and 75 are presented as downward-pointing hollow triangles in the figure. Interestingly, these corrections—made forty years ago—fall almost precisely on the G curve generated by the data for 88 through 156. Durand's recalculations and the backward projections of the G-based analysis for later, less questionable dates conform and support each other.[2]

If this back-projection is approximately correct, China between 2 and 57 lost (or lost control over) somewhat over half of her population to revolt, flooding, and invasion and the likely famine, disease, and disruption of family life that accompanied or followed these trying events. This represents demographic disaster slightly greater in proportion than that in Ireland between 1841 and 1900, but a good deal less than the 70 percent to 95 percent declines observed as the peoples of the Americas and the Pacific were invaded. If such atrophy proceeded along the historically usual D trend of population decline between the known points of years 2 and 57, the Chinese population stood at about 41 million in the year 23: That is, about 31 percent of the population present in the year 2 disappeared in the revolution and flooding and accompanying difficulties that took place before the new regime was put together, while another 24 percent was lost over the next three and a half decades in the aftermath of these early troubles and during the invasions that followed the creation of the new dynasty. Perhaps scholars of ancient China will be able to verify whether these implications of the elsewhere standard D curve for demographic atrophy are correct or not.

For three and a half centuries of the long, demographically undocumented era of 156–606, the country broke into smaller political units, beginning with the fall of the Han dynasty around 220. The Sui (581–618) brought many of the pieces back together again (including territory as far south as Annam), but with a population somewhat smaller than that of 156. During the troubles that saw the Sui replaced by the T'ang, household numbers for 606 and 627 indicate another major population loss for China (Durand 1960, 23). Whether this was demographic in nature or instead mostly jurisdictional or reflective of a deterioration in how head-counting was administered will have to be decided by the experts; but recorded households shrank by two-thirds, if not more, in a very short time. By the middle of the 7th century, though, the T'ang regime had again brought Korea, Manchuria, Mongolia, and Turkestan under Chinese control. As in other historical situations previously observed, continental conquest had much to do in generating the G curve of increase for households in "China" 639–705 that appears in the middle panel of Figure 7.1a and in part A of Table 7.1. With the G growth of 726–755 that followed, the number of households ruled by the T'ang finally reapproached the scale reported in the second century for the Han dynasty (which also had controlled large outlying areas surrounding China proper).

After 755 there appears still another collapse in the data, nominally from about 53 million persons in 755 to about 17 million in 760. Though "China was torn by revolts which were suppressed with bloody force" at this time, Durand joins the group of scholars who believe that 36 million lives were unlikely to have been forfeit to these events (Durand 1960, 223–24). The very steep D curve for 755–772 in the figure, in other words, suggests real population loss (in terms of households) only as it was significantly magnified by collapse in administration. The people who remained were just not counted properly. What a more realistic trend for the actual demographic decline may have been, however, is hinted at by household numbers for 755, 756, 780, and 812. These indicate a flatter D curve, which depicts a drop not from 8.9 million households to 1.2 in five years but decay from 8.9 million to 2.4 over a period of almost six decades. This estimate of 73 percent decline may still include some jurisdictional losses as well, since the height of T'ang power came in earlier years. Subsequent growth

Figure 7.1a
Probable Trends in the Population of China since 2 A.D.: Across Twelve Centuries Preceding the Mongol Conquest

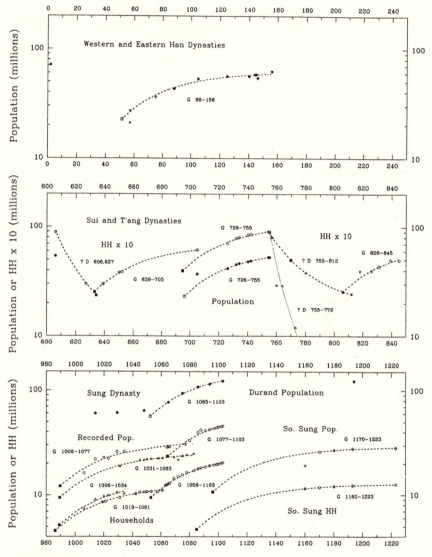

Source: Table 7.1.

Figure 7.1b
Probable Trends in the Population of China since 2 A.D.:
Seven Centuries from Genghis Khan to the People's Republic

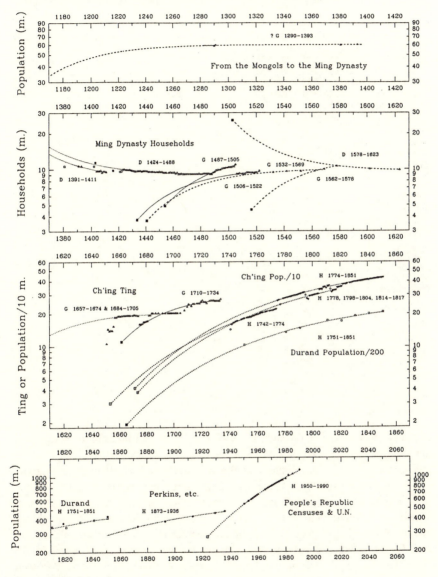

Source: Table 7.1.

Table 7.1
Two Distinct Demographic Epochs in China

A. A Giant Restrained				B. Bursting Malthus's Bonds		
Population	88-156	G	51	Pao-Chia	1742-1774	H 1654
Households	606,627	?D	634			
"	639-705	G	633	P.-C. high	1775-1851	H 1671
"	726-755	G	695	P.-C. low	1778-1817	H 1673
Population	726-755	G	696	Durand Pop.	1751-1851	H 1665
Households	755-812	?D	765			
"	826-845	G	806			
Pop. high	1006-1077	G	990	Perkins	1873-1936	H 1751
Pop. low	1031-1083	G	989			
HH high	1006-1034	G	989			
HH low	1019-1061	G	986			
Population	1077-1103	G	1064	Census/U.N.	1950-1990	H 1923
Households	1058-1103	G	1053			
Sung Pop.	1170-1223	G	1096			
Sung HH	1160-1223	G	1085			
Population	1290-1393	?G	1152			
HH low	1391-1411	D	1347			
HH high	1424-1488	D	1351			
Households	1487-1501	G	1454			
"	1506-1522	G	1433			
"	1532-1569	G	1441			
Households	1562-1578	G	1516			
"	1578-1623	D	1503			
Ting	1657-1705	G	1586			
"	1710-1734	G	1662			

Sources: Durand 1960; Ho 1959; Perkins 1969; Tien 1973; *Stat. Ybk. of China* 1986; U.N. *Demo. Ybk.* 1993.

in the G form from 812 through 845 took the number of households back up to the level of the late 600s, not the Han-rivaling peak of 755.

The end of the T'ang dynasty in 906 was followed by about three-quarters of a century during which China again splintered into warring states. For the first four decades of the Sung, who once more reunited most of the usual territory and ruled until the country was overrun by Jurchen and then Mongol armies in the 13th century, population records do not survive. Beginning in 1006, however, figures for both population and households become available. These are shown in the bottom graph of Figure 7.1a. The recorded population represents only a very low multiple of household numbers. In Durand's view, it is likely that only males were calculated, and not all of them.[3] For the years 1065–1103 a G trend with base year at 1052 closely approximates the path of his revisions (249). This is because the official household numbers take the G form in 1058–1103 with t_0 at 1053, as Table 7.1 and the bottom panel of the figure indicate. Durand simply applied a constant multiplier to them.

For the 11th century, however, the recorded Sung data almost certainly mix two distinct populations or ways of measuring the same population. That is, numbers for a larger territory seem intermingled with those for a smaller one; or counts of higher reliability alternate with those representing less complete coverage. The figure shows this most clearly, a phenomenon Durand might have perceived had he graphed the available information and fitted trends to it. The two G's for reported population, for example, have base years at 989 and 990; but the level for the higher data evident across the period 1006–1077 is 30 percent above that for the lesser numbers recorded during the span of 1031–1083. There is less difference for households. Here too, though, the figures for 1006–1034 follow a G path of increase that is noticeably above the data for 1019–1061, but closely parallel in deceleration. In short, our new approach reveals more about the direction of demographic change in China over the century between 1006 and 1103 than Durand was able to eke out, including the quite consistent patterning that in fact underlies the seeming changeability of the data. This finding should assist future scholars in determining the types of census-taking or collation of information that were apparently alternating over most of the 11th century. Was there, for instance, an ongoing debate among officials in the Sung administration about who should be counted (perhaps involving how taxes should be calculated and collected)?

By 1127 invading Jurchens had seized much of northern China, establishing a Chin regime. Only a severely shrunken empire of the Sung remained in the South. Once the territory controlled had been reduced, population in this rump domain apparently increased in G form to 1223. The first recorded estimate for population is low (and not fitted to the curve); but the G pattern for the number of *households* is very clear from 1160 onward, as the bottom panel of Figure 7.1a indicates. Estimates for the Chin empire of the north are available for only 1187, 1190, and 1195, too short a span to trend.

The Chin demographic evidence is brief for good reason. By 1212 enemies far more dangerous and powerful than the preceding Huns, Tibetans, and Jurchens fell upon China. Genghiz Khan overran most Chin domains as far south as the Yellow River by 1215 and died (1227) during the further campaigns that brought the rest of Chin holdings under Mongol control by 1234. In the few years in between, he went off to conquer Turkestan, Transoxania, and Afghanistan and raid Persia and southern Russia. Under the image-astute leadership of the "perfect warrior," whole populations of Chin cities that resisted were put to the sword as an object lesson for centers yet to be besieged. The epidemic and famine that followed such heavy-handed conquest, and the destruction of administrative systems that might have aided the stressed population, killed many more. Later, in 1258–1259, Genghiz Khan's grandsons launched a three-pronged attack upon the southern Sung and quickly broke the power left to this dynasty. In that second wave of invasion in the south, however, live subjects to pay taxes were apparently at last valued more than dead enemies to serve as examples of power. The demographic losses were now much less severe. Of Genghiz's grandsons, first Mangu and then Kublai became rulers of China. A new dynasty commenced; it would last until 1368.[4]

The Yuan dynasty data on population are scant; but when put together with evidence from the early years of the Ming (an indigenous leadership which finally got rid of the Mongols), they indicate a likely G trend from 1290 or earlier through 1393 (Durand 1960, 229, 231–32). This is shown in the top panel of Figure 7.1b. The Ming administration, like that of the Sung preceding the Mongol conquest, soon vacillated and grew careless in how the population was reported.[5] Still, as the second panel of the figure and Table 7.1 together demonstrate, the D curve of decline for households in 1391–1411 closely parallels the higher D for 1424–1488 that succeeds it. The same bend of change is indicated. Meanwhile, out-of-line early data for 1402 and 1403 in fact bracket the higher D path for whatever form of reporting characterized the later period of 1424–1488; and figures around 1420 for a while take an intermediate and parallel track of slow decline at this apparent point of transition from one form of recording to the next. Once again, fitting the relevant G-based trends throws further light on what was happening to census-taking as well as on how the size of the population was altering.

From 1487 through 1505 surviving records show decline giving away to substantial growth of the G type in the Chinese population. Then either census-taking or the size of China degenerated again, so that households reported in 1506–1552 were substantially fewer than those for 1487–1505, though somewhat slowing or flattening expansion in the G pattern continued. Another, though smaller, drop in coverage appears around 1530. Here, though, the subsequent G for 1532–1569 is even more parallel to its predecessor than the 1506–1522 trend was to the data for 1487–1505. In the light of these patterns, it seems likely that actual household numbers swelled along the same G track from 1506 through 1569; quite possibly, a single G path pertained all the way from 1487 through 1569, with departures from that path representing only variations in the quality of reporting. Does that interpretation make sense in terms of what is known of the administrative and social history of the Ming era?

Brief more robust growth, possibly in G form, followed for the years 1562–1578. Subsequently, data for 1578–1623 indicate that the number of households ruled by the Ming declined somewhat—in the familiar D pattern—across several decades before this dynasty, too, was overthrown.

Once again China was overrun by invaders, this time from the northeast. The Manchu established their rule after taking Beijing in 1644; but remnants of the Ming dynasty were not destroyed until 1662, and disorders in the South persisted until 1682 (Durand 1960, 234, 236). From Beijing the Ch'ing dynasty governed China until 1912. Up to 1734, the Manchu administration counted "*ting*," whose meaning has been debated. Still, it is the view of Durand that the number of *ting* "might give a rough indication of the trend of population growth during the second half of the seventeenth century and the first decades of the eighteenth."[6]

From 1651 through 1656 enumerations apparently covered larger and larger areas as Ch'ing authority was extended southward. Then, for most of the time through the early 1700s, the number of *ting* increased along a G curve, as indicated in the third panel of Figure 7.1b and in Table 7.1. In the exceptional years of 1675–1683 almost certainly significant territory was not included in the survey, since several princes who had been allowed to rule semiautonomously in the south revolted in 1674 and were finally overcome only in 1682. The alignment of these temporarily disrupted data with the G trend of fresh expansion in *ting* for 1710–1734 is probably coincidental. Also, as Durand suspected (237), the numbers around 1700 may indeed represent just lazy repetitions of earlier computations. The *ting* figures from 1710 through 1734, on the other hand, fairly clearly reflect new G-shape growth in the Chinese population.

One of the accomplishments of Emperor Ch'ien Lung (r. 1736–1796), under whom early modern China attained its maximum extent,[7] was to reform the collection of population statistics. The system did not always work well.[8] The third panel of Figure 7.1b, however, shows that in spite of the deficiencies it is possible to establish rather clearly how Chinese population grew between 1741 and 1851, when the Taiping Rebellion severely disrupted national administration–and directly or indirectly killed off millions of people.

In essence, demographic expansion took place according to one long H trend for these eleven decades. The simplest evidence is in Durand's recalculations of population, shown as hollow squares on the graph. But Ch'ing official totals (the solid inverted triangles) show very much the same thing, taking into consideration how the statistical system is reputed to have dropped out or picked up areas during certain periods. As part B of Table 7.1 summarizes, *pao-chia* enumerations for the high years from 1775 through 1851 and the low numbers for 1778–1817 form almost exactly parallel H curves; Durand's recomputations for 1751–1851 climb in a very similar fashion (with base year at 1665 compared with 1671 or 1673); and the *pao-chia* totals for 1742–1774 follow an H with t_0 nearby at 1654. Given the problems known to have existed in the system, it is probably best to conclude that the Chinese population grew in a single H trend from the early 1740s to the Taiping Rebellion until fresh evidence proves otherwise.

This finding has the interesting result that, demographically, in the later 18th and early 19th centuries China was expanding in very much the same way as Norway, Russia, and Spain (Table 5.1). In other words, her demographic increase resembled that of countries that, though not at the center of modern economic development in the West like Britain, nonetheless resided at least on the margins of such change and not in the real backwaters of economic development. In the 19th century, in short, bellicose and greedy European nations forced their trade upon a China whose economy was already growing well enough to support robust, only slowly decelerating population growth. The "backwardness" of China in this era has probably been substantially exaggerated in Western perception.

Furthermore, twice again since 1851 China has been able to sustain demographic growth along an H track. First, though, disaster had to be overcome. China probably lost about 20 percent of her people (approximately 85 million) during the Taiping revolt that followed the intervention of Western powers to promote their opium trade. This protracted rebellion in the heart of central China devastated the nation's crucial food-distribution systems, spreading starvation and disease that far outpaced the military losses. Then, however, from 1873 through 1936, the records indicate new H growth that persisted through the end of the empire, the shaky years of the new republic, the first phase of invasion by Japan, and unstable, divided rule under warlords, the Kuomintang, and the budding Communist Party.[9]

After more demographic losses during the main Japanese invasion, World War II, and the civil war of the 1940s in which the Communists drove the Kuomintang out to Taiwan, the population of China has—in spite of all the policy aimed at restraining it—resumed growth in the H form, as censuses since 1953 and U.N. estimates around them demonstrate.[10] Unlike, say, what happened in Norway or Russia following World War II, the modern sequence of successive H growths—begun in 1741—has not yet come to an end in China. There remains great pressure upon China's economy and social services to support her people. Presumably at some point soon, this H path, as we have seen in other countries around the world, will give way to a more rapidly decelerating and economically feasible G trend of future increase. What clues can be found, within China or in comparison with other historical transitions from H to G expansion, that will divulge when and how that change of course will take place?

If China has for many personified the Malthusian apocalypse of demographic potential kept in hand only by massive crises of death and disaster, Tokugawa Japan up to the Meiji revolution of the 1860s exemplifies a population fine-tuned by restraint to stick close to the carrying capacity of a given way of life within a fixed domain of resources. From 1721 through 1852 there are figures only for the number of commoners; but these, without samurai and outcasts, represented the overwhelming majority of the population.[11] Figure 7.2 shows how their numbers remained for almost a century and a half between 25 and 27 million. This majority of the Japanese population, however, did (if Tokugawa record-keeping was relatively stable in practice over the long haul) rise through the 1720s, decline during 1732–1780 and again—more steeply—during 1780–1792, then mount slightly again between 1792 and 1852. Even within the narrow confines of such limited flexibility, trends of G, D, D, and G shape seem to have occurred in Japan, as the figure illustrates. Table 7.2 summarizes the patterns identified in this and other Asian nations.[12]

Earlier on, demographic growth during the first century of the Tokugawa era had been considerably more robust. There were about 30 million people in Japan in 1721. If in 1600 the country contained approximately 8 million persons, the midpoint of Hayami's range of 6.2 to 9.8 million, then demographic increase in

Figure 7.2

Growth Patterns in Other Large Asian Populations with Long Records: Japan, Java/Indonesia, and Some Peoples of the Indian Subcontinent

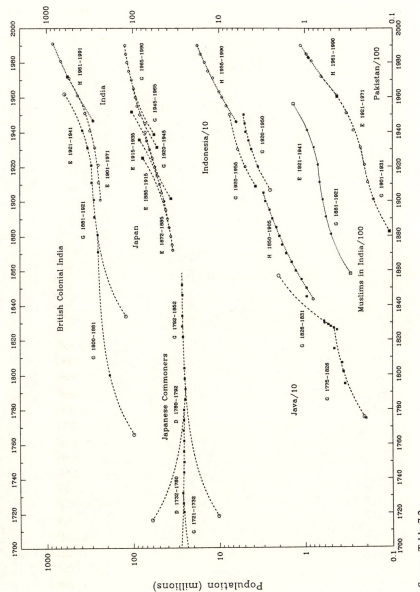

Source: Table 7.2.

Table 7.2
Patterns of Population Growth in Modern Asia

A. The Middle East

Kuwait

1957-1990	G 2001

Qatar

1950-1970	G 1990
1970-1990	G 2003

Oman

1975-1990	G 1999

Yemen

1950-1975	G 1937
1980-1990	G 1997

Bahrain

1941-1965	E 1955
1965-1981	E 1963
1971-1990	G 1994

Cyprus

1881-1901	?G 1860
1901-1921	?G 1884
1931-1973	G 1926
1980-1990	G 1952

Turkey

1927-1950	G 1921
1950-1970	G 1955
1970-1990	G 1970

Lebanon

1960-1990	rG 1934
1950-1963	G 1971

South Yemen

1960-1990	G 1973

Saudi Arabia

1950-1980	G 1966
1980-1990	?E 1971

Iraq

1867-1905	?G 1860
1905-1927	?G 1888
1930-1947	G 1937
1947-1990	F .

Iran

1867-1920	G 1873
1910-1950	E 1960
1956-1990	F .

Syria

1931-1946	G 1950
1960-1990	H 1882

Jordan

1950-1961	G 1954
1961-1975	E 1965
1975-1990	E 1986

B. The Indian Sub-Continent

India

1800-1881	G 1766
1881-1921	G 1834
1901-1971	E 1972
1961-1991	H 1947

Pakistan

1901-1931	G 1883
1921-1971	E 1960
1961-1990	H 1983

Bangladesh

1951-1970	E 1966
1961-1991	H 1967

Burma-Myanmar

1872-1901	G 1849
1901-1931	G 1877
1921-1973	E 1971
1963-1990	H 1942

Ceylon-Sri Lanka

1850-1891	G 1848
1901-1921	G 1879
1921-1963	E 1957
1963-1990	G 1956

Nepal

1963-1981	E 1981
1975-1990	G 1979

Bhutan

1963-1980	G 1975
1975-1990	E 2001

250

Table 7.2 (Continued)

C. Southeast Asia

Java-Indonesia	Brunei	Sabah	Singapore	Malay Peninsula
1850-1905 H 1844	1911-1947 H 1879	1911-1931 G 1894	1871-1901 G 1883	1921-1947 G 1920
1920-1950 G 1907	1947-1990 H 2001	1948-1960 G 1965	1911-1931 G 1921	1955-1980 G 1960
1955-1990 H 1946		1960-1980 H 1990	1947-1985 G 1960	

Philippines	Tatwan	Thailand	Sarawak	Cambodia	Laos	Vietnam
1876-1918 G 1897	1905-1920 G 1883	1911-1937 E 1936	1948-1963 G 1948	1921-1950 E 1954	1921-1946 E 1958	1931-1950 G 1920
1918-1948 H 1899	1920-1935 E 1935	1929-1947 G 1929	1963-1980 H 1958	1958-1975 G 1967	1960-1990 G 1960	1950-1970 G 1958
1939-1960 E 1956		1947-1990 H 1957		1980-1990 G 1979		1970-1990 G 1974

D. Northeast Asia

China	Japan	Hong Kong	Korea-S. Korea	North Korea	Mongolia
1578-1623 D 1503	1600,1721 ?G 1610	1871-1901 E 1880	1920-1935 E 1954	1960-1990 G 1967	1969-1989 G 1975
1657-1705 G 1586	1721-1732 G 1649	1901-1931 E 1919	1955-1990 G 1957		
1710-1734 G 1662	1732-1780 D 1623	1961-1980 G 1963			
1742-1851 H 1665	1780-1792 D 1716				
1873-1937 H 1741	1792-1852 G 1719				
	1872-1885 E 1925				
	1885-1915 E 1935				
	1915-1935 E 1952				
1950-1990 H 1923	1920-1945 G 1902				
	1945-1965 G 1931				
	1965-1990 G 1939				

Sources: Table 7.1; notes 11, 13, 15–17; Mitchell 1995; U.N. *Demo. Ybk.*

the country might have surged along a constantly decelerating G path based at about 1610. By the 18th century this trend would have reached a near-stationary phase of the curve, which is compatible with the slight movement after 1721 shown in Figure 7.2. Such G-shape interpolation between 1600 and 1721, based upon only two points of information, is very speculative indeed; but it resonates well with the historical story of how feudal Japan was consolidated and given peace. What a G curve hypothesized from the estimates for 1600 and the 1720s implies is that the new stability of this Tokugawa Shogunate provided a significant demographic opportunity. The response would have been most rapid in the early years, however. By 1670, when the registration from which population for 1721–1852 is deduced was installed (as a system of religious control aimed at stamping out Christianity and supporting Buddhism), the proposed G path implies that the Japanese population would have approximately tripled since 1600. Across the next half century, in contrast, the people of the country would have increased less than 20 percent. The question posed here for scholars of Tokugawa Japan is whether such a decelerating pattern of population increase makes more sense against what is known of other aspects of the history of the country in this era, and better fits demographic growth as it appears in the local evidence for 17th century upon which they are so fruitfully working, than the linear increment between 1600 and 1720 suggested by Hayami (1968, 22, 1, 23).

With the era of Meiji reform, more modern census-taking began in Japan (Taeuber 1958, 45, 48; Japan, Statistics Bureau 1994, 36–37). The jump in level between 1852 and 1872 for the population in Figure 7.2 probably mostly reflects only how the new counts became more complete; hence, different symbols are used on the graph. Between 1872 and the years following World War I, however, the people of Japan seem to have expanded along what can best be described as two or three E-type surges of accelerating population explosion: 1872–1885, 1885–1915, and probably again 1915–1935, though a decelerating G for 1920–1945 overlaps and might replace this last upswing, the way tendencies to "explode" by now have often been seen to come to an end in Latin America and Europe. Experiencing successive E surges between about 1870 and World War II in this manner means that the population of Japan increased across the period very much like that of Germany (Table 5.1 in Chapter 5), another aggressive member of the community of nations during the era. The difference was that by the 1930s the Japanese demographic growth was beginning to slow down while the German did not.

Since World War II, increase in the Japanese population has apparently followed two G curves, up to and after the middle 1960s. The reason for a change in course at that point may well have something to do with the impact of the war on age structure. But providing the best answer will have to be left to local demographers.

India, under British colonial rule, had a much larger population than Japan, but an appreciably less well documented one historically. Across the 19th century, the people of the subcontinent apparently multiplied along a rather more vigorous path than was evident in Japan, but not in the robust H pattern characteristic of China following the Taiping Rebellion. The likely G curve for India, which depends upon an upwardly revised estimate by Kingsley Davis for 1800, is shown in the top plot of Figure 7.2.[13] A fresh phase of G-shaped growth more certainly ensued across the four decades up to 1921. By then, however, demographic expansion in India began to accelerate, taking an E trajectory that would persist past World War II. A parallel series for the present-day territory of India without Pakistan, indeed, displays the E shape from 1901 all the way through 1971 (India, Cent. Stat. Org. 1982, 21–22). Since the 1960s, though, demographic growth in India has started to decelerate. This process has taken the slowly slowing H form followed in China instead of the G pattern pursued in Japan. In fact, as students of contemporary population well know, the Indian expansion has been even stronger.[14] For better or for worse, India is on her way toward having the largest national population in the world. Comparable trends appear in Figure 7.2 and part B of Table 7.2 for the Muslim peoples of India, inhabitants of the territory of modern-day Pakistan, and the population of Bangladesh (formerly East Pakistan).[15]

Within Dutch colonial Indonesia, Java, the most populous area, probably experienced something like G growth from 1775 to the 1820s (Nitisastro 1970, 12, 31, 33, 35, 54, 67, 75, 163; Mitchell 1982, 43). As Dutch administrators pushed for the development of colonial cash crops such as sugar, the population of Java seems to have started off in a new, very strong G curve for a few years in the later 1820s, only to stall out soon into a more sustainable trajectory of growth. This path, followed from about 1850 through 1905, took the H form; but it was very much steeper than the H for the population of China that has been observed between the Taiping Rebellion and World War II. Then from the end of World War I to the end of World War II, Java—and the future Indonesia as a whole (the Dutch East Indies)—experienced new but now more rapidly decelerating G-type increase. Since the 1950s, though, the people of Indonesia have again expanded in a modern H pattern almost identical to that of India.

For six other Asian societies whose records reach back into the 1800s both parallels and local variations in demographic growth are illustrated in Figure 7.3. The patterns include 20th century "Third World" E-type surges in the Philippines, Sri Lanka (formerly Ceylon), Myanmar (Burma), and Iran (Persia). Slow deceleration in the H form appears in the Philippines while a U.S. colony but also in present-day Myanmar parallel to neighboring India. Even the F pattern occurs: not for "frontier" conditions but in Iraq ever since the 1940s, Iran since the 1950s, and perhaps briefly in the Philippines 1960–1980. Still, G trends are the most frequent. Exceptions to them all emerged after 1920; and in Cyprus there has been nothing but a sequence of G patterns since 1881.[16] Table 7.2 makes these findings part of an overall regional framework for understanding what kind of demographic increase occurred when and where across the heavily

Figure 7.3
Other Asian Countries with Data since the 1800s: The Philippines, Ceylon,
Burma, Iraq, Iran, and Cyprus

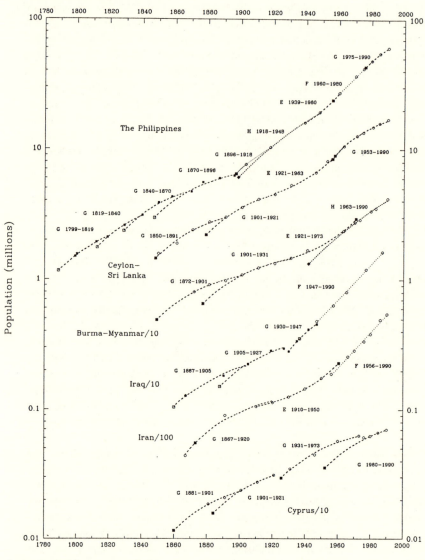

Source: Table 7.2.

populated terrain of Asia. Just shorter demographic histories are known else-where on the continent, sometimes beginning only after World War II. Still, the table shows how growths in 39 Asian countries have followed paths character-ized by the G family of curves.[17]

In all, G-based curves effectively outline the history of societal population growth and decline in Asia, as they have for the Americas, Australasia, Oceania, and Europe. Once again G itself is the predominant form of increase; but there have been quite a few cases of population explosion in Asia, and also slowly decelerating H-type expansion. Not unexpectedly for another part of the Old World, constant proportional multiplication of the F type has again been rare. A few countries, though, have had such growths in their recent pasts, not in typical "frontier" conditions but more like modern Mexico or Guatemala (Table 4.4). Demographic decline along the D path is not evident at the national level in Asia since 1800, unlike the several instances seen in Europe. In China, how-ever, loss in this form was apparently recurrent across the preceding twelve centuries,[18] while the Japanese population contracted more gently along D tra-jectories twice in the 1700s.

Beneath these generalities, though, there stands out in the summary of Table 7.2 considerable differentiation of pattern from place to place and over time. In the Middle East and on the Indian subcontinent (parts A and B of the table), no less than 15 of 16 trends that had come to an end by 1950 were simply G's, the one exception being an E for 1910–1950 in Iran. As in China across the centuries from 2 A.D. to 1740, and in what is known of Japanese demographic expansion up through 1850, growth in premodern conditions has meant the rapid deceleration of G—nothing else. The slowly decelerating, long-rising H trends found quite frequently in Europe, especially northern Europe, from as early as the 1500s onward did not come to Asia until this present century, with the two exceptions of China and Dutch colonial Java. True, E's were beginning to gather steam before World War II in several places on the Indian subcontinent (India, Pakistan, Burma, Ceylon, Nepal); but the swerve of incipient explosion upward did not yet thrust itself into the faces of demographers as it was to do in the 1950s and 1960s.

In contrast to these populations living between the Hellespont and the road to Mandalay, almost half the 31 documented trends ending before 1950 in north-eastern and southeastern Asia (parts C and D of Table 7.2) were something other than G. In Japan, Korea, and Hong Kong no less than 6 E trends are evident in this era. Taiwan, Thailand, Cambodia, and Laos similarly saw E explosions that came and went by 1950. Meanwhile, the population of China had expanded along two sustained H paths between 1742 and 1937; and Java, Brunei, and the Philippines—as Dutch, British, and American colonies respec-tively—had also experienced this distinctive form of demographic increase in H trends that had run their course by 1950. Following World War II, moreover, growth of the H type has been shared by Indonesia and the neighboring terri-tories of Brunei, Sabah, and Sarawak in one geographical clustering of countries and India, Pakistan, Bangladesh, Myanmar, and Thailand in another. Elsewhere in Asia, only China and Syria have supported H growth recently. What economic and social changes have fostered such sustained robust demographic expansion in these places but not others? What cost or gain has been passed back from such expansion to the living standards of the people?

Among seven trends for northeastern Asia that lasted or arose *past* 1950, in contrast, the only non-G is the H for post-revolutionary China. Even if some of the curves were very steep at first, as among the small petroleum principalities, a substantial majority of the recent trends in the populations of southeastern Asia and the Middle East also took the strongly decelerating G form. Half of the exceptions were E's. In Bahrain and the Philippines such explosions have given way to G-type slowing in growth by now; but in Jordan and Saudi Arabia they have not, still threatening stability with accelerating demographic increase. Since World War II, four nations in Southeast Asia and the Middle East have even experienced the exceptional steady pressure of Franklin-Malthus steady proportional growth at the F rate. In Taiwan and the Philippines, such taxing expansion has been replaced by G deceleration; in Iraq and Iran it has not, with rather aggressive consequences. Only four populations in these two Asian regions, meanwhile, have seen increase in the slowly slowing H shape. In all four—Indonesia, Sabah, Thailand, and Syria—the H patterns continue today.

Among the peoples of the Indian subcontinent, finally, far differently from Southeast Asia and the Middle East, G deceleration has been rare since 1950. Only in Sri Lanka and Nepal have mid-century E explosions cooled out this way. In Bhutan, postwar G growth has to the contrary just recently given over to E-type acceleration. Exploding patterns also persisted into the 1970s in India, Pakistan, Bangladesh, and Myanmar. While in those four countries deceleration has now at last appeared, it comes in the much more slowly slowing H form, not G. The resources of the subcontinent will still have to stretch considerably to take care of so many more people, even though the threat of *accelerating* demographic doom is not hanging over everyone's head as it was a quarter of a century ago.

Other particulars of Table 7.2 catch the eye. Examples include the way H expansion currently is shared by the resource-rich areas of Sabah, Sarawak, and Brunei on the northern coast of Borneo along with Thailand and Indonesia but not other parts of Southeast Asia; how Korea and Taiwan, both then under Japanese occupation, experienced E-type explosion resembling that of Japan in the early 1900s; the lack of any such acceleration in Viet Nam in contrast to her neighbors (were her demographic practices more French, or was recurrent war the key factor?); and the recognizable imprints of oil and refugees upon the population histories of various countries of the Middle East. In several ways the comparative framework of the table enriches our global understanding and suggests avenues of further investigation into the causes and consequences of the movements noted.

G-BASED FORMS OF CHANGE IN POPULATION SIZE
FOR SOME REGIONS WITHIN ASIAN COUNTRIES

As in Europe, the Americas, Oceania, and Australasia, it is useful to examine the behavior of regional populations within at least a few better-documented Asian nations. Such disaggregation makes it possible to perceive better what kinds of historical conditions in this part of the world contributed to generating the forms of growth that are encountered. Examples selected for full analysis here include China and Japan, which offer regular or fairly frequent regional records since the 1740s, and India, whose local totals cover only the recent century but whose demographic detail represents what has happened under quite different circumstances. Some additional evidence from peninsular Malaysia, the Philippines, Sri Lanka (Ceylon), Thailand, Indonesia, and the Ottoman Empire is noted briefly as well.

What can be culled from several sources in English concerning demographic growth (or decline) in the provinces of China since 1749 is summarized in Table 7.3 and illustrated in Figures 7.4a and 7.4b.[19] There are some conflicts among the sources, doubts about the quality of certain counts (especially for 1771 and 1964), and possible boundary changes among provinces that I cannot pretend to master. More expert hands will have to make some revisions in the proposed patterns and in the tentative conclusions drawn from them here. Nevertheless, it would seem that some useful outlines of similarity and dissimilarity in population trends begin to appear across provinces. These can help in understanding somewhat better how the world's largest human population has evolved over the past two and a half centuries.

From the beginning, it is necessary to understand the widespread tendency for data series to be discontinuous between 1851 and 1873. Chiefly reflected here is the great disaster caused by the Taiping Rebellion of 1850–1864. Through revolt, disruption of farming and trade, starvation, and repression this upheaval caused severe demographic losses in several provinces while it added refugees to a few.[20] At about the same time, moreover, other problems adversely affected population in various parts of China: from Muslim revolt in the Northwest to flooding along the lower Yellow River to heavy emigration from the European-disrupted Southeast—which created "Chinatowns" all around the world.[21] Taking these shifts into account, it becomes possible to pattern and comprehend provincial trends before and after that crisis era in the demographic history of China.

Prior to the 1740s, the population of the country as a whole has been seen to increase in G form, no other shape (Figure 7.1 and Table 7.1). For the some two dozen provinces of which the country was composed that continued to be mostly the case also for the next century, from 1749 to 1851. Table 7.3 demonstrates how only six regions experienced any other shape of demographic

Table 7.3
Trends of Expansion and Contraction across Two and a Half Centuries in the Provincial Populations of China

A. G-Expanding Regions of the South and North

Guangxi	Hunan	Fujian	Jiangxi	Tibet
1771-1851 G 1750	1749-1851 G 1745	1749-1787 G 1736	1749-1851 G 1754	
		1812-1851 G 1785		
....	....	....	....	
1851-1893 G 1827	1873-1913 G 1839	1873-1933 C 2003	1873-1933 C 2015	1819-1964 C 2037
1893-1933 G 1876	1913-1964 G 1865			
1933-1964 G 1898				
1964-1987 G 1973	1964-1987 G 1960	1953-1987 G 1959	1953-1987 G 1959	1964-1987 G 1965

Shaanxi	INNER MONGOLIA:	Suiyan	Chahar
1749-1851 G 1725			
....			
1851-1893 C 1915			
1893-1933 G 1836	1873-1933 G 1838	1873-1933 G 1863	1893-1933 G 1867
1953-1987 G 1959	1953-1987 G 1967		

MANCHURIA:	Jilin	Liaoning	Heilongjiang
1749-1787 G 1757		1771-1787 G 1718	
1819-1873 G 1803	1776-1819 G 1799	1787-1851 H 1772	
....	....	....	
1913-1953 G 1915			
1953-1987 G 1962	1953-1987 G 1957	1953-1987 G 1956	1953-1987 G 1970

B. Provinces with H-Type Growth

Hebei	Gansu	Shanxi	Ningxia	Xinjiang
1749-1812 H 1689	1749-1776 G 1768	1749-1787 G 1713		
1819-1873 G 1748	1776-1851 rG 1695	1776-1819 E 1841		
....	....	....		
1873-1933 H 1739	1873-1913 H 1750	1851-1893 D 1814	1873,1893 ?G 1808	
1893-1953 E 1973		1933-1976 H 1910	1933-1964 H 1928	1933-1957 F ·
1953-1987 G 1950	1933-1987 G 1945	1964-1987 G 1956	1964-1987 F ·	1957-1987 H 1976

Jiangsu	Anhui	Guangdong	Sichuan	Yunnan
1749-1851 H 1669	1749-1819 H 1649	1749-1851 G 1757	1749-1787 G 1768	1749-1787 H 1707
			1812-1851 G 1814	1787-1851 G 1783
....	....	....	....	....
1873-1913 E 1947				
1893-1933 H 1785	1873-1933 H 1787	1873-1953 G 1852	1873-1964 H 1792	1873-1964 H 1834
1953-1987 G 1943	1953-1987 G 1947	1953-1987 H 1924	1964-1987 G 1960	1964-1987 G 1967

Table 7.3 (*Continued*)

C. Areas with Accelerating E Growth, But No H or F Trends

Qinghai			Shandong			Henan		
			1787-1851	G	1760	1749-1851	G	1735
			....			....		
1873-1933	?G	1852	1873-1933	G	1831	1873-1913	G	1805
1933-1982	E	1970	1893-1964	E	1990	1933-1976	E	1981
1964-1987	G	1974	1953-1987	G	1952	1964-1987	G	1961

Hubei			Zhejiang			Guizhou		
1776-1851	G	1773	1771-1851	G	1754	1749,1771	G	1702
						1776-1851	G	1695
....			....			....		
1873-1933	E	1960	1873-1933	E	1979	1873-1957	E	1977
1953-1987	G	1951	1953-1987	G	1950	1964-1987	G	1970

Source: Note 19.

Figure 7.4a
Demographic Growth and Decline in the Provinces of China since 1749: Five Northern Provinces

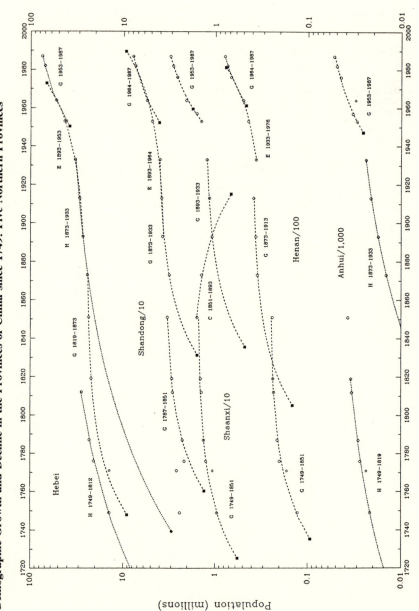

Source: Note 19.

Figure 7.4b
Demographic Growth and Decline in the Provinces of China since 1749: Five Southern Provinces

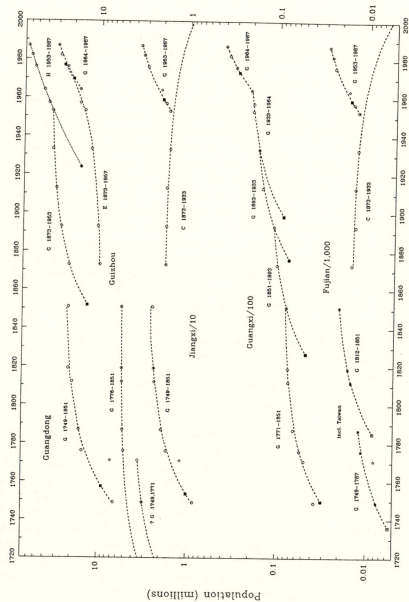

Source: Note 19.

increase preceeding the Taiping Rebellion. (To facilitate following this continuity from province to province before 1851, Table 7.3 divides trends before and after this critical point by broken lines.) The 1740–1850 H pattern for China as a whole (Figure 7.1b) came about, that is, mostly because G trajectories from province to province followed different timings. In the same fashion, predominantly G-shaped increases in the states of the United States have been seen to generate aggregate H expansion there for 1850–1940 through their staggered timing.

Of the six exceptional trends, the most unusual appeared in Shanxi Province. Here, explosion of the E type apparently occurred for 1776–1819, the table shows. A possible dynamic in this process is the growth of the Muslim population, which was soon to come into conflict here with the ruling Chinese. Or was it the intrusion of Chinese settlers themselves that expanded in provocative, accelerating fashion and touched off intercultural crisis? The appearance of this lone E trend, on the other hand, could just be coincidental.

Still further westward into the heartland of Asia, in pre-Taiping Gansu (part B of Table 7.3), meanwhile, occurred another historical instance in which very vigorous G growth (1749–1776) was replaced by suddenly flatter demographic increase in the G form (1776–1851). This phenomenon (rG), first encountered in the Great Plains of North America, has been associated in many places and at many times historically with overambitious attempts to develop new territory. "Gansu" at this administrative stage included the populations of several of China's farflung northern and western frontiers. Does the retrogressive succession of G trends here in the 1770s similarly signify how an over-zealous effort by the current dynasty to colonize and develop the northern and western fringes of the empire in the middle of the 18th century collided with a ceiling of actual potential?

The most common exceptions to G-type population growth in the provinces of China before 1851 were the five instances of local H-type expansion. Three cases occurred in territories astride the leading centers of China's economic development and trade: in Hebei, home of the Manchu capital, Beijing, and its port Tianjin; in Jiangsu, site of Shanghai at the outlet of the Yangtze; and in Anhui, where the south-north artery of the Grand Canal intersected with the west-east trade of the Yangtze (Perkins, 149). As Table 7.3 indicates, all three of these provincial H's roughly paralleled that for China as a whole 1750–1850 (Table 7.1), a not surprising result for the capital region and the chief centers of business in a growing society (like New York and Pennsylvania within the United States in the 19th century, as observed in Chapter 2). The tendency of populations in Hebei and Anhui to expand in the national H form, however, came to an end by about 1820. In Jiangsu, in contrast, it took the Taiping Rebellion to break the pattern. What does that say about the role of Shanghai and its environs in the mid-19th century development of China? The other two provincial H trends before 1851 show up in what might be called developmental frontiers: in Liaoning, across the Gulf of Chili from Hebei, which embraced the militarily and economically sensitive centers of Port Arthur, Dairen, and Mukden, and in Yunnan, China's wedge for expansion into Southeast Asia. The Yunnan H lasted only to 1787 and was generally parallel to that for the capital province of Hebei and of China as a whole. Did this shared pattern of growth result from some formal push by the central administration to develop the South? In Liaoning, in contrast, the slope of the local H of 1787–1851 was appreciably steeper than in the other four provinces with growth of that shape during this era, more like the H path taken by China as a whole for 1873–1936 than the country's contemporary H trend for 1750–1850. These nearer parts of Manchuria, rich in soybeans, coal, and harbors, were becoming prime territory for economic and military development; and a contest to out-expand the southward-encroaching Russians was on.

Elsewhere—in the vast majority of provinces for all or most of the time—between 1749 and 1851 population multiplied locally across China only according to the basic, rapidly decelerating path of G. In some places, however, such demographic increase via the G curve was flatter than in others (had earlier base years in the formula). On the geographical margins Shaanxi in the Northwest, Guizhou in the South, and Liaoning and Shanxi (both just to 1787), Table 7.3 shows, had flatter G's (with earlier base dates) than Guangxi, Guandong, Hunan, Jiangxi, Fujian, Zhejiang, Henan, and Hubei—which compose China's great belly that sags southeastwards into the Pacific—or Shandong. In Jilin, Manchuria as a whole, Sichuan, and Yunnan (after 1787), all dynamic developmental frontiers of pre-Taiping Chinese society, G growth steeper than the norm occurred. On the whole, relatively parallel G-shaped increases in population prevailed among certain types of provinces, with just enough variation in timing across these groups to make Chinese demographic growth as a whole accumulatively take an H path from 1750 to 1850.

Following the crises of the 1850s and 1860s, in contrast, patterns of provincial population growth across China became appreciably more varied. In the first place, population in four provinces systematically atrophied.[22] In neighboring Fujian and Jiangxi (Figure 7.4b) from 1873 into the 1930s numbers started to decline slowly, but then dropped off faster and faster in the rare C pattern that accelerates downward towards extinction. What was it about life in this region that put that unusual form of demographic decay into motion? It is perhaps easier to comprehend why population shrank in such an increasingly more rapid trajectory amid the harsh conditions of Tibet from 1819 through 1964. The deleterious effects of Chinese invasion in the 1950s seem to have continued a demographic decay that had been under way for decades. How even steeper C-type population loss occurred in Shaanxi, in the north, between 1851 and 1893 may reflect the way Muslim-Chinese conflict there unfolded over time; or it may instead have helped cause that tension. Neighboring Shanxi, with many of the same cultural and environmental problems, was the one province of China in the past two and a half centuries to see its population drop off in the globally more common decelerating D path of demographic decline. Local scholars will have to sort out the particulars; but some interesting questions arise from these similarities and distinctions in forms of local population loss, which are reminiscent of recent variations among certain rural departments of France in part C of Table 6.3.

Elsewhere since 1873, provincial populations across China have only expanded. Unlike the era before the Taiping Rebellion, though, all the familiar G-based forms of increase have now appeared with some frequency over the past century.

The F slope emerged in the 20th century in Xinjiang and Ningxia. Asian continental frontiers could support the same kind of constant proportional population growth as American ones or Siberia to the north.

Appreciably more common, however, has been expansion in the slowly decelerating H trajectory. Between 1873 and 1933 this type of demographic increase appeared in Hebei and Gansu in the north and, more steeply, in Jiangsu and Anhui on the lower Yangtze. Multiplication for Sichuan in the southwest followed a parallel H, with base year at 1792, for the longer period from 1873 all the way to 1964; and in Yunnan next door, contemporaneous H growth for 1873–1964 was stronger still (with t_0 at 1834). Since the 1930s, furthermore, phases of H expansion have also emerged in Shanxi and Ningxia in the north, Guandong on the southern coast, and Xinjiang in far inland China. Most of these provinces would seem to have been involved at the time in considerable economic (and/or military) development, a condition apparently associated historically with such a trajectory of demographic increase around the world, though the details of such connections in these parts of China will have to be spelled out by someone more familiar with local history.

Population explosion, common for Japan and other countries within Asia but totally absent in the national demographic expansion of China, has also unfolded locally in several provinces. One belt of territories with E curves was draped across southern China northeastwards from Guizhou in the deep interior through Hubei out to Zhejiang and Jiangsu on the central coast. Another group of provinces, which had later-starting and later-timed E trajectories of accelerating population growth, was located in the northeast: in Hebei, Shandong, and Henan, as Table 7.3 summarizes. The E trend for Qinghai in the far west resembled this pattern. Just why these 8 provinces experienced accelerating demographic increase, not the 19 others for which records exist concerning at least part of their growth patterns since 1873, will have to be worked out by someone else. But certain guiding questions seem obvious for such further inquiry: For instance, were combinations of local changes in birthrates and deathrates that underlay these provincial E trajectories in modern China comparable to what can be found for "exploding" nations and regions in Europe, elsewhere in Asia, or—say—in Latin America? Were agricultural change, migration, and industrialization once again important and distinctive factors in producing accelerating demographic increase, as apparently they have been in the explosions of European nations and regions?

In all other trends of population size since 1873 in the 27 provinces of

China—or temporarily aggregated groupings of territories forming Inner Mongolia and Manchuria (Ningxia, Suiyan, and Chahar; Liaoning, Jilin, and Heilongjiang)—the shape has been the basic G. To begin, 15 such paths of increase have been identified over the years before World War II, compared with 20 F, H, or E trends just described and 4 trajectories of sustained decline. That constitutes a much more diverse mix of pattern than the 19 G's, 5 H's, 1 E, and no systematic declines which appear across the provinces across the hundred years up through 1851. As China's total population increased in a new H trajectory from 1873 up to about 1940, distinctively different contributions to the whole were made by the various regions of the country. Even the timings of the G trends were more widely dispersed during this next demographic era, though provincial parallels as well as divergences continue to be informative.[23]

G growth between 1873 and 1940, as the population of China as a whole surged ahead again in H form, was mostly a phenomenon of the northern rim of the country (Qinghai, Ningxia, Shaanxi, Henan, Shandong, Suiyan, Chahar, and Manchuria) or a small area in the southeast (Guangxi three times, Hunan twice, and Guandong). Chinese demographers and economic historians ought to be able to isolate what it was that gave these regions the basic, quickly decelerating form of G increase in their populations while most provinces of the country saw demographic expansion take more unusual forms.

In marked local convergence, however, since World War II population virtually all across the provinces of China has expanded in G form. An H trend in Guandong—China's main international outlet—and short sequences of H increase and F multiplication in the westernmost Inner Mongolian territory of Ningxia and the far northwestern province of Xinjiang are the only exceptions.[24] Even more than between 1749 and 1851, H expansion for China as a whole since the Revolution has depended upon just differences of timing among the various provincial G patterns. And this lagging has been regionally very simple in pattern: In an almost solid triangle of provinces from Jilin and Liaoning in Manchuria down the coast through Hebei, Shandong, Jiangsu, and Zhejiang to Fujian and tapering back inland through Jiangxi, Anhui, Hubei, Shaanxi, and Shanxi to a point at Gansu, the G curve had in all but one case begun by 1953 and had a base year by 1957 or earlier. Elsewhere, the postwar G's have been later and more robust, beginning after 1953 and having their t_0's in the 1960s and 1970s. Whether for reasons of tighter political control (including limitation of births) or due to variations in economic development, the most constricted recent population growth in China has been in the thirteen provinces of the core wedge. Faster, less restrained demographic increase has characterized the flanks of this inner triangle to the south and the north.

In sum, during all three broad eras of modern Chinese demographic history—1740–1850, 1850–1940, and from 1950 to the present—provincial population trends have followed G-based patterns. These movements open up and structure fruitful courses for further investigation, of population dynamics but also of economic and social change.

Earlier, from the later 1300s to the later 1500s it seems as though the rise

Table 7.4

Between the Mongols and the Manchu: Apparent Population Trends for the Ming Provinces from 1381 through 1578

	1381-1491				1491-1578	
CHINA	1391-1488	D 1350		CHINA	1487-1569	G 1440
Hubei+Hunan	1381-1491	D 1332		Hubei+Hunan	1491-1578	G 1424
Jiangxi	1381-1491	D 1345		Jiangxi	1491-1578	D 1413#
Anhui+Jiangsu	1391-1491	D 1352		Anhui+Jiangsu	1491-1578	G 1452
Guangdong	1381-1491	D 1362		Guangdong	1491-1578	G 1427
Fujian	1381-1542	D 1365*		Fujian	1491-1578	?C 1622#
Zhejiang	1381-1542	D 1370*		Zhejiang	1542,1578	G 1462
				Yunnan	1391-1578	?G 1443
Shaanxi	1381-1491	G 1294		Shaanxi	1491-1578	G 1443
Shandong	1381-1491	G 1317		Shandong	1491-1578	G 1447
Guangxi	1381-1491	G 1325		Guangxi	1491-1578	G 1488
Henan	1381-1491	G 1348		Henan	1491-1578	G 1480
Hebei	1381-1542	G 1364*		Hebei	1491-1578	E 1626
Gansu+Shanxi	1381-1542	G 1365*		Gansu+Shanxi	1491-1578	E 1640
Sichuan	1381-1542	G 1365*		Sichuan	1491-1578	E 1630
				Guizhou	1491-1578	E 1642

* Early G or D lasts to 1542 rather than 1491.
\# Two provinces with decline 1491–1578.

Source: Notes 25–27.

and fall of provincial populations also moved in G-based forms. The evidence is widely spaced and is sometimes contested among informed authorities, in part because they employ differing Chinese sources (Durand 1960, 250–51; Perkins 1969, 207; Ho, 1959, 258). Nonetheless, surprisingly simple and suggestive regional clusters of G and D patterns appear, as Table 7.4 demonstrates for two eras that generally divided the demographic experience of the Ming dynasty, which ruled China across the long epoch from the ouster of the Mongols to the Manchu invasion of the 1600s. The curves are only approximated by template, but the details should be close to the mark.

From the end of the 14th century to the last years of the 15th, the territories of eight modern provinces—Hubei with Hunan and Anhui with Jiangsu (which were paired administratively at the time) and also Jiangxi, Guangdong, Fujian, and Zhejiang—saw the number of their inhabitants dwindle away along D paths very much like the population of China as a whole at the time (Figure 7.1b). In the cases of Fujian and Zhejiang this decelerating type of decline lasted on to about 1540.[25] In contrast, meanwhile, the populations of nine other areas (Shaanxi, Shandong, Guangxi, Henan, Hebei, Sichuan, Yunnan, and Gansu with Shanxi) expanded forward from the 1380s along G curves with base years in the early to middle 1300s. In four instances this trend lasted to the 1540s.[26] Table 7.4 shows how most of these G's were virtually vertical mirror images of the D's of the eight other territories. How could the Chinese people as a whole then atrophy in D form during 1391–1488? The answer is that the shrinking provincial populations were much *larger* than the growing ones: As of 1381 about 41 of 59 million people lived where atrophy was to take place. Population decline from the 1380s to the 1490s occurred in the rice-producing regions from the lower Yangtze southward, where most people resided. What changes in the early decades of Ming rule set off depopulation there (and therefore in China as a whole), while regions to the north and west experienced demographic increase? Did overeager taxation depopulate China's breadbasket? Did disease or change in landholding or government policies of regional development pull and push people to relocate to the north and west?

Subsequently, from about 1491 through 1578, all but two of China's provinces saw their peoples expand. The exceptions were neighboring Fujian and Jiangxi, on the southeast coast opposite Taiwan. Local historians should be able to determine what cut back population here while mostly it multiplied across China from the late 15th century until the late 16th. Begging special explanation is the apparent tendency of Fujian's people to contract in the rare, slowly starting but accelerating C trajectory while Jiangxi (just inland) lost people in the more familiar faster-starting but soon slowing D form. What was going on in these provinces? Or is there just some fluke in the data?

In most areas, population increased across the 16th century in G paths very similar to what has been found for China as a whole for 1487–1569.[27] Only Guangxi and Henan display appreciably steeper G curves for the period. Across an arc of northern and western frontiers ranging from Hebei, next to Manchuria, through Shanxi, Gansu, and Sichuan to Guizhou just north of Annam, however, the number of people seems to have expanded in accelerating E explosion 1491–1578. Were these local build-ups around the fringe of Chinese society driven by migration (perhaps some of it forced) or by natural increase encouraged through open-ended settlement and economic development? Or are widely spaced data points leading our trending astray?

Still earlier in Chinese history, several provinces that were not ravaged by the Mongols saw their numbers of households grow in G patterns during the 11th, 12th, and 13th centuries approximately parallel to the G for China as a whole for 1058–1103 (base year at 1053) and the G for the Sung South 1160–1223 ($t_0 = 1085$) in Table 7.1. The counts in Guangdong and Guangxi together, Fujian, and Zhejiang all probably increased from 1080 to 1173 and from there to about 1280 in G form with base year near 1040 (Perkins, 195). In Jiangxi and Hunan, growth parallel to this seems to have occurred between 1080 and 1173. Then, though, refugees from the Mongol devastation of the North almost doubled the household numbers reported in these provinces by 1280. From 1080 to 1173 household numbers in Hebei and Sichuan (then including modern Yunnan and Guizhou) also increased in a manner that could have followed G curves with t_0's just a little later, in the 1070s.[28] Meanwhile, Anhui and Jiangsu and

Hubei may have held only half as many households by 1173 as in 1080. Whether this resulted from actual losses in the Jurchen invasion of northern China or from how control over these two territories (three provinces today) was divided between the Sung, who kept the relevant records, and the Chin, who apparently did not, will have to be determined by somebody else. So will the validity of such drastic regional decreases. In all, though, provinces that were not overrun by Jurchens or Mongols or flooded by refugees from these invasions all seem to have gained population in very common form. So did other territories, up to the point where their growth was violently disrupted.

In short, for China throughout most of the past nine centuries, regional as well as national population growth (or decline) is insightfully organized in terms of G-based trends. Such patterning seems to make sense within the context of some of the broader outlines of familiar Chinese history and should stimulate, probably assist, study of how demographic movements of this sort were rooted in and in turn did much to shape the social and economic development of the varied regions contained within this most populous nation of the world.

In Japan as a whole, demographic growth during the second half of the 18th century and the first half of the 19th was very different from that in China. No robust H pertained; instead, numbers first fell slightly via D for 1732–1780 and 1780–1792, then rose somewhat via G for 1792–1852, to leave the population on the eve of the Meiji Restoration roughly the same size as it had been approximately a century and a half before (Figure 7.2 and Table 7.2). This tendency to equilibrate did not, however, eliminate variation of pattern among the regions that composed Japan.

Population trends for the *do* or divisions during the last century of the Tokugawa regime show simultaneous atrophy and growth. Forty years ago, Irene B. Taeuber, whose data are reexamined here, argued that local fluctuations over the period 1750 to 1800 gave way to general demographic increase for the next half century.[29] That does not quite seem to be the case.

Actually, demographic decline in a large and crucial part of Japan, the south face of the main island from the eastern end of the Inland Sea to somewhat above Tokyo (the *do* of Kinai, Tokaido, and Tosando-shima), continued well past Taeuber's "divide" at the turn of the century along D trends already at work by 1750.[30] In the northern portion of the main island, Tosando-kami, the size of the population for all practical purposes remained flat for the century between 1750 and 1852. Thus four large regions, which contained over half of Japan's population in 1804 (midway through the hundred years studied), fail to conform with the sustained population increases that Taeuber claimed to be general for the first half of the 19th century. Meanwhile, across the later 1700s, G trends of increase, rather than decline, prevailed in Sanyodo, Sanindo, and Saikaido-shimo—respectively the southern and northern coasts of Honshu west of Kyoto and the lower part of Kyushu. Those G-type increases persisted all the way to 1852. The trends for these *do* neither fell and then rose nor climbed as steeply in the 1800s as did the patterns for Japan as a whole. The growth of population across the first half of the 19th century leading up to the Meiji Restoration that Taeuber attributed to "early commercial and industrial developments" can be found only in four *do*: It is most evident in Hokkaido, the thinly populated, northernmost island, on which Japan's aboriginal population, the Ainu, still outnumbered settlers in 1800. Also experiencing fresh demographic expansion of the G form in the first half of the 19th century were Nankaido, the southwestern island behind which runs the Inland Sea; Hokurokudo, "the cold and humid western coast of Honshu"; and Saikaido-kami, the "upper" part of Kyushu. Perhaps the sea trades of these regions and the tempting forests and mines of Hokkaido spurred systematic new demographic growth across the first half of the 19th century, extending up to the Meiji Restoration. But Japan's leading centers of commerce and industry were not generating comparable G surges of demographic increase in their *do* at this time.

In fact, only one *do* in eleven, Saikaido-kami—representing the upper end of Kyushu, the bottom island of Japan—roughly paralleled the country as a whole in population movement both before and after 1800. While identifying the regional G and D trends of later Tokugawa Japan confirms some of the basic points Taeuber made looking at these same data four decades ago, it offers significant extension and revision of her interpretation.

Past the Meiji reforms of the later 1800s, the population of Japan as a whole has been observed to multiply for several decades in a very different and more challenging form (Figure 7.2). Repeated trends of the proportionally accelerating E type appear for 1872–1885, 1885–1915, and possibly 1915–1935 before a sequence of decelerating G's takes over to last until the present time. What regional movements underlay such trends? How uniformly did the changes in births and deaths and migration that netted out into such patterns for the nation generate parallel surges of population at more local levels?

Existing records make it possible to follow demographic increase or decline in eleven regions of Japan, including Okinawa, from 1903 through 1992 (Figure 7.5).[31] Distinct patterns of movement stand out for different parts of the country, and none of these slavishly followed the trends for Japan as a whole. As discovered for the century preceding the Meiji Restoration, quite dynamic and diverse regional histories have continued in modern times to underlie the broad national outlines of Japanese population change.

Along the southeastern side of the outward bow of the big island, Honshu, eastward from Kinki (the Tokugawa division of Kinai) around Kobe, Kyoto, and Osaka through the prefectures of Tokai (Mie, Aichi, and Shizokua) to Kanto (Tokyo and its environs), Figure 7.5 and Table 7.5 show that relatively parallel sequences of G growth have occurred since 1903. The one exception in this heartland of modern Japanese development appeared in Kinki, where in the early 1970s the shared path of expansion following World War II could no longer be sustained, and a retrogressively timed rG trajectory—more like the one for 1920–1940—was followed instead. What kind of ceiling did demographic increase in the environs of Osaka Bay encounter at this time?

Figure 7.5
Population Trends in the Regions of Modern Japan

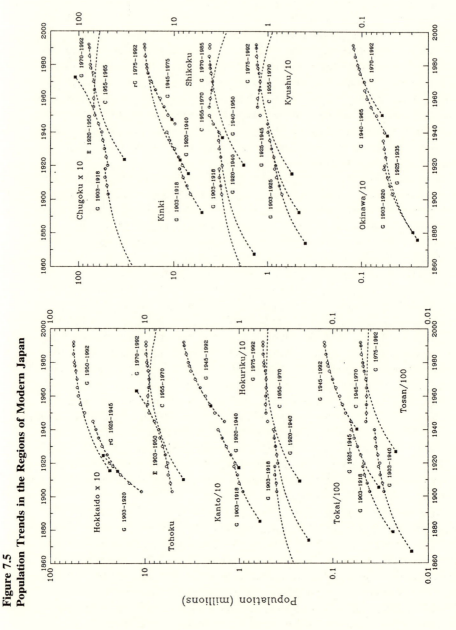

Source: Note 31.

Table 7.5
Growth and Decline in the Regions of 20th Century Japan

A. Eastern Central Honshu: The Modern Heartland

Kanto		Kinki		Tokai	
1903-1918	G 1885	1903-1918	G 1892	1903-1918	G 1879
1920-1940	G 1917	1920-1940	G 1915	1925-1945	G 1906
1945-1992	G 1954	1945-1970	G 1947	1945-1992	G 1940
		1975-1992	rG 1923		

B. The Rest of Honshu

Tosan		Hokuriku		Tohoku		Chugoku	
		1903-1918	G 1841			1903-1918	G 1853
1903-1940	G 1867	1920-1940	G 1853	1903-1950	E 1963	1920-1950	E 1973
1945-1965	C 2090	1950-1970	C 2092	1955-1970	C 2046	1955-1965	C 2054
1970-1992	G 1927	1970-1992	G 1909	1970-1992	G 1910	1970-1992	G 1923

C. The Southern Islands, Okinawa, and Hokkaido

Shikoku		Kyushu		Okinawa		Hokkaido	
1903-1918	G 1846	1903-1925	G 1874	1903-1920	G 1880	1903-1920	G 1925
1920-1940	G 1867	1925-1945	G 1892	1925-1935	G 1876	1925-1945	rG 1915
1940-1950	G 1937			1940-1965	G 1938		
1955-1970	C 2018	1955-1970	C 2022				
1970-1985	G 1920	1975-1992	G 1915	1970-1992	G 1950	1950-1992	G 1916

Source: Note 31.

For the rest of Honshu, a distinctly different pattern for population size has pertained since World War II. Tohoku, comprising the northern third of the island above Tokyo, Tosan and Hokuriku respectively inland and along the other coast west of the capital, and Chugoku, the bottom end of Honshu below Kobe, all saw their peoples atrophy in the unusual slow-starting but accelerating C form after the war. So did the western islands of Shikoku and Kyushu. Chugoku and Tohoku, at the opposite ends of the big island, had experienced accelerating E expansion for three or more decades up to 1950, the only *regions* of the country to display such an exploding pattern at any time. In Tosan and Hokuriku and on Shikoku and Kyushu, in contrast, a quick jump in numbers is evident between 1940 and 1950 (Figure 7.5) that offset simultaneous loss of population in Kanto, the region of the severely bombed capital, Tokyo, and Kinki, around Osaka and Kobe. Such war-era shifts were not sustained and began to erode faster and faster in C fashion. By about 1970, though, all six areas saw their populations increase once more. These growths took largely parallel G form, though not as strong as was evident in Kanto, Kinki, and Tokai (with base years more like 1917 than the 1947 average for those three other areas).

Besides the unusual E surges of Tohoku and Chugoku, patterns preceding World War II indicate both parallels and contrasts in the timing and steepness of G trends. It was primarily these mixes that generated successive E trajectories for Japan as a whole across the early decades of the 1900s. In all, though, regionalism in this century's population growth in Japan is quite simple to pattern. The resulting G-based trends of Figure 7.5 and Table 7.5 show both continuity and contrast, which should be easy to explain in terms of the demographic dynamics and economic and social histories of the regions involved.

As within Japan and China, it is possible to follow demographic growth and decline across the states and territories that compose India, the second most populous country of the world. Figures for administrative units used since independence and the separation of Pakistan have been officially reconstructed for the 1901–1941 years of the British colonial Raj to yield consistent local series across the present century.[32] Table 7.6 compares the sequences of pattern that emerge from graphing and curve-fitting. Figure 7.6 plots the trends for some of the larger regions.

The first thing to note is that ten adjoining, mostly large states listed in part A of Table 7.6 saw their populations expand between 1901 and 1991 in a sequence very like the pattern for India as a whole: G growth in the early years of the century was followed by E explosion for several decades and then by slowly decelerating H increase since about 1960. These states included about two-thirds of India's total population of 361 million as of 1951, halfway through the era studied. In the majority of the country, in other words, whatever interplay of fertility, mortality, and migration produced this sequence of G, E, and H trends, it was shared from state to state.

That degree of commonality, whether deriving from national policy or from some other convergence of local demographic behavior, is very different from what has been found in modern China and Japan. In those two other major Asian nations, going back as far as 1381 and 1721 respectively, provinces or districts have exhibited much more variety within the country-wide framework. Only a small minority of local patterns followed the national outline. The implication is that India has experienced much less social and economic change through regional transformations.

In five other large states of India (part B of Table 7.6), furthermore, demographic expansion both in the early 20th century and since 1960 or so has also tended to follow the country-wide pattern, save that no population explosion of the constantly proportionally accelerating E sort is needed for modeling demographic increase across the middle of the 1900s.[33] Of this group, Madhya Pradesh, Bihar, Orissa, and West Bengal (next to Bangladesh) form a block of four large states that constitutes the eastern quarter of the diamond shape that represents India minus her nearly isolated eastern territories. Among these remote eastern districts, too, bounded by Bangladesh, Myanmar, and China, E explosion has been mostly absent. Unlike the states of section B in the table, though, these even more eastern-placed territories of part C are distinguished from India as a whole also by their very recent patterns of demographic increase. Several are currently experiencing rapidly decelerating G growth in their populations, not the more slowly slowing H's of the large states of sections A and B of Table 7.6. In contrast, though, Tripura, Meghalaya, Manipur, and Arunachal Pradesh—confronting Bangladesh, Myanmar, and China—through purposeful settlement policy or for some other reason have populations that are now multiplying at the constant .03 rate of the F trend. They are behaving, in other words, like demographic as well as political and military frontiers. In the West (part D of the table), finally, several scattered territories—mostly small ones—also have failed to conform to the general and widely shared regional growth patterns for India.

In sum, while varying local trend sequences around the fringes of the country have emerged, the main challenge is to explain how so much area-by-area homogeneity characterized the demographic expansion of India, in contrast to the local variety that has been found within China and Japan. It would also be insightful to comprehend just how Kerala, Madhya Pradesh, Orissa, Bihar, and West Bengal may have avoided the E-type population explosion that was so widespread across most larger states of the country during the middle of the century. Even within the largely common demographic patterning of Indian regional history, G-based trends reveal provocative and insightful differences as well as shared movements.

Less extensive evidence for a few other Asian countries merits at least some preliminary analysis, estimated by just fitting curve templates by eye. Clues are culled from Sri Lanka, the Philippines, Peninsular Malaysia, and Indonesia.

In Ceylon/Sri Lanka following World War II, all but two of the nineteen districts or pairs of subsequently divided districts indicate G growth roughly similar to that for the country as a whole (Peebles 1982, 30–31, 33). Such uniformity was hardly the case previously. One group of districts, which lay mostly in the mountainous southeastern portion of the island, saw their populations expand across the late 1800s and early 1900s only via successive G trends. Southern and western coastal sectors of the island, meanwhile, contained districts that experienced two surges of E-type population explosion between 1871 (when records begin) and the 1960s. Local scholars should easily establish the factors that generated these divergent patterns of demographic growth and their consequences in regional social and economic life.

The population of the Philippines as a whole grew in H form under American colonial rule. Subsequently, it exploded across the middle of the century in accelerating E fashion before settling into log-linear F increase for the period 1960–1980 and then dropping off into G deceleration since the 1970s (part C

Table 7.6
Population Patterns in the States and Territories of India since 1901

A. States Largely Following the Sequence for All India

<u>INDIA</u>
1850-1921 G 1834
1901-1971 E 1972
1961-1991 H 1947

<u>Tamil Nadu</u>
1901-1921 G 1856
1921-1971 E 1970
1961-1991 H 1924

<u>Karnataka</u>
1901-1921 G 1807
1921-1971 E 1970
1961-1991 H 1946

<u>Andhra Pradesh</u>
1901-1921 G 1857
1921-1941 G 1900
1941-1971 E 1979
1971-1991 H 1949

<u>Maharashtra</u>
1901-1921 G 1843
1901-1971 E 1968
1961-1991 H 1951

<u>Uttar Pradesh</u>
1901-1921 C 2000
1921-1941 E 1969
1941-1981 E 1982
1971-1991 H 1955

<u>Jammu & Kashmir</u>
1901-1941 E 1967

<u>Gujarat</u>
1901-1921 G 1855
1901-1961 E 1961
1961-1991 H 1953

<u>Rajasthan</u>
1921-1941 E 1962
1941-1961 E 1972
1971-1991 H 1971

<u>Punjab</u>
1911-1941 E 1958
1951-1981 H 1921

<u>Himachal Pradesh</u>
1911-1981 E 1982
1941-1991 H 1944

<u>West Bengal</u>
1901-1921 G 1816
1931-1951 G 1917
1951-1991 H 1951

B. Major States without Sustained Population Explosion

<u>Kerala</u>
1901-1921 G 1874
1921-1941 G 1912
1951-1991 H 1931

<u>Madhya Pradesh</u>
1901-1921 G 1861
1931-1951 G 1904
1961-1991 H 1954

<u>Orissa</u>
1901-1921 G 1845
1921-1951 G 1895
1951-1991 H 1932

<u>Bihar</u>
1901-1921 G 1812
1921-1951 G 1900
1961-1991 H 1942

C. Distinctive Patterns in the Eastern Regions of India

<u>Nagaland</u>
1921-1941 G 1890
1951-1971 G 1974
1981,1991 G 1999

<u>Mizoram</u>
1901-1921 G 1863
1921-1941 H 1903
1951-1971 G 1956
1971-1991 G 1989

<u>Assam</u>
1901-1931 E 1935
1931-1961 E 1958
1961-1991 G 1968

<u>Sikkim</u>
1931-1961 H 1855
1961-1981 E 1985
1961-1991 G 1984

<u>Andaman & Nicobar Is.</u>
1961-1981 E 1975
1961-1991 G 1991

Table 7.6 (Continued)

Tripura	Meghalaya	Manipur	Arunachal Pradesh
1911-1931 G 1915	1901-1921 G 1877	1901-1951 H 1855	
1931-1951 G 1935	1931-1951 G 1909		
1951-1971 G 1974			1961-1981 G 1975
1961-1991 F .	1961-1991 F .	1951-1991 F .	1951-1991 F .

D. Varied Trends in More Western Locations

Lakshadweep	Goa, Daman, Diu	Dadra & Nagar Haveli	Pondicherry
1921-1961 H 1872	1921-1961 G 1882	1901-1951 G 1890	1921-1971 E 1978
1961-1991 H 1960	1961-1991 G 1967	1951-1971 G 1959	1971-1991 E 1982
		1971-1991 G 1982	

Haryana	Chandigarh	Delhi
1901-1921 D 1847	1901-1921 D 1874	1911-1941 E 1931
1931-1951 G 1905	1931-1951 G 1905	1941-1971 G 1971
1951-1991 H 1961	1961-1991 G 1996	1971-1991 G 1991

Source: Note 32.

Figure 7.6
Patterns of Demographic Growth and Decline in Some Larger States of India

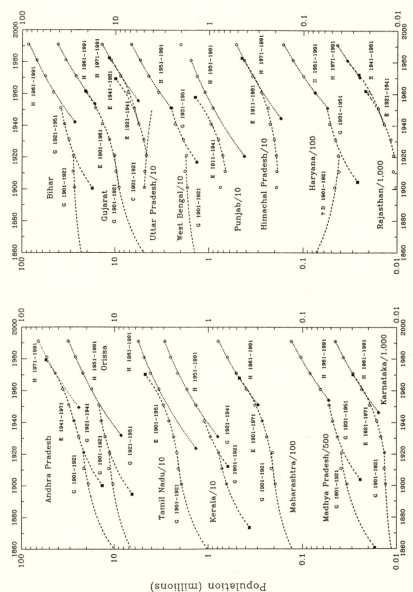

Population (millions)

Source: Note 32.

of Table 7.2). Recently, as in Sri Lanka, populations in 11 of 13 divisions of the Philippines have been expanding in G trends comparable to that for the nation as a whole (Philippines, *1988 Stat. Ybk.* 24–30). Earlier, more diversity is evident. The likely F trend for the country across the 1960s and 1970s arose out of varied timing among the G curves evident in most regions. Similarly, the H-type expansion of the Philippine population as a whole up through 1948 received support from H trends in only four regions (Western Visayas and three parts of Mindanao) that faced southwestward to the Sulu and Celebes Seas. Then the accelerating E growth that gave the country population explosion, while common to eight regions of the Philippines between 1939 and 1970, failed to emerge in Southern and Northern Mindanao, Northeast Luzon, Metropolitan Manila, and Western Visaya. In all, one sees a growing cross-regional convergence of demographic behavior in the Philippines: least during the national H trend of 1918–1948 (under U.S. colonial development and administration), more during the E surge of 1939–1960 that accompanied World War II and independence, and most of all during the G growth of recent decades.

On the Malay penisula (the mainland portion of the present state of Malaysia, formerly the British colony of Malaya), as of 1980 no similar homogenizing of state patterns of demographic growth with the national one had occurred with time (Saw 1988, 50, 57). To the contrary, regional population histories have, if anything, *diverged* since reliable records began in 1911. The country has split into an eastern region of four states (Jahore, Pahang, Kelantan, and Trengganu) that have had mid-century population explosion, which still continues or has led to local F-type constant multiplication, and a western zone of seven states in which demographic increase is decelerating. In three cases, growth is flattening rapidly via the basic G curve (as for Peninsular Malaysia as a whole for 1955–1980); in four of these areas (Kedah, Perak, Penang, and Selangor) the more slowly slowing H is the model. In four of the states situated along the Malacca coast, furthermore, no E-type explosion has occurred at any point since 1911.

This regional distribution means that the central western portion of Peninsular Malaysia has had demographic growth through the course of the present century much like Java, the most developed part of the large nation of Indonesia, not far away—or resource-rich Brunei and Sabah on Borneo (Table 7.2). In contrast, Malaya's eastern zone has had its population expand more as on less-developed Sumatra, the big island at Indonesia's northwestern end, near Malaya's Malacca coast in geography but apparently unlike it in social and economic history. As in Sumatra, E then F sequences of population growth have appeared across recent decades on meagerly developed Irian Jaya, the Indonesian end of New Guinea, and Kalimantan, the bulk of Borneo that is part of Indonesia. E followed by G or H deceleration has been the norm in Sulawesi (the Celebes) and West and East Nusa Tenggara (the Flores Islands, Timor, etc.). Perhaps largely due to tourism, population on Bali has expanded since 1961 in a slowly slowing H trend resembling that for Java, while the far-flung Molucca Islands at the eastern end of Indonesia (Maluku) have witnessed constant proportional population increase of the F type over the past three decades (Indonesia World Bank 1994, 169). The regional data from Indonesia, though scant, especially when connected with evidence from neighboring Malaysia and the Philippines usefully expand the sense of what sort of places within the countries of southeastern Asia have experienced the different G-based patterns of population increase and how local movements have followed, or failed to follow, national ones.[34]

Regrettably, regional historical evidence for the *western* end of Asia is more difficult to come by with one notable exception (Karpat 1985).[35] Though brief in chronological range and beset by boundary changes and some apparently faulty official reporting, this compilation of Ottoman censuses, as supplemented with some corrections by its author, makes it possible to acquire at least a general sense of what kinds of growth patterns prevailed across the last several decades of this extensive, if shrinking, empire—how demographic expansions in what became parts of Turkey, Greece, Yugoslavia, Albania, Syria, Lebanon, Palestine/Israel, and Iraq compared with each other. This pathbreaking work makes it quite clear that between the 1870s and World War I regional populations all across the Ottoman Empire predominantly increased in G form, and virtually nothing else.[36]

There appears, furthermore, to be no broad regional system to the timing of these curves. From limited data available, it seems likely that the populations of documented territories all expanded in roughly parallel G trajectories from 1831 or sooner to 1878. Among G's across later years the steeper ones are scattered all across the empire: from Suriye (Syria) in the south to Bitlis near the Caucasus, and from there to Istanbul. Quite local circumstances are needed to explain how later, more robust G surges occurred in these places rather than elswhere.

Certain distinctive movements in the data clearly reflect Balkan wars, boundary changes, and ethnic and religious separations of the period (in Iskodra, Yanya, Manastir, Salonik, Edirne, and the Aegean Islands). The notorious repression of Armenians produced something like a D curve along which the population of Van was cut in half between 1878 and 1906. Other shifts or bounces in local numbers seem to entail erratic record-keeping, as in undercounts for neighboring areas (Jerusalem with Syria and Bitlis with Diyarbekir in 1906; Jerusalem, Beyrut, and Zor in 1878) or shifts of population between them (Bitlis and Diyarbekir after 1878; the environs of Bursa between 1874 and 1893). As it has done in other historical contexts, G patterning helps order the data and elucidate likely errors and ambiguities even beyond the notable achievements of a scholar like Karpat.

For the Ottoman Empire in its waning decades, for Peninsular Malaysia and the Philippines since the 1910s, for Ceylon/Sri Lanka beginning in the 1870s, for India across the past century, for both modern and Tokugawa Japan, and for China over much of the last thousand years, it has been possible to compare and contrast demographic growth or decline from region to region, as earlier chapters have done for local territories within Europe and the Americas. In Asia as elsewhere, internal movements within parts of national populations have articulated in quite diverse ways with overall country-wide trends. Once again, furthermore, the identification of types of changes in population size with parts of nations known to have certain local histories or characteristics helps towards understanding what is likely to underlie the dynamics of the different forms of G-based trends that are so universally observed. At the same time, in the continuing dialogue between evidence and systematization, patterning by means of the G-related curves has demonstrated connections and distinctions among regions that are not emphasized in the literature to date and has thrown further light upon certain problems of quality and reliability in the available data.

ONCE AGAIN DARKEST AFRICA: DEMOGRAPHIC INCREASE AMONG THE PEOPLES WE KNOW LEAST

Insensitive colonialism, lingering tribalism, and erratic administration have conspired to divide Africa into more than fifty countries whose demographic records are mostly short in time and weak in reliability and frequently cover populations smaller than those found for regions within substantial nations elsewhere. Still, it is essential to see what order and insight emerge from the countrywide counts and estimates that do exist. Table 7.7 groups the national patternings according to (A) territories that have seen only G growth, (B) nations whose peoples have recently expanded in the less usual F or H trajectories, and (C) populations that have exploded via the E curve but have not experienced the F or H paths of demographic multiplication.[37] Figure 7.7 plots the G-related trends that seem to fit demographic increase and decline in some of the countries of modern Africa. Most have patterns only for the present century.

There is little question about what kinds of places have had only G growth since their records begin. Most lie off the coast of the continent (the Seychelles, Mauritius, Reunion, and the Comoros to the east and the Cape Verdes to the west) or embrace just small areas of Africa's near-equatorial littoral on the Atlantic or Indian Ocean sides. That recently tragic Rwanda and Burundi have similarly seen only G growth may in part derive from their short population records. But they are also small countries, which like every territory but Ethiopia in section A of Table 7.7, lie roughly along the diagonal that traverses Africa and its insular appendages from the Cape Verdes, at about 15 degrees north on the west side of the continent, in the Atlantic, to Mauritius and Reunion at 20 degrees south on the east, in the Indian Ocean.

In contrast, several countries across the North of Africa, here and there dipping down deep across the great Sahara desert, have experienced in recent decades the more robust H and F forms of G-related demographic growth. This group (subset 1 in part B of the table) includes Egypt and Sudan to the east and Morocco, Algeria, Tunisia, and Niger to the west, but for some reason not Libya and Chad in between. Another cluster of peoples in southeastern Africa (subset

Table 7.7
Known Patterns of Growth in Fifty-One Populations of Africa

A. Territories with Only Decelerating G Growth

1. Islands. etc.

Comoros	Seychelles	Mauritius	Reunion	Cape Verde	Equit. Guinea	Sao Tome & Principe
	1891-1931 G 1882	1862-1931 G 1810			1920-1950 G 1917	1921-1960 G 1862
	1931-1960 G 1920					
1966-1975 G 1962	1963-1990 G 1955	1944-1990 G 1953	1954-1990 G 1958	1950-1990 G 1958	1950-1990 G 1943	1963-1975 G 1966
1975-1990 G 1992					1975-1990 G 1980	

2. Mainland Populations Strung Southeastwards from Cape Verde to the Indian Ocean

Senegal	Guinea-Bissau	Ivory Coast	Rwanda	Burundi	Ethiopia?
1931-1950 G 1912					
1950-1970 G 1961		1950-1960 G 1942	1960-1975 G 1967	1960-1980 G 1953	1956-1975 ?G 1970
1970-1990 G 1981	1970-1990 G 1984	1960-1990 G 1986	1975-1990 G 1988	1980-1990 G 1983	1975-1990 ?G 1990

B. Populations That Have Expanded in F or H Form

1. In Northern Africa

Egypt	Morocco	Tunisia	Algeria	Niger	Sudan
			1872-1886 G 1881		
			1886-1906 E 1919		
1882-1927 H 1849	1921-1931 G 1915	1911-1926 G 1871	1911-1948 E 1959		
	1931-1960 G 1932	1926-1946 E 1948	1948-1963 E 1977		
1917-1966 E 1962	1960-1980 F .	1946-1970 E 1976	1963-1980 G 1971	1960-1975 G 1977	1950-1970 F .
1960-1990 H 1956	1971-1990 G 1972	1966-1985 F .	1970-1990 F .	1970-1990 F .	1973-1990 F .
		1975-1990 G 1976			

2. In Southeastern Africa

Kenya	Tanzania	Zambia	Zimbabwe	Malawi	Madagascar
		1904-1931 E 1929	1901-1911 G 1917	1901-1926 G 1903	1921-1950 G 1891
1921-1949 E 1940	1921-1957 H 1905	1921-1950 G 1923	1911-1950 E 1947	1926-1945 G 1927	
1949-1975 H 1975		1950-1969 G 1971	1950-1963 G 1986		1950-1970 E 1969
1975-1990 E 1973	1957-1990 F .	1969-1990 F .	1963-1990 F .	1945-1990 F .	1970-1990 F .

280

Table 7.7 (*Continued*)

3. Along the Guinea Coast

Gambia		
1901-1921	G	1922
1931-1963	E	1973
1963-1980	G	1979
1970-1990	F	.

Guinea		
1950-1970	F	.
1970-1983	E	1975
1980-1990	?G	1927

Liberia		
1950-1974	E	1972
1960-1990	F	.

Ghana		
1911-1948	G	1924
1948-1970	G	1962
1970-1990	F	.

Togo		
1922-1950	E	1970
1959-1990	F	.

C. Populations with Explosions, But No F or H Expansions

1. Currently or Recently (?) Exploding

Libya?		
1931-1951	G	1925
1954-1970	E	1955
1970-1984	E	1965

Chad		
1931-1970	G	1949
1970-1990	E	1991

Central African Rep.		
1936-1980	E	1969
1980-1990	E	1988

Cameroon		
1924-1949	E	1937
1960-1970	E	1958
1970-1990	E	1983

Congo		
1921-1936	G	1941
1950-1970	E	1961
1970-1990	E	1977

Uganda		
1911-1970	E	1955
1970-1990	E	1978

Swaziland		
1904-1936	G	1900
1921-1966	E	1951
1966-1990	E	1981

Somalia?		
1931-1963	G	1941
1950-1980	E	1971

Mauritania		
1931-1950	E	1926
1950-1976	E	1971
1976-1990	E	1994

Upper Volta		
1950-1980	E	1979

Sierre Leone		
1901-1963	G	1894
1963-1975	E	1978
1975-1990	E	1995

Benin		
1920-1936	E	1930
1936-1970	E	1967
1970-1990	E	1983

2. Decelerating after Explosion

Libya? (Botswana)		
1921-1946	G	1930
1946-1971	G	1957
1971-1990	E	1971

Mali		
1921-1936	G	1898
1950-1970	E	1975
1963-1990	G	1968

Nigeria		
1902-1931	G	1884
1931-1963	E	1951
1963-1980	E	1969
1975-1990	G	1986

Gabon		
1921-1975	E	1969
1970-1990	G	1975
1960-1985	G	1972

Zaire		
1921-1940	G	1924
1947-1970	E	1959

Angola		
1900-1931	?C	1939
1940-1975	E	1983
1975-1990	G	1983

Namibia		
1921-1952	E	1949
1946-1963	G	1949
1963-1990	G	1989

Lesotho		
1891-1921	G	1902
1946-1970	E	1969
1970-1990	G	1981

Mozambique		
1928-1963	G	1922
1960-1980	E	1971
1970-1990	G	1983

Source: Note 37.

281

Figure 7.7
Some Discernible Population Trends in Africa

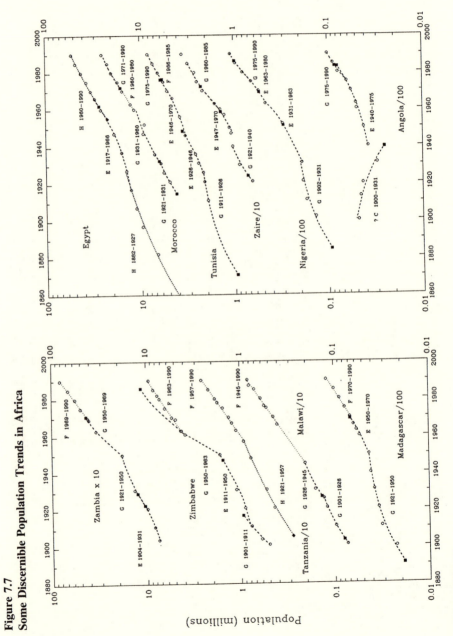

Source: Note 37.

2)—in Kenya, Tanzania, Zambia, Zimbabwe, Malawi, and on the great island of Madagascar—similarly have seen F or H trends of population increase lately, or both. Finally, the F trend of constant proportional multiplication has also appeared along the Guinea Coast—from Gambia in the far west, opposite the Cape Verdes, eastward through Guinea, Liberia, Ghana, and Togo.[38]

In these three regional clusters across Africa, the H pattern, which has been the rarest growth shape in Africa, occurring in only 3 among 51 countries of the continent, seems to have emerged here and there. Local scholars will have to make the final decisions, but the apparent worldwide association of H-type expansion in population with economic development would not seem necessarily to be violated by trends of this sort in Egypt 1882–1927 and 1960–1990, Kenya 1949–1975, and Tanzania 1921–1957. In contrast, Tanzania—not the other two—has joined Algeria, Niger, Sudan, Zambia, Zimbabwe, Malawi, Madagascar, Gambia, Liberia, Ghana, and Togo in F trajectories of demographic expansion that have continued into the 1990s. How are these burgeoning populations going to be supported? Where is the "room" for continued doubling about every 23 years? Is epidemic AIDS going to make the trends start to decelerate? Morocco and Tunisia (part B of the table), in contrast, may have found the way out of such pressures; their F trends began to give way to decelerating G's in the 1970s. Guinea, however, at about the same time went from F multiplication into apparent E-type explosion, though it seems as if this pattern, too, is now curving out into a G.

Such relief of accelerating population pressure has not yet come to the ten or more countries in which E trends have continued into the 1990s. These are listed in the first section of part C of Table 7.7. For Libya and Somalia, evidence for the 1990s suggests that the recent explosions may be ending, though the nature of the next path of growth is not yet evident. In eight other countries it is fairly clear that recent E trends have swung out into decelerating G's, as shown in the second section of part C of the table.

Altogether, no less than 32 of 51 African countries recorded—almost two-thirds of them—seem to have had one or more phases of population explosion in the 20th century. The timing of these trends, furthermore, indicates that certain types of populations on the continent have gone through that kind of demographic adjustment very much together. Among eleven societies with early E trends regional groupings stand out (1) Dahomey/Benin, Cameroon, and Nigeria; (2) Swaziland, Southwest Africa (Namibia), the Rhodesias (Zambia and Zimbabwe), Uganda, and Kenya; and (3) Tunisia and Mauritania. Later E trends clustered in Congo, Zaire, Cameroon (in its second E surge by 1960), and the Central African Republic, on the one hand, and in Egypt, Libya, and Algeria, on the other. Explosions mostly persisting past World War II, some of them second local surges in this form, then were focused in Tunisia, Algeria, and Libya; Gabon, Nigeria, Benin, Togo, Upper Volta, Mali, Liberia, Sierra Leone, Guinea, Gambia, and Mauritania; and down the eastern flank of Africa from Somalia, Kenya, and Uganda through Mozambique and Madagascar to the South

African satellites of Botswana, Lesotho, and Swaziland. Finally, Angola, Congo, Cameroon, the Central African Republic, and Chad—and also Benin, Sierra Leone, and Mauritania scattered out to the West—have experienced even later E trends. Except in Angola, which has been in chronic revolution, as of 1990 these trajectories of accelerating growth continued still, putting pressure on national resources and making political stability more difficult to sustain. Such shared E-type explosions, as in the case of more exceptional H or F growths, raise fruitful questions that should assist in structuring further inquiry as to how the various G-based trends come about and how different populations have followed them.

For one part of Africa, Egypt from 20 through 1440 A.D., something is known about population size well back in time. The estimations are indirect, based upon tax records; and trends can for the most part only be speculative because of the infrequency of calculations (Russell 1987, 75–98). Nonetheless, it is insightful to examine the kinds of demographic movements that are implied and to think about what they might mean relative both to what is known of the history of Egypt across the first fifteen centuries of the present era and to trends that have been observed for other parts of the world during this long span of thinly evidenced time.

Figure 7.8 shows the kinds of movements—probably only G or D in shape—that the scattered data suggest. The G's for 300–530, 639–680, 743–869, and 1189–1315 and the D for 869–1090 have a little more evidence to support them than the other proposed curves, which are intimated by only two data points each. Still, the whole possible set of ebbs and flows is worth considering.

In the first place, the potential population movements seem compatible with at least some of the history that is known to have unfolded around them. Rome, for instance, from the time of first intervention there by Pompey and Caesar, used Egypt as a granary, drawing off large shipments to feed various parts of her domain. To whatever extent this Roman exploitation hurt Egyptians, to whatever degree a non-plague pestilence that afflicted the empire in the second century was the culprit instead, Egyptian population declined about 30 percent between 20 and 300 A.D. (Russell 1987, 78, stresses disease). Along what track this loss occurred can only be speculative; but if it was continuous and decelerating from the time Egypt came under Roman control, the path might have looked something like the hypothesized D in the top panel of the figure.

According to Russell, "modest revival" of Egyptian population from the 4th to the 6th century is supported by a known extension of the area under cultivation and by the way trade with the East strengthened during this epoch. The G for 300–530 in the second part of Figure 7.8 involves a demographic increase of about 11 percent and includes an estimate at 460, partway through the span periodized by Russell. Then plague hit Egypt hard in 542–600, followed by low water in the Nile and a submergence of large parts of the delta that covered much land with lakes. By the time of the Arab conquest in 639, the next date

Figure 7.8
Possible Population Trends for Egypt between 20 and 1440 A.D.

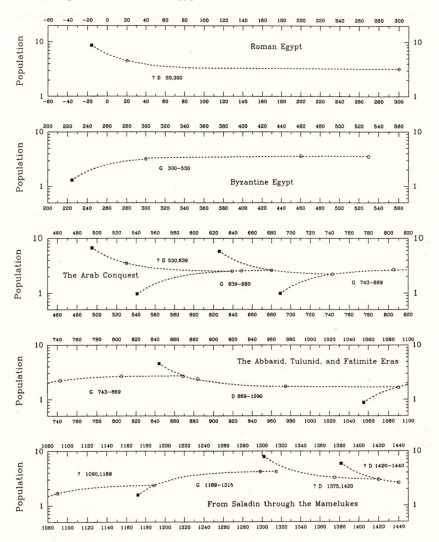

Source: Russell 1987, 75–98.

for which there is an estimate, the population had shrunk by almost 30 percent (Russell 1987, 79). There is evidence from Europe, some of it recapitulated in Table 7.8, that a major plague epidemic like this one does work its way through a population along a D path. Though scarcely exact, because it rests upon only two dates, the proposed curve from 530 through 639 in the middle panel of Figure 7.8 may roughly but insightfully capture the kind of decline involved.

Under early Arab rule, the population of Egypt edged back up slowly during the era 639–680 but somehow fell again before 743. It may be just coincidence, but Table 7.8 shows that the population of China also swelled via G after 639, though more robustly—after likewise shrinking more steeply in the early 600s, increasing via one G surge for 639–705 and another for 726–755 (Figure 7.1). Was there plague in China, too, around 600, or just other forms of disaster that contributed to the collapse of the Sui dynasty and the succession of the T'ang? From about 642 through 731 the water level of the Nile was low, reducing the fertile flooding that was the basis for Egyptian agriculture (Russell 1987, 80–82).

The recovery of the Egyptian population between 743 and 869 is known to have occurred in a period of ample flooding and strong rule under the Abbassids (which started in 750). The decline that followed across the next two centuries, a movement also of fairly confident outline, began with a century of low water and witnessed a revival of the Byzantine empire that reduced Egyptian trade through warfare. The rule of the Tulunids and the Fatimites did not elevate population numbers before 1090. In general, there was a weakening of Islam in this period, which allowed some early success to the Crusades (Russell 82–84).

Some sort of demographic increase, however, then occurred across the century between 1090 and 1189. In part, loosely held southern territory was brought back under Egyptian control; but the Delta gained population, too. Table 7.8 suggests that demographic expansion may have in fact been intercontinental at this time, with approximately parallel G trends or possible G trajectories in China (the country as a whole, then the part left to the Sung), Egypt, and England. The era of fresh population growth that followed, from about 1200 through the 1340s, involved further international parallels; and these were based upon more certain G trends—in Mongol-dominated China, in Egypt from the rule of Saladin into the reign of the Mamelukes, in England under three Edwards from Evesham to Crécy, and in the south of France.[39]

Then came another attack of plague. China seems to have been spared for the time being; but Egypt, England in general, the Duchy of Cornwall, and towns of southern France like Montpellier (Languedoc) and Périgueux (Guienne) experienced substantial D-shape population loss from the 1340s forward. Table 9.5, later, displays parallel atrophy in many locales from England through Languedoc, Provence, and Dauphiné on to Tuscany. Apparently, as in Egypt, the plague took a second bite out of European populations in the later 1300s and the 1400s, which D's with similar base years illustrate across the bottom of

Table 7.8

Possible Trend Comparisons for Egypt with China and Europe between 20 and 1488 A.D.

China	Egypt	England	Cornwall	Montpellier	Other Europe
88- 156 G 51	20, 300 ?D 16BC				
?	300- 530 G 225				
606, 627 ?D 634	530, 639 ?D 495				
639- 705 G 633	639- 680 G 542				
	680, 743 ?D 626				
726- 755 G 695	743- 869 G 690				
755- 812 ?D 765					
1006-1077 G 990	869-1090 D 844				
1077-1103 G 1064 C	1090,1189 ?G 1055	1086,1260 ?G 1081			
1190-1223 G 1096 S					
1290-1393 G 1152	1189-1315 G 1172	1260-1340 G 1228		1249-1340 G 1219 B	
	1375,1420 ?D 1302	1348-1374 D 1340	1337,1358 ?D 1324	1347-1382 D 1362	1340-1415 D 1333 Pi
					1366-1400 D 1335 Pé
1391-1488 D 1350	1420,1440 ?D 1382		1371-1473 D 1361	1386-1446 D 1378	1400-1434 D 1393 Pé
					1412-1481 D 1355 G
					1371-1443 D 1365 M
					1384-1415 D 1351 V

C = China, S = Sung area only, B = Barjols, Pi = Pistoia, Pé = Périgueux, G = Diocese of Geneva,
M = Montalcino, V = Valdelsa

Source: Note 39.

Table 7.8. Whether from plague or for some other reason, early Ming China now once more suffered parallel losses.

In all, the population of Egypt for about 1,400 years rose and fell very much in line with what known histories of epidemics, Nile-dependent agriculture, and changes in regime might suggest. Often G and D curves, thinly documented though they may be, seem to capture the movements. The Egyptian demographic system did not hold so close to one equilibrium size as that of Tokugawa Japan; but it swung less steeply up or down than that of contemporary China (Figures 7.2 and 7.1). Between about 1100 and 1450, though, some close parallels in growth and decline appear in Asia, northern Africa, and Europe. Over the previous millennium only between 600 and 750, another time-span following plague, did Egyptian and Chinese trends potentially move somewhat together. As of about 1100, across an era of Crusades, invasions from Central Asia, increased cultural diffusion, and enhanced long-distance trade, something of an intercontinentally shared demographic regime seems to have appeared and lasted into the later 1400s. The dissemination of disease seems to have played a key role in these movements, while relatively unchanging agricultural method made populations vulnerable to alterations in their environments, whether military or climatological. As of about 1500, economic development—both international and internal—did more to shape trends in the size of various populations, as this and preceding chapters have indicated.

Evidence from Asia and Africa shows how the little G-based family of related formulas now can be said to model change of population size quite all over the world, across a wide variety of societies and extensive periods of recorded time. This set of six curves on the whole appears adequate to represent effectively and simply virtually all historical trends of demographic growth or decline, for regional as well as national populations. In addition, as has been found repeatedly in other parts of the world as well, looking at movements from these new perspectives helps evaluate and select among incomplete or uncertain data in ways that clear up ambiguities in the available information.

These far-reaching claims will be, and should be, bombarded by questions and criticisms from those who know local facts best. Beyond doubt, some improvements in local particulars can be made. Nonetheless, there have been so many useful and insightful applications here of the G-based family of models that it does not seem excessive to propose that the set of six formulas for growth and decline will henceforth prove to be a reliable and generally indispensable tool of demographic analysis.

The findings for Asia and Africa do more than just complete the circle of the world. They carry forward understanding of what kind of increase occurred where, and why.

To begin, premodern change in size of population—whether in Rome, China, Egypt, England, Japan, or the Ottoman Empire as late as 1914—only expanded via G or shrank via D. Whether growing actively and suffering major crises from time to time or maintaining an equillibrium close to no change at all, populations of premodern societies simply do not seem to have experienced the less frequent F, H, and E paths of growth that require some modification of G.

In the West, H-type increase initially emerged for the Dutch maritime provinces, England, and Sweden in the 1500s, then diffused to various other parts of Europe. By the middle of the 1700s the total population of China and a few of her provinces and the peoples of some parts of the New World could be found also expanding in this slowly slowing fashion, followed in time by other regions of Asia, other societies of the Americas, and Egypt, Tanzania, and Kenya within recent Africa. The pattern generally seems to have been associated with societies that developed economically as their populations increased.

Yet demographic increase in that one particular shape is not *necessary* for economic growth, it appears. Japan, now one of the most economically advanced nations of the world, has never seen its population or that of any of its major regions expand in H form. Instead, Japan industrialized across the later 1800s and early 1900s while her population enlarged in successive E surges. That association is not so foreign, however, since the populations of England and several other European countries and regions have done the same since the 1700s. So, perhaps, did the residents of five Chinese provinces as early as the 1500s, at the height of Ming culture. And "Third World" countries like Mexico and India have experienced fundamental economic change along with their population explosions in recent decades. Some of yesterday's underdeveloped, defenseless victims of population explosion have become today's "Little Tigers."

Apparently more than one relationship between demographic increase and economic development can occur. The E form seems historically more associated with conditions in which population is cut loose to be available for a particular kind of economic change (as in factory work), while expansion in the H pattern involves more prolonged and complex feedback between demographic multiplication and a *variety* of economic developments. What makes one interaction occur rather than the other? What are the contributions of births, deaths, and migration to each? Why are both these forms of expansion only relatively modern phenomena historically? Meanwhile, G growth remains the way that most fresh opportunity for support is occupied or used up by a population, while the F trend seems to entail extension of a type of life—either geographically, as in agriculture during continental settlement, or occupationally, as in the expansion of a modern manufacturing system to fresh labor markets—without accumulative transformation of the nature of the economy. These historical patternings frame new agendas for an already lively area of the social sciences.[40]

NOTES

1. The principal gaps remain between 156 and 606 and from 845 to 1006.

2. He estimates about 27 million on the basis of plausible growth rates to 88. Similarly, he considers the official figure for 75 to be about 2 million too low (Durand 216,

219). As for what constituted "China" at the time, returns by area for the years 2 and 140—at both ends of the evidence of the first panel of Figure 7.1a—indicate that parts of Manchuria, Korea, Mongolia, Turkestan, and Viet Nam are included in the numbers across the era covered here. The area that became the future province of Fujian is not (221).

3. His recomputation of population for the period 1014–1103 is based upon a ratio of 6.0 persons per household rather than the 2.3 or so indicated by the official figures (Durand 226–27).

4. Though Kublai's campaigns to gain control of Japan, southeastern Asia, and Indonesia failed. Perhaps the best brief, demographically oriented account of the Mongol conquest is in Perkins (1969, 197–99). He accepts that in the erstwhile Chin provinces of Hebei, Shanxi-Gansu, Shaanxi, Shandong, and Henan the post-conquest population was perhaps only a quarter of what had been there in the early 1200s. Durand thinks that even the consequences of conquest, conversion of farmland to pasture, and flight of farmers to the South did not produce such heavy losses (1960, 229–30).

5. Durand (233) shows convincingly how surviving numbers for both persons and households for 1413–1420 were at some stage of the recording process almost certainly copied from those for 1404–1411.

6. They seem to have been neither taxpaying individuals nor households (as some scholars have assumed) but "conventionalized fiscal units defined with reference to the amount and quality of land held by the registered households as well as the numbers of their adult male members" (Durand 1960, 237). The expert analysis of the data for the Ch'ing era is in Ho 1959.

7. Including territory from north of the Amur River south through Indo-China and west through Turkestan. Mongolia, Tibet, Nepal, and Burma were held as vassal states.

8. As of 1741 the numbers were to be gathered annually through this *pao-chia* three-layered procedure that began with units of ten households. Doubtless there were problems with how this system operated. Irene Taeuber and Wang Nai-Chi argued that there was a tendency for a province to carry forward its current number until prodded to do better, while some areas periodically dropped in and out of the national total, significantly affecting its level ("The Population Reports of the Ch'ing Dynasty and the Growth of China's Population," American Association for the Advancement of Science, Section K, Chicago, 1959, as cited by Durand 1960, 239).

9. Perkins (1969, 212) is used for 1873, 1893, and 1913; Ho 1959 (86) is the source for 1928 and 1936. The graph shows, furthermore, how the figures of Perkins for 1819 and 1851 parallel the H curve for the calculations of Durand for 1751–1851 and indicate that Durand's low total for 1821 is an aberration distorted by a dip in the level of reporting for *pao-chia* at this time (as shown in the third panel of Figure 7.1b).

10. In hindsight, the annual U.N. projections from the 1970s slowed increase down more than they should have, given what the censuses of 1983 and 1990 have subsequently shown.

11. Numbers for 1726–1852 and the Japanese sources are in Taeuber 1958, 22. The figure for 1721 is from J. I. Nakamura, "Social Structure and Population Change: A Comparative Study of Tokugawa Japan and Ch'ing China" (paper presented to the Columbia University Seminar on Economic History, March 1, 1979, 6). Akira Hayami (1968, 3) estimates that the total Japanese population about 1720 was approximately 30 million. This makes counted commoners roughly four-fifths of the total. For 1873 and 1903–1918, Taeuber 1958, 45, 48, 195; for 1920–1992, *Japan, Stat, Ybk.* 1994, 36–37.

12. To facilitate comparison and contrast, part D of the table repeats particulars on trends since 1578 in China as well as presenting the patterns for Japan and other countries. It consolidates all Chinese information for 1742–1851 (given in Table 7.1 and Figure 7.1b) into what, as partial series seem to be indicating, was the underlying overall movement across that long era.

13. K. Davis 1951, 25–27. His calculations are followed to 1921; thereafter, those in Mitchell 1982, 43.

14. In the new mode of trend analysis used here, the H curve for India since the 1960s has a base year almost a quarter of a century more recent than the comparable but flatter H trajectory for China (1947 vs. 1923).

15. Lal 1973, 125; K. Davis 1951, 193; Afzal 1974, 2; *Pakistan Stat. Ybk. 1985*, 33.

16. Mitchell 1982, 47, 45; *Philippines Stat. Ybk.* 1988, 24. El Attar 1979, 16. The dip of population level on Cyprus in the late 1970s is the result of political division.

17. All of these have been plotted and analyzed the usual way in developing Table 7.2. See also: Taiwan, *Stat. Ybk. 1985*, 2; *Korea Stat. Ybk. 1993*, 35; Kim 1992; *Econ. Soc. Stat. Singapore* 1983, Table 2.5; *Ybk. of Stat. Malaysia 1991*, Table 3.1.8; *Stat. Ybk. of Turkey* 1987, 33, 1991, 52.

18. And possibly occurred between 1851 and 1873, accompanying the Taiping Rebellion.

19. Durand 1960, 251; Perkins 1969, 207, 212; Ho 1959, 283 (for 1787); Mackerras and Yorke 1990, 175, 177 (censuses of 1964 and 1982, and 10 percent sample for 1987). For continuity of recent figures with the past, the cities of Beijing and Tianjin are included in Hebei Province and Shanghai in Jiangsu, rather than listed separately. Estimates for 1976 are incorporated in the figure and the trend fitting where they seem in alignment with surrounding data (Kaplan et al., 1980, 16).

20. The uprising was based on the lower Yangtze River valley in the provinces of Anhui, Jiangsu, Zhejiang, Jiangxi, and Hubei. As of 1873 the estimations of provincial population that Perkins made (1969, 209, 210) indicate losses ranging from 62 percent in Anhui to 28 percent in Jiangxi relative to the levels of 1851. During the revolt, the lower Yangtze was cut off from grain that had ordinarily been supplied by Hunan and Sichuan. Similarly, the Hangzhou-Xi'an grain route that fed the northwest was broken. Northern Zhejiang remained a defiant area for some time and suffered retribution accordingly. Because Zhejiang, Anhui, Jiangsu, and Jiangxi supplied three-quarters of the grain tribute to Beijing, up the Grand Canal, their problems in turn caused trouble for Hebei (Perkins, 153, 149, 150).

In neighboring Henan and Hunan, populations increased 46 and 12 percent respectively. That relocation involved about 16 million persons, according to Perkins. Some 20 million, though, are "conservatively" estimated to have died from the revolt directly, and quite probably another 20 million disappeared due to the indirect impact of rebellion-related crises of sustenance and health upon the birthrates and deathrates in this part of China and other areas whose way of life was affected.

21. Anhui and Jiangsu were further hurt when the Yellow River, after 800 years of emptying out down the lower Huai River, altered course again (Perkins 1969, 210–11). Muslim revolt in Gansu, Shanxi, and Shaanxi provinces in the 1860s and 1870s was "ruthlessly put down," though only after the insurgents themselves had slaughtered many nonbelievers. Drought was another problem for that region in this era (Perkins 1969, 211; Ho 1959, 247–48). Up through 1851 data for Xinjiang, Ningxia, and possibly Xinghai are included with Gansu. Excluding these would make the demographic decline for

Gansu Province proper more like 43 to 48 percent, not the 64 percent indicated by the data of Perkins (Perkins 1969, 211; Durand 1960, 252, note n; Ho 1959, 248).

Taiwan, part of Fujian up through 1851, was now administratively severed. Thus, much of an apparent loss of 6 million people from the province between 1851 and 1873, which Perkins considers excessive, never really took place (Durand 1960, 252, note n). A more modest actual decline there and the 24 percent demographic loss indicated for Guandong are probably very much in line with the substantial overseas migration characteristic of southern China in the middle of the 19th century and with contemporaneous movement into China's southern interior, which swelled populations in Guangxi and Guizhou in the hinterland of Guangdong (Canton).

22. More idiosyncratically, Shanxi and Gansu also lost some people between 1913 and 1933. Perkins attributes this decline to their being "areas of considerable war lord activity of a particularly brutal sort, in addition to which the two provinces were heavily hit by drought" (1969, 211, 213).

23. In the late 1800s Henan and Ningxia had, or probably had, very flat G-type population increases. Somewhat steeper, and mostly lasting into the 1930s, were G's for Guangxi, Shandong, Hunan, Shanxi, and Inner Mongolia. Still stronger were the decelerating growths of populations in Qinghai and Guandong 1873–1933, while the expansions of Suiyan and Chahar within Inner Mongolia and fresh G increases in Hunan and Guangxi involveed t_0's between 1863 and 1876. Guangxi saw a third G surge before World War II (with base year at 1898); and collectively the provinces of Manchuria saw even steeper increase in G form for 1913–1953, mostly under Japanese control.

24. H's begun in the 1870s did continue in Sichuan and Yunnan to 1964 as well.

25. The rather different 1393 figures in Durand for Hubei and Hunan, Jiangxi, Zhejiang, Fujian, and Guangdong are not used, as both 1381 and 1391 data line up with the proposed D curves. Ho's numbers for Fujian and Zhejiang in 1542 are employed (page 258).

26. The Yunnan trend probably persisted to 1578 and appears in the right portion of the table. Here 1391 numbers for Shandong, the evidence in 1393 for Henan and Guangxi, and both 1391 and 1393 figures for Sichuan and Hebei are omitted for the curve-fitting, while the correction of van der Sprenkel for Shaanxi in 1391 that Durand mentions (1960, 252, footnote 1) is employed. His amendations for Zhejiang in 1391 and Gansu-Shanxi in 1491 are not accepted, however.

27. Ho's figures for Anhui and Jiangsu ("Nan-Chili"), Gansu and Shanxi, and Sichuan are used for 1542, but not his number for Hebei ("Pei-Chili"), which seems about a million too much, dragging the level first up and then down between 1491 and 1578. The dangers in all these figures are illustrated by the 2,041,000 for Guangdong in 1578 preferred by van der Sprenkel from one Chinese document (and followed by Durand) versus the 5,041,000 of another source, which is almost certainly a modest 3 million or 150 percent too high from a simple numerical error!

28. The numbers for Hebei derive from a different source (Perkins 1969, 195). Other northern provinces (Gansu and Shanxi, Shaanxi, Shandong, and Henan) seem not to have kept comparable records around 1173, probably because of the Jurchen (Chin) takeover of a substantial portion of Sung domains in 1127. No trend can be estimated for these regions.

29. These territories were organized around the roads that connected the fiefs to the

Shogun's capital at Edo (now Tokyo). Taeuber (1958, 23) contains the data on commoner population in the *do*, descriptions of those regions, and her Japanese sources. Though not presented in a figure, the trends discussed here have been fitted mathematically.

30. Kinai, the Inner Provinces, was the region around Kyoto and Osaka. Data from Hanley and Yamamura (1977, 91) allow us to trace the D curve in the crucial area of the Kinai both earlier and later than elsewhere, from 1721 to 1872, and to have numbers at more dates with which to verify the shape of the trend. Tokaido, the Eastern Sea Road Division, stretched from Kinai up the coast to include the horseshoe of land that forms Tokyo Bay. Tosando, the Eastern Sky Road Division, ran northeastward up the spine of the main island behind Tokaido. "Shimo" designates its lower portion, the mountains strung up and down the center of Honshu.

31. Data for 1903–1918 come from Taeuber (1958, 48); she also (70) groups prefectures by region, which allows similar aggregation for the 1920–1992 information available in Japan Statistics Bureau 1994, 36–37. The 1978 figure is taken from the 1979 edition of this yearbook, 16.

32. India, *Stat. Abs. 1982*, 21–22; *India 1993*, 10. Data for Mizoram through 1971 and a check on poorly printed numbers in the 1982 edition come from *Stat. Abs. 1975*, 6.

33. The interested reader who tries out his or her own fits, however, will find that E trends are *possible* for Kerala 1931–1961, Madhya Pradesh 1941–1971, Orissa 1951–1971, and Bihar 1951–1971. Only for West Bengal is there truly *no* chance of at least a brief E. The point, though, is that such relatively short E curves, while possible, are not *required*—unlike the G's leading into them and the H's leading out.

34. Growth trends for the half-dozen principal regions of Thailand could also be determined.

35. The principal tables employed here are to be found on pages 150 (for 1894–1914), 121 (for 1878), 117 (for 1872 and 1874), 109–15 (for 1831), and 202–08 (for Istanbul 1830–1882). Trends have been fitted to the models proposed.

Though brief in chronological range and beset by boundary changes and some apparently faulty official reporting, this compilation of Ottoman censuses, as supplemented with some corrections by its author, makes it possible to acquire at least a general sense of what kinds of growth patterns prevailed across the last several decades of this extensive, if shrinking, empire. We learn how demographic expansions in what became parts of Turkey, Greece, Yugoslavia, Albania, Syria, Lebanon, Palestine/Israel, and Iraq compared with each other. They are based, however, on short strings of data and numbers about which there is occasionally some question. Our discussion should thus be regarded as just a preliminary suggestion of likely relationships from region to region for readers willing to work further with the data themselves. The interpretation can doubtless be improved.

36. Besides the regions covered regularly by Karpat, Lawless (1972, 98) shows G-shape growth for 1890–1919 in the central portion of what became modern Iraq (around Bagdad) and for 1867–1905 and 1905–1935 in the southern section (around Basra).

37. Unless otherwise noted, the data come from Mitchell 1982, 38–42, or U.N. *Demo. Ybk.* 1992. Patterns for South Africa and for Mauritius before the middle 1800s have been covered in Chapter 3.

38. Early data for Algeria and Ghana cannot be modeled at present.

39. Figures 7.1, 5.3; Tables 7.1 and 9.4 and 9.5 (in Chapter 9). Barjols is just one of several villages of Provence that displays a pre-plague G growth like this.

40. A subsequent phase of this study explores such "demonomic" relationships of demographics and economics in several insightful historical contexts.

Chapter 8

The Growth of Cities and the Spread of Urbanization

If a few trends based on the G formula have repeatedly and generally characterized the growth and decline of populations in nations and in substantial regions within countries around the world from the beginning of recorded demographic history to the present, as Chapters 2 through 7 have indicated, questions then arise as to just how *locally* such patterns apply. Do they also adequately represent the increase or atrophy of cities, for example? What of small areas within major regions, like counties? How about growth or decay in very limited and local populations, such as those of villages or hamlets? Do the same six shapes of trend constantly reappear in small territorial and demographic units as well as big ones? Do they suffice to model their growth and decline, or are further shapes needed? And what happens to the mixes or frequencies for the members of the G family of curves as the focus on population increase or loss becomes geographically narrower and narrower?

These are the topics of this chapter and the next one. Unlike nationwide populations, however—or even well-recorded regional data sets that have considerable chronological depth—there is available a virtually infinite number of series for local populations, especially over recent years. While it is possible to follow fairly completely the development of the few well-recorded leading metropolises for which population estimates reach back across three or four centuries prior to the present, in modern times there exist even too many large cities around the world, let alone smaller urban centers, to cover or even to sample substantially. Some examples, chosen to illustrate circumstances in different eras of history in different parts of the world, must suffice. It is hoped that these selections will demonstrate that there is merit in investigating further the way G-based trends have also characterized local population growth and decay.

HOW CITIES DEVELOPED IN THE WESTERN HEMISPHERE

Figures 8.1a, 8.1b, and 8.1c show how recorded or estimated population increase and decline in twenty cities and/or metropolitan areas of the Western Hemisphere have followed G-type patterns across their histories.[1] Figure 8.1a presents the trends for five older eastern cities of the present United States, for which records exist since the 1600s or 1700s.[2] In Philadelphia, New York, Providence, and Charleston, sequences of expansion in the basic G pattern have predominated, the two exceptions being brief log-linear F increase in Providence 1820–1840 and perhaps also New York 1870–1890. In New Orleans, gateway to the vast, fruitful Mississippi-Ohio-Missouri watershed, E-type demographic explosion seems to have occurred during 1769–1810 and possibly appeared again across the first four decades of U.S. control of the city, as investment and settlers flooded into the Mississippi watershed. After 1797, however, save for the outlier of 1840, the demographic expansion of New Orleans could—as illustrated in the figure—also be represented by just a sequence of G trends.

Do the successive stages of expansion in Figure 8.1a fit what is known of local urban history? The shift from one phase of G growth to another in Philadelphia and New York (and probably in Providence) around 1740, for example, conforms well to a new acceleration of colonial trade during the decades preceding the Revolution in which these ports and their hinterlands are recognized to have participated (Harris 1989, 291). The fresh G increase for 1787–1840 in Charleston, on the other hand, fits appropriately the dissemination of short-staple cotton across the Carolina interior after Whitney's invention of the gin. F-type expansion in Providence 1820–1840 plausibly may have been driven by the extensive water-powered industrialization of the Blackstone River Valley in these years following the War of 1812, while similar exceptional log-linear increase in New York's population for 1870–1890 is timed with the massive receipt of immigrants by this port after the Civil War and the explosion (and incorporation) of the surrounding boroughs.

It is well known that in recent decades the inner cities of the United States have decayed. Figure 8.1a shows how such atrophy in population probably took the D pattern in the city of Providence 1950–1980 and quite possibly followed this familiar G-based curve of decline also in Philadelphia 1970–1990, New York 1950–1990, and New Orleans 1960–1980. In contrast, broader metropolitan areas, which include not only these cities but also their suburban environs, continue to gain population in G trends that began about the time of World War II. Examples are given in the figure for Philadelphia, New Orleans, and Charleston.

Figure 8.1b demonstrates that not just cities of the United States have fol-

Figure 8.1a

Increase and Decrease in Major Urban Populations of the Western Hemisphere: Some Early-Documented Cities and Metropolitan Areas of the United States

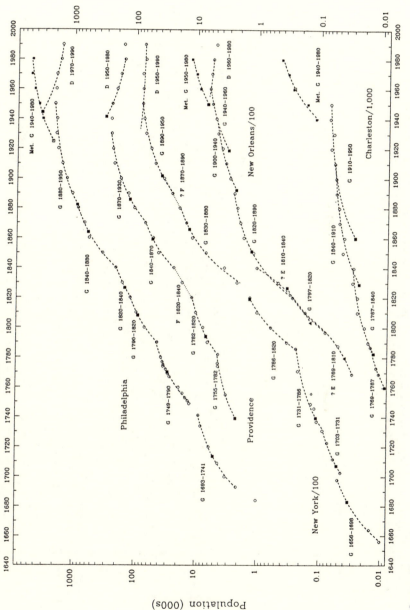

Source: Notes 1 and 2.

Figure 8.1b

Increase and Decrease in Major Urban Populations of the Western Hemisphere: Some Early-Documented Cities and Metropolitan Areas Elsewhere in the Americas

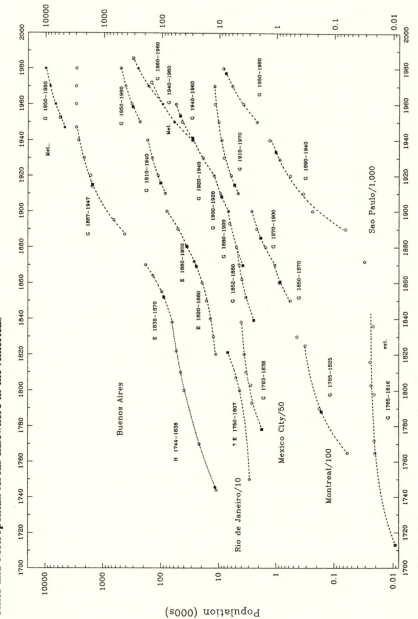

Source: Mitchell 1993, 44–56.

Figure 8.1c
Increase and Decrease in Major Urban Populations of the Western Hemisphere: Selected Cities with Shorter Data Series

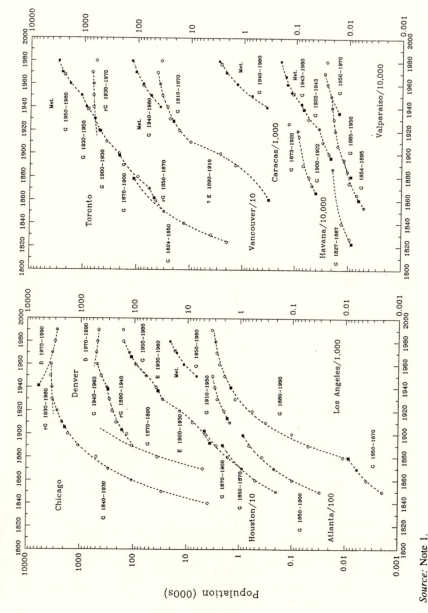

Source: Note 1.

299

lowed these patterns of demographic growth. Mexico City, Montreal, and São Paulo have since the 1700s expanded in just sequences of successive G growths.[3] For Rio de Janeiro, in contrast, population increase in the proportionally accelerating E form is clear for 1820–1880 and likely for 1750–1807 and 1880–1900 as well. Since 1910, though, two stages of decelerating G growth characterize the expansion of this no longer quite so bumptious urban center. Buenos Aires, on the other hand, introduces the possibility that a city, like a country or region, can have its population expand in the slowly decelerating H form (1744–1838). While the population of Argentina as whole multiplied in H patterns for 1778–1809 and 1809–1839 (the latter with a base year of 1764 compared with 1746 for Buenos Aires), to have an H trend like this in a city population proves to be truly exceptional: the one example of that type of growth among about 350 trends in more than a hundred cities examined. Demographic growth for Brazil took this form, but not for São Paulo or Rio. While the H trajectory fits U.S. population increase from the 1850s to about 1950, no major city of the country displays this pattern. What, then, was distinctive about the way in which Buenos Aires expanded through the late 18th and the early 19th centuries and how this was related to the growth of her hinterland?

Subsequently Buenos Aires, like Rio, experienced E growth in the late 1800s, then G increase in its population up to World War II. Since 1947, the city proper has begun to lose some population (though the trend is not yet clear) while—as for many cities of the United States—the broader metropolitan area has enjoyed significant new G-shape growth.

Figure 8.1c, finally, displays the trends in ten more cities of the Western Hemisphere. The great mid-continental hub of Chicago expanded from 1840 all the way through 1930 (in spite of the famous fire) along a single G track for ninety years. With the advent of the Depression, however, further demographic increase to 1960 could only follow a much slower, retrogressively timed rG curve—the kind of setback or capping of growth experienced previously in several midwestern farm states. Since 1970, Chicago proper has lost population in a D pattern, like Philadelphia (Figure 8.1a). St. Louis, Milwaukee, and Minneapolis (not graphed) appear similarly to have shifted into appreciably slower rG growth about 1920 or 1930 and then actually to have shrunk in D form since 1960 or 1970. Broader dynamics of midwestern urbanization in the 20th century appear to be involved.

As in Chicago, steep G-type initial growth in Denver was replaced by retrogressively timed, slower decelerating rG increase—not in the 1930s, but about 1890. For the state of Colorado, this kind of retrograde shift between G's came near 1910 (Figure 2.2c). The difference in timing probably reflects the Denver area's particular early dependence on the mining of precious metals, whose market broke in the 1890s. World War II set off another phase of G increase in Denver's population. Since about 1970, however, the number of people in the city has eroded away along the same kind of D path found in many eastern urban centers.

Houston expanded in two G growths across the second half of the 19th century, but then saw its population increase accelerate in E form through the first three decades of the 1900s, as oil fueled the life of southeastern Texas. Of a few dozen largest U.S. cities examined at least tentatively for this study, Houston is the only one to approximate population explosion in the modern era. It did so a second time, furthermore, between 1930 and 1960. In recent years, however, the city proper has had only decelerating G growth and may have stopped expanding altogether since 1980.[4]

In the Southeast, the population of Atlanta enlarged along a single G curve from 1850 to 1900 as if the Yankees had never ravaged Scarlett's fair city. A shift upward in the size of this important center occurred for some reason between 1900 and 1910; then new G growth through 1950 followed. The more broadly cast metropolitan area has experienced even fresher G-type demographic increase since that time, though evidence for the old boundaries of Atlanta shows decline in the D pattern for 1970–1990 (not graphed). Similar recent D-type atrophy after successive G growths has appeared in other southeastern cities such as Birmingham, Louisville, Richmond, and Baltimore.

In the West, Los Angeles expanded moderately from 1850 through 1870 as a southern center for the new state of California. But as the land of Zorro became first the terminus of the Southern Pacific Railway and then the back lot of celluloid make-believe, the population of the city surged along one great and lasting G curve all the way from 1870 to 1990 or later. The 1890s saw somewhat weaker growth than this pattern; the 1920s were a time of expansion rather stronger than the underlying trend. Still, the fundamental model has endured through smog, traffic jams, ethnic strife, and earthquakes for more than a century.

Elsewhere in the West, the history of urban growth has been quite different. Salt Lake City, San Francisco, Seattle, and Portland all have expanded in four different trend sequences of their own. Each sequence, however, has been composed of just G increases and D declines.

Also shown in Figure 8.1c are five additional cases from cities in Canada and Latin America. As Vancouver, becoming the railhead to and from the East, displaced ocean-encircled Victoria as the western terminus for Canada, the population of this great-city-to-be exploded from 1890 through 1910 in the kind of E trend observed in the early years of New Orleans or Rio. From 1910 through 1970, then, the growth of Vancouver took relatively flat G form, though—as everywhere—the metropolitan area expanded more robustly than the core city. By 1980 population loss was beginning to appear even in this glittering money-magnet of Canada's Pacific Rim.

Whereas Toronto, an earlier base for westward expanding transportation and trade, has seen its population mount solely in a series of G trends, such growth has not continued without interruption. About 1850, in a retrogressive shift, slower G expansion replaced faster—rather than the other way around—as population increase in Upper Canada, Toronto's hinterland, hit a ceiling near 1860

(Figure 3.1). Once again, in a later era, the expansion of Toronto proper stalled out—about 1930. This time the new G was even flatter relative to the preceding one; and the trend lasted to 1970, where the city's population began to decline (as is seen so frequently in the cities of the United States), though numbers[5] for the broader metropolitan area of Toronto continued to climb vigorously along successive G paths, first for 1930–1950 and then for 1950–1980.

Havana, Cuba, and Valparaiso, Chile, have constituted more quietly growing cities than, say, Buenos Aires and São Paulo in Figure 8.1b. Each has seen its population expand along a series of G curves without interruption by some other pattern. Valparaiso began to lose people in the 1970s; but the metropolitan area of Havana kept right on expanding demographically in G form until 1980 or later. The population of Caracas, Venezuela, increased not unlike that of Valparaiso until about 1920. Then it, especially the metropolitan area, began to take off in further modern growth.

There can be no proof of universality here. Only samples of evidence are offered. Together, though, these graphed and otherwise cited background cases from the Western Hemisphere strongly suggest that the G family of curves effectively represents the ways in which the major cities of the New World have enlarged. Within this small set of related mathematical functions, moreover, urban growth according to G itself has overwhelmingly constituted the predominant form of demographic expansion. Sometime, though, cities—like the regions around them—have had to abandon overambitious paths of G growth for flatter ones. The E trend has occasionally appeared in unusual situations of open opportunity (mostly early in the history of a city), while F and especially H paths of demographic increase have been very rare indeed. Decline in urban populations, a frequent phenomenon of center cities in recent years, has meanwhile tended to follow the G-based D shape, though the brevity of many trends observed so far keeps any diagnosis of the form of urban decay rather tentative.

Some hints about the role of G-based movements in the history of urbanization already begin to emerge, such as the conditions that may occasionally encourage forms of increase in cities that are alternative to the basic G equation, the relationships between the expansion of urban centers and the growth of their hinterlands, and the shift from core cities to suburbs. Generalization should not proceed too far, however, until patterns of growth in cities of the Old World are explored.

URBANIZATION IN EARLY MODERN EUROPE

Figure 8.2a plots increase and atrophy in the populations of six European cities for which records begin early and reach over long periods of time.[5] To start with the most extended patterns, three phases of G growth are evident for Amsterdam across the two centuries from 1400 to 1600.[6] The province of Holland increased in importance during the 15th century. Though trailing behind Flanders and Brabant in population and wealth and at first having no outstanding city, this part of the Netherlands by 1477 was the most urbanized region. Within that broader environment of regional growth, specialization in the North Sea fisheries and the bulk-carrying trade of the Baltic apparently swelled the population of Amsterdam along a G path from about 4,000 in 1400 to around 8,000 as the century came to a close.[7] The city then expanded further in a fresh G trend during 1494–1546 after the Netherlands passed to the Hapsburgs. This tie allied Amsterdam trade with the markets of the worldwide domains of the future Emperor Charles V, who became King of Spain in 1517. The province of Holland benefited from increasing integration in the northern regions of the Netherlands 1516–1549; and the population of Amsterdam seems to have enlarged in a new G trend.[8]

As Hapsburg control of the Netherlands began to crumble, the peopling of Amsterdam pushed forward again, the city becoming now twice the size of provincial competitors like Haarlem and Delft and pulling ahead of Leiden and Utrecht, though still remaining appreciably smaller than the preeminent centers of the southern Netherlands (modern Belgium). Leading up to and during the struggle for Dutch independence, however, the number of people in the city rose from 13,000 in 1546 to 22,000 in 1557, 27,000 in 1562, and some 50,000 by 1600.[9] Now Amsterdam served as the business center of a new nation, gathering refugees from Antwerp, her ravaged predecessor at the head of northern European trade, and other parts of the southern and eastern provinces still in Spanish hands; the city branched out into new commerce, industry, and finance while the surrounding countryside developed some of the most advanced agriculture in Europe. The new, strong G trend of 1546–1600 is easily understandable within this context of regional and urban development.

Though there exist only two data points upon which to base a judgment, it appears that Rotterdam, Holland's future preeminent port at the mouth of the Rhine, saw its population expand much like that of Amsterdam between 1560 and 1630. Subsequently, from the early 1600s into the early 1800s, as Figure 8.2a makes quite clear, Amsterdam and Rotterdam did share very much the same pattern of demographic increase, though Rotterdam remained only about one-quarter the size of Amsterdam, the new star of northern European commerce. The growth paths followed G curves with base years at 1612 and 1614 respectively, which in both cases lasted about two centuries! In this new surge, significant fresh demographic expansion occurred across the early 1600s, the glory years for Dutch fleets and Dutch merchants. Thanks to the prolonged G-type deceleration involved in these trends, however, by the latter part of the century urban growth in both centers had almost totally stagnated. The leading cities of the Netherlands, once hearths of worldwide trade and military might that reached from Pernambuco and Manhattan to Batavia and Nagasaki, now rested upon past gains and lived off activities like finance and brokering that drew no additional people into urban life. Along these G curves of first fresh demographic growth then lingering stagnation from about 1600 to 1820 in the central places of the Netherlands, the Dutch Golden Age came and went.[10]

Figure 8.2a
Urban Population Growth and Decline in Europe: Six Cities with Early Records

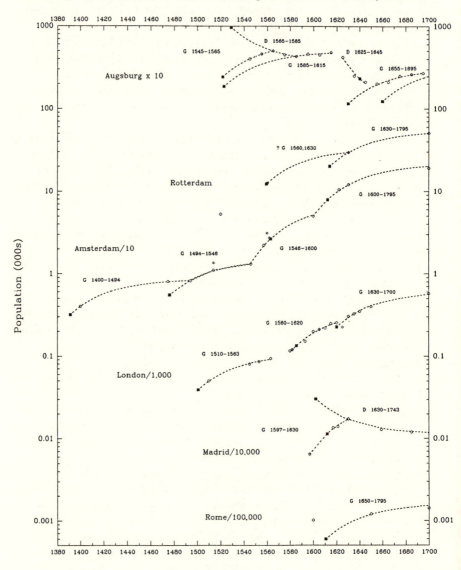

Figure 8.2a (*Continued*)

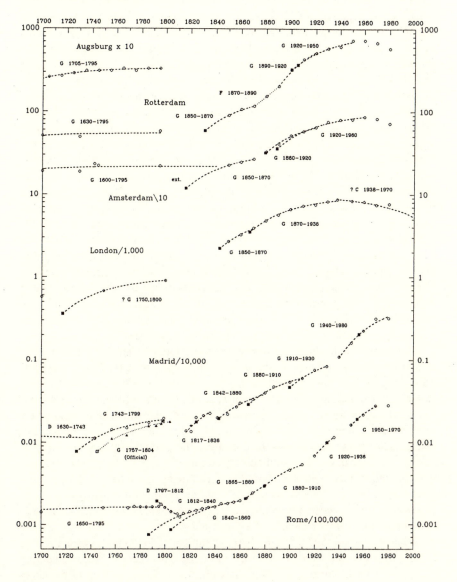

Source: Note 5.

In London, the capital and primary trading center of Holland's brash would-be competitor across the North Sea, successive G growths appeared for 1510–1563 and then from 1580 to 1620. The first of these periods involved an early Tudor era from the beginning of Henry VIII's reign to the accession of Elizabeth; the second embraced England's age for rediscovering expansion and international involvement—no longer in France but in Ireland, the western Atlantic, the Netherlands, and ultimately India. These growths lagged behind Amsterdam's trends for 1494–1546 and 1546–1600. But England, too, was elbowing her way into farflung global opportunities; and her increasingly dominant metropolis was expanding apace. As of 1630 or so, the urban parallel across the North Sea drew closer still, as London entered a new phase of G-shaped population increase with base year at 1620 compared with the 1612 for Amsterdam's trend. Figure 8.2a graphs this similarity from the available data; Table 8.1 summarizes the particulars of the two curves. While pushing upward steadily through the Civil War, the Restoration, the Great Fire, the plague, and the Glorious Revolution, this London growth—as in the leading centers of the Netherlands—continued to decelerate decade after decade, becoming flatter and flatter. Data for the 1700s are scant; but the 17th century G for London may well have lasted into the 1740s. Between 1750 and 1800, however, in London unlike Amsterdam, Rotterdam, and The Hague, Table 8.1 indicates, new population increase occurred. The G drawn on the figure here is only speculative; but its two underlying data points suggest fresh growth beginning near 1740 and running until about 1820 before being replaced by still further expansion, an increase in line with what is known of Britain's wealth and power across these decades.

London and the leading commercial cities of Holland were not the only urban centers to share a common G-shaped pattern of growth beginning in the early 1600s. Figure 8.2a also shows how from about 1650 to 1795 the population of Rome expanded along a G curve with t_0 at 1611. Not only was Rome located in an entirely different part of Europe; it was not, like Amsterdam, Rotterdam, or London a rising center of colonial trade. Meanwhile Augsburg, in Bavaria, had ceased by the later 1600s to constitute the commercial hub it had been during the glory days of the bullion-backed Fuggers and Welsers. Yet here, too, the population increased for 1655–1695, following the disaster of the Thirty Years War, via a G trend with base year at 1630, only slightly later (and therefore a little steeper) than the other European centers reviewed so far. And in Madrid, the inland capital of Castile—and of Spain and her now far-flung possessions—from 1597 through 1630 the number of inhabitants began to surge along a G trajectory with a t_0 of 1612, the same base year as for contemporary G-type growth in Amsterdam. The crisis of government and drain of resources into foreign wars that so weakened once mighty Spain in the 17th century is then reflected in systematic D-shaped population loss for the capitol from 1630 through about 1740, a period through which—in contrast—major northern European cities grew. When Madrid did expand again, however, across the second half of the 18th century up to the Napoleonic invasion, the fresh peopling of

Table 8.1
Shared Patterns of Growth and Decline before 1800 in Thirty European Cities

Phases:	I	II	III	IV	V	VI
Amsterdam	1400-1494 G 1391	1494-1546 G 1476	1546-1600 G 1563	1600-18427 G 1612	....	....
Rotterdam			1560,1630 ?G 1559	1630-1796 G 1614	....	....
The Hague*				1630-1796 G 1626	....	....
London		1510-1563 G 1501	1580-1620 G 1586	1630-17307 G 1620	?	1750,1800 ?G 1717
Nottingham			1550-1650 G 1539	1700-1710 G 1630	1710-1745 G 1696	1745-1765 G 1728
						1760-1801 (E 1798)
Frankfurt**	1440-1550 G 1400	1512,1550 ?G 1504 –	1600-1610 G 1608 –	1638-1800 – 1639	....	?
Würzburg*		1506-1550 G 1460	1571-1631 G 1614	1650-1750 G 1617	....	....
Leipzig**		1550,1580 ?G 1515 –	1558-1623 G 1556 –	1637-1699 G 1637	1700-1802 G 1678	
Munich		1600-1620 G 1573	1600-1620 G 1573	1620-1650 [D 1593]	1660-1700 G 1637	1700-1800 G 1667
Augsburg		1545-1565 G 1532	1625-1645 [D 1640]	1655-1695 G 1630	1705-1795 G 1660	
–		1565-1585 [D 1529] 1585-1615 G 1523				
Geneva		1560-1590 [D 1541]		1660-1700 G 1625	1700-1800 G 1673	
–		1590-1610 G 1542				
Zürich		1529-1580 G 1524	1610-1650 [D 1573]	1650-1800 G 1623	1700-1800 G 1673	
–		1580-1600 [D 1555]				
Basel		1540-1563 G 1502	?	1629-1666 G 1604	1669-1699 G 1638	
–		1563-1595 [D 1518]			1693-1783 G 1675	
Strasbourg				1600-1700 G 1586	....	....
Koblenz				1600-1750 G 1584	1700-1800 G 1647	1742-1792 G 1711
Paris**				1650-1795 G 1611	....	....
Marseilles**			1550-1650 G 1550	1650,1700 ?G 1615	?	....
Rome			1550,1600 ?G 1520 –	1597-1630 G 1612	?	1750-1850 G 1719
Naples				1650-1800 G 1614	1630-1743 [D 1602]	1743-1799 G 1728
Madrid				1650-1800 G 1614		
Lisbon** (w/o 1750)					....	....
Copenhagen**				1650,1700 ?G 1598	1650-1800 G 1663	1749-1800 G 1704
Stockholm**			1600,1650 ?G 1560	1700,1750 ?G 1677	1700,1750 ?G 1667	?
Vienna**			1600,1650 ?G 1560	?	1700,1750 ?G 1677	?
Warsaw**			1600,1650 ?G 1570	1620-1700 G 1586	1700,1750 ?G 1676	?
Bruges			1550-1620 [D 1510]	1610-1690 G 1590	1700-1740 (C 1769)	1750-1790 (E 1846)
Ghent			1550,1610 [D 1531]	1650-1710 G 1602	1700-1760 [D 1646]	1770-1790 G 1725
Mechelen		1550,1590 [D 1555]	1590-1640 G 1584	1600-1660 G 1599	1710-1780 [D 1679]	....
Aalst District			1570,1580 G 1616	1600-1660 G 1599	1660-1700 [D 1610]	1730-1790 G 1706
–				1610-1670 G 1608	1700-1730 G 1676	
Evergem			1570-1610 G 1548	1680-1700 G 1631	1700-1750 G 1673	1750-1790 (E 1814)
–						

*Fitted, but not in Figure 8.2; **Roughly estimated; – Drop before next growth phase.

Source: Notes 5–18.

Figure 8.2b
**Urban Population Growth and Decline in Europe: Other Northern Centers in the
16th, 17th, and 18th Centuries**

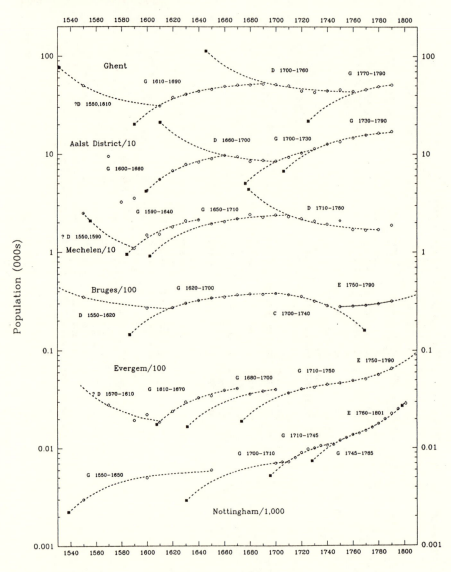

Sources: van Houtte and van Buyten 1977, 83; Chambers 1965, 351; de Vries 1984, 270.

the city more resembled the path of increase for London than the languid, late-stage G growth of the Dutch centers, Rome, or Augsburg. The vigor of 18th century Madrid serves as still another reminder that the strength of trans-Atlantic Spanish society in the 1700s may have been more resilient than is often recognized.

Data in Figures 8.2b and 8.2c from some other cities for which frequent evidence is available between 1500 and 1800 extend the impression of how general the pattern of urban growth was in the 1600s (Phase IV of Table 8.1). Munich, Frankfurt, and Leipzig expanded from the middle 1600s through 1700 along G trends very parallel to Augsburg, slightly behind (and year-by-year therefore slightly faster) than the five other urban centers of Figure 8.2a (Elsas 1936, 1: 79; 2B: 85, including Würzburg). Meanwhile growth in Würzburg, Geneva, Zürich, and Basel was timed more parallel with that in Amsterdam, Rotterdam, London, Madrid (up to 1630), and Rome (Mattmüller 1987, 209, 211, 204–08). Particulars of the curves are related most readily through Table 8.1. Even further afield from the best-known concentrations of European economic growth at this time, Nottingham, north of London in eastern England, probably expanded in similar form, judging from evidence that unfortunately becomes frequent only as of 1700.[11] From 1710 through 1745 and 1745 through 1765, fresh G growths and then some E-type accelerating population increase to 1791 or 1801 made provincial Nottingham enlarge proportionally much more than did London. The metropolis for the time being gave back to provincial centers (not just Nottingham, but the likes of Manchester, Birmingham, and Leeds) some of the additional proportion of England's population she had gathered to herself across the 1500s and 1600s.

On the continent, meanwhile, Leipzig, Munich, Augsburg, Geneva, Basel, Strasbourg, Paris, Copenhagen, Stockholm, the Aalst District and Evergem in Belgium, and perhaps also Vienna and Warsaw shared the kind of early 18th century G trend found in Nottingham (Phase V in Table 8.1). Outside of the Low Countries and the Mediterranean area such growths were common. Rather fewer cities, though, participated in the type of fresh expansion after 1750 that appeared in London and briefly in Nottingham (for 1745–1765). Among thirty urban examples, only the scattered centers of Koblenz, Naples, Madrid, Stockholm, Ghent, and the Aalst District display that pattern, as greater local distinctions once more characterized the expansion of European cities.[12]

The remaining five centers graphed on Figure 8.2b lay in the southern or Spanish Netherlands, now modern Belgium, the territory that the Hapsburgs held onto after the Dutch Revolt. As of 1600, the old medieval cities of Ghent and Bruges were still twice the size of Rotterdam, though Amsterdam had achieved their scale during the later 1500s. Bruges, Ghent, the Aalst District, Evergem, and Mechelen all lost population, mostly in the D form of decline it seems, during the wars for Dutch independence in the late 1500s.[13] By controlling the estuary of the Scheldt and even holding Ostend for several years before 1604, the Dutch struck a heavy blow to the erstwhile commercial preeminence of the

Figure 8.2c
Urban Population Growth and Decline in Europe: Some Cities of Southern Central Europe

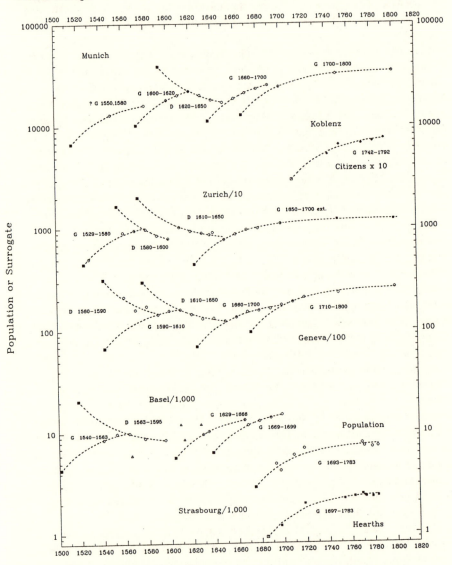

Sources: Dreyer-Roos 1969; François 1982; Elsas 1936; Mattmüller 1987; Mitchell 1992.

southern Netherlands. This economic damage came on top of devastation from the fighting itself, including the mayhem wreaked on Antwerp by unpaid Spanish troops in 1576. But first Mechelen, in Limbourg, then the other towns in Figure 8.2b—which are located more in the northwest of what is now Belgium, between Bruges and Antwerp—expanded from the early 1600s forward in G trends that were very parallel with the experience of other European cities in Phase IV of Table 8.1.

Subsequently, however, the populations of first Aalst and then Ghent and Mechelen—starting in 1660, 1700, and 1710 respectively—shrank once more along D paths for periods of 40 to 70 years. In this behavior they, most closely Aalst, join Madrid in Phase V of Table 8.1. The decline of Spain's capital accompanied similar loss of population in some cities the Hapsburgs held in the Low Countries. Just how widespread across their large, diverse realm was this urban atrophy, and were the local causes linked or coincidental?[14] In Bruges, in contrast, the pattern of demographic decay from 1700 through 1740 followed a different course: the rare downwardly accelerating C trend. In Bruges and Evergem, finally—as in England's Nottingham—demographic increase across the last decades of the 18th century appeared in the accelerating E form, while in Ghent and Aalst new G growth followed decline and in Mechelen the population was apparently still atrophying as late as 1780.

Earlier, as cities of the Southern Netherlands lost population during the Dutch Revolt, the demographic health of Augsburg and Würzburg in southern Germany and of Geneva, Zürich, and Basel in Switzerland also deteriorated. In Basel and Geneva, the culprit of the 1560s was plague (Mattmüller 1987, 204–5, 209). Was that biological dynamic general for urban decline in southern Central Europe during the later 16th century? Did Spanish armies carry the disease to Belgium? Some decades later, when Leipzig, Frankfurt, Munich, Augsburg, Geneva, and Zürich lost population between 1610 and 1650 (Phase III in the table), several armies *were* thrashing around Central Europe. In disaster as in demographic good health, considerable parallelism—sometimes regional, sometimes virtually continental—appears in the growth and decay of European cities during the early modern era. Curves of G and D shape almost universally suffice to capture the trends.

PATTERNS OF GROWTH IN EUROPEAN CITIES SINCE ABOUT 1750

The period after 1750 or so, de Vries and others have correctly argued, ushered in a new era of urban and economic history for the continent. Trending for some centers whose records begin later than the examples of Figure 8.2 are added in Figures 8.3a and 8.3b.[15] Table 8.2 then draws upon these two figures to summarize and compare patterns in the modern growth of their sampling of European hubs.

First of all, Table 8.2 shows how before most modern core cities started to

Table 8.2
Patterns of Growth in Selected European Cities since 1750

Era: I

Stockholm	1749-1800	G 1704
London	1750,1800	?G 1717
Naples	1750-1850	G 1719
Madrid	1743-1799	G 1728

II

Copenhagen	1780-1850	G 1757
Lisbon	1800-1876	G 1761

II

Stockholm	1810-1841	G 1780
Warsaw	1800-1863	G 1782
Rome	1812-1840	G 1787
Vienna	1800-1857	G 1792

III

Helsinki	1800-1870	?G 1802
Madrid	1817-1836	G 1825
Kuibyshev	1811-1867	G 1844
Rome	1840-1860	G 1805
Amsterdam	1850-1870	G 1816
Prague	1850-1880	G 1824
Rotterdam	1850-1870	G 1831
Naples	1861-1890	G 1832
Gorky	1850-1867	G 1832
Madrid 2	1842-1880	G 1843
Athens	1850-1870	G 1844
London	1850-1870	G 1844
Stockholm	1845-1880	G 1846
Copenhagen	1850-1870	G 1848
Marseilles	1850-1890	G 1851
Paris	1850-1920	G 1854
Rome 2	1865-1880	G 1864
Vienna	1857-1890	G 1874
Warsaw	1860-1890	G 1883

IV

Athens	1870-1900	G 1887
Helsinki	1870-1890	G 1892
Prague	1880-1910	G 1858
Madrid	1880-1910	G 1867
Gorky	1867-1910	G 1876
Rome	1880-1910	G 1880
Vienna	1890-1910	G 1886
Copenhagen	1880-1910	G 1887
Warsaw	1890-1910	G 1902
London	1870-1930	G 1867
Marseilles	1890-1954	G 1870
Amsterdam	1880-1920	G 1879
Lisbon	1890-1930	G 1883
Stockholm	1880-1925	G 1887
Naples	1900-1950	G 1887
Kuibyshev	1867-1926	G 1891
Rotterdam	1890-1920	G 1905

V

Prague	1910-1970	G 1897
Madrid	1910-1930	G 1900
Copenhagen	1911-1950	G 1903
Helsinki	1900-1930	G 1918
Athens (C)	1900-1960	G 1924
Amsterdam	1920-1960	G 1889
Rotterdam	1920-1950	G 1900
Warsaw	1920-1946	G 1908
Lisbon	1920-1960	G 1911
Stock'm (C)	1935-1960	G 1928
Rome	1920-1936	G 1930
Helsinki 2	1930-1970	G 1932
Kuibyshev	1926-1980	G 1956
Gorky	1920-1940	G 1965
Athens (M)	1928-1960	G 1956
Stock'm (M)	1940-1970	G 1951
Madrid 2	1940-1980	G 1956
Naples	1950-1970	G 1923
Marseilles	1954-1968	G 1949
Gorky 2	1959-1980	G 1949
Rome 2	1950-1970	G 1955
Warsaw 2	1950-1980	G 1966
Athens (M)	1960-1980	G 1963

II   Second appearance in this column.
(C)   Center city.
(M)   Metropolitan area.

Sources: Mitchell 1988, 72-75; de Vries 1984, 270-78; notes 5-22.

shrink—beginning with Vienna and Paris after World War I (Figure 8.3b)—wave after wave of growth everywhere took the basic G form. Meanwhile, slowly decelerating H increase is entirely missing from the histories of the more than two dozen leading modern European centers covered in the graphs. E acceleration is almost absent.[16] So, too, is the F trajectory or any other form of log-linear expansion except for Rhine-mouth Rotterdam in the brief period 1870–1890 (Figure 8.2a). City by city, modern growth across Europe has adhered consistently—almost totally—to just G trends, as has already been found to be the case for urban centers of the continent whose records have permitted investigation back further in time.

The second point is that there are many parallels among these G patterns that should help identify the forces which underlay, which drove, modern urbanization in Europe. Some of these resemblances in trend may be coincidental, of course; but many of the similarities and differences observed seem to offer clues as to why and how certain cities, and cities in certain regions, have grown at particular times. To facilitate comparison, Table 8.2 groups patterns for individual urban centers first roughly by when trends started (as under the roman numerals I through V), then clusters them within these columns by years covered in the G trends and by the timing of the base points of those curves.

Across the later 1700s and early 1800s, fresh growth appeared in cities around the fringes of Europe: London, Copenhagen, Stockholm, Naples, Madrid, and Lisbon, joined rather later by Warsaw, Vienna, and Rome (parts I and II in the table). Meanwhile, centers down the old economic and cultural spinal cord of the continent from the Low Countries to Italy tended to stagnate along late stages of G curves begun in the early 1600s.[17] Munich, Augsburg, and Leipzig also fairly much ceased expanding as the momentum of somewhat later G trends petered out towards 1800.

The national data provided by de Vries (1984, 30, 39, 45) likewise show the least relative urban growth either in number or in proportion living in cities of 10,000 or more between 1750 and 1850 in Italy, France, Belgium, and the Netherlands, accompanied by Portugal. Meanwhile Scotland, England, Ireland, and Germany, along with Poland, urbanized the quickest either by number of city dwellers or in terms of their percentage of total population. Spain, Austria and Bohemia, and Scandinavia came in between, with middling rates for population growth in the cities of 10,000 or more persons and for the increase of such centers as a proportion of all their people. The fortunes of sample cities graphed in Figures 8.2a, 8.2b, 8.3a, and 8.3b here and the aggregate evidence of de Vries by country paint very much the same picture of once again regionally distinct urban changes across the continent between 1750 and 1850.

That epoch of geographical distinctiveness in the development of cities came to an end in the middle of the 19th century as several for-the-time-being quiescent centers now joined metropolises all over Europe in the fresh G-type expansions that are listed in column III of Table 8.2. Of the eighteen cities traced, only Lisbon missed out on this surge in the middle 1800s. There, a G

Figure 8.3a
Population Growth and Decline in Selected European Cities: Centers with Mostly Recent Evidence

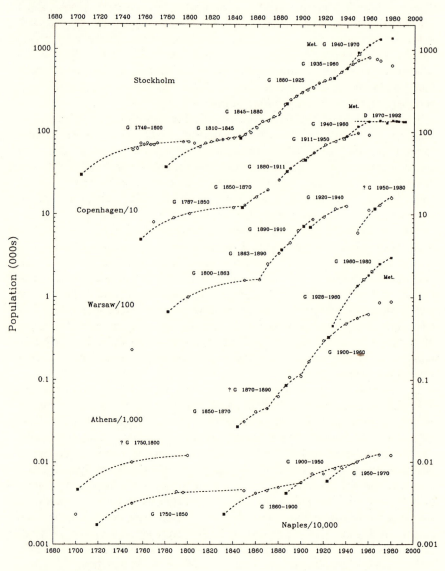

Source: Mitchell 1992, 72–75.

Figure 8.3b
Population Growth and Decline in Selected European Cities: More Centers with Mostly Recent Evidence

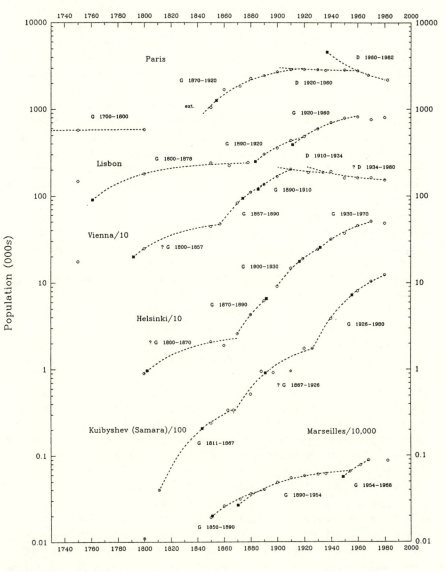

Source: Mitchell 1992, 72–75.

growth begun in 1800 lasted through to 1876 or later. Elsewhere, from London across Scandinavia to the Russian cities of Gorky (Nizhne Novgorod) and Kuibyshev (Samara), from the Low Countries through France and down the boot of Italy, and from Athens northward to Vienna, Prague, and Warsaw, one major urban center after another shared in the G-shape surge of big cities at this time. The steepness of the curves for the period, however, rose appreciably from Rome to Warsaw in the table, from a base year at 1805 to one at 1883.[18] Helsinki, Kuibyshev, and Madrid began their trends of this type earlier than other cities, near the start of the century.

For explaining such general international urban growth, which runs right across the leading cities of Europe following about 1850, diffusing industrialization almost certainly plays a central role. This was a time at which the chief source of power shifted from water to steam, and railroads readily carried coal to population centers in order to exploit their cheap labor, supplementing operations established at waterfalls or mine heads without much regard for prior peopling.

Growth patterns for two production centers of Germany's Rhine watershed illustrate such impacts of economic change. Barmen was a locus of early industrialization in the dynamic Wupperthal; later-developing Gelsenkirchen lay north of Essen in the Ruhr district (Köllmann 1965, 588–607). In the Wupper watershed around Barmen, the shift from craft to industrial means of textile production began right after the Napoleonic Wars. Population swelled in G form in 1818–1850 as Barmen's employers strove to compete with English and Belgian rivals. Then two successive stronger G surges between 1858–1895 and 1895–1910, resembling the growths seen widely in column IV of Table 8.2, appeared as local manufacture diversified from textiles into buttons, mechanical engineering, and chemicals. In the Ruhr around Gelsenkirchen, factory development took off only in the 1850s. But then the population of Gelsenkirchen multiplied approximately eighty-fold between the 1840s and 1910 along a G path with its t_0 at 1912. Still a rural town of some 3,000 residents in the 1850s when an Anglo-Belgian company sank the first mine, the city had matched Barmen's 169,000 inhabitants by 1910 (Köllmann 1965, 591).

In less distinctively industrial areas of Europe, too, cities below the largest size also enlarged in G form across the 19th century. Calabria, the toe region of Italy, is not noted for its economic growth. Of its three chief urban centers, Cosenza expanded along a single G path from 1815 though 1881. In contrast, Reggio di Calabria and especially Catanzaro, while similarly swelling across the early 19th century, experienced fresh increase in G form from about 1860 to 1901, with t_0's near 1840—like the big cities of column III in Table 8.2 (Izzo 1965, 249, 301, 349).[19] Patterns of demographic expansion elsewhere across Europe in this era should reflect local variations in how, and how much, regions engaged in the processes of industrialization. But G-type trends seem to be the norm for all degrees and all phasings of such involvement.

The country-by-country findings of de Vries for the first four decades (1850–

1890) of this next century-long period show urbanization (in cities over 10,000) quickening almost everywhere in contrast to 1750–1850. The exceptions were in England, Wales, and Scotland, leaders of the previous era, where already high levels of urbanization made it difficult for proportionately more people to keep on concentrating in cities, while Ireland joined Italy and Portugal to constitute the laggards of documented European city growth for 1850–1890. Most aggressive in rates of urbanization at this time were the countries of Central Europe: Austria and Bohemia, Germany, Switzerland—and also Scandinavia. Belgium, the Netherlands, and France saw the rate of their urbanization revive enough to make them about average participants in the pace of further city growth. In general, after 1850 something of an evening-up process seems to have been going on, in contrast to the more marked regionalization of 1750–1850.

Widely shared expansion in the leading cities of Europe persisted into the early years of the present century, as column IV in Table 8.2 indicates. Except for Paris, which kept to her previous G path until 1920, all eighteen preeminent urban centers being followed (and Barmen with them) experienced comparable new G-form increase cross the last years of the 1800s and the early 1900s. Finally, from about World War I to World War II, or somewhat later, thirteen of the cities studied display still a third wave of shared G-type growth (Prague through the first entry for Gorky in column V of the table).[20] Marseilles and Naples, however, continued to follow G trends begun in 1890 and 1900 all the way through World War II. The urban cores of Vienna, Paris, and London, meanwhile, already had begun to *lose* population between the wars, as Figures 8.3b and 8.2a indicate. In spite of these exceptions, though, surprisingly similar growth histories appear across the leading centers studied here through three phases of G-type expansion between about 1850 and 1950.

De Vries (1984, 47) helpfully provides further evidence of such convergence at the national level, above and beyond what is demonstrated by the individual cities of Table 8.2. As of 1980, on average 47 percent of the populations of England and Wales, the Netherlands, and France lived in cities of 100,000 or more as did 32 percent of the residents of Spain, Switzerland, Germany, Scandinavia, Scotland, Belgium, Italy, and Poland, in that order. Exceptionally, in Ireland and in Austria and Bohemia the figure reached only about 21 percent, and just 11 percent in Portugal. The diversity of urban concentration from country to country, though still evident, was for the most part no longer so great as it had been in earlier eras.

Very recently, chiefly since some time after World War II, many major European cities have been losing population. Vienna and Paris began noticeably earlier, around World War I, and London during the Depression. In part, cities have just overflowed their boundaries in suburbanization, though even metropolitan Stockholm seems to have begun to shrink. Inner cities in general have clearly declined on this continent as well as in the Americas. Following World War II, nonetheless, seven European centers in Table 8.2 can be seen to have enjoyed significant further growth before constriction began. Naples, Rome, Marseilles, and Madrid cluster in the western Mediterranean.[21] In the East, Warsaw joined Gorky and Kuibyshev in the kind of stronger post–World War II expansion of urban population to be found near the bottom of column V of Table 8.2.[22] There are at least hints here that regional shifts and geographical differentiation among growth patterns may be returning since 1950 among the major centers of Europe, as has been observed during the previous epochs of approximately 1750–1850 and 1550–1650.

Such ebb and flow of similarity across parts of Europe between the 1400s and the present can best be identified and understood alongside what is known of economic change from era to era. That analysis forms one task of a later volume of this study. In the meantime, though, it is evident that for individual cities just G and D curves account for the overwhelming majority of urban growth and decline recorded on this continent ever since city populations can first be traced. Patterning urban change by such G-based trending, furthermore, fruitfully both confirms and refines previous insights concerning how European cities have evolved over the past five hundred years or so.

OUTLINES OF MODERN URBAN DEVELOPMENT IN ASIA AND AFRICA

Reliable evidence on urban populations in either Asia or Africa does not reach back very far in time. Even contemporary estimates tend to be approximate and variable. Nonetheless, so many cities of substantial size exist in these parts of the world that it is important to investigate their growth in at least some preliminary manner. As of the early 1990s, for example, China alone contained 373 cities of 100,000 or more inhabitants, India another 303, and Japan 214 (U.N. *Demo. Ybk. 1993*, 278–86).

To begin to sample this vast array of urban centers, Figure 8.4a graphs change of population size in eight selected cities each from China and Japan, mostly since the end of the 19th century. Figure 8.4b plots trends in six urban centers of India and eleven others elsewhere in Asia. These thirty-three cities are chosen in part for their preeminence, in part to represent central places of varied location and function. Table 8.3 summarizes and compares the patterns found in this sampling.[23]

First of all, in China across a period since 1900 that has included two revolutions, invasion, and other major breakdowns of government and supply, only Beijing and Shanghai have fairly consistently enlarged. Expansion even in the metropolitan areas of these two famous cities, though, hit ceilings of retrogressive rG succession: Beijing in the late 1950s and Shanghai in the middle 1970s, as Figure 8.4a shows. Specific policies not to let the administrative capital of the new People's Republic multiply excessively or its commercial capital get out of hand would seem involved in these two sharply capped growths.[24] De-

Figure 8.4a
The Modern Growth of Urban Centers in Asia: Some Cities of China and Japan

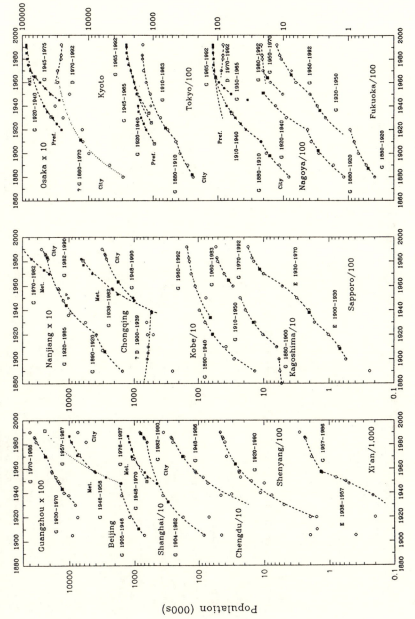

Table 8.3
Trends for Certain Asian Cities since Their Records Began

Phases:	II	III	IV	V	VI
China					
Beijing (met.)	1905-1950 G 1911			1957-1987 rG 1971	1948-1958 G 1991
Shanghai		1904-1982 G 1933			1982-1990 G 1989
Nanjiang	1890-1920 G 1906		1920-1982 G 1944		1982-1990 G 1983
Guangzhou (Canton)		loss	1930-1970 G 1943		1970-1986 G 1970
Chengdu		loss		1948-1986 G 1970	
Shenyang (Mukden)		loss		1920-1990 G 1964	
Xi'an		loss	[1938-1957 E 1911]	1957-1986 G 1958	
Chongqing	(1900-1939 D 1841)			1948-1990 G 1963	
Ürümqi (est.)			[1938-1953 E 1914]		1958-1990 G 1980
Lanzhou (est.)			[1920-1948 E 1930]		1953-1990 G 1980
Japan					
Tokyo	1880-1910 G 1898	1910-1940 G 1934		1950-1970 G 1964	(1970-1992 D 1925)
Osaka	1880-1910 G 1911	1920-1940 G 1931		1945-1975 G 1965	(1970-1992 D 1929)
Kobe	1880-1910 G 1882	1890-1940 G 1920	1960-1990 G 1934		
Kyoto	1880-1920 G 1902	1910-1983 G 1922			
Nagoya	1880-1900 G 1826	1910-1950 G 1930	1920-1940 G 1951	1950-1970 G 1964	1980-1992 rG 1909
Kagoshima	1880-1920 G 1887	1930-1950 G 1936		1960-1983 G 1965	
Fukuoka		[1900-1930 E 1908]		1950-1992 G 1966	
Sapporo			[1930-1970 E 1938]		1970-1992 G 1974

Table 8.3 (*Continued*)

Phases:	I	II	III	IV	V	VI
Other Countries						
Bombay	1881-1931 G 1876	1901-1921 G 1898		1931-1971 G 1948	1941-1961 G 1964	1961-1991 G 1974
Calcutta	1871-1910 G 1865	1911-1931 G 1899			1931-1971 G 1957	1971-1991 G 1971
Kanpur	1881-1921 G 1850		1921-1941 G 1916		1941-1971 G 1962	1971-1991 G 1973
Madras	1891-1911 G 1866	1911-1931 G 1904			1931-1961 G 1957	1971-1991 G 1971
Ahmedabad	1881-1901 G 1891	1901-1931 G 1911				1961-1991 G 1980
Karachi	1881-1901 G 1883	1911-1931 G 1896				1941-1981 G 1983
Rawalpindi (est.)	1871-1891 G 1854	1901-1931 G 1900		1931-1951 G 1945		1961-1981 G 1981
Colombo (est.)				1946-1971 G 1940		
Teheran				1920-1940 G 1946	1950-1980 G 1969	1940-1986 G 1984
Istanbul (est.)	1890-1910 G 1871				1950-1965 G 1966	1965-1983 G 1979
Izmir (est.)	1860-1900 G 1826*					1950-1993 G 1989
Ankara			1919-1947 G 1937		1947-1970 G 1965	1936-1990 G 1983
Bangok (est.)			1920-1936 G 1919			
Seoul					1947-1971 G 1960	1960-1967 G 1986
Pyongyang					1968-1991 rG 1969	
Taipei			1911-1947 G 1934	1910-1931 G 1947	1947-1971 G 1967	
Kuala Lumpur			1911-1931 G 1921	1920-1950 G 1952	1947-1985 G 1960	
Singapore	1871-1901 G 1883					
Hong Kong	[1871-1901] E 1880]	[1901-1931] E 1919]	[1911-1941 E 1931]		1961-1980 G 1963	1971-1991 G 1991
Delhi			1911-1931 E 1941		1941-1971 G 1971	1960-1985 G 1981
Djakarta		[1891-1911] E 1927]	[1900-1930 E 1941]		1930-1960 G 1968	1960-1980 rG 1956
Bandung			[1910-1957 E 1945]		1930-1960 G 1966	
Rangoon	1880-1920 G 1890		[1921-1971 E 1938]		1953-1983 G 1978	1971-1991 G 1988
Visakhapatnam	1881-1921 G 1865		[1910-1970 E 1945]			1970-1993 G 1975
Damascus						

Source: Note 23.

Figure 8.4b
The Modern Growth of Urban Centers in Asia: Selected Cities in Other Countries

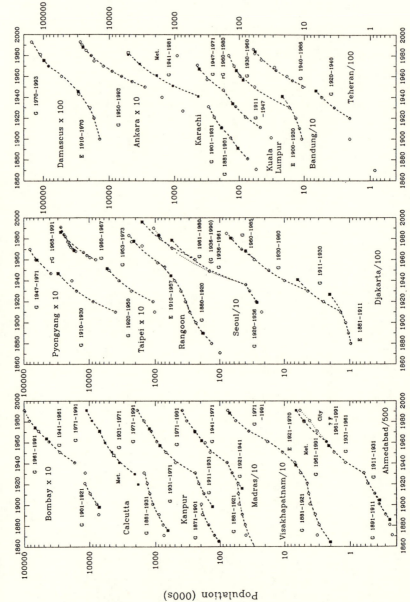

Population (000s)

Source: Note 23.

mographic evidence for Shanghai proper in the 1980s suggests that the old G trend of 1904–1948 for the core city kept on slowing for three decades thereafter. Nanjiang (Nanking), meanwhile, lost population for a time as the Nationalists fled their capital for Taiwan, though evidence before and after the early 1950s suggests a long-term G-type expansion for 1920–1982 which resembles that of inner Shanghai 1904–1982.

Even in relatively modern times, the cities of China have been vulnerable to major disasters. While only Chongqing shows systematic D-shape decline on the graph for a significant period of time—across the first four decades of this century, presumably as China's hold on her western interior weakened in the era that produced and followed the 1911 revolution—Xi'an after 1904 and Chengdu after 1921 also lost many inhabitants before engaging in vigorous modern growth. Xi'an lay in warlord country for much of the period between the world wars. Guangzhou (Canton) decayed more gently through combative years up into the 1930s, during which this city gave birth to both the Communists and the Kuomintang. In spite of losses in the early 1900s, for Shenyang (Mukden) since World War I only a change of hands at the end of World War II significantly reduced population below what has otherwise been a strong, sustained G-shaped thrust of expansion for this leading industrial center.

In Japan, Tokyo and Osaka—and to a lesser extent Kobe and Nagoya—visibly lost much population in World War II from casualties during massive bombings and from flight to escape them.[25] Kyoto, the culturally protected old imperial city, and the less tempting provincial targets of Kagoshima, Fukuoka, and Sapporo avoided such demographic setbacks. In Tokyo and Osaka prefectures, the broader administrative areas incorporating the cities proper, robust recovery after World War II hit a ceiling near 1970; and the new rG trends thereafter are flatter than the ones before. Such setbacks in these two metropolitan districts apparently occurred without the central government policies associated with similar phenomena in Beijing and Shanghai. Available recent data indicate, meanwhile, that systematic urban demographic decay in D form has been the norm since about 1970 in both Tokyo and Osaka center cities, much as in Philadelphia and Chicago (Figures 8.1a and 8.1c) or Paris and Vienna (Figure 8.3b).

In Sapporo, on the northern island of Hokkaido, the growth of the central place for this late-developing region of Japan displays a proportional *acceleration* not witnessed for this part of the country as a whole. One such explosion began just before the Russo-Japanese War; the second, as Japan armed further in the 1930s. By now, however, decelerating G growth has replaced the E trend of 1930–1970, as in the Chinese city of Xi'an since 1957 (and as in New Orleans about 1800, Vancouver around 1910, or Houston in the vicinity of 1960, as Figures 8.1a and 8.1c indicate). Similar Chinese urban successions from E to G trends appeared in Lanzhou and Ürümqi about 1950 (not graphed but estimated by inspection for Table 8.3). The former lies along the upper Yellow River on the old trade routes to Central Asia further west and north of Xi'an, while

Ürümqi is situated still farther out, almost in Kazakhstan. This accelerating E-type growth in certain cities seems very much associated with the development of China's vast northwestern interior. Qinghai Province just west of Lanzhou, for instance, experienced demographic explosion from 1933 until the 1970s before swerving into a G path. In several northeastern regions, in contrast, provinces had accelerating growth but not their cities. These findings suggest some interesting lines for further analysis concerning how population explosion appears exceptionally in a few cities, in the Old World as well as the New.

Table 8.3, which summarizes the evidence of both graphs and some additional information that is not plotted in them and Figure 8.4b show that certain other Asian cities also exploded demographically at one point or another in their recorded histories. This happened in Visakhapatnam in southern India, Delhi in northern India, Rawalpindi in Pakistan, Djakarta and Bandung in Indonesia, Rangoon in Myanmar (Burma), Hong Kong, and Damascus.[26] How is such urban growth in the E form to be explained in terms of improved health, persisting high fertility, and migration—and the relationships of those forces with economic development? Or are these several trends of that shape perhaps only coincidental?

Meanwhile, likely retrogressive or rG successions appear in Taipei and Bandung to accompany the ceiling encounters of Beijing, Shanghai, Tokyo, and Osaka. For the recent demographic history of most Asian cities, however, repeated, successively renewed G sequences are the norm. Table 8.3 indicates, moreover, how during certain periods of time closely similar G trends have been shared across many cities in many different parts of Asia.

Most notably, following World War II, 5 of 10 sample cities of China, 5 of 8 Japanese centers, and 16 of 25 cities drawn from the rest of Asia—or 26 of 43 cases in all (approximately 60 percent across the board)—experienced growth in G trends that had their base years clustered around the early 1960s (Phase V in the table). In Ürümqi and Lanzhou in northwestern China and Sapporo, Karachi, Teheran, Ankara, Seoul, Visakhapatnam, and Damascus elsewhere in Asia, the G-type growths since World War II have been steeper, with t_0's averaging more like 1982 (Phase VI). Meanwhile, Beijing, Shanghai, Nanjiang, Ghangzhou, Bombay, Calcutta, Delhi, Kanpur, Madras, Ahmedabad, Rawalpindi, Izmir (Smyrna), and Djakarta have seen their populations increase in *second* postwar G expansions that have had much the same timing. In Calcutta, Guangzhou, Nanjiang, the core cities of Shanghai and Kyoto, Nagoya, and perhaps Colombo, in contrast, relatively flatter G trends begun before World War II continued substantially thereafter. In all, many parallel trends appear in Figures 8.4a and 8.4b and Table 8.3. To what extent have cities strung across Asia in fact been subject since the 1940s to common medical, social, and economic changes that might produce such similarities of pattern in growth or decline? What can be gained from studying their parallel growths?

Earlier, during the period between the wars (III and IV in the table, and an occasional trend from II), Asian patterns of urban growth were more diverse.

Five of the sample cities lost population one way or another for a time. All of these were in unstable China. Ten cities experienced population explosion. Nine increased demographically in relatively strong G form (IV) and 13 more slowly but along curves of the same shape (III).

Back still further in time, among the Asian urban histories for which trends can be established before World War I, once again greater similarity among centers appears. While there is some variation in timing among the G trends listed in Phases I and II of the table, which cover that period, of the 26 sample cities whose populations can be tracked before 1914 only declining Chongqing and exploding Hong Kong, Bandung, and Djakarta did not swell according to one or two G paths.[27]

For Africa, cities whose population size can be followed for some substantial span of time are less numerous. Still, Figure 8.5 presents a dozen cases for illustration. These are selected so as to cover different parts of the continent, to take advantage of centers with the longest records, and to represent diverse types of change in urban demographic increase.

As in Asia, since World War II there has been considerable parallelism in African urban growth. In particular, Lagos in Nigeria, Casablanca in western Morocco, Accra in the Gold Coast, Nairobi in Kenya, and Maputo (Lourenço Marques) in Mozambique have been expanding recently over rather similar G trends. Dar es Salaam in Tanzania followed a similar G path to about 1960 before taking up a fresh, stronger one. So did Suez up through 1966. Somewhat flatter G paths in Cairo 1947–1992, Algiers to 1966, Durban to 1960, and possibly Oran to 1966 or later also rather resemble each other. In contrast, city populations as diverse as those of Casablanca, Cairo, Lagos, and Maputo recently were exploding—for Maputo and Casablanca both into World War II and out of it as well. Each of these two hubs, indeed, has witnessed two E-type trends of accelerating demographic increase since about World War I, accompanied by 1930–1952 growth in this form in Lagos. In Cape Town the years following the attainment of self-government, 1910–1936, saw the F trend of population increase that is so rare in cities.[28] No H trends appear in these African centers, though, any more than in the Asian examples; and in general urban population increase across the continent has once again mostly involved just sequences of G-shape enlargements.

In sum, of more than 350 growth trends observed by this study in cities around the world, approximately 90 percent are of only the G form. Among the cases presented in the tables and figures of this chapter, the predominance of this pattern ranges from 99 percent in Europe since the later 1700s, to 95 percent in Europe before 1750, 87 percent in the Americas, 88 percent in Asia, and 81 percent for the limited, mostly recent cases from Africa. Generally speaking, the more settled the society the more completely its cities grew in G form. The H trend has been found only once, in Buenos Aires between 1744 and 1838. Log-linear F appears just four times: in Providence, Rhode Island, during two de-

Figure 8.5
The Expansion of a Dozen African Cities

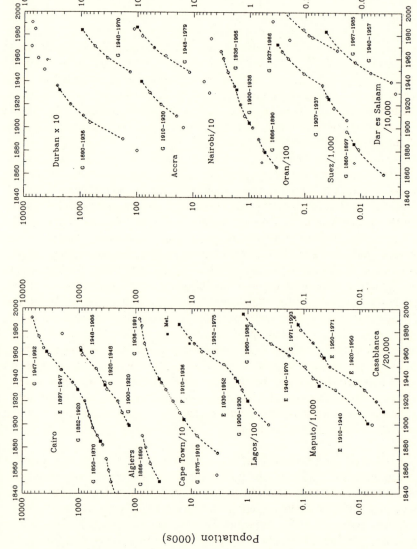

Sources: Mitchell 1982, 66; U.N. *Demo. Ybk.* 1983, 1993.

cades of rapid early 19th century industrialization; perhaps in New York 1870–1890 as immigration surged through her harbor; in Cape Town for a quarter century following the Boer War; and equally briefly as Rotterdam took off in 1870–1890 as entrepôt for the Rhine artery into western Europe.

The main exception to G-type expansion, accelerating increase in the E pattern, amounts to 23 percent of the trends identified for Africa, 12 percent for Asia, 10 percent for the Americas, 5 percent for Europe before 1800, and not a single observed instance on that continent thereafter. In the Western Hemisphere, such explosions occurred in the early days of New Orleans and Vancouver, in Buenos Aires after independence, in Rio perhaps three times between 1750 and 1900 (but never in São Paulo), and twice in the oil boom center of Houston across the first half of the 1900s. How similar or dissimilar were the historical contexts of these once "go, go" cities to the conditions of Cairo, Lagos, Casablanca, and Maputo in recent times? Or Hong Kong, Delhi, Djakarta, Xi'an, and some other Asian hubs earlier in the 20th century? In Europe, meanwhile, only Bruges, Evergem, and Nottingham clearly show the E pattern, all three in the years between 1750 and 1800, a time of population explosion and early industrialization in England and probably also in Belgium.

In conclusion, the G form of demographic expansion predominates historically for cities even more generally than it does among the populations of nations or regions that previous chapters have studied. Where and how the 10 percent of exceptions occur, furthermore, would seem easy to explain with a little local research. Apparent parallels in the historical contexts of these unusual growth trends are highly suggestive. Meanwhile, the more local the populations that are being examined—here the individual city in contrast to the region or the whole nation—the more infrequent growth forms other than G become, or C exceptions to the usual D-type demographic decay. The implication is that G and D may be the fundamental building blocks of change in population size, whereas other members of their small family of curves depend upon the way in which local changes of G and D shape sum up to compose a broader whole. So far we have still been reaching down to deal only with quite large populations in major cities, however. Does the predominance of basic G growth and D (1/G) decline become even stronger when the analysis focuses even more finely upon the peoples of still smaller demographic units? The next chapter addresses that question.

Meanwhile, we must recognize that the growth of cities represents one frequent way in which people relocate—within a society or from one to another. Thus to have urban development follow G-based forms so generally implies strongly that *migration* may do so as well. This finding raises the fundamental question of whether the other two dynamics that shape population size and structure—*fertility* and *mortality*—also themselves move along G paths—and if so, why. Those issues form the topics of the next volume of this comprehensive historical study.

NOTES

1. Mitchell 1993, 44–56. For the United States 1990: *1990 Census Profile*, 4; and *Stat. Abs.* 1993, 34–36. Supplemental early data are cited where used.

2. For the additional center of Boston 1680–1790, see Figure 1.3 in Chapter 1. Philadelphia to 1790: Harris 1989, 274; New York to 1790 (New York County or Manhattan Island): Rossiter 1909, 170, 181–83; Providence to 1790: Rossiter, 163; Charleston to 1790: Rossiter, 11. Early New Orleans estimates come from Mitchell 1993, 46.

3. Supplementary early estimates for São Paulo City come from Marcilio 1973, 119.

4. Dallas, in contrast, has had no E-type demographic increase in its history. From 1970 to 1990, however, Dallas without the expansion that included Fort Worth went into retrogressive rG growth along a much flatter curve than the one for 1940–1970. Decline did not set in, as for Denver and several midwestern cities; but an unsustainable trajectory of local urbanization was surrendered in favor of more modest increase. San Antonio, meanwhile, saw its G surge of 1900–1930 halt as the size of the city stagnated for a decade during the Depression. The new G trend that began in 1940 has, unusually, persisted right into the 1990s.

5. A general source for this section is: Mitchell 1988, 72–75. In addition, *Augsburg*: Elsas 1936, 1: 79; *Rotterdam*: van Houtte and van Buyten 1977, 82; *Amsterdam*: ibid., 1982 display of the City of Amsterdam Museum, and Lambert 1971, 204. *London*: 1510, 1545, 1553, 1563, and 1582 from Russell 1948, 298; 1580 and 1593 (City and Liberties) from Finlay 1981, 60; 1600 and 1650 from Wrigley 1967, 37, 44–51; other dates from 1605 to 1640 come from Finlay, 60 (City, Liberties and Out-Parishes).

Madrid: Data for 1597 and 1630 and for 1757 through 1799 are "selected estimates" by Ringrose (1983, 28); numbers for 1617 and 1621 and for 1685 and 1723 represent his calculations of inhabitants from communicants (28); figures for 1659 and 1743 are inhabitants as reported in primary sources (27). Official figures for 1757–1804 are also graphed for comparison with Ringrose's amendments for 1743–1799. His preferred estimate for 1821 is inserted as a filled diamond in the official series for 1817–1836. The rest of the information on Madrid consists of official numbers reported by Ringrose or Mitchell. The preferred estimates of Ringrose for 1842, 1850, and 1860 differ only slightly from this series.

Rome: Estimates for 1600, 1650, 1700, and 1750 are from Felloni (1977, 5–7); Friz (1974, 29–31) presents calculations for 1770 through 1870. Officially registered persons reported residing in the city as of Easter are employed 1770–1795 to match what seems to be the nature of preceding numbers; from 1797 through 1870 calculations to include other individuals as well are utilized.

A few figures are taken from de Vries 1984, 270–78.

6. The diamond symbols on the graph represent estimates not employed in the curve-fitting.

7. Israel (1995, 15) puts Amsterdam—along with Delft, Leiden, and Haarlem—in "the ten to fifteen thousand range" by 1477; this is a level that van Houtte and van Buyten say the city reached only in the 1500s.

8. Israel, 32–33, 55–73. The ca. 1520 figure of 13,500 from van Houtte and van Buyten seems high relative to other sources—in particular, 11,000 for 1514.

9. The 30,900 of van Houtte and van Buyten for "ca. 1560" is, it appears, once more somewhat high relative to the rest of the data for this period.

10. A closely parallel G for The Hague 1630–1795 fortifies the generality of this conclusion about the fate of Dutch cities. That extra evidence is in van Houtte and van Buyten (1977, 82).

11. Chambers 1965, 351. An estimate of about 6,000 for Nottingham in 1650 from de Vries (1984, 270), would make the base year for the curve there even more like the 1612 for London.

12. Additional sources for Figure 8.2c and Table 8.1 include: Dreyer-Roos 1969, 57 (hearths [feux] and total population for just the city of Strasbourg proper are employed); François 1982, 44 (only the number of citizens in Koblenz is given).

13. The Aalst District instead lost about two-thirds of its population in a very short period around 1575 (van Houtte and van Buyten 1977, 83). Estimates for Bruges, Ghent, and Mechelen around 1550 from de Vries (1984, 272) are included in Figure 8.2b. They should be regarded as only approximate, as comparison of his 1600 estimates with more finely timed data series for these cities indicates.

14. In addition, the size of Antwerp shrank significantly between 1698 and 1755, a second loss following decline between 1560 and 1630 and growth between 1630 and 1698. Meanwhile, Mons and Namur, located in the south central region of Belgium, suffered no such subsequent drop (though they had lost population along with the Belgian centers covered in Table 8.1 during the later 1500s); but Leiden, in southern Holland northwest of Rotterdam, did (van Houtte and van Buyten, 82). Local scholars should be able to determine what dynamics brought about these declines of the 1700s in certain cities of the Low Countries but not others, in particular losses from warfare and from shifts of trade and industry, especially textiles.

15. Except for Gorky and Prague, which were examined as extra cases to help comprehend patterns for the East but not graphed.

16. Though Nottingham and the two Belgian cities of Bruges and Evergem in Table 8.1 and Figure 8.2b show signs of E-type explosion in the late 1700s. There is a possibility that London expanded the same way between 1750 and 1850. More data are needed to decide that, however. It may not be the case.

17. For instance (in Table 8.1), Amsterdam, Rotterdam, The Hague, Paris, Frankfurt, Würzburg, Strasbourg, Zürich, and Rome (before 1812). An exception to that geographical pattern appears, however, in relatively small Koblenz on the middle Rhine (Phase VI in Table 8.1). Growth of one form or another in medium-sized centers of Belgium in Table 8.1 (Bruges, Ghent, Evergem, and the Aalst district) across the later 1700s would seem to involve reaction to previous decline in these places and perhaps also a gain by secondary centers at the expense of bigger neighbors as the leading cities of the Low Countries on one side and Paris on the other approached stagnation. While growth in Amsterdam and Rotterdam and the Hague virtually came to a halt in the 18th century, Antwerp and Leiden actually lost substantial population—between 1698 and 1755 and 1700 and 1795 respectively (van Houtte and van Buyten 1977, 82–83).

18. Figure 8.3b indicates how the 1870–1920 curve for Paris cuts back through the size of the city at 1850, though Paris apparently swelled above that trend temporarily before the conquest of 1870.

19. Somehow Reggio lost significant population suddenly in the 1850s.

20. Trends of expansion for greater Athens and greater Stockholm are included in the table, as in Figure 8.3a, for illustration of growth not impeded by the geographical limits set by political boundaries, but do not figure in the analysis of trends of increase in cities per se.

21. In her growth of 1940–1980, Madrid was in large part rebounding from the effects of the Spanish Civil War.

22. The strong surge of Kuibyshev (formerly Samara, in Russia's near-Ural region) had begun by 1926. In Gorky, new growth since 1959 has in fact been along a retroactive G trend, rather flatter than that for 1920–1940. Warsaw was recovering from her harsh treatment in the war.

23. Mitchell 1982, 67–72; U.N. *Demo. Ybk.* 1983, 1984, 1992, and 1993; Wriggins and Guyot, eds., 1973, 43.

For specific countries, *People's Republic of China*: State Stat. Bureau 1986, 75; Mackerras and Yorke, eds., 1990, 177; Kaplan et al. 1990, 12; Chandrasekhar 1960, 50; Tien 1973, 358–59; *Japan*: Stat. Bureau 1990, 30–35; *India*: Res. and Ref. Division 1993, 18; Central Stat. Org. 1982, 15–20; *Turkey*: State Institute of Stat. 1987, 38.

24. See, for instance, Ian Buruma, "The 21st Century Starts Here," *New York Times Magazine*, February 18, 1996.

25. Prefecture data give the most regular series for recent years in Tokyo and Osaka, though for the latter inner-city numbers fell proportionally even more in the mid-1940s.

26. Delhi and Hong Kong have been examined in Chapter 7.

27. While no trend can be established, Guangzhou, Shenyang, and Xi'an also lost population in some form before World War I.

28. In Durban, another South African city, similar expansion may have followed World War II; but Figure 8.5 indicates some shift around 1980 from more inclusive counts to more limited numbers.

Chapter 9

The Local Generality of the Simplest G-Shaped Trends: Cross-Cultural Examples over Time

Turning to examine population units smaller than cities requires becoming even more selective and illustrative. Still, it is important to acquire some sense of how well G-based trends account for changes in the size of local populations that demographic historians have established within many kinds of societies across diverse periods of time. It will be insightful to learn what happens to the relative frequencies of the six curves within this small set of formulas as the populations studied become narrower and narrower in scope.

For these purposes, some samples of three types of local demographic units are explored. The first composes counties and similar geographical areas, which in aggregate compose the regions, provinces, or states within nations that have been discussed in previous chapters. The second group of local populations involves towns: units of demographic concentration on the whole considerably smaller and less central than the cities of Chapter 8. The data for some of these communities embrace surrounding rural districts. Finally, at the most local level of all, growth and decline in the populations of some manors, villages, hamlets, pueblos, and tiny isolated Pacific atolls are examined.

In sampling the many historically described local populations available, there has been an effort to cover evidence from the widest possible ranges of time and type of society and to discuss some total data sets now and then, lest it be thought that only friendly examples are chosen. It is hoped that the offered illustrations will inspire readers themselves to contribute towards assessing how G-related trends fit change in the size of local populations, either by providing fresh data or simply by drawing further on the voluminous existing detail that cannot all be covered in this one study.

POPULATION INCREASE AND DECAY IN COUNTIES AND SIMILAR LOCAL AREAS

Historical patterns of demographic growth and decline for fairly small areas within societies can be studied for quite a few parts of the world. Samples from the Americas, Europe, and Asia are examined here.

Figure 9.1 shows how between 1698 and 1790 the populations of the counties of New York generally grew along two successive G paths, with the transition mostly around 1750 (Rossiter 1909, 170, 181–83).[1] The areas along the coast all increased most flatly. Demographic stagnation in Albany County in the 1740s reflects the hazards of King George's War. In all, the figure indicates considerable parallelism in the growth of counties that experienced comparable conditions.

Meanwhile, the five counties of Rhode Island all grew across the early 1700s via G curves with base years near 1740 (Rossiter 1909, 163; fitted but not graphed here). Then Providence County (which included much more than just the town of that name) experienced fresh, stronger G-type expansion beginning about 1750 as northwestern Rhode Island and neighboring parts of Massachusetts and Connecticut were settled by Yankee farmers, while the other four areas held the colonial G trend to the Revolution. Newport, occupied and besieged, lost people during the war; but then the reduced population of the county resumed growing to 1840 along a path identical in timing with its pre-Revolutionary trend (and what Kent perpetuated to 1810). Washington, across Narragansett Bay from stagnating Newport, after a wartime jump shed inhabitants along a D path to 1840. Providence County, which felicitously straddled the lower Blackstone River with its falls, saw its population explode along an E curve of constant proportional acceleration from about 1790 to 1840 as water-powered industrialization filled up the region, though by 1840–1860 *decelerating* G growth had taken over. Bristol saw demographic expansion, in three successive G curves, punctuated by what happened there in the Revolution and another loss of residents around 1820 during the early days of industrialization at nearby Fall River.

In short, the demographic growth and occasional decline of all these fifteen counties of New York and Rhode Island for substantial periods of time are simply and sufficiently modeled by trends from the G family of curves. Only three of these patterns seem necessary, moreover. No signs of F or H growth or C decline appear. The E pattern of explosion occurs only once, in rapidly industrializing Providence County from 1790 to sometime between 1830 and 1850. In sum, of 17 growths in New York and 15 in Rhode Island that one E pattern is the single exception to G-type expansion. Even more than among the cities examined in Chapter 8, in other words, population increase at the county or comparably local level seems to have been very much a matter of growth in the G trajectory alone. Work presented elsewhere on trends among taxables for

Figure 9.1
The Growth of County Populations in New York, 1698–1786

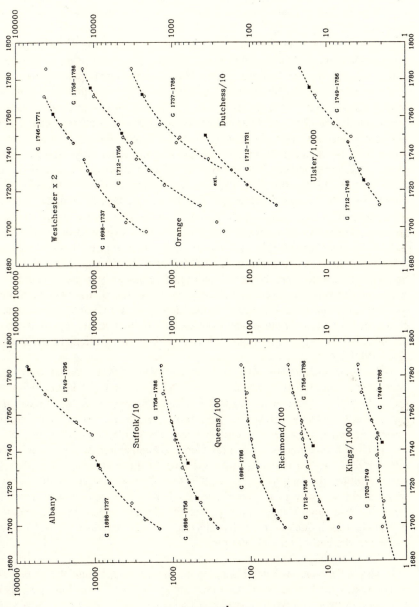

Source: Rossiter 170, 181–83.

the several dozen counties of Virginia and Maryland, on the one hand, and various zones of Pennsylvania and New Jersey surrounding Philadelphia, on the other, reenforces the impression that throughout the Thirteen Colonies and the early United States local populations over and over again grew in just G form (Harris 1983; 1989, 297).[2]

Some additional data from the Spanish frontier settlements of the upper Rio Grande and from provinces within Peru indicate comparable patterns for locales within colonial Iberian America. In New Mexico, the total population increased in three successive G paths from 1749 through 1776, 1776 through 1829, and probably from 1829 to the war in which this territory was seized by the United States (Gutiérrez 1991, 167).[3] The Spanish invaders and their descendants multiplied via steeper G segments during 1746–1776 and 1776–1829 to outnumber the natives by about three to one, rather than the other way around, as the balance had stood about 1750. From 1749 through 1776 the population of Indians declined in D form. Then their number recovered slowly in a shallow G path from 1776 through 1820 or later that in no way kept up with the increase of residents who were classified as "Spanish." After 1829, however, the "Indian" segment of New Mexico's population seems to have expanded in parallel fashion. Meanwhile, around El Paso to the south a similar, if rather flatter, D-shaped decline for the native population appeared from 1750 through 1790. People of Spanish and mixed origin, however, multiplied very steeply in that area in 1747–1760, only to slip into much slower, retrogressively timed G growth from there to 1800. This cluster of settlement further down the Rio Grande seems to have constituted yet another historical frontier that could not live up to its early promise, in contrast to the fruitful valley of more northern colonial New Mexico (Hall 1989, 145).

Tributarios or *contributyentes* in some provinces of Peru reported by P. Macera likewise multiplied between 1731 and 1821 via G paths (Sánchez-Albornoz 1974, 113). For Tinta in the Urubamba valley above Cuzco in the southern Sierra and Conchucos perched in the northern Sierra east of modern Trujillo, numbers swelled in parallel G form between about 1780 and 1820. In Castrovirreina south of Lima in the central Sierra, a comparable curve was followed after 1802, though a flatter G from 1754 up to that point is also evident. A rough plotting of demographic increase in five other areas suggests that G paths of local expansion were the norm across all the major geographical zones of Peru, but had quite diverse timing: that the dynamics that drove population growth in this mountain-divided society apparently remained quite local—at least until the end of the colonial period.

In another mountain-divided population, Switzerland, Figure 9.2 displays—in contrast—just how parallel the trends of growth were over long periods of time among three contiguous districts of the canton of Solothurn, an area south of Basel (Schluchter 1990, 26). From 1514 through 1633 the peoples of Gösgeramt, Niederamt, and Werderamt enlarged along very parallel G trends. Thereafter, the presence of data for only two years—1692 and 1739—makes

Figure 9.2
Population Growth in Three Districts of the Swiss Canton of Solothurn, 1514–1633 and 1795–1980

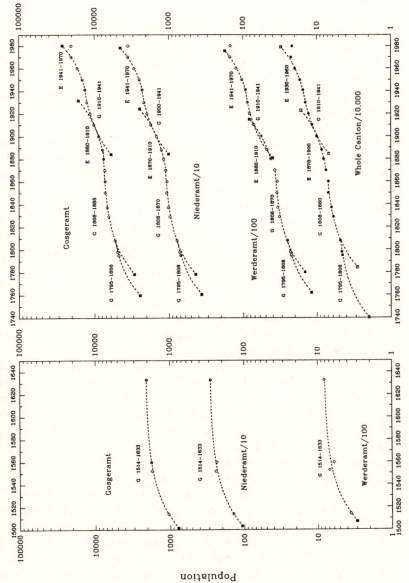

Source: Schluchter 1990, 26.

further trending impossible before 1795. But from 1795 onwards, as the right-hand part of the figure shows, demographic increase in all three of these districts and the Canton of Solothurn as a whole once again moved in very parallel fashion through a series of mixed G and E trends. Referring back to patterns for Switzerland as a whole in Table 5.1, however, it can be seen that neither the canton nor its districts produced the kind of H trend found for the population of the entire country during 1837–1888. Other localities expanding in other ways were needed to generate that composite national curve. Since 1880, however, the local demographic trends of Solothun have largely resembled the national ones. Both in modern times and as early as the 16th century, in short, the population movements of these particular Swiss districts have been more integrated into a single demographic regime than those found in New York, Rhode Island, New Mexico, or Peru.

Figure 9.3 reaches further afield across time and space to illustrate the recurrence of G-based trends in the growth and decline of quite disparate local populations. Närke was a province "situated in the border area between Eastern and Western Sweden." After virtually no change from 1691 through 1710 and a brief dip for 1711–1715 following plague and famine in 1709 and 1710, its people multiplied substantially in G form until 1750 or later (Utterström 1965, 538–39).

New G-shape growth is also apparent in the early 1700s (following some form of much flatter expansion since 1660) for a dozen Worcestershire parishes (Eversley 1965, 404). After heavy mortality in the 1720s (slightly later and more severe than in Närke) cut back this local English population considerably, from 1740 forward it increased in proportionally *accelerating* fashion via three successive explosions to 1830 or later. The first parallels the E-type increase observed northeastward across the Midlands in Nottingham 1760–1801 (Figure 8.2b and Table 8.1). The second and third (1776–1800 and 1800–1830) are both gentler than the 1726–1806 E surge for the English population as a whole, but carry the accelerating form of growth to a somewhat later date than what the nation experienced. As during considerably more modern times in Switzerland, it is seen that "population explosion" could be a local phenomenon in 18th century England, not the aggregate consequence of some national summation of local expansion in other forms. That finding should prove helpful in determining just how populations take off in this ever faster way.

Similar explosion is evident in Rhineland Mark 1722–1780 (Pounds 1979, 100). The E trend for this compact territory astride the Ruhr almost exactly parallels the contemporary proportional acceleration in the population of England from 1726 to 1806 (Figure 5.1a). It also resembles very closely the E trend for 1759–1802 in Württemberg, in southwestern Germany. In discussing demographic increase for the major regions of Germany in Chapter 6 (Table 6.4 and Figure 6.4a), we speculated that undocumented downriver Rhineland territories probably gained people in the 18th century, like Württemberg, in the fashion of northwestern European countries such as England, Scotland, Ireland,

Figure 9.3
Demographic Increase and Decline for Various Localities within Europe, 1665–1850 and 1337–1473

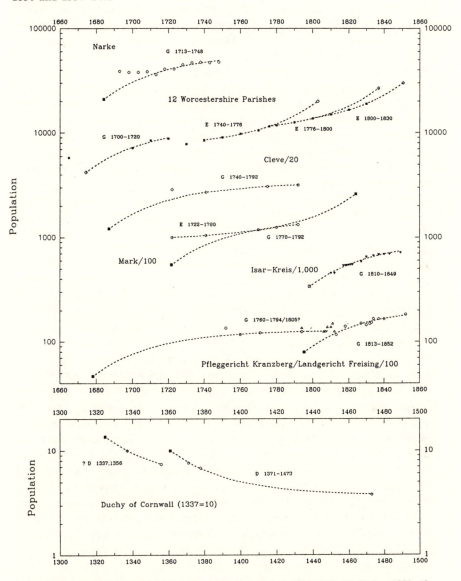

Sources: Utterstrom 1965, 538–39; Eversley 1965, 404; Pounds 1979, 100; W. R. Lee 1973, 13; Russell 1948.

the Netherlands, and Denmark (Table 5.1). Here in Mark lies evidence that this regionalizing hypothesis was correct. In relatively small Mark, however, further increase after about 1780 took a G form that was appreciably flatter than that in Württemberg (or Hannover, or Oldenburg, or Hesse). And, up to 1792 at least, there is no sign in Mark of the H trends that appeared in Rhineland and Westphalia after the Napoleonic wars (Table 6.4) and in several nations of northern Europe rather earlier. This territory, which embraced soon-to-be industrialized Barmen and Gelsenkirchen, did not pick up the H pattern of demographic growth until the 19th century. Instead, it followed the path taken to 1800 by the populations of other, more eastern Prussian holdings such as Neumark, Pomerania, and East Prussia (part A of Table 6.4).

In Cleve, further downriver from Mark where the Rhine enters the Netherlands, no E surge appeared. Instead, following some loss after 1722, population growth from 1740 through 1792 pursued a relatively flat G with base year back in the 1680s (Pounds 1979, 100). This trend apparently paralleled the pattern of demographic increase not only in nearby Overijssel across the Dutch border to the north (Table 6.3) but also in the more distant area around Freising in upper Bavaria (at the bottom of the top panel in Figure 9.3)

In the Pfleggericht Kranzberg (which with some boundary changes became the Landgericht Freising in 1803), after some decline during the war years of the 1750s, the population increased from 1760 through 1794 along a G curve with its t_0 in the late 1670s (W. R. Lee 1977, 13). Quite probably this trend continued into the early 1800s, when the boundary changes were taking place.[4] From 1813 through 1852, however, it is fairly clear that the same population is being measured. This swelled along a fresh G trend with base year at about 1795. That is almost exactly the same timing of G reported for the Isar-Kreis, the part of Oberbayern that contained Kranzberg/Freising, which lay just north of Munich and east of Dachau (W. R. Lee 1977, 21) and also what has been found for the early 1800s in Bavaria as a whole, Baden, Württemberg, and many other major regions of Germany (Table 6.4). Furthermore, the preceeding flat G of the later 1700s in both Cleve and Kranzberg/Freising continues trends of this shape that Württemburg, Silesia, and Neumark abandoned about 1760 for more robust growth. Data from Mark and Cleve near one end of western Germany and from Kranzberg/Freising near the other thus helpfully fill out knowledge of where and how population in Germany increased—in some places aggressively, in others much more quietly—during a period for which only a few major regions are demographically documented.

Several small, scattered principalities of the German Empire whose populations are recorded from 1816 through 1910 also all grew demographically only via G paths: Schwarzburg-Sondershausen, Lippe-Detmold, Schaumburg-Lippe, Schwarzburg-Rudolstadt, Reuss-Schleiz, Reuss-Greiz, and Waldeck and Pyrmont (Köllmann 1980, 82–84, 220–22, 232–34, 238–40, 244–46, 278–80, 284–86, 314–16, 320–22; Germany, *Stat. Jahrbuch* 1914, 2–3). Across a somewhat earlier span of time, meanwhile, G curves also constituted the universal shape of change in the size of populations for the *arrondissements* of Savoy between 1756 and 1848 (Rousseau 1960, 180–221).[5] From 1756 to 1776 all seven areas expanded very much together along G paths. From 1776 to 1848 there was still much similarity, but now more variation in timing.

Throwing local light upon a considerably earlier age in Europe, the shallow panel at the bottom of Figure 9.3 plots demographic decline of the era of the Black Death in Cornwall, the southwesternmost tip of England (Russell 1948, 266). Noticeably, there was some initial loss between 1337 and 1356, during which about one-quarter of the population disappeared. Whether the D trend tentatively fitted just to 1337 and 1356 is approximately accurate can be questioned; starting downward in the late 1340s, after the arrival of plague, might be more suitable. Yet it will be seen from very local evidence further on in this chapter that demographic decline in two successive D trends, starting before the bubonic pandemic, could well have been actual experience. On the broader historical stage, meanwhile, the number of surviving heirs per deceased heiress from various English sources fell off 15 percent from 1255–1300 to 1300–1348 before dropping away more drastically in D form from 1348 into the early 1400s (Russell 1948, 244–45). Chapter 4 has shown that a "double dip" of this sort was quite common when the natives of the Americas encountered strange diseases in the 1500s.

Growth in just G form and decline via D have existed for several centuries among local populations in Asia, Figure 9.4 indicates. The upper left panel begins by showing demographic expansion in three counties of southeastern China between 1371 and 1578 (Ho 1959, 17–20). That epoch embraces the two centuries that followed the expulsion of the Mongols by the Ming. After about 1472 officials in Ch'ang-shu County seem to have started just copying earlier reports. Previously such corruption of the records appears less likely; and from 1371 through 1432 and then from 1432 through 1472 the Ming data in fact seem to reflect two successive G trends of demographic expansion in this locale. In Wu-chiang County of southern Jiangsu province between 1391 and 1412 reporting officials clearly changed the way they counted "mouths," whose number dropped significantly relative to households. Still, under the old system in 1371–1391 and according to the new procedures in 1412–1486 the population seems to have grown via successive G trends. The base dates of these are close enough to each other that the best working hypothesis probably should be that the actual number of people in Wu-chiang multiplied slowly in one extended G path from 1371 through 1486, being only counted by different rules or with different accuracy before and after about 1400. In Lien-chiang County of Fujian Province, finally, similar omission of many individuals differentiates population reports of 1482 and later from the census procedures of 1381. Persons per household fell off drastically as "mouths" more and more reflected taxable persons only. But from 1482 through 1578 the number of households in the county increased in G form with base year at 1402. This suggests a pattern of demo-

Figure 9.4
Some Trends of Local Population Size in Southeastern China, Anatolia, and Japan between 1371 and 1872

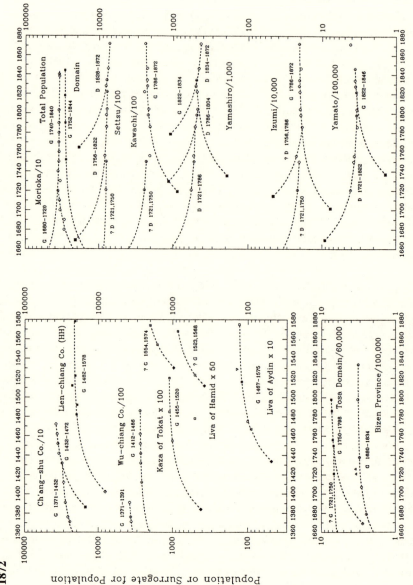

Population or Surrogate for Population

Sources: Ho 1959, 17–20; M. A. Cook 1977, 11; Hanley and Yamamura 1977, 49, 91, 148–50; Hanley 1968, 627.

graphic expansion not unlike that found in Ch'iang-shu County 1432–1472 (with its t_0 at 1386). A reasonable working hypothesis again might be that the populations of these two counties increased in parallel fashion across most of the 15th century and possibly some of the 16th. The corruption of these three local census series, as the purpose of counting focused on new modes of taxation, does not in the end conceal G-shape trends that probably took place in actual local population growth. For substantial stretches of time these demographic landscapes loom out through the fog of mandarin administration that threatens to obscure them.

Turning to the other end of Asia, the same panel of Figure 9.4 displays G-type trends in population growth for three areas of Anatolia across overlapping periods of time between 1455 and 1575 (M. A. Cook 1972, 11).[6] This epoch runs from just after the defeat of the Crusader army at Varna and the fall of Constantinople to just after the death of Suleiman the Magnificent and the naval battle at Lepanto, the era over which the Ottoman Empire reached its prime, not only militarily and politically but economically and culturally. Up to about 1520 estimated population in all three districts of Anatolia expanded relatively flatly, but in the Kaza of Tokat and the Liva of Aydin clearly along the later stages of G curves. Across the next half century the peoples of Tokat and the Liva of Hamid multiplied in vigorous fresh growth, possibly along relatively parallel new G paths, though Aydin kept its G trajectory of the 1400s all the way to 1575. Was the relative stagnation of Aydin somehow connected with a peaking out of Turkish sea power, shipbuilding, and Mediterranean trade?

For Japan under the Tokugawa Shogunate, it is possible to follow quite local patterns of demographic increase for areas that are situated across a considerable swathe of the island group. Data begin in the later 1600s and run almost two centuries to 1872.

The population of Tosa, a province (*kuni*) on the ocean side of the southwestern island of Shikoku, enlarged very gently between 1721 and 1750, then slightly more vigorously via a G trend across the second half of the 18th century (Hanley and Yamamura 1977, 49).[7] Bizen Province, which lay across the Inland Sea from Shikoku on the main island of Honshu, experienced demographic growth along an intermediately timed G trend that lasted all the way from 1680 through 1834 (Hanley 1968, 627).[8] On the domain of Morioka situated in the Tohoku region of northeastern Honshu, meanwhile, population from 1752 through 1844 increased along a G path with base year at 1644 that closely resembled the trend in Bizen. This is shown at the top of the righthand panel of the figure. Estimated total population for Morioka, however, including persons not living on land directly controlled by the domain, grew much like this from 1680 through 1720 but then flattened out more, probably even going into D-shape decline from 1740 through 1840 (Hanley and Yamamura 1977, 148–50).[9]

The other five Japanese provinces appearing in the righthand graph of Figure 9.4 were situated in the Kinai, mostly within 25 miles of Osaka. In this traditional hearth of Japanese cultural and economic life, unlike areas to the east and the west that have just been examined, population *loss* was common, especially across the 18th century (Hanley and Yamamura 1977, 91). The figure shows how such atrophy followed, or could have followed ("?"), D patterns. And when most of these provinces began to grow again around the turn of the century, they did so via G paths.[10] These findings urge us to know better how local areas both well to the southwest and far to the northeast of the Kinai—like Tosa, Bizen, and Morioka—grew as the Kinai shrank and gained population in closely similar movements. How did the periphery gain demographically against the old core during this period of Japanese history?

Within the compact region of the Kinai and elsewhere that demographic historians of China, Turkey, and Japan allow the amateur to browse in English, globally familiar patterns of change in population size stand out. First of all, in every example of Figure 9.4 from Asia, local population either increased in G form or declined via D. No other trends appear necessary to model the data. This finding underscores the need to understand how growth in a *few* locales in the West, from northwestern Rhode Island to Worcestershire to Switzerland, upon rare occasions took the unusual E trend of accelerating expansion. Meanwhile, in southeastern China under the Ming, in parts of Anatolia during the golden age of Ottoman expansion, and in late Tokugawa Japan, both local similarities and dissimilarities among G-based trends offer—as in Europe or the Americas—valuable insights into the social, economic, and demographic change that was taking place.

THE GROWTH PATTERNS OF TOWNS

Even more local than counties or comparable geographical areas have been the towns into which people have clustered across recorded history in order to enjoy benefits from division of labor, concentrated defense, and sociability. Sometimes the reporting units of these lesser centers have included parts of the surrounding countryside, not unlike smaller counties or districts. Sometimes such communities have grown large enough to blur into the category of cities discussed in Chapter 8, making distinction rather arbitrary in this respect, too. Nonetheless, it is useful to look at a few samples of towns: demographic units rather smaller than counties or big cities but rather larger than the minimal gatherings of people into villages, manors, or hamlets.

Figure 9.5 presents, in its lefthand panel, trends in certain frontier settlements of the Americas. Santiago de Guatemala, having lost population up to about 1600 in typical fashion for early Spanish America, saw its its Indian (tributary) and non-Indian residents and its total population augment in G trends for the next century and a half (Lutz 1994, 65). The total population of the town increased over the century from 1655 through 1755 in G form with t_0 in the 1590s, rather more flatly than the tributaries of the Quinizilapa Valley and the Cuchu-

Figure 9.5
Expansion and Contraction in Some Towns in the Americas between 1574 and 1860

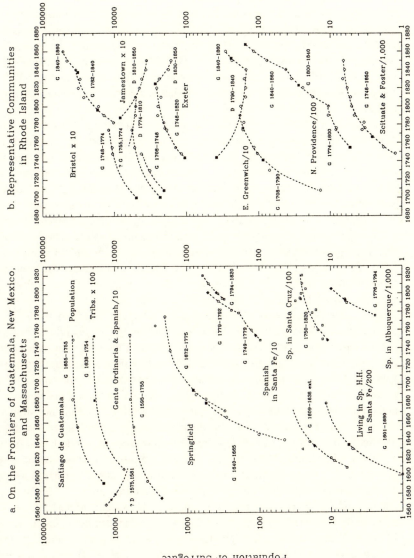

a. On the Frontiers of Guatemala, New Mexico, and Massachusetts

b. Representative Communities in Rhode Island

Sources: Lutz 1994, 65; Gutierrez 1991, 92, 170; Innes 1983, 469; Rossiter 1909, 163.

matán Highlands elsewhere in Guatemala (Figure 4.3 in Chapter 4), but probably not unlike the people of the southern Mexican highlands of the Mixteca Alta between 1660 and 1720 (Figure 4.2a).

Much the same kind of demographic growth, though later and steeper, characterized European elements in the fringe settlements of Santa Fe, Santa Cruz, and Albuquerque up the Rio Grande Valley of New Mexico during the 1700s and early 1800s, and both Spanish and all people living in Spanish households in Santa Fe during the early colonizing period that preceded the great Pueblo uprising of 1680 (Gutiérrez 1991, 170, 92).[11] All of these trends have G shape, though that for Santa Cruz involves considerable fluctuation and the 1630 figure for Spaniards in Santa Fe (the hollow triangle) seems to be something of an outlier.

On another American frontier, meanwhile, thrusting up into a native-populated interior along another river that provided good farmland and a key position for trade, Springfield was established in the Connecticut valley of western Massachusetts in the late 1630s. The inhabitants of this frontier town multiplied in a G path across the quarter-century from 1640 through 1665 that was very similar to the trend of growth for Massachusetts as a whole from 1640 to 1710 in Figure 2.1b (Innes 1983, 469) The flattening out between 1665 and 1672, when a new, slightly steeper G trend began, probably reflects some adjustment of boundaries or new town–founding out of Springfield's original territory. A crisis for "the Valley" during the French and Indian War temporarily turned Springfield into a refuge aroud 1760, interrupting a G curve that otherwise ran across the hundred years from 1672 through 1775.

This curve, with its base year in the early 1690s, was representative of growth in other parts of New England, Table 9.1 indicates: with Newport, Portsmouth, and Little Compton, Rhode Island slightly earlier in the timing of their G trends and with Jamestown, Bristol, Warren, and South Kingstown slightly later (Rossiter 1909, 163). Trends for all twenty-seven communities (or pairs that later became divided towns out of a single original community) have been examined and computed to give the reader the sense of the full set of data, not simply my choices. Plots for six locations are illustrated in part b of Figure 9.5. Several parallel changes of population size for particular areas of Rhode Island between 1707 and 1860 appear. Overall, these 27 communities of Rhode Island display 53 G trends of expansion in their populations up into the early 1800s, not counting curves hypothesized upon just two data points (with "?" before the G). Not a single F, or H, or E pattern of increase is evident. Meanwhile, at some point in their pre-1860 history, several towns experienced demographic decline. In each of the 12 cases, though, loss took the D form. No other pattern of sustained decline occurred, though a community such as Bristol could lose a few people suddenly during the Revolution just as a Jamestown could pick up additional inhabitants between 1748 and 1755 as boundary rearrangements took place.

More evidence accumulates that just G and D were the *local* forms of increase

Table 9.1
Population Trends in Twenty-Seven Rhode Island Towns

Newport County

Newport	1639-1708 G 1681	1708-1774 G 1724	1776-1840 G 1754	–
New Shoreham	1708-1748 G 1683	–	1748-1810 G 1753	1810-1830 G 1816
"				1840-1860 G 1822
Portsmouth	1708-1748 G 1692	1755-1850 G 1720	–	–
Jamestown*		1708-1748 G 1708		
"		1755,1774 ?G 1701	1774-1810 [D 1717]	1810-1850 [D 1788]
Middletown		1748-1774 G 1722	1790-1810 G 1755	1810-1840 [D 1755]
Tiverton			1748-1830 G 1753	1840-1860 G 1845
Little Compton	1748-1774 G 1680			
"	1790-1820 G 1680?	–	–	1820-1840 [D 1790]

Bristol County

Bristol*		1748-1774 G 1700	1782-1840 G 1796	1840-1860 G 1837
Warren		1755-1776 G 1700	1782-1810 G 1788	1830-1850 G 1838
Barrington			1790-1840 [D 1748]	1840-1860 G 1850

Washington County

North Kingstown		1708-1860 G 1721	–	–
South Kingstown		1730-1755 G 1702	1755-1850 G 1745	–
Exeter*			1748-1820 G 1744	1830-1850 [D 1825]
Charlestown			1748-1790 G 1746	1790-1860 [D 1782]
Richmond			1748-1790 G 1765	1790-1840 [D 1746]
"				1840-1860 G 1839
Westerly & Hopkinton		1708-1748 G 1740	1748-1800 G 1765	1790-1840 [D 1758]
"				1840-1860 G 1848

Kent County

East Greenwich*		1708-1790 G 1742	1790-1840 [D 1744]	1840-1860 G 1852
Warwick		1730-1774 G 1744	1782-1820 G 1780	1820-1860 G 1827
West Greenwich		1755-1790 G 1744	1790-1810 [D 1772]	1820-1860 [D 1806]
Coventry			1748-1850 G 1763	–

Providence County (w/o city)

Cranston		1755-1790 G 1717	1800-1840 G 1790	1850,1860 ?G 1874
Scituate & Foster*			1748-1850 G 1765	–
Gloucester & Burrillville			1748-1830 G 1762	–
Cumberland			1748-1810 G 1754	1820-1850 G 1835
Johnston			1748-1820 G 1758	1820-1850 G 1823
Smithfield		1755,1774 ?G 1753	1782-1810 G 1778	1820-1860 G 1834
North Providence*		1774-1800 G 1755	1800-1840 G 1823	1840-1860 G 1867

*Example graphed in Figure 9.5b.

Source: Rossiter 1909, 163.

and decay in colonial New World populations. These local patterns, though, could either parallel broader ones (like the D declines among communities of Washington County in the early 1800s) or sum up to produce exceptional forms (like the E for Providence County 1790–1860, a pattern that no individual town of the area itself followed).

In Europe, too, demographic increase and decline at the town level seem to have involved movements only in G or D (1/G) form. Three sets of illustrations are offered: Figure 9.6 presents patterns for five communities with unusually long records: one from Spain, one from France, one from Germany, and two from Belgium. Table 9.2 goes further to summarize fitted trends for ten northern European towns from the 1700s to the 1900s. Figure 9.7 then demonstrates population growth and atrophy in five medieval centers between about 1320 and 1550: three from northern central Italy and two from southern France.

Cuenca, situated about half way between Madrid and Valencia, lost some population during the later 1500s[12] and then considerably more between 1597 and 1644 (Reher 1990, 20) (Figure 9.6). The hypothetical D curve for the latter contraction, with base year at 1601, resembles the evidence for Spain as a whole between 1589 or 1610 and 1648 in Figure 5.1a of Chapter 5, while the tentatively proposed G curve between 1644 and 1693 (with t_0 around 1590) closely follows that for baptisms for the town's home region of New Castile from 1645 through 1745 (Table 6.1). In short, while suspected trends of decline and then recovery for Cuenca between 1597 and 1693 rest upon just three data points in all, they conform to what is likely to have been happening in the region and in the country as a whole. Then, between losses to British occupation in one war and to Napoleonic occupation in another, the population of Cuenca expanded along an enduring G path for 1719–1801, a local pattern now departing from those of New Castile and Spain as a whole. Further disaster hit the people of the town between 1836 and 1844, at a time of widespread international epidemics and economic depression. In all, the probable and possible D and G trends identified for Cuenca both fit what is known of local history and help place that experience in the context of regional and national demographic change for Spain in the 16th, 17th, 18th, and early 19th centuries.

In Meulan, down the Seine from Paris, from 1685 through 1726 population shrank in D form (Lachiver 1969, 40–41). This curve in Figure 9.6 is appreciably steeper than the D for France as a whole for 1675–1700 indicated in Figure 5.1b. The trajectory does, though, support the hypothesis in Chapter 5 that France joined Spain, Italy, England, and Ireland in experiencing demographic atrophy during the 17th century but that such loss appeared later and lasted longer in France. It also suggests that the relatively flatter trend for the society as a whole derived from its being a composite of places like Meulan that had more marked local decline and communities that probably suffered no demographic loss at all.

Whatever had happened before, the people of Meulan expanded in G form

Figure 9.6
Demographic Increase and Decline in Five European Towns with Long Records

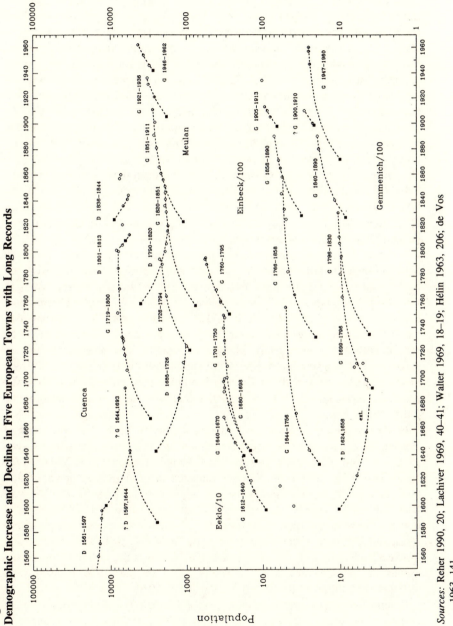

Sources: Reher 1990, 20; Lachiver 1969, 40–41; Walter 1969, 18–19; Hélin 1963, 206; de Vos 1963, 141.

from 1726 through 1794 more robustly than in France as a whole, and along a single G path rather than two successive ones (Figure 5.1b). But then a substantial proportion of local population was lost during the turbulent years between the early 1790s and about 1820. Ironically, this was precisely the brief period in which the people of France collectively display accelerating E growth like several northern European neighbors. The pattern for Meulan reenforces the conclusion arising from the earliest calculable trends for a dozen selected departments of France in part C of Table 6.3: It was the biggest urban centers of the country whose populations exploded at this time. Did many smaller towns pay as much of a price as Meulan while neighboring big cities expanded? Or was this particular secondary center just exceptionally close and vulnerable to the growth of Paris? All four trends for Meulan since the early 19th century take G form, punctuated by losses in the two world wars. The path for 1820–1851 resembles growths of G shape in several French departments covered by Table 6.3. So does the G of 1851–1911. The G-form recovery following World War I, however, was unlike any trend among the dozen sampled departments at this time, though beginning in the 1940s the population of Meulan came back along a G path typical of several zones of the nation.

Einbeck, on the Leine north of Göttingen, during the Thirty Years War fell twice to Imperial armies and also suffered major fires in 1628 and 1641. Of 1,189 residences in 1619, some 646 remained in 1644; and of these only 411 were fully inhabitable. It is estimated that the population dropped from about 6,000 in 1616 to more like 2,500 as of 1644 (Walter 1969, 18–19). From 1644 through 1756, Figure 9.6 then shows that the population of Einbeck recovered substantially, if not completely, along a G path that resembles contemporary expansions of Augsburg 1655–1695, Munich 1660–1700, Leipzig 1637–1699, Frankfurt 1638–1800, and the Duchy of Württemberg 1639–1679 (Tables 8.1 and 6.4), German cities and territories that had likewise been devastated by the Thirty Years War.

Einbeck again lay in harm's way during the Seven Years War (the battle of Minden took place nearby). Local population dropped about a quarter between 1756 and 1766. From 1766 through 1858, though, the town probably enlarged once more along the kind of G track depicted in the figure, somewhat flatter than contemporary growth in the surrounding state of Hanover 1816–1871 (part B of Table 6.4). Then, from 1858 forward the population of Einbeck enlarged in new G form, while Hanover and much of northwestern Germany experienced accelerating growth of the E type (part C of Table 6.4). Still later local G-form increase leading up to World War I, however, presages the path of demographic expansion that Hanover as a whole would follow in 1900–1939. It also resembles the trend followed by French Meulan 1921–1936.

Gemmenich, just south of Aachen (Aix-la-Chapelle), lost about a quarter of its people between 1624 and 1658 (Hélin 1963, 206), not in the manner of Belgian cities already recovering from the Dutch Revolt by the 1620s (Figure 8.2b), but like Einbeck and several larger centers of Germany hit by the Thirty

Years War. A century of demographic recovery in G form then blessed Gemmenich from 1699 through 1796. Subsequent G-type growths, now parallel to those in Einbeck, occurred in 1796–1830, 1840–1890, and 1905–1913. Communities of eastern Belgium and northwestern Germany seem to have been sharing some common demographic dynamics.[13] Though Gemmenich's province of Liége (Table 6.3) expanded rather more strongly than the town up to 1830 and then somewhat more weakly across the middle of the 19th century—and also following World War II—considerable integration of economic and demographic change across the this part of Europe is indicated.

Eeklo, at the other, western end of Belgium—in East Flanders, north of Ghent and near the border with Dutch Zeeland—escaped demographic damage during the Thirty Years War, but suffered in later conflicts of the 1670s and around the turn of the century (de Vos 1963, 141). Otherwise, the figure indicates, local population would have increased from 1640 to 1750 along a G trend parallel to that of Einbeck. When still further G-shaped growth came to Eeklo 1760–1795, it was stronger than comparable new trends for the nearby city of Ghent (Figure 8.2b), Gemmenich over near the German border, or Einbeck in Hanover.

Starting in the middle of the 18th century, records become available for other European towns. As in Table 9.2, these help place the movements of Figure 9.6 within a broader context of demographic increase and decay across at least a substantial area of northwestern Europe. Husum and Lübeck lay at the north end of western Germany, above Einbeck. The first had been a prominent commercial center on the North Sea coast of Schleswig-Holstein in the 17th century, but in modern decline became better known for its cattle market (Momsen 1969, 52–53); the second, sitting east of Denmark on the Baltic, was one of the smaller historic Hanseatic ports (Köllmann 1980, 256–58). Olne and Chênée were located in the Belgian province of Liège, southwest of Gemmenich (Hélin 1963, 203–05); Evergem and Zomergem were towns of East Flanders, situated south of Eeklo (Deprez 1963, 157). Together with Eeklo, Gemmenich, Einbeck, and Meulan from Figure 9.6, these six additional communities provide a sampling of ten towns in an arc sweeping southwestward from Germany's Danish border across Belgium to the Channel, including one example from north-central France. Table 9.2 summarizes the trends of demographic expansion within this belt.

To begin, all eight communities recorded this early enlarged in G form in roughly parallel fashion beginning in the later 1700s. G growth of comparable timing has also been found for the later 18th century in five parts of Prussia (part A of Table 6.4 in Chapter 6). Together these patterns suggest relatively common local demographic expansion for the later 1700s and early 1800s right across the northern rim of sub-Scandinavian Europe, from the Channel to the Baltic coast and along it to East Prussia—dipping south to Silesia and perhaps also the Île de France, if Meulan was typical for this territory, and including the poor rural inland province of Drenthe in the Netherlands 1764–1794 (Table 6.3, part A).

Table 9.2
Patterns of Growth and Decline in Ten Northern European Communities

Community					
Meulan	1726-1794 G 1723	1820-1851 G 1758	1858-1911 G 1873	1921-1936 G 1906	1946-1962 G 1942
Gemmenich	1796-1830 G 1735	–	1840-1890 G 1827	1900,1910 ?G 1899	1947-1960 G 1872
Eeklo	1760-1795 G 1751	–			
Einbeck	1766-1858 G 1732	–	1858-1890 G 1828	1905-1913 G 1898	
Husum	1769-1845 G 1706	–			
Chênée	1740-1811 G 1703	1831-1856 G 1837	1866-1910 G 1873		1920-1957 G 1872
Olne	1757,1789 ?G 1716	1805-1890 G 1768	1868-1880 G 1862	1890-1910 G 1888	
Lübeck		1815-1862 G 1770			1900-1960 [D 1873]
Zomergem	1796-1846 G 1728	1796-1846 G 1752	1846-1876 [D 1817]	1890-1947 G 1789	
Evergem		–	1846-1876 [D 1799]	1876-1890 G 1824	1900-1947 G 1870

Sources: Lachiver 1969, 40–41; Hélin 1963, 203–06; de Vos 1963, 141; Walter 1969, 18–19; Momsen 1969, 52–53; Köllmann 1980, 256–58; Deprez 1963, 157.

By the early 1800s, however, growth in the communities of Table 9.2 began to take more divergent courses. Husum, Einbeck, Gemmenich, and Evergem stayed with the relatively flat G trajectories that their populations had followed in the later 1700s. In contrast, appreciably stronger G-type expansion appeared in new growth in Meulan and Olne, joined by similarly timed first-known trends in Lübeck and Zomergem. The Belgian provinces of East Flanders and Liège, which contained six of the ten towns of Table 9.2, similarly gained population in G paths with t_0's near 1770. So did West Flanders and—for a while—Hainaut (part B of Table 6.3). Meanwhile, the French departments of Haute Marne, Sâone et Loire, Calvados, Hautes Alpes, and Landes (five of seven rural zones sampled for part C of Table 6.3) saw their inhabitants multiply along similar G curves, joined by Bouches du Rhône, the region of Marseilles, and also Dutch Limburg, dangling down above Liège. This somewhat later-timed G paralleled the trend of Belgium's Limbourg province next door but also movements in the provinces of Luxembourg, Namur, Brabant, Antwerp, and Hainaut (after 1816) within Belgium and the departments of Loiret and Vendée in France. In Germany, meanwhile, a dozen states experienced G increase across the early 1800s with t_0's between 1765 and 1793, including Hanover, the region of Einbeck, Schleswig-Holstein, the region of Husum, which also bordered Lübeck, and Oldenburg lying in between. In effect, all areas of far northwestern Germany gained people in that manner. Within this far-ranging context, the slower continuing demographic expansions of Gemmenich, Einbeck, Husum, and Evergem become insightful exceptions whose demographic dynamics would be worth understanding well and contrasting systematically with what seem to have been the movements of the bulk of the population in northwestern Europe.

Then across the second half of the 19th century (the middle column in Table 9.2), the sample towns went still more distinct ways in their demographic histories. In East Flanders, Evergem and Zomergem lost population for a while in familiar D-shape decline, though the province itself gained people in fresh G form in 1876–1910. So, starting in the 1870s, did the province of Liège whose three recorded towns display three different patterns of demographic expansion for the period: Olne continuing its trend from the first half of the 19th century; Gemmenich swelling not unlike the province as a whole; but Chênée abandoned such a trend in the 1860s for the stronger type of G increase found in Meulan and Lübeck. In all, eight towns of Table 9.2 that have records for the later 19th century followed four different growth patterns, trends often not conforming to the demographic increase of the regions in which they were located. Considerable migration and urbanization is indicated.

Meanwhile, as of the 1860s, all the western regions of Germany (Table 6.4, part C) were producing E-shape accelerations of demographic expansion, a form found in none of these towns, including Einbeck and Lübeck. The origins of those explosions for broader territorial populations thus seem to have been phenomena of aggregation, not simple reflections of local movements. Meanwhile, the out-of-the-way northern rural provinces of Friesland and Groningen, alone within the Netherlands, developed comparable G trends (resembling expansion in Einbeck and Gemmenich), though among the nine provinces of Belgium (Table 6.3) no less than seven display the kinds of movements found in the middle column of Table 9.2. Some of the sampled rural departments of France shrank along D curves not unlike those of the towns of Zomergem and Evergem in Flanders; but others took the unusual C shape (Table 6.3, part C). It was several major French urban districts that had G growths resembling those of Gemmenich and Einbeck. This juxtaposition of town and regional evidence highlights how during the significant economic change of the later 1800s migration connected local patterns of demographic increase into regional and national ones.

In the early years of the 20th century, except for Zomergem in East Flanders, where much slower growth occurred, parallelism seems to have returned to local demographic expansion in northwestern Europe. From Meulan in France, to Gemmenich in eastern Belgium, to Einbeck and Lübeck in northwestern Germany, comparably timed G trends appear. Some similarity has characterized still more recent periods as well: in the Belgian towns of Gemmenich, Chênée, and Evergem, into the 1950s and 1960s. But Olne lost people in D form across most of this past century, while growth after World War II in Meulan, just down the Seine from Paris, was of a very robust sort compared with the other towns of Table 9.2, though in a timing of G similar to that of the departments of Lyon and Marseilles and stronger than for Seine, the whole broader area around Paris.

Some of the best insight into the mechanisms by which different kinds of rural areas generated different patterns of demographic expansion in the 17th, 18th, and early 19th centuries comes from a study of ten districts of the canton of Zürich (R. Braun 1978, 301). For these clusters of villages and other settlements outside the city, widely spaced data points unfortunately render trending before the 1770s only speculative. But available data from 1635 through 1671 indicate that each of the ten may have followed G curves resembling those of the city of Zürich, Basel, Geneva, and several other centers across Europe in the middle and later 1600s (Table 8.1). Subsequently, population loss between 1671 and 1700 in eight of the cantonal districts resembles decay that was happening in Meulan and in France as a whole at the time (later than in Spain, Italy, and England in Figure 5.1a), again indicating generality within Switzerland for trends found elsewhere. Further population loss in the 1760s, in contrast, appears to be distinctively local on the basis of other towns, cities, and regions covered in this study. Only Horgen and Hinwil along the southern fringe of the canton escaped this demographic decay from epidemics of dysentery in 1763 and 1768 and from famine in 1770–1771 (Braun 1978, 331).

Meanwhile, between 1700 and 1762 all districts except Regensberg gained population, the areas with domestic textile manufacture more steeply than the richer farming zones for reasons so nicely laid out by Braun. If these growths took G paths, those curves resembled the trends for Cuenca, Eeklo, and Einbeck in Figure 9.6. Meanwhile, the movements for the highland textile zones of the canton were more like the 1699–1796 G for Gemmenich, located in a eastern Belgian region that was also known for its domestic cloth industry. Such economically based zonal distinctions tended to disappear after the 1770s, however, as now well-documented G growths up to 1812 or 1836 became quite tightly parallel across 9 of 10 districts of Canton Zürich. After about 1790, there was more population increase in the farming settlements of the canton than in the textile districts, the reverse of Braun's argument about the demographic impact of textiles, unless such activity—now perhaps including factories—was coming down from the mountains to exploit supplies of labor closer to the city.

For some towns and smaller cities in Europe, finally, it is possible to examine demographic increase and decline across a still earlier period, from about 1350 to 1550. These medieval modelings often must be based upon the number of hearths taxed in a community, not counts of actual persons. Nonetheless, they offer a fundamental sense of how settlements of intermediate size shrank with the inroads of the plague in the later 14th century and then recovered in the 15th and early 16th centuries.

Figure 9.7 presents six examples, four from the northern regions of central Italy, one from southern France, and one from Switzerland. Montalcino perched in the mountains south of Siena (Cortonesi 1984, 159). Perugia was a substantial town or small city in the upper Tiber Valley, amidst the Appenines west of Siena (Grohmann 1984, 272). The settlements of Valdelsa, somewhat north of Siena, collectively contained about two thousand hearths (Muzzi 1984, 137, note 9). Montpellier lay in Languedoc, west of the Rhône delta and near the Mediterranean coast (Russell 1987, 163). Pistoia was a substantial town northwest of Florence (Herlihy 1967, 75–76, 105).[14] Geneva occupied the southwestern tip of Switzerland (Le Roy Ladurie 1987, 27). Russell's estimates for England as a whole are graphed in Figure 5.3 and for Cornwall in Figure 9.3. While some of these series cover only limited periods of time, the overall latticework of available evidence in Table 9.3 indicates considerable interregional continuity for population trends during the later Middle Ages.

While the series is short and variable, the number of hearths in Aix-en-Provence seems to have expanded in a G trajectory between 1321 and 1345 only somewhat more robust than that for the population of England 1260–1348, and then contracted between 1345 and 1356 somewhat more steeply (Baratier 1961, 128–29). The initial decline of population in Montpellier 1347–1362 followed D form very parallel to the decline of Aix; but the first atrophy of possible D shape in Valdelsa was flatter, more resembling the probable trend for Cornwall and the single 1340–1415 D in Pistoia. In Valdelsa and Montpellier second decays with D trajectory appear in the later 1300s and early 1400s (Figure 9.7). The first available evidence for Montalcino and Perugia and for the Diocese of Geneva indicates parallel movements that may have been second rather than first waves of demographic decline.

This "double dip" phenomenon has been noted elsewhere around the world as various new diseases struck populations at certain times. The implications for

Figure 9.7
Growth and Disaster in Some Medieval Communities

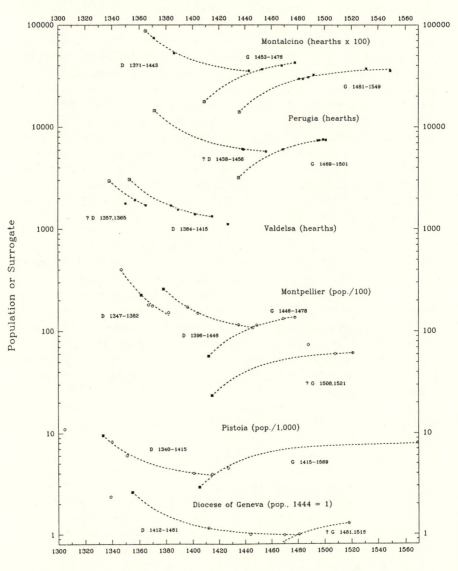

Source: Table 9.3.

Table 9.3

Comparing Medieval Population Movements from England, France, Switzerland, and Italy

Location	Pre-Plague	1st Decline	2nd Decline	1st Recovery	2nd Recovery
All England	1260-1348 G 1228	1348-1374 D 1340	?		
Cornwall		1337,1356 ?D 1324	1371-1473 D 1361		
Valdelsa		1357,1365 ?D 1338	1384-1415 D 1351	1469-1501 G 1438	1481-1549 G 1436
Perugia		?	1438-1456 D 1372	1453-1478 G 1409	
Montalcino		1340-1415 D 1333	1371-1443 D 1365	1415-1569 G 1405	
Pistoia					
Montpellier	1321-1345 G 1259	1347-1382 D 1362	1396-1446 D 1378	1446-1476 G 1412	1508,1521 ?G 1415
Aix-en-Provence		1345,1356 ?D 1371			
Diocese of Geneva		?	1412-1481 D 1355		1481,1518 ?G 1448

Sources: Russell 1948, 1987; Herlihy 1967, 75–76, 105; Cortonesi 1984, 159; Grohmann 1984, 272; Muzzi 1984, 137; Le Roy Ladurie 1987, 27.

AIDS in our own era is worth thinking through carefully. For students of demographic disaster, the locations of these events, the duration of each D decline,
the proportions of people lost, and the comparative timing of trends of decay
from place to place that appear in this study should help frame further investigations of how generational transitions, the economic and social consequences
of death and disease, and other discontinuities created such patterns of double
or multiple demographic atrophy in some historical contexts, though not in
others.

Then, as these medieval populations began to recover, growth took familiar
G form. This began earlier in Pistoia, Montalcino, and Montpellier than in Perugia and Geneva. Both Montalcino and Montpellier, however, then suffered
sudden demographic drops around 1480 (Figure 9.7). These were followed by
new G trends quite similar to those that had pertained before. Just what happened
at that time in towns so far apart? Redefinition of community boundaries or
methods of record-keeping are possibilities, along with abrupt consequences of
war, famine, or sickness. Pistoia and Perugia, meanwhile, seem to have re-
expanded demographically via G without any such cutback, and the population
of Geneva rebounded only considerably later.

Susan B. Hanley's study of the districts that composed Bizen province in
Tokugawa Japan offers a complete set of data on local demographic increase
and decline for one territory across almost two centuries. Figure 9.8 plots the
patterns that emerge from her calculations. It also includes a modeling for a
roughly contemporaneous series from the town of Hirano, which was located
eastward in the Kinai (Hanley 1968, 626–37; Hanley and Yamamura 1977, 108).

Across the late 17th century and into the early 18th, all ten local populations
increased, most in clear G form and with Wake, Iwanishi, Akasaka, Tsutaka,
Mino, and Kojima expanding closely together, with t_0's around 1640.[15] This is
how Bizen province as a whole increased in population from 1680 through 1834
(Figure 9.4) and resembled the short 1704–1726 G for Hirano in another part
of Japan.[16] Castle Town, however, enlarged very slowly between 1679 and 1721,
along a G trend whose base year would fall way back in the middle of the
1500s. The growth of Kamimichi and Oku between 1679 and 1707 would fit
G's with base years in the 1610s, in between the t_0 for Castle Town and those
for the majority of the districts of the province, though fresh G-shape expansion
occurred in the two districts from 1707 to 1726.

For the hundred years following the 1720s, Castle Town most steeply, but
also Akasaka, Wake, and Oku, lost people in D form. So did Hirano, and apparently Tsutaka and Iwanishi—but via two successive D curves: one parallel
to the other four local trends, one appreciably later. D patterns for the early 18th
century with base years lying between about 1660 and 1690 have previously
been encountered in Yamashiro, Yamato, and probably Kawachi and Izumi
provinces of the Kinai (Figure 9.4). Among the Tokugawa *do*, D-type demographic decay in the Kinai as a whole was somewhat more moderate than this,

Figure 9.8
Growth and Decline in the Castle Town and the Eight Districts of Bizen Province and in Hirano in the Kinai

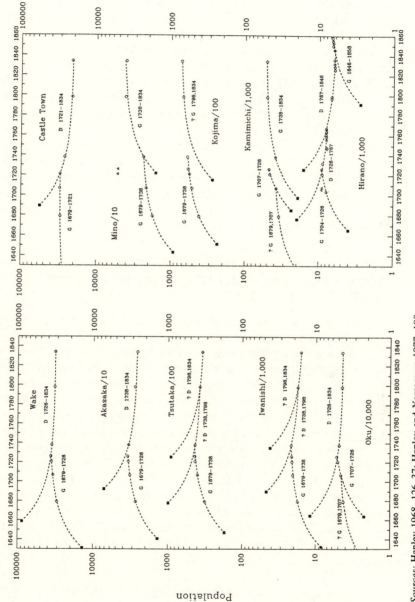

Sources: Hanley 1968, 126–37; Hanley and Yamamura 1977, 108.

along with Saikado-kami; but D's very much like those of these Bizen districts pertained for the populations of Tokaido and Tosando-shima between 1750, where our data begin, and 1840. In contrast, Kamimichi—after a drop between 1726 and 1738–gained inhabitants over the next century in G shape. So did Mino, and apparently Kojima also, though probably starting fresh growth only in the 1760s. New increase came to Hirano, too, but only after 1846. These local G-type expansions of population were steeper than trends that can be found in any of the broad regional *do* across the years before the 1800s or in Morioka or Tosa (Figure 9.4); but they resemble increase in the commoner population of all Japan 1792–1852, whose t_0 came about 1720 (Figure 7.2 and part D of Table 7.2). Isumi and Kawachi gained people this way after 1786, but not the other provinces of the Kinai (Figure 9.4).

What made some of the local populations within Bizen province grow while others declined? What parts did migration and natural increase and economic change play in these contrasts? How did parallels of demographic loss or gain occur both within the province and relative to places far outside it? The G-based mode of analysis reframes such questions fruitfully for pursuing them beyond the insights that the original studies provided.

EXPANSION AND ATROPHY AT THE GRASS ROOTS: THE EXPERIENCE OF VILLAGES, MANORS, PUEBLOS, HAMLETS, AND ATOLLS

The finest-drawn units for analyzing demographic growth or decline, the narrowest collective components above individual households that historical tools can isolate and grasp, are villages, manors, hamlets, or simple clusters of rural settlement. Distinctive New World evidence comes from the pueblos of colonial New Mexico. For Europe, various records from English manors and from villages in Dauphiné, Provence, Guienne, Languedoc, and Tuscany allow insight into such very local trends during the later Middle Ages and the transition to early modern life. Later European evidence from villages, estates, or parishes helps establish illustrative patterns for grassroots demographic expansion or contraction as local peoples in Germany, England, Austria, France, and southern Italy evolved through the 17th, 18th, and 19th centuries. In Asia, a few well-documented cases from China and Japan, mostly since the later 1600s, support comparable conclusions about population growth and decline at the lowest collective level observable there. Atolls of the South Pacific provide some final examples for this survey of very local demographic movements in world perspective.

Between Spanish reoccupation in the early 1700s, following Pope's Rebellion, and the middle of the 1800s, when the United States seized New Mexico by force of arms, population figures for twenty-one pueblos are known for much of the time (Gutiérrez 1991, 172). The numbers have much short-term variability in them, representing as they do calculations for clusters of a few hundred people who were simultaneously living on the brink of natural disaster, incorporating refugees from collapsed or attacked neighboring settlements, and confronting systematic pressure to accept foreign ways (resistance to which could entail just disappearing for a while). Still, the longer and more stable series offer some useful insight into the demographic expansion and contraction that appeared locally during this colonial era in New Mexico.

It would seem that G and D paths alone suffice to summarize the movements. Further, certain parallels or contrasts in trend from place to place are indicated. These should be of help to historians, archaeologists, anthropologists, and others who study the course of pueblo life in New Mexico. For instance, growth across the 1700s in Cochiti, Isleta, Laguna, and Zia (to 1760) followed largely parallel G curves. In Santo Domingo, Galisteo, and Taos (after a drop to 1750), increase in G form also took place; but it was much flatter. Meanwhile, Tesuque, Pecos, Santa Clara, Zuni, and—after 1760—Zia lost inhabitants. Later, 19th century atrophy appeared in Zuni after the recovery of 1760–1800, and in Cochiti. Starting in the 1750s, Zia and Pecos experienced second D-shaped declines in population. In fact, these probably represent their third phases of loss, considering what untrendable evidence for the early 1700s indicates in each place.

What changes in resources, health, the strength of local culture, and external pressures or attractions that might have moved individuals out of the native community produced these particular patterns from place to place? While the evidence is erratic compared with series available elsewhere, it would seem to provide some insight on how native American populations were affected by colonization, as well as further indications that at the most local level human increase and decline across many kinds of cultures and epochs has tended to follow just the G and D forms.

Thanks to generations of scholars who have been interested in the fate of small communities, for Europe there now exists considerable evidence on such population trends from the 1200s to the present. Sampling the earlier data, Figure 9.9 presents findings for three localities from England and four from Dauphiné, in southeastern France.

For Halesowen, a manor located just west of Birmingham in Worcestershire, trends of population size have been approximated from the number of males appearing in the court rolls in various successive groups of years. Half a century ago Josiah Cox Russell used falling returns of frankpledge (a form of taxes only indirectly related to population) as a surrogate for demographic decline on three manors in Essex. The number of tenants (male or female) to be found at various times on Hakeford Hall manor of Coltishall township in eastern Norfolk, just north of Norwich, provides a third English perspective. Yet another, for males age 12 and older, comes from a revisit by Lawrence R. Poos to Great Waltham and High Easter, locales previously explored by Russell, and several surrounding communities of central Essex. Poos employed tithingpenny data to estimate

Figure 9.9
Some Local Trends in Medieval England and Dauphiné

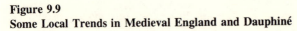

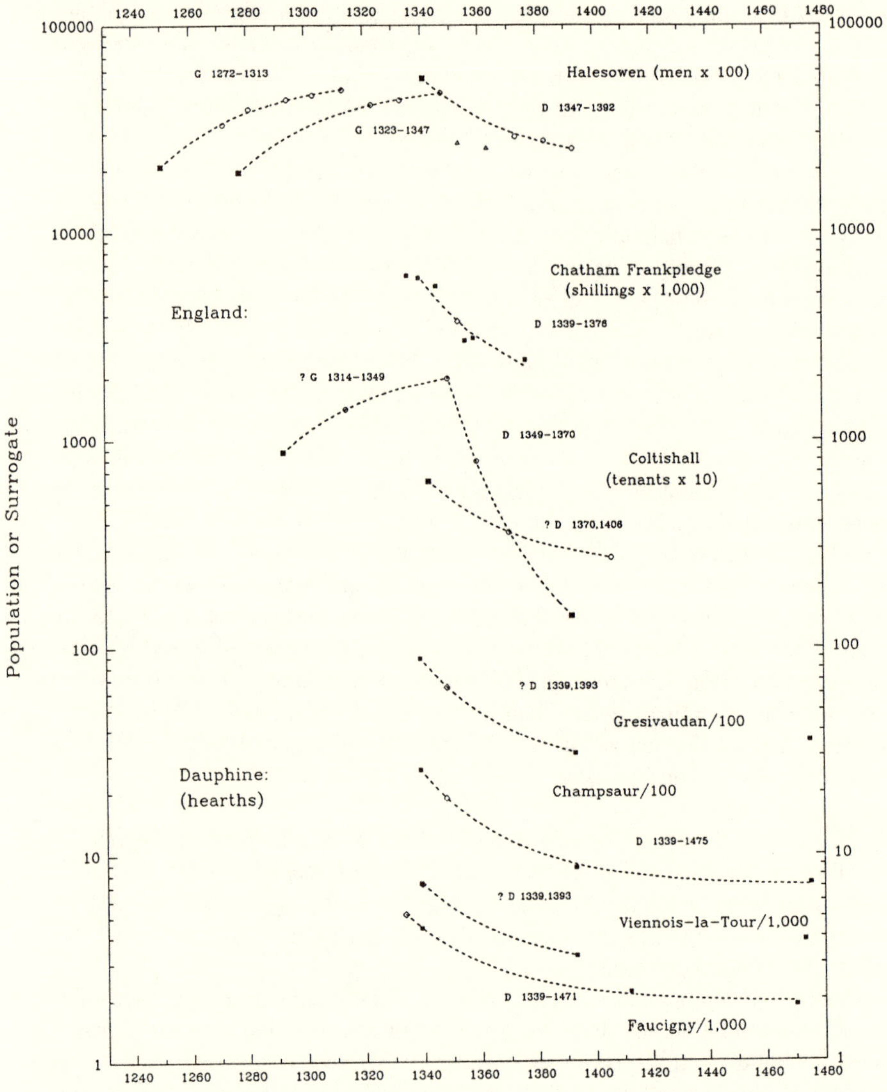

Sources: Note 17; Dupâquier et al. 1988, 332.

trends for male population aged 12 and above. The results are graphed (in arithmetic scale) in his book.[17]

From 1272 to 1313 the Halesowen evidence indicates that local population grew along the kind of G curve Russell estimated for England as a whole for 1260–1348 (Figure 5.3). The local difference is that somehow between 1313 and 1323 a significant atrophy occurred, though somewhat steeper G growth at a lower level resumed from 1323 to the arrival of the Black Death. The drop in the 1310s would seem to confirm the view of M. M. Postan that divisions of land in the late 13th century had rendered the English population vulnerable to a Malthusian crisis. This arrived, he said, with the "great famine" of 1315–1317 (Razi 1980, 27, note 1). Significant growth, with or without that kind of interruption, apparently also occurred in Coltishall between 1314 and 1349. In contrast, the evidence of Poos for his two larger and more complex communities of Great Waltham and High Easter, his only locales with evidence before the early 1300s, stays generally level in the long run between the 1260s and 1310. The pattern then diverges markedly from what is known elsewhere—for Worcestershire, Norfolk, and England as a whole—by falling about a third between 1310 and the eve of the Black Death. The decline in Great Waltham, according to Poos, accelerated through the 1320s, 1330s, and 1340s, which makes the plague look like just the *coup de grace* at the end of a four-decade C-shaped trend of progressively acclerating demographic decline.

In this scenario, losses after the plague struck came to only about 15 percent as of the 1370s and 40 percent as of the 1390s (35 and 35 in High Easter). Some set of unusual local circumstances or a divergence that originates from the kind of data used as a surrogate for population change seems indicated. Meanwhile, the Chatham frankpledges that Russell utilized declined 60 percent between 1339 and 1376, about four times as much as Poos's population estimates for the manor of Great Waltham, of which Chatham was a part. The kind of deep demographic cut in the very first years of the plague, which Poos finds for his two foremost Essex communities, is evident also in Halesowen, Russell's calculations for England, his frankpledge series for Chatham, and probably also Coltishall. In all these other places, however, after a decade or two of shock-response, demographic decline settled into sustained D paths with base years clustering around 1340.

Among the thirteen other Essex communities graphed by Poos only one, Hatfield Broadoak, also clearly displays comparable strong decline *before* the Black Death, the phenomenon that Poos stresses for his regional interpretation. In Berden, Witham, and Boreham there exists evidence before 1349; but gaps in the data thereafter would allow either the pattern Poos posits or the greater post-plague D-shaped loss found elsewhere in England. For four of his communities, moreover—Chatham Hall (as Russell determined using another indicator), Margaret Roding, Birdbrook, and Writtle—it seems highly likely that the heaviest decline likewise took D form from the 1340s onward, after the plague struck, not before. For the other six Essex places studied via tithingpence there is insufficient information for even roughly estimating trends in the 1300s (Poos 1991, 96–103). Thus students of medieval England simultaneously confront questions of how the method of estimation may affect population numbers and the possibility that three or more communities of central Essex, perhaps a minority even within that region, were indeed especially hard hit by the problems of the early 1300s, such that the aftermath of the plague failed to generate there the deep demographic loss in D form that characterized 14th century atrophy of population elsewhere in Essex, England, and across Europe.

That kind of deep-cutting, long-term trend is what seems to have emerged in Dauphiné, as the bottom part of Figure 9.9 indicates (Dupâquier et al., 1988, 332).[18] Meanwhile, studies of taxable hearths in Périgueux in Guienne and S. Quirico d'Orca in Tuscany and cadastral population in Pourrières, Digne, and Tourves in Provence indicate very parallel D curves of decline from the 1360s or later into the early 1400s, like the recorded post-plague atrophy of most communities covered in Table 9.4.[19]

Trends in the number of hearths in some communities of Provence, to the south between Dauphiné and the Mediterranean, confirm just how common were patterns of population growth before the plague as well as demographic decay thereafter (Baratier 1961, 128–29). These villages held from a few dozen to a few hundred hearths over the years leading up to the onset of plague, but only between 16 and 200 by the middle of the 15th century. Figure 9.10 shows how the numbers of hearths in Barjols, Forcalquier, Moustiers, and Colmars all expanded in G trends from the 1200s to the arrival of the Black Death. The regional town of Aix-en-Provence enlarged along a G trend timed at 1259 (Table 9.3). In Apt, the fifth village sampled, demographic increase before the plague apparently was considerably flatter.

When the plague struck Provence, the number of hearths taxed also generally shrank in parallel fashion from community to community, though some local variations appear in particular villages. Colmars and Moustiers—and to a lesser extent Apt—display quick drops below the long-term curve for recorded hearths in the 1350s and 1360s (as has been found for some English series in Figure 9.9). These especially low points are designated with triangles in the figure in lieu of the usual symbol for the data. In general, though, all five villages for the long run experienced D-shape demographic atrophy that lasted from the 1340s to the 1430s or later. Indeed, recovery emerges before 1480 only in Moustiers and Barjols, further evidence that the demographic impact of the Black Death was decidedly not a short-term matter easily shrugged off. Other Provençale hearth evidence from Baratier displays similar trends. Patterns for Aups, Esparron-du-Verdon, Ferrières, Riez, and Saint-Maximin, though not graphed, have been estimated for Table 9.4. These decelerating declines were quite parallel both from place to place within Provence and internationally, the table indicates. So was post-plague demographic atrophy in Languedoc, as Figure 9.11 illustrates from the famous study of Le Roy Ladurie (1966, 1: 189–90, 194, 567–68, 571). D trends for Lunel, Lodève, and possibly Gignac adhere to

Table 9.4
Estimated Population Trends in Some European Communities with Data before 1600

Phase:	Pre-Plague	First Decline	Later Decay	First Recovery	Subsequent Growth	Later Expansion
Barjols (P)	1249-1340 G 1219	1340-1436 D 1349				
Forcalquier (P)	1299-1340 G 1222	1340-1469 D 1350				
Moustiers (P)	1249-1344 G 1228	1344-1439 D 1360		1439-1471 G 1408		
Apt (P)	1263-1345 G 1166	1345-1471 D 1362				
Collmars (P)	1263-1344 G 1239	1344-1471 D 1332				
Riez* (P)	1300-1315 G 1240	1340-1430 D 1354				
Saint-Maximin* (P)	1315-1340 G 1268	1340-1471 ?D 1330				
Faucigny (D)		1339-1471 D 1334				
Viennois-la-Tour (D)		1339,1393 ?D 1339				
Champsaux (D)		1339-1475 D 1348				
Gresivaudan (D)		1339,1394 ?D 1348				
Halesowen (E)	1272-1313 G 1250	1347-1392 D 1341				
-	1323-1347 G 1278	1339-1376 D 1353				
Chatham (E)						
Coltishall (E)	1314,1349 ?G 1292	1349-1370 D 1392				
Périgueux (G)	1321,1339 ?G 1305	1366-1400 D 1335	1400-1434 D 1393			
Esparron-du-Verdon* (P)	1263-1306 G 1302	1341-1365 ?D 1349	1434-1454 D 1437	1454-1467 G 1485	1477-1492 G 1497	
Aups* (P)	1323,1341 ?G 1327	1341-1436 D 1338	1420-1471 D 1429			
Ferrières* (P)	1323-1344 G 1335	1344,1365 ?D 1374	1393-1412 D 1392			
S. Quirico d'Orcia (T)		1404,1443 ?D 1351	1452-1509 D 1370	1509-1550 G 1455	1537-1642 G 1510	
Pourrières (P)		1368-1387 D 1359	1387-1430 D 1375	?		
Digne (P)		1407-1465 D 1336		1465-1481 G 1443	1493-1511 G 1486	
Tourves (P)		1400,1418 ?D 1336		1440-1480 G 1399	1497-1645 G 1497	
Gignac (L)		1390,1462 ?D 1340			1519-1596 G 1505	1655,1672 ?G 1624
Lodève (L)		1400-1540 ?D 1335		1540-1586 G 1532	1589-1655 ?G 1495	1602-1662 G 1563
Lunel (L)		1396-1528 D 1339			1528-1602 G 1500	
Bessan (L)				1502-1539 G 1493	1539-1611 G 1512	
Sérignan (L)				1521,1550 ?G 1483	1550-1664 G 1522	1654-1776 G 1596
Ariane (L)					1526-1644 G 1523	1644-1744 G 1602
Fontès (L)					1539-1604 G 1519	
					1693-1714 G 1612	1754-1784 D 1719

*Estimated from graphing, not computed. P = Provence, D = Dauphiné, E = England, G = Guienne, T = Tuscany, L = Languedoc.

Sources: Baratier 1961, 128–29; Dupâquier et al. 1988, 332; Razi 1980, 25; Russell 1948, 226–27; B. Campbell 1984, 93, 96; Higounet-Nadal 1978, 190–91; Cortonesi 1984, 161–62; Le Roy Ladurie 1966, 189–90, 194, 567–68, 571.

Figure 9.10
Growth and Decline in Five Villages of Provence, 1246–1471

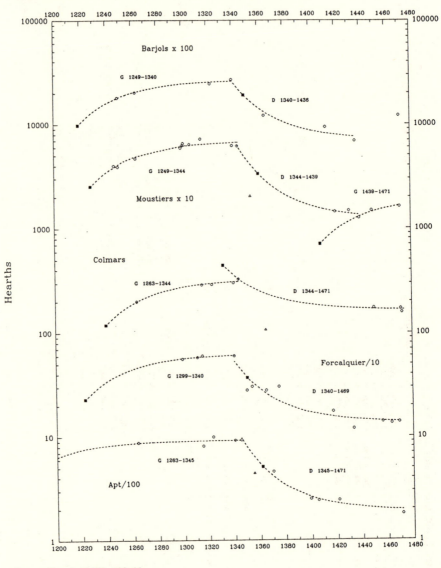

Source: Baratier 1961, 128–29.

Figure 9.11

Transition of Epoch in the Languedoc of Le Roy Ladurie, 1390–1790: Six Communities with Early Records

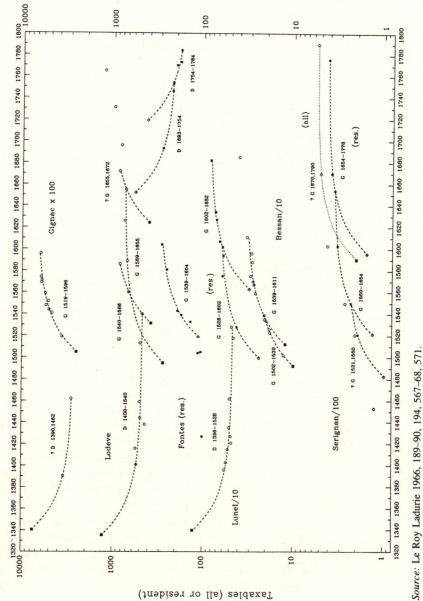

Source: Le Roy Ladurie 1966, 189–90, 194, 567–68, 571.

the common timing of the second column of Table 9.4. While some communities covered in the table experienced second, even third, declines of D shape before recovery set in (most obviously Périgueux), a shared impact of the Black Death seems to have been common across Europe. Studies that show different results should explore carefully the reasons for such local distinctiveness.

As "l'eruption démographique" (Le Roy Ladurie) refilled communities in the 15th and 16th centuries, more variation in timing occurred for first waves of recovery than in trends appearing after about 1480. The latter all had base years between 1483 and 1532, with most marked parallelism among population growths that were contemporaneous to the long-lasting inflation of the 16th century. Clusterings of local G (and D) patterns continued through the 1700s.[20] On the whole, though, the communities of Languedoc rebounded demographically noticeably later than other regions for which evidence exists. By 1465 G trends of recovery were already at work in Moustiers, Digne, and Tourves in Provence across the Rhône and in Périgueux to the north in Guienne.

As the life of rural Europe moved from the early modern era towards the present time, small communities continued to grow in G trends or lose population along D paths. Figure 9.12 presents examples from Germany, England, Switzerland, and France.[21]

Neckarhausen, between Tübingen and Stuttgart on the Neckar, like the surrounding Duchy of Württemberg fared badly from the Thirty Years War, losing perhaps 85 percent of its inhabitants between the 1620s and the 1640s. Subsequent recovery was strong. In spite of some setback in the 1680s, when the armies of Louis XIV attacked nearby parts of the Empire, carrying disease and disorganization with them, the G trend of 1645–1675 was, in effect, just continued at a lowered level for 1685 through 1755, following a hitch downward that is not noted by Sabean. As he does mention (Sabean 1990, 41), however, outright demographic decline appeared in Neckarhausen in the 1760s, the time of the Seven Years War. Then the population of the village expanded again, first during 1775–1805 and then from there to where the study terminates.

In Lambsheim, a village in the Palatinate, north and west of Neckarhausen on the other side of the Rhine watershed, population had been increasing slowly before the Thirty Years War, perhaps along the kind of G curve suggested in Figure 9.12 from local data for 1551 and 1618. But that conflict proved comparably disastrous here: of about 975 residents of 1618, only some 200 remained two decades later, a loss of about 80 percent from the fighting and from the starvation and disease that devastated the countryside as armies moved over it (or from flight to escape these disasters). Across the remainder of the 1600s and the early 1700s, the population of Lambsheim rebounded more slowly than that of distant Neckarhausen, along a G curve for 1638–1709. Then its expansion became more robust for the period between 1709 and 1774. In the 1720s the level of Lambsheim's population for some reason dropped downward; but the timing and curvature of the G for 1735–1774 very much resembled what would

Figure 9.12
Trends since 1600 for Certain Communities in Württemberg, the Palatinate, Bavaria, Solothurn, Bas Quercy, and Hertfordshire

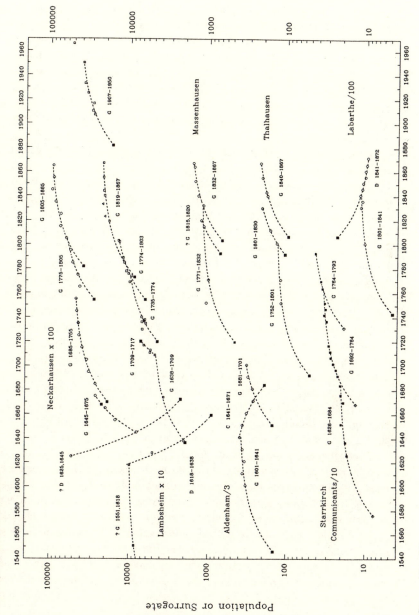

Source: Note 21.

be the G for 1709–1717, suggesting a shift in the area reported or what kinds of people were counted rather than a change in underlying growth trend for the community. Subsequently, Lambsheim expanded very parallel to Neckarhausen along two successive G trends, first into the Napoleonic years and then to the 1860s.[22] At least two communities of southwestern Germany seem now to have been responding demographically in comparable ways to the social and economic change taking place around them. (A similar curve was followed by the population of all Württemberg from 1816 through 1877, Table 6.4 has previously shown.) G-shape growth in the 20th century is also evident in Lambsheim from 1907 through 1950, with some new pattern of increase starting between there and 1966.

Comparably, the local Bavarian communities studied by W. R. Lee expanded in G-type trends between the middle 1700s and the 1860s. Massenhausen and Thalhausen were estates, one ecclesiastical, one secular, in the Pfleggericht Kranzberg of Oberbayrn (Figure 9.3). The population of Massenhausen—the larger, more complexly structured and open estate—after some loss at the time of the Seven Years War (through a decline in births) probably expanded rather more rapidly across the last decades of the 18th century than that of Thalhausen, a smaller holding controlled by a single lord. Each estate, though, gained residents somewhat more robustly in this period than the surrounding Pfleggericht Kranzberg as a whole (Figure 9.3). New growth came to both communities in the early 1800s. The tendency in each case was for the population to enlarge along a steeper, later G than seen in Neckarhausen or Lambsheim at the time. Also in each case, more markedly in Thalhausen, such expansion was interrupted in the 1820s or early 1830s, when births declined and deaths increased. Then both estates experienced new and very parallel G growth into the 1860s. In effect, in the early 1800s the two communities started to expand demographically in the fashion of the Landgericht Freising as a whole 1813–1852—and also the even broader Isar-Kreis 1810–1849 (Figure 9.3)—but were somehow cut back in these ambitions and had to start over in the 1830s.

Aldenham was a parish fifteen miles north of London near Watling Street, the old Roman artery northwestward through Leicester. G-type expansion of local population across the early 1600s ended with the Civil War. From 1641 through 1671 the demographic size of the parish perhaps shrank in the unusual proportionally accelerating C pattern, a very rare case of demographic decline in this form among hundreds of local trends examined. The number of household heads in the parish, however, declined over 1651–1671 in D rather than C mode, raising some questions concerning what assumptions were made about the data and how ratios of various parts of the population to each other were handled. Subsequently, though, G-shape recovery that began near 1671 was common among heads of households and married males as well as for the parish totals shown in Figure 9.12.

The number of communicants form the basis for estimating population trends in Starrkirch, a parish in the Werderamt district of the canton of Solothurn

(Figure 9.2). Their numbers expanded in three successive G curves for 1626–1684, 1692–1764, and 1764–1793. These are years through which little evidence exists for the Werderamt in its entirety or for the other two Solothurn districts examined by Schluchter. Thus the Starrkirch data fill in a chronological gap for the broader area around the parish as well as providing at least one example of very local growth patterns in Switzerland for comparison with findings elsewhere.

The final, bottom-most plot in Figure 9.12 displays 19th century growth and decline in Labarthe, a commune of Bas-Quercy somewhat north of Toulouse in southwestern France. The kind of G growth to about 1840 and D decline thereafter that appears here also characterizes trends of population size for the period in two other nearby communities studied by Sangoï: Molières and Vazerac. Similar G and D trends for the era have also been identified among selected rural departments of France examined in Table 6.3.

Overall, the seven examples in Figure 9.12 show how the populations of small European communities from the early modern era into recent times, like their medieval predecessors, almost exclusively swelled along G paths or shrank in D form. Those movements sometimes paralleled trends for the broader regions that contained these settlements. In other cases, particular patterns of local change in demographic size differed from paths for the regional aggregate, raising questions of just how local variations interacted together to create the whole or to fit collectively within its parameters.

Figure 9.13, finally, examines population trends in 10 of the 424 communes of the province of Calabria for which data between 1815 and 1901 are readily available (Izzo 1965, 247–352). Places were selected to illustrate the various mixes of growth and decline involved as southern Italy underwent the social and economic changes of the 19th century, including much emigration. Two locales even display rG growth as over-vigorous post-Napoleonic expansion was curbed.

In all, data for small European communities from the 1200s to the present time, across almost eight centuries and several distinctive kinds of societies, show almost exclusively expansion in G trends and contraction along D paths. The reasons for these two fundamental, simple, and related patterns should thus yield very basic understanding of how populations expand or shrink. There remains also the question of how these local movements aggregate into regional and national trends in which the G or D paths have different timing than that found in particular localities or compound into H, E, or F growths—patterns that are not found locally. Meanwhile, similarities and dissimilarities in how particular local populations have changed size in G or D form open up insights into how they shared—or did not share—in certain social and economic changes of their place and time, a valuable tool for many types of historical analysis.

Local historical data for Asia comes almost wholly from China and Japan, particularly the latter. Figure 9.14 first of all displays the pattern of population

Figure 9.13
Expansion and Atrophy in Some Communities of 19th Century Calabria

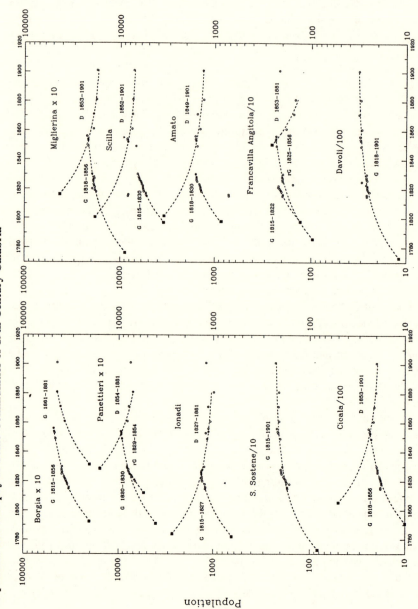

Source: Izzo 1965.

Figure 9.14
Examples of Very Local Growth and Decline in China and Japan

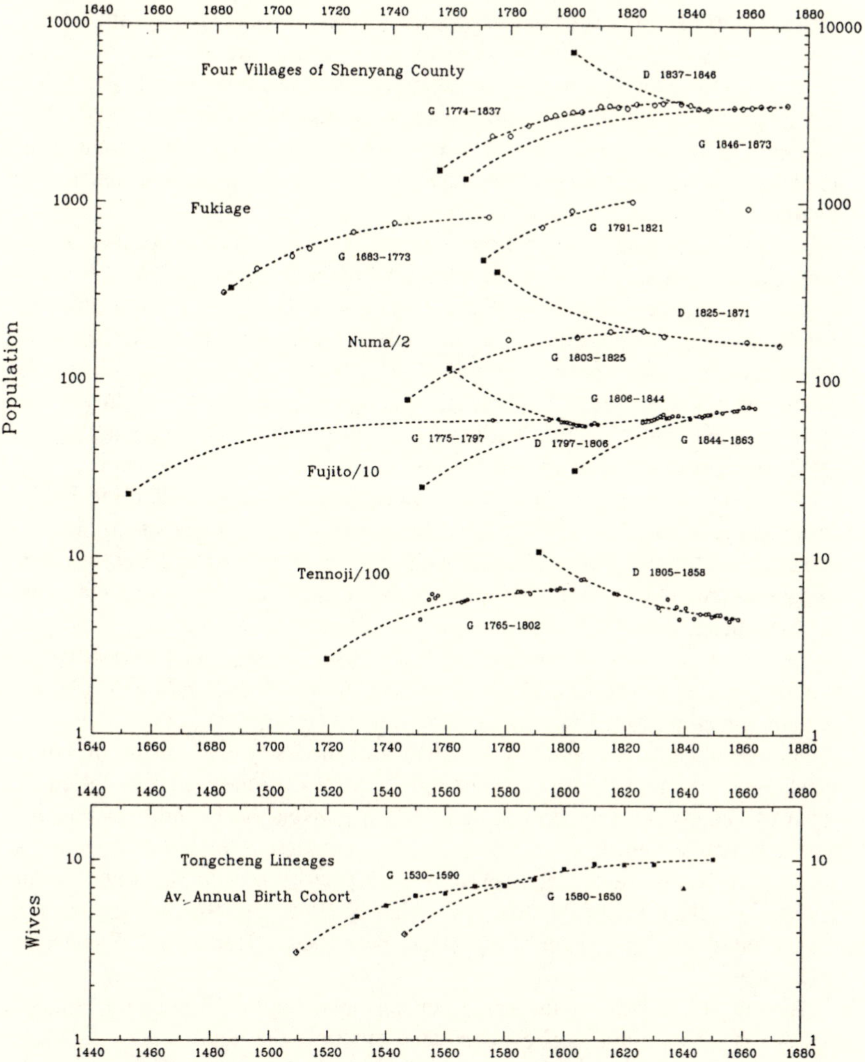

Sources: J. Lee et al. 1995, 164–69; Telford 1995, 48–51, 69; Hanley 1985, 198–99, 203–4; Hanley and Yamamura 1977, 106–7.

growth in four villages of Shenyang County over the century from 1774 to 1873. This county surrounded the capitol of Liaoning (formerly Fengtian) Province in southern Manchuria. The villages lay to the north of the city (J. Lee et al., 1995, 164–69). Very simply, the total population of the villages expanded in G form over 1774–1837, declined for nine years via D during the troubled middle of the 19th century, then grew along another G path from 1846 through 1873. The base years of the two G's are close enough (1756 and 1765) to conclude that before and after the contraction of 1837–1846 the way growth decelerated was identical. For all practical purposes the pattern of ever slower expansion just continued at a lower level after the break.

In the shallow panel at the bottom of the figure is some further local evidence from China. Graphed, by birth cohort, are the number of wives found in thirty lineages of Toncheng County between 1530 and 1650 (about 11,500 women in all). Tongcheng, situated on the north bank of the Yangzi in Anhui Province, is considered to have been a peripheral area of the Lower Yangzi region, in which there was underdeveloped land onto which populations could expand during the era studied (Telford 1995, 48–51, 69). From 1530 through 1580 or 1590, the number of births of females who would live to become wives recorded in these lineages increased along a G trajectory with base year at 1509. Fresh, stronger growth in G shape for girl babies who would show up as lineage spouses then followed from 1580 through 1630 or 1650. This had its t_0 at 1546. Suggested are not one but two eras of opportunity for establishing extra families in Tongcheng, a distinction not made by Telford. The drop at 1640 involves females born in the troubled years of 1635–1644, during which wars between the Ming and the Qing (the Manchurian invaders who would rule to 1911) and regional rebellion roiled the life of the county (Telford 1995, 73).

Fujito, Fukiage, and Numa were villages of the Okayama domain of Toku-gawa Japan. Fujito was a farming community located on the road from the castle town of Okayama's southermost district to a port on the Inland Sea. Fukiage was a fishing settlement on the sea, next to a community that was becoming a major port. Numa was a "landlocked village" that "lacked the opportunities for economic expansion" of the other two (Hanley 1985, 198–99, 203–4). Tennoji was a village of Settsu *kuni* in the Kinai, near Osaka (Hanley and Yamamura 1977, 106–7).

Though situated all in the same general area, Fujito, Numa, and Fukiage had—in spite of some parallels that stand out from the figure—quite different histories of population growth and reasons for their expansion. The authors cite the fate of ports, reclamation of land, and the textile industry as causes of the observed movements. Nonetheless, each community swelled or shrank in just G or D paths. Tennoji, a village near Osaka, lost much population across the early 1800s by failing to stay competitive in cotton manufacture relative to villages that were located further out into the countryside from Osaka and other urban centers (Hanley and Yamamura 1977, 106). It would appear that Fujito, on a main thoroughfare in Okayama, may have been one of those gaining settlements.

On the whole, it seems as if the G and D trends underlying the data of these exemplary historical studies help sort out better in time and place the explanations that the authors give for demographic increase and decline.

The most extensive work on local populations in the Tokugawa era, employing the registers that were devised by the Shogunate to eradicate Christianity (the *shumon-aratame-cho*), has been conducted by Akira Hayami and his associates, following the earlier initiative of Kanetaro Nomura. Figure 9.15 presents illustrations of demographic movements in villages of a few dozen to a few hundred people in Suwa County (Hayami and Uchida 1972, 478–85). Suwa lay inland northwest of Edo (Tokyo) in Shinano Province, which sat astride the mountainous backbone of Honshu, the big island of Japan. In all, local population series are available for 38 small communities in the county for various time spans between the 1670s and the 1860s. Selected for illustration in the figure are some of the longer and more continuous sets of data.[23]

Among these communities, all situated in one county, some insightful similarities of demographic G-shaped growth and D-form decline appear, but also substantial differences. The researchers cite terrain (mountainous, plain, volcanic slopes), sector of the county, and newness of settlement as factors uniting or distinguishing the demographic behavior of villages. The examples of Figure 9.15, however, attest that location did not simply determine demographic growth and decay. The patternings—sometimes shared, sometimes divergent—would seem to suggest further ways to organize and understand local demographic atrophy and expansion across the villages of this one Japanese county between the 1670s and the 1860s, extending the valuable insights already provided by the authors.

Figure 9.16, finally, examines patterns of increase and atrophy in the modern populations of ten atolls of the South Pacific.[24] These small, scattered peoples experienced D-form declines and G-shape recoveries without the more complex E and F types of G-based trends that sometimes appeared in the larger populations of Oceania (Figure 4.7 and Table 4.7).

Being more remote from main routes of communication and less attractive to those who were exploring and exploiting the South Seas, some of these atolls saw their initial depopulation start quite late and then last to about 1900—as on out-of-the-way Takuu, Nukuria, and Nukumanu, which lay northeastward out to sea off the Solomons. On similarly located Ontong Java the devastation of contact with the outside world did not end until 1940. One can follow the deep, sometimes two-dip declines of these remote atoll peoples fairly much across their full extent. Elsewhere, the demographic cost of invasion and intrusion in various forms had apparently largely worked its course by the first dates for which numbers exist, as on Makin or Nukuoro. Anthropologists of Oceania may continue to debate the causes of such losses; but their existence, extent, and form are quite clear. So is the G shape in the recoveries of these island populations, from the gentle increase on Nukuria 1907–1939 to the proportionally

Figure 9.15
Demographic Expansion and Decay in Twelve Communities of Suwa County in Tokugawa Japan

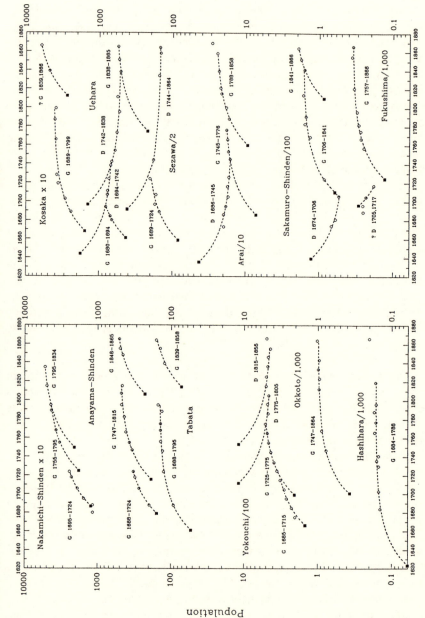
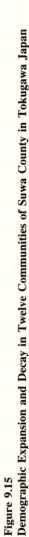

Source: Hayami and Uchida 1972, 478–85.

Figure 9.16
Growth and Decline on Ten Atolls of the South Pacific between 1830 and 1972

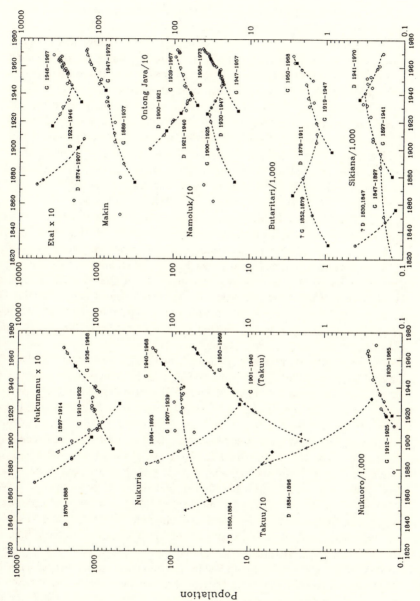

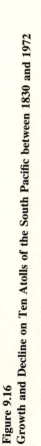

Source: Note 24.

enormous surge on Takuu between 1901 and 1940 and the roughly parallel G growths that then appeared on Nukumanu, Nukuria, and Takuu after World War II.

In some places, population size vacillated substantially up and down in certain eras: for instance on Namoluk and Etal in the Central Carolines in the third quarter of the 19th century. For one thing, the former seems to have been re-populated from the latter during the later 1800s. Immigrant origins are clear for all eight modern clans on Namoluk, though further loss of population occurred in the 1930s and 1940s. On Etal, meanwhile, if the first estimate—of missionary origin—is correct (which it may not be), substantial demographic growth be-tween 1862 and 1874 in spite of war in the Mortlock Islands must somehow be explained. More certain figures thereafter indicate that well-known typhoons, food shortages, and "labor recruiting" cut down the Etal population by about 75 percent between 1874 and 1907. By 1925, however, the newly governing Jap-anese reported 309 residents, about twice the number for 1907, though this population south of Truk in turn shrank again into the 1940s.

While Makin and Butaritari cluster together in the Gilbert Islands, north of Tarawa of World War II fame, the numbers of people on Butaritari for some reason fluctuated noticeably more. Both Butaritari and Makin suffered less from "blackbirding" for Peru and from somewhat less involuntary labor recruiting for the cotton farms of Fiji, the coconut plantations of German Samoa, and the sugar fields of Hawaii than did some of the more outlying and vulnerable Gil-berts. They also endured fewer local wars and periods of drought and starvation. Why the population of Makin resisted decline in the later 19th century more than that of Butaritari is not explained, however.

Sikiana, finally, sat northeast of Guadalcanal at the northern end of the Great Eastern Passage, a north-south route between the Solomons and the Santa Cruz Islands that was apparently much taken by whalers in the 19th century. By 1840 or so the islanders had already been heavily exposed to ships that provisioned there and to the diseases and vices that these vessels carried. Bayliss-Smith estimates a 58 percent loss, possibly along a D trend that resembles declines on Western Samoa, U.S. Samoa and the Northern Cook Islands and among the native people of Tasmania in Table 4.7. The G-shaped recovery on Sikiana 1847–1897 is also very much like first G growths on U.S. Samoa 1853–1900, Western Samoa 1853–1900, and Tahiti 1848–1881. Not geographical proximity, as between Sikiana, on the one hand, and Nukumanu, Nukuria, and Takuu, on the other, but similarity of exposure to outside contact shaped the timing and the extent first of demographic decay and then of population recovery on the once-isolated islands of the South Pacific. The same conclusion has been reached about various regions of central Mexico three centuries before, as the Spanish intruded to a greater or a lesser extent upon their ways of life. Population loss after World War II is attributed by Bayliss-Smith mostly to out-migration to take advantage of the "towns, plantations, and schools" of the main Solomon

Islands; but poor health conditions remained a factor in holding down the number of Sikiana's residents.

This evidence from small atoll populations of the South Pacific joins local findings coming from all around the world, and from widely different epochs since the 13th century, to extend significantly the importance of G-based forms for analyzing demographic growth and decline.

First of all, adding this grassroots evidence to what has been learned from larger populations examined in Chapters 2 through 8 has now produced a few thousand historical instances in which G-based curves visibly suit population trends over substantial spans of time. Since samples of very localized data appear to follow the standard patterning as well, the implication is that probably tens if not hundreds of thousands of recorded trends of population growth and decline (the usable records explode for recent times) could be effectively represented by the limited set of G-based models, overwhelmingly by G and D patterns alone.

Second, the simple G and D trends, which by themselves most of the time reliably and simply summarize how national and regional populations have swelled and atrophied historically, seem even more completely to account for change in the size of the many times more numerous local demographic building blocks of which those bigger units are composed. The "atoms" of population, so to speak, expand and contract in just G and 1/G (D) form. Other kinds of G-based trends appear only in composite demographic "molecules"; they are compounded out of these "atoms."

Third, while in many individual historical cases to change the span of time considered or to introduce some different formula might (often will) produce a better trend fit, the real question is whether as much evidence can be accounted for in all observed instances as simply as by G and D and their more unusual relatives H, F, E, and C. "Simply" comes to bear in two respects. On the one hand, are other models introduced for alternative fitting as uncomplicated in their structure, in their number of parameters, and in their connectedness to each other as the little G-based family of curves? On the other hand, how many different competing formulas have to be employed to do the enormous historical work that is performed by the G-related set of six, and principally just G and D?

Meanwhile, the modelings of demographic increase and atrophy offered in these chapters over and over again seem to make sense relative to the histories through which the fitted populations lived. Sometimes conventional interpretations based upon very different kinds of materials are confirmed or extended by looking at related demographic movements in G-based terms. Sometimes they are fruitfully revised. A useful feature of the kind of patterning proposed, furthermore, is that at times it helps to identify and understand corrupted or inconsistent data, which are frequently a problem in working with historical sources. In short, one must ask: Does a proposed alternative way of patterning the demographic evidence do as well in enriching the historical interpretation?

Finally, the fact that the smallest grassroot populations seem universally to increase in G form and decay via D, not following the four other curves of the G-related family, indicates that the underlying demographic behavior that produces growth or decline through births, deaths, and migration is likely to take even fewer paths than the resultant expansion or contraction of populations, especially larger and more complex ones. In particular, multiplication in the H and F modes seems to reflect how local growths in G shape, timed in different ways, sum up. The implication is that as the next stage of this inquiry turns to historical changes in the fertility, mortality, and migration that determine the path of population size, the basic demographic dynamics will be found to alter only via G and its three simple transpositions of D, E, and C.

NOTES

1. New York County appears as New York City in Figure 8.1a.

2. The former piece identifies 157 G trends, without any alternative pattern, in the increase of taxables for dozens of counties and parishes of Maryland and Virginia over the century and a half that preceded the Revolution. Taxables were generally white males 16 and above and both male and female slaves of comparable age or somewhat younger.

3. The figure for 1746 is not employed in these calculations, since the number of Indians seems seriously undercounted at this time.

4. The way the two G trends approach each other in the early 1800s may help clarify Lee's data with respect to just what area was being counted in the records of the years of transition. The transition-era data points denoted with triangles are not included in any curve fitting.

5. Data for 1756–1776 must omit children under five. From 1776 forward, total population is reported. Counts for 1858 and 1861 mostly do not appear to be comparable to previous figures and are not trended.

6. His calculations are based upon fiscal surveys (Cook, 10, note 1). The parts of Aydin covered lay near the southwestern Mediterranean coast of Turkey between the Gulf of Antalya and the Aegean. The selected zone of Hamid perched just inland to the north, among the lakes that form at the western end of the Taurus Mountains. The Tokat area employed sat near the north-central Black Sea coast of Anatolia, part way between Kastamonu and Trabzon. The population sizes are given by Cook relative to a base of 10.

7. The domain totals are selected as being more complete than the Bakufu data for the province.

8. The high figures for 1721 and 1726 clearly depend upon inflated numbers for the district of Mino in those years. The location of the *kuni* are given in Hanley and Yamamura, 62.

9. They prefer the direct domain data, among other reasons on grounds that other series seem to overdramatize deaths from famous famines.

10. Settsu was the area west of Osaka within which Kobe lay. Yamashiro was the site of the Imperial Residence at Kyoto, and Kawachi the province of Osaka. South of Osaka

along the shore, sat Izumi, the province surrounding Sakai, while Yamato, the province of Nara, Japan's first capital, occupied the peninsula east of Izumi.

11. Apparently some reduction in the count for Spanish people in Santa Fe occurred in the early 1790s. While the number drops, very much the same timing of G trend continues thereafter. Local historians should be able to identify and explain the change in record-keeping that took place at this time.

12. The D-shape trend from 1561 through 1597 furthers suspicion that the C pattern of atrophy in baptisms for New Castile 1585–1645, and others like it in Table 6.1 of Chapter 6, appear because a *birth* surrogate is employed to estimate the atrophy of *population*.

13. Even Meulan, in northern France, shared parallel G growths from the 1820s to the 1930s, Figure 9.6 indicates.

14. An 8,000 calculation for 1399 (but 4,000 for 1401) implied by one chronicler makes no sense relative to the much lower data around it and the steady trend for the surrounding countryside for 1383, 1392, 1401, and 1404.

15. The triangular entries for Mino in 1721 and 1726 are almost certainly errors. The 30,000 extra persons for these two dates make it seem as though the Castle Town had been added in by mistake (Hanley 1968, 627 and 626).

16. Without the two high counts of 1708 and 1710 that are marked with triangles. If these are correct and the figure for 1704 wrong, then growth in Hirano paralleled the G for the Castle Town of Bizen and was not unlike the hypothesized G for 1721 and 1750 for the domain of Tosa in Figure 9.4.

17. Razi 1980, 25; he usefully reviews the debate on late medieval movements, especially the impact of the Black Death, and the sources upon which various positions are based (1–2 and 27–32, 99–101). Russell 1948, 226–27; B. Campbell 1984, 93, 96; Poos 1985, 522; 1991, 93–103.

18. Dupâquier et al., 1988, 332. Recovery had apparently set in by the 1470s in Gresivaudan and Viennois-la-Tour.

19. Higuounet-Nadal 1978, 190–91; Cortonesi 1984, 161, 162 (note 31); Baratier 1961, 50.

20. Besides the Languedoc examples presented in Table 9.4, Bassan, Montperoux, Saint-Georges-d'Orques, and—briefly—Portiragnes shared G trends with base years near 1550; Maraussan, Marsillargues, and Portiragnes joined Aniane and Serignan in G's with t_0's near 1600.

21. Sabean 1990, 41; Rembe 1971, 15–18; W. R. Lee 1977, xxix–xxxi, 15–17; Newman-Brown 1984, 407, 410; Schluchter 1991, 30–31; Sangoï 1985, 21.

22. In this later growth the numbers for 1823 and 1833, denoted by triangles, for some reason lie above the the calculated curve but parallel to it.

23. The simple extended G trend for Kamisugasawa-Shinden is presented elsewhere (Harris 1989, 302).

24. Bayliss-Smith 1975a, 320, 300–05; 1975b, 430. Carroll 1975b, 344–50. Marshall 1975, 163–69. Nason 1975, 122–30. Lambert 1975, 214–15; 220–28.

Conclusion

A small set of repeated trend shapes has been identified according to which populations of many types from all recorded eras have expanded or contracted historically. These six related curves based upon the constant .03 proportional deceleration of G account for every sustained form of change in human numbers that demographic theorists have proposed, from classics of the 1700s to analyses of the present time. They represent the actual movements of the data of population history more accurately, simply, interconnectedly, and insightfully than those prior interpretations.

To consider even such sweepingly demonstrated international empirical generalizations to be "laws" that apply universally rather than just crop up ubiquitously must await the usual consideration, application, and criticism by others. In the meantime, though, enough evidence has been produced from enough different historical contexts to indicate that these propositions should be taken seriously and evaluated carefully. Already it appears worthwhile to take systematic stock of how each of the six related forms occurs and to develop a strategy for getting to understand why these particular patterns emerge so regularly.

The first step is to summarize what kinds of G-based movements have shown up in what kinds of historical contexts. Some of this information appears in Table C.1. Table A.2 of the Appendix holds further detail. Covered are all trends of growth or decline that have been fitted for this study, including those not appearing in graphs or tables in the interests of space. On the other hand, graphed patterns of few or erratic observations that have been designated as uncertain with a "?" are *not* counted. While the numbers could easily be changed

Table C.1
The Percentages of Various G-Based Trends of Growth and Decline at Different Levels of Population

	G*	E	H	F	Growths	[no.]	D	C	Declines	[no.]
Global	29	29	42	0	100	[7]	-	-	-	[0]
Continents	40	20	33	7	100	[15]	-	-	-	[0]
Nations	59	21	13	7	100	[499]	100	0	100	[13]
Provinces, States	72	14	12	2	100	[1,598]	81	19	100	[150]
Ethnic Sub-Populations	85	9	4	2	100	[109]	80	20	100	[20]
Cities	91	8	0	1	100	[360]	92	8	100	[24]
Counties, Districts	86	14	0	0	100	[93]	100	0	100	[10]
Towns, Villages, Manors	100	0	0	0	100	[238]	98	2	100	[98]
All Trends Identified	75	13	10	2	100	[2,897]	89	11	100	[315]

*Includes rG trends.
Excludes tentative trends denoted "?" in figures and tables.

Source: Table A.2, Appendix.

by fresh information on certain trends or by accepting possible alternative patternings, the relative frequency of the different G-related trend types set forth in Table C.1 is likely to remain stable.

G itself models the large majority (75 percent) of all 2,900 or so historical *growth* trends encountered. The smaller or narrower the population unit being examined, the stronger this predominance is: 59 percent in data for nations, 72 for regions, 89 for ethnic subpopulations, cities, and local districts such as counties, but universal (238/238) among trends of expansion for towns, villages, manors, and other small demographic units that have been examined. Correspondingly, for each growth pattern alternative to G the frequency declines with size of population: 21, 14, 7, and 0 percent for accelerating or "exploding" E; 13, 12, 1, and 0 percent for G's slowly decelerating cousin H; and 7, 2, 1, and 0 percent for constant proportional F. Meanwhile, when populations have *declined* across time historically, D has been the path taken even more generally than G among growths: 89 percent of the time. The frequency of C, however, displays no unidirectional relationship to population size of the sort found for the three paths of expansion alternative to G. It has been most common in populations of intermediate size, least evident for nations and for the smallest demographic units.

There is a clear chronological dimension to the prevalence of simple G as well. Besides the scale of population unit being considered, *earlier* historical populations expanded in just G form more frequently than modern ones, as Table C.2 demonstrates. For Rome, medieval England, China to 1740, and Japan prior to the Meiji reforms, *all* observed growth trends have taken only G shape. The same is true for county and other modest-sized districts in premodern China and Japan, Europe to 1700, and colonial Spanish America. No H or F patterns appear in Chinese provinces to 1740, Japanese *do* to 1870, and regions of the Ottoman empire to 1914. Just 4 probable E-type accelerations of the 16th century in Chinese provinces and 1 such regional surge within the Ottoman Empire around 1900 are to be found among 111 growths of premodern populations surveyed.[1] E, H, and F are patterns not only of larger, more complex demographic units; they also have occurred historically in developed or developing populations of only relatively modern times.

An examination of regional and local patterns within documented societies has demonstrated how growth trends for larger units—especially the F, H, and E forms—mostly reflect the way local movements with different timings, principally G's, sum up. Figure C.1 displays recent trends of aggregate population increase at an even higher international level: by continent and globally, including U.N. projections to 2025 (Livi-Bacci 1992, 201, 149, 204). Here the basic G form is noticeably less predominant. In fact, just 29 percent of global trends and 40 percent of continental ones in Figure C.1 are of G shape, says Table C.1.

In effect, total human population since 1850 has gone through the kind of sequence found in England between 1686 and 1861, another period of about a

Table C.2
The Simplicity of Pre-Modern Trends (Percentages)

	G	E	H	F	Growths	[no.]	D	C	Declines	[no.]
NATIONS:										
Rome & Medieval England	100	0	0	0	100	[7]	100	0	100	[3]
China to 1740	100	0	0	0	100	[13]	100	0	100	[2]
Japan to 1850	100	0	0	0	100	[2]	100	0	100	[2]
Subtotal:	100	0	0	0	100	[22]	100	0	100	[7]
REGIONS:										
Chinese Provinces to 1740	84	16	0	0	100	[25]	87	13	100	[8]
Japanese "Do" to 1870	100	0	0	0	100	[10]	100	0	100	[6]
Ottoman Regions to 1914	96	4	0	0	100	[26]	100	0	100	[1]
Subtotal:	92	8	0	0	100	[61]	93	7	100	[15]
COUNTIES, DISTRICTS:										
Pre-Modern China & Japan	100	0	0	0	100	[14]	100	0	100	[7]
Europe to 1700	100	0	0	0	100	[3]	100	0	100	[2]
Colonial Spanish America	100	0	0	0	100	[11]	100	0	100	[1]
Subtotal:	100	0	0	0	100	[28]	100	0	100	[10]
TOTAL:	95	5	0	0	100	[111]	97	3	100	[32]

Source: Table A.2, Appendix.

Figure C.1
Recent and Expected Global Demographic Expansion

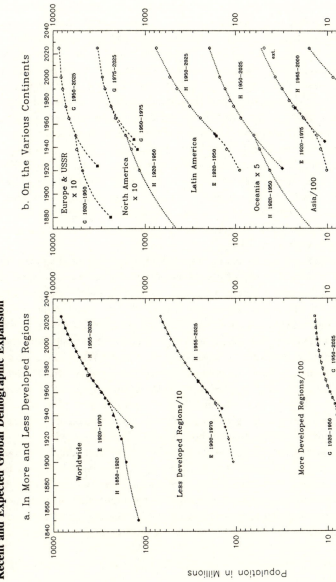

a. In More and Less Developed Regions

b. On the Various Continents

Source: Livi-Bacci 1992, 201, 149, 204.

century and a half: an H succeeded by an E, then another H, all three trends being of several decades in duration. Has this demographic patterning been accompanied by the same kind of sequencing in economic development? For the England of the era in question that first meant domestic industry and urbanization supported by improved agricultural productivity, followed in the 18th century by the expansion of factories in a few industries (particularly textiles), followed by the application of the new knowledge and techniques to a wide range of productive enterprises in the 19th century. Other countries or regions within them like Ireland, Scotland, Denmark, Belgium, and certain provinces of the Netherlands have been seen to have shared the historic demographic sequence along with England; still other European populations display fragments of it—from the Atlantic to the Urals, from Norway to Italy and Serbia.

For most of the 20th century, however, for England, Europe, and the more developed regions of the world collectively (Figure C.1), further demographic expansion took only the G form. This does not mean that economic growth has stopped; but what continues ceases to swell population in the historically exceptional H and E fashions. The gains go into higher standards of living instead of more people to share (and generate) the resources. The transition back to basic G increase for all North America took place alongside the second European trend of that sort as of about 1950.

It is the developing regions of the world, with their vast populations, that have imprinted E then H trends up the expansion of *homo sapiens* as a whole since the early 20th century. The peoples of Latin America and Asia have each surged this way—the former changing path around 1950, the latter in the 1960s.[2] In Africa, population explosion from the 1920s into the 1960s was followed by the one known instance of F-type expansion on a continental scale from there to the present, though projections suggest that slow deceleration in H form is finally beginning, in part due to the unhappy consequences of AIDS. "Oceania" combines Australia and New Zealand with many islands of the South Pacific. The H pattern for 1920–1950 resembles that of North America for the same years. The subsequent, current H—weighted with vigorous recent Polynesian demographic increase—is like that for human population as a whole.

In essence, less developed parts of the world, whether individually as countries or collectively as continents, have in the 20th century been following Europe through a familiar demographic sequence, one apparently linked closely to the dynamics of modern economic growth. Put the other way around, at an earlier time Europe and countries and regions within that continent themselves behaved like "developing" nations. To say that the processes that generate these trend sequences belong to some distinct "Third World" aggregate of modern societies is to misunderstand their nature and to throw away the advantages of knowing some history.

Our survey of growth and decline across various types of populations, cultures, and periods of time, in short, sketches out a blueprint for comprehending how the six different kinds of G-based paths for change in population size come about. Where and when the distinctive trend types have occurred suggests how they may have unfolded.

G, to begin with, is the primary building block of demographic increase. However expansion happens to be set in motion—by fresh resources to support more people (or attract them from one place to another), by health improvements that reduce mortality, or by economic, social, or cultural changes that induce higher fertility—populations, from the tiniest to the largest ones, from ancient times to the present, across all varieties of cultures, social orders, and economies, generally use up the opportunity presented to them via a G path of constantly proportionally slowing growth. Collectively, without certain other accompanying developments, the inducements for further expansion peter out via G. That is why G is by far the most frequent trend, whose predominance becomes even greater as more local populations are examined or those with simpler economies.

Usually the succession from one G trend to another is from a flatter phase of the pattern to a steeper one, from a curve with earlier base year to one with a later t_0. For Europe, Latin America, and Africa almost no exceptions have been found. In a certain kind of historical setting, however, the reverse can be true: The second, slower G presents a ceiling that the preceding curve cannot penetrate. Such retrogressive G succession, rG, has generally occurred where once promising resources for development have not lived up to the expectations made of them, predominantly along the farming, grazing, mining, and timbering frontiers of the United States, Canada, Australia, and New Zealand (including several major cities of North America dependent upon such growth). But it has also appeared here and there in other historical settings of overenthusiastic or disappointed expansion such as Barbados around 1650 in the early days of West Indian sugar, the Danish West Indies near 1740, Gansu Province of northwestern China around 1776, Beijing and Shanghai under anti-cosmopolitan policies of the People's Republic, shattered Lebanon in the 1960s, the Kinki region of Japan in the 1970s along with Osaka, Tokyo, and Nagoya and other Asian cities like Bandung, Taipei, and Seoul.

In all, Verhulst, Quetelet (whose reasoning about competition Verhulst adopted), and others who have taken up the concept of shrinking returns to further demographic expansion like Reed, Pearl, and Lotka have begun on the right track. Where they have lost the way is, first of all, in conceptualizing everlasting or long-enduring maxima or "carrying capacities" that do not change. In fact, economic growth, altering values, and environmental improvements of various sorts *frequently* set off new eras of demographic expansion. The ceiling can be raised in several ways. The second shortcoming of those analysts has been failing to recognize that new population levels in these simplest and most common contexts of demographic increase are approached always via the constant $-.03$ proportional deceleration of G. Some mechanism channels increase into the one path over and over again, not into the infinite array of rates of slowing that are allowed in the logistic thinking of Verhulst and his followers.

How such change in just the one form is repeatedly generated by demographic dynamics is the topic of the next phase of our inquiry, the volume that follows this one.

Similarly, negative blows to populations—by war, epidemic, starvation, the introduction of birth controls, aging, or the departure of young people who might otherwise bear children locally—are absorbed via D, the upside-down transposition of G. Among historical declines of population that lasted any length of time, D has been even more universal than G among growths. Example of population loss in this shape have been noted from the 5th century B.C. struggles of the Roman Republic with her neighboring cities and invading Gauls and the mortal 3rd century conflict with Carthage and from the later 8th century collapse of the Tang Dynasty in China, the 13th century disasters of Mongol invasion, and 15th century atrophy under the Ming. This last trend proves to resemble very closely the path of recorded population losses in Europe following the arrival of the Black Death in the late 1340s, whose evidence stretches from England to southern France to Switzerland to Italy. In more modern times, the D form captures the infamous losses of Amerindian population with Iberian conquest in the 1500s and early 1600s, the wasting by plague, war, and famine of much of Europe in the 17th century, the less drastic downward adjustments by means of which Tokugawa Japan retained about the same size across two centuries, the decimation of Pacific populations by contact with outsiders from the 1700s to the 1900s, the Irish diaspora triggered in the 1840s, the flight and discouragement of East German youth after World War II, and the decay of many 20th century inner cities. Lotka in 1925 realized that the logistic formula might be turned on its head to capture population decline, but did nothing more with the idea. Around 1970 Cook and Borah almost identified the D curve in their analysis of demographic disaster following the Spanish invasion of Mexico. The simple fact that sustained population loss over and over again takes the 1/G or D form has in the end, however, so far eluded demographic historians and students of contemporary population.

The F and H patterns apply not to local growths but to broader aggregates of them. Mostly they can be observed to occur as local increase in G form with divergent timings, sum up to generate constant or just slowly slowing expansion, trajectories that escape or weaken the drag of G's rapid deceleration. In these agglomerations migration—to new settlements, to cities, or from less promising to more promising regions—is an important element. Both both F and H patternings thus entail certain kinds of economic change and an interplay of demographic processes with them. But the two curves would seem to involve fundamentally different relationships of economic and demographic growth.

Franklin, and after him Malthus, grasped much about the nature of the F exception to G-type increase in population. Before very recent decades this pattern was indeed usually a phenomenon of territorial expansion and new settlement, not only in British North America and neighboring New France, but in South America, the European population of 19th century South Africa, Tsarist

Siberia, some 20th century provinces of China's deep continental frontier, the current Amazon interior of Brazil, and a few present-day territories of India's easternmost borders. An emptied space could also refill for a while via F, as in west central Mexico in the 1700s or Tahiti and Fiji in the 1900s.

Rather further afield from the Franklin-Malthus interpretation, however, are several F growths of recent times in what are often called "Third World" or developing countries. These have appeared in places like Mexico, Ecuador, the Dominican Republic, and several other societies of Central and South America; in Iran, Iraq, Taiwan, Sumatra, and the Philippines; in Tanzania, Malawi, Morocco, Liberia—in all, 14 of 51 recorded countries of Africa. In these contexts, generally emerging after 1960, constant proportional demographic expansion in the F form would seem to have been supported by a rather different kind of economic extension in lieu of simple geographical colonization. Settlement no longer spread to meet the needs of metropolises and their markets, as in the political colonies and frontiers of old. Nevertheless, the opportunity to fulfill similar functions for "core" developed economies located elsewhere, whether in cheap labor or in commodities like bananas or petroleum, for a while sustained constant demographic growth in certain peripheries that were blessed with improved conditions (and often the optimism of postcolonial empowerment).

That this steady proportional F expansion of population always takes the .03 rate, not the infinite array of log-linear trajectories allowed in stable population theory, appears to reflect how smaller demographic units that contribute to the overall trend themselves grow via G and how G-based growth connects economies and populations. The latter relationships are pursued in subsequent phases of this investigation, published separately. Already, though, three important things are evident about this longest-known member of the family of six G-related curves.

First, F is a relatively modern phenomenon, evident initially in mainland British North America and New France in the 1670s, the recovery of west central Mexico in the 1740s, the burgeoning slave populations of Cuba and Puerto Rico as of 1770, South Africa's Cape Colony from 1820, and Argentina along with Brazil's state of Sao Paulo starting in the 1850s. All other appearances of F that have been located so far are still more recent.

Second, no other log-linear form of demographic expansion appears, only G-based F with the .03 rate of increase. Builders of stable population theory from Euler in the 1760s to Lotka and Kuczynski in the early 1900s and Coale and his associates after World War II have instead argued or implied an infinite range of possible "r"s. That theoretical assumption is just not historical reality. Actual trends of growth (or decline) simply do not turn out that way.

Third, contrary to what Malthus maintained, the F trend does not appear, as in Franklin's New World evidence upon which he relied, because it is the natural, uninhibited, maximum rate for the multiplication of mankind. To the contrary, our evidence has identified three ways in which human increase his repeatedly exceeded the .03 rate. Most frequently, this has been in *new* populations following G trends. At any stage of G growth before year 0 proportional expansion is faster than .03. The same is true for any H trend, though fewer growths before the t_0 in this model have been observed. Finally, the most threatening trajectory of all, the E of constantly *accelerating* population explosion had frequently gone past the .03 pace before starting to slow down. The cause of the F pattern must derive somewhere else—though our inquiry does go on to identity a different kind of "natural" base for all G-related patterns, founded upon mortality and its impact upon age structure rather than upon fertility.

The historical evidence that this survey manages to cover indicates that H has been every bit as rare among *local* populations as F. It is likewise a recent phenomenon, first appearing in the Dutch maritime province of Holland and in England and Sweden in the middle 1500s, followed by Spain, Portugal, Norway, and Ireland along Europe's "Atlantic Rim" by about 1650. During the 1700s the H pattern spread to the New World: Brazil, Argentina, recovering regions of west central Mexico, Cuba, St. Domingue, Jamaica, Virginia, South Carolina, New Jersey, and French Canada. It also emerged in Russia by the 1760s and China by the 1740s. Aside from Dutch colonial Java as of about 1850 and Egypt after 1880, nonetheless, the H form seems absent in Oceania, Africa, and Asia (other than China) before the 20th century. In the 1800s, H trends emerged in the United States as whole and in her middle Atlantic states, anew in Brazil and Argentina now joined by Chile and Mexico. The century also saw H growths spread across Europe in successive geographical waves (Chapters 5 and 6), linking many countries and regions through their demographic patterns to the spread of economic development.

In the 1900s the H form appeared once more in southern South America and the United States. Within Asia, Indonesia as a whole, Java, the north coast of Borneo, and parts of peninsular Malaysia have participated in H-typed demographic expansion along with China, the Philippines, South Asia (from Pakistan through India and Bangladesh to Myanmar), former Soviet Central Asia, and Egypt's one-time partner, Syria. In Africa, however, so far only Kenya and Tanzania have accompanied Egypt in having H growth at some time in the 20th century. Meanwhile, early homes of H-type expansion have ceased to produce the form. That change had been most notable in Europe, where no national or regional evidence exists of current population growth via H, but pertains also to southern South America and Canada. The United States and China provide the exceptions in which sequences of H trends begun one-and-a-half to two-and-a-half centuries ago presently continue. Collectively, though, the population of all developing or less developed countries is continuing to expand in an H trend, including the continental people of Africa, Asia, Latin America, and Oceania. The aggregate population of more developed countries is not—including the peoples of Europe and of North America as a whole. Since developing populations currently far outweigh developed ones, global numbers of *homo sapiens* are at present swelling in H fashion.

Such historical patterning, spreading outward from northwestern Europe in the 1500s to many Atlantic-facing regions of the continent in the 1600s, to the American colonies of these nations in the 1700s (plus geographically expanding Russia and commercially blossoming China), and further extending across Europe and within the Western Hemisphere in the 1800s, brings to mind where and when the foundations for modern economic growth were laid historically. This process has involved new trade, new industry, increased urbanization, and the agricultural resources to support the additional population involved. The absence of H-type demographic increase almost everywhere in Asia, Africa, Oceania, and equatorial Latin America until the 20th century and its modern disappearance from former hearths of the phenomenon in Europe and the Americans both further underscore the connection of H-type population increase to global economic development. So does local analysis that pinpoints where and when the H patterns appeared from region to region within various countries.

In contrast to F and H, the patterns E and C are—like D—simple transpositions of G, not modifications of the curvature of that basic trend. Both paths spell potential disaster for populations. E accelerates toward unsupportable infinity; C heads ever more rapidly downward toward zero.

The historical evidence on C is quite simple. First, it is the rarest of all six G-related patterns of change in population size. Further, it seems to occur in situations where populations are progressively losing their niche, their way of life and system of support. Examples have appeared in West Indian islands whose grasp on the sugar market was slipping; Prince Edward Island 1891–1931, Depression-era Saskatchewan 1931–1951, and perhaps Arkansas 1940–1960; the two challenged cities of Bruges in the 1700s and London in the middle 1990s; Tibet 1819–1964; Fujian, Jiangxi, and Shanxi provinces of China in the 19th century; and the Tohoku, Hokuriku, Tosan, and Chugoku regions of Japan since World War II. Especially insightful, finally, is the way C seems to be connected with falling birthrates: in several regions of Spain in the later 1500s and early 1600s (Table 6.1), in the sampled rural departments of Hautes Alpes, Calvados, and Loiret as France came to "face depopulation" in the early 1900s through declining fertility, and earlier in scattered local situations such as Crulai and Tourouvre-au-Perche in northern France across the 1600s and 1700s and Aldenham in Hertfordshire 1641–1671 (Gautier and Henry 1970, 58; Charbonneau 1970, 60–61; Newman-Brown 1984, 407, 409). This demographic connection of the C pattern of population decline will receive systematic further examination as historical changes in birthrate and fertility are soon explored.

"Population explosion," proportionally accelerating demographic increase (not just any rapid growth), turns out to take the form of G inverse (G^I), G reversed both top to bottom and horizontally with respect to time. This systematically quickening E phenomenon existed in many populations across more than two centuries before it was noticed and labeled by demographers in the 1960s.

Like the other H and F exceptions to G, E seems to be associated historically with a certain kind of economic change. For this phenomenon, too, an insightful distribution can be traced geographically. Among known data the main European threads begin in England, Scotland, Ireland, Iceland, Denmark, the Netherlands, France (briefly), Rhineland Mark, and Württemberg in the 1700s and early 1800s. Tendrils run during the later 19th century to most of the rest of Germany, Limburg and West Flanders in Belgium, Spain and Portugal, Switzerland, the Czech lands, Austria and a few adjacent Hapsburg holdings, Romania, and a regionally distinguishable network of Russian provinces. Finally they extend in the early 20th century to Hungary, Macedonia, Albania, the Caucasus, and Soviet Central Asia. Much of this patterning of place and time smacks of the spread of early phases of industrialization, in which the premium was on cheap mass labor, often collected into new factory locations. Traditional rural values, practices, and pressures that regulate marriage and reproduction tend to weaken with these dislocations, pushing up fertility as long as minimal conditions for survival are maintained and families do not yet begin to trade having more children for better living standards. It is in these kinds of circumstances, a stage not only of economic development but of what is called "demographic transition," that E-type population surges have occurred historically.

Twentieth century cases of such population explosion are well known in Asia, Africa, and Latin America, though this form of accelerating growth starting in the later 1800s in Hong Kong and in Jiangsu, Zhejiang, Hebei, Shandong, and Guizhou provinces of China (or beginning in the 1930s in Henan and Qinghai) has not been noted. Modern Third World E trends, like their European predecessors, seem to be associated with a cheap labor type or phase of economic development. So may certain outlying historical examples.

The earliest probable cases of the E pattern noted in this study, for instance, come from a few provinces of Ming China between 1491 and 1598—from Hebei and from Shanxi and Gansu (reported together) in the North and Sichuan and Guizhou in the Southwest. What kind of economic development was occurring there in the 16th century? Later and elsewhere, the few *urban* E trends that have been located mostly seem associated with boom cities on current frontiers: from Rio and early New Orleans in colonial Latin America to the 18th century hinterland of Potemkin's Odessa, to Houston and Vancouver in the early 20th century, to China's gateway cities for the interior of Asia (Xi'an, Lanzhou, and Ürümqi) in the 1930s and 20th century Sapporo along with her northern Japanese hinterland of Hokkaido. The inhabitants of Nottingham and Bruges in the 1700s, like those of Providence Country in Rhode Island 1790 to 1850, would seem to have been multiplying via E along with local industrialization of the time. As demographically devastated populations of west central Mexico began recovery in the late 1600s and early 1700s, E was the first path taken. What was happening to the economy here? Or was fertility beginning to build up on its own? These questions arise equally from the E trends for *births* in Spain's regions of Catalonia 1595–1625 and León 1685–1755.

In short, among the four G-based demographic growth trends, G itself is the fundamental building block, the usual form—especially in local populations and before modernization reached different parts of the world, variably between the 16th and the 20th centuries. F, one of three modern exceptions to G, has been associated historically with extensions of existing economic systems into new resource areas—of raw materials or of labor—often regions for the time being expanding peripheral service to the core without themselves representing foci of economic development. Population increase via H, in contrast, escapes the rapid deceleration of G by means of economic growth. While the G pattern reflects the impact of a particular opportunity that allows or inspires demographic increase, but whose advantage is quickly exhausted by additional people, the H trend seems characteristic of historical situations in which not one but a series of favorable changes make room for (even require) more population, for instance through the complex effects of urbanization or accumulative technological change. Slowly starting but accelerating growth via E, on the other hand, has generally occurred with labor-intensive phases of economic growth, most evidently early industrialization—especially situations where restraints on human reproduction are relaxed, the problem Malthus emphasized, though he failed to perceive the *accelerating* seriousness of the threat (the E form, not F).

Along with two types of demographic decline—one, D, decelerating as a disaster or shock is absorbed progressively by a population; the other, C, accelerating toward total collapse as some flaw of the local system begins to prove more and more serious—we end up with six mathematically related laws of sustained change in the size of populations. While many historical examples have been invoked, the validity of these empirical generalizations can ultimately be determined only by having others use and test them. Meanwhile, though, besides eliciting intimations of universality, we have begun—by analyzing the historical settings in which the six trend types appear—to identify how these forms might be generated. Such theorizing inevitably involves how demographic behavior and life conditions, many of them economic in nature, interact in combined "demonomic" systems.

At times these interrelationships can seem impossible to unravel, a frustratingly Gordian challenge. Yet the survey presented here already produces some important clues as to how best to proceed. First, it seems very *unlikely* that all economic changes, even separated into categories associated with G, F, H, E, D, and C patterns, *for their own reasons* always take such G-based shapes and thereby give demographic trends their repeated curves. Too many historical eras, social and cultural settings, levels of demographic unit, and varieties of economy are involved. The likelihood that the six trends always take the same forms for economic reasons is even further reduced when acts of nature like disease or climate and other interventions of humanity such as war or birth control are added to economic inputs as external stimuli. Instead, something *internal to the dynamics of populations* must carry and replicate the G shape and its five transformations throughout so many and so varied historical conditions.

Thus the next phase of this study, the next volume, advances to examine the behavior of demographic factors that are known to contribute towards shaping trends in population size. Already, the growth of particular cities, more general patterns of urbanization, and the paths of expansion observed in new settlements or colonies demonstrate that G-related trends are in the least deeply imbedded in, if not universal to, *migration*. Meanwhile, reactions of population size in periods of known epidemic, ravaging by war, and starvation make it clear that the effects of *mortality* can also play out significantly in G-based forms. Finally, C and E birth movements that have been noted along with certain trends of demographic atrophy or increase historically suggest that *fertility*, too, follows paths rooted in the G formula. Meanwhile, the sequencing of H and E trends by place and time that has been followed around the world is as much reminiscent of the diffusion of "demographic transition" as it is of the travels of modern economic growth.

If the curve shapes are caused by internal demographic dynamics, however, why is there so much historical association with economic growth and change? First, *which form* of G-based path is going to be followed by population increase, as well as *when it will start*, seems to depend upon the kind of economic, medical, military, or cultural developments that serve as stimuli or triggers for initiating a new phase of expansion or atrophy. We have argued that some types of economic growth have different consequences for alterations in population size than others; and the nature of continuing interaction between demographic and economic change, how they do or do not feed off each other, has much to do with the kind of G-based path followed. Conversely, however, since economies are made by the actions of people, if the numbers of producers and consumers expand or contract over and over again in certain standard patterns for demographic reasons, there will be imprints of these trends, direct or indirect, upon many if not most economic processes. These connections offer important fresh perspective on how economic changes unfold, and social and cultural developments as well. A third stage of this study thus employs some of the rich matching economic and demographic history available to demonstrate how such demonomic interactions seem to work.

What this first volume had done is to simplify, revise, and integrate available theories and findings on how populations have increased or atrophied historically. The six G-based curves capture such changes appreciably better than past conceptualizations, from the population classics of the 18th century to interpretations of the present time such as stable population theory, explosion, or demographic transition. They account for known data patterns form the fifth century B.C. to the 1990s, for movements in all kinds of societies and at all levels of population.

Such findings, which suggest that the possible trend shapes are determined by the dynamics of populations themselves, place demography at the heart of all studies of change in human life. For other social scientists, notably economists, models are simplified and constraints are set upon the variety of paths along which change moves, even though economic inputs remain significant for starting population gain or loss and determining which of the six G-based types of trend will be followed. Demonomic interaction—long stressed by theorists of population—is not eliminated; but particular roles of the component demographic and economic contributions are more properly prescribed. In practical terms, meanwhile, policy makers, participants in the marketplace, and students of social developments all around the globe should be helped in understanding how trends in their field of interest have unfolded and also what paths they are likely to follow in the future—though simple projection without understanding the conditions and forces at work or changes that might occur remains as foolish as ever.

NOTES

1. The colonies of North and South America and the Caribbean from the 1600s forward are considered in this conclusion to be appendages of developing Europe.

2. The 2025 projection for Asia may be low; or it may signal that this part of the world is currently making the transition from H into G expansion.

Appendix

Table A.1
Applying Some New and Some More Familiar Models to the Historical Growth Patterns of American Colonies/States

A. G Trends in the Earliest Areas of Settlement

Place and Time:		Measure:	Fixed G	Open G (G_0)	Logistic	Line
Virginia	1607-1710	F	3,092	1,345	651	49
		Rank	1			
		Exponent		.0277		
Virginia	1780-1870	F	309	190	127	191
		Rank	30			
		Exponent		.0217		
Virginia	1870-1930	F	234	336	171	711
		Rank	680			
		Exponent		.0149		
Connecticut	1650-1700	F	8,330	6,334	6,774	6,806
		Rank	48			
		Exponent		.0339		
Connecticut	1700-1740	F	1,780	699	898	935
		Rank	4			
		Exponent		.0329		
Connecticut	1750-1840	F	990	487	361	189
		Rank	15			
		Exponent		.0270		
Connecticut	1900-1940	F	427	148	2,319	170
		Rank	944			
		Exponent		.0216		
Connecticut	1970-2010	F	54	21	–	51
		Rank	2			
		Exponent		.0187		
Pennsylvania	1890-2025	F	2,547	1,764	1,108	123
		Rank	3			
		Exponent		.0267		
So. Carolina	1780-1870	F	529	269	192	272
		Rank	21			
		Exponent		.0254		
So. Carolina	1870-1940	F	1,041	506	330	279
		Rank	21			
		Exponent		.0267		

B. H Trends in the Earliest Areas of Settlement

Place and Time:		Measure:	Fixed H	Open H (H_0)	Logistic	Line
Virginia	1670-1710	F	1,407	876	294	227
		Rank	17			
		Exponent		.0166		
Virginia	1940-2025	F	4,719	4,788	7,250	5,056
		Rank	1,650			
		Exponent		.0389		

Table A.1 (*Continued*)

Place and Time:		Measure:				
Pennsylvania	1830-1880	F Rank Exponent	5,785 17	2,177 .0294	939	456
So. Carolina	1720-1770	F Rank Exponent	8,878 1,053	3,493 .0279	3,557	113

C. G Trends in Later-Settled States

Place and Time:		Measure:	Fixed G	Open G (G_0)	Logistic	Line
Illinois	1810-1890	F Rank Exponent	2,023 4	1,351 .0378	603	89
Illinois	1890-1940	F Rank Exponent	384 14	171 .0243	93	274
Illinois	1950-2025	F Rank Exponent	182 1,316	92 .0205	57	147
Oregon	1870-1940	F Rank Exponent	1,207 2	526 .0279	285	543
Louisiana	1950-2025	F Rank Exponent	388 17	193 .0240	126	217
Iowa	1910-2025	F Rank Exponent	197 28	195 .0159	120	188
Utah	1850-1940	F Rank Exponent	5,693 17	2,847 .0282	3,098	687
Utah	1970-2025	F Rank Exponent	1,314 1	580 .0283	520	531

D. H Trends in Later-Settled States

Place and Time:		Measure:	Fixed H	Open H (H_0)	Logistic	Line
Oregon	1940-2025	F Rank Exponent	3,380 3	1,670 .0343	1,024	2,502
Louisiana	1870-1940	F Rank Exponent	2,053 1	897 .0334	510	1,493

Sources: Selected trend segments from Tables 2.1 and 2.2 fitted via 3,000+ *TableCurve* models.

Table A.2
Numbers of Various G-Based Trends of Growth and Decline Found for Different Levels and Locations of Population

	G*	E	H	E	Growths	D	C	Declines	All Trends
GLOBAL	2	2	3	0	7	0	0	0	7
CONTINENTAL	6	3	5	1	15	0	0	0	15
NATIONAL:									
U.S.A. and Canada	6	0	3	2	11	0	0	0	11
Australia, N.Z., S. Africa	16	0	0	1	17	0	0	0	17
Latin America	45	14	9	10	78	0	0	0	78
Europe	87	20	36	0	143	8	0	8	151
Asia	73	23	16	4	116	5	0	5	121
Africa	65	49	4	16	134	0	0	0	134
Total:	292	106	68	33	499	13	0	13	512
REGIONAL:									
U.S.A. and Canada	249	3	18	5	276	4	2	6	282
West Indies	93	3	2	1	99	7	4	11	110
Australia, N.Z., S. Africa	61	1	0	0	62	5	0	5	67
Larger So. Pacific Is.	29	6	0	3	38	19	0	19	57
Latin America	87	30	26	6	149	43	0	43	192
Europe	404	115	103	2	624	36	11	47	671
Asia	225	67	49	9	350	7	12	19	369
Total:	1,149	225	198	26	1,598	121	29	150	1,748
ETHNIC AND RACIAL GROUPS:	93	10	4	2	109	16	4	20	129
LOCAL POPULATIONS:									
Bigger Cities	328	28	1	3	360	22	2	24	384
Counties, etc.	80	13	0	0	93	10	0	10	103
Towns	109	0	0	0	109	33	0	33	142
Villages, Manors, Hamlets, Atolls	129	0	0	0	129	64	1	65	194
Total:	646	41	1	3	691	129	3	132	823
GRAND TOTAL:	2,180	382	271	64	2,897	279	36	315	3,212

*Includes rG.

Sources: Tables and figures for Chapters 1–9 and other curves fitted for their development.

Bibliography

GOVERNMENT PUBLICATIONS

Australia

Cameron, R. J. 1982. *Year Book: Australia* 66. Canberra: Australian Bureau of Statistics.
Knibbs, G. H. 1915. *Official Yearbook of the Commonwealth of Australia* 8. Melbourne: Commonwealth Bureau of Census and Statistics.

Brazil

Fundaçao Instituto Brasileiro de Geografia e Estatŝtica. 1988. *Anuário estatístico do Brasil*. Rio de Janeiro: IGBE.

Canada

Department of Agriculture. 1876. *Censuses of Canada 1665 to 1871*. Ottawa.
Dominion Bureau of Statistics. 1953. *9th Census of Canada*. Ottawa.
Leacy, F. H., ed. 1983. *Historical Statistics of Canada*. 2nd ed. Ottawa: Statistics Canada.
Ministry of Supply and Services. 1981. *Canada Yearbook*. Ottawa.
Statistics Canada. 1991. *Canada: 125th Anniversary Yearbook, 1992*. Ottawa.
Urquhart, M. C., ed. 1965. *Historical Statistics of Canada*. Cambridge: The University Press.

Czechoslovakia

Czechoslovakia: Statistical Abstract. 1968. Prague: Orbis, ed. Libuse.
Manuel Statistique de la République Tchécoslovaque. 1932. Prague: Edition de l'Office
    de Statistique.

Finland

Tilatokeskus. 1991. *Suomen tilastollinen vuosikirja 1991* (Central Statistical Office of
    Finland, *Statistical Yearbook of Finland*). Helsinki, n.s., 86.

Germany

Kaiserlichen Statistische Amt. 1914. *Statistisches Jahrbuch für das Deutches Reich.* Ber-
    lin: Verlag von Puttkammer and Mühlbrecht [K. Stat. Amt].

Greece

National Statistical Services. 1971. *Statistical Yearbook of Greece 1971.* Athens.

Hungary

Hungarian Central Statistical Office. 1991. *Hungarian Statistical Yearbook 1990.* Bu-
    dapest.

India

Central Statistical Organization. 1982. *Statistical Abstract: India 1982.* New Delhi: De-
    partment of Statistics, Ministry of Planning, n.s., 26.
Research and Reference Division. 1993. *India 1993: A Reference Annual.* Delhi: Ministry
    of Information and Broadcasting.

Indonesia

World Bank. 1994. *Indonesia: Sustaining Development.* Washington, D.C.

Ireland

Central Statistics Office. 1991. *Ireland: Statistical Abstract 1991.* Dublin: Stationery
    Office.

Italy

Instituto Centrale di Statistica. 1976. *Sommario di statistiche storiche dell'Italia 1861–1975*. Rome.
————. 1991. *Annuario statistico Italiano*. Rome.

Japan

Statistics Bureau. 1990 and 1994. *Japan, Statistical Yearbook*. Tokyo: Management and Coordination Agency.

Luxembourg

Service Central de la Statistique et des Études Économiques. 1990. *Statistiques historiques 1839–1989*. Luxembourg: Ministère de l'Économie.

Malaysia

Department of Statistics. 1992. *Buku Tahunan Perangkaan Malaysia 1991 (Yearbook of Statistics Malaysia 1991)*. Kuala Lumpur.

New Zealand

Department of Statistics. 1992. *New Zealand Official 1992 Yearbook (Te Pukapuka Houanga Whaimana o Aotearoa)*. Auckland.

Norway

Statistisk Sentralbryå. 1978. *Historisk Statistikk 1978 (Historical Statistics 1978)*. Norges Officielle Statistikk XII 291. Oslo.

Pakistan

Federal Bureau of Statistics. 1985. *Pakistan Statistitical Yearbook 1985*. Islamabad.

People's Republic of China

State Statistical Bureau. 1986. *Statistical Yearbook of China 1986*. Oxford: Oxford University Press.

Philippines

National Statistical Coordination Board. 1988. *1988 Philippine Statistical Yearbook*. Manila: Republic of the Philippines.

Singapore

Department of Statistics. 1983. *Economic and Social Statistics, Singapore 1960–1982.*
    Singapore.

South Africa

Central Statistical Service. 1990. *Suid-Afrikaanse Statistieke.* Pretoria.
Department of Foreign Affairs. 1985. *Official Yearbook of the Republic of South Africa.*
    11th ed.

South Korea

Republic of Korea. 1993. *Korea Statistical Yearbook 1993.* Seoul: National Statistical
    Office.

Spain

Institutio National de Estadística. 1991. *Annuario Estadístico 1990.* Madrid.

Sweden

Statistika Centralbyrån. 1969. *Historisk statistik för Sverige* (National Central Bureau of
    Statistics. *Historical Statistics of Sweden*). Part 1, *Population*, 2d ed., 1720–1967.
    Stockholm: AB Allmänna Förlaget.

Taiwan

Government Information Office. 1985. *Statistical Yearbook, Republic of China 1985.*
    Taipei.

Turkey

State Institute of Statistics. 1987. *Türkiye istatistik yilligi: Statistical Yearbook of Turkey
    1987.* Ankara: Prime Ministry.
————. 1991. *Türkiye istatistik yilligi: Statistical Yearbook of Turkey 1991.* Ankara:
    Prime Ministry.

United Kingdom

Office of Population Censuses and Surveys. 1991a. *1991 Census: Preliminary Report
    for England and Wales.* London: HMSO.
————. 1991b. *Population Trends.* No. 66, London: HMSO.

United Nations

Demographic Yearbook. 1975, 1980, 1985, 1990, 1992, 1993 (1995). [*Demo. Ybk.*]

United States

U.S. Bureau of the Census. 1975. *Historical Statistics of the United States, Colonial Times to 1970.* 2 vols. Washington, D.C.: U.S. Department of Commerce, [*Hist. Stat.*].

———. *Statistical Abstracts.* Washington, D.C.: U.S. Department of Commerce, 1977, 1985, 1991, 1993, 1997 [*Stat. Abs.*].

———. 1991. "Metropolitan Areas and Cities," *1990 Census Profile,* No. 3. Washington, D.C.: U.S. Department of Commerce.

SECONDARY WORKS

Adams, Donald R., Jr. 1986. "Prices and Wages in Antebellum America: The West Virginia Experience." *Journal of Economic History* 52: 206–16.

Afzal, Mohammed. 1974. *The Population of Pakistan.* Islamabad: Pakistan Institute of Development Economics.

Alba, Francisco. 1982. *The Population of Mexico: Trends, Issues, and Policies.* Trans. by Marjory Mattingly Urquidi. New Brunswick, N.J.: Transaction Books.

Andersen, Otto. 1979. "Denmark." In W. R. Lee, ed. 1979, 79–122.

Appleman, Philip, ed. 1976. *Thomas Robert Malthus, An Essay on the Principle of Population.* New York: W. W. Norton and Company.

Baratier, Édouard. 1961. *La démographie Provençale du XIIIe au XVIe siècles.* Paris: S.E.V.P.E.N.

Barón Castro, Rodolpho. 1978. *Población de El Salvador.* San Salvador: UCA/Editores; first published Madrid, 1942.

Bayliss-Smith, Tim P. 1975a. "The Central Polynesian Outlier Populations since European Contact." In Carroll, ed. 1975, 286–343.

———. 1975b. "Ontong Java: Depopulation and Repopulation." In Carroll, ed. 1975, 417–84.

Bell, E. T. 1965. *Men of Mathematics.* 2nd ed. New York: Simon and Schuster.

Bloomfield, G. T. 1984. *New Zealand: A Handbook of Historical Statistics.* Boston: G. K. Hall & Co.

Boserup, Ester. 1965. *The Conditions of Agricultural Growth: The Economics of Agrarian Change under Population Pressure.* Chicago: Aldine Publishing Company.

———. 1983. *Population and Technology.* Oxford: Basil Blackwell Ltd.

Bourgeois-Pichat, J. 1965. "The General Development of the Population of France since the Eighteenth Century." In Glass and Eversley, 474–506; first published in *Population* 7 (1952): 319–29.

Braun, M. 1976. *Differential Equations and Their Applications: An Introduction to Applied Mathematics.* New York: Springer-Verlag.

Braun, Rudolf. 1978. "Protoindustrialization and Demographic Changes in the Canton of Zürich." In Charles Tilly, ed., *Historical Studies of Changing Fertility.* Princeton: Princeton University Press, 289–334.

Brunt, P. A. 1971. *Italian Manpower 225 B.C.–A.D. 14.* Oxford: The Clarendon Press.

Campbell, Bruce M. S. 1984. "Inheritance and the Land Market in a Fourteenth-Century Community." In R. Smith 1984, 87–134.

Carillo Batalla, Thomas Enrique. 1967. *Analisis Cuantitativo y Cualitativo de la Economia de la Población Venezolana.* Caracas: Comision Nacional del Cuatricentenario de la Fundacion de Caracas.

Caritat, Marie Jean Antoine Nicolas, Marquis de Condorcet. 1795. "The Tenth Stage: The Future Progress of the Human Mind." In *Sketch for a Historical Picture of the Progress of the Human Mind,* 173–202. Trans. by June Barraclough. London: Weidenfield and Nicolson, 1955. (Facsimile, Ann Arbor: University Microfilms, 1975).

Carroll, Vern. 1975. "The Population of Nukuoro in Historical Perspective." In Carroll, ed. 1975, 344–416.

Carroll, Vern, ed. 1975. *Pacific Atoll Populations.* Honolulu: University Press of Hawaii for the East-West Population Institute; Association for Social Anthropology in Oceania Monograph No. 3.

Centro de Estudios de Población y Desarrollo. 1972. *Informe Demografico Peru–1970.* Lima. CEPD.

Chambers, J. D. 1965. "Population Change in a Provincial Town: Nottingham 1700–1800." In Glass and Eversley, 334–53; first published in L. S. Presnell, ed. *Studies in the Industrial Revolution: Essays Presented to T. S. Ashton.* London: Athlone Press, 1960.

Chandrasekhar, S. 1960. *China's Population.* 2nd ed. Hong Kong: Hong Kong University Press.

Charbonneau, Hubert. 1970. *Tourouvre-au-Perche aux XVIIe et XVIIIe siècles.* I.N.E.D. *Travaux* 55. Paris: Presses Universitaires de France.

———. 1975. *Vit et Mort de nos Ancêtres.* Montreal: University of Montreal.

Childe, V. Gordon. 1951. *Man Makes Himself.* New York: New American Library. First published 1936.

Cippola, Carlo. 1965. "Four Centuries of Italian Demographic Development." In Glass and Eversley 1965, 570–87.

———. 1979. *The Economic History of World Population.* Harmonsworth, Middlesex: Penguin Books. First published 1962.

Coleman, David. 1986. "Population Regulation: A Long-Range View." In Coleman and Schofield 1986, 14–41.

Coleman, David, and Roger Schofield, eds. 1986. *The State of Population Theory: Forward from Malthus.* Oxford: Basil Blackwell Ltd.

Comadrán Ruiz, Jorge. 1969. *Evolucion Demografia Argentina Durante el Periodo Hispano (1535–1810).* Buenos Aires: Editorial Universitaria de Buenos Aires.

Comba, Rinaldo, Gabriella Piccinni, and Giuliano Pinto, eds. 1984. *Strutture familiari epidemie migrazioni nell'Italia medievale.* Naples: Edizioni Scientifiche Italiane.

Connell, K. H. 1975. *The Population of Ireland 1750–1845.* Westport, Conn.: Greenwood Press. First published Oxford: The Clarendon Press, 1950.

Cook, James. 1821. *The Three Voyages of Captain James Cook Round the World.* 7 vols., London: Longman, Hurst, Rees, Orme, and Brown.

Cook, M. A. 1972. *Population Pressure in Rural Anatolia 1450–1600. London Oriental Series* 27. London: Oxford University Press.

Cook, Noble David. 1981. *Demographic Collapse: Indian Peru, 1520–1620. Cambridge Latin American Studies* 41. Cambridge: Cambridge University Press.

———. 1993. "Disease and the Depopulation of Hispaniola, 1492–1518." *Colonial Latin American Review* 2: 213–45.

———. 1998. *Born to Die: Disease and New World Conquest, 1492–1650.* Cambridge: Cambridge University Press.

Cook, Sherburne F., and Woodrow Wilson Borah. 1971, 1974, 1979. *Essays in Population History: Mexico and the Caribbean.* 3 vols. Berkeley: University of California Press.

Cortonesi, Alfio. 1984. "Demografia e popolamento nel contado di Siena: Il territorio Montalcinese nei secoli XIII–XV." In Comba et al., 1984, 153–81.

Cullen, L. M. 1976. "Economic Trends, 1660–91." In T. W. Moody, F. X. Martin, and F. J. Byrne, eds. *A New History of Ireland*, 3: 387–407, *Early Modern Ireland.* Oxford: The Clarendon Press.

———. 1986a. "Economic Development, 1691–1750." In T. W. Moody and W. E. Vaughan, eds. *A New History of Ireland*, 4: 133–58, *Eighteenth-Century Ireland.* Oxford: The Clarendon Press.

———. 1986b. "Economic Development, 1750–1800." In T. W. Moody and W. E. Vaughan, eds. *A New History of Ireland*, 4: 159–95. *Eighteenth-Century Ireland.* Oxford: The Clarendon Press.

———. 1994. "The Irish Diaspora of the Seventeenth and Eighteenth Centuries." In Nicholas Canny, ed. *Europeans on the Move: Studies on European Migration, 1500–1800*, 113–49. Oxford: Clarendon Press.

Darwin, Charles. 1859. *The Origin of Species by Means of Natural Selection, or the Preservation of Favored Races in the Struggle for Life.* 7th ed. New York: D. Appleton and Company.

———. 1898. *The Life and Letters of Charles Darwin.* Ed. by Francis Darwin. 2 vols. New York: D. Appleton and Company.

Daultrey, Stuart, David Dickson, and Cormac Ó Gráda, 1981. "Eighteenth-Century Irish Population: New Perspectives from Old Sources." *Journal of Economic History* 41: 601–28.

Davis, Kingsley. 1951. *The Population of India and Pakistan.* Princeton: Princeton University Press.

Davis, Ralph. 1973. *The Rise of the Atlantic Economies.* Ithaca: Cornell University Press.

Deerr, Noel. 1949, 1950. *The History of Sugar.* 2 vols. London: Chapman and Hall.

Del Panta, Lorenzo. 1979. "Italy." In W. R. Lee, ed. 1979, 196–235.

Deprez, Paul. 1963. "De bevolking van Evergem, Knesselare, Ronsele en Zomergem in het licht van de volkstellingen van 1796/1798." In Van Assche-Vancauwenbergh et al. 1963, 151–93.

———. 1979. "The Low Countries." In W. R. Lee, ed. 1979, 236–83.

De Vos, A. 1963. "De omvang en de evolutie van het Eeklose bevolkingscijfer tijdens de XVII$_e$ en de XVII$_e$ eeuw." In Van Assche-Vancauwenbergh et al. 1963, 123–48.

De Vries, Jan. 1974. *The Dutch Rural Economy in the Golden Age, 1500–1700.* New Haven: Yale University Press.

———. 1984. *European Urbanization 1500–1800.* Cambridge, Mass.: Harvard University Press.

De Vries, Jan, and Ad van der Woude. 1997. *The First Modern Economy: Success, Failure, and Perseverance of the Dutch Economy, 1500–1815.* Cambridge: Cambridge University Press.

Drake, Michael. 1969. *Population and Society in Norway 1735–1865*. Cambridge: The University Press.

Dreyer-Roos, Suzanne. 1969. *La population Strasbourgeoise sous l'Ancien Régime. Publications de la Société Savante d'Alsace et des Régions de l'Est* 6. Strasbourg: Librarie Istra.

Dunn, Richard S. 1972. *Sugar and Slaves: The Rise of the Planter Class in the English West Indies, 1624–1713*. Chapel Hill: University of North Carolina Press.

Dupâquier, Jacques. 1979. *La population française aux XVIIe et XVIIIe siècles*. Paris: Presse Universitaires de France.

Dupâquier, Jacques, et al. 1988. *Histoire de la population française*. Vol. 1. *Des origines à la Renaissance*. Paris: Presses Universitaires de France.

Durand, John D. 1960. "The Population Statistics of China, A.D. 2–1953." *Population Studies* 13: 209–56.

Dyrvik, S. 1972. "Historical Demography in Norway, 1660–1801: A Short Survey." *Scandinavian Economic History Review* 20: 27–44.

Eichengreen, Barry, and Ian W. McLean. 1994. "The Supply of Gold under the Pre-1914 Gold Standard." *Economic History Review* 47: 288–309.

El Attar, Mohammed E. 1979. "Population Growth and Redistribution in Iraq." *Demography India* 8: 13–29.

Elliott, J. H. 1977. *Imperial Spain, 1469–1716*. New York: New American Library. First published London: St. Martin's Press, 1963.

Elsas, M. J. 1936. *Umriss einer Geschichte der Preise und Löhne in Deutschland vom ausgehenden Mittelalter bis zum Beginn des neunzehnten Jahrhunderts*. 2 vols. Leiden: A. W. Sijtoff.

Euler, Leonhard. 1760. "Recherches générales sur la mortalité et la multiplication du genre humaine." *Memoires de l'Académie Royale des Sciences et Belle Lettres* (Berlin) 16, 144–64. Trans. by Nathan and Beatrice Keyfitz. In D. Smith and Keyfitz 1977, 83–91. It is attributed there to the Belgian Académie Royale.

Eversley, D. E. C. 1965. "A Survey of Population in an Area of Worcestershire from 1660 to 1850 on the Basis of Parish Registers." In Glass and Eversley, 394–419. First published in *Population Studies* 10, 1957.

Felloni, Giuseppe. 1977. "Italy." In Wilson and Parker 1977, 1–36.

Fernández, Mario E., Annabelle Schmidt, and Victor Basauri. 1977. "Anexo: La población en Costa Rica." In Louis Demetrio Tinico, ed., *Población de Costa Rica y Origenes de los Costarricenses*. San José: Editorial Costa Rica for the Biblioteca Patria, 215–86.

Finlay, Roger. 1981. *Population and Metropolis: The Demography of London 1580–1650*. Cambridge: Cambridge University Press.

Fournier, Louis A. 1969. "Población y Balances Naturales en Centro America." In Rodrigo Gutiérrez and Ferdinand Rath, eds., *Población y Recursos en Centroamerica: "El Desafio del Siglio XX,"* 11–35. Ciudad Universitaria "Rodrigo Facio": Universidad de Costa Rica.

François, Etienne. 1982. *Koblenz im 18. Jahrhundert: Zur Sozial-und Bevölkerungsstruktur einer deutschen Residenzstadt. Veröffentlichungen des Max-Planck-Instituts für Geschichte* 72. Göttingen: Vandenhoeck and Ruprecht.

Franklin, Benjamin. 1751. "OBSERVATIONS concerning the Increase of Mankind, Peopling of Countries, &c." In Leonard W. Labaree, ed., *The Papers of Benjamin Franklin* 4: 227–34. New Haven: Yale University Press.

Friz, Giuliano. 1974. *La Popolazione di Roma dal 1770 al 1900*. Rome: Edindustria Editoriale.

Gates, Paul W. 1962. *The Farmer's Age: Agriculture 1815–1860*. New York: Holt, Rinehart and Winston.

Gautier, Etienne, and Louis Henry. 1970. *La population de Crulai Paroisse Normande: Étude historique*. Institut national d'études démographiques *Travaux et Documents* 33. Paris: Presses Universitaires de France.

Gemery, Henry A. 1980. "Emigration from the British Isles to the New World, 1630–1700: Inferences from Colonial Populations." *Research in Economic History* 5: 179–231.

Gille, H. 1949. "The Demographic History of the Northern European Countries in the Eighteenth Century." *Population Studies* 3: 3–65.

Glass, David V., and D. E. C. Eversley, eds. 1965. *Population in History: Essays in Historical Demography*. Chicago: Aldine Publishing Company.

Godwin, William. 1797. "Of Avarice and Profusion." In *The Enquirer: Reflections on Education, Manners and Literature*. London: G. G. and J. Robinson; reprinted New York: Augustus M. Kelley, 1965.

Gompertz, Benjamin. 1820. "A Sketch of the Analysis and Notation Applicable to the Value of Life Contingencies." *Philosophical Transactions of the Royal Society* 110: 214–94.

———. 1825. "On the Nature of the Function Expressive of the Law of Human Mortality, and on a New Mode of Determining the Value of Life Contingencies." Ibid., 115: 513–85.

———. 1862. "A Supplement to the Two Papers of 1820 and 1825." Ibid., 152: 511–59.

Goubert, Pierre. 1965. "Recent Theories and Research in French Population between 1500 and 1700." In Glass and Eversley 1965, 457–73.

Grobbelaar, J. Q. 1985. *The Population of Natal/KwaZulu 1904–2010*. Natal: Natal Town and Regional Planning Commission.

Grohmann, Alberto. 1984. "Entità dei focolari e tipologie insediative nel contado Perugino del sec. XV." In Comba et al. 1984, 269–89.

Gutiérrez, Ramón A. 1991. *When Jesus Came, the Corn Mothers Went Away: Marriage, Sexuality, and Power in New Mexico 1500–1846*. Stanford: Stanford University Press.

Hall, Thomas D. 1989. *Social Change in the Southwest, 1350–1880*. Lawrence, Kansas: University Press of Kansas.

Hanley, Susan B. 1968. "Population Trends and Economic Development in Tokugawa Japan: The Case of Bizen Province in Okayama." *Historical Population Studies, Daedalus. Proceedings of the American Academy of Arts and Sciences* 97, no. 2.

———. 1985. "Family and Fertility in Four Tokugawa Villages." In Hanley and Wolf 1985, 196–228.

Hanley, Susan B., and Kozo Yamamura. 1977. *Economic and Demographic Change in Preindustrial Japan 1600–1868*. Princeton: Princeton University Press.

Hanley, Susan B., and Arthur P. Wolf, eds. 1985. *Family and Population in East Asian History*. Stanford: Stanford University Press.

Harrell, Stevan, ed. 1995. *Chinese Historical Microdemography*. Berkeley: University of California Press.

Harris, P. M. G. 1969. "The Social Origins of American Leaders: The Demographic Foundations." *Perspectives in American History* 3: 159–344.

———. 1983. "Settling the Chesapeake: The Growth, Spread, and Stabilization of a European Population." Paper for the Seminar of the Philadelphia Center for Early American Studies, Nov. 18.

———. 1989. "The Demographic Development of Philadelphia in Some Comparative Perspective." *Proceedings of the American Philosophical Society* 133: 262–304.

———. 1992. "Economic Growth in Demographic Perspective: The Example of the Chesapeake, 1607–1775." In *Lois Green Carr: The Chesapeake and Beyond—A Celebration*, 55–92. Crownsville, Md.: Maryland Historical and Cultural Publications.

Hayami, Akira. 1968. "The Population at the Beginning of the Tokugawa Era." *Keio Economic Studies*, 4: 1–28.

Hayami, Akira, and Nobuko Uchida. 1972. "Size of Household in a Japanese County throughout the Tokugawa Era." In Peter Laslett and Richard Wall, eds., *Household and Family in Past Time: Comparative Studies in the Size and Structure of the Domestic Group over the Last Three Centuries in England, France, Serbia, Japan and Colonial North America, with Further Materials from Western Europe.* Cambridge: The University Press.

Helczmanovzski, Heimold. 1979. "Austria-Hungary." In W. R. Lee, ed., 1979, 27–78.

Helczmanovzski, Heimold, ed. 1973. *Beiträge zur Bevölkerungs-und Sozialgeschichte Österreichs.* Vienna: Verlag für Geschichte und Politik.

Hélin, E. 1963. "Croissance démographique et transformation des campagnes: Chênée, Olne, et Gemmenich aux XVIIIᵉ et XIXᵉ siècles." In D. Van Assche-Vancauwenbergh et al. 1963, 195–240.

Henripin, Jacques. 1972. *Trends and Factors of Fertility in Canada.* Ottawa: Dominion Bureau of Statistics.

Henry, Louis, and Yves Blayo. 1975. "La population de la France de 1740 à 1860." *Population*, special issue: *Démographie Historique*, 71–122.

Herlihy, David. 1967. *Medieval and Renaissance Pistoia: The Social History of an Italian Town, 1200–1430.* New Haven: Yale University Press.

Higuounet-Nadal, Arlette. 1978. *Périgueux aux XIVᵉ et XVᵉ siècles: Étude de démographie historique.* Bordeaux: Federation historique du sud-ouest.

Ho, Ping-ti. 1959. *Studies in the Population of China 1368–1953.* Cambridge, Mass.: Harvard University Press.

Hofstadter, Richard. 1955. *The Age of Reform: From Bryan to F.D.R.* New York: Vintage Books.

Hofstee, E. W. 1981. *Korte demografische geschiedenis van Nederland van 1800 tot heden.* Haarlem: Fibula-Van Dishoeck.

Hofsten, Erland, and Hans Lundström. 1976. *Swedish Population History: Main Trends from 1750 to 1970.* Urval VIII, Stockholm: Allmänna Förlaget.

Hughes, Robert. 1987. *The Fatal Shore: The Epic of Australia's Founding.* New York: Alfred A. Knopf.

Hume, David. 1752. "Of the Populousness of Antient Nations," Discourse X, *Political Discourses.* In *The Philosophical Works of David Hume.* 4 vols. Boston: Little, Brown and Company, 1854.

Innes, Stephen. 1983. *Labor in a New Land: Economy and Society in Seventeenth-Century Springfield.* Princeton: Princeton University Press.

Israel, Jonathan I. 1995. *The Dutch Republic: Its Rise, Greatness, and Fall 1477–1806.* Oxford: Clarendon Press.

Izzo, Luigi. 1965. *La popolazione Calabrese nel seccolo XIX: demografia ed economia.* Naples: Edizioni Scientifiche Italiane.

Jones, F. Lancaster. 1970. *The Structure and Growth of Australia's Aboriginal Population.* Canberra: Australian National University Press.

Juttikala, Eino. 1965. "Finland's Population Movement in the Eighteenth Century." In Glass and Eversley 1965, 549–69.

Kabuzan, Vladimir M. 1971. *Izmeneniia v Razmescheshchenii Naseleniia Rossii v XVIII-pervoi polovine XIX v.* Moscow: Izdatelstvo "Nauka."

Kaplan, Fredric M., Julian M. Sobin, and Stephen Andors, eds. 1980. *Encyclopedia of China Today.* Updated ed. Fair Lawn, N.J.: Eurasia Press.

Karpat, Kemal H. 1985. *Ottoman Population 1830–1914; Demographic and Social Characteristics.* Madison, Wis.: The University of Wisconsin Press.

Kellenbenz, Hermann, and assistants. 1977. "Germany." In Wilson and Parker 1977, 190–225.

Keyfitz, Nathan. 1968. *Introduction to the Mathematics of Population.* Reading, Mass.: Addison-Wesley Publishing Company.

———. 1985. *Applied Mathematical Demography.* 2d ed. New York: Springer Verlag. First published New York: Wiley, 1977.

Kim Doo-Sub. 1992. "Sociodemographic Determinants of the Fertility Transition in Korea." In Calvin Goldscheider, ed., *Fertility Transition, Family Structure, and Population Policy,* 45–46. Boulder, Colo.: Westview Press.

Klein, Kurt. 1973. "Die Bevölkerung Österreichs vom Beginn des 16. bis zur Mitte des 18. Jahrhunderts." In Helczmanovzski 1973, 47–112.

Köllmann, Wolfgang. 1965. "The Population of Barmen Before and During the Period of Industrialization." In Glass and Eversley, eds. 1965, 588–607.

———, ed., 1980. *Quellen zur Bevölkerungs-, Sozial-, und Wirtschaftsstatistik Deutschlands 1815–1875.* Vol. 1, Antje Kraus, *Quellen zur Bevölkerungsstatistik Deutschlands 1815–1875.* Boppard am Rhein: Harald Boldt Verlag.

Labaree, Leonard W., ed. 1961–. *The Papers of Benjamin Franklin.* New Haven: Yale University Press.

Lachiver, Marcel. 1969. *La Population de Meulan du XVIIᵉ au XIXᵉ siècle (vers 1600–1800): Étude de démographie historique.* Paris: S.E.V.P.E.N.

Lal, K. S. 1973. *Growth of Muslim Population in Medieval India (A.D. 1000–1800).* Delhi: Research Delhi.

Lambert, Audrey M. 1971. *The Making of the Dutch Landscape.* London: Seminar Press.

Lambert, Bernd. 1975. "Makin and the Outside World." In Carroll, ed. 1975, 212–85.

Lamur, H. E. 1973. *The Demographic Evolution of Surinam 1920–1970: A Socio-Demographic Analysis.* Verhandelingen van het Koninklijk Instituut voor Taal-, Land-, en Volkenkunde 65. The Hague: Martinus Nijhoff.

Lawless, R. I. 1972. "Iraq: Changing Population Patterns." In J. I. Clarke and W. B. Fisher, eds., *Populations of the Middle East and North Africa: A Geographical Approach.* London: University of London Press.

Leasure, J. William, and Robert A. Lewis. 1966. *Population Changes in Russia and the USSR: A Set of Comparable Territorial Units.* Social Science Monograph Series 1, no. 2. San Diego: San Diego State College Press.

Lee, James, Cameron Campbell, and Lawrence Anthony. 1995, eds. "A Century of Mortality in Rural Liaoning, 1774–1873." In Harrell 1995, 163–82.

Lee, W. R. 1977. *Population Growth, Economic Development and Social Change in Bavaria 1750–1850.* New York: Arno Press.

———. 1979. "Germany." In W. R. Lee, ed., 1979, 144–95.

———, ed., 1979. *European Demography and Economic Growth.* New York: St. Martin's Press.

Le Roy Ladurie, Emmanuel. 1966. *Les paysans de Languedoc.* 2 vols. Paris: S.E.V.P.E.N.

———. 1987. *The French Peasantry 1450–1660.* Berkeley: University of California Press; trans. by Alan Sheridan.

Lewis, Robert A., Richard H. Rowland, and Ralph S. Clem. 1976. *Nationality and Population Change in Russia and the U.S.S.R.: An Evaluation of Census Data, 1897–1970.* New York: Praeger Publishers.

Livi-Bacci, Massimo. 1977. *A History of Italian Fertility during the Last Two Centuries.* Princeton: Princeton University Press.

———. 1992. *A Concise History of World Population.* Trans. by Carl Ipsen from *Storia minima della popolazione del mondo,* 1989. Cambridge, Mass.: Blackwell Publishers.

Lotka, Alfred J. 1925. *Elements of Physical Biology.* Baltimore: Williams and Wilkins.

Lovell, W. George. 1981. "The Historical Demography of the Cuchumatán Highlands of Guatemala, 1500–1821." In Robinson, ed. 1981, 195–216.

Ludwig, Armin K. 1985. *Brazil: A Handbook of Historical Statistics.* Boston: G. K. Hall and Co.

Lutz, Christopher. 1981. "Population Change in the Quinizilapa Valley, Guatemala, 1530–1770." In Robinson, ed. 1981, 175–94.

———. 1994. *Santiago de Guatemala, 1541–1773: City, Caste, and the Colonial Experience.* Norman, Okla.: University of Oklahoma Press.

Mackerras, Colin, and Amanda Yorke, eds. 1990. *The Cambridge Handbook of Contemporary China.* Cambridge: Cambridge University Press.

Makeham, William M. 1867. "On the Law of Mortality." *Journal of the Institute of Actuaries* 13: 325–67.

Malthus, Thomas Robert. 1798. *An Essay on the Principle of Population.* London: J. Johnson: reprinted New York: Augustus M. Kelley, 1965.

———. 1872. *An Essay on the Principle of Population.* 7th ed. In Gertrude Himmelfarb, ed., *On Population: Thomas Robert Malthus,* 145–594. New York: The Modern Library, 1960.

Mansfield, Edwin. 1961. "Technical Change and the Rate of Imitation." *Econometrica* 29: 741–66.

Marcilio, Maria-Luiza. 1973. *La Ville de Sâo Paulo: Peuplement et population, 1750–1850 d'après les registres paroissiaux et les recensements anciens.* Paris: Presses Universitaires de France, Publications de l'Université de Rouen.

Marshall, Mac. 1975. "Changing Patterns of Marriage and Migration on Namoluk Atoll." In Carroll, ed. 1975a, 160–211.

Mattmüller, Markus. 1987. *Bevölkerung der Schweitz, Teil I: Die frühe Neuzeit. Basler Beiträge zur Geschichtswissenschaft* 154. Basel: Verlag Helbing and Lichtenhahn.

Mauro, Frédéric, and Geoffrey Parker. 1977a. "Spain." In Wilson and Parker 1977, 37–62.

————. 1977b. "Portugal." In Wilson and Parker 1977, 63–80.

McArthur, Norma. 1967. *Island Populations of the Pacific.* Canberra: Australian National University Press.

McCusker, John J. 1970. *The Rum Trade and the Balance of Payments of the Thirteen Colonies, 1650–1775.* Ph.D. thesis, 2 vols., University of Pittsburgh.

McCusker, John J., and Russell R. Menard. 1991. *The Economy of British America, 1609–1789.* Chapel Hill: University of North Carolina Press; first published 1985.

Menard, Russell R. 1980. "The Tobacco Industry in the Chesapeake Colonies, 1617–1730: An Interpretation." *Research in Economic History* 5: 109–77.

————. 1989. "Slave Demography in the Lowcountry, 1670–1740: From Frontier Society to Plantation Regime." *Working Papers of the Social History Workshop.* Department of History, University of Minnesota.

Merrick, Thomas W., and Douglas H. Graham. 1979. *Population and Economic Development in Brazil, 1800 to the Present.* Baltimore: The Johns Hopkins University Press.

Mitchell, Brian R., ed. 1962. *Abstract of British Historical Statistics.* Cambridge: Cambridge University Press.

————. 1980. *European Historical Statistics 1750–1975.* 2nd ed. New York: Facts on File.

————. 1982. *International Historical Statistics: Africa, Asia.* New York: New York University Press.

————. 1992. *International Historical Statistics: Europe 1750–1988.* 3rd ed. New York: Stockton Press.

————. 1993. *International Historical Statistics: The Americas 1750–1988.* 2nd ed. New York: Stockton Press.

————. 1995. *International Historical Statistics: Africa, Asia and Australasia 1750–1988.* 2nd rev. ed. New York: Stockton Press.

Momsen, Ingwer Ernst. 1969. *Die Bevölkerung der Stadt Husum von 1769 bis 1860: Versuch einer historischen Sozialgeographie.* Kiel: Geographischen Instituts der Universität Kiel.

Morgado, Nuno Alves. 1979. "Portugal." In W. R. Lee, ed. 1979 319–39.

Muzzi, Oretta. 1984. "Aspetti dell' evoluzione demografica della Valdelsa Fiorentina nel tardo medioevo (1350–1427)." In Comba et al. 1984, 135–52.

Nadal, Jordi. 1984. *La Población Española (Siglios XVI a XX).* Corrected and enlarged edition, Barcelona: Editorial Ariel, S. A., first published 1966.

Nason, James D. 1975. "The Strength of the Land: Community Perception of Population on Etal Atoll." In Carroll, ed. 1975, 117–59.

Neiva, Artur Hehl. 1966. "The Population of Brazil." In Pan-Am. Assembly 1966, 33–60.

Newman-Brown, W. 1984. "The Receipt of Poor Relief and Family Situation: Aldenham, Hertfordshire 1630–90." In R. Smith 1984, 405–22.

Nitisastro, Widjojo. 1970. *Population Trends in Indonesia.* Ithaca: Cornell University Press.

Pan-American Assembly on Population 1966. *Population Dilemma in Latin America.* Washington, D.C.: Potomac Books.

Pearl, Raymond A., and Lowell J. Reed. 1920. "The Rate of Population Growth in the United States since 1790 and Its Mathematical Representation." *Proceedings of the National Academy of Science* 6: 275–88.

Peebles, Patrick. 1982. *Sri Lanka: A Handbook of Historical Statistics*. Boston: G. K. Hall and Co.

Perkins, Dwight H. 1969. *Agricultural Development in China 1368–1968*. Chicago: Aldine Publishing Company.

Poos, Lawrence R. 1985. "The Rural Population of Essex in the Middle Ages." *Economic History Review*, 2nd s., 38: 515–30.

———. 1991. *A Rural Society after the Black Death: Essex 1350–1525*. Cambridge: Cambridge University Press.

Pounds, N. J. G. 1979. *An Historical Geography of Europe 1500–1840*. Cambridge: Cambridge University Press.

Rashin, Adolph G. 1956. *Naselenie Rossii za 100 Let (1811–1913gg.): Statisticheskie Ocherki*. Moscow: The State Statistical Publishing House.

Razi, Zvi. 1980. *Life, Marriage and Death in a Medieval Parish: Economy, Society and Demography in Halesowen 1270–1400*. Cambridge: Cambridge University Press.

Recchini de Lattes, Zulma, and Alfredo E. Lattes. 1975. *La Población de Argentina*. Buenos Aires: Instituto Nacional de Estadística y Censos.

Reher, David Sven. 1990. *Town and Country in Pre-Industrial Spain: Cuenca, 1550–1870*. Cambridge: Cambridge University Press.

Rembe, Heinrich. 1971. *Lambsheim: Die Familien von 1547 bis 1800. Beiträge zur Bevölkerungsgeschichte der Pfalz* 1. Kaiserslautern: Heimatstelle Pfalz.

Ringrose, David R. 1983. *Madrid and the Spanish Economy, 1560–1850*. Berkeley: University of California Press.

Rivarola, Domingo M., et al. 1974. *La Población del Paraguay*. Asunción: Centro Paraguayo de Estudios Sociologicos.

Roberts, G. W. 1966. "Populations of the Non–Spanish-Speaking Caribbean." In Pan American Assembly 1966, 61–85.

Robinson, David J. 1981. "Indian Migration in Eighteenth-Century Yucatán: The Open Nature of the Closed Corporate Community." In Robinson, ed. 1981, 149–73.

Robinson, David J., ed. 1981. *Studies in Spanish American Population History. Dellplain Latin American Studies 8*. Boulder, Colo.: Westview Press.

Ross, Robert. 1975. "The 'White' Population of South Africa in the Eighteenth Century." *Population Studies* 29: 217–30.

Rossiter, W. S. 1909. *A Century of Population Growth: From the First Census of the United States to the Twelfth, 1790–1910*. Washington, D.C.: U.S. Bureau of the Census.

Rousseau, Raymond. 1960. *La population de la Savoie jusqu'en 1861*. Paris: S.E.V.P.E.N.

Rowse, A. L. 1957. "Tudor Expansion: The Transition from Mediaeval to Modern History." *William and Mary Quarterly*, 3rd ser., 14: 309–16.

Russell, Josiah Cox. 1948. *British Medieval Population*. Albuquerque: University of New Mexico Press.

———. 1987. *Medieval Demography*. New York: AMS Press, Inc.

Sabean, David Warren. 1990. *Property, Production, and Family in Neckarhausen, 1700–1870*. Cambridge: Cambridge University Press.

Sánchez-Albornoz, Nicholás. 1974. *The Population of Latin America: A History*. Trans. by W.A.R. Richardson. Berkeley: University of California Press.

Sangoï, Jean-Claude. 1985. *Démographie paysanne en Bas-Quercy 1751–1872*. Paris: Editions du CNRS.

Saw, Swee-Hock. 1988. *The Population of Peninsular Malaysia.* Singapore: Singapore University Press.

Schama, Simon. 1987. *The Embarrassment of Riches: An Interpretation of Dutch Culture in the Golden Age.* New York: Alfred A. Knopf.

Schluchter, André. 1990. *Das Gösgeramt im Ancien Régime: Bevölkerung, Wirtschaft und Gesellschaft einer Solothurnischen Landvogtei im 17. und 18. Jahrhundert. Basler Beiträge zur Geschichtswissenschaft* 160. Basel: Verlag Helbing and Lichthahn.

Schmitt, Robert C. 1968. *Demographic Statistics of Hawaii: 1778–1965.* Honolulu: University of Hawaii Press.

Sheridan, Richard B. 1974. *Sugar and Slavery: An Economic History of the British West Indies, 1623–1775.* Baltimore: The Johns Hopkins University Press.

Simon, Julian L. 1977. *The Economics of Population Growth.* Princeton: Princeton University Press.

Simonsen, Roberto C. 1962. *História Econômica do Brasil.* 4th ed. São Paulo: Companhia Editora Nacional; first published 1937.

Slicher van Bath, B. H. 1963. *The Agrarian History of Western Europe* A.D. *500–1850.* Trans. by Olive Ordish. London: Edward Arnold (Publishers) Ltd.

Smith, Adam. 1776. *An Inquiry into the Nature and Causes of the Wealth of Nations.* 2nd ed. Edited by James E. Thorold Rogers, 1880. Oxford: Clarendon Press.

Smith, David, and Nathan Keyfitz, eds. 1977. *Mathematical Demography, Selected Papers.* Berlin: Springer Verlag.

Smith, Richard M., ed. 1984. *Land, Kinship and Life-Cycle.* Cambridge: Cambridge University Press.

Spengler, Joseph J. 1938. *France Faces Depopulation.* Durham, NC: Duke University Press.

Stone, Lawrence. 1947. "State Control in Sixteenth-Century England." *Economic History Review* 17: 103–20.

Taeuber, Irene B. 1958. *The Population of Japan.* Princeton: Princeton University Press.

Telford, Ted A. 1995. "Fertility and Population Growth in the Lineages of Tongcheng County, 1520–1661." In Harrell 1995, 48–93.

Tien, H. Yuan. 1973. *China's Population Struggle: Demographic Decisions of the People's Republic, 1949–1969.* Columbus: Ohio State University Press.

Utterström, Gustaf. 1965. "Two Essays on Population in Eighteenth-Century Scandinavia." In Glass and Eversley, eds. 1965, 523–48.

Van Assche-Vancauwenbergh, D., et al. 1963. *Cinque études de démographie locale (XVIIᵉ–XIXᵉ s.).* Brussels: Pro Civitate, Collection Histoire, no. 2.

Van Houtte Jan A., and Léon van Buyten. 1977. "The Low Countries." In Wilson and Parker 1977, 81–114.

Verhulst, Pierre-François. 1838. "Notice sur la loi que la population suit dans son accroissement." *Correspondences Mathématique et Physique,* 10: 113–17 Brussels: A. Quetelet.; trans. by David Smith in Smith and Keyfitz 1977, 333–37.

―――. 1845. "Recherches mathématique sur la loi d'acroissement de la population." *Nouveaux Mémoires de l'Académie Royales des Sciences* (Brussels) 18: 3–40.

―――. 1847. "Deuxième mémoire sur la loi d'acroissment de la population." *Nouveaux Mémoires de l'Académie Royale des Sciences* 20: 1–32.

Villamarin, Juan, and Judith Villamarin. 1981. "Colonial Censuses and Tributary Lists of the Sabana de Bogotá Chibcha: Sources and Issues." In Robinson, ed. 1981, 45–92.

Von Foerster, H., P. M. Mora, and L. W. Amiot. 1960. "Doomsday: Friday, 13 November, A.D. 2026." *Science* 132: 1291–95.

Vorzimmer, Peter J. 1969. "Darwin, Malthus, and the Theory of Natural Selection." *Journal of the History of Ideas* 30: 537–42.

Wallace, Robert. 1809. *A Dissertation on the Numbers of Mankind in Antient and Modern Times*. 2d ed. Edinburgh: Archibald Constable and Co.; reprinted New York: Augustus M. Kelley, 1969.

Wallerstein, Immanuel. 1974. *The Modern World-System I: Capitalist Agriculture and the Origins of the European World-Economy in the Sixteenth Century*. New York: Academic Press, Inc.

———. 1980. *The Modern World-System II: Mercantilism and the Consolidation of the European World-Economy, 1600–1750*. New York: Academic Press, Inc.

Walter, Hubert. 1969. *Bevölkerungsgeschichte der Stadt Einbeck*. Hildesheim: August Lax Verlagsbuchhandlung.

Wilson, Charles, and Geoffrey Parker, eds. 1977. *An Introduction to the Sources of European Economic History 1500–1800*. Ithaca: Cornell University Press.

Winsor, Charles P. 1932. "A Comparison of Certain Symmetrical Growth Curves." *Journal of the Washington Academy of Sciences* 22: 73–84.

Wriggins, W. Howard, and James F. Guyot, eds. 1973. *Population, Politics, and the Future of Southern Asia*. New York: Columbia University Press.

Wrigley, E. A. 1967. "A Simple Model of London's Importance in Changing English Society and Economy 1650–1750." *Past and Present* 37: 44–70.

Wrigley, E. A., and R. S. Schofield. 1981. *The Population History of England 1541–1871: A Reconstruction*. Cambridge, Mass.: Harvard University Press.

Index

About the Author

P. M. G. HARRIS is Professor Emeritus of History at Temple University. He has published essays and articles on the historical social origins of American leaders, the relationship of local and regional settlement in early America, the demographic expansions of the Chesapeake and the Delaware valley in the colonial era, connections between population change and economic development in early Maryland and Virginia, and the trends of prices in the American colonies.